green REPUBLICAN

green REPUBLICAN

JOHN SAYLOR AND

THE PRESERVATION OF

AMERICA'S WILDERNESS

Thomas G. Smith

UNIVERSITY OF PITTSBURGH PRESS

Published by the University of Pittsburgh Press, Pittsburgh, PA 15260

Copyright © 2006, University of Pittsburgh Press

All rights reserved

Manufactured in the United States of America

Printed on acid-free paper

10 9 8 7 6 5 4 3 2 1

Library of Congress Cataloging-in-Publication Data

Smith, Thomas G.
  Green republican : John Saylor and the preservation of America's wilderness /
Thomas G. Smith.
      p. cm.
  Includes bibliographical references and index.
  ISBN 0-8229-4283-6 (cloth : alk. paper)
  1. Saylor, John P. (John Phillips), 1908-1973. 2. Conservationists—United States—
Biography. I. Title.
  QH31.S317S65 2006
  333.72'092—dc22
                          2006001973

for Sandra

contents

Acknowledgments   ix

Trailblazer   1

1. Headwaters   7

2. Political and Environmental Trailhead   24

3. Maverick Republican   43

4. Dinosaur Canyons   57

5. Big Dam Foolishness   78

6. Wilderness and Park Advocate   95

7. Coal, the C&O Canal, and Kinzua   119

8. The Rainbow Connection   142

9. Passage of the Wilderness Bill   158

10. The Battle to Save Grand Canyon   180

11. Wild and Scenic Rivers   206

12. Base Camp   222

13. Greening America   237

14. Saving the Redwoods   250

15. Congressman for Conservation   266

16. Alaska   285

17. Trail's End   307

Notes   321

Bibliography   377

Index   393

Photographs follow page 236
Courtesy Special Collections and Archives, Stapleton Library,
Indiana University of Pennsylvania.

acknowledgments

DURING the decade it has taken me to complete this study, I have amassed enormous scholarly debts. I am grateful, first, to the Saylor family. Anna Catherine Saylor Bennett, a radiant octogenarian, guided me to family haunts and homesteads and spoke spiritedly about her brother. John Saylor's daughter Susan, son Phil, son-in-law Russell, and nephew David also took time to talk with me. So, too, did former congressional colleagues, staff members on the House Interior Committee, federal officials, and Saylor's legislative and personal assistants.

Former leaders of the environmental community, who hold Saylor in esteem, continuously offered encouragement and support for this project. In the spirit of former Wilderness Society president Olaus Murie, one even offered the use of his retreat. This act of generosity gave my wife, Sandra, and me our first chance to stay in a "gated community," the gate protecting a five-mile-long logging road that led to a lone cabin on the edge of a national wilderness area. The cabin lacked electricity but had plenty of firewood, an adjacent meandering stream, and an assortment of wildlife neighbors. Our host had instructed us to help ourselves to the contents of the "refrigerator," which turned out to be a large, hollowed-out, shaded stump well stocked with cooled beverages appropriate for a campfire celebration of our wedding anniversary.

As most writers realize, librarians are national treasures. From Boston to San Francisco, the archivists with whom I worked were gracious and knowledgeable. Phil Zorich and his successor, Theresa McDevitt, who now heads Special Collections at Indiana University of Pennsylvania, where the Saylor Papers are housed, could not have been more gracious or accommodating. Although I am sure I tried their patience, Jim Douglas and Laura Robinson at the Nichols College Library never balked at my requests for material, and Jim helped me with computer issues. Other archivists, too numerous to mention here, also helped guide my research.

Members of the tightly knit Nichols College community also offered encouragement. Academic dean Alan Rinehardt, with good humor and a poet's heart, has championed this project from the beginning, as have colleagues Jim

Conrad, Paul Lambert, Don Leonard, Karen Tipper, and Ed Warren. I am indebted to my friend and officemate Don Leonard for advice and fun-filled diversions, especially at his place on Cape Cod. Andrea Becker and Kathy Piniarski cheerfully provided an assortment of administrative support. I am also grateful to the college for twice granting me yearlong sabbatical leaves and for financial assistance. The college is blessed with a trustee, Robert Kuppenheimer, who has established a fund that allows faculty members to attend conferences and conduct research. Besides the "Kuppy Fund," I have benefited from a Morris K. Udall Research Grant.

I would be remiss if I did not express gratitude to three outstanding "trail guides": Wayne Bowdish, a high school English teacher, encouraged my earliest feeble attempt at biography; the late Ralph Adams Brown at SUNY Cortland inspired me to become a teacher; and the University of Connecticut's Thomas G. Paterson, my mentor and friend, is an exemplar of the history profession.

I am indebted to the editors of the following publications for giving me permission to reprint portions of previously published articles: "Voice for Wild and Scenic Rivers," *Pennsylvania History* 66 (Autumn 1999): 554–79; and "John Kennedy, Stewart Udall, and New Frontier Conservation," *Pacific Historical Review* 64 (August 1995); 326–62.

Cynthia Miller, director of the University of Pittsburgh Press, encouraged my proposal early on and sent a supportive e-mail at an important time. Kendra Boileau Stokes, who guided the project for a year before moving on to another press, was a patient, skillful, good-natured editor. Deborah Meade, Carol Sickman-Garner, and the other editors at the University of Pittsburgh Press deftly and thoughtfully shepherded the book to publication. The anonymous reviewers offered valuable suggestions. And my son Tom Jr., who works for a publisher, read the entire manuscript and improved it immeasurably. Any errors and shortcomings that remain are mine alone.

My four children, their spouses, my in-laws, and my sister have been stalwart in their support. My six young grandchildren, like some of my students, have been sources of joy and comic relief, simultaneously exhausting and energizing me. My everlasting gratitude goes to my wife, Sandra, for her many sacrifices, for her laughter and loving support, for saving the manuscript from errors, and for trying to save me from myself. To her I dedicate this book.

green REPUBLICAN

Trailblazer

SOME READERS MAY CONSIDER the title of this book, *Green Republican,* a contradiction in terms. In recent history, the Republican Party has (probably fairly) gained a reputation for putting economic development far ahead of environmental issues. But the Republican Party, as historians and other observers have noted, has a rich conservation tradition. At the turn of the twentieth century, President Theodore Roosevelt championed the wise use of natural resources, rather than their plunder. Through executive action, the Roosevelt administration set aside wildlife refuges and millions of acres of timberland as national forests and promoted aesthetic conservation by preserving natural scenic treasures such as Grand Canyon. John Saylor, a congressman representing a western Pennsylvania coal-mining district from 1949 to 1973, built upon this earlier Republican legacy.[1]

John Saylor was an exceptional member of Congress who championed conservation and environmental initiatives during the three decades following World War II. He was far more vigorous in his support for national parks, wilderness, and environmental protection than most of his congressional colleagues. Indeed, Saylor was one of the most important environmentalists of his generation and the leading conservationist in Congress in the twentieth century. Morris Udall (D-AZ), Frank Church (D-ID), Henry "Scoop" Jackson (D-WA), and Clinton Anderson (D-NM) also established strong records, but they lacked Saylor's pioneering spirit and commitment to the cause.

Saylor believed that once national parks and monuments had been established, they became sacrosanct. During the 1950s and 1960s, when federal dam building flourished, he helped block proposals by the powerful Bureau of Reclamation to build dams in Dinosaur National Monument and Grand Canyon. He was also a fervid protector of wilderness areas. In the House of Representatives, he was the driving force behind legislation establishing the National Wilderness Preservation System in 1964 and the National Wild and Scenic Rivers System of 1968. Known as a maverick and pioneer, he battled for national parks and wilderness at a time when such positions were unpopular.[2]

Several factors shaped Saylor's evolution as an environmental activist. His parents instilled in him a love of nature, John inheriting from his father a passion for hunting and angling. They also provided him with a strong religious base that emphasized earth stewardship. America's natural wonders, he once said, stood "as special monuments to the Divine Being": "To permit the despoilment of our natural resources would be to desecrate a divine inheritance. It is thus incumbent upon us to make provisions . . . to safeguard for succeeding generations the natural endowments that are our trust." Protecting natural splendors, he believed, would bring present and future generations closer to the Creator.[3]

A World War II veteran, Saylor was intensely nationalistic and patriotic. He believed that America's sublime landscapes, especially its national parks, glorified the country's people, as well as God. A 1950 *New York Times* editorial reflected his sentiments, he said, when it spoke of the national parks as the citizenry's wisest investment: "It is an investment in health, recreation, education and in something as simple and as profound as love of country—love of the unique and wonderful natural fabric that is the foundation of America." This equation of patriotism and conservation was a pillar of Saylor's perspective. He was unstinting in his support of wilderness preservation, believing that the noted historian Frederick Jackson Turner was right when he asserted in the early 1890s that America's distinct democratic, enterprising, individualistic spirit had been shaped by the wilderness experience. Because wilderness had helped forge the American identity, large tracts should be preserved to inspire future generations.[4]

Like many wilderness advocates of his era, Saylor viewed wilderness as an uninhabited and untamed natural landscape, downplaying or ignoring the fact that Native Americans had earlier inhabited and abandoned these wild areas. Indeed, as historian Mark Spence has shown, in creating some of the earliest national parks, such as Yellowstone, federal officials dispossessed Native people so that the reserves would be more "wild." Saylor, although typical of his time in insisting that new parks and wilderness areas be uninhabited, did not advocate the dispossession of Native Americans.[5]

Theodore Roosevelt served as Saylor's political and environmental hero. Like Roosevelt, Saylor sought as a policy maker to strike a balance between the use and the preservation of federally controlled natural resources, insisting that the two goals were not inherently in conflict: "Through wise planning and use we can both preserve and develop. The problem with which we are faced is, of course, how to achieve the requisite planning and proper use for the greatest benefit." Too often, he maintained, federal planners slighted the goal of preservation.[6]

Saylor took a proprietary interest in public lands. Though located mainly in the West, these 750 million acres, he insisted, belonged to the American people, not just to the residents of the states where the lands were located. Given constitutional authority to make laws and regulations relating to these lands, Congress, he said, should act in the national interest. Representatives should not allow the public domain in the West to be ravaged as it had been in the East. Paved roads, commercial enterprises, cities, and modern conveniences are "good," he once said, "but they are not good enough." Americans also need natural landscapes for beauty, inspiration, and solitude; consequently, large tracts of unspoiled Western terrain should be preserved for aesthetic and recreational purposes.[7]

Early in his career, Saylor had some encounters with nature that reinforced his commitment to the protection of national parks and wilderness areas. His most enriching experience occurred in 1953 when he visited Dinosaur National Monument on the Colorado-Utah border. After rafting down the Yampa and Green rivers, he became convinced that a proposed federal dam would desecrate "one of the most impressive wilderness areas in all the world . . . with its tremendous canyons of unparalleled beauty." At the conclusion of that raft trip, river guide Bus Hatch informed the Sierra Club's David Brower: "I think Congressman Saylor is going to help us out." As Brower later recalled, "Never did the word 'help' have so much territory to cover as in what was about to be done to save rivers, national parks, wilderness, and an over-all sane view towards a beautiful planet." Saylor thus helped save the Dinosaur canyons and several other primeval landscapes.[8] Over the next two decades, Saylor acted as a towering figure in environmental policy making. He could be intimidating:

he was blunt, forceful and—at six feet, four inches—physically imposing. But he was also well liked and respected on both sides of the aisle as an affable, hardworking congressman who was knowledgeable about environmental issues. Generally bipartisan, he worked comfortably with Democrats and Republicans, conservatives and liberals, and was adept at compromise and coalition building.[9]

Throughout his legislative career, Saylor served on the House Committee on Interior and Insular Affairs. This committee, dominated by Westerners, held jurisdiction over legislation relating to Native Americans, public lands, conservation, national parks, and irrigation. During the 1960s and early 1970s, Saylor, as the ranking minority member on the committee, wielded great influence. During this time period, as political scientist Richard F. Fenno has observed, regional differences outweighed party affiliation on the committee. Even though Saylor was one of the few Easterners on the committee, Westerners were forced to cooperate with him because they were vastly outnumbered on the House floor. If Saylor opposed a committee bill, he could round up enough Republican and non-Western votes on the floor to kill it.[10]

Since there were no Native Americans, federal lands, or national parks in his district, Saylor could generally vote his conscience on environmental legislation. "Of course," as one former legislator observed, "every Congressman likes to vote his convictions when he can, but he also wants to keep his seat." Thus, like all successful politicians, Saylor also worked diligently to retain his position.[11]

As the representative of a major coal-producing area, he had to balance his concern for wilderness and the environment with his goal of protecting the economic livelihood of his constituents. Fortunately for Saylor, preservation concerns at large often coincided with interests at home. He opposed federal hydroelectric and atomic power plants, in large measure, because they competed with coal as an energy source, referring to them as "miner displacement programs." In 1962 alone, he pointed out, the Bureau of Reclamation built hydroelectric plants that produced 1.8 million kilowatts of electricity: "As a consequence, the coal industry will lose about 6 million tons of business, with a wage loss of $12 million to miners." The industry was further injured by public power plants constructed by the Army Corps of Engineers and the Atomic Energy Commission. Saylor, a Westerner grumbled, "is against hydropower dams as much as a man can be. He is against them 24 hours a day, seven days a week, forever and ever. He is against hydropower dams because they ostensibly do violence to pretty canyons. But he also is against them because they allegedly compete with coal-fired electric plants fed by his state's coal diggers who live in his district. And he would not be much of a congressman if he was any other way either."[12]

Nevertheless, while Saylor was a fervent defender of coal and private power, his environmental activism went far beyond the narrow scope of his district. He loved the rugged outdoors and was passionate about defending national parks, preserving wilderness, and protecting the environment. He supported air and water quality legislation even though it proved burdensome to the coal, steel, and utility industries. In short, Saylor's environmentalism was genuine, rooted in his patriotism, his religion, and his upbringing.

In spite of his membership in the Republican Party, Saylor's commitment to the cause was seldom, if ever, doubted by conservation leaders, who developed a friendly working relationship with him. He was especially close with Joe Penfold of the Izaak Walton League, Charles Callison of the National Wildlife Federation and later the Audubon Society, Howard Zahniser of the Wilderness Society, and David Brower of the Sierra Club. During the late 1960s and early 1970s, Saylor also built a trusting relationship with Stewart Brandborg and Michael McCloskey, who succeeded Zahniser and Brower in leadership positions with the Wilderness Society and the Sierra Club. Saylor communicated with these individuals, read their organizations' publications, and rarely departed from the positions they took. Indeed, national conservation leaders often met in Saylor's office: "People would leave messages there for us, we would leave them for others, and we would get news and advice from Mr. Saylor's top assistants, Ann Dunbar . . . and Harry Fox," Brower recalled. "Then Coach Saylor would come in and we would talk about our plans and hopes and learn of his, and why ours might or might not work. There is nothing uncommon about this relationship," he continued, "but it becomes extraordinary when it goes on for two decades, and when you count up the conservation victories that simply would not have happened without the counsel, encouragement, and loving kindness . . . that John Saylor gave."[13]

While this book carries no political agenda, it is difficult to resist speculating on how Saylor would view the modern conservation movement. He most assuredly would be displeased with the degree of rancor and partisanship that has beset congressional discourse. He would certainly berate zealous environmentalists who engage in monkey wrenching and other acts of eco-violence. And he would be disenchanted with his party's environmental record over the past three decades. He decried the lack of funding for the National Park Service as a member of Congress, deplored attempted raids on the national parks by timber companies, and opposed drilling in the Arctic National Wildlife Refuge during the energy crisis of the early 1970s; it is safe to assume he would probably maintain these positions today. Above all, he would no doubt encourage Democrats and Republicans to put aside party differences and work to protect the national park system, wilderness, and the planet. And he would be pleased if Democrats and Republicans alike took inspiration from his environmental record.

one

Headwaters

A WEATHERED METAL SIGN depicting grazing livestock marked the dirt road to Bellevue Farm in the elegant horse and cattle country of northern Virginia. A stocky, eighty-seven-year-old man with lush white hair emerged from the ranch house to greet the visitor and direct him to the garage. The inside of the building was empty except for the walls, which were covered with framed photographs of prominent political personalities of the 1950s and 1960s. "This is my rogue's gallery, and here is the chief rogue," declared Floyd Dominy, pointing to Republican representative John P. Saylor of Pennsylvania. The picture featured a smiling Saylor holding a clenched fist in Dominy's face. That image, Dominy recalled, perfectly captured Saylor's "bombast and amicable nature." Unlike some leading conservationists of the day, Dominy observed, Saylor was "earthy, unsanctimonious, likable, and a real man" who liked to hunt and fish. While good-natured, Saylor was also strong in his convictions and impossible to bully.[1]

During the 1950s and 1960s, Dominy and Saylor represented opposite positions in the American conservation movement. As head of the Interior Department's Bureau of Reclamation, Dominy generally favored the development of public resources, especially federally constructed hydroelectric dams on Western rivers. Saylor, on the other hand, championed the inviolability of the national park system, the preservation of wilderness, and the protection of the environment, long before any of these causes became fashionable. From the mid-1950s to the mid-1970s, he was the preeminent preservationist in the House of Representatives and probably all of Congress. And since his death in 1973, perhaps no national legislator—and certainly no Republican—has been so avid and active in the pursuit of earth stewardship.

John Phillips Saylor was born on July 23, 1908, on a farm in Conemaugh Township, about five miles outside Johnstown, Pennsylvania. His persecuted English Mennonite forebears, led by Christian Saylor, had migrated to Philadelphia by way of Switzerland in 1684, three years after the establishment of William Penn's colony. Over the centuries, the family sprawled out geographically until by the mid–nineteenth century it had reached Johnstown in western Pennsylvania.[2]

Located in Cambria County about sixty miles east of Pittsburgh, Johnstown is nestled at the foot of the Laurel Highlands region of the Allegheny Mountains. Three rivers converge there in the shape of a lazy Y. The Little Conemaugh River tumbles down the steep hillside from the northwest, while the Stony Creek River descends from the northeast. The junction of these two streams forms the Conemaugh River, which stretches southwest to form the tail of the Y. Downtown Johnstown is laid out in the wedge-shaped area between the two upper rivers.

Johnstown's natural setting proved a blessing and a curse. The surrounding mountainsides brimmed with ore deposits, and the area became a center for the coal, iron, and steel industries. The Cambria Iron Company was established along the Conemaugh River in 1852, and under subsequent organizational entities—Cambria Steel Works (1898), Midvale Steel and Ordnance (1916), and Bethlehem Steel—it served as the major industry in the region for more than a century. Bethlehem operated the mills in Johnstown from 1923 until the mid-1980s.[3]

While the rivers supplied water for industrial, household, and recreational use, however, they also made the city prone to floods. On the afternoon of May 31, 1889, the earthen South Fork Dam fourteen miles up the Little Conemaugh River crumbled, sending a torrent of water hurtling through Johnstown. Homes and businesses were flattened, and more than twenty-two hundred people died. Nonetheless, the three decades after the infamous Johnstown flood were characterized by economic growth for the steel industry and general prosperity for the city.[4]

John Saylor's antecedents were among the flood's fortunate survivors. John Phillips, Saylor's maternal grandfather, was a miner, and his paternal grandfather, also named John Saylor, worked at the Cambria Iron Company. Neither lost his home or any loved ones. Saylor's parents, Tillman and Minerva Phillips Saylor, of English stock, were teenagers during the flood. Born in Johnstown, they both graduated from Johnstown High School and went on to college, Tillman attending the Indiana Normal School (now Indiana University of Pennsylvania) and Minerva the Millersville Normal School (now Millersville University of Pennsylvania). After graduating, both became teachers in Johnstown area schools, where they met. Tillman aspired to become an attorney, eventually attending the University of Michigan Law School and returning to Johnstown after graduation in 1904 to start a law practice. Three years later, he married Minerva Phillips. Minerva was a highly intelligent woman who relished teaching, but following the custom of the times, she gave up her career to raise a family. Besides the oldest child, John, the marriage produced Anna Catherine (1911), Margaret (1914), and Tillman Jr. (1917).[5]

The family first lived in a home built by Grandfather Phillips at 327 Lincoln Street. John attended the Adams Street School, where his mother had taught, then transferred to the Roxbury School when his father built a new red brick house in an orchard near the residence of Grandfather Saylor. The family stayed in this home on Saylor Street until 1921, when John's seven-year-old sister Margaret died of diphtheria. After her death, Minerva insisted upon relocating, so Tillman erected a new yellow brick house on an adjacent property up the road. With a flourishing law practice, Tillman eventually moved the family into a newly constructed fieldstone dream house on the adjoining lot.[6]

John Saylor, then, grew up in upper-middle-class comfort. His father was a successful attorney, owner of three houses, and a member of the Johnstown and Sunnehanna country clubs. A Republican, Tillman eventually entered local politics, serving as city solicitor during the 1930s. Prosperous and prominent, Saylor's parents were loving disciplinarians who set high ethical and moral standards for their children. They insisted upon religious instruction. The Mennonite faith, at least for the Saylors, had long ago given way to the Dutch Reformed Church and then the United Church of Christ. The children were required to attend Sunday school and regular Sunday services. John remained an active member of St. John's United Church of Christ throughout his life, raising his two children in that faith, teaching adult Sunday-school classes, and being elected president of the congregation.[7]

As former teachers, the Saylors also prized education. Their three surviving children, who went to religious-affiliated colleges, all obtained advanced degrees. Perhaps John, practical minded, fun loving, and likable, was the least intellectually gifted of the siblings. Although academic courses were a struggle for him, he graduated from Franklin and Marshall College and the Dickinson College School of Law. His younger brother, Tillman, invariably described as "brilliant," graduated from Haverford College and Harvard Law School. Anna Catherine received her undergraduate degree from Hood College in Frederick, Maryland, and her master of arts degree from Columbia University, where she studied with famed historians Allen Nevins and Carleton J. H. Hayes. She planned to go on for her doctorate in political science but abandoned that goal when she married and had a child. After her family had been raised, she became an associate professor of political science at the University of Pittsburgh at Johnstown.[8]

In the 1910s and 1920s, when John Saylor was a young man, Johnstown offered glorious entertainment choices for the affluent. Luna Park in Roxbury, near the Saylor home, was a summer amusement facility that featured a boardwalk, boating pond, harness racetrack, merry-go-round, and roller coaster. The Majestic and Cambria theaters in downtown Johnstown offered plays, concerts, and vaudeville acts. Silent movies captivated audiences at the Nemo, the State, the Globe, the Grand, and other theaters. The Auditorium lured crowds with dances, roller-skating, boxing matches, and big band music. One could buy peanuts and popcorn from street vendors or purchase sandwiches and ice cream at the Elite Candy Store and Kredel's Drugstore. More substantive meals were available at the Green Kettle Room or at hotels such as the Fort Stanwix. In the summer there was plenty of baseball, employers such as Bethlehem Steel fielding teams in amateur hardball leagues. In the mid-1920s, the city built Point Stadium at the juncture of the Stony Creek and Little Conemaugh rivers, future stars such as Rip Collins and Joe Cronin playing professional minor league baseball for the Johnstown Johnnies in the Middle Atlantic League. And if one wanted a change of pace, only a few miles' travel would provide opportunities to fish, hunt, hike, picnic, and commune with nature.[9]

Indeed, John Saylor's preservationist perspective was shaped during his formative years in Johnstown. He had ample opportunity to experience nature on his uncle Sam and aunt Maggie's farm in Somerset County. Moreover, his mother revered nature, and his father was an avid angler and hunter who instilled a passion for these outdoor activities in his sons. In later years, John would say that his love for nature derived from his "first memory of walking through woods with [his] father." Tillman often went big-game hunting in

Alaska and the American West, and the Saylor homes were adorned with trophy animals. In the 1920s, Tillman Sr. helped establish a sportsmen's association that purchased a hunting and fishing camp near Cook's Run in Potter County, and throughout his life John took periodic refuge at "Lost Cabin." Mr. Saylor also helped nurture his son's love for national parks. John Saylor recalled that his father took him at age twelve to Yellowstone National Park, noting that this experience helped to mold him into a lifelong champion of wilderness and the national park system.[10]

Tillman Sr. also claimed Gifford Pinchot as a friend, thus passing along to his son the conservationist viewpoint that had emerged during the first two decades of the twentieth century, when Progressives, led by President Theodore Roosevelt and Pinchot, his Pennsylvanian chief of forestry, championed the efficient use of natural resources. Their utilitarian viewpoint held that experts in the federal bureaucracy could scientifically manage the public domain to eliminate waste and plunder by special interests. Progressives also gave heed to preservation: scenic lands were to be set aside to serve humankind by providing recreation, refreshing the spirit, eliminating stress, and transforming "sissies" into virile outdoor participants. As a member of Congress, John Saylor especially identified with the preservationist impulse and was consequently labeled a "Teddy Roosevelt Conservationist."[11]

The teachings of John's religious parents also reinforced his preservationist outlook. They emphasized the notion of stewardship more than human dominion over nature: natural scenic treasures were sublime examples of God's handiwork that should not be defiled by humans. This viewpoint was also voiced in the writings of John Muir, who had cofounded the Sierra Club and helped establish Yosemite National Park in the 1890s. While there is no evidence that the Saylors were familiar with Muir's work, their Nature-as-God's-Temple philosophy was similar to his.[12]

Like his hero Theodore Roosevelt, John Saylor was intensely nationalistic. National parks and other areas of scenic beauty glorified the nation, and these patriotic symbols should not be corrupted by commercial enterprises. His children tell the story of the time he took them to see the Petrified Forest. There Saylor spotted a man pilfering a petrified rock as a souvenir and ordered the culprit to put it back because it belonged to the American people. If every visitor took a souvenir, he scolded, the park's beauty would be diminished. He believed that the federal lands belonged to the American people and that it was the duty of Congress to protect the public estate from despoliation. To be sure, public lands outside national preserves should be open to grazing, mining, lumbering, and dam building, but not to commercial use exclusively. Some of these areas should be set aside as additional parks or wilderness.[13]

John Saylor's urban, industrial environment also may have influenced his outlook. Author Malcolm Cowley, a Pennsylvania native, described Johnstown as "one of the grimiest small cities in the world." Area coal mines and steel mills blighted the landscape, fouled the rivers, and smudged the air, but industrial degradation may have made Saylor more appreciative of primeval lands, sparkling streams, and abundant wildlife. Remarkably, and perhaps not coincidentally, western Pennsylvania produced four nationally renowned environmentalists during the middle decades of the twentieth century. Along with Saylor, the preeminent preservationist in Congress, Howard Zahniser, who grew up along the upper Allegheny River in Tionesta, served as executive secretary of the Wilderness Society and dedicated his life to the enactment of legislation preserving pristine areas. Rachel Carson, who triggered the modern environmental movement by exposing the dangers of pesticides in *Silent Spring,* was born and raised along the lower Allegheny River. And the environmental cult hero Edward Abbey, before moving to Arizona to write literary classics such as *Desert Solitaire* and *Appalachian Wilderness,* grew up as a Saylor constituent in Indiana County.[14]

In spite of his eventual prominence, however, John Saylor's academic record gave few hints of his future success as a legislator and preservationist. At Johnstown High School from 1920 to 1924, he performed well in history classes but struggled with Latin and physics, an overall C student. But he was personable, outgoing, and active in extracurricular affairs. At six feet four inches he towered over his classmates, but he was exceedingly thin and not very athletic, shunning basketball in favor of track and the rifle team. He was a member of the student council and appeared in five plays with the Dramatics Club. The high school yearbook, *The Spectator,* took note of his "gift of gab," listing "red hair" among his likes and his favorite expression as "where's Flo?" "Flo" was Florence McConaughy, an attractive, red-haired classmate and fellow dramatist who drew the attention of several boys, not just Saylor. She listed her likes as "boys," her dislikes as "teachers," and her goal as "to get out of J.H.S." Saylor named "walking" as a dislike, his pastime as "acting," and his goal as "to become a lawyer."[15]

The yearbook also carried one of Saylor's short stories. It tells of a young man left alone at his family's large, three-story home in a desolate area outside of town. He tries to occupy himself with reading and solitaire but begins to see shadows and hear noises. Frightened, he gets his father's revolver and proceeds to investigate. Nervously he examines the rooms on the first two floors without result, then moves to the third floor and slowly opens a door. Two "eyes" glare at him in the darkness. He cocks the gun and prepares to shoot but first flips on the light. The "eyes" turn out to be bottles of phosphorous on his father's laboratory shelf. Relieved, he descends the stairs, soon learning that the shadows he had seen were his own. One is tempted to read lessons into this story about most fears being unjustified and life's mysteries having logical explanations. But the story probably best serves as an example of Saylor's sense of drama. As a husband, parent, and member of Congress, he enjoyed surprises and histrionics and was always a bit of a ham.[16]

Only sixteen at graduation, Saylor was sent to Mercersburg Academy for additional preparation before college. Those recommending him to the school included the family minister, J. Harvey Mickley, and high school English teacher Kathryn Ulery. Mickley had baptized the candidate and considered him "a young man of good parts and character." He urged the headmaster to provide Saylor with "helpful advice as to what studies he should take and give him sufficient to keep him busy." The minister also let the academy know that the boy's father was a prominent attorney who at that moment was serving as a delegate to the Republican national convention in Cleveland.[17]

Ulery observed that the applicant had a fine mind but that "somewhere in his work he had poor preparation or failed to apply himself." This lack of preparation included the subject of English. But John was "sunny-tempered, honest in his convictions and devoted to friends." He also came from a fine family: "While his parents hold their children responsible for home duties and impose necessary restraints, the family intercourse is that of affectionate comradeship," the teacher noted. She concluded that the academy and Saylor would mutually benefit from their association.[18]

The boyhood home of President James Buchanan, Mercersburg was a tidy town of fifteen hundred people located in south-central Pennsylvania, near the Maryland border. Affiliated with the Reformed Church, Mercersburg Academy was a boarding school for boys. As an educational institution, it traced its roots to 1836, when it was part of Marshall College. It was established as a private boys' preparatory school in 1893 by Dr. William Mann Irvine.[19]

Headmaster Irvine was a strait-laced, quirky man who used new terminology for the equivalent of grades nine through twelve. Freshmen were "juniors," sophomores were "lower middlers," juniors were "upper middlers," and seniors were "seniors." Believing religion to be the "Queen of all Sciences," he made weekend morning chapel mandatory, as well as prayer before each evening meal in the dining hall. The hymn "Onward Christian Soldiers" routinely played at academy functions such as the opening of the fall term. Smoking was prohibited in all college buildings. And Irvine recoiled at the use of the words *bathroom, toilet,* and *lavatory,* so if nature called, one asked to use "the Ten" (for the number painted on the doors of all lavatories). Students had to abide by a code of conduct. Serious violations such as drinking or gambling brought expulsion, and lesser infractions resulted in walking guard—a weekend detention that required the offender to pace around the campus for hours at a time. Breaking the smoking ban, for example, brought ten hours of walking.[20]

Irvine was beginning his thirty-second year when John Saylor enrolled as an upper middler. (One of his schoolmates was future film star Jimmy Stewart, from Indiana, Pennsylvania.) Accepted as an upper middler, Saylor made an arrangement with the registrar whereby he would take senior courses and if successful would graduate with the class of 1925. Tall and stick-thin, Saylor posed in suit and black bow tie with the ninety-nine members of the class of 1925. Except for one young man from the Canal Zone in Panama, all were white. The school's restriction against women, its religious affiliation, and the annual cost of one thousand dollars made the academy a bastion for white male Protestants. Blacks were excluded until 1964 and women until 1969. On occasion, the school admitted Hispanic and Native American students. It imposed a strict quota for Jews.[21]

The school year began in mid-September under a cloud. The previous July, President Calvin Coolidge's son, Calvin Jr., who would have been a member of the class of 1925, had died of blood poisoning. The academy yearbook, *The Karux,* was dedicated to him, a memorial service held in mid-November. Irvine described the president's son as "manly and clean in habit and mind, and in character . . . earnest, direct, true and strong."[22]

In preparing its students for admission into Princeton, Dartmouth, Yale, and other top colleges, the academy required a liberal arts curriculum with courses in math, history, English, science, and language. Saylor's fall courses, under his special arrangement, consisted of Virgil, solid geometry, trigonometry, upper middler French, and senior English. The school also emphasized oratory, with public speaking including debates and formal presentations. Based on experience, effort, and talent, speakers were divided into three categories: Scrub, Prelim, and Proper. Scrubs were the least able, Propers the most talented. Already stigmatized, Scrubs were also restricted to campus study hall on Saturday evenings. As a Scrub, Saylor took the negative on the topics "Resolved: That the United States Government Should Own and Operate the Railroads" and "Resolved: That the United States Government Should Own and Operate the Coal Mines." Promoted to Prelim, Saylor took the affirmative on the topic "Resolved: That the United States Government Should Grant Statehood to Alaska and Hawaii." Preparing for this debate, he later claimed, made him an advocate of statehood for these territories as a member of Congress. Saylor eventually achieved promotion to Proper in the spring of 1925.[23]

The school tried to keep its young men occupied outside the classroom, offering football, baseball, track, swimming, boxing, and wrestling. Saylor, however, did not participate in sports. Nor did he join the Drama Club or any other organization. Periodically, the academy held formal dances and brought young women to campus from Penn Hall in nearby Chambersburg. Off the dance floor, couples were restricted to a certain plot of ground and were carefully chaperoned. Occasionally, Mercersburg brought special guests to talk to the young men about sex. One speaker advised that they might thwart glandular yearnings by hanging "a portrait of Roosevelt up on the wall, and when temptation comes, look up and inquire, 'How about it, Teddy?' I can't think of Theodore Roosevelt in connection with sex wrongdoing."[24]

On Saturdays, if students were not gazing at images of Teddy Roosevelt, they could walk into the town of Mercersburg to watch a movie at the Star Theater or snack and play pinball at McLaughlin's. The school newspaper also recommended hunting as an autumn diversion. While the school prohibited smoking, drinking, gambling, and on-campus dating, it did permit students to possess shotguns. "A great deal of pleasure can be had by going for a short hunt before morning roll call," the paper advised, adding, "It is surprising the amount of territory one can cover between sunrise and seven o'clock." An all-day Saturday hunt was possible if a student obtained permission to miss chapel and dinner, and one could also hunt all day on Thanksgiving. Bagged game could be given to Steigers, the dining hall director, so that "the fruits of his labors" could "be enjoyed by the sportsman."[25]

Recreational diversions were dependent upon good conduct and passing grades. Those who were not successful academically were said to have "conditions," and their Saturdays were spent getting extra help from teachers. Whether from homesickness, the hospitalization of his mother, or a lack of preparation,

Saylor had conditions every term. At the end of the fall term, he had received insufficient grades in every subject except geometry. He was dropped from the senior class and given less advanced courses in French and Latin, while continuing to take geometry, trigonometry, and senior English. He failed every course in the winter and spring terms. The academy instructed him to remain on campus for additional study, tutoring, and makeup exams from June 4 to June 13, at a cost of three dollars per day. If he refused, he would not be permitted to return in the fall.[26]

These instructions prompted a visit from Tillman Saylor Sr. He learned that his son had been "loafing all year." One teacher told him that John had been "jazzing around campus when he ought to have been studying," and another coldly advised the father "to take him out and put him to work." "Considerably exercised," Tillman Saylor withdrew John on June 6 and "took him home and gave him a job with a pick and shovel."[27]

After receiving a bill for the unpaid balance of the short summer session, John's father sent a stern letter protesting the charge of eighteen dollars and the fact that he had not been kept informed of his son's lack of effort and academic progress. Headmaster Irvine replied that the registrar had informed him that the bill had been a mistake and that the money would be refunded or credited to the account when the student returned in the fall. Irvine was perplexed, however, by the charge that the school had been remiss in keeping the father apprised of his son's academic standing. Ten progress reports, all discouraging, had been mailed to the parents. Additionally, at a spring meeting, the father had been told that the boy "had been poorly prepared and that possibly he was not very brilliant." Given John's level of effort, the registrar informed the father, it would take three years for him to complete his studies at Mercersburg. The issue of his return became moot, however, when he was accepted at Franklin and Marshall College. Saylor seemed to walk away unscarred by his experience at Mercersburg. He always claimed to be a graduate of the academy and, despite his lackluster record, became a member of its board of regents in 1962.[28]

Affiliated with the Reformed Church, Franklin and Marshall College was located in Lancaster, Pennsylvania. Franklin College, founded in 1787, had merged with Marshall when that college relocated from Mercersburg to Lancaster in 1853. Like Mercersburg Academy, F&M was mainly a school for white male Protestants. There was no quota for non-Protestants, but in reality few Catholics and Jews attended the college. The first African American graduated in 1950, and women were not enrolled until 1969.[29]

Dr. Henry Harbaugh Apple, the college's popular president, was determined to expand the enrollment and reputation of F&M. He recruited a large freshman class of 256 in 1925, thus bringing the total enrollment to 656, more than doubling the student body of 1920. Over the next four years, he expanded the offerings and facilities in science and business, and the student body climbed to more than 750. In twenty years, from 1909 to 1929, Apple had increased the number of buildings from six to fifteen, enlarged the faculty from thirteen to forty-four, and grown the endowment from two hundred thousand dollars to more than one million. Apple, the student newspaper noted, was proud of the growth and "radiated happiness about the Campus to the extent that, for the period of his administration, their [sic] has been a constant wholesome and happy life led by the students."[30]

The students, of course, were not always happy. They cheered the elimination of compulsory Sunday-morning chapel in favor of a voluntary monthly vesper service, but they decried Saturday-morning classes and a mandatory Wednesday-afternoon convocation. The convocation was thought to be gruesome because it forced students to endure announcements and boring speeches for an hour. To fill the time, they also had to sing songs, and there were only so many times they could happily sing "Old Black Joe." The students even threatened to strike when the Christmas break was shortened in 1928. And the ban against Victrolas in dormitory rooms also brought protests: Why could students play musical instruments but not Victrolas? Would it not make more sense, the school paper asked, to establish a curfew against loud noise? Some students, doubtless those who had already met the standard, complained when the Latin requirement for liberal arts majors was reduced from four to two years. John Saylor probably was not one of those protesting the change.[31]

Following his pattern at Mercersburg, Saylor avoided membership in campus clubs. He did join Chi Phi fraternity and as a sophomore played one season of varsity football. A scrawny lineman on a twenty-six-player squad, Saylor suffered through a disastrous season. As a member of the Eastern Collegiate Athletic Association, F&M scheduled games against Ursinus, Muhlenburg, Gettysburg, Dickinson, and Albright, along with games against the likes of Army. Saylor and his mates posted a record of no wins, eight losses, and one scoreless tie. They were shut out in seven of nine contests and outscored 190 to 13. Saylor terminated his football career after that one dreadful season.[32]

Academically, Saylor showed marked improvement over his performance at Mercersburg. Of course, this was not difficult. He was an English major but received his best grades in four history classes. As always, Latin gave him trouble, and he had to repeat a course in Horace and Juvenal. The year he played football, he managed to fail a two-semester physical education class, which he was forced to repeat his senior year. He also struggled with French and chemistry. His scholastic difficulties, as usual, resulted from a lack of effort and too much "jazzing around." The college yearbook noted that "his intimate knowledge of the town is indeed astounding, in contrast to his lack of knowledge in Latin class. His generosity to the girls is well known to all, and he is always present at the bigger and better social functions of the town." Saylor, the yearbook continued, believed that F&M "cramps his style" and planned to seek brighter lights "and to study a little law on the side."[33]

In the fall of 1929, just a month before the stock-market collapse, Saylor enrolled at the University of Michigan Law School, his father's alma mater. This experience proved disappointing, his grades substandard, and he was asked to leave in June. Saylor rarely mentioned this setback, but it may have helped shape his future. The scarcity of jobs in the depressed economy also may have served as a sobering influence. Whether out of economic desperation or intellectual maturation, Saylor eventually committed himself to the serious pursuit of a law degree.[34]

Saylor was one of fifty-eight men and two women who entered the Dickinson School of Law in the fall of 1930. The law school had been established in 1834, but the college was founded in 1783 and was claimed to be the twelfth-oldest in the United States. Dickinson is located in Carlisle, Pennsylvania, a city of about ten thousand people tucked in the Cumberland Valley, about seventeen miles southwest of Harrisburg.[35]

Saylor attended Dickinson from 1930 until 1933, the worst years of the decadelong depression. The budget was so tight at the law school that it did not publish a yearbook in 1933. But for those with the wherewithal, education costs were reasonable. The tuition was $250 yearly, plus another $340 for room and board at a nearby private residence. The three-year course of study consisted of classes in such subjects as contracts, criminal law, torts, property, constitutional law, and moot court. Saylor did not excel academically, but he was one of thirty-five members of his entering class of sixty to graduate. And fortunately, he had a job waiting for him.[36]

Saylor returned to Johnstown to work at his father's law firm, launching his career at a time when Johnstown, like other American cities, was undergoing economic disruption, political turmoil, and labor strife. Johnstown had the additional burden of being devastated by another flood.

Even cities with diverse economies were ravaged by the Great Depression, but Johnstown was generally a one-company town. In its coal mines and steel plants, Bethlehem employed nearly fourteen thousand laborers out of the city's labor force of seventeen thousand, accounting for 72 percent of the town's total wages. Bethlehem was wounded but not incapacitated by the Depression. To survive, it curtailed production, idled some mills, chopped wages, and reduced the full-time workforce, with only 15 percent of the company's workforce laboring full-time by the late 1930s. Part-timers worked one or, if they were lucky, two days per week. Between 1929 and 1932, wages were slashed by 64 percent. Then came another 50 percent reduction in 1932. The average weekly wage had plummeted from $36.07 in 1925 to $12.77 in 1932.[37]

Less income meant that workers and merchants had to struggle to get by economically. To attract customers, some businesses, such as Glosser Brothers Market, extended credit and issued coupons offering a five-cent discount on a single total purchase. To earn extra income, women did sewing and served as laundresses, maids, cooks, and dishwashers outside the home. At nearby farms, men and older children bartered their labor for milk, eggs, potatoes, and other produce. Desperate souls picked through garbage and coal-slag heaps, and some stole redeemable bottles from front porches. Nearly five thousand people left Johnstown during the early years of the Depression, and another six thousand county families had to go on relief to obtain a four-dollar weekly food allowance.[38]

Those people who could not pay their taxes or meet mortgage payments faced the possibility of losing their homes. Bethlehem allowed its mortgagees to restructure their payments, and the state of Pennsylvania gave abatements for penalties and back interest if the delinquent agreed to satisfy unpaid taxes in five annual payments. Still, many lost their homes to the bank and the county. John Saylor's sister recalled that a family she knew lost their home even though they had paid off 80 percent of their mortgage. She complained to her father about the injustice of foreclosure, but he said, "My dear, until the final payment is made, it's just rent."[39]

Without financial records or personal correspondence for the period, it is difficult to generalize with any certainty about John Saylor's standard of living. But even with the sorry state of the economy, his practice seems to have prospered. After all, he worked for a prestigious firm whose clients included

Bethlehem Steel and the Pennsylvania Railroad. Saylor was successful enough to purchase a new home in downtown Johnstown in 1937, becoming a partner in the firm by the end of the decade.[40]

Politics did not initially beckon to Saylor, perhaps because city government seemed so ineffective. Historically, Johnstown had been an obstinately Republican city, but the incumbent mayor, O. Webster Saylor, John's uncle, was under siege. In hard times, desperate citizens looked for answers, and the Republican mayor did not seem to have them. In the mayoral race of 1931, the community turned to Edward "Eddie" McCloskey, an irascible, demagogic newspaper publisher who ran as an independent.[41]

McCloskey was a self-taught former prize-fighter who established the *Derby* in 1927. In his newspaper and later in his mayoral campaign, he attacked "the interests"—mainly Bethlehem Steel. Johnstown, he said, should diversify its economy so that the community would not be so dependent on and beholden to Bethlehem. He charged that its executives were overpaid and its laborers underpaid. Its tax rate was too low and its influence too pervasive. It controlled the city's two major newspapers, the police department, and local politicians. He called the Chamber of Commerce the "Chamber of Comics" and demanded "fewer cops." He also pushed national and local public works projects as a remedy for the Depression.[42]

At first, McCloskey was popular. He made city council meetings open to the public, reduced the size of the police force, rarely used his power as magistrate to administer fines, increased the tax on property, and persuaded the city to go into debt to fund the construction of sewers as a works project.

But McCloskey was not effective. Citizens grew tired of his combative style and his constant battles with the city council. Plus, hard times persisted, and Bethlehem threatened to relocate some of its plants outside the city. In 1935, he did not seek reelection, and Johnstowners turned to Daniel Shields, another independent. Shields promised to bring order, stability, and civility to the city. He got along with the city council and ingratiated himself with Bethlehem and many middle-class city residents by lowering the tax rate. Mayor McCloskey's city solicitor had openly advocated the overthrow of capitalism, but Shields appointed a dignified conservative, Tillman Saylor Sr., to serve as the city attorney. Saylor's job, which his son John would later inherit, consisted of advising the mayor and city council on legal issues, representing the city in court cases, clearing liens for unpaid taxes, and defending the mayor's dispensation of justice on appeal.[43]

The new administration had been in office less than three months when Johnstown was clobbered by another flood. Days of rain had swollen the rivers, and they sloshed over their banks on St. Patrick's Day, covering the city with fourteen feet of water. The flood took twelve lives, knocked out telephone and electrical service, capsized cars, collapsed bridges at Franklin and Poplar streets, and destroyed seventy-seven buildings. In all, damages amounted to a total of forty million dollars.[44]

In addition, New Deal legislation affected labor relations in Johnstown. In 1935, Congress passed the National Labor Relations Act—generally referred to as the Wagner Act—granting workers the right to unionize and barring employers from undermining organizational activities in their plants. The National Labor Relations Board was established to oversee factory elections, recognize duly elected unions, and investigate charges of unfair employer practices such as terminating workers for attempting to organize. In short, it became unlawful for employers to ban the formation of unions.

In 1935, the Congress of Industrial Organizations (CIO), headed by John L. Lewis, set out to organize unskilled workers in key industries such as automobiles and steel. Using sit-down strikes, the union was recognized by General Motors and Chrysler in 1937, with Ford holding out until 1941. In 1937, U.S. Steel accepted the union, instituting a wage increase and a forty-hour week. "Little Steel," such as Republic and Bethlehem, went along with the wage hike and the eight-hour day but refused to recognize the union. At Republic in Chicago on Memorial Day 1937, violence broke out between police and picketers, leaving ten people dead and forty wounded. Johnstown also seemed to be on the verge of violence. In mid-June 1937, the CIO attempted to unionize Bethlehem's Johnstown facility, but that strike brought violence and martial law, ultimately failing. Workers did not unionize at Bethlehem and other Little Steel companies until World War II.[45]

It is difficult to gauge how the tumultuous events of the 1930s affected Saylor's political outlook. There is no evidence to indicate that either he or his father joined the efforts to break the strike against Bethlehem Steel. When Saylor became a member of Congress, representing a heavily unionized coal-mining district, he became a champion of organized labor. As a rock-ribbed fiscal conservative, he deplored the growth of federal bureaucracy and massive government spending, but he accepted the major thrust of the New Deal, especially emergency make-work programs. He considered the Civilian Conservation Corps "one of the best things the Government has ever done." As a national lawmaker, he supported public housing, the food stamp program, the antipoverty campaign, and increased Social Security benefits. He judged people by the quality of their character, not the color of their skin, and endorsed most civil rights legislation.[46]

Despite the St. Patrick's Day flood, Saylor did not become a champion of publicly financed multipurpose dams, in the tradition of the New Deal. Controlling floods was a legitimate concern of the federal government, but he was less enthusiastic about reclamation and power production. Irrigating arid Western lands, though noble in purpose, was extremely costly and added crops to an already glutted domestic agricultural market. And federally financed hydroelectric power competed with privately produced fuels like Pennsylvania coal. Massive hydroelectric dams also clogged free-flowing rivers and sometimes flooded natural panoramic treasures. But these political and environmental issues were in the future; Saylor's main concerns in the mid-1930s were his law practice and his efforts to win the heart of Grace Doerstler, the daughter of a Pennsylvania Railroad brakeman.

While a student at Franklin and Marshall College, John Saylor had met Grace Doerstler of Rohrerstown, Pennsylvania. Of Pennsylvania Dutch ancestry, she attended nearby Millersville State, the same college that John's mother received her degree from in 1895. After graduation, the two dated while John attended law school in Carlisle and she taught school in Columbia, Pennsylvania. The seven-year courtship ended in 1937 when the couple exchanged vows in the chapel of the Union Theological Seminary, across the street from F&M College. They bought a home at 179 Orlando Street in Johnstown, living there until the 1950s.[47]

The year after the wedding, Tillman Saylor Sr. died from a heart attack at the age of fifty, and John succeeded him as city solicitor, a post he held until 1942. With America's entry into World War II after the bombing of Pearl Harbor, John volunteered his services. The decision to enlist was difficult because it meant leaving Grace and his infant son John Phillips Jr., born in 1941. But there was never a doubt about which military branch he would join. Given his surname, he later joked, he felt compelled to join the U.S. Navy.[48]

As a lieutenant (junior grade), Saylor trained at a variety of East Coast facilities before being sent to the San Francisco Naval Base to serve as a communications officer aboard the newly commissioned U.S.S. *Missoula.* Nicknamed "Miserable Mike," the *Missoula* was a troop transport vessel that was destined to participate in major beachhead assaults in the Central Pacific in 1945, including the invasion of Iwo Jima.[49]

On February 19, the morning of the beachhead assault, Captain Alex C. Kopper called Saylor to his quarters and asked him to provide a flag for the Marine assault battalion. As communications officer, Saylor was custodian of the ship's flags, so he and the Marine battalion's communications officer selected a small boat flag that could be carried with the assault troops. After three days of gruesome fighting, a unit from E Company of the Second Battalion, Twenty-eighth Regiment, Fifth Marine division, scrambled to the top of Mount Suribachi and hoisted a U.S. flag on a twenty-foot pipe. Though tiny, that fluttering symbol brought cheers and inspiration to the men ashore and at sea. Shortly thereafter, the small flag was lowered and replaced by a larger one acquired from another landing craft. Associated Press photographer Joe Rosenthal captured a picture of five Marines, one of them Michael Strank from Johnstown, raising the larger replacement flag. That posed picture won the Pulitzer Prize and became the most admired of the war.[50]

Following the fall of Suribachi, the *Missoula* supplied reinforcements for the invasion of Okinawa in early April. After deploying these forces, the ship was ordered to the southern Philippines to pick up a battalion for an invasion of Japan. Near Japan, the crew learned of the surrender on August 14, and the troops were unloaded at Yokohama to serve as occupational forces. The *Missoula* then returned to the Philippines to pick up more troops for the occupation of nuclear-blasted Hiroshima. After being roughed up by a typhoon, "Mike" was given instructions to return home, arriving in San Francisco on Thanksgiving Day 1945. Saylor went on to Philadelphia, where he was separated from the Navy, then proceeded to Johnstown, where he was reunited with Grace and his young son "Phil" in 1946. The following summer, Susan Kathleen was added to the Saylor family.[51]

In Johnstown, Saylor resumed his legal career but never seemed fulfilled by the practice of law. He remained in the Naval Reserve, joined veterans' and fraternal organizations, and became active in local politics. When the district congressional seat became vacant owing to the death of the incumbent representative, Saylor sought the Republican nomination as a candidate in the special election. He was about to embark on a new and exciting career in politics.[52]

two

Political and Environmental Trailhead

Colonel Robert Coffey Jr. was a war hero. Piloting a P-47 Thunderbolt with the Army Air Force during World War II, the Johnstown native completed ninety-seven missions over Europe and destroyed fourteen enemy planes before being shot down over Germany. Avoiding capture, he worked his way into France and fought with the underground. After the war, the three-time recipient of the Distinguished Flying Cross resigned from active military service in 1948 to enter politics and was elected to the U.S. House of Representatives. Coffey had represented Pennsylvania's Twenty-sixth District for less than four months before dying on a training flight in New Mexico. A special election was scheduled on September 13, 1949, to select a successor. District Democrats nominated Curry Coffey, the mother of the deceased incumbent. The Republicans named John P. Saylor.[1]

Pennsylvania's Twenty-sixth Congressional District included Armstrong, Cambria, and Indiana counties. Armstrong and Indiana were essentially rural and Republican. Cambria, which included Johnstown, was industrial and narrowly Democratic. In 1949, Republicans held a slight 7,000-vote edge in registered voters. In the special election of 1949, however, Mrs. Coffey had the backing of organized labor, and about one-third of the district's 155,000 registered voters belonged to unions.[2]

A native Alabaman with a southern drawl, the fifty-five-year-old Coffey enjoyed public sympathy, but she faced an attractive and formidable opponent in John Saylor. His once lanky frame had filled out to 225 pounds, and his expansive personality matched his imposing physical presence. A navy veteran with a creditable war record, he was engaging, articulate, and energetic, his gender giving him a further advantage. To be sure, World War II had been a turning point for women in terms of securing employment outside the home, but national political office, like most upper-management business and professional positions, remained a male bastion. Of 535 members of Congress in 1949, only one woman, Margaret Chase Smith of Maine, held a seat in the U.S. Senate, and only nine women served in the House of Representatives.[3]

Once nominated as a congressional candidate, Saylor decided not to assail Coffey directly. Instead, he assailed the Truman administration for high taxes, mounting deficits, and an expansive and intrusive federal bureaucracy. In short, he argued that Truman was a dangerous radical who was trying to impose on Americans "a socialistic welfare state."[4]

Coffey, on the other hand, portrayed herself as a liberal who strongly supported President Harry S. Truman's Fair Deal domestic policies, especially his repeal of the Taft-Hartley Act. Passed in 1947 over Truman's veto, the Taft-Hartley measure reflected growing sentiment against labor unions and liberalism. It had outraged labor by outlawing the closed shop, in which only union members could be employed. It also prohibited union financial contributions to federal political races, obligated union leaders to sign non-Communist pledges, and authorized the president to call an eighty-day cooling-off period in strikes that endangered national security. By supporting repeal of Taft-Hartley, Coffey won the endorsement of the United Mine Workers (UMW), the American Federation of Labor (AFL), and the CIO.[5]

Saylor attempted to steer a middle course on labor issues. He defended labor's right to organize, bargain collectively, and strike; to his mind the Taft-Hartley Act provided an acceptable, if not perfect, set of guidelines. Work stoppages, he believed, should not be allowed to threaten the national economic interest, so he supported the provision granting the president injunctive powers to temporarily halt a strike. But he opposed the prohibition against the closed shop and considered the loyalty pledge meaningless because, he said, Communist union leaders would lie.[6]

Saylor was a tireless campaigner. Going door-to-door, he estimated that he visited with thirty thousand people, about one in five voters in the district. He worked at a frantic pace and often stopped at corner groceries for quick meals of kielbasa and raw hamburger. He loved people and excelled at recalling names and faces, his captivating personality and good humor an advantage. One of his House colleagues later recalled that Saylor possessed "a naturally grand manner that had a way of transforming even a simple greeting into a special occasion." And a Pennsylvania journalist declared that Saylor was "a guy who could charm a vote out of rock."[7]

In spite of a steady drizzle, about 110,000 of 155,000 registered voters, or 71 percent, visited the polls on September 13, helping Saylor defeat Coffey by nearly 8,500 votes, winning by large margins in Armstrong and Indiana counties and narrowly losing in Cambria County. Asked for her reaction to her husband's victory, Grace Saylor said that she was "thrilled to death for John. He worked so hard." The successful candidate seemed humbled by the "tremendous responsibility" that awaited him and pledged to do everything possible "to live up to the trust placed in me by the voters." He admitted to being exhausted and planned to relax with rod and reel before heading to Washington.[8]

With considerable exaggeration, the Saylor-for-Congress Committee called the win "one of the most pointed and significant political developments of the decade," producing a booklet demonstrating how it had been accomplished. Most important, the booklet advised, "the truth was told—and the truth shall keep you free." As the only off-year congressional contest, the election received considerable national attention, especially from Republicans. House minority leader Joseph Martin (R-MA) called Saylor's victory "a conclusive demonstration that the march toward state socialism can be stopped." The *Chicago Daily Tribune* gave a front-page headline to Saylor's win and the next day followed with an editorial about how the victory served as a repudiation of nearly two decades of "thinly veiled socialism." The *New York Herald Tribune, Baltimore Sun,* and other Republican newspapers also played up Saylor's victory.[9]

Although voters in western Pennsylvania had concerns about Taft-Hartley, big government, and the threat of Communism, other factors better explain Saylor's victory. He was an attractive, amiable, hardworking male candidate with a respectable war record, running in a district that was predominantly Republican. He also had the support of most district newspapers. His victory should not have been a surprise. A Johnstown newspaper reporter summed up the results accurately when he wrote a friend that "the national significance of John's victory was greatly over-emphasized. He did not win on national issues—his victory is just a tribute to his own personality, popularity and vigorous campaigning. It has been many years since such an effective campaigner has appeared on the local scene."[10]

Saylor was sworn in on September 28, 1949, only three weeks before the end of the first session of the Eighty-first Congress. The House chamber was under repair, so the ceremony took place in a nearby room with the congressman's wife, children, brother, sister, and friends looking on from a rear corner. The House of Representatives comprised 261 Democrats, 171 Republicans, and 1 American-Laborite (Vito Marcantonio of New York), with two positions vacant. Conservative Texas Democrat Sam Rayburn, whom Saylor would grow to revere for the discipline he imposed upon the proceedings, was the House Speaker. Joseph Martin of Massachusetts was the minority leader. Three of Saylor's colleagues—John F. Kennedy, Richard Nixon, and Gerald Ford—would become presidents. He was proud to be joining such an august political institution whose duty was public service.[11]

At the end of his first day in office, Saylor attended a dinner party given in his honor by Republican House leaders Joseph Martin of Massachusetts and Charles Halleck of Indiana. Guests included state GOP leaders, the Pennsylvania Republican congressional delegation, and other selected members of the House and Senate. Asked to say a few words, Saylor spoke forthrightly, earning himself a reputation for being blunt, prickly, and independent minded. He called party leaders a "bunch of snobs" who too often sought votes in board rooms instead of mines and factories. The party, he said, might take a lesson from his victory—namely, that to be successful GOP candidates needed to be more sensitive to the needs of ordinary workers and seek their votes aggressively. The audience took offense at the upstart's advice and gave him only a smattering of applause, Martin so incensed that he waited three weeks before giving Saylor a committee assignment. Saylor complained to the press that he was being given "the run around," but eventually he was appointed to the Committee on Public Lands.[12]

Normally, Grace Saylor might have been able to rein in her headstrong husband at a dinner party, but she had returned to Johnstown with son Phil, age eight, and daughter Susan, age two. Grace disliked Washington and politics and wanted to raise the children in Johnstown. "I married a lawyer, not a politician," she said. So John spent weekdays in Washington, where he lived in an apartment near the Hill, and drove four and a half hours to Johnstown each Friday, returning to Washington on Sunday. At first he drove himself, but eventually he had one of his assistants, Johnstown native William Lohr, chauffeur him. Back in Johnstown, Saylor often remained an absentee father. On Fridays he usually had a speech to deliver or a political function to attend, and on Saturdays he went to his congressional office at Ebensburg or Johnstown to make himself available to constituents. Sundays he usually spent with his family, at home and at church, returning to Washington in the evening.[13]

Saylor's staff included Ann Dunbar and Harry Fox. A Johnstown native and graduate of the University of Pittsburgh, Dunbar had served as a secretary in Saylor's law office; she remained his chief legislative assistant until her death in 1972. Harry Fox, an Armstrong County native who had served with Saylor on the *Missoula*, also remained with Saylor until the end. When Dunbar became terminally ill in the early 1970s, Richard Gentry would be added to the staff. Although eager to serve, Saylor had little opportunity to contribute initially, with only three weeks left before the recess. But he used his first vote, on the day he was sworn in, to oppose the Mutual Defense Assistance Bill, which sought a one-year appropriation of $1.5 billion in military aid for Europe and Korea.[14]

The second session of the Eighty-first Congress began on January 3, 1950, and continued for twelve months. The year was dominated by U.S. participation in an undeclared but United Nations–sanctioned police action against North Korea. That same summer Senator Joseph McCarthy, Republican of Wisconsin, ranted against Communists who had allegedly infiltrated the U.S. government and virtually every other area of American society.

Saylor too was concerned about the Communist threat abroad and at home. Like most Americans during the early Cold War, he believed that Communism was a Soviet-directed monolith that had bullied its way into Eastern Europe and China. He supported the Truman administration's effort to contain the "Red Menace" in Europe through the $12 billion Marshall Plan and the creation of a defensive military alliance, the North Atlantic Treaty Organization (NATO). But like hardliners from both parties, he bashed the Truman administration for losing China and making South Korea vulnerable to Communist aggression by pulling out U.S. forces in 1949. When war erupted in Korea in June 1950, Saylor blamed Truman for inviting the North Korean attack but supported the U.S. military's commitment to containing the spread of Communism.[15]

Much of Saylor's time was devoted to more domestic committee work. Republican minority leader Martin had assigned him to the Committee on Public Lands, a forerunner of the House Committee on Interior and Insular Affairs. Besides public lands, the committee dealt with legislation affecting territories; Native Americans; irrigation and reclamation; national parks and forests; and mines, mining, and natural resources. As a member of this committee, he worked to protect the economic concerns of Pennsylvania so long as they did not conflict with the national interest. In terms of tariff policy, he was a protectionist who opposed low tariffs because they tended to cost American laborers, especially union workers, their jobs. He spoke out against the importation of cheap foreign oil, especially residual fuel oil, because it competed with Pennsylvania-produced bituminous coal and its availability drove miners out of work. By harming the coal industry, Saylor claimed, the Truman administration was endangering national security.[16]

As a committee member, Saylor was known as a friend of the territories. He supported successful legislation that provided a civil government for Guam and another measure authorizing the residents of Puerto Rico to establish a written constitution. He also favored statehood for that Caribbean island if it was the will of the Puerto Rican people. He developed a close friendship with Joseph Farrington, the Hawaiian delegate to Congress, and championed statehood for that Pacific island and for Alaska. The House passed bills granting statehood to both Hawaii and Alaska, but the Senate resisted for nearly a decade. Still, statehood advocates in both territories knew they could always rely on Saylor to support their cause.[17]

Saylor seemed to delight in his job. His independence sometimes exasperated GOP House leaders, but he was popular with colleagues on both sides of the aisle. He proved a good sport by agreeing to become the catcher on the Republican congressional baseball team. When he made the commitment, newspapers quoted his son Phil as saying, "Gee, Dad, they must have been awfully hard up for players." Saylor was also fond of constituent service and mingling with voters. He especially enjoyed making appointments to military-service academies, and when other members of Congress did not use their allotments, he requested them. He took full advantage of the publicity that accompanied human-interest stories in his district, such as the ninety-two-year-old justice of the peace from South Fork who made the *Guinness Book of Records* by getting elected to another six-year term after fifty-three years of service.[18]

On a more serious note, coal miners in the district had gone on strike, and Saylor worked successfully to obtain potatoes, dried milk, and other surplus food for needy families from the U.S. Department of Agriculture. This gesture helped Saylor win favor with the UMW and later made him an advocate of the federal food stamp program. By the end of his first year in Congress, a local newspaper noted that he had done an excellent job of looking after the interests of the people of his district. He won reelection in 1950, defeating Lewis Evans, a former coal miner and labor organizer, by 6,300 votes.[19]

In 1951, as Saylor began his first full term, he had yet to find his way as a legislator or conservationist. He would do so as a member of the Public Lands Committee, renamed the House Interior Committee in February 1951. Saylor eventually became immersed in Western water issues and developed a reputation for being unfriendly toward federal reclamation and publicly financed hydroelectric dams. There were no national parks, national forests, wilderness, or federal lands in Pennsylvania, so Saylor, unlike Westerners on the committee, could resist the demands of grazing, mining, timber, and irrigation interests to vote his conscience on natural resource issues. His antagonistic attitude toward federal dam building initially derived from his fiscal conservatism, fear of big government, and solicitude for the Pennsylvania coal industry. The Rochester & Pittsburgh Coal Company, with its offices and mines in Indiana County, was a major employer in Saylor's district. Its mines, and those of smaller concerns in the district, produced coal for homes, blast furnaces, and electricity-generating stations in the East. Although little Pennsylvania coal went to markets in the West, Saylor, of political necessity, had to guard against public power projects that weakened the coal and utility industries in general. He insisted that federal reclamation projects be financially sound and serve the main purpose of irrigation. If the principle objective of federal dams was the production of public power, he opposed them. His hostility to big dams and public power dovetailed with his belief in the inviolability of the national park system.[20]

At midcentury, Saylor was concerned more with preserving the wonders of capitalism than with preserving the wonders of nature. He was particularly distressed by the Bureau of Reclamation's ravenous appetite for dam building and its expanding role within the Interior Department. During Franklin Roosevelt's presidency, the bureau's scrawny workforce of two thousand had bulked up to nearly twenty thousand. In the first three decades of the century, the bureau had spent about $9 million yearly erecting small dams in the arid West that impounded water mainly for the irrigation of family farms. But under Roosevelt's public works spending program during the Depression years, the bureau's annual expenditures climbed to $52 million, the central purpose of federal dam building shifting from reclamation (making arid lands arable) to the generation of public power. In the 1930s, the bureau constructed Hoover Dam on the Colorado River and secured congressional authorizations to build

Shasta Dam on the Sacramento River in California's Central Valley and Grand Coulee Dam on the Columbia River—all massive multipurpose facilities that could produce hydroelectricity; control floods; and provide water for domestic use, irrigation, and recreation. Moreover, the sale of power made them self-liquidating. The electricity produced on the Columbia River at Grand Coulee Dam and at the downstream Bonneville Dam, erected in 1938 by the Army Corps of Engineers, enabled the Pacific Northwest to become the center of the aircraft industry in World War II.[21]

There was a modest falloff in dam building during World War II, but planners at the Bureau of Reclamation and Army Corps of Engineers were not idle. To prevent Western streams from "wasting to sea," a popular expression in the early postwar years, they would treat river systems as a whole and plan for the comprehensive development and use of water resources. Large hydroelectric facilities, called "cash register dams" or "paying partners," would finance projects throughout an entire river basin: irrigation works no longer would have to pay for themselves. The revenues from hydroelectric dams in a river basin could also be used to help fund numerous watershed projects. The plan was attractive because it virtually compelled the bureau to build hydroelectric dams to fund reclamation works.[22]

Federal engineers devised plans for the maximum economic utilization of major Western river basins. After studying more than one hundred sites on the Colorado River, they determined that the most suitable locations for mighty hydroelectric dams were Bridge Canyon near Grand Canyon National Monument, Glen Canyon on the Utah-Arizona border, Flaming Gorge on the Wyoming-Utah line, and Echo Park on the Utah-Colorado boundary. The bureau and the Army Corps of Engineers also developed ambitious plans for the Columbia, Missouri, and Rio Grande river basins. To Saylor, these schemes were harbingers of socialism, and he became hostile toward the federal agencies that advanced them, particularly the Bureau of Reclamation and its leader, Michael Straus.[23]

A former journalist, Straus was a wealthy, liberal, idealistic, rumpled New Englander. After becoming the first nonengineer commissioner of the bureau in late 1945, he was driven by the goal of implementing the organization's river-basin development plans. During the war years, expenditures on reclamation totaled $330 million. Under Straus, during the height of the Cold War (1947–51), they reached $1.2 billion. But even more lavish projects were in the works. The bureau pushed its plan for the Bridge Canyon Dam on the lower Colorado

River and the Colorado River Storage Project, which called for the construction of ten dams, including Echo Park, Flaming Gorge, and Glen Canyon, on the upper main stem of the river and its tributaries. The bureau and the Army Corps of Engineers also worked jointly to develop the Columbia. The bureau had already constructed Grand Coulee, the largest power-producing dam in the world, and by 1951 had Hungry Horse and Palisades dams under construction. The Corps of Engineers had completed Bonneville and by the early 1950s had started work on six more dams. Additionally, the two agencies combined had received congressional authorization for a dozen other multipurpose projects throughout the river basin. But the government's craving for dam building on the Columbia had not been sated. Pronouncing the Columbia River basin "still relatively undeveloped," Interior Secretary Oscar Chapman and Straus sought legislative approval for the Hells Canyon project, the only piece of the comprehensive Columbia River development plan that had yet to gain congressional authorization.[24]

Coming from flood-prone Johnstown, Saylor saw a legitimate need for the Army Corps of Engineers to build dams to control floods and improve rivers for navigation. He also supported sound federal reclamation projects. But he opposed federally financed multipurpose projects such as Hoover Dam on the Colorado River and the Grand Coulee Dam on the Columbia River, which were designed mainly to produce electricity. The production of public power offended his faith in private enterprise. A newspaper reporter summarized his position as "Billions for Defense but Not One Cent for Public Power." Saylor would later oppose federal dam building because it plugged free-flowing rivers, endangered wilderness, and threatened the sanctity of national parks, but his initial objections were grounded upon fiscal and political conservatism and regional economic self-interest.[25]

Drafted by the Interior Department and introduced in October 1951 by Thomas Murdock (D-AZ), chairman of the House Committee on Interior and Insular Affairs, Hells Canyon was a gaudy project even by Bureau of Reclamation standards. It called for the construction of the tallest and third-largest dam in the world, behind Grand Coulee and Hoover. "The world's highest dam in the continent's deepest canyon," newspapers reported. Located on the Snake River near the Oregon border, the 742-foot-high dam would impound nearly 3.8 million acre-feet of water (an acre-foot totals 325,850 gallons) in a 90-mile reservoir between the cities of Lewiston and Weiser, Idaho. The facility would produce 1,124,000 kilowatts of electricity: 688,000 on site and another 436,000 at existing and authorized plants downstream. The sale of power over fifty years would cover nearly 90 percent of the $357 million cost. The remaining costs, mainly in the form of flood-control benefits, would be borne by taxpayers. The project would inundate Idaho Power and Light's proposed Oxbow facility 20 miles upriver and foil that private company's plan to build four additional hydroelectric dams.[26]

Almost immediately, Hells Canyon became an issue of public versus-private power development. Proponents of the project, mainly the Interior Department and New Deal Democrats, argued that only the massive federal facility could produce enough power to meet future defense and civilian needs. The Hells Canyon project would yield 1,124,000 kilowatts, compared to 530,000 kilowatts from private development, and thus save 600,000 kilowatts that otherwise "would be lost forever." The abundance of cheap electricity would attract the metallurgical industry and enable chemical companies to produce fertilizer from one of the nation's largest untapped phosphate beds. Unlike the private proposal, the federal project was multipurpose, improving navigation, providing flood control and recreation, and ultimately irrigating nearly 4 million acres. Proponents claimed that there would be no injury to fish and wildlife and expressed no concern about blocking a free-flowing river or flooding one of the nation's wildest and deepest canyons. "If the last frontier actually exists within the borders of the United States, it is the great trench carved by the Snake River," wrote Oregon state senator Richard Neuberger. Yet Neuberger advocated harnessing the "rapids and whirlpools" in order "to establish a new industrial empire between the Rockies and the Pacific Ocean." Despite claims of its being multipurpose, however, the project's overriding concern was the generation of power.[27]

When the bill came before the House Subcommittee on Irrigation and Reclamation, Saylor, who had already made up his mind, was ornery. Convinced that a bureau engineer was attempting to dodge a question, he said, "Can't you get it through your head that I don't like evasive answers?" He grilled Interior Secretary Chapman on aspects of irrigation and forced him to concede that the bill provided no irrigation benefits at all. Idaho lands would have to be irrigated by future projects, Chapman explained. Saylor and other Republican committee members pointed out that this was the first attempt by the Bureau of Reclamation to develop a project without any irrigation benefits.[28]

Opponents of the Hells Canyon project, such as Saylor and the Idaho congressional delegation, preferred private power development. Idaho Power and Light could build five low dams at no cost to taxpayers. Moreover, the private utility would pay taxes on its facilities. While the power yield would not be as copious as in the federal project, it would be sufficient to attract industry to Idaho. "Taxpaying" power companies even bought a full-page ad in the *Saturday Evening Post* to remind readers that private development would help thwart the advance of socialism: "Those who want a socialistic America know that when a government takes over electricity, it is a step toward the control of every business, farm and family." Small dams, too, would be less prone to attack by saboteurs and enemy bombers in the event the Korean conflict escalated into a global war, said Idaho governor Len Jordan. Within a decade, preservationists would also decry big dams because they gagged natural-flowing waterways. But in 1952, there were few champions of wild rivers, especially if they were located outside national parks. Governor Jordan had spent twenty years as a rancher along the Snake but seemingly had no sentiment toward preserving its natural course through the canyon. "Our goal in Idaho is to dry that river up at the Hells Canyon site," he declared to the committee, "to use it all over the land." John Saylor's preservationist ethic, too, had yet to be shaped.[29]

After nine days of hearings, testimony on the Hells Canyon project was indefinitely postponed when committee members realized that the bill had no chance of being reported favorably. It would resurface, however, in upcoming congresses, and Saylor would continue to oppose it.[30]

Although public power development was his major lament, Saylor had misgivings about the entire federal reclamation program. Enacted in 1902, the National Reclamation Act, sometimes called the Newlands Act, sought to promote family-sized farms of 160 acres in the seventeen states and territories of the arid West. The Interior Department then established the Reclamation Service, renamed the Reclamation Bureau, to construct and operate irrigation projects. Water users were to reimburse the government for construction costs, at no interest, in ten annual payments. Over decades, the law had been adjusted until by the early 1950s water users were permitted to take fifty years to meet this obligation.[31]

By 1950, the bureau had spent nearly $2 billion constructing 110 storage dams, 65 diversion dams, and more than 16,000 miles of channels that irrigated 5.6 million acres. Most Westerners considered federal reclamation essential to their region's economic development and hailed the program as a success. Residents from humid regions, especially fiscal conservatives, were less enthusiastic. Saylor had several concerns about the program. Too often, he complained, the public power tail wagged the reclamation dog. In theory, irrigation was supposed to be the bureau's main purpose, but in practice, especially after World War II, power generation had instead become its main objective. By 1950, bureau dams were producing 3.5 million kilowatts of electricity, a figure that would more than double with the completion of authorized plants. Increasingly, revenues from "cash register" dams were used to defray the costs of irrigation. In the Columbia River basin, for example, water users had to meet only 28 percent of costs because revenues from Grand Coulee hydropower paid the remainder. Shasta Dam provided similar benefits for farmers affected by the Central Valley project in California.[32]

Saylor also doubted that the program contributed to the nation's general economic welfare. Irrigated lands in the arid West often produced crops such as grains and cotton that were also grown in humid states, thus adding to an existing agricultural surplus. And federal hydroelectricity competed with privately produced fossil fuels as an energy source. Moreover, taxpayers had to pay the interest charges on irrigation construction costs, and with the repayment period extended from ten to fifty years, this feature of the program constituted a sizable federal subsidy. Then, too, the bureau had become a powerful, arrogant bureaucracy that too often proposed projects irrespective of their financial feasibility. Consequently, taxpayers became burdened with boondoggles—expensive, impractical, interest-free works whose costs might never be repaid.

Saylor's assault on the bureau led to his first encounters with Floyd Dominy. Born in Hastings, Nebraska, Dominy attended the University of Wyoming, where he majored in economics. He served in Wyoming as a county agent with the Department of Agriculture, became a Western field agent for the Agricultural Adjustment Administration, and then worked for the Inter-American Affairs Bureau during World War II. After the war, he took a job with the Bureau of Reclamation. He was hot tempered, hard drinking, profane, philandering, brash, and blunt. He was also bright, hardworking, ambitious, and advancing rapidly. Indeed, he had risen to the post of commissioner in only thirteen years.[33]

In 1952, as the bureau's assistant director, Dominy appeared before the House Subcommittee on Irrigation and Reclamation to renegotiate the contracts of three water districts in Montana that could not keep up with their payments. Water users of Frenchtown on the Clark Fork River in western Montana sought a ten-year extension on a forty-year contract that had been negotiated in 1935. Dominy pointed out that the district's soil was poor and that only 2,800 out of 4,800 acres could be irrigated. "I want to know when the

Bureau came to this phenomenal viewpoint," Saylor interjected, "that you can get into a situation that their schedules are beyond the ability of the people to pay, under the highest market prices in our nation's history, because if it is true in this case, in this small instance, what is it going to be like when we get to some of the big ones?" Dominy reminded Saylor that section 7 of the Reclamation Law of 1939 permitted the secretary of the interior, with the consent of Congress, to renegotiate contracts based upon the users' ability to pay. He also pointed out that even if the water users defaulted, the product would continue to be delivered.

This paternalistic and fiscally lax policy incensed Saylor. He informed the committee that he had requested from Interior Secretary Chapman "a complete list of every project that the Bureau of Reclamation has had since its inception, down to date. I am satisfied in my own mind that all is not well in the Bureau of Reclamation, and I do not believe that the members of this committee and the Members of Congress are in a position to deal properly with this matter piecemeal." The bureau, he charged, deliberately recommended unsound projects "as a means of building up a bureaucracy down there which is probably the most vicious in Washington."[34]

Dominy also rewrote the contract terms for the Malta and Glascow districts on the Milk River in northeastern Montana. The state's Republican congressman, Wesley D'Ewart, conceded that the project had been ill considered. If there were errors that were not made, he said, "I don't recollect what they were." The heavy clay soil was not water absorbent, and about the only crop that could be grown was bluestem hay, which had little market value. The impoundment dam was located near the Canadian border, and in winter the irrigation pipe froze, thus delaying the flow of water to the lands 400 miles downstream. To offer district farmers a longer growing season, the bureau had built another reservoir farther downstream, but this in turn increased the amount of indebtedness. "Was the project designed when they had engineers at the head of it or when they had newspapermen at the head of the Bureau?" Saylor inquired.

Ignoring the jab at his boss, Dominy informed the subcommittee that the project was begun in 1903 as one of the earliest reclamation efforts. In its formative years, he explained, the bureau's policy was to establish a project in every Western state. Asked what proportion of these early developments had been successful, Dominy estimated about half: the projects in high-altitude states were less successful because of poorer soil and shorter growing seasons.

But he refused to admit to any failures. As a son of the West, he averred that Congress had not wasted money in any instance. To be sure, some projects could have been "more prudent and better administered," but every development had been worthwhile.[35]

Saylor was incredulous. Water users in both districts had been making payments for four decades. Now Dominy proposed extending the contracts by 106 years for one district and 116 years for the other. Saylor wondered how this could not be viewed as a bad investment, especially when taxpayers would have to pay interest charges over all these years. Dominy reiterated the point that reclamation had helped settle the West and produced indirect benefits such as development of the railroads. Westerners also bought Eastern-manufactured products. He reminded the committee that in recent projects the sale of power was subsidizing the cost of irrigation. Saylor was hardly comforted by this reminder, as he wanted to reform the system, but for the present he reluctantly joined his subcommittee colleagues in unanimously recommending renegotiation of the contracts.[36]

One of the most ambitious reclamation proposals of the early 1950s was the Central Arizona Project (CAP). Its House sponsor, Arizona Democrat Thomas Murdock, considered the CAP bill "so vital to the State of Arizona" that he felt compelled to "put all the energy and influence that I possess into its enactment." Its overriding objective was to provide irrigation for a large swath of farmland in the Salt River valley near Phoenix. Arizona's capital and most populous city had nearly doubled in size, its population reaching 106,000 in the 1940s. But except for Phoenix and Tucson, which had grown from 36,000 people to 45,000 during the same decade, Arizona was essentially an agricultural state. Using mainly underground water, farmers in the corridor had placed approximately 700,000 acres under irrigation by 1950, but the subterranean resource had been nearly "mined out," and Arizonans wanted to replenish it with a plentiful and perpetual supply from the Colorado River, more than 200 miles away. Arizona's designs on the Colorado worried Californians because the city of Los Angeles, with a population of 1.2 million in 1950, wanted all the water the river could produce. The massive project also alarmed Saylor.[37]

Planned by the Bureau of Reclamation, the CAP called for the construction of an open concrete aqueduct that would carry 1.2 million acre-feet of water annually to Phoenix-area farmers. Lake Havasu, the reservoir at existing

Parker Dam on the Colorado, would supply the water, which four giant turbines would lift 985 feet to an aqueduct; it would then flow 241 miles downhill to Phoenix. The turbines would be powered by hydroelectricity from a newly constructed high dam at Bridge Canyon near Grand Canyon National Monument, about 270 miles upriver from Parker Dam. The Bridge Canyon Dam was the centerpiece of the CAP because it could provide both energy and cash. It would produce 4.6 billion kilowatts of electricity yearly (more than Hoover Dam), one-third of which would be used to power the Havasu pumping plants. The remainder would be sold commercially to pay off all but a small portion of the $788 million cost in seventy-five years.[38]

At first glance, the CAP's prospects appeared promising. The dam would inundate a majestic canyon and create a reservoir that might intrude upon Grand Canyon National Monument, but most conservationists did not appear overly concerned. Indeed, the Sierra Club, then a modest regional organization of five thousand members, initially endorsed the CAP. The U.S. Senate had already approved a bill that was nearly identical to the House version, and Thomas Murdock chaired the House Committee on Interior and Insular Affairs, where the bill was sent for hearings. But Saylor recoiled at the measure's expense and taxpayer-subsidized public power, and Californians, including three on the committee, objected to Arizona's attempt to use Colorado River water that might benefit their state.[39]

Given rising construction costs and the bureau's spotty record on project estimates, Saylor predicted that the CAP would probably cost three times the projected $788 million. He also questioned its irrigation benefits. When pressed, bureau officials admitted that virtually no new lands would be irrigated; the project would simply replace central Arizona's nearly depleted existing water supply. Bureau witnesses also conceded that thousands of lush acres would not turn to dust if the project was not approved. Saylor also questioned the necessity of Bridge Canyon Dam. Couldn't other sources of energy—coal, fuel oil, natural gas, atomic reactors—power the Havasu turbines? Proponents countered that other forms of energy might be able to spin the turbines, but they could not whirl the cash registers. Bridge Canyon Dam was necessary to fund the project.

But Saylor could not be persuaded. Even if the power could be purchased by Arizona industry, would that not then attract more people, who would place additional strains on the water supply, thus prompting more requests for reclamation projects? Perturbed by Saylor's skepticism, Arizonans pointed out that the state of Pennsylvania benefited from taxpayer-subsidized flood-control projects, while Western water users had to reimburse the government for reclamation developments. Provoked, Saylor revealed that over the past two years, Pennsylvanians had paid $6.4 billion in federal taxes, while Arizonans had contributed less than $500 million. Moreover, the CAP would cost more than all the money Arizona had paid in federal taxes since it had become a state. If a double standard existed, Westerners should change the law.[40]

The objections of fiscal conservatives were hurdles enough, but CAP proponents also had to surmount obstacles put up by Californians. The states of California and Arizona had been arguing over the division of Colorado River water for thirty years. Unless that squabble was settled, California committee members Clair Engle and Sam Yorty, both Democrats, and Norris Poulson, a Republican, were not about to consent to any plan that might deprive their state of water.

Delegates from the seven states forming the Colorado River system had attempted to craft a water-apportionment plan at Santa Fe, New Mexico, in 1922, arbitrarily partitioning the stream into two basins at Lee's Ferry, Arizona. The upper basin included Colorado, New Mexico, Utah, and Wyoming, while the lower basin consisted of Arizona, California, and Nevada. The Bureau of Reclamation had estimated the annual flow at 17.5 million acre-feet, so the delegates distributed 7.5 million acre-feet to each basin and 1.5 million acre-feet to Mexico, with the extra, if any, going to lower basin states. Besides losing out on leftover water, upper basin states would have to make sure that 75 million acre-feet of flow reached the lower basin every ten years. The legislatures of six basin states ratified the Colorado River Compact, but Arizona balked. Fearful that the more populous and economically mature California would utilize most of the water, Arizona insisted upon dividing the lower basin entitlement before ratifying the compact.[41]

But Arizona's defiant stance did not deter California's efforts to harness the river. In 1928, Congress authorized the building of Boulder Dam on the Colorado River near Las Vegas. Later renamed Hoover Dam, the facility, once completed in 1935, provided power for Nevada and Los Angeles; protected southern California from devastating floods; and created a large reservoir, Lake Mead, which served as a recreational wonderland. The legislation also called for the construction of the All-American Canal, finished in 1942, which carried water from Hoover Dam to the Imperial Valley of California. And as a way of settling the dispute between Arizona and California, it suggested apportioning the water of the lower basin, California receiving 4.4 million acre-feet, Arizona 2.8 million, and Nevada 300,000. Arizona went to the Supreme Court, arguing that the project could not be undertaken until it had approved the Colorado River Compact, but it lost.[42]

With its surging population and booming economy, California continued to press for more water. In 1941, the Bureau of Reclamation constructed Parker Dam, 155 miles downstream from the larger Hoover facility, which produced electricity and created a reservoir, Lake Havasu, that would supply Los Angeles with water from a 242-mile-long Colorado River aqueduct. The $220 million project was financed by Los Angeles and twelve other cities comprising the Metropolitan Water District of California.[43]

Not wishing to be left behind, Arizona approved the Colorado River Compact in 1944 and entered into a contract with the secretary of the interior to utilize 2.8 million acre-feet of Colorado River water. Almost half its allotment would be used for the CAP, its counterpart to the Hoover and Parker dams. But there was a problem of supply. Reclamation officials had badly overestimated the stream's annual flow, and it was doubtful if there was enough water to satisfy the demands of both states. So in the committee hearings, Engle, Yorty, and Poulson all criticized the Arizona project as unnecessary and economically extravagant. Chairman Murdock used a folksy analogy in an attempt to portray California's position as unreasonable and illogical, asking the committee to imagine that he and his "close friend and neighbor" Clair Engle had each deposited $1,000 in the same bank. Imagine further, he said, that Murdock had announced to the committee that he was going to the bank to withdraw his money. Would it make sense for Engle to yell: "No, you don't. Do not touch it. It is my money"?[44]

Saylor and other critics of the CAP held that even if the "accounts" of both parties could be verified, the "bank" might not have the wherewithal to meet both obligations. Most committee members were not persuaded by assurances from the Bureau of Reclamation that the Colorado would provide at least 7.5 million acre-feet for both basins and another 1.5 million acre-feet for Mexico. "The Bureau goes into a district or an area and draws down figures to prove what they want, without actually taking the facts," Saylor scolded.[45]

After nineteen days of hearings, it was clear that the CAP had no chance of being reported favorably. Saylor introduced a motion to adjourn the hearings until the Supreme Court or the two states themselves had apportioned the waters of the lower river. Arizona governor Howard Pyle accused Saylor and other supporters of adjournment of caving in to California's political clout, but the motion carried handily. Arizonans would long resent Saylor's opposition to their pet project. In 1953, the Supreme Court decided to hear the case of *Arizona v. California,* but it waited eleven years to hand down a ruling. With the water rights issue eventually settled in its favor, Arizona again sought congressional authorization for the CAP. But by the mid-1960s, the wilderness movement had blossomed, and preservationists, with Saylor at the forefront, protested the construction of Bridge Canyon Dam because it threatened to violate Grand Canyon National Monument.[46]

Back in Pennsylvania, few of Saylor's constituents took an interest in Western water problems. They were concerned, quite naturally, with issues that directly affected them. Fortunately for Saylor, organized labor was generally satisfied with his performance. In 1952, he supported a successful mine-safety bill that permitted federal inspectors to shut down mines they deemed unsafe. He also pleased unions when he denounced President Truman's executive order authorizing the federal government's seizure of mills during a steel strike. Like most conservatives, and many liberals, Saylor was horrified by what he regarded as an unconstitutional act by an imperious president. "I do not fear a steel strike nearly as much—even under present world conditions—as I do government seizure," he told a reporter. Truman eventually helped forge an agreement between management and labor that ended the seven-week strike, and Saylor was relieved over the outcome, but the steel takeover reinforced his belief that Democrats had to be ousted from power to avoid the onset of a socialistic government like that of Great Britain.[47]

Like most Republican candidates in 1952, Saylor hammered Truman for Korea and hammered Democrats in general for being war-prone and soft on Communism. Indeed, he capitalized on the anti-Communist hysteria gripping the nation. When Republican vice-presidential candidate Richard Nixon was accused of benefiting from an illegal slush fund, Saylor defended him: "The people who would like to get Dick Nixon are the same people who tried to get him to lay off Alger Hiss, the Communist." The threat of internal subversion, he cautioned, "is a clear-cut issue in this campaign, and Nixon is responsible for putting Hiss behind bars. Don't forget that Stevenson was one of those who testified what a sterling character Alger Hiss was."[48]

When Republican presidential candidate Dwight Eisenhower visited Johnstown, Saylor was pictured on the front page of the city's newspapers campaigning with him. Saylor was delighted with his party's platform, especially its opposition to the further establishment of "all-powerful Federal socialistic valley authorities." Endorsed by most newspapers and labor unions, Saylor won reelection comfortably, capturing more votes in the district than Eisenhower. The election of 1952 was a romp for Republicans, who won the White House and both houses of Congress. Saylor looked forward to working with the new president and the Republican-dominated Congress to decentralize government, devolve power back to the states, slow federal reclamation projects, and enhance opportunities for private enterprise. And with his district growing increasingly distressed, he would concentrate his efforts in the next Congress on improving the economic prospects of western Pennsylvania.[49]

three

Maverick Republican

JOHN SAYLOR wanted to celebrate his mother's seventy-ninth birthday with his colleagues on the House Interior and Insular Affairs Committee. He ordered platters of ham and turkey and an assortment of liquor and approached newly appointed Republican committee chair A. L. Miller about holding the event in the House Interior Committee meeting room. A teetotaling physician from Nebraska, Miller agreed to the request so long as no liquor was served. "Doctor, what is a party without a highball?" Saylor inquired.

Determined to proceed, Saylor sent out the invitations. Miller became incensed at Saylor's defiance and sought guidance from Republican House speaker Joseph Martin. Even though alcohol was commonly served at social functions in federal buildings, Martin supported the liquor ban, perhaps because he too was a nondrinker. Miller sent a letter to Saylor reminding him of their earlier conversation: "I am assuming you are using the room for a social get-together minus hard liquor. If such is not the case, you do not have my permission to use the committee room. If the room is used in violation of this letter, I would expect to take the case to the floor of the House for an airing. The resulting publicity could cut two ways." Saylor decided to call off the party but thereafter held "no-cocktail Miller" in disdain. Indeed, he was often at odds with party leaders, including Martin and President Eisenhower, especially on economic and natural resource policy. And when it came to issues affecting his district and federal reclamation projects, Saylor was not as quick to back down as he was with the cocktail party.[1]

In his personal habits, Saylor was a moderate drinker. He usually had a cocktail before dinner and sometimes wine with his meal. He drank socially and was indifferent about whether he consumed beer or mixed drinks, rarely if ever overindulging. His children do not recall ever seeing him intoxicated and point out that he always gave up alcohol during Lent.[2]

Saylor was less disciplined about eating. He enjoyed preparing and consuming food and often cooked for his staff, dinner guests at his home, or companions at the hunting camp in Potter County. And he seldom scrimped on quantity and portions. A nondiscriminating and robust eater, he eventually bulked up to nearly 250 pounds. He never smoked, but his excess weight and poor nutrition may have contributed to the heart disease that plagued him in his later years. Except for brief visits to emergency rooms following minor traffic accidents and a weeklong hospital stay for an appendectomy, he enjoyed robust health prior to the onset of heart disease.[3]

Saylor's husky physique and booming voice made him an imposing and at times intimidating figure. "He was a large man, with a large voice, and he liked to use it," recalled House Interior staff member Pat Murray. For some associates, his image sprang to mind when the radio carried the popular 1950s Jimmy Dean hit "Big John." Saylor was never called "Jack," always "John," "Big John," or later "Uncle John" and "St. John" by conservationists. When he became angry, he could grow caustic and explode in a torrent of swearing. But even when he was not agitated, he swore casually. "Hello, you little bastard," he would address Representative John Dingell of Michigan. "Hello, you big bastard," Dingell would respond. At one point, Saylor became so disgusted by his own habit that he decided to fine himself ten cents each time he cursed at work. Would he still be effective? a reporter wondered. "You'd be surprised," he responded, "how emphatically I can express myself without using a single cuss word." In spite of Saylor's disclaimer, however, the experiment proved inhibiting and was soon abandoned.[4]

When vexed, Saylor could be "prickly" and a "crusty old son-of-a bitch," but generally he was even tempered and quick to laugh. He was a captivating storyteller, his affability, ebullience, frankness, and sense of humor making him popular on both sides of the aisle. Indeed, one of his closest associates was Democrat Dingell.[5]

Perhaps because he had such high regard for his mother, sister, and wife, Saylor was always courteous toward women. He was polite without being patronizing, recalled one female acquaintance. A female constituent noted that he "is a gentleman. He is not arrogant nor insulting toward women." Saylor appreciated female intellect and beauty, but Grace was the one love of his life, and there is no evidence that he ever dishonored his wedding vows.[6]

Saylor had few hobbies. Like most Pennsylvanians, he got caught up in the excitement when the Philadelphia Phillies "Whiz Kids" edged out the Brooklyn Dodgers in the final game of the 1950 season to capture the pennant. And he inserted tributes in the *Congressional Record* to western Pennsylvania athletes such as the baseball star Stan Musial. But Saylor was not a dedicated baseball or football fan, nor did he participate in many sports. He joined the Johnstown country club, but he did not golf or play tennis.[7]

When his hectic schedule permitted, he liked to hike, fish, and hunt. He carried his fishing gear in his car and held licenses in several states. He prized landing a twenty-five-inch, nine-pound, nine-ounce black bass that he took with a fly rod on the St. John River in Florida's Ocala National Forest. He and Dingell occasionally escaped to the Eastern shore to hunt birds. Saylor also made periodic excursions to the hunting camp in Potter County, although he cooked and socialized at "Lost Cabin" more than he hunted. When he did take to the woods, he almost always reported seeing prey, but his companions do not recall that he ever returned with game—only stories.[8]

For relaxation, he played bridge, poker, and canasta, the rage of the 1950s. His taste in literature turned to light reading—outdoor and nature magazines —rather than books. He relished stories about the American frontier experience and appreciated Western art, particularly works by Charles Russell and Frederic Remington. His romantic (and debatable) view that the frontier served as the forge of American individualism and democracy no doubt contributed to his advocacy of wilderness protection. He developed a close association with the leaders of what were then relatively insignificant conservation organizations— the National Parks Association, the National Wildlife Federation, the Izaak Walton League, the Audubon Society, the Sierra Club, and the Wilderness Society—making himself available to their officials and reading their magazines and newsletters.[9]

When the House was not in session, Saylor tended the flower garden at his home at 411 Orchard Street in Johnstown. Sometimes he was mistaken for the gardener, visitors driving by and asking if the congressman was at home. Saylor would direct them to the entrance and delight in their reaction when he greeted them at the door in his gardening clothes.[10]

He also enjoyed traveling. In the summer, he frequently drove his family cross-country to visit national parks. At Grace's insistence, however, lodging consisted of motels instead of tents. Saylor's spirit of adventure also lured him to far-flung destinations such as Hawaii, Alaska, Guam, Samoa, Vietnam, and Antarctica. As an officer with the Naval Reserves, he visited both the North and South Poles, the first member of Congress to do so.[11]

Like most politicians, Saylor thrived on attention and publicity. Photo opportunities included poses with President Eisenhower, Senator Joseph McCarthy (before his downfall), and a variety of other national and local notables. Press photos featured him in parka and mukluks behind a dogsled, in a baseball uniform, and in mining garb. Democratic Representative D. R. "Billy" Matthews of Florida envied Saylor's penchant for publicity: "If I could get my pictures in the papers of the 8th Congressional District of Florida one half as often as you get yours in all of the great periodicals throughout the country, I would never be worried again about any opponent."[12]

But Saylor's trips did not always gain favorable publicity. A Pennsylvania journalist, for example, could not understand how a visit to Antarctica could possibly benefit the district. Angry enough "to spit tacks," Minerva Saylor urged her son to ignore the criticism and "don't mention [the] South Pole unless asked about it. I can still play politics even at [age] 83. So just ignore it and keep making friends."[13]

With his penchant for publicity, Saylor made certain that he capitalized on surviving gunshots. As the House deliberated a farm bill in early March 1953, three Puerto Rican nationalists from the visitors' gallery opened fire on the members below. Saylor escaped unscathed, but five of his colleagues were wounded. He agreed to write a firsthand account of the attack for the *Johnstown Tribune-Democrat* and provided verbal renditions for several other district newspapers, describing the assault as his most frightening peacetime experience and demanding swift justice for the perpetrators. The 231 members who were on the House floor were fortunate, he said, that the attackers were not armed with hand grenades. On a lighter note, Saylor expressed regret that the incident forced the cancellation of a White House party because it was his wife's first visit to Washington that term.[14]

Politics served as Saylor's vocation and principle avocation. He had a knack for remembering people's names and seemed to savor conversations with constituents. Appearances at county fairs, school commencements, building dedications, patriotic celebrations, and political rallies seemed to energize rather than exhaust him. His thunderous voice, hearty laugh, and storytelling ability made him a popular speaker, and he seemed to delight in providing constituents service, whether helping an individual deal with federal bureaucracy, nominating a young man to one of the service academies, securing federal funds for a highway, or obtaining trout from the Interior Department's Fish and Wildlife Service for stocking Pennsylvania streams. And no constituent request seemed trivial: he told the story of a woman who, late one evening, telephoned her representative at home to complain about an odorous dead cat in an alley. The representative expressed sympathy and advised her to telephone the Department of Sanitation in the morning. "Oh, I would never think of bothering them with something so trivial," she responded.[15]

He was also adept at convincing his constituents that they were his top priority. He declined an invitation to socialize with the president and party chieftains in Gettysburg, a district newspaper reported, because he had made a commitment to speak in Johnstown. This may have been true, but it should be noted that the 1954 congressional election was only a week away, and Saylor had grown exasperated with Eisenhower on the issues of taxes, tariffs, and federal reclamation. At any rate, the *Johnstown Tribune Democrat* portrayed him "as one of the most independent, hardest-working and ablest members of the House of Representatives of whom any district would be proud."[16]

Saylor looked forward to Republican rule, but the Eisenhower administration, in many ways, disappointed him. In 1954, for example, Eisenhower's advisers recommended a revision in the general tax code. The administration bill gave businesses greater latitude in claiming depreciation costs and slashed the tax on stock dividends. It also made it easier for individuals to take deductions for medical treatment, child care, and charitable contributions.[17]

Sounding like a Democrat, Saylor claimed that the administration bill did more for corporations than it did for ordinary working people. He preferred to reform the tax code by increasing the personal exemption from $600 to $1,500, plus $1,000 for each dependent. It was time, he said, for Congress to show wage earners that "'of the people, by the people, for the people'" was "taking precedence over the phrase 'from the people' which has become a truism in years past." He pushed his bill personally with Eisenhower but had no success. Realizing that without the president's support his own bill stood little chance for approval, Saylor came out in support of a Democratic proposal that raised the personal exemption from $600 to $700. Eisenhower went on television to oppose this modest proposal as a budget breaker, and Republican House leaders pushed hard for party unity on the administration bill. To support the Democrats' substitute, they declared, would constitute a "vote against Ike." Saylor was unconvinced, becoming one of only ten Republicans to support the Democratic proposal, which failed by a vote of 210 to 204. While Saylor's vote was unpopular among party chieftains, it pleased his constituents and enhanced his reputation as an independent-minded congressman dedicated to the interests of miners, steelworkers, and other ordinary working people.[18]

Saylor also proved antagonistic toward Eisenhower's foreign economic policy because its approach too closely resembled that of the New and Fair Deals. In terms of foreign aid and tariffs, Saylor generally adhered to traditional Republican doctrine. He grudgingly supported the 1954 $4.5 billion foreign aid bill, mainly because much of the assistance went to help the French fight Communism in Indochina, but he reversed himself the following year because U.S. taxpayers needed relief. Besides, he noted, U.S. generosity was shoring up the European coal industry and permitting foreign operators to undersell Pennsylvania producers. He regretted the fact that the Marshall Plan of 1948 had not required aid recipients to purchase a certain amount of American-produced coal.[19]

Eisenhower's advocacy of lower tariffs, Saylor insisted, was another departure from traditional Republican economic policy. Eisenhower, like most internationalists, believed that freer trade fostered prosperity and world peace. When the president in 1953 asked for a one-year extension of the Reciprocal Trade Agreements Act, protectionists like Saylor proved unreceptive, believing that over the years lenient trade policies had damaged industries in their districts. Saylor contended that the coal industry had been devastated by the importation of cheap residual fuel oil, mainly from Venezuela. Pennsylvania miners who dug the coal and railroaders who transported it had been thrown out of work because power stations increasingly were being fueled by cheap foreign oil. He called for a quota, claiming that "we do not need foreign residual oil in this country. Not a drop of it. We have coal to supply the energy requirements of our industries."[20]

While Saylor was more conservative than Eisenhower on tax and tariff matters, he was slightly more liberal than the president and House leaders on social issues. Representing a working-class district, Saylor generally aligned himself with liberal Democrats in his support for public housing, increased pay for postal workers, Social Security expansion, and civil rights. Unlike Eisenhower, he heartily supported the 1954 Supreme Court decision in *Brown v. Board of Education*, which declared segregated public schools unconstitutional. He also favored a court decision mandating the desegregation of public housing and held in contempt those members of Congress, mainly from the South, who used color as a reason to deny statehood to Alaska and Hawaii.[21]

In a decade of conformity, consensus, and intense patriotism, Saylor, following a recommendation from the president, introduced successful legislation inserting the words "under God" into the pledge of allegiance. The inclusion of that phrase, he declared, "will reaffirm the principle that this great nation was created and preserved under God." He also favored the establishment of a prayer room in the capitol building and the printing of "In God We Trust" on currency and postage stamps.[22]

Saylor was generally weak in defense of civil liberties. He approved the continuation of programs first implemented by Truman to remove alleged subversives from government offices, especially the State Department. Like Eisenhower, he refused to publicly denounce Senator Joseph McCarthy's scattershot charges of disloyalty, which endangered civil liberties, destroyed reputations, and created a climate of fear. In May 1954, shortly after McCarthy had demonstrated his viciousness and recklessness in the televised Army hearings, Saylor gave a speech in his district saying: "Let us not be afraid to speak of whatever we wish without having someone who disagrees with us call us names." In another address, he said that "no one disagrees with Senator McCarthy's ends, which are to get rid of communists in government, but rather people disagree [on] how he goes about it. No one should hide behind the Fifth Amendment for immunity—especially if they are in government service."[23]

But Saylor exacerbated the canker of McCarthyism when he parroted the senator's charges that the lenient and economically injurious trade policies of the 1930s and 1940s had resulted from treachery in the State Department. "The planned deterioration of American industry and American wage standards began when carefully-placed individuals in important positions in the State Department succeeded in making those offices a veritable infiltration plant for Soviet intrigue," he declared. "A horde of State Department dandies—looking like adult Lord Fauntleroys bound for an international cotillion—would hopscotch from one conference to another searching for representatives of other countries ready and willing to accept handouts . . . in the form of trade concessions." Like McCarthy's, Saylor's charges were unsubstantiated and ridiculous.[24]

At the request of a religiously affiliated athletic organization, Saylor invited McCarthy to be the keynote speaker on Catholic Day in Johnstown. A local Democratic newspaper wondered why the congressman would want to identify himself with such a mean-spirited figure, a local Republican insisting that McCarthy's presence would bring the party into further disrepute, but Saylor pressed ahead. He kept his introductory remarks brief, emphasizing McCarthy's popularity as a speaker to the crowd of fifteen thousand at Ideal Park. McCarthy spoke to the charge that he had used unsavory methods in searching out Communists. "You can't hunt skunks with top hats and lace handkerchiefs," he declared. "I have yet to hear one person say that we should not hunt out Communists." Three months later in December, the Senate completed its investigation of McCarthy by condemning his cruel and reckless tactics. Discredited, McCarthy became a tragic figure and died three years later.[25]

Initially, Saylor was enthusiastic about the Eisenhower administration's stance on resource and power development. In his first State of the Union address in February 1953, Eisenhower advanced a partnership approach toward resource development. "The best natural resources program for America," he asserted, "will not result from exclusive dependence on Federal bureaucracy. It will involve a partnership of the States and the local communities, private citizens, and the Federal Government, all working together. This combined effort will advance the development of the great river valleys of the nation and the power they can produce."[26]

To manage the program, Eisenhower appointed Douglas McKay secretary of the interior. A conservative Republican, McKay had been a car salesman, mayor, and two-term governor of Oregon. His supporters, including Saylor at first, believed that he would downsize the department, chop spending, curtail the reclamation program, and encourage private and local participation in resource development. Detractors, such as independent Republican senator Wayne Morse of Oregon, feared that McKay would be a stooge of special interests.[27]

Eisenhower also planned to name Assistant Commissioner Goodrich Lineweaver to succeed Michael Straus as head of the Bureau of Reclamation. Saylor considered Lineweaver "more dangerous to our country than his predecessor" and vehemently opposed the change. He provided evidence, probably supplied by Floyd Dominy, assistant director of the bureau, demonstrating Lineweaver's "unfitness" for the office. In 1951 and 1952, Dominy had prepared memoranda admitting that in the past the bureau had undertaken some ill-advised projects. Those "honest mistakes," Dominy asserted, should not be compounded by trying to rescue failed irrigation projects, such as Riverton in Wyoming and Heart River in North Dakota. To Dominy's and Saylor's dismay, Lineweaver allegedly responded to the memoranda by expunging them from the files and pushing ahead with the projects. Their protests, however, were enough to block Lineweaver's chances, and the appointment went to Wilbur Dexheimer, a native Coloradan and career bureau engineer who would serve until 1959, when he was replaced by Dominy.[28]

Initially, Saylor was pleased with the performance of McKay and Dexheimer. In his first year in office, McKay slashed the department's work force by 10 percent, claiming that some of the casualties were "screwballs," a term used by McKay to identify alleged subversives. In a wartime economy move, Truman had already downsized the Reclamation Bureau from twenty thousand to seventeen thousand employees. McKay made additional cuts that left the agency with thirteen thousand workers. In addition, Congress continued its policy of paring the bureau's budget, which had been shrunk from $364 million to $165 million between 1950 and 1955. The Budget Bureau also issued Circular A-47, which advised all federal agencies to use restraint in the pursuit of water and power projects. Moreover, in 1953 Congress created a special task force, chaired by ex-president Herbert Hoover, to review federal resource policy. Not surprisingly, perhaps, its report called for minimal federal involvement in reclamation and power projects.[29]

As he had promised during the campaign, Eisenhower, early in his first term, urged congressional leaders to enact legislation transferring to the individual states ownership of the offshore lands within their "historic boundaries." Often referred to as the tidelands, these submerged lands were rich in resources, particularly oil. In the so-called tidelands decision of 1947, the Supreme Court had established federal title to submerged lands on the outer continental shelf but remained vague on the rights to lands within three miles of the seashore. In 1952, Congress had enacted legislation granting ownership of these submerged lands within a three-mile limit to the states, but Truman vetoed it. In the spring of 1953, the Eighty-third Congress again took up the issue. Some legislators, especially those from noncoastal states, denounced the bill as a raid on a national resource; others argued that state historic boundaries extended beyond the three-mile limit. Saylor, for example, claimed that the Treaty of Paris ending the Revolutionary War in 1783 had established the offshore boundaries of the thirteen original states at twenty leagues, or more than sixty miles. Congress decided to enact two separate bills. One granted state title to submerged lands three miles offshore (ten and a half miles in the cases of Texas and Louisiana), and the other recognized federal ownership of submerged lands beyond state historic boundaries. Saylor supported both measures.[30]

The administration also announced two policy decisions that enraged advocates of public power. In 1953, McKay withdrew the Interior Department's objections to private power development on the Snake River at Hells Canyon. The year before, Secretary Chapman had thwarted the attempt by Idaho Power and Light to obtain a license to build three small hydroelectric dams by informing the Federal Power Commission of the Reclamation Bureau's plan to build a single high dam. McKay's decision, however, now removed a major obstacle to private development. The following year, Eisenhower erected another hurdle in the path of "creeping socialism" by instructing the Atomic Energy Commission to deal with a private concern, Dixon-Yates, instead of the Tennessee Valley Authority, to provide energy for the city of Memphis. Opponents denounced the Dixon-Yates, Hells Canyon, and tidelands decisions as "giveaways," tagging McKay with the title "Giveaway McKay." Saylor had supported McKay's moves but soon became disenchanted because decentralization had not gone far enough. He wanted the federal government to step in when it came to protecting domestic industries in his district from foreign competitors but to step aside when it came to the development of water resources. The irony of this position seems to have escaped him.[31]

Early in his presidency, Eisenhower had cautioned that some development projects were too massive for companies, communities, or states to undertake. One of those projects was the St. Lawrence Seaway. The seaway scheme had been in the plans of engineers and politicians for decades. The United States and Canada would jointly finance the construction of a twenty-seven-foot-deep channel along the St. Lawrence River to permit ship traffic from the Atlantic Ocean to the Great Lakes. Representatives from Eastern states had heretofore blocked legislation creating the seaway because they believed it would take traffic away from their ports and railroads. By 1953, however, three factors made the project more palatable to U.S. legislators. First, iron ore supplies in the Great Lakes had been nearly depleted. Second, new ore nests had been discovered in Labrador that could feed Canadian and Midwestern U.S. steel plants. And third, Canada had threatened to proceed unilaterally. Thus, in April 1953, Eisenhower came out in favor of the $105 million project, pushing hard for its approval as a matter of national security.[32]

Saylor vigorously opposed the seaway because it would bring further injury to the already distressed economy of his district, facilitating the importation of cheap foreign oil and thus posing "a direct and serious threat to the security and well-being of the bituminous coal industry." He was not persuaded by Eisenhower's argument that the giant ditch would strengthen U.S. security. By neglecting the American coal industry, he warned the president, "you are greatly injuring the national defense." Saylor voted against the proposal, but it passed the House by a vote of 241 to 158 and became law in May 1954. Following passage of the bill, Saylor, again with his constituents' interests at heart, urged Eisenhower to relieve youth unemployment in Pennsylvania by reviving New Deal Civilian Conservation Corps camps, but the administration balked because the problem was regional, not national, in scope. Saylor and other representatives also met with Eisenhower to renew their requests for relief of the bituminous coal industry by a rate hike on imported foreign oil. Other than a photo with the president in the Rose Garden, however, their appeal came to nothing. Saylor's stance on the seaway, reciprocal trade, and relief for the coal industry was appreciated by the Rochester and Pittsburgh Coal Company of Indiana, Pennsylvania, and other employers in his district. One constituent hailed him as "the best friend the miners ever had."[33]

Saylor also conflicted with the Eisenhower administration over wilderness issues. Initially, the administration seemed to appreciate the tradition of national park inviolability. When plans emerged to reduce the acreage of Everglades and Olympic national parks, for instance, Secretary McKay spurned them, as did Saylor. As a member of the House Interior Committee, he toured Olympic Park; attended field hearings in Port Angeles, Washington; and decried the assault on the park by timber companies. His passionate defense of Olympic Park convinced one Sierra Club member that he was "a true supporter of our National Park System." Saylor and McKay also proved unreceptive when the Bureau of Reclamation and Democratic Montana congressman Lee Metcalf sought to revive a plan, earlier discarded by the Truman administration and the Army Corps of Engineers, to build a dam on the North Fork of Montana's Flathead River. That project would have submerged twenty thousand acres of Glacier National Park.[34]

The threat to Glacier prompted the first of what would be many Saylor speeches in defense of the national park system. He denounced the proposal, scolding Metcalf for revisiting it. The plan, he reminded Metcalf, had already been proposed and dismissed. Why waste taxpayers' money on new studies? Did Metcalf know that the proposed dam would destroy an elk and deer refuge? Did he realize that Glacier National Park was one of the premier wilderness areas remaining in the continental United States? Did he understand that the dedicated area belonged to the people of the United States and not to the state of Montana? "Have not the people a right to hold just a few spots in this great country of ours for their own enjoyment and call it their own?" he asked. Those familiar with national parks, he counseled, "expect them to be defended and protected against destruction by small groups of individuals who seek temporary or local gains of a limited nature." He implored his House colleagues to "make sure that our generation does not go down in history as the generation that destroyed the finer things in life and deprived our children and our children's children" of their wilderness heritage. Similar criticisms from conservationists helped persuade McKay to suggest constructing a dam beyond the park boundaries.[35]

While pleased with McKay's stance against dam building in national parks, Saylor grew disgruntled with the administration's reclamation program. In spite of reductions in bureau staff and appropriations, its projects seemed to abound. Saylor introduced legislation to contain costs. One bill proposed revoking congressional authorization for all projects that had not yet been started; another sought to make it a criminal offense for the Bureau of Reclamation and Army Corps of Engineers to contract for work in excess of the total amount authorized for any project. Neither bill got out of committee.[36]

Eisenhower had promised Westerners in his first State of the Union address that "soundly planned projects already initiated should be carried out." Aside from authorized projects, the administration proposed and Congress approved fifty-three new ones between 1953 and 1961. Eisenhower would later boast in his memoirs that "we efficiently carried on one of the greatest reclamation programs in our history." Floyd Dominy, an assistant under Dexheimer in the 1950s, would portray the administration's promise to slow reclamation as a sham. In reality, he recalled, neither the Democrats nor the Republicans in the 1950s and 1960s sought "to discredit" the reclamation effort.[37]

Saylor was not duped by the administration's retrenchment rhetoric. When Secretary McKay boasted about restraining the bureau's activities, Saylor shot back a discomfiting reply: "I am sorry to notify you that as far as I am concerned, I can find no change whatsoever in the Bureau of Reclamation. The projects presented today are as fantastic, if not more so, as those presented by the Democrats. . . . Dexheimer is continuing the strategy of Mr. Strauss [*sic*]."[38]

One of the most "fantastic" of the bureau's schemes was the upper Colorado River Storage Project (CRSP). Bureau historian Michael Robinson has described the CRSP as the agency's "most dramatic application of basinwide planning and development concepts." After years of study, the bureau proposed in 1950 the construction of ten dams on the Colorado River and its tributaries to provide flood control, water storage, reclamation, hydroelectricity, and recreation for the upper basin states of Colorado, Wyoming, Utah, and New Mexico. Two of the proposed dams were to be built at Echo Park and Split Mountain in Dinosaur National Monument on the Utah-Colorado border. Interior Secretary Chapman held hearings on the proposal at the Interior Department in 1950. Conservationists and the department's National Park Service director, Newton Drury, protested that the reservoirs created by the two dams would mar the park's scenic grandeur and thus violate the principle of preservation. Chapman approved the CRSP in June 1950 but later reversed his decision because of the intensity of conservationists' protests.[39]

The Korean conflict stalled the project for three years, but with the end of the war, Secretary McKay revived it in late 1953, Eisenhower providing his endorsement the following spring. Several factors explain Eisenhower's commitment to the scheme. First, the project retained some elements of private enterprise. The Reclamation Bureau would construct the generating plants, but private companies would string the transmission lines and market the power. For this reason, private utilities generally supported the CRSP. Second, Eisenhower did not wish to alienate voters and legislators of the intermountain West, who wholeheartedly supported the endeavor as an economic boon to their region. Third, Eisenhower perhaps had exchanged his support for the CRSP for backing of the St. Lawrence Seaway project by Western representatives. Finally, on matters relating to natural resource development, Eisenhower usually followed the advice of McKay. "He sees no newspapers, no magazines, and has not the slightest understanding of conservation (or any other nonmilitary and nonforeign) issues," groused the conservationist Irving Brant. "His inclination will be to do whatever McKay asks him to do."[40]

When the CRSP bill came before Congress in 1954, Saylor served as its foremost critic in the House of Representatives. He denounced it as an economic extravagance and a menace to the sanctity of park preservation. As he was already hostile toward reclamation, it was not difficult for Saylor to sympathize with conservationists who saw the project as a threat to the principle of national park inviolability. During the battle over the CRSP, Saylor allied himself with park defenders and wilderness champions and for the first time made his mark as a preservationist.

four

Dinosaur Canyons

THE PROSPECT OF rafting wild Western rivers appealed to Saylor's sense of adventure, so he accepted an invitation from Joe Penfold, Western representative of the Izaak Walton League, to run the Yampa and Green rivers through Dinosaur National Monument on the Colorado-Utah border. Besides excitement, the voyage would provide an opportunity for Saylor and Democratic Colorado representative Wayne Aspinall, both members of the House Interior and Insular Affairs Committee, to see firsthand the primitive sandstone canyon country that would be submerged if Congress approved the Colorado River Storage Project. All in all, the two-day wilderness experience proved a turning point in Saylor's evolution as a preservationist, heightening his appreciation for pristine lands and national parks and exposing him to an influential conservation leader. Already a foe of big dams for philosophical and economic reasons, he would spearhead the campaign in the House against the CRSP mainly because it would despoil a nationally protected scenic wonderland. During the battle for Dinosaur he established a national reputation as a champion of the national park system and wilderness preservation.

Dinosaur National Monument was established in 1915 as an 80-acre preserve to protect Jurassic dinosaur remains. In 1938, President Franklin D. Roosevelt expanded the small fossil quarry to some 210,000 acres when he gave protection to the remote Green and Yampa river canyons on the Colorado-Utah border. Dinosaur had become an immense preserve, but it was generally

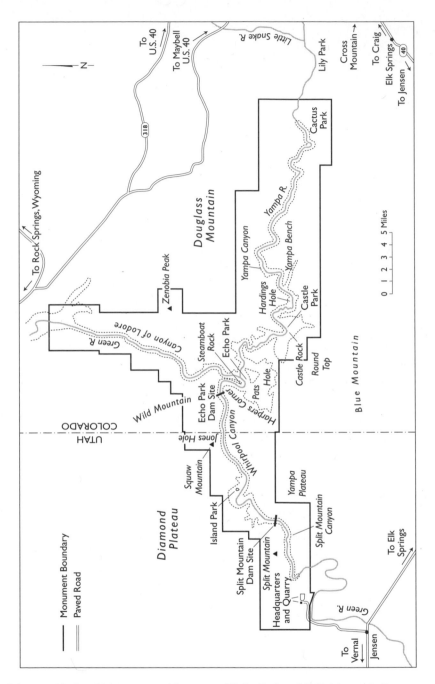

Dinosaur National Monument with proposed Echo Park and Split Mountain Dam Sites. Mark W. T. Harvey, *A Symbol of Wilderness*. Copyright 1994. Reprinted by permission of the University of New Mexico Press.

unknown and unfrequented until conservationists in the early 1950s learned of the Bureau of Reclamation's plans to flood its primeval and federally protected canyonlands.[1]

The fight over Dinosaur emerged at about the same time that the conservation movement was undergoing a transformation initiated by World War II. In the four decades before the war, American conservation had been driven essentially by the imperatives of efficiency and aesthetics. At the turn of the century, Progressives, notably President Theodore Roosevelt and his chief of forestry Gifford Pinchot, espoused the efficient use of natural resources. This utilitarian perspective affirmed that experts in the federal bureaucracy could scientifically administer the public domain to minimize waste and plunder by special interests. In giving heed to aesthetics, Progressives believed that scenic treasures were to be preserved, not for their ecological value, but to serve humankind by providing recreation, regenerating the spirit, and relieving stress. But when utilitarian and preservationist interests conflicted, as they did, for example, with a controversial proposal to invade Yosemite National Park with the Hetch Hetchy Dam in the 1910s, aesthetic values usually gave way.[2]

In 1916, shortly after the loss of the Hetch Hetchy valley, Congress attempted to placate preservationists by creating the National Park Service (NPS) within the Interior Department. The NPS was authorized to promote and administer federal preserves—parks, monuments, and reservations—which had been created "to conserve the scenery and the natural and historic objects and the wildlife therein, and to provide for the enjoyment of the same in such a manner and by such means as will leave them unimpaired for the enjoyment of future generations." It often became difficult for the NPS to balance the conflicting goals of public enjoyment (recreational use) and scenic preservation (aesthetics). To what extent should roads and trails be carved in public preserves? Should portions of parks be set aside as wilderness refuges? And would the creation of artificial lakes impair natural grandeur or enhance recreational opportunities and promote visitation?[3]

Owing to economic and national security reasons, the NPS was unable to block intrusions into federally protected areas during the Depression and war years. Companies with defense contracts gained access to critical mineral resources in Grand Canyon, Shenandoah, and Yosemite national parks. In addition, despite the strenuous objections of the National Parks Association (NPA), a private organization formed in 1919 to protect federal parks and monuments, President Roosevelt in 1938 authorized the Colorado–Big Thompson Plan. Completed eight years later, this Bureau of Reclamation project transported water from the west to the east slope of the Colorado Rockies via a thirteen-mile tunnel under Rocky Mountain National Park.[4]

After World War II, however, the movement to protect wilderness gained momentum. Conservationists began to question resource policies that seemed to be more concerned with life's riches than with the enrichment of life. The use of nuclear weapons had demonstrated the fragility of humankind: unrestrained scientific advances might endanger the human species. Surges in population and tourism, the economic emergence of the American West, and the press for natural resources to fuel the military-industrial establishment during the Cold War threatened existing national preserves. Conservationists began to reassess the relationship between human beings and their planet. Increasingly they were drawn to an ecological concept that emphasized that humans were not lords of the environmental realm, but just a part of the web of life.

Conservationists also reevaluated the works of John Muir, who had cofounded the Sierra Club and helped establish Yosemite National Park in the 1890s. Muir championed the intrinsic value of nature and wilderness preservation. Similarly, the ecological message of Aldo Leopold's *Sand County Almanac,* which appeared in 1949, urged readers to cease viewing nature as a commodity and to practice earth stewardship. People belonged to the land, not vice versa.[5]

With the end of the war, conservationists expected the relaxation of demands on national parklands; instead, pressures mounted. Timber companies sought unsuccessfully to harvest pine stands in Olympic National Park. The Army Corps of Engineers proposed Glacier View Dam, which would have submerged twenty thousand acres of Glacier National Park. And the Bureau of Reclamation wanted to erect Bridge Canyon Dam on the Colorado, which may have infringed upon Grand Canyon National Park and Monument. But the greatest menace to the national park system was the bureau's plan to erect dams in the primeval canyons of Dinosaur National Monument. The controversy over this proposal, according to historian Mark Harvey, "was the first major clash between preservationists and the dam builders in the postwar American West."[6]

Conservation groups understood that defense of the Dinosaur canyons would require a major effort, and their campaign consisted of four simultaneous movements. First, they challenged the necessity of the dams. Second, they played upon the fears of southern Californians, who worried that the project might deprive them of Colorado River water. Third, they played to the economic concerns of Easterners and Southerners, who recoiled at the hefty cost—

a billion dollars—of a project that might add to the farm surplus. And finally, they launched a publicity effort designed to inform citizens of the threat to a federally protected scenic treasure.[7]

In July 1950, Utah-born historian Bernard DeVoto moved thousands of readers with an article in the *Saturday Evening Post*. Subsequent articles extolling the scenic glories of the monument and the sanctity of the park system appeared in the early 1950s in *Living Wilderness, National Parks Magazine,* the *Sierra Club Bulletin,* and the *New Republic.* When proponents of the dams pointed out that most defenders of the monument had not actually seen it, because of its remoteness, conservation organizations sought to familiarize their members and the general public with the endangered canyon through hikes and raft trips.[8]

River running had not yet emerged as a popular outdoor pastime in the postwar years. Between 1945 and 1950, the Green and Yampa rivers attracted on average fewer than sixty adventurers per year. In 1952, however, the Sierra Club's seventy-four-year-old Harold Bradley and his two sons ran the rivers and, following their suggestion, the Sierra Club began sponsoring raft trips in 1953. That year nearly two hundred people floated the rivers with the Sierra Club, and another three hundred, including John Saylor, experienced the canyon country with smaller groups.[9]

The Saylor-Aspinall river trip was coordinated by Joe Penfold, a lean, bespectacled, pipe-smoking, crew-cut Coloradan who served as the Western representative of the Izaak Walton League. Mild mannered and professorial in appearance, Penfold from the beginning had been a forceful opponent of dams at Echo Park and Split Mountain in Dinosaur National Monument. He had first run the rivers in the summer of 1951 and considered the canyons unrivaled in their "sheer breath-taking beauty." He realized that the economic development of the West would require some sacrifice of scenic landscapes, but he pooh-poohed as "pure poppycock" the argument of dam proponents that a reservoir would provide greater boat access and therefore greater scenic and angling enjoyment for more people. The dams would dry up stretches of the river and ruin fishing pools, he argued. And experiencing the "roar of the rapids" on a live river ultimately would prove more appealing to tourists than motorized rides on placid, "fluctuating, second-rate reservoirs." Besides, he reasoned, national preserves should be inviolate. Penfold maintained that the dams could be constructed on alternative sites outside the federally protected areas.[10]

On the day of departure, Penfold picked up the congressmen from their motel in Vernal, Utah, and drove them over rough unpaved roads through the monument, stopping at some scenic overlooks before launching at Mantle Ranch. The two-boat party consisted of Penfold and his fourteen-year-old son Mike, Saylor and his twelve-year-old son Phil, Aspinall, monument superintendent Jess Lombard, and the father and son master river guides Bus and Don Hatch.

The weather was ideal—clear without oppressive heat. The group drifted down the Yampa beneath spectacular sheer cliffs, including Steamboat Rock, which stood as an eight-hundred-foot sandstone sentinel at Yampa's juncture with the Green River. At this confluence, the adventurers followed the Green past the Echo Park dam site in Whirlpool Canyon and then camped for the night at Jones Hole. At their camp, they fished, identified wildlife tracks, and spotted deer and eagles. The next day, Bus Hatch, to Saylor's delight, allowed the young boys in his raft to direct the oars, except through the rapids. Generally, the river was low, which was a relief to Penfold because Aspinall, who could not swim, was terrified of the water. In the afternoon, they bobbed past the Split Mountain dam site and reached monument headquarters, where their journey ended.[11]

Penfold pronounced the trip a success to conservation leaders. Saylor, he reported, "had a thorough-going time," having remarked that his two days on the river were among the best in his memory and that the farther he drifted downriver the more he believed that the dams should not be built. Penfold sensed that conservationists may have found a political ally in Saylor, describing him as "a very fine sort of fellow, good-natured, a bit on the blustery side. He has the reputation on the Committee as a bull in a china shop," an image that "he apparently enjoys and lives up to as best he can." Moreover, Penfold continued, the congressman "very obviously despises" chairman A. L. Miller, "which might be useful to us sometime." He also possessed a "fundamental distrust" of the Reclamation Bureau "and its gargantuan projects." "I think we can very definitely count on him as a restraining influence in his Committee," Penfold speculated.[12]

Penfold was less optimistic about Aspinall. He had proved to be "a good sport" and appeared to be taken with the grandeur of the canyons, but he also seemed politically committed to the CRSP. Still, he had given Penfold some hope by saying that if other sites could be found, he would agree to the removal of the Echo Park and Split Mountain sites from the project. Overall, Penfold was buoyed by the trip and considered it "time well spent." Saylor seemed to have been won over to the cause, and Penfold informed the president of the Sierra Club that he thought they had "better than a fighting chance" of preserving the canyons. Conservation leaders agreed with this assessment and praised Penfold for having achieved a coup for their cause.[13]

Secretary Douglas McKay asked Interior Undersecretary Ralph Tudor to make a recommendation relating to the Dinosaur dams. "It is another hot one and may cause almost as much excitement as the Hells Canyon affair," Tudor noted in his diary. Accompanied by reclamation commissioner Wilbur Dexheimer and National Park Service director Conrad Wirth, he took a raft inspection trip to the proposed dam sites in mid-September 1953. Like Saylor, Tudor was impressed by the splendor of the canyons, but not enough to save them. In late November, he advised McKay to endorse the Echo Park dam site, but to hold off on the construction of Split Mountain Dam until a later date. The Echo Park site was crucial to the project because its steep and narrow canyon walls would save 100,000 to 200,000 acre-feet yearly in evaporation losses, compared to alternative sites outside the monument. The evaporation-loss figures were hardly inconsequential because even an annual savings of 100,000 acre-feet would be sufficient to furnish all the water needs of a Denver-sized municipality.[14]

Interior Secretary McKay announced his support for the CRSP on December 12, 1953. He proposed the construction of two initial dams—Echo Park inside the monument and Glen Canyon outside the preserve in northern Arizona. Several other dams, including Split Mountain, would be built later. He also advanced Tudor's evaporation-loss argument to help explain his approval for the controversial Echo Park dam site. McKay's announcement disappointed, but hardly surprised, most conservation leaders, who also expected approval by the budget bureau and the president. The real fight to save Dinosaur monument, they knew, would have to be won in Congress, and they pressed Saylor to oppose the dam at Echo Park "with every fiber of your being."[15]

The House Subcommittee on Irrigation and Reclamation held hearings on three similar Colorado River Storage Project bills from January 18 to January 28, 1954. Chaired by Republican William Henry Harrison of Wyoming, the subcommittee included Republican William Dawson of Utah, a sponsor of one of the bills; Wayne Aspinall; John Saylor; and twenty other members of Congress, mainly from Western states.

Tudor, the lead witness, anticipated some difficult questioning because groups like the Sierra Club had been "putting on the heat" and disseminating "a lot of misleading information." During his testimony before a standing-room-only audience, Tudor frankly admitted that the Interior Department faced a predicament: on the one hand, it had an obligation to protect national parks and monuments; on the other, it was expected to promote the economic development of the arid West through reclamation. Alternative sites to Echo Park were not an option because of greater evaporation losses. The choice, then, was "simply one of altering the scenery of Dinosaur National Monument without destroying it in a basin which is and will remain rich in scenery, or of irreplaceably losing enough water to supply all the needs of a city of more than 600,000." The department had chosen the former.[16]

During the question period, Saylor left no doubt that he believed the Interior Department had made the wrong choice. He began by trying to lead Tudor away from the evaporation question, asking him to refer to a map and point to those proposed CRSP dams that would be used primarily for irrigation. Tudor preferred to have subsequent bureau witnesses answer this question. When Saylor insisted that Tudor answer, Representative Dawson interrupted with a suggestion that it would be "better procedure" to allow reclamation officials to address this inquiry. "I do not want to be told what will be better procedure," Saylor snapped. The Interior Department had devised a multi-dam plan for the upper basin states, Saylor declared, and the government's first witness should be able to reveal which ones were for water storage and which were for power. Instead, Tudor had focused on the evaporation issue to justify the controversial Echo Park Dam. When Tudor admitted that he was not familiar with all the details of the plan, Saylor turned to another issue: the sanctity of the national park system.[17]

Were not most federal parks and monuments established because they possessed grand scenery? Saylor asked. Tudor admitted they were. Were not federal reserves owned by the people, not just by a few states, regions, or basins? Again, Tudor conceded. And was it not the responsibility of the Interior Department to protect national parks and monuments? It was, the undersecretary answered, but when it came to a choice between losing scenery and losing water resources, the department had decided that some landscape could be sacrificed. But would not a reservoir at Echo Park flood the glorious Dinosaur canyons? Saylor pressed on. True, Tudor replied, the canyons would be filled with two hundred to three hundred feet of water, but the monument would not be ruined, only "more accessible to more people." What about the rapids they had both run the previous year? Saylor asked. Would they not be covered by a "placid pool"? Yes, Tudor responded, but then you would not have to drag your boat in low water. When Tudor revealed that his party could not get to Split Mountain canyon because of low water, Saylor countered that Tudor should have been smart enough not to run the river during the dry season. All in all, Saylor announced, Tudor had not made a convincing case for the construction of Echo Park Dam.[18]

Tudor and dam proponents in general were taken aback by Saylor's bellicosity. Tudor considered him "uncouth" and "rough at times" as he proceeded to "climb all over my frame." Saylor's losing his temper was not an act, Tudor concluded, "because even after the hearings he came down off the rostrum and started to tear into me again." Tudor could not understand why Saylor was so adamant in his defense of the national park system, incorrectly concluding that Saylor "was actually carrying the ball for Southern California," whose inhabitants opposed the CRSP "because it would indirectly have some effect on them."[19]

Saylor also grilled expert witnesses from the Bureau of Reclamation. Indeed, he became so relentless that subcommittee chair Harrison sought to place a limit of five minutes for questioning on each member. Saylor, however, objected on the grounds that a $1 billion project should not be rushed. He did agree to a ten-minute limit when other members of the committee ceded him their time.[20]

Through his questions and observations, Saylor attempted to portray the bureau as arrogant, inflexible, and sloppy in its use of data. Whether it was estimating the annual flow of the Colorado River, the cost of a project, power revenues, acres to be irrigated, or losses due to evaporation, "its figures were unreliable." By focusing on greater evaporation losses to justify the Echo Park Dam, the bureau was creating a "bugaboo" to divert attention away from suitable alternative sites, he argued. "I think it is incumbent upon your Bureau," he instructed Commissioner Dexheimer, not to dictate to the committee "where the project has to be built."[21]

Until opponents had the opportunity to testify during the last three days of hearings, Saylor pressed the argument against the CRSP virtually alone. During this time, he had long discussions with conservation leaders such as David Brower of the Sierra Club, Howard Zahniser of the Wilderness Society, and Fred Packard of the National Parks Association, and they familiarized him with the anti-dam position.[22]

Proponents maintained that the CRSP would serve literally and figuratively as an "oasis" for the upper basin. It would provide a vital resource for irrigation and domestic consumption and supply power to develop mineral resources such as phosphates, which were important to national defense. The lower basin states had been assisted in the development of the Colorado River, and now it was time for the federal government to help the upper basin. Saylor, however, would have none of it. He held that the Colorado River had been "overworked" and that there was not enough water to supply both basins. As for reclamation, the Echo Park and Glen Canyon dams would produce not "one drop" of water for irrigation because they were essentially power facilities, and, Saylor maintained, federal taxpayers should not subsidize the production of power. Proponents held that Echo Park Dam was the "wheelhorse" of the team of dams because it would produce enough power to make the project economically sound. But while Saylor admitted that the precipitous canyon made an ideal dam site, he maintained that "it is a national monument and I am opposed to it." Besides, the bureau had not looked hard enough at sites outside the monument.[23]

Dam proponents played down the loss of scenery, but Saylor knew better from firsthand experience. Democratic representative Ken Regan of Texas, for example, noted that Dinosaur was seldom visited and stated that in setting it aside as a preserve the National Park Service had "perpetrated a hoax on the people of the United States because there is not a darn thing to see." Saylor countered that "a great deal of grandeur and glory" would be lost by plugging the waterway. Moreover, the "only way to actually appreciate and understand the beauties of the Yampa Gorge is to actually go down in it." More than five hundred people had floated the river in 1953, and they probably had become better acquainted with its scenic wonders, Saylor sarcastically observed, than Regan had by whooshing over it in an aircraft. But Wayne Aspinall, who had drifted through the canyons with Saylor, reached a different conclusion: there were more than a hundred places in his congressional district alone, he said, that surpassed Dinosaur National Monument in scenic value. Saylor let this remark pass, but later in the hearings he reminded Aspinall of their wonderful experience together in a special place "that will be gone if you build this dam."[24]

Supporters of the project also denied that building Echo Park Dam would establish a precedent for invading federal preserves. Republican senator Wallace Bennett and Representative William Dawson of Utah claimed that when President Roosevelt expanded the monument in 1938, he had recognized the legitimacy of a 1904 bureau claim that it could construct a dam within the monument. Saylor pointed out that Roosevelt had referred specifically to a site in the northern reaches of the monument known as Brown's Park; he had not given the bureau carte blanche to erect dams anywhere in the monument. True, a dam at Brown's Park would have submerged a small portion of the monument, but not the Echo Park and Split Mountain sites. In other words, Saylor and other preservationists argued, the bureau could develop the site at Brown's Park, but no other site within the monument.[25]

Proponents also claimed that the precedent for dam building within national parks and monuments had been set at Hetch Hetchy in 1913 and in legislation creating subsequent preserves such as Rocky Mountain National Park (1915) and Hawaiian Volcanic National Park (1916). Saylor countered by pointing out that since the creation of the NPS in 1916 no dam had been erected in a federal park or monument. In the early 1950s, however, gung-ho federal engineers in the Bureau of Reclamation and the Army Corps of Engineers had concocted fantastic plans to impound water not only in Dinosaur National Monument but also in Glacier National Park, Mammoth Cave National Park, and Grand Canyon National Monument.[26]

Dam supporters accused Saylor of exaggerating Reclamation's designs on national preserves. Republican representative John Rhodes of Arizona conceded that federal engineers had plans to intrude upon Grand Canyon monument with a dam but stated that the intrusion would be inconsequential because the impoundment would only raise the water level by twenty-five feet, not flood the monument. In Saylor's opinion, however, raising the water level by more than twenty feet constituted flooding: "If I were not to assume that was a flood, I might report that water that occurred in Johnstown in 1889 was only a slight dampness, that all that it was was an elevation of the water about 25 feet."[27]

Saylor also challenged advocates of the project when they maintained that building dams in Dinosaur had overwhelming support in Western states. He declared that "for the first time since I have been a Member of the Congress the Post Office Department is delivering mail to me in sacks." Much of that mail, he disclosed, was from residents of the upper basin states, and sentiment was running fifteen-to-one for preservation of the monument. In truth, most residents of the intermountain West probably favored Echo Park Dam, but non-Westerners did not. By February 1954, the committee had received 53 letters supporting the dam and 4,678 in opposition.[28]

Westerners on the committee wondered about Saylor's sudden solicitude for raw country. Concern for wilderness, Representative Dawson observed, became keener the farther away an individual lived from it. Representative Rhodes of Arizona pointed out that Pennsylvanians had despoiled their landscape by digging oil wells and coal mines and now wanted to prevent Westerners from developing their natural resources. "I feel as a member of this committee," Saylor said in response, "that it is incumbent upon us to preserve inviolate the limits of our national parks and monuments." Rhodes asked Saylor how he would have reacted had he been a member of parliament in the eighteenth century during a discussion "about developing the wilds of Pennsylvania." Saylor insisted that he would have taken the same position. Admittedly Pennsylvanians had made some environmental mistakes, he said, but "we have seen what has happened back East and we are going to see to it that the same thing does not happen to the folks out West. In other words, we are going to save you from yourselves."[29]

During the final three days of the hearings, opponents of Echo Park Dam had an opportunity to testify. They reiterated and expanded upon points they had coached Saylor on during the first seven days of testimony. Representatives from the Izaak Walton League, the Sierra Club, the National Wildlife Federation, the National Parks Association, and several other groups stressed the inviolability of the park system. They would support the CRSP, but only if Echo Park and Split Mountain dams were deleted from the project.[30]

David Brower, executive director of the Sierra Club, proved to be the most unsettling witness to proponents of Echo Park Dam. He spoke eloquently of the beauties of the monument and ridiculed the idea that a reservoir would only alter them. Drowning the Dinosaur canyons would "only" alter the scenery in the monument in the same way that toppling centuries-old giant trees "would only alter Sequoia National Park."[31]

Brower's most important contribution was giving added impetus to the argument that the Dinosaur canyons could be preserved by utilizing another site. He did this by exposing the errors of the Bureau of Reclamation in calculating the rates of evaporation between the Echo Park site and a larger than planned dam at Glen Canyon. The committee, Brower counseled, should not "rely upon the figures presented by the Bureau of Reclamation when they cannot add, subtract, multiply, or divide." Using "ninth-grade arithmetic," he demonstrated that the difference in evaporation losses between Echo Park Dam and a larger Glen Canyon Dam was not 165,000 acre-feet, as the Bureau claimed, but only 70,000 acre-feet. Bureau experts tsk-tsked Brower's lack of mathematical sophistication, but they could not erase the doubts that had been planted in the minds of dam proponents and committee members.[32]

Preservationists also had high praise for Saylor's "spirited opposition" to dams in Dinosaur. Brower noted privately that "Republican Saylor of Pennsylvania has really been carrying the ball in cross examining the Interior witnesses—badgering might be a better word." And the Sierra Club Conservation Committee characterized Saylor as "our best friend on the Committee to date. He has an excellent grasp of the situation and has been giving the Bureau of Reclamation a very hard time." After ten days of hearings, conservationists were upbeat about their chances of killing Echo Park Dam in subcommittee or on the House floor. But they realized that victory depended upon winning over members of Congress, especially in the East. Saylor could not "do that whole job himself," noted one preservationist, but he could "serve as a damn fine general" of the forces.[33]

The House subcommittee was not scheduled to go into executive session on the CRSP until April, so preservationists used the interim to try to excise Echo Park from the bill. The bureau's evaporation-loss argument seemed to be weak, and conservationists slammed it. Saylor requested evaporation-loss data from the bureau for more than 150 potential dam sites. If nothing else, he was using this tactic to buy time: "Saylor has been loading the Bureau up with work; he wants lots more reports on lots of subjects which will take them time to prepare," Brower noted privately.[34]

Other conservationists recruited experts to recalculate the evaporation data. They had already received assistance from Ulysses S. Grant III, an engineer with the Army Corps of Engineers, but now they also turned to Luna Leopold, with the U.S. Geological Survey, and to Richard "Ric" Bradley, a Cornell University physics professor and son of a former Sierra Club president. Bradley in particular was asked to help Brower show that the evaporation losses between Echo Park Dam and a thirty-five foot-higher Glen Canyon Dam would be insignificant.[35]

Conservationists also worked feverishly to win over the American public to the viewpoint that their national parks and monuments were sacrosanct. They showed films, such as *Wilderness River Trail* and *Legends of Lodore,* that touted the wonders of the Dinosaur canyons. Saylor showed these films at the conclusion of the hearings, but only a few committee members attended. Conservationists also extolled park and wilderness values in publications such as *Harper's,* the *New Republic,* the *Sierra Club Bulletin, Living Wilderness,* and *National Parks Magazine.* An obliging Saylor inserted some of these articles into the *Congressional Record.* Conservationists also blitzed Secretary McKay and President Eisenhower with wires and telegrams urging protection of the monument. But to no avail. Following a favorable recommendation from the Bureau of the Budget, Eisenhower came out for the project on March 20, 1954. The president was swayed by the argument that the CRSP would provide both economic benefits and greater accessibility and recreational opportunity within the monument.[36]

Conservation leaders were furious. "I think the President is weak and hopeless," declared the artist Ansel Adams. Saylor tried to set up a meeting with the president, but Eisenhower put him off. He also sent a reproachful letter to budget director Joseph Dodge. How could he justify flouting the long tradition of national park inviolability, especially when alternative sites seemed suitable given the bureau's faulty evaporation-loss analysis? Additionally, Saylor said, Dodge had failed to inform the public about the "hidden subsidies" that would be provided to irrigation beneficiaries, thus hiking up the project's total cost.[37]

These "hidden subsidies" consisted of extra interest taxpayers would have to pay on borrowed money. Prevailing reclamation law, Saylor pointed out, required water users to repay, without interest, the cost of irrigation works in forty yearly installments. But the CRSP would lengthen the repayment period to fifty years. Water users would escape interest payments, but the federal government would not, being charged interest on the money borrowed to build the irrigation structures. This hidden subsidy, now increased by ten years, amounted to millions of dollars that taxpayers would be required to satisfy. Then, too, irrigation projects were not self-liquidating. Construction costs were so high that water users could not repay them, so the deficit was met by the sale of power. In the case of the CRSP, water beneficiaries would be expected to pay on average only 15 percent of the irrigation expense. The remaining 85 percent would come from power revenues that could be stretched out for fifty years. This generous repayment program, Saylor said, was another subsidy that elevated the interest costs on the borrowed money.[38]

Dodge downplayed Saylor's criticism. The Budget Bureau had recommended approval of the CRSP because it was convinced that when the monument had been enlarged in 1938, provision had been made to erect a dam, not just at Brown's Park, but at any locale in the monument. Nor did he believe that the bureau's evaporation-loss figures had been discredited. He conceded Saylor's point that the project involved a "considerable subsidy as a result of deferred interest free repayments," which he estimated at $135 million, but he still regarded the project as economically sound. Final project approval, he reminded Saylor, was up to Congress.[39]

For nearly a month, from mid-April to early May, the House subcommittee met in executive session to consider the CRSP legislation. Saylor caused a "row" by offering a spate of monument-saving amendments. The first proposed deleting Echo Park Dam from the bill, but it was defeated twelve to five. Californian Clair Engle, who supported Saylor's amendment, observed that it was going to be difficult to pass the bill with Echo Park and wondered why proponents insisted upon its inclusion. Aspinall replied that if upper basin lawmakers proceeded with the measure without Echo Park it would encourage conservationists to continue their battle for park preservation for the next twenty-five years or more. Conservation leaders, who learned of this remark from Saylor, interpreted it to mean that Westerners had plans to invade other federal preserves.[40]

Failing to remove Echo Park from the CRSP, Saylor next offered a series of amendments proposing alternative dam sites, including New Moab, Dewey, Low Gray Canyon, High Desolation Canyon, High Glen Canyon, Cross Mountain, and Flaming Gorge. All were rejected. Saylor then tried to save Echo Park through some backdoor amendments. One would have forbidden the construction of any project that did not directly serve the purposes of irrigation; another would have prevented the construction of power plants that could not produce electricity at market value or less. Yet another proposed that all revenues yielded by the CRSP be funneled into the general treasury instead of funding irrigation projects. None was accepted. His one successful amendment raised the appropriation from $950,000 to $1 billion, probably to make the project more objectionable to thrift-minded members of Congress. On May 3, in spite of Saylor's work, the subcommittee recommended the CRSP to the full House Committee by a vote of twelve to nine.[41]

Although they were unsuccessful, Saylor's efforts drew raves from conservation leaders. Saylor, observed Fred Packard of the NPA, "has been of tremendous help to us on the committee, and has been fighting valiantly to get Echo Park Dam out of the project." "I thank God for Pennsylvania which produced you (I assume) and which had the good sense (I know) to send you to Congress," wrote Brower. "I hope you know how widespread is the admiration felt for you all over the country owing to the magnificent part you are playing in the battle," Brower wrote again a month later. Penfold congratulated him on his "grand fight," and Harold Bradley, whose son Richard was working with Brower to dispel the evaporation-loss argument, hailed Saylor's "fine work" and "courage and statesmanship." A fellow Republican, Bradley believed that

Saylor, "perhaps better than any other man," could help save the administration from the mistake of invading Dinosaur: "And on the floor of Congress—we need a David—armed with the hard pebbles of truth and conviction, to drive back Reclamation's Goliath." Saylor proved worthy of this challenge.[42]

During the two-week interval between the end of the subcommittee hearings and the beginning of the deliberations of the full committee, Saylor worked closely with conservation leaders to shore up the preservationist position on the Dinosaur canyons. In cooperation with Brower, Saylor issued a "Dear Colleague" letter to all members of Congress that attempted to refute point by point an earlier pro-dam letter that Representative Dawson had disseminated. Saylor's letter essentially reiterated the argument that the monument was nationally protected and thus sacrosanct, that an impoundment would transform "a unique place into a trite one," and that alternative dam sites existed that would produce the same economic benefits and leave the magnificent Dinosaur canyons unmarred.[43]

Saylor also sought to dispel the notion, perpetuated mainly by the Utah congressional delegation, that shooting the rapids in Dinosaur monument was a perilous undertaking. Republican Utah representative Douglas Stringfellow told House colleagues of a California couple who had been misled about the joys of rafting Dinosaur's canyons. They had read stories in *Sunset* and *National Geographic* and decided to take a raft trip themselves in a folding kayak, but their craft was ripped apart by the rapids, and they barely escaped with their lives. Expert river guides such as Don Hatch decried the attack on their sport and asked Saylor to defend it. He obliged. In remarks before the House, he lambasted the California couple for foolishly trying to negotiate the river without a qualified pilot. He had taken the same excursion with Don Hatch and had experienced no mishaps: "When people venture into fields for which they are ill-equipped, unprepared, and fail to use the simple rules of safety practiced in everyday life, they find themselves sometimes in very embarrassing positions." He then inserted into the *Congressional Record* letters from river guides who detailed the California couple's mistakes and lack of common sense. Still, conservation groups feared a tragedy that might damage their cause and urged river runners to forego kayaks and challenge Dinosaur's waterways only with experienced guides.[44]

Saylor also continued to probe the evaporation-loss angle. Because evaporation loss varied according to water depth and surface area, Saylor asked the Reclamation Bureau to provide data on "water surface area at mean operating level" for Echo Park and thirteen other reservoirs under study for the CRSP. Ric Bradley, who had directed the evaporation-loss study for conservationists, was growing "less hopeful that this evaporation study is going to lead to anything spectacular." Then in mid-April he received a letter from assistant reclamation commissioner Floyd Dominy revealing that the bureau had erred in its earlier evaporation-loss estimates. The difference in evaporation losses between a high Glen Canyon Dam and dams in the Dinosaur canyons was a negligible 25,000 acre-feet. Dominy released this information, he later recalled, suspecting that "the shit would hit the fan." Tudor threatened to fire the person who had embarrassed him, but Dominy owned up to it without any repercussions. Indeed, Tudor resigned shortly thereafter.[45]

Bradley and Brower promptly seized upon the importance of Dominy's letter, Brower informing Saylor that he had obtained a letter of "immediate importance and usefulness." Brower disclosed the bureau's error in a Sierra Club press release, and the *New York Times*, to the chagrin of the Interior Department and CRSP proponents, carried the story in early May. Undersecretary Tudor was infuriated by the turn of events. On March 9, he had written William Henry Harrison, chair of the House Subcommittee on Irrigation and Reclamation, to disclose that the evaporation-loss differential between a large Glen Canyon facility and the Echo Park and Split Mountain dams should have been 70,000 acre-feet, not 165,000, as he had stated in his January testimony. Then, after learning from the bureau of still another error, he had to write Harrison again two months later to say that the evaporation-loss figure should have been 25,000 acre-feet, not 70,000. He conceded "that this error in the evaporation calculations for the high Glen Canyon Dam Reservoir may cast doubt as to the reliability of the calculations for other reservoirs." Consequently, he instructed the bureau to undertake another review of the figures.[46]

On May 13, the day Tudor sent his second mea culpa letter to Harrison, the full House Interior and Insular Affairs Committee met to consider the CRSP. Believing they had countered the evaporation-loss argument, preservationists became hopeful that the full House committee would remove the Dinosaur dams from the bill, and as usual, they looked to Saylor to lead the way. He introduced an amendment removing Echo Park Dam from the bill, but it lost by a vote of thirteen to ten, and five days later, the committee approved the CRSP by a vote of thirteen to twelve.[47]

Saylor bristled at the outcome of the vote and the maneuvers of committee leaders Miller and Harrison. The committee, he said, had voted for a project "without considering serious evaporation errors admitted by the Bureau of Reclamation." Before the committee acted on the measure, he noted, he had attempted to make the bureau's miscalculations part of the record, but Harrison and Miller had "refused to take official cognizance of this crucial evidence of error, which throws an entirely new light on the Echo Park Dam controversy." The committee's indifference, he fumed, "was typical of the high-handed manner in which this vast billion-dollar project has been approached" and "indicates how frightened and frantic Echo Park proponents are." He went to the floor to bring the bureau's evaporation errors to the attention of the full House, inserted Tudor's admission of errors into the record, and made another demand for a high Glen Canyon Dam as a substitute. He also prepared a minority report for the House committee that scored the CRSP for violating the sanctity of a national monument and for its hidden subsidy of $2,700 per acre for lands that would be irrigated in future projects.[48]

In his effort to save Dinosaur monument, Saylor had come up short again. But his tenacious battle and dedication to park values won the admiration of preservationists. "I have nothing but the highest praise for your splendid continuing efforts to defeat the construction of Echo Park Dam," wrote Richard Bradley. Brower referred to Saylor as "our champion." And in a Denver speech, Penfold hailed Saylor's "dogged determination at the hearings and . . . skilled cross-examination of witnesses." The closeness of the vote in the full committee, he said, was attributable in large measure to Saylor's "strong leadership." Penfold found it remarkable that, with most of the grand scenery located in the West, a Pennsylvanian should emerge as "the vigorous and able new champion of the national park system."[49]

Dam supporters fulminated against both Saylor and the Interior Department for its evaporation-loss miscalculations. Without mentioning Saylor by name, a *Denver Post* editorial expressed concern that the intermountain region's economic interests might be "sacrificed to false economy and the appeasement of rebellious non-Western elements within the Republican party." Wayne Aspinall expressed gratitude that "attempts by known opponents of the bill to amend it so that it would become completely unpalatable failed." And David Brinegar, the executive secretary of the Central Arizona Project, declared that he "might feel Saylor was a champion of something good were it not for the fact that I have seen Angelenos' arms around him." Saylor's primary reason for opposing the CRSP, he suspected, was to protect southern California's claim to its share of Colorado River water. Saylor had come to his position, according to Brinegar, out of friendship for Norris Poulson, a former House colleague who had become mayor of Los Angeles. With good reason, Arizonans believed that Californians were attempting to block their development of the Colorado River. And since Saylor had opposed the CAP in the early 1950s, they believed he was in league with California. Even some conservationists wondered if Saylor would demand from them some political price for defending national parklands. But Saylor objected to federal hydroelectric dams because they competed with privately produced fossil fuels as a source of power, burdened taxpayers, and often encroached upon nationally protected wild country.[50]

While "girding their loins" for a tough battle on the House floor, preservationists had received some welcome support from the media. In the summer of 1954, the *New York Times*, the *Christian Science Monitor*, and the *Washington Post* editorialized against Echo Park Dam. Eleanor Roosevelt opposed Echo Park in her syndicated "My Day" column. John Oakes carried articles against the invasion of the monument in his conservation column in the Sunday *New York Times*. Martin Litton of the *Los Angeles Times* wanted to know who on the committee had voted for the CRSP so he could "get something sarcastic out on those who are the wrong thinkers." And former New Dealer Raymond Moley, who had become an editor for *Newsweek*, used his widely read "Perspective" column to denounce the CRSP on economic grounds, singling out Saylor for praise and using the Pennsylvanian's "hidden subsidy" argument to decry the excessive irrigation costs. Some preservationists considered Moley difficult and less than committed to the cause of preservation, but Bernard DeVoto said, "there is no reason why a bastard should not be used when he's on our side—and his pieces have impressed a lot of people." Indeed, the economic arguments of Saylor and Moley convinced some conservationists that the entire CRSP was "unsound," not just the Echo Park feature.[51]

Dam opponents were heartened by public opposition to the defilement of Dinosaur monument. "I don't think the God damn stupid bastards currently known as the Administration will get any major legislation through Congress this session," predicted the historian and journalist Bernard DeVoto. And if Congress did not enact the CRSP in 1954, he continued, it probably never would because "we have really raised the country." Another optimistic preservationist told Brower that "if the dam is blocked I think I'll hafta go out and celebrate by getting drunk."[52]

The anticipated floor fight did not occur. Even though the CRSP received a favorable rule, Speaker Martin refused to call up the legislation for floor action. In the Senate, the Interior Committee added more irrigation projects, which drove up the cost to $1.5 billion, but the upper chamber delayed action on the measure until 1955.

Having achieved a temporary victory, conservation leaders decided to give special recognition to Saylor "for his outstanding work in behalf of Dinosaur National Monument." Fred Packard of the NPA initiated and coordinated the affair. The NPA would present Saylor with an award—the first in its long history—but other conservation groups were expected to participate in the ceremony. "Every effort should be made for the organizations to be represented," Packard directed, "if possible by the ranking official of the organization."[53]

Saylor was honored at the Sunnehanna Country Club in Johnstown on October 14. More than sixty people attended the luncheon, including Saylor's mother, who was celebrating her eightieth birthday. Ira Gabrielson, president of the Wildlife Management Institute, served as master of ceremonies, and representatives from fifteen conservation groups were also in attendance, including Packard of the NPA, Zahniser of the Wilderness Society, Penfold of the Izaak Walton League, and Brower of the Sierra Club.

Sigurd Olson, president of the NPA, presented the award and gave the keynote address, describing Saylor as "one of the most thoroughly informed, honest, and deep-thinking conservationists in Congress." He had "advanced his reputation across the country" by his energetic defense of Dinosaur monument against the substantial threat of Echo Park Dam. He also shared with most conservation leaders the dream of wilderness preservation: "He is one who knows the dream, who has the courage, vision, knowledge, and foresight to recognize the deep significance of the issues he has fought for." Olson concluded by presenting Saylor with honorary lifetime membership in the NPA and a plaque from more than a dozen conservation organizations "for distinguished service in behalf of the National Parks and Monuments of the United States." This ceremony was one of the highlights of Saylor's congressional service up to that point.[54]

With their tribute to Saylor coming only two weeks before the congressional election, conservation leaders hoped it would give a boost to his bid for reelection. The *Pittsburgh Press* had reported that Saylor was particularly vulnerable in 1954 because of severe unemployment in western Pennsylvania—nearly 22 percent—and because he had disagreed so often with Republican national leaders.[55]

Democrats nominated Johnstown attorney Robert Glass to oppose Saylor. He criticized Saylor for being too cozy with the special interests; he was often pictured in newspapers, Glass observed, "shaking hands with one of three generals—General Motors, General Eisenhower, or General Electric." Moreover, he had failed to rebuke Defense Secretary Charles Wilson for insulting the unemployed when he said that he had always preferred bird dogs to kennel-fed dogs. Not only had Saylor tolerated insensitive remarks, Democrats charged, but he had not done enough to relieve unemployment. Instead of demanding a tax on imported oil, he should have been looking for "new uses and new markets" for Pennsylvania coal.[56]

However, although most Democrats found him wanting, Saylor received considerable blue-collar support. He was endorsed by the Railway Workers Union and the United Mine Workers, labor official John T. Jones asserting that the UMW owed Saylor "a debt of gratitude for his leadership in the fight to pass a mine safety law and against the Reciprocal Trade Act and the St. Lawrence Seaway project. His labor record is one of the best."[57]

Most district newspapers endorsed Saylor, as did two nationally syndicated columnists. In *Harper's Magazine,* Bernard DeVoto lauded Saylor's conservation record. And after two requests from Saylor, Raymond Moley of *Newsweek* sent an "entirely unsolicited" endorsement to the *Johnstown Tribune-Democrat,* calling Saylor "the most effective fighter in either House of Congress" against the waste of taxpayers' money on "unwelcome reclamation projects in the West." His reelection and continued opposition to the CRSP, Moley continued, would save Pennsylvania taxpayers millions of dollars.[58]

Saylor won reelection by a comfortable 5,000-vote margin. His victory even prompted one discouraged Democratic newspaper columnist to urge his candidacy against the incumbent GOP senator Edward Martin in 1956. Saylor, the writer noted, would make an excellent candidate for the position, and "the local Democratic organization might have a chance to elect a Democratic congressman." Besides, the journalist concluded, Saylor had done more for the district in one year than Martin had done in six.[59]

In the next Congress, Saylor would continue to battle against Echo Park Dam and other reclamation projects that, to his mind, defied sound economy or debauched the national park heritage. Many Westerners, especially residents of the intermountain states, denounced him as a "stooge" of wilderness preservationists who was determined to emasculate the reclamation program and block their economic progress. But conservationists portrayed "Uncle John" as a stalwart in the defense of the national park system.[60]

five

Big Dam Foolishness

By 1955, Saylor's antipathy toward the Bureau of Reclamation had been well established among his colleagues on the House Committee on Interior and Insular Affairs. Californian Clair Engle charged that Saylor had "developed such a spleen against the Bureau of Reclamation" that he had forgotten that there had been an election a few years ago and that a Republican secretary of the interior now headed that organization.[1]

Saylor claimed not to be motivated by partisan politics when it came to the bureau. That agency, he insisted, was engaged in an audacious program of dam building. "Those who run the Bureau of Reclamation—and it does not make any difference what administration is in charge," he stated, come before Congress seeking to erect "gigantic projects as memorials to themselves." Two western Colorado projects in particular galled him: the CRSP and the Fryingpan-Arkansas. But less expansive works also drew his ire. He fought to restrain the bureau's building plans but met with only limited success.[2]

The Colorado River Storage Project was the most ambitious but not the only upper basin reclamation proposal to stir political controversy. In January 1953, Representative J. Edgar "Ed" Chenoweth, a Republican from Trinidad, Colorado, introduced legislation proposing the Fryingpan-Arkansas project. On the surface, the plan seemed reasonable: divert water from the lush western side of the Colorado Rocky Mountains to the parched eastern slope. The origins of this water-diversion scheme dated back to the 1930s. Following a severe drought, water users along the 300-mile-long Arkansas River Valley in eastern

Colorado had urged the Interior Department to provide them with a supplemental water plan. Rarely thinking in moderation when it came to moving rivers around, the Bureau of Reclamation, after years of study, responded in 1950 with the Gunnison-Arkansas plan. Under this proposal, about 900,000 acre-feet of water annually would be transferred from the Gunnison River on the west slope of the Rockies to the Arkansas River Valley, at a cost of $780 million. When this grand scheme faltered within the Interior Department for political and economic reasons, the bureau offered a scaled-down version called the Fryingpan-Arkansas project.

Through a cluster of canals, tunnels, ditches, and reservoirs, water from two Colorado River tributaries, the Fryingpan and the Roaring Fork, near Aspen in Pitkin County, would be carried to eastern-slope irrigation farmers and to the residents of Pueblo, Colorado Springs, and other municipalities. The project would deliver nearly 70,000 acre-feet of water annually at a total cost of $172 million. Though much smaller than its orphaned progenitor, the Fryingpan-Arkansas project also met resistance, especially from the residents of Pitkin County.[3]

In August 1951, opponents organized the Pitkin County Water Protection Association, objecting to the project on several grounds. First, they suspected that it was really only the initial phase of the more grandiose Gunnison-Arkansas project. Second, a projected reservoir near Aspen would flood some private dwellings, including the ranch of the assistant secretary of the Navy, James Smith. Third, the reservoir would mar the scenic splendor of the region and degrade trout and other wildlife habitat. Finally, and most important, if any surplus water existed, it would be needed by the residents of the western slope. Chenoweth recalled encountering some hostility when he visited the site of the proposed reservoir near Aspen. He had gone without lunch, and as he passed a fruit stand he snatched a peach. An observer hollered: "You can steal a peach but don't try to steal any of our water."[4]

Pitkin County residents appealed to national conservation organizations to support their position, but without success. The project did not intrude upon national parks or federally designated wilderness areas, so the Sierra Club and other groups were reluctant to intercede. Moreover, they did not want to detract from their defense of Dinosaur National Monument by appearing to be opposed to all Western water-development projects.[5]

Politically, opponents had little clout. About 300,000 people lived in the Arkansas River valley, compared to 1,600 in Pitkin County. The project was pushed hard by its sponsors, Ed Chenoweth and the state's senior U.S. senator,

Republican Eugene Milliken, and had the support of the governor and of the state's water conservation board. Outside Pitkin County, west-slope residents were mainly indifferent. Even Wayne Aspinall, who represented Pitkin County in Congress, supported the Fryingpan-Arkansas project, but only after the CRSP with Echo Park Dam had received congressional approval. Pitkin County residents, then, were delighted when John Saylor championed their cause.

The House Subcommittee on Irrigation and Reclamation held hearings on the Fryingpan project from June 8 through June 10, 1953, near the end of the session. As would become his custom, Saylor grilled proponents about the economic and reclamation features of the proposal and usually found their answers wanting. The cost of the irrigation works alone, he observed to one proponent, was estimated at $60 million. But irrigation users would pay about $250,000 yearly for the use of the diverted water. Over the course of forty years, the time when reclamation projects were routinely expected to be paid off, the yield from irrigation customers would be roughly $5 million, leaving a short-fall of $55 million. "Is there anything wrong with the mathematics we teach back in Pennsylvania?" Saylor asked. "I always understood that 2 and 2 were 4 anywhere in the country, and I am at a loss. I am only trying to . . . find wherein this is supposed to be feasible." Proponents explained that additional revenue would come from municipal and industrial water users and from the sale of power. This prompted Saylor to conclude that the main purpose of the bill was not reclamation, but municipal water use and power production. If Easterners were not permitted to ask Washington to build them a water supply, why should Westerners be allowed to do so? Finally, Saylor predicted that the project would cost taxpayers more than the estimated $172 million because, "regardless of party or when the project was authorized, the Bureau of Reclamation never builds within their estimated costs. They do not even have one they can point to and say that is the exception."[6]

Because it was late in the session and not all the witnesses had been heard, the subcommittee delayed action on the Fryingpan proposal until the following year. By then, Saylor had been battling the CRSP for months and had grown more adamant in his opposition to big reclamation projects. In May 1954, the subcommittee reported the Fryingpan bill favorably. Proponents hoped the full committee would unanimously report the bill to the Rules Committee, but they were disappointed when Saylor submitted a "scathing" minority report. "I did my best to talk Mr. Saylor out of the idea of filing minority views," wrote Chenoweth. "I cannot understand just why he is taking such an active interest in opposing our project."[7]

Joined by Republican Craig Hosmer of California and six Democrats, Saylor denounced the project for several reasons. First, the Budget Bureau had not endorsed it. Second, the measure modified existing reclamation policy by using the "Collbran formula": under what was to have been a one-time-only repayment arrangement adopted by Congress in 1952 for a project in Collbran, Colorado, water users were permitted to take longer than fifty years to satisfy their financial obligation. As applied to the Fryingpan project, this formula allowed 60 percent of the investment to be paid after the fifty-year deadline. Saylor estimated that the delayed repayment would cost taxpayers about $425 million in interest. In addition, he estimated that the cost of bringing water to about 309,000 acres would be $1,375 per acre, nearly six times the value of irrigated land in the area. Furthermore, he perceived potential engineering problems, including the freezing over of open canals at an elevation of 7,000 feet, and feared that the plan was a precursor to the more robust Gunnison-Arkansas project. Finally, the people of Pitkin County, who were to supply the water, did not want the project.[8]

Saylor advanced these same arguments with Sherman Adams, an assistant to President Eisenhower. Before their meeting, Adams was counseled that Saylor "is usually carrying on a running feud with the Bureau of Reclamation" and that he should be handled "with great care as an important bill is coming up on the House side . . . and presently Saylor is voting for the bill." After meeting with Saylor, and then with Assistant Interior Secretary Ralph Tudor, who conceded that the department had been hasty in recommending a "boondoggle," the administration decided not to push for the project with House leaders.[9]

During the rules debate, Saylor doubtless caused some muffled titters when he came out against the project "not as an enemy of reclamation, but as a friend of reclamation." Economically sound projects, he said, were worthy of support, but the Fryingpan did not come close to measuring up. Indeed, "as compared to the Fryingpan-Arkansas project, the upper Colorado River Storage Project . . . smells like a bed of roses." In its economic, engineering, and irrigation aspects, Saylor asserted, the Fryingpan project resembled a Rube Goldberg contraption. If approved, he predicted grave consequences for taxpayers. Switching analogies, he compared the measure to "a Trojan horse which will allow the entire Gunnison-Arkansas project to become a reality."[10]

Proponents worked to counter Saylor's assault. A. L. Miller, chair of the House Committee on Interior and Insular Affairs, said Saylor should be as concerned with wasted water as he was with wasteful public spending. The "greatest waste in this country," he declared, "is permitting water to run into the ocean before it is used." He also reminded Pennsylvanians that they had been the recipients of nonreimbursable federal flood-control programs and should therefore be supportive of Western reclamation. For his part, Chenoweth was perturbed that only three of Pennsylvania's twenty-six-member House delegation voted for the bill: "It is obvious that the influence of Mr. Saylor was largely responsible for this situation. However, I was a little surprised and disappointed that he was able to obtain so many votes against a project that was of great importance to the people of Colorado. I think this is the first time I have seen a member of congress take such an interest in defeating a project in another state, in which his own people had not the least interest or concern." He labeled Saylor's economic assessment of Fryingpan as "fantastic and absurd" and assured colleagues that Fryingpan was an independent project, not the first step toward Gunnison-Arkansas. He further claimed that Saylor's opposition "was based on a personal desire for publicity and a feeling that increased water in Colorado might take industries away from the East." The latter charge had some merit: Saylor was an opponent of federally financed hydropower, and one of the main beneficiaries of industrial water and power would have been the Pueblo-based Colorado Iron and Coal Company, the largest corporation in the state and the nation's ninth leading producer of steel.[11]

Owing in large measure to Saylor's criticisms and the opposition of Californians who feared that the project might diminish the quantity and quality of water flowing into the lower basin from the upper Colorado River watershed, the Fryingpan measure failed to obtain a rule by a vote of 195 to 188. "Stunning Blow to Colorado," stated an editorial in the *Rocky Mountain News.* The *Denver Post* attributed the defeat to water-hungry Californians, with "the vocal assistance of an arch-enemy of all reclamation, Rep. John Saylor of Pennsylvania, an antediluvian Republican."[12]

But not all Coloradans were disappointed with the outcome. Residents of Pitkin County hailed Saylor as their "best friend in Washington," demonstrating their gratitude with their votes even though Saylor's name never appeared on a Colorado ballot. During the September primary for the Fourth Congressional District, the Democratic incumbent Wayne Aspinall ran unopposed. But when the ballots were counted in Pitkin County, Saylor, as a write-in-candidate, received eighty votes, Aspinall fifty, and Charles Wilson fourteen. For years, that vote served as a source of good-natured ribbing between Aspinall and Saylor. For conservationists, the vote would take on more serious connotations. Over the next two decades, it would come to symbolize in a general way the different environmental perspectives of the two most powerful men on the House Interior Committee. Though this portrayal was oversimplified, Aspinall was seen as being pro–resource development, often at the expense of wilderness, while Saylor was seen as a foe of big dams and as preservationist minded.[13]

When Representative Chenoweth reintroduced the Fryingpan project in 1955, he reduced its estimated cost by 10 percent, to $156 million. But in spite of pleas from Coloradans to change his position, Saylor continued to oppose Fryingpan because the residents of Pitkin County did not want it, because he believed that it would cost more than the projected $156 million, and because it was "the camel's nose under the tent," "the first step" in the gargantuan Gunnison-Arkansas plan. Once again, Saylor's objections helped to kill the Fryingpan legislation for the 1955 session.[14]

The battle over Fryingpan, however, was but a trickle compared to the torrent of controversy that surrounded the CRSP. Having blocked passage of the CRSP in 1954, conservationists debated their future course of action. Some, such as Bernard DeVoto of *Harper's* and Martin Litton of the *Los Angeles Times*, suggested opposition to the entire project, not just Echo Park Dam. "No Colorado Project, no Flaming Gorge, no Glen, none of it [is] sound, give Utah nothing, make 'em pay like L.A., let 'em starve," Litton wrote privately. "Our star is on the ascendancy, the snowball may well be underway, this is no time to be conciliatory, finish off the enemy before he can regroup."[15]

Conservation leaders sympathized with this position but dared not risk having their organizations obstruct development of the upper basin if they wanted any conservation gains in the future. "I think our strength in the future lies in being positively for a sound program in the Colorado," Penfold advised Brower. The potency of the argument against Echo Park Dam had surprised project proponents, and "for the first time we have them looking at their hole card." Conservationists, then, would cooperate, but they planned on "exacting a price—and a stiff one—for dropping opposition to the whole project."[16]

But they were undecided on what that price should be. At bottom, the Dinosaur canyons had to be saved. Brower suggested having Saylor resurrect legislation, first introduced in 1952 by Republican California congressman Leroy Johnson, that proposed saving the area by either upgrading its status from monument to national park or prohibiting the construction of dams in any national monument. But Saylor proved unreceptive to this scheme, since congressional protocol dictated that such legislation be offered by members of Congress from the affected area.[17]

Brower also wanted to save Glen Canyon in northern Arizona. In April 1954, he had urged Saylor to offer a high Glen Canyon dam as a substitute for Echo Park, but by the summer Brower had changed his mind. He had not yet visited the gorge, but some conservationists, such as the photographer Charles Eggert, described it as perhaps more stunning than Dinosaur and worthy of national park status. Brower proposed removing Echo Park and Glen Canyon from the CRSP and retaining the Flaming Gorge, Cross Mountain, Navajo, and Curecanti dam sites. Saylor, on the other hand, considered saving Glen Canyon a peripheral and potentially divisive issue, one that detracted from the main argument that national preserves were sacrosanct. "John Saylor advises us," Packard wrote Brower, "to stick as closely as possible to our fundamental purpose of objecting to the Echo Park Dam because it invades the National Park system."[18]

Most conservationists realized that Glen Canyon could not be saved, despite its spectacular scenery. It was not part of a national park or monument, and the proposed dam there would produce the bulk of the water storage and hydropower for the CRSP. They grew concerned when the bureau divulged that impounded water at Glen Canyon—from either a high or a low dam— might crawl to the base of Rainbow Bridge National Monument in southern Utah, but instead of opposing the construction of Glen altogether, they decided to hold bureau engineers accountable for protecting Rainbow Bridge with a barrier.[19]

Thus, conservation groups decided to support the CRSP if the Echo Park dam was removed from the bill. Saylor, however, announced early in 1955 that he planned to oppose the entire project for a variety of reasons. First, he considered it unsound economically. If the upper basin states wanted the project, they should fund it themselves, not burden Eastern taxpayers. Second, he echoed the sentiments of Colorado governor Ed Johnson, who held that the Colorado River Compact of 1922 forbade basin states from erecting hydroelectric dams when stored water could not be put to agricultural or domestic use. The reservoirs at Glen Canyon and Echo Park, Saylor insisted, would be used to produce power that would pay for irrigation works hundreds of miles upstream. Third, he criticized the project because these irrigation projects would produce crops already in surplus. Finally, he had concerns about the safety of the proposed Glen Canyon dam. Late in 1954, Reclamation engineers had opposed a high Glen Canyon dam as a substitute for the Echo Park facility because the rock structure might not be able to hold the additional weight. If this was the case, Saylor asked, then would the rock base be able to support the original structure, which was only thirty-five feet lower?[20]

"SAYLOR SPOUTS AGAIN," noted a headline in a Colorado newspaper. Although residents of the intermountain West were annoyed by Saylor's opposition, they still expected the CRSP to be enacted by the Eighty-fourth Congress in 1955. In January, President Eisenhower endorsed the CRSP in his budget message and State of the Union address. The same month *Time* ran an article favorable to the construction of the project, including Echo Park Dam. Moreover, Western members of Congress, with the exception of those from California, were pressing for a united front on the CRSP, for fear that its loss might jeopardize the future of the entire reclamation program. Leaving little to chance, proponents of Echo Park Dam also formed the Upper Colorado River Grass Roots, Inc., or Aqualantes, a water vigilante group that sought to publicize the CRSP, lobby Congress, and raise money for the cause.[21]

Saylor could not resist ridiculing the Aqualantes. Like most of the vigilantes of the Old West, he said, the Aqualantes were misguided. They told people that the CRSP would cost $1.5 billion, but its final cost, according to Saylor, would be $3 billion. They claimed that the project would provide irrigation but did not reveal that the crops to be produced were already in surplus. They touted the recreational opportunities of the proposed Echo Park reservoir without mentioning that a national monument and wilderness canyon would be flooded. "The Aqualantes are not riding to save the West's water," Saylor charged. They "are riding to raid the Treasury of the United States; the Aqualantes are riding to force through congress a gigantic scheme for improving their own lot; a scheme that is agriculturally unsound, economically unjustified, and absolutely unnecessary. Hi Ho, Aqualantes!"[22]

While Saylor blasted the Aqualantes on the floor of the House, a small group from the Aspen area formed the "Angrilantes" to show their displeasure with the Fryingpan project and the CRSP. The major conservation groups also formed lobby groups—the Trustees for Conservation, the Council of Conservationists, and the Citizens Committee on Natural Resources—to fight Echo Park Dam. Conservationists flooded the White House and Congress with letters and telegrams protesting the proposed dam at Echo Park. Preservationists also continued to push the glory of the Dinosaur canyons in such publications as *This Is Dinosaur*. Edited by Wallace Stegner and published by Alfred A. Knopf, this powerfully written and elegantly illustrated volume was sent to each member of Congress. Finally, the campaign against Echo Park Dam was aided when journalist Raymond Moley published *What Price Reclamation,* a scathing fiscal attack on the CRSP and other costly reclamation projects.[23]

The Eighty-fourth Congress, now controlled by Democrats, convened on January 5, 1955. As expected, the $1.5 billion Senate bill, which included Echo Park and Glen Canyon dams, plus thirty participating irrigation projects, met little resistance, passing by a vote of fifty-eight to twenty-three on April 20. The major battle for the project took place in the House, where five bills were introduced. All contained the Echo Park and Glen Canyon dams, but they differed in terms of the number of participating irrigation projects. House Interior Committee chair Claire Engle scheduled five days of hearings in March and April under the direction of Wayne Aspinall, who headed the Subcommittee on Irrigation and Reclamation.[24]

As he had the previous year, Saylor served as the point man for the opposition forces. Aggressively and persistently, he attempted to discredit government witnesses during the hearings. He forced assistant secretary of the interior Fred Aandahl to admit that the department had miscalculated the evaporation loss at Echo Park by 600 percent. He pressed Bureau of Reclamation officials to explain the need for Echo Park, given the fact that evaporation loss was no longer a factor. Would not a "high" dam of 615 feet at Glen Canyon serve as a suitable substitute for Echo Park Dam? No, replied Commissioner Dexheimer, because a high dam at Glen would back water into Rainbow Bridge National Monument, lose more water to evaporation because of its larger surface area, and perhaps be structurally unsafe.

Saylor jumped on the safety issue. If the bureau had doubts about the safety of a high dam of 615 feet, could they assure the subcommittee that a low dam of 580 feet would be secure? Hadn't the commissioner implied last fall that a low dam might not be structurally sound? What studies had the bureau conducted at the Glen Canyon site in the last six months? Had core drillings been made? Had porosity levels been examined? Dexheimer promised to provide the information for the record, but Saylor was not satisfied since the bureau had reneged on such promises in the past or had provided information that was erroneous or unresponsive to questions. Throughout the hearings, Saylor peppered bureau officials with questions concerning geological structure, evaporation losses, the cost per acre of irrigation, and the organization's tendency to build without regard for cost or the sanctity of parklands. Dam proponents accused Saylor of "badgering" bureau witnesses, but opponents lauded him for asking probing questions.[25]

While aggressive and sarcastic toward government witnesses, Saylor handled private proponents with civility and humor. For example, a Vernal, Utah, resident testified that he was nauseated by Sierra Clubbers who wanted to save the natural wonders of the state for future generations. Utahans, he read from his written testimony, did not want to be "saved[,] they wanted to be damned." Saylor suggested changing the word to *dammed* in order to spare so many good people from eternal punishment.[26]

Saylor was also not above grandstanding to demonstrate a point. Dam proponents had long argued that a reservoir at Echo Park would eliminate rapids and spare river rafters injury or death. To counter this argument, Saylor used the testimony of an experienced river runner, Kim Bradley, the eleven-year-old granddaughter of a former Sierra Club president: "Did you go down the terribly dangerous river where only the hardy are able to survive?" "Yes." "How old were you?" "Nine." "How many days were you on the river?" "Six." "Six days. Did you get dumped out into the water at any place along the line?" "No." "And you completed the trip, would you like to go back?" "Yes." Saylor concluded by remarking that those "who want to talk about the horrors of the river and [say] that it is only right for foolhardy individuals, should see [the] shining example of this young lady who went down and would like to go back again."[27]

Saylor's ardent defense of the Dinosaur canyons and his grasp of Western reclamation impressed friends and foes alike. Preservationists like Brower praised him for "a top job of questioning" and suggested additional discrepancies and weaknesses in the pro–Echo Park Dam argument. Indeed, his knowledge of Western water problems prompted one Denver resident to reassess the image of Saylor as "some kind of green-eyed monster with only venom for the West."[28]

During and after the hearings, preservationists consulted frequently with Saylor on tactics. Following April passage of the CRSP by the Senate, Saylor helped convince conservation leaders that the only way to save Echo Park, at least in 1955, was to oppose the CRSP. If conservationists withdrew their opposition in return for the deletion of Echo Park, he warned, then a Senate-House conference committee might reinsert the dam in a compromise bill, and he would be unable to kill it. After talking with Saylor, William Voigt of the Izaak Walton League advised all conservationists "to work like the very devil now to try to kill the bill in the House and kill it in its entirety."[29]

Preservationists also relied on Saylor to help counter what they regarded as distortions or misinformation propagated by dam proponents. Recent pronouncements by Republican Utah senator Arthur Watkins especially riled them. During the House subcommittee hearings, Watkins had issued new documentary evidence purporting to prove that the Interior Department and Federal Power Commission had filed claims to eleven potential hydroelectric power sites, including Echo Park, that predated Roosevelt's expansion of the monument in 1938. Moreover, the Federal Power Commission asserted that these claims were still in effect. Put simply, Watkins contended, the proposed dam did not intrude upon a national monument; rather, the expansion of the monument to the Echo Park area in 1938 had intruded upon a prior existing water-power claim.[30]

Caught off guard, conservationists scrambled to deflect Watkins's argument. During the hearings, Saylor's only retort was to say that preservationists would oppose any attempt to violate a national monument. Fred Packard of the National Parks Association and Richard Leonard of the Sierra Club prepared memoranda for members of Congress and the major newspapers countering Watkins's argument, but they seemed to have little effect. Packard and Zahniser then asked Saylor to refute Watkins's points on the House floor. Supplied with briefs from Leonard and William Norris, a Washington attorney, Saylor accepted the challenge.[31]

He began by upbraiding Watkins for maligning conservationists by asserting that they had deliberately deceived the American public by claiming that national parks and monuments were inviolate. Conservationists, Saylor said, were "sincere and honest Americans" who regarded national preserves as sacrosanct. He agreed with Watkins that legally Congress could authorize a dam at Echo Park; indeed, Congress "could destroy every inch of our national parks and monuments if it wanted to," he declared, but fortunately, precedent and good judgment dictated against such a narrow-minded move.

He challenged Watkins's point that power-site withdrawals were "solemn reservations" that were legally binding. "A power withdrawal is merely a precautionary measure to assure that prospective power development sites do not pass to private ownership under the public land laws," he argued. "A power withdrawal does not guarantee to anyone that the site will be developed for power purposes. Many, many more power withdrawals are made than power dams are built." Moreover, the presidential proclamation of 1938 by implication superseded all prior power claims. In short, Roosevelt had considered the wonders of scenery more important than the potential for power. By concentrating on legal subtleties, he concluded, Watkins and other dam proponents had failed to grasp the notion that the proposed facility at Echo Park would not only obliterate "a magnificent stretch of natural scenery" but also establish an alarming precedent by intruding upon the national park system. "This is an argument that has never been answered," he said, "because it is unanswerable."[32]

Having satisfactorily rebutted Watkins's argument, at least as far as conservationists were concerned, Saylor then used the House floor to assail the argument that the reservoir created by Echo Park Dam would improve the scenery and provide citizens with additional recreational opportunities. During a speech in Los Angeles, Interior Secretary McKay, whom Saylor despised, had envisioned a road-accessible serene lake at Echo Park to provide enjoyment for anglers, boaters, picnickers, and swimmers. "What has been done on Lake Mead is what we have in mind in Dinosaur National Monument," McKay had declared.

Saylor used McKay's analogy as a springboard to lampoon Lake Mead. Created by Hoover Dam, the reservoir was hardly a scenic or recreational mecca, he said. In fact, he declared, it "has nothing whatsoever to offer." It was encircled by "uncounted miles of mud flats. Great reaches of ashen silt deposits bake and crack under the desert sun. The recreational areas are far removed from water, standing forlorn and useless," he continued. Hardly a playground, Lake Mead might more accurately be described as "a gigantic desert enjoyed exclusively by lizards and insects." By contrast, Dinosaur National Monument was one of the more spectacular wilderness areas on the planet. Trying to enhance its beauty "by making it another Lake Mead would be like applying an air hammer to the chiseled features of the Venus de Milo, or using a house-painter's brush on a Rubens masterpiece." Those remarks left many Nevadans, who were proud of their Lake Mead, aghast. Republican congressman Clifton Young claimed that Saylor's comments would have "a more forceful social and economic impact upon southern Nevada than all of the nuclear devices which have exploded there thus far." Moreover, he stated, to contend that Lake Mead "has nothing to offer is like saying Marilyn Monroe has no feminine charms."[33]

Having offended Nevadans by denigrating Lake Mead, Saylor next turned his scattergun on the Hetch Hetchy reservoir of California. Congress had made "a great mistake" in 1913 when it transformed the "breathlessly beautiful" Hetch Hetchy valley of Yosemite National Park into a reservoir. Like Lake Mead, this site had little to offer. Saylor described the lake and its surroundings as "sordid," "a tragic picture of splenetic emptiness," a "ghastly monument to the 1913 model anticonservationists." The product of eager reclamationists who believed they could improve upon nature, Hetch Hetchy had become a half-empty bathtub ringed by "scattered stumps of once proud trees" and permeated by the "stench of drying, stinking muck." A similar fate would await the Dinosaur canyons if dam builders got their way.[34]

On June 6, 1955, the House subcommittee met to consider the CRSP. Saylor introduced an amendment deleting Echo Park, but it lost. Two days later, however, the subcommittee reversed itself and excised Echo Park Dam from the bill. At the same time, however, it agreed to an amendment recommended by Aspinall that would create a panel of engineers to compare all other dam sites with Echo Park and then forward their conclusions to the president by the end of 1958. In short, Echo Park Dam still had a chance.[35]

A week later, the full House Interior Committee met to consider the bill. Saylor and preservationists were uneasy over the Aspinall amendment, Saylor calling it a "time bomb" because it would allow Echo Park Dam to be reinserted into the CRSP at some future date. In late June, however, the House committee chopped the Aspinall amendment, approving the measure without Echo Park Dam, recommending a $760 million bill that included storage dams at Glen Canyon, Flaming Gorge, and Navajo on the San Juan River in New Mexico. It also approved eleven irrigation works. By contrast, the Senate bill was nearly twice as expensive, recommending large dams at Navajo, Glen Canyon, and Echo Park, plus thirty irrigation projects.[36]

Although Echo Park Dam had been deleted from the House bill, conservation leaders were not satisfied, fearing that the dam would be revisited by a Senate-House conference committee. This fear seemed remote when Engle and Aspinall announced that they were withdrawing their support for Echo Park Dam and vowed to block any effort to reintroduce it in the conference committee. Still, conservationists hesitated to go along with the House bill until the Senate and the Bureau of Reclamation agreed to eliminate the dam and pledge to protect Rainbow Bridge National Monument from the waters of Glen Canyon reservoir. For his part, Saylor continued to blast the entire project as economically unsound, with or without Echo Park Dam. Realizing that the CRSP could not survive a vote by the full body, House leaders decided to reconsider the bill in 1956. The Dinosaur canyons had been spared again.[37]

Brower and Zahniser gave much of the credit for the reprieve to Saylor. Just before departing on a Sierra Club excursion to the Tetons, Brower congratulated Saylor for the "magnificent job" he had done. "I suspect those upper basin boys will be back swinging come January, but somehow I think you've taken the sting out of their swing," he wrote. "I've said it before and I'll say it again. If it hadn't been for John Saylor, those boys would be hard at it right now messing up one of the finest parts of our entire National Park System. Long may you live to fight the kind of battle we can be sure we'll be confronted with again and again—and will win again and again so long as we have men of your stature up there on the hill."[38]

Brower may be excused some exaggeration: he was, at least in part, trying to nurture Saylor for future battles. Several forces had coalesced in 1954 and 1955 to block the construction of Echo Park Dam. The most important players, as historian Mark Harvey has noted, were conservation organizations, especially the Sierra Club, with Brower at its head, which helped direct public attention to the threat to the national park system. Indeed, in 1955 the NPA bestowed upon Brower the same award it had given Saylor the year before. The California congressional delegation had also contributed to the resistance movement, as had individuals such as Wallace Stegner, Bernard DeVoto, and Raymond Moley.[39]

But the impact of Saylor's leadership must not be understated. He was one of the first and certainly the foremost critics of the project in the House, and his assistance to conservation groups proved invaluable. He served as their legislative eyes and ears, obtained hard-to-get data from government agencies, offered advice on tactics, inserted anti-dam speeches into the *Congressional Record*, helped show the fallibility of Reclamation Bureau specialists with tough questions, worked ardently to remove Echo Park Dam from the bill in subcommittee, and probably won over several of his colleagues with his passionate defense of the park system. By 1955, he had earned additional accolades for his zealous efforts to protect national parklands. The battle to protect Dinosaur National Monument may have been won without him, but it would have been far more difficult and time consuming.[40]

Although the Fryingpan and the CRSP were the most controversial, other similar reclamation projects demanded the attention of the House Committee on Interior and Insular Affairs in 1955. On occasion, Saylor supported reclamation proposals when he considered them economically sound. The Trinity River project in California was one that won his blessing. This $225 million Bureau of Reclamation project proposed diverting 700,000 acre-feet of water annually, about 17 percent of the river's flow, from northern California to the Sacramento River valley, where it would be used for hydropower and irrigation. Water users would repay their share of the cost, about $68 million in forty years, and the power costs, approximately $157 million, would be repaid at 3 percent interest over twenty-six years. The measure also offered the possibility of partnership in the production of electricity, a principle that was dear to conservatives like Saylor and the Eisenhower administration. The partnership arrangement meant that private companies would build four power stations and sell the electricity. Besides funding the power houses, they would pay the federal government for the privilege of using the falling water to generate the power and also pay taxes to the local community.

Trinity proved less controversial than Fryingpan and the CRSP. It was less costly and intruded upon no national preserves. It had nearly unanimous support in California, including the counties from which the water would be diverted. It was also dear to Clair Engle, the Californian who chaired the House Committee on Interior and Insular Affairs. Indeed, Engle had initially pushed the CRSP—at least until he realized that it was doomed with the presence of Echo Park Dam—because he did not want to endanger Trinity and other reclamation projects.

Trinity also received a boost when Saylor endorsed it. "What I have to say will probably come as a distinct shock to some of the members," Saylor said on the House floor, but "this is the best reclamation project that they will ever be privileged to vote upon." He supported the project because it would produce crops such as grapes, nuts, and fruits that were not in surplus; because it would be self-liquidating; and because of the power partnership arrangement. His "benediction" came as a shock to some representatives. "Even Rep. John Saylor, who habitually rips into the Bureau of Reclamation at the drop of a gavel, stepped out of character long enough to urge support of the Trinity," observed Democrat Stewart Udall of Arizona. The Trinity project passed the House by a vote of 230 to 153. The large number of negative votes from the South, Midwest, and East, however, did give pause to supporters of more controversial projects, such as the CRSP.[41]

By mid-1955, both preservationists and members of the House Interior Committee were frustrated by the prospect that the CRSP threatened to become a "hardy perennial." Proponents of the CRSP were also growing impatient, as their chances for success seemed to be slipping away. Realizing that a bill with Echo Park Dam would never get through the House, upper basin state senators met in Denver on November 1, 1955, and issued a pledge that the proposed dam at Echo Park would be removed in the next legislative session. That same month Interior Secretary McKay announced that the department had discarded plans to invade the Dinosaur canyons.[42]

These assurances were welcome, but not quite good enough for preservationists. They insisted that the legislation itself contain assurances that Dinosaur National Monument would be protected from any dams and that Rainbow Bridge National Monument would be shielded from the impounded waters of Glen Canyon Dam. Their additional demands exasperated upper basin state representatives, but they eventually agreed, and conservationists in January 1956 declared their support for the CRSP.[43]

Saylor, however, continued to oppose the project. He considered it unsound economically, especially since the revenue-producing power dam at Echo Park had been axed from the project. He proposed an amendment that would have provided an outright gift of $420 million for the project so long as the upper basin states agreed never to approach Congress again for more money for the irrigation component of the bill. The upper basin state representatives, however, said they did not want handouts, and the amendment was defeated. Saylor also decried the fact that the measure altered the historic pattern of reclamation law by increasing the traditional repayment period for the construction of power works from forty to one hundred years, for municipal water works from forty to fifty years, and for irrigation works from forty to fifty years. Too, the irrigation structures would produce crops that would add to the agricultural surplus. The House dealt with this objection by adding an amendment that forbade the growing of six major crops on the newly irrigated acres for a period of ten years. On March 1, the House approved the CRSP by a vote of 256 to 136, Saylor voting with the minority. The following week, the House-Senate conference committee, which included Saylor, deleted Echo Park from the measure and endorsed two provisos protecting the national park system from any CRSP dams and guarding Rainbow Bridge National Monument from the sprawling waters of Glen Canyon Dam.[44]

Although unsuccessful, Saylor's spirited opposition to the CRSP gained national attention and the gratitude of conservation groups. Preservationists hailed Saylor as the "outstanding champion of park protection" and worked for his reelection to Congress in 1956. Fiscal conservatives praised his opposition to costly federal reclamation projects. Democratic representative James Haley of Florida described his colleague as an "inspiring" leader whose "dedicated, unselfish, and courageous efforts" helped to protect a national monument and saved taxpayers the expense of building a $500 million dam at Echo Park. He had not achieved a total victory, Haley continued, "but he has won the admiration and respect of even the most aggressive of his foes."[45]

The depiction of Saylor as a feisty defender of the national park system and fiscal conservatism was on the mark, but Saylor also served sectional and local economic interests. Like most members of Congress east of the Mississippi, he was concerned that Western reclamation projects would yield crops that competed with those produced in surplus in his own state. Moreover, as a representative from a major coal-producing region, he was determined to protect his district's miners from imported foreign oil, nuclear-generated energy, and hydroelectric power. In future sessions of Congress, he would continue to battle for their interests, for the protection of national parklands, and for the preservation of wilderness.[46]

six

Wilderness and Park Advocate

DURING THE FRACAS over the CRSP, newspaper writer and Sierra Club member Martin Litton shared an anecdote that illustrated the growing concern of many conservationists over the threats to wild areas by dam builders and other developers. Long ago in the snowy wilds of Siberia, a sleigh was surrounded by ravenous wolves. To buy time and save the passengers, the driver cut loose one of the horses, and it was devoured. This desperate act provided only temporary relief, and the sleigh soon came under attack again. Another horse was released, then another, and with each sacrifice the sleigh was slowed until ultimately the entire group was lost.[1]

The message of this anecdote was not lost on preservationists. They understood that the fight for Dinosaur National Monument meant more than safeguarding two pristine canyons and upholding the inviolability of the national park system. The proposed dam at Echo Park, as Howard Zahniser cautioned John Saylor, posed a "threat to any hope we have of preserving any of our land in its natural, unspoiled beauty. It is a threat to our wildlife refuges, a threat to all our State and city parks, a threat to our wilderness areas, our national forests, and to all the areas that we have sought to set aside for special preservation purposes by the device of land classification. It is a threat to these because it endangers what has been deemed to be the safest of all such systems of land classification, the national park system." Put simply, if a national monument could not be protected, then any wild area could be ravaged by the wolves of commercialism.[2]

Indeed, as the historian Mark Harvey has shown, the fight to protect Dinosaur National Monument represented the first significant confrontation between developers and preservationists in the postwar American West and was a pivotal event in the American conservation movement. After the successful campaign to spare Echo Park, national preserves became less susceptible to development, but they were not immune. Conservation groups such as the National Parks Association, the Wilderness Society, and the Sierra Club dedicated themselves, in the postwar decades, to giving added protection to vast reaches of national wilderness preserves. Already skeptical of federal reclamation projects, and a fervent defender of the sanctity of national parklands, John Saylor became an early recruit in this emerging wilderness crusade.[3]

Along with economic development, the postwar population and tourism boom in the American West also worried those who sought to preserve wild areas. Demands for roads, hotels, parking areas, restaurants, souvenir shops, and recreational facilities to accommodate visitors might doom primitive areas in national parks, forests, and monuments just as surely as bulldozers would. Fred Packard of the National Parks Association summed up concern over overpopulating the parks when he wrote that "the emphasis in park matters should be on re-creation, as contrasted with recreation. There is a conflict of viewpoint here that may be irreconcilable." This assessment proved accurate, especially in the arid West during the postwar years. Most Westerners believed that there was scenery and wilderness aplenty and that "true" conservation meant prudent resource development and recreation. While not renouncing public recreation and wise use, conservationists like Packard, Brower, Zahniser, and Saylor held, in contrast, that primitive areas in national preserves were endangered by "civilization" and that measures should be taken to preserve them.[4]

Shortly after the victory at Dinosaur, Howard Zahniser called upon Saylor to discuss wilderness preservation. At Zahniser's urging, Saylor and Democratic senator Hubert H. Humphrey of Minnesota agreed to sponsor legislation creating a national wilderness system. Introduced in June, late in the session, the legislation stood little chance of success, but it did launch a spirited debate over the issue of locking up natural resources that would last for nearly a decade.[5]

The idea of having the national government set aside areas of scenic and rugged splendor had been partially realized during the late nineteenth and early twentieth centuries. Congress established Yellowstone National Park in 1872 and

Yosemite National Park in 1890. The Antiquities Act of 1906 authorized the president, through executive order, to protect areas of scientific, historical, and scenic significance as national monuments. President Theodore Roosevelt proclaimed as national treasures the Muir Woods and Lassen Volcanic Peak in California, Devil's Tower in Wyoming, and the Petrified Forest and Grand Canyon in Arizona. He also used executive authority, subsequently approved by Congress, to establish national wildlife refuges. In 1916, Congress created the National Park Service, within the Interior Department, to administer, promote, and protect national parks and monuments. Congress also allowed for the conservation of timberland in 1891 by authorizing the president to establish forest reserves. Almost immediately, President Benjamin Harrison set aside 13 million acres, President Grover Cleveland contributed 21 million, and President Theodore Roosevelt reserved another 132 million.[6]

The U.S. Forest Service, within the Department of Agriculture, was established in 1905 to supervise these reserves. Gifford Pinchot, its first chief, championed wise resource use. Downplaying preservation, the Forest Service made the timber, grasses, water sites, and ores of its reserves available to commercial interests, although it guarded against overuse. Trees, for example, were regarded as a crop that needed to be harvested and then replenished. Despite this "tree farm mentality," to borrow a phrase from Craig Allin, some Forest Service employees, such as Arthur Carhart, Aldo Leopold, and Robert Marshall, emerged in the years after the Great War to champion the preservation of some forest-land in its primeval condition.[7]

The years between World War I and World War II, as historian Paul Sutter has convincingly argued, were central to the formation of the modern wilderness crusade. During these years, Americans had more leisure time and spent some of it engaging nature by automobile. Aided by federal road building, auto-camping and motor touring boomed during the interwar years, as did the enterprises that sought to meet the consumer demands of the nature-seeking public. Increasingly, roadside landscapes became cluttered by billboards, gas stations, motels, campgrounds, restaurants, and souvenir shops. The federal government also brought trails, roads, and campgrounds to national parks and forests, especially with its work relief programs of the 1930s. Some conservationists, particularly the men who founded the Wilderness Society in the mid-1930s, believed that motorized outdoor recreation posed a greater threat to pristine landscapes than did logging, mining, and dams. Consequently, they worked to preserve sizable natural expanses that were unencumbered by roads, automobiles, and recreational and commercial development. In short, roadless-ness and solitude became essential components of their wilderness idea.[8]

Shortly after World War I, the Department of Agriculture hired Arthur Carhart as a landscape architect to design structures in forest reserves that would be rented out by the Forest Service. Sent to Trappers Lake in the White River National Forest of Colorado to plan the construction of summer homes, he recommended against development in order to keep the area roadless and pristine. His superiors agreed. He also recommended against intruding upon the Superior National Forest in upper Minnesota. This unspoiled lake region, now known as the Boundary Waters Canoe Area, should be held as wilder-ness, he counseled, because it would prove to be "as priceless as Yellowstone, or the Grand Canyon—if it remained a water-trail wilderness." Again, Carhart's recommendation was approved by the secretary of agriculture, and eventually, in 1930, Congress preserved 1.2 million acres as the Superior Roadless Area, the first national wilderness preserve.[9]

Aldo Leopold was an assistant district forester in New Mexico. Like his friend and confidant Carhart, he believed that large spans of wilderness should be undeveloped, mainly to protect fish and animal habitat. He recommended, and the Forest Service approved, the preservation of nearly 575,000 acres of wilderness in the Gila National Forest of New Mexico. After leaving the Forest Service in the early 1920s, Carhart and Leopold continued as outsiders to push for the preservation of wild country.[10]

Influenced by the arguments of Carhart and Leopold, and concerned by the efforts of the National Park Service to acquire scenic national forestland, Chief of Forestry William B. Greeley ordered a study of existing wilderness areas. This inventory led to the 1929 issuance of Regulation L-20, which au-thorized the chief of forestry to establish areas for public appreciation and recreation where primitive conditions would prevail. Yet these "primitive areas" were not immune from commercial use "since the utilization of such resources, if properly regulated, will not be incompatible with the purposes for which the area is designated." (Indeed, by 1937, of the seventy-two primitive regions in ten Western states, encompassing nearly 135 million acres, only four zones of approximately 300,000 acres were free from logging, grazing, and roads.)[11]

Robert Marshall was yet another Forest Service official who worked to preserve additional acres of wilderness and make existing primitive areas less susceptible to development. He was instrumental in having the Forest Service adopt two new regulations in 1939, U-1 and U-2, which gave added protection to about 14 million acres of unspoiled timber country. Regulation U-1 authorized the secretary of agriculture, upon recommendation of the Forest Service, to designate thirty expanses of 100,000 acres or more as "wilderness areas." These pristine regions would be closed to mechanized vehicles and virtually all development, except for mining and grazing. Hiking, camping, and hunting would be permitted. The agriculture secretary could lift the cloak of protection, but only after public hearings. Regulation U-2 provided for the establishment of forty-two "wild areas" of less than 100,000 but more than 5,000 acres. These regions would remain primeval and noncommercial, except for mining and grazing, unless the chief of forestry reclassified them. The primitive areas, established earlier by regulation L-20, would retain their status pending a review by the Forest Service. (Eventually, thirty-eight of these areas were classified as "wilderness" or "wild" areas.) By 1939, then, the Forest Service had designated four categories of pristine forest reserves: "wilderness," "wild," "roadless" (the two areas in the Minnesota lake country), and "primitive."[12]

In 1935, Marshall, Leopold, and six other men founded the Wilderness Society, their purpose "to secure the preservation of wilderness, conduct educational programs concerning the values of wilderness, encourage scientific studies, and mobilize cooperation in resisting the invasion of wilderness." Upon his early death in 1939, Marshall left $400,000 to the organization so that it could carry on its work.[13]

While the new Forest Service regulations appeared to have perpetuated wilderness, the Wilderness Society and other preservationists feared that the Forest Service might attempt to open protected areas to economic development. Their fears seemed justified. Following Marshall's death, the Forest Service returned to its focus on timber production, including clear-cutting entire stands of trees and dragging its feet on reclassifying primitive areas as "wilderness" and "wild." Preservationists became alarmed that the Forest Service might succumb to the demands of lumber companies to open up or declassify previously designated "wilderness" and "wild" areas. This concern, coupled with the Bureau of Reclamation's attempt to intrude upon wilderness at Dinosaur National Monument, prompted demands for legislative protection for untamed areas in all national preserves. This goal became the main responsibility and life's work of the Wilderness Society's Howard Zahniser.[14]

Like John Saylor, Zahniser was from western Pennsylvania. After graduating from college in 1928, he worked as a conservation writer for the U.S. Fish and Wildlife Service and then during the war headed the Division of Information in the Department of Agriculture. After the war, he joined the Wilderness Society as executive secretary (later executive director) and edited its quarterly magazine, the *Living Wilderness*. Besides their western Pennsylvania origins, Zahniser and Saylor also shared a dedication to wilderness preservation and the sanctity of the national park system. During the battle over Dinosaur monument, they became friendly and developed a close working relationship, although the two men were a contrast in personalities. While Saylor could be irascible, intemperate, impatient, brash, and bombastic, Zahniser was even tempered, forbearing, contemplative, courteous, and unassuming.

Zahniser had been considering wilderness legislation since 1949 but delayed preparing a draft until he knew the outcome of the Echo Park conflict and had reached agreement on the need for a bill among conservationists. By the spring of 1956, he had crafted the bill mentioned earlier, with the help of other conservation leaders, and asked Saylor and Humphrey to introduce it in the House and Senate respectively.[15]

Cosponsored by several other legislators, the Humphrey-Saylor companion bills sought to create a statutory shield for publicly owned wilderness areas so that federal agencies, such as the Forest Service, could not open them by whim to development through declassification. In these bills, wilderness was defined as "an area where the earth and its community of life are untrammeled by man," where the individual "is a member of the natural community who visits but does not remain and whose travels leave only trails." The legislative canopy would cover forty-nine pristine areas in national parks and monuments; twenty in wildlife refuges and ranges; fifteen on Indian reservations (with the approval of tribal representatives); and eighty in national forests, including fifty-nine "primitive" zones that would be absorbed once the Forest Service classified them as "wilderness" or "wild" over the next ten years. In all, the bill proposed protection for 163 backcountry areas totaling 55 million acres. The specific areas to be included only survived the first few drafts, the final bill leaving it up to the agencies to survey and make their recommendations.[16]

To avoid swelling the national bureaucracy, wilderness areas would continue to be administered by existing federal agencies. Each agency was charged with maintaining the wilderness character of each sanctuary and recommending to Congress additional areas for inclusion in the system. Commercial activities were virtually banned: there would be no lumbering, grazing, prospecting, mining, motoring, or road or dam building. There were exceptions, however. Where use had already been established, grazing, and in a few instances motorboat and aircraft operation, would be allowed. No forest areas where logging operations were under way were brought into the program. Following existing policy, hunting would be permitted in wilderness areas administered by the Forest Service, but not in territory under the jurisdiction of the Park Service. Early versions of the measure also called for the creation of a National Wilderness Preservation Council made up of six private citizens appointed by the president and several designated federal officials to maintain records and provide public information.[17]

Shortly after introducing the bill, Saylor gave a House speech, ghostwritten by Howard Zahniser, explaining why it was important to save wilderness. Abundant natural resources, he said, helped make the United States prosperous, powerful, and ethnically diversified: "We are a great people because we have been so successful developing and using our marvelous natural resources, but, also, we Americans are the people we are largely because we have had the influence of the wilderness in our lives." Like the famous historian Frederick Jackson Turner, he believed that the frontier or wilderness experience had helped promote democracy, self-reliance, opportunity, creativity, and other characteristics that made Americans unique. Saylor also shared Theodore Roosevelt's belief that interacting with wilderness helped produce people who were physically and mentally vigorous. Losing wild areas might soften Americans and make them susceptible to conquest by hardier outsiders. And like Zahniser and other preservationists, Saylor believed in the intrinsic value of wilderness. The beauty, expanse, and solitude of unspoiled landscapes, he asserted, refreshed the human spirit by relieving stress and providing a sense of wonder and inspiration and a realization that individuals are part of the web of life who should serve as stewards, not masters, of the planet. After recounting the contributions to the wilderness idea of such individuals as Henry David Thoreau, John Muir, Theodore Roosevelt, Aldo Leopold, Robert Marshall, and others, Saylor closed by saying that the traditional policies of prudent resource use and recreation should be continued while simultaneously assuring "that some of our land is preserved as nearly as possible untouched by any kind of civilized development [and] as God made it."[18]

Saylor's speech was well received and widely distributed by conservation groups, the Wilderness Society alone sending out 48,000 copies and reprinting it in the *Living Wilderness*. But as expected, the legislative session ended without either chamber acting on the wilderness bills.[19]

After Congress adjourned, Saylor solicited suggestions on the bill from hundreds of "friends of conservation." He forwarded the overwhelmingly positive responses he received to the Wilderness Society and discussed with Zahniser the objections a few people had to the legislation. "It is a great pleasure to be privileged to work along with you on these problems and a great encouragement to know of your championship of wilderness preservation," Zahniser wrote Saylor.[20]

With the opening of the Eighty-fifth Congress in January 1957, Humphrey and Saylor resubmitted slightly amended versions of their wilderness bills. The principal change related to primitive areas in the national forests, which would be instantly brought into the system and protected from development pending the ten-year review by the agriculture secretary. Both the Senate and House Committees on Interior and Insular Affairs held hearings in June, but neither reported the legislation. But Zahniser was not discouraged: little acrimony had been demonstrated, and few people spoke out against the principle of wilderness preservation. His strategy, as he had informed Saylor months before, was to proceed slowly to promote understanding, careful deliberation, and ultimately consensus.[21]

While not vociferous, however, opposition to the bill was brisk. Wayne Aspinall of the House Committee on Interior and Insular Affairs, who would prove a bane to wilderness advocates, let Joe Penfold know privately that he was cool toward the measure. Timber, oil, grazing, mining, and water interests objected to the legislation because it would lock up resources they might need in the future. Forest-product representatives were also concerned that wilderness areas would not be protected against fires, insects, and disease. The Park Service and Forest Service withheld their support, believing that wilderness was sufficiently protected. Park Service director Conrad Wirth wondered about the propriety of including Indian reservation lands and wildlife sanctuaries in the program and doubted that a national wilderness preservation system would give as much protection to unsullied landscapes as would national park status. Wirth was also more receptive to roads than were wilderness advocates: "As we build a road into Wonder Lake in Mt. McKinley National Park that does not mean that the park is no longer a wilderness," he stated. "The road is a wilderness road, to bring people into the wilderness." The Forest Service too showed little enthusiasm for the proposal; it would hinder them from determining the best use for a specific national forest.[22]

Both federal agencies disliked the establishment of a National Wilderness Preservation Council, fearing it would serve as a "super agency" or Bureau of Wilderness Preservation that would monitor and perhaps rebuke their determinations relating to wilderness and serve as a special advocacy group in the government for wilderness values. Consequently, they portrayed such a council as a slab of bureaucracy that would come between themselves and Congress.[23]

Others viewed the wilderness proposal as privileged legislation that would benefit only an elite minority. Instead of serving a variety of purposes, wilderness territory would be set aside for the use of those who had the time and money to hike, camp, watch wildlife, and commune with nature.[24]

Finally, some conservation leaders privately expressed doubts about the bill. Arthur Carhart, for example, considered a wilderness system useless unless policy makers also devised an overall plan for land, recreation, and resource use. Devereux Butcher, former editor of *National Parks Magazine,* worried that those segments of the national parks and monuments not categorized as wilderness would be opened to roads, hotels, saloons, and other comforts of civilization.[25]

Wilderness proponents worked doggedly to deflect criticism of the bill. Saylor asserted that the preservation of wilderness had the overwhelming approval of the American people, inserting into the *Congressional Record* excerpts from hundreds of letters of support that he had received. He and Zahniser also sought to placate the Forest Service, the Park Service, and others with concerns about the Wilderness Council. This body would hold no administrative jurisdiction and would be essentially powerless. It would serve mainly as a record-keeping and information-distribution center. Moreover, an amendment would reduce the number of citizen representatives from six to three.[26]

Proponents also emphasized the conservative aspects of the nonpartisan legislation. Its purpose, Zahniser repeatedly declared, was "to accomplish wilderness preservation without disturbing the status quo." The federal agencies would continue to administer the wilderness areas under their jurisdiction. But legislation was necessary to prevent future bureaucrats from yielding to the pressure of commercial interests to unlock wild areas. Delicately, supporters of the bill pointed out that the Forest Service had recently shaved 53,000 acres from the Three Sisters Wilderness in Oregon when it was reclassified in 1957. Moreover, no measures protected national parks and monuments from roads and motorized recreation. Indeed, many preservationists were concerned by the Park Service's Mission 66 plan to obtain increased congressional appropriations for improving roads and other facilities by the year 1966, the fiftieth anniversary of the agency's founding.[27]

Wilderness proponents also sought to counter other objections. Wilderness areas on Indian reservations would be sanctioned by Native Americans.

Existing uses on national forestlands, namely grazing, would be honored. Timber harvesting on designated wilderness national forestlands was not presently allowed, so the lumber industry would not lose privileges. Only mining and water development was excluded, and Congress, in the national interest, could always open protected areas to dams, mining, grazing, or lumbering. Nor was the wilderness proposal elitist. Like national art, science, and history museums, wilderness preserves were natural galleries open to all. Moreover, one could be nourished and comforted by wild territory without actually visiting it. Zahniser acknowledged the need for a master plan on land use and recreation but agreed with Saylor, "our good Republican sponsor in the House of Representatives," who cautioned that wild country was rapidly disappearing, stating that "the purpose of the Wilderness Bill is to protect something that is in great need of protecting, even while we are making broad studies of all our outdoor recreational needs and opportunities."[28]

Throughout the year, wilderness advocates pushed for the proposal in a variety of ways. They emphasized the nonpartisan nature of the bill and wooed pivotal legislators such as Aspinall and Clinton Anderson of the Senate Interior Committee. They worked hard to win over officials in the Park Service and the Forest Service. They sought to counter misinformation about the measure that appeared in newspapers and magazines. They distributed copies of Saylor's "Saving the Wilderness" speech and published articles supporting the proposal in magazines such as the *Living Wilderness, Audubon, National Parks Magazine,* and the *Sierra Club Bulletin.* And they made speeches.[29]

In an address celebrating National Wildlife Week, Saylor pointed out that setting aside backcountry was important to the survival of endangered species such as grizzly bears, whooping cranes, and California condors and for the psychological health of the harried human species. And in an appearance before the Wilderness Club of Philadelphia, Saylor stressed the difference between conservation and preservation: the former focused on using resources wisely and preventing abuses such as overlogging, overgrazing, overhunting, overfishing, stream pollution, littering, and soil erosion; the latter stressing setting aside wild country for its own sake and for the re-creation of humans. "Man does not live by bread alone," he admonished. "His soul hungers for a sustenance that only Nature's grandeur can offer." Moreover, wilderness was "the oldest resource of all, the raw material for our civilization." He admitted that wilderness was evocative and sometimes hard to define. He spoke of the time a teacher had asked a pupil to explain a vacuum. "I have it in my head," the student said, "but I just can't express it." He admired the definition worked out by Zahniser: wilderness was a sanctuary where "the earth and its natural life community are untrammeled by man." Humans should visit by foot, canoe, or horseback and then depart, leaving minimal traces of their travels. Saylor closed by admonishing that "God's handiwork" would soon be a distant memory unless Congress acted to protect it.[30]

Wilderness proponents, at the suggestion of the Forest Service, made minor concessions in order to improve the bill's chances for success in 1958. One permitted the president to authorize prospecting, mining, and dam building in wild areas when such uses were patently in the national interest. Another made it more difficult to add wilderness territory to the program by requiring the approval of both houses of Congress. The original bill had permitted the appropriate federal agency to add land to the wilderness system so long as neither House disapproved. This slight alteration helped ease the fears of the Forest Service that it would lose an excessive amount of its holdings to preservation, and the modifications were sufficient to win the guarded support of the Park and Forest Services. But opposition from commercial interests and Western politicians remained strong.[31]

As usual, preservationists tried to placate the opposition, especially stock growers and the forest-products industry. Zahniser reminded both groups that no existing rights on public lands would be lost, and Saylor appealed to those in the lumber industry to continue to serve the cause of conservation. "There is no one who loves the woods and wild country more than a lumberman," he said. "Who then could be more interested in seeing that some of this grand country is preserved for his kids to see as it was in the early days?" It was incorrect, he asserted, to portray timber concerns as despoilers who were out to cut and run; most of them favored a dual policy of use and preservation. Most public forestland should be open to economic use, but some should be left unspoiled. Preservationists agreed that "we can have both commodity production and wilderness preservation in this wonderful land of ours." If there should ever come a time, Saylor declared, that there was an economic need for the 2 percent of forestland that had been set aside as wilderness, then "both our wild areas and America are doomed."[32]

Some Wilderness Bill proponents grew impatient with the efforts to accommodate the opposition. Existing rights such as grazing should not be countenanced, asserted a University of Utah botany professor. And Brower became disturbed when resource managers in the private and public sectors were acknowledged as conservationists. He did not want the term to lose its meaning, as it would "if a pulp man calls himself a conservationist. If he is one, who isn't?" But Zahniser, Saylor, and most preservationists realized that politically they would probably be required to make further concessions because they would not prevail if they sought a perfect bill. This viewpoint found support after the Senate twice held hearings but did not report the bill favorably. The proposal did not have enough support in the House to schedule hearings. But wilderness advocates understood that "this was no little fight" and that it "might take several years" to win.[33]

Actually, the Wilderness Bill might have been given greater consideration had another conservation measure not been given priority. In 1957, Saylor and others had introduced legislation to establish a national Outdoor Recreation Resources Review Commission (ORRRC). The proposal was conceived and partially drafted by Joe Penfold, Saylor's river-rafting companion of the Izaak Walton League. Worried that future generations would not have enough fishing, hunting, boating, hiking, camping, picnicking, and wildlife-watching opportunities, he proposed the creation of a fifteen-member panel to scrutinize the existing availability of recreation resources, determine needs in the decades ahead, and devise a strategy to meet those future requirements. Their report was to be submitted to Congress by January 1960, later extended to January 1961. Held up for a year because the Park Service and some legislators believed that the ORRRC would conflict with the Mission 66 plan, the bill passed in 1958. Chaired by Laurance Rockefeller, the Recreation Commission was made up of seven individuals from the private sector and eight members of Congress, including Saylor. Although there was a genuine need for such a review, preservationists became disgruntled when Aspinall and other opponents worked to stall action on the Wilderness Bill until the submission of the ORRRC report in 1961.[34]

Shortly after the Eighty-sixth Congress convened in 1959, Humphrey and Saylor again introduced identical wilderness bills. Other legislators either co-sponsored the bill if they were in the Senate or submitted separate measures if they were in the House. The new legislation contained additional concessions, especially to federal agencies. The agriculture secretary, for example, was granted authority to control fire, insects, disease, and animal overpopulation in designated wilderness areas, and the amount of time given to the Agriculture Department to reclassify primitive areas was increased from ten to twenty years. In addition, both the agriculture and the interior secretaries could name associates to represent them on the National Wilderness Preservation Council. Finally, to mollify Western commercial interests, the revised bill eliminated language stating that the preservation of wilderness superseded all other uses. The modified proposal, declared Wilderness Society president Olaus Murie, "has been so dressed down to meet so many objections that certainly no one, among stockmen or others, with any sense of democracy, could have any objections to its present form." Murie was mistaken.[35]

The revised bill fared no better than earlier versions. The proposed Wilderness Preservation Council and the inclusion of Indian reservation territory continued to prove troublesome. Western economic interests also continued to oppose the bill, as did some important leaders on the Senate and House Interior Committees. Senator Clinton Anderson of New Mexico, the second ranking majority member, was miffed because conservation leaders had not consulted him when they drafted the original bill. He used the pending ORRRC report, due in 1961, to delay action on the bill until it could be made more attractive to Western interests. Wayne Aspinall, who became chair of the House Interior Committee in 1959 when Clair Engle was elected to the Senate, was openly hostile to the Wilderness Bill. He wrote Brower a "perfectly frank" letter cautioning "that until the sponsors of the Wilderness bill are able to get together with the other users of public lands in the West and assure them that the Wilderness bill supporters are not endeavoring to destroy already established uses (which include water resource development, mining, grazing, etc.), I shall continue to be opposed to the legislation." And like Anderson, Aspinall preferred to await the report of the ORRRC before moving on the wilderness legislation.[36]

Saylor and other preservationists worked doggedly to wear down resistance to the bill. Zahniser wrote dozens of letters, even drafting some for Saylor's signature, assuring cattle growers and the forest-products industry that the proposal did not threaten their interests. Saylor wrote a widely distributed article entitled "The Conservation Legacy of Theodore Roosevelt," which stressed the wilderness preservation features of that "far-sighted" president who had set aside the first wildlife refuge, several national monuments, and 100 million acres of national forests. The Wilderness Bill, Saylor asserted, was merely "an extension of the policies established by Theodore Roosevelt."[37]

The Wilderness Bill enjoyed considerable support and picked up endorsements from several newspapers and magazines, but it could not get out of committee. The Senate Interior Committee held hearings on the bill but postponed a vote at the request of committee member Joseph O'Mahoney, a Democrat from Wyoming, who had been ill. O'Mahoney also had reservations about locking up resources that might be needed during the Cold War. Congress, he insisted, should be given greater control over wilderness areas than the present measure allowed. In the House, meanwhile, Aspinall declined to hold hearings. Nevertheless, while Saylor was unsuccessful in obtaining House action on the bill, his fervency in behalf of wilderness proved gratifying to preservationists. "I thank God there is a conservationist like you in Congress," wrote one constituent.[38]

By late 1959, Zahniser, who had a history of heart trouble, was exhausted and exasperated. When Wilderness Society president Murie seemed to lose zeal for a bill that had been diluted by amendments and scolded him for running up a deficit of more than $30,000, Zahniser offered to resign. After Murie sent him a letter of support and reassurance, however, he agreed to stay on even though it might "require a continuing effort, perhaps an enlarged one." Zahniser tried to be optimistic. Maybe their opponents were also tired. The bill had some strong advocates in Congress and had been endorsed by twenty-two national groups and fifty-six other organizations. And additional modifications would no doubt also have to be made.[39]

Already slowed by the ORRRC bill, wilderness preservation also had to compete with the 1960 Multiple Use–Sustained Yield proposal. Pressed by commercial interests and fearful of losing some of its majestic holdings to national parks, the Forest Service asked Congress to give legislative sanction to the long-established practice of multiple use—logging, hunting, grazing—in national forests, proposing that its lands be managed for "outdoor recreation, range, timber, watershed, and wildlife and fish purposes." Saylor and other preservationists gave their support to the measure so long as it was understood that it did not obviate the need for wilderness preservation legislation, and the Forest Service agreed. Preservationists also wanted equal billing for wilderness preservation as one of the listed multiple uses, but they had to settle for a phrase stating that "the establishment and maintenance of areas of wilderness are consistent with the purposes and provisions of this act."[40]

With public support mounting, as evidenced by endorsements from the *San Francisco Examiner* and other publications, preservationists had hopes that wilderness legislation would be enacted in 1960. They sent each member of Congress a copy of Saylor's "Saving the Wilderness," an *Audubon* article entitled "Land Forever Wild," Ansel Adams's *This Is the American Earth,* and a letter urging support for the bill. Once again their hopes were dashed. The preservation measure, complained John Oakes in the *New York Times*, "has been subjected to the most stubborn opposition of special interests and their representatives who wish to leave the way open for future exploitation—for timber, grazing or power purposes—of lands already designated as wilderness by the Federal Government."[41]

Reservations raised by O'Mahoney and Republican senator Gordon Allott of Colorado during the previous year, however, now necessitated further adjustments in the wilderness proposal. On July 2, 1960, late in the second session, Saylor and James Murray (D-MT), chair of the Senate Interior Committee, who had announced that he was leaving Congress, introduced yet another version of the Wilderness Bill, proposing three major changes. First, it eliminated the National Wilderness Preservation Council. Second, it excised from the system any Indian reservation land. Finally, it allowed Congress to add territory to the program after the initial fifteen-year period only when federal agencies recommended areas for inclusion. This modification was designed to satisfy O'Mahoney and timber companies that feared that a majority of forestland might be included in the system.[42]

Introduced on the last day before summer recess, the measure received scant consideration when Congress reconvened in August. Preservationists were bitterly disappointed with the "do-nothing" Eighty-sixth Congress. "Thanks to Senators O'Mahoney of Wyoming and Allott of Colorado," Oakes groused, it had "failed to act on one of the most important conservation bills to come before any recent Congress, the Wilderness Bill." Even the normally staid *Saturday Evening Post* endorsed the bill with the reminder that "once the wilderness is gone, none of man's technological genius can restore it. It is gone forever— and with it a sanctuary of our heritage." Preservationists were not about to give up. Zahniser remembered a supporter telling him in 1956 that "we may need to work four or five sessions of Congress before passage and should go into battle with the attitude that we will win and not give up on a first or second defeat." Fortunately, preservationists had Saylor in the House and Clinton Anderson in the Senate to serve as legislative field marshals for this coming battle.[43]

The battle for wilderness legislation coincided with a campaign by preservationists to gain national park designation for Dinosaur National Monument.

The upgrade in status, they reasoned, would make that remote canyon country less vulnerable to future economic development. National parks differed from monuments in that they were created by legislative action instead of presidential proclamation and generally were regarded as having greater protection against development. Only Congress could change the boundaries of a national park, while a president, by proclamation, could adjust the size of a monument, as Roosevelt had done in Dinosaur in 1938. Conceivably, another president could reduce the boundaries of the monument so that the Dinosaur canyons would someday be excluded from protection. Moreover, the general public understood that national parks were hallowed national treasures but was less sure about the status of national monuments.[44]

The bulk of Dinosaur National Monument was located in Wayne Aspinall's district, so his cooperation was considered critical. Fortunately for the redesignation effort, Aspinall had committed to the proposal as part of the CRSP compromise. Privately, however, preservationists questioned the sincerity of his support and looked to Saylor to spearhead the Dinosaur National Park effort in the House. A few conservationists wanted to delay action until an upper basin state senator could be found to sponsor the legislation. Delay would also avoid the appearance of rubbing in the loss of Echo Park Dam. But most preservationists believed they should move while they had momentum and while Dinosaur was in the public mind. In 1956, Saylor and Aspinall introduced identical Dinosaur National Park bills, calling for the expansion of the preserve by some 27,000 acres; the gradual end of grazing and construction of access roads; and the cancellation of any dam sites (Brown's Park) that had been recognized when the monument had been expanded in 1938.[45]

The measure had widespread public and editorial support, but the Utah congressional delegation, still smarting over the loss of Echo Park Dam, proved reluctant to support a bill introduced by "one of the most vociferous foes of the whole Upper Colorado Program and reclamation in general." Utah representative William Dawson said that intermountain Westerners were still "bitter" over the loss of Echo Park Dam and now were being asked to support a park proposal that would eliminate grazing. Utah senator Arthur Watkins accused preservationists of a "disturbing breach of faith." They had agreed, he said, to take no steps to make Dinosaur a national park until the Interior Department had undertaken studies seeking alternative locations within the monument for a dam.[46]

Preservationists were astounded by Watkins's interpretation of the CRSP compromise. Saylor called this a "silly accusation," pointing out that preservationists "would never have agreed to a temporary withdrawal of Echo Park Dam which this amounts to." He then inserted into the *Congressional Record* statements from various conservation groups denying that they had ever agreed to hold off on park status for Dinosaur pending a review of alternative dam sites by the Interior Department.[47]

When Congress failed to act in 1956, Saylor and Aspinall reintroduced the legislation the following year. Meanwhile, Fred Smith, director of the Council of Conservationists, had persuaded Colorado's Gordon Allott to introduce a bill in the Senate, promising that his lobbying group would back it to the hilt. Unfortunately, the Allott bill was so controversial that it caused a rift among conservationists that proved fatal to the legislation.[48]

As a supporter of Echo Park Dam, Allott, like Aspinall, seemed an unlikely candidate to sponsor national park legislation for Dinosaur National Monument. He did so, he explained, because upgrading Dinosaur to park status would increase congressional funding for roads in the preserve, draw more tourists, and boost the economy of northwestern Colorado. Privately, he may have viewed the park bill as a backdoor way of someday gaining a hydroelectric dam in the protected area.[49]

The House and Senate bills were similar except for one key feature: language in the House legislation made it clear that the proposed park would forever be free from dams. Allott took the position that one Congress could not bind another and made no mention of power dams. His bill, however, did contain a clause that permitted the interior secretary, under the authority of the federal reclamation laws, to conduct studies of potential reservoir and canal sites in the protected area. No dams or other developments, however, could be undertaken without the express approval of Congress. Allott claimed that this clause was routine and that without it the Interior Department would never give a favorable report on the bill.[50]

For Saylor and other preservationists, the Allott bill was hardly routine: it seemed to violate the CRSP pledge against dams in Dinosaur National Monument. They became even more suspicious when representatives from the upper basin states continued to press for the construction of Echo Park Dam. These urgings enraged Saylor and helped reinforce his suspicion that from the start "there was absolutely no sincerity at all in the people from the west saying that they would take the Colorado River project without Echo Park. That was only an expedient for the time being." He pledged to continue to uphold the sanctity of the national park system: "We might as well have a showdown once and for all on whether national parks and national monuments shall be used for the benefit of all the people or for the sole benefit of the local people." Colorado governor Stephen McNichols denounced Saylor for being "one of the most selfish legislators" in Washington. "It is a sad day," he continued, "when reclamation [has] to depend on Saylor."[51]

Concerned preservationists sought to modify the Allott bill through Fred Smith. After all, Smith and the Council of Conservationists had been instrumental in the defeat of Echo Park Dam and seemingly would not wish to reinstate it. Fred Packard of the National Parks Association informed Smith that conservation groups preferred the Saylor bill because it disallowed water development in the proposed park, while the Allott bill "means continued efforts to build Echo Park Dam." The Allott proviso authorizing the interior secretary to investigate reservoir sites "would give dam builders an excuse for claiming that this modifies the intent of Congress as expressed in the Colorado River Project Act, and would also lay us open to the charge that we conservationists who formerly insisted Echo Park Dam not be built are now taking the position of agreeing to studies for the dam if the status of Dinosaur is changed to that of a national park. We would thus be giving up achievements of the past to secure national park status for the monument." The NPA became the first of many conservation groups to come out against the Allott bill.[52]

Smith was infuriated and lashed out. He informed Packard's superiors, the trustees of the National Parks Association, that their "ridiculous position" would deny park status for Dinosaur. Heretofore the NPA had done nothing to promote a park designation for Dinosaur, he scolded. Now, owing to the "determined and picayune objections" of its executive secretary, it had become the only national conservation group to oppose the Allott bill. Moreover, conservationists were misguided in asking Saylor to introduce the Dinosaur National Park bill; Allott should have been given that honor.[53]

Smith's attack on Packard astonished conservation leaders. Packard considered it "one of the most extraordinary documents I can imagine originating from the head of a public relations firm." Brower maintained that a Dinosaur park "with the Allott 'escape clause' would be easier to break into than the present monument." When Brower, Penfold, and Zahniser defended Packard and also came out against the Allott bill, Smith retaliated by removing all three of them from the executive board of the Council of Conservationists.[54]

Some conservationists, such as the publisher Alfred Knopf, supported Smith, but others questioned his emotional state because he seemed "intemperate," "muddleheaded," and "psychotic." Fearful that wrangling and backbiting might derail the park proposal and other legislation such as the Wilderness Bill, Zahniser and other preservationists attempted to reconcile the House and Senate bills. But a compromise could not be reached, and the Eighty-fifth Congress ended in 1958 without action on the Dinosaur park bill.[55]

Early in 1959, Saylor and Allott reintroduced their respective bills. Aspinall, who had been appointed chair of the House Interior and Insular Affairs Committee in the new Congress, introduced a separate bill that initially drew little support. It proposed a modest expansion of the boundaries, access roads in the area, and the gradual termination of grazing rights, but it dodged the issue of water development and retained Dinosaur's status as a national monument. Allott's bill retained language giving the interior secretary authority to make withdrawals for power dams. "We lost the early battle" at Echo Park, Allott wrote Aspinall, "but I have no intention of losing the war."[56]

Seeing the park proposal slipping away, Smith pursued two courses of action, neither of which included being less bellicose toward those who disagreed with him. First, he asked conservation leaders to lift their objections and permit the Allott bill to pass the Senate. Then the House could amend it to its liking. If two different versions emerged, then House and Senate conferees could work out a compromise park bill. Second, he persuaded Horace Albright to approach Saylor about being more accommodating. A Republican who had served sixteen years in the National Park Service, including four as its director during the Hoover administration, Albright was highly respected by Saylor and other conservationists. Describing Saylor as "a great conservationist in the right place," Albright expressed regret that the Dinosaur park bill had not yet reached the House floor. One of the reasons for the bill's lack of progress was that the interior secretary had not issued a favorable report on it. Could not Saylor take some action, he suggested, that would move the bill along?[57]

Refusing to take the bait, Saylor notified Albright that the Allott bill was unacceptable and that he would not compromise. Moreover, he insisted that Allott accept his version of the bill. "I will not endorse, support or lend any influence to the establishment of the Dinosaur National Monument as a national park until I receive a firm commitment from Senator Allott and others that the language contained in S. 160 is deleted and the language as written in my own bill, H.R. 951, is substituted," he wrote. He claimed to have "no pride of authorship" over the legislation, but he would not sacrifice principle for political expediency. He and preservationists were alarmed by the Allott proviso authorizing the study of reservoir sites in the park because the Bureau of

Reclamation "has a strange habit of making investigations which suddenly become full scale plans for completed projects."[58]

Then he dropped a bombshell. He stated that earlier in the year, during a telephone conversation, Allott had admitted to him that the controversial language relating to reservoir studies had been inserted in the bill "for the express purpose of insuring that Echo Park Dam would be built." He also accused Smith of trying to have a House-Senate conference committee determine the issue because such a group would be dominated by Westerners, and the language of the Allott bill would prevail. Saylor thus vowed to oppose "any and all bills which I feel in any way will jeopardize our national park system, or which will provide the opening wedge for the proponents of Echo Park Dam." Saylor sent copies of his response to conservation leaders, stiffening resistance to the Allott bill and making reconciliation nearly impossible.[59]

Proponents of the Allott bill assailed Saylor for fantasizing. Smith characterized Saylor's letter to Albright as "an incredible concoction" that must have been prepared by "somebody other than an intelligent Congressman." Saylor's charge that Allott supporters were scheming to have a House-Senate conference committee determine the outcome of the park bill was preposterous; the only legislative strategy that existed was to obtain park status for Dinosaur. And only the Allott bill stood a chance of success: it was a "pipedream" to believe that a House member from Pennsylvania could push a bill through Congress to establish a park in Colorado.

Saylor's accusation that Allott had admitted to having introduced the Dinosaur National Park bill in order ultimately to reinstate Echo Park Dam was "an insidious, unqualified, damned lie," according to Smith. Allott also denied having made this statement to Saylor. Supporters of the Allott bill also scolded Saylor for insisting upon a pure park. No upper basin state representative, they declared, could endorse Saylor's anti–water development section in the bill and expect to survive politically. Indeed, Utah senator Arthur Watkins had lost his bid for reelection in 1958, they claimed, because he had failed to secure Echo Park Dam. They pointed out that earlier in the century conservationists had gone along with the creation of national parks and monuments that permitted mining, grazing, and other so-called impure commercial activities. They asserted that the interior secretary currently had the power to conduct studies of potential reservoir sites in any national park or monument. Finally, they blasted Saylor for distributing his Albright letter to conservation leaders, thus knocking the "living bejesus" out of a chance to pass a park bill.[60]

Saylor remained unmoved, and on balance, his position seems reasonable. Representatives from the upper basin states had not given up hope of resurrecting the Echo Park Dam project; the governors of Wyoming, Utah, and Colorado had openly declared their support for the dam. Utah Democrat Ted Moss, newly elected to the U.S. Senate, told the river guide Don Hatch that he would support a Dinosaur National Park bill, "provided we are able to build Echo Park Dam." Allott, on the other hand, was less forthright. Whether he had actually admitted to Saylor that he had introduced the park bill to gain Echo Park Dam is difficult to verify. Brower claimed to have seen a transcription of the telephone conversation between the two men and assured conservation leaders that Saylor's version was accurate. Moreover, Allott's written statements demonstrate that he had not given up on Echo Park Dam. "I do not intend to preside over the internment of that dam," he informed Fred Packard. "Lest there be any doubt," he wrote a Colorado newspaper journalist, "I have not given up on the dam." He told another preservationist that he believed that a dam at Echo Park was "most unlikely" in the "foreseeable future," but he defined "foreseeable future" as ten to twenty years. And he assured a constituent that "no bill will be approved by the Senate Interior Committee which forever precludes the building of a dam in Echo Park or in the Dinosaur Monument. I believe there is a crying need for one."[61]

During the "Great Dispute," as it came to be called, the vast majority of preservationists sided with Saylor and urged him to stand his ground. Like Saylor, they were convinced that the Allott bill was an underhanded attempt to circumvent the no-dam pledge of the CRSP compromise. True, the interior secretary presently had the authority to launch reservoir-site studies in national parks and monuments, but why was there a need to specifically reiterate that authority in the Allott bill unless there was an ulterior motive? It was also true that impure national preserves had been established in the past, but by the mid-1950s preservationists had enough political clout to be more demanding when creating new national parks and monuments. Moreover, the Pinchot school of thought, which favored the prudent use of resources, was falling out of favor: "I think we have two different parties (not political) in national park matters—those who feel use is more important than preservation, and those who think the opposite," Brower wrote Albright. When it came to upholding park values, Saylor clearly came down on the side of preservation and took pride in being labeled a "purist." Having defeated the Echo Park Dam proposal once, he and most preservationists were not about to support any legislation that might resurrect it, even if this meant foregoing national park status for Dinosaur National Monument.[62]

Meanwhile, both bills stalled in their respective committees pending a report from the secretary of the interior. The Interior Department supported park designation for the monument but had misgivings about each bill. By voiding existing or potential reclamation sites, Saylor's bill would be unpopular with the Bureau of Reclamation and with Westerners. The Allott bill, on the other hand, seemed to make the park vulnerable to water development, which upset preservationists and the National Park Service. In an attempt at reconciliation, the interior secretary recommended passage of both bills so long as the controversial provisions relating to water development in each were dropped in favor of a reconciling amendment. He suggested wording stating that with congressional statutory approval any lands in the park could be made available for "nonpark purposes" when such uses were deemed to be of a greater public necessity than the purposes for which the park was created. In other words, Congress could always enact legislation to build a dam in the park. This amendment proved unacceptable to most preservationists because it still seemed to leave an opening for a dam. They preferred a strong park bill or none at all. Saylor, Smith sneered, was "willing to die a hero in this matter."[63]

Ultimately, Saylor and the preservationists concluded that the best way to safeguard the Dinosaur canyons was to abandon park designation in favor of the Aspinall bill. A compromise, the Aspinall measure proposed adjusting the boundaries of Dinosaur to make it more unified topographically. Some 20,000 acres would be added and another 22,000 acres deleted for a net loss of about 2,000 acres, but without altering the character of the reserve. The most important feature of the bill related to the status of the preserve. It would remain a monument, but it would now have permanent protection because it would be established by Congress instead of presidential proclamation. The bill called for the building of entrance roads, and the gradual termination of grazing, but it remained silent on the issue of water development.[64]

Whisked through the House Interior Committee, the measure reached the House floor, where it was debated briefly and passed by voice vote in late June 1960. The Senate also passed the bill after adding two amendments. The first removed 3,000 acres from the monument because it was prime Utah deer-hunting country. The second inserted the wording recommended earlier by the Interior Department relating to Congress's authority to use lands in the monument for nonpark purposes if dictated by public necessity. When the

Calling the proposed Echo Park dam a "crime" against nature and the national park system, Saylor brought this 1955 Daniel Patrick cartoon to the attention of the House during a speech on the floor. Two years later, he recommended upgrading the monument to national park status to further protect it against commercial development.
St. Louis Post-Dispatch Editorial Cartoon Collection. Used by permission, State Historical Society of Missouri, Columbia.

House rejected both amendments, conferees were appointed to settle the impasse. Saylor was one of five House conferees, and Allott was one of three from the Senate. The committee compromised by accepting the first amendment, dealing with the removal of hunting territory, but rejected the second, relating to the possible use of monument lands for nonpark purposes. Both houses accepted the conference report, and the Dinosaur National Monument bill became law in early September 1960.[65]

Saylor and preservationists were pleased with the outcome. They would have preferred park designation, but not at the risk of jeopardizing the canyons. Under congressional authority, Dinosaur National Monument now seemed safe from development. While the legislation pleased both sides, it did not patch over cracks within the conservation movement. Even though Aspinall had crafted the compromise that successfully settled the contentious campaign over park status for the Dinosaur canyons, preservationists gave him little credit. He was seen, at heart, as a development-minded Westerner who was never enthusiastic about wilderness nor about park designation for the monument. Saylor, on the other hand, was portrayed as a heroic figure who battled doggedly for wilderness protection and the sanctity of the national park system, two principles that had become dear to preservationists by the late 1950s. Packard described Saylor as the "leading champion of national park integrity in the House," and Brower called him "one of the best friends conservation ever had in Congress." The Sierra Club honored Saylor with a lifetime membership, and the Izaak Walton League, the Wilderness Society, and several other conservation organizations joined in honoring him with an award for distinguished service. Though often at loggerheads, he and Aspinall, as the senior members of their respective parties on the House Interior and Insular Affairs Committee, helped craft legislation that made the 1960s a landmark decade in the environmental movement.[66]

seven

Coal, the C&O Canal, and Kinzua

TESTIFYING BEFORE a House subcommittee, Sigurd Olson of the National Parks Association was asked if he believed that preservation constituted the wise use of natural resources. He answered in the affirmative, explaining that there were occasions when a society had to choose between intangible and material values. He then told an anecdote about a Chinese gentleman who was given two pennies by a benefactor. When asked if he planned to use both coins for food, he said no because he had decided to spend one for food and the other for hyacinths to nourish his soul. For Olson, Saylor, and many other preservationists, the federal government was not doing enough in its conservation program to nurture hyacinths.[1]

Saylor in particular continued to be provoked by "promiscuous" federal dam building. "We have spent billions of dollars in this country building huge mainstem dams on our rivers," he asserted in a speech in April 1960. "This has been done in the name of conservation. The people and organizations backing these big dams claim to be conservationists. But are they?" To Saylor, the answer clearly was no. It was unfortunate, he said, that more people did not take an active interest in preserving free-flowing rivers and unsullied landscapes. But the "big dam program goes on in the name of conservation while true conservation takes a back seat."[2]

Having battled proposals to build massive hydroelectric projects at Echo Park and Hells Canyon in the West, Saylor was equally determined to block big flood-control facilities in the East. Two projects suggested by the Army

Corps of Engineers proved especially galling. One proposed a dam on the Potomac River at Great Falls, outside Washington, DC, that would have flooded a portion of the historic Chesapeake and Ohio Canal. He and other preservationists sought instead to make the canal a national historical park. The other proposed an impoundment on the Allegheny River in western Pennsylvania that would have inundated part of the Seneca Indian reservation. Besides fighting these two dams, Saylor battled to include Arctic wilderness and lake and ocean shorelines as part of the national park system. And, as always, he had to balance his zeal for wilderness preservation with the more immediate goal of improving the economic fortunes of his congressional district, which had fallen on hard times by the mid-1950s.

Although the phrase "all politics is local" had yet to be coined, Saylor understood the necessity of taking care of his congressional district. At home, he and his staff downplayed his involvement in national conservation issues even though these issues consumed most of his time and energy. Through speeches and press releases, Saylor created the image of being a tireless battler for the economic well-being of his district. And no issue was more important to his constituents and to his political future than the health of the coal industry. Throughout his career, he was a trade protectionist who sought high tariffs and quotas on imported residual oil in order to make coal competitive as a source of power. His hostility to Western hydroelectric dams stemmed, in part, from his fear that these facilities would draw industries from the East, thus leaving coal operators in Pennsylvania with fewer utility plants to supply. And while many preservationists looked to emerging nuclear energy sources as environmentally preferable to both coal and hydroelectric dams, Saylor remained resistant. Atomic-powered electrical plants, he declared, would be "anathema to everyone who depends upon the production of coal, oil, and gas for a livelihood." Moreover, publicly constructed nuclear plants would further "enlarge the federal government's holdings in the electrical power business." Then, too, nuclear reactors might pose health and safety risks and prove more contaminating to humans and the environment than coal. When Congress established a committee to study ways that the Atomic Energy Commission could make practical use of nuclear power, Saylor responded in 1956 by pushing a resolution through the House of Representatives creating a similar study group for the coal industry.[3]

Chaired by Ed Edmondson of Oklahoma, the Special House Subcommittee on Coal Research and Development held six field hearings in February and March 1957. As a salute to Saylor for having established the special subcommittee, its first hearing was held at the Ebensburg Courthouse near Johnstown, Pennsylvania. Edmondson hailed Saylor's "sincere and fighting interest in the problems of the coal industry" and gave him the honor of chairing that day's hearings.[4]

Witnesses who appeared before the subcommittee painted a gloomy picture. Coal had been "left an orphan," according to a union official with the United Mine Workers. Increasingly, private utilities were using domestic and foreign oil to power their plants, and in the near future nuclear reactors would likely generate electricity, thus further diminishing the consumption of coal. Moreover, owing to city ordinances against excessive smoke emissions, coal-fired steam locomotives had been replaced by diesel engines.[5]

Statewide, the consumption of bituminous coal was down, but Saylor's district had been hit particularly hard. In Armstrong, Cambria, and Indiana counties, coal production dropped from 52 to 37 million tons between 1947 and 1956. During these same years, the number of employed coal miners decreased by nearly fifteen thousand, a 52 percent loss. To be sure, some of this decline resulted from mechanization, but underconsumption was the main contributor, according to state and union representatives. In 1953, the U.S. Department of Labor had declared Saylor's district a surplus-labor—or economically distressed—area, meaning the unemployment rate had exceeded 6 percent for more than eighteen consecutive months. It would remain a distressed area for the next two decades.[6]

Field hearings elsewhere in Pennsylvania and in other coal-producing states showed a similar pattern of decline. Experts testified that there was plenty of coal for several decades to come, but most of it would remain in the ground unless further demand could be stimulated. Specialists speculated that additional research might show that coal could be used to make by-products such as liquid fuel, plastics, chemicals, tar, and road-building materials. The special subcommittee recommended legislation establishing an independent coal research and development commission made up of representatives from the public and private sectors. Saylor introduced a bill, but no action was taken during the Eighty-fifth Congress.[7]

Saylor, Aspinall, and several other members of Congress from coal states reintroduced the Coal Research Bill in 1959. It passed both houses, but President Eisenhower vetoed it, preferring to give responsibility for coal research to the Interior Department, rather than create another layer of federal bureaucracy with an independent commission. The following year, a new bill was introduced giving responsibility for coal research to the Interior Department's

Bureau of Mines. This measure passed both houses, and Eisenhower signed it into law.[8]

Meanwhile, the jobless rate in Saylor's district persistently topped 6 percent, sometimes reaching 15 percent in the Johnstown area, and Saylor pushed several measures to relieve economic hardship. He attempted to raise the personal income tax exemption from $600 to $750, but the bill never got out of committee. He supported a hike in the minimum wage from $1.00 to $1.25 per hour, but this legislation too was voted down until 1961. He joined a majority of his colleagues in extending unemployment benefits from twenty-six to thirty-nine weeks and reinstituting the World War II food stamp program. Allowing low-income families to acquire food with stamps at a retail grocery was more dignified, he asserted, than requiring them to go to warehouses, union halls, or railroad depots for surplus agricultural products. Representative Leonor K. Sullivan (D-MO) later recalled that when she introduced the first food stamp legislation in 1957, Saylor was the only Republican to vote for it.[9]

Saylor also sought to protect the jobs of Pennsylvania workers by restricting foreign aid and imports. He decried the practice of providing vast amounts of economic assistance to friend and foe alike, while American communities went unassisted, becoming incensed, for example, when the Eisenhower administration contributed two hundred jet aircraft and other military equipment to Marshal Tito, the Communist leader of Yugoslavia. Assisting that "Red Gangster," he asserted, was an affront to the jobless, taxpayers, and "all Christianity."[10]

The import of large quantities of residual oil also irked Saylor. "The detrimental effect of an oversupply of alien commodities entering American markets is an obvious factor in Pennsylvania's economic problems," he fumed. Oil imports totaled 182 million barrels in 1958 and threatened to reach nearly 295 million barrels the following year, the equivalent of 70 million tons of bituminous coal. Imported oil, he stated, threatened not only American jobs but also national security: "Who among us would dare to depend upon foreign oil that must travel over the lonely seaways that even now may be infested with Red submarines?" President Eisenhower shared Saylor's concern and issued an executive order in March 1959 placing an upper limit on imported residual oil. While pleased with this action, Saylor pressed for greater restrictions, but without success.[11]

Concerned by chronic unemployment and wretched living conditions in their districts, members of Congress from western Pennsylvania and the other Appalachian coal-producing states spearheaded a drive to obtain federal assistance. They were joined in their efforts by colleagues representing economically distressed areas in the rural South and Eastern industrial centers. Long before the 1962 publication of Michael Harrington's landmark *Poverty in America,* these members of Congress decried poverty in the midst of general affluence: if the federal government could devise programs such as the Marshall Plan and Point Four to relieve economic stagnation abroad, then it could enact an economic recovery plan for needy Americans.

In consecutive congresses (1957–59), Saylor introduced what came to be known as Area Redevelopment Assistance bills, proposing modest public works projects and tax breaks for corporations establishing businesses in economically depressed areas. His measures, neither of which got out of committee, were in line with the president's recommendation for assistance in the form of $50 million in low-interest loans and $1.5 million in grants.[12]

Several members of Congress, mainly from distressed mining states, introduced more ambitious bills. A 1960 Senate bill proposed $380 million in assistance. A House amendment, which Saylor supported, lowered the cost of the package to about $200 million in loans and $50 million in grants to enable economically depressed farm and industrial areas to attract new businesses and retrain the jobless. In supporting the bill on the House floor, Saylor tried to shame cost-conscious colleagues into supporting it. If they could approve the president's request for $4 billion in foreign aid, he said, then they could hardly balk at an aid package "for our own people in our own country."[13]

Unwilling to risk the wrath of voters, both houses passed the bill. But Eisenhower vetoed it as he had a similar proposal two years before. Disappointed, Saylor blamed Democrats for forcing the veto by insisting upon a bill that was five times more costly than Eisenhower was willing to accept. He vowed to keep fighting for the legislation, and a four-year, $394 million bill was passed in 1961 and approved by President John F. Kennedy.[14]

Saylor's fervent concern over the economic problems of his district left him conflicted about the damaging environmental impact of extracting and burning coal. He was embarrassed by strip-mining operations that left "hideous" scars on the "fetching" western Pennsylvania landscape; this disfigurement was "even more appalling," he asserted, "when you are a conservationist." Most of the damage had been done during World War II, when production was more important than protection of the landscape. Indeed, the state of Pennsylvania had waited until 1945 before enacting legislation requiring strip-mine operators to backfill their excavations.

Since restoring the pits would require considerable expense, Saylor sought federal assistance. After all, if Congress could reclaim arid lands in the West, why could it not redeem pockmarked lands in the East? As an initial first step toward this goal, he introduced a bill requesting that the Interior Department study the extent of strip mining; assess its impact on health, safety, and the economy; and report its findings to Congress. The bill died in committee.[15]

Saylor demonstrated less concern over the fumes, odor, and smoke produced by coal burning. Living in Johnstown, he was acutely aware that smokestack emissions blackened the sky, fouled streams, and smudged the air, but he initially believed that air pollution was essentially a local problem and that communities in western Pennsylvania were making excellent progress in reducing air contaminants. Even many Pennsylvanians, however, did not share this view. In Saylor's own district, for example, state officials attempted to do away with unsightly heaps of coal slag (boney piles) by burning them. The state Department of Health examined these smoldering piles and stated that the fumes were not a health hazard. The editor of the *Apollo News-Record* sarcastically noted, "It may be that sulfur dioxide that blisters paint and injures the finish on automobiles is not injurious to human health."[16]

The U.S. Public Health Service also had concerns about the effects of coal burning and requested a congressional appropriation of $2 million yearly to study this "increasingly serious" issue. Saylor opposed this request as "extravagant" and unnecessary: "There is positively no need to set up a giant office in Washington to determine what laws are best to keep air clean in the communities in our land." Such an agency, he no doubt reasoned, might restrict the use of coal and further damage the region's ailing economy.[17]

When he was not pushing the economic interests of his Pennsylvania district and wilderness preservation, Saylor was performing the routine duties expected of a member of Congress. He delivered speeches, attended picnics and county fairs, appeared at testimonial dinners and commemorative celebrations, crowned local beauty contest winners such as the "Pennsylvania Cherry Blossom Princess," and assisted constituents with federally related problems.[18]

In the late 1950s, he also had to deal with some personal health issues. His eyesight began to deteriorate, so he began to wear black "Buddy Holly–style" glasses. His weight soared, so he dieted and shed 50 of his 275 pounds. He also experienced two automobile accidents. On one occasion, his car was rear-ended, and he was hospitalized for a week with a neck injury. The other left him nearly impaled when a metal rod was dislodged from a vehicle and sliced through his car's windshield.[19]

Throughout his political life, Saylor, like most politicians, made every effort to obtain publicity. After Stan Musial excelled in major league baseball's 1956 All-Star Game, Saylor paid tribute to the St. Louis Cardinals star and noted his western Pennsylvania origins. Saylor also piqued the interest of football-crazed Pennsylvanians when he denounced a 1957 U.S. Supreme Court decision declaring that professional football, unlike baseball, was a business, not a sport, and therefore bound by the Sherman Anti-Trust Act.[20]

Saylor also associated himself with prominent people from the present and the past. When Hollywood star Jimmy Stewart appeared in Indiana, Pennsylvania, at the opening of an airport named in his honor, Saylor was present for the ceremony and a photo opportunity. He also made the keynote speech in the town of Cresson when the U.S. Postal Service issued a stamp commemorating the fiftieth anniversary of Admiral Robert Peary's discovery of the North Pole. As he was credited as one of the legislative architects of the Alaska Statehood Bill, Saylor's photograph appeared in several state newspapers accepting a U.S. flag with forty-nine stars. And for Saylor's efforts to bring the territory of Hawaii into the union, President Eisenhower presented him with one of the pens he used to sign the Hawaii Statehood Proclamation.[21]

Saylor perhaps drew the most local and national publicity by visiting the continent of Antarctica in late 1957, becoming the first member of Congress to fly over the South Pole. As a member of the Naval Reserve, he toured the McMurdo Sound Naval Air Base, prepared shrimp cocktail for sailors from a seventeen-year-old cache of canned goods that had recently been discovered, and posed for photos in a dogsled.[22]

Although he was fascinated by the frozen expanse of Antarctica, however, Saylor was more interested in the pristine landscapes of the United States. Besides pressing for enactment of the Wilderness Bill, he worked in the late 1950s to add more scenic, recreation, wildlife, and historic areas to the national park system. He ardently supported legislation, recommended to Congress by Interior Secretary Fred Seaton, to establish the Arctic National Wildlife Range. Containing nine million acres, about four times the size of Yellowstone National Park, the refuge was proposed to protect grizzly and polar bears, caribou, wolverines, Dall sheep, and other animals that inhabited the remote northeastern corner of Alaska. The legislation had widespread support in Congress, but the Alaska governor and congressional delegation opposed it because the area might be needed someday for commercial development. Unwilling to break the precedent of abiding by the will of state congressional members when establishing national preserves, Congress refused to act. Nevertheless, in December 1960, Seaton announced that the executive branch had set aside the area as a national wildlife range.[23]

Between 1958 and 1960, Saylor introduced legislation to preserve threatened stretches of lake and ocean shoreline at Indiana Dunes; Oregon Dunes; Cape Cod, Massachusetts; Point Reyes, California; and Padre Island, Texas. The battle to preserve the Indiana Dunes on Lake Michigan was not won until 1968, and efforts to safeguard the Oregon Dunes failed. But Congress did pass bills, introduced by legislators from the affected states, to establish Cape Cod National Seashore in 1961 and Padre Island and Point Reyes national seashores the following year, for the first time adding units to the national park system by authorizing the purchase of private lands.[24]

Eager to provide more open space and recreation opportunities for overcrowded Easterners, Saylor also sponsored legislation to create the Chesapeake and Ohio Canal National Historical Park near Washington, DC. This proposal brought Saylor and other preservationists into conflict with capital-region municipal and commercial leaders who wanted to build a water storage and hydroelectric dam on the Potomac River that would flood part of the proposed park. Given his protectionist stance on coal and his environmental views, Saylor, not surprisingly, considered it more important to establish a park than to build a dam.

The history of the C&O Canal dated back to 1828. Paralleling the Potomac River, the canal was supposed to connect the Atlantic Ocean with the Ohio River, but mountainous terrain forced construction to stop in 1850 at Cumberland, Maryland, some 186 miles distant. The canal was used heavily during the Civil War and the postwar decades, but the emergence of railroads and later highways had made it impractical by the early twentieth century, and it was abandoned. In 1938, the federal government purchased the canal, hand-hewn stone locks, and towpath from the B&O Railroad for $2 million. The 186-mile right-of-way, in some places only 30 feet wide, in others nearly 1,000, contained barely 5,000 acres. The first twenty miles of the canal, from tidewater to Seneca, Maryland, were generally well preserved and watered, and the government gave jurisdiction over this section to the National Capital Parks. The longer upstream section, badly in need of repair, was turned over to the National

Park Service. Although the canal in most places was in rough shape, an official with the Park Service described its right-of-way as "one of the most scenic, one of the most picturesque riverside trails in the United States," adding that "the canal generally is in the best preservation of any of the large old canals of that era."[25]

The canal area was used by hikers, bird watchers, canoeists, and picnickers. In 1950, however, the recreation retreat was jeopardized when the National Park Service released a plan to build a four-lane parkway from Washington, DC, to Cumberland, Maryland. In places, the highway would come within 100 yards of the canal. U.S. Supreme Court Justice William Douglas, the editors of the *Washington Post*, and representatives from conservation groups staged a protest against the proposed parkway in 1954, hiking the entire 186-mile length of the canal in eight days. Eventually, the Park Service scrapped the highway plan and recommended making the entire right-of-way into a national historical park.[26]

In 1957 and 1958, members of Congress from Maryland introduced bills in the Senate and House proposing the creation of the Chesapeake and Ohio Canal Historical Park. Both the Senate and the House bills contained provisions permitting the future construction, should the need arise, of a multipurpose dam on the Potomac that might flood a portion of the park.

The Senate bill passed, but the water-development provisions proved unsettling to preservationists and unsatisfactory to commercial interests. During hearings held on both bills by the House Subcommittee on Public Lands in the summer of 1958, Saylor argued that the provisions for future dams would establish a precedent for invading national parks. On the other hand, Western representatives on the subcommittee and officials representing electrical cooperatives and power groups maintained that the recent battle over the proposal to construct Echo Park Dam in Dinosaur National Monument had convincingly demonstrated that once a national preserve had been established, it was off-limits to development. For them, the bills did not give enough assurance that a dam on the lower Potomac River would be built.[27]

Democratic subcommittee member Al Ullman of Oregon pointed out that Saylor was "an opponent of dams most any place, and that he does not take a very good look in many instances at some of our rivers in the West." He was referring to Saylor's opposition to renewed efforts to build the Hells Canyon Dam on the Snake River. In 1957, the Senate had passed a bill authorizing construction of the massive power dam, but Saylor labeled the measure "dead as a Dodo" and used his influence to make sure it never got out of the House Interior Committee. For Ullman, national survival depended upon maximizing the development of water and other natural resources, including the Potomac River. Saylor replied that some rivers and other natural landscapes should be left unspoiled to provide humans with a sense of beauty, inspiration, and wonder. He asked Aspinall to recall their enjoyable float trip to Steamboat Rock in Dinosaur National Monument and reminded Ullman of Isaiah's admonition to the children of Israel in the Old Testament: "Woe unto any nation that builds door to door and house to house until there is no room in the land for the people." Congress adjourned before acting on any of the bills.[28]

At the opening of the Eighty-sixth Congress in January 1959, Saylor and newly elected Democratic Maryland representative John Foley introduced similar C&O park bills. Each measure had three objectives: to restore dilapidated portions of the canal and towpath and designate the entire 186-mile swath a national historic park; to construct a 25-mile-long skyline road on the ridge high above the canal and the Potomac River gorge in the uppermost reaches of the park; and to acquire about 10,000 additional acres for the roadway and for scenic buffer lands. In all, about $12 million would be needed for the restoration work, the additional land, the roadway, and trailside facilities. The two bills differed in one key respect: the Foley bill allowed Congress to authorize the construction of a dam for water storage or electricity that would flood part of the park, while Saylor's version contained no qualifying language or mention of a possible dam.[29]

Neither bill proved satisfactory to commercial interests or to the municipal leaders of the District of Columbia, who realized that the U.S. Army Corps of Engineers was undertaking a study of the Potomac River and might recommend the construction of a major dam at River Bend, near Seneca, Maryland. Saylor's bill seemed to exclude water development altogether, and Foley's measure left the development door slightly ajar, but the recent Echo Park Dam controversy in the Dinosaur canyons had shown that Congress would not authorize dam construction in an area that had been designated a park or monument. Consequently, Maryland Democratic representative Richard Lankford and, strangely enough, Foley introduced identical legislation as an alternative to the first two bills. Besides proposing a historical park and skyline roadway, the alternative bills held in limbo thirty-five miles of the proposed park nearest Washington. No canal restoration work could be undertaken along that stretch in order to give the Corps of Engineers up to three years to complete a water-development plan for the Potomac River basin. Furthermore, the interior secretary could not spend money for any recreational facilities without first consulting with the secretary of the army and the commissioners of the District of Columbia. In other words, the Army Corps of Engineers was expected to recommend a dam that would flood twenty to thirty-five miles of the proposed park, so money should not be wasted on improvements.[30]

To preservationists, the alternative bills were unacceptable because they seemed to presume the construction of a dam. They also expressed doubts about Foley's sincerity in proposing the park, labeling the second bill "Foley's Folly" and blasting the congressman for trying to play both sides of the preservationist/development issue. On the other hand, those who fretted about the District's future water supply criticized Saylor for being more interested in park purity than water purity. As with so many conservation issues in the postwar years, it was difficult to find a balance between the development and preservationist positions.[31]

Chaired by Democrat Gracie Pfost of Idaho, the House Subcommittee on Public Lands held hearings on the four bills in Washington, DC, during mid-March and mid-April 1959. Aspinall had undergone surgery, so Pfost, Saylor, and Ullman did the bulk of the subcommittee work on the C&O proposals. Throughout the hearings, support for the park was nearly unanimous. However, considerable friction developed between witnesses who preferred to create a park without any qualifying provisions and those who wanted to leave open the possibility of future water development. The National Park Service, conservation organizations, sportsmen's groups, and garden clubs supported the Saylor bill. The U.S. Army Corps of Engineers, municipal leaders of the District of Columbia, and representatives from public power groups favored the Lankford and second Foley bills.

Following an explanation of the four bills, officials from the National Park Service gave a ringing endorsement to the Saylor bill. This measure, they said, would create a park immediately that would provide recreational opportunities to nearly nineteen million people who lived within a 150-mile radius of the nation's capital. Asked by Ullman and Pfost if they would be satisfied with a strip that covered only 145 or 150 miles of the canal, they replied that they would prefer to forego the park rather than have part of it covered with a reservoir. Pfost and Ullman took offense at this all-or-nothing position and immediately let it be known that the Saylor and first Foley bills were in trouble. Water was the "lifeblood" of their region, and they believed it was "highly unusual policy" on any river to make water development subservient to recreation. "I come from the West," said Ullman. "I am imbued with a multi-purpose concept of water development."[32]

Perhaps sensing payback by Pfost and Ullman for his opposition to Hells Canyon and other Western dams, Saylor seemed more testy than usual when witnesses spoke in favor of the alternate bills. He was particularly eager to demonstrate that studies and recommendations by the Army Corps of Engineers were fallible and should not be accepted blindly. Like the historian Irving Brant, Saylor believed that the corps was "nearer omnipotence than omniscience."[33]

Colonel George Sumner stated that the corps could support any of the bills, except Saylor's, but preferred the two that excluded thirty-five miles of the proposed park until the Corps of Engineers had completed its study of potential reservoir sites on the river. Sumner also pointed out that the corps was responsible for providing the water needs of the District of Columbia, so the main focus of the study would be water supply and pollution abatement.[34]

Saylor asked whether the corps in the recent past had conducted a study of the Potomac River basin. Sumner stated that it had done so in 1944, recommending the construction of fourteen dams, seven on the main stem and seven more on tributaries. Saylor inquired if the head of the Corps of Engineers in 1944 had approved this recommendation, and Sumner replied, "There was considerable opposition." Saylor demanded: "Answer that question. Did he or did he not approve it?" "He did not, that is correct." Saylor then asked if the current head of the corps had approved the recommendation, and Sumner pointed out that the 1944 report had been shelved. "Do you mean to tell me," Saylor retorted, "that the Army Engineers who are interested in building dams all over the country, and who have their headquarters up here in Baltimore, and who have people that make up their staff pass over the Potomac every time they leave Washington and go to the Pentagon, have been so lax in their interest in something right under their noses that from 1944 to 1956 they did not think about it?" Before Sumner had an opportunity to answer, Saylor blasted the fourteen-dam plan as preposterous: it would flood nearly the entire length of the Potomac River basin.[35]

Saylor also tried to discredit other witnesses, especially Albert Herling of the Potomac River Protective Association. Rural electric cooperatives and public power groups, which under law had priority in obtaining federally produced power at subsidized rates, supported the Lankford and second Foley bills because they favored the construction of a hydroelectric dam at River

Bend. To appear less self-serving, the electrical power groups had formed a dummy organization—the Potomac River Protective Association—and hired Herling, a California lobbyist, to represent their interests.

Herling said that his group favored a multipurpose park bill because it was concerned about the economic development and future water needs of the capital region. Saylor pressed him for details about his organization. What were its objectives or mission? Herling had difficulty explaining. Who were the officers? Herling could not name them. How many members did it have? He did not know. How would someone go about joining the organization? "You are doing an excellent job of getting me flustered," Herling replied. "I cannot even think straight. I am astounded at my own failure in memory at the moment." "So am I," Saylor shot back. At that moment, Gracie Pfost whispered in Saylor's ear, then promptly informed the audience that she had told Saylor that he was much more likable when he was not "so cantankerous." With this bit of comic relief, Herling was excused.[36]

Successful in exposing the Potomac River Protective Association as a sham, Saylor had more difficulty discrediting the arguments of individuals who expressed concerns over the future water supply of the District. An engineer representing the commissioners of the District of Columbia believed that setting aside the entire 186-mile canal as a park would "preempt the future development of the river from the standpoint of supply water for a rapidly expanding metropolitan area." On the other hand, the River Bend Dam would address the District's water problem in two ways: first, it would provide a reservoir of potable water; second, releases from the reservoir would flush or dilute pollutants downstream, thus providing yet more water for domestic and industrial use.[37]

Saylor used several arguments to counter the water-supply issue. First, the Potomac was polluted because the states of Maryland and Virginia permitted communities to dump untreated sewage and industrial contaminants into the river. State laws should thus be enacted to correct the situation. Second, the Washington Aqueduct at Great Falls, Maryland, had been providing water through conduits for more than a hundred years, and if river pollutants were treated, it could continue to supply the District for decades to come. Third, District commissioners had exaggerated the problem of water quality and supply. Indeed, if the situation were as grave as they claimed, it should have been addressed long ago, and they should be removed from office for having failed to do so. Fourth, if studies showed that reservoirs were needed to provide water for the region, then dams could be built on Potomac tributaries that would not mar the park. Finally, if the need became urgent, Congress could always authorize the construction of a dam to flood a part of the park.[38]

District commissioners and Representative Ullman were not convinced by Saylor's arguments. They pointed out that once a park had been established, Congress, since 1916, had never permitted an intrusion. Consequently, declared Ullman, "we should not do anything to foreclose the water supply of the metropolitan area." He favored one of the alternative bills establishing a park for 150 miles of the canal upstream, leaving the remaining swath downstream in abeyance until the Corps of Engineers had finished its water-needs study.[39]

Saylor became angry when the focus of the hearings shifted from the establishment of a park to the water needs of the District of Columbia. The hearings, he said at one point, had "gone completely berserk." They "have no more relation to the establishment of a park, in my humble opinion, than they do to a tax problem." He also lashed out at the second Foley bill, claiming it was really an underhanded attempt to set a precedent for invading a national preserve: "This is the fifth column technique which Mr. Franco made so popular in recent years. It is nothing new. This is just being the old wolf in new clothing." Not surprisingly, Foley took offense at being linked with a Spanish Fascist and wanted the record to show that it was not his intent to undermine the national park system.[40]

The hearings ended in mid-April with conservation groups hailing the Saylor measure and declaring that they wanted a pure park bill or none at all. Ullman warned them to compromise, saying that most Americans were more interested in "survival and water supply" than in "paths through the woods."[41]

Eventually, the Interior Department suggested an amendment to the first Foley bill that in effect reasserted Congress's authority to use any portion of the 186-mile park for nonpark purposes when those purposes were in the greater public interest. After gaining approval from the House Interior Committee and the Rules Committee, the proposal went to the floor, where it was rejected. Saylor and other proponents were unable to convince their colleagues that the park would not block water development at River Bend and that the anticipated costs of the land and construction of the skyline roadway would not exceed $12 million.[42]

Though Saylor and other C&O Canal Historic Park supporters were disappointed by the vote, they would ultimately prove victorious. On January 18, 1961, two days before leaving office, President Eisenhower designated the 165-mile strip of canal between Seneca and Cumberland, Maryland, a national monument. The remaining 21-mile section remained under the jurisdiction of the National Capitol Parks. But a decade later, to Saylor's great satisfaction, Congress designated the entire 186-mile pathway a national historic park. Recognizing Saylor's long-time advocacy and the fact that the House had used his measure as a template, Representative Roy Taylor (D-NC) declared on the House floor that "no one deserves more credit for this bill than the gentleman from Pennsylvania."[43]

While pleased that the historic C&O Canal had been spared from inundation, Saylor was distressed by another river-development proposal by the U.S. Army Corps of Engineers that affected his home state. To the dismay of the Pennsylvania congressional delegation, Saylor in 1957 came out against the Kinzua Dam on the Allegheny River in western Pennsylvania.

Following the St. Patrick's Day flood in Pittsburgh that claimed forty-seven lives and $50 million in property damage, Congress had passed the Flood Control Act of 1936. This measure authorized the construction of a series of dams along 200 miles of the Allegheny River above Pittsburgh. Kinzua, the uppermost of the nine scheduled dams, was to be located ten miles north of the town of Warren, near the New York state border. Congressional appropriations for the Kinzua project had been delayed because of World War II and because Seneca Indians objected to having their homes, burial grounds, and farmland submerged by impounded water. In all, the project would inundate about 9,000 productive acres on the Allegany Reservation in southeastern New York and about 700 acres on the Cornplanter Grant in northwestern Pennsylvania. The 28-mile-long reservoir would force the relocation of about seven hundred Senecas. The Seneca Nation argued that the government was bound by the Pickering Treaty of 1794, which entitled them to their lands in perpetuity.[44]

The Omnibus Public Works Bill of 1957 contained a provision calling for an initial $1 million for the $120 million Kinzua Dam project. Saylor decried the size and cost of the proposed dam. When the Army Corps of Engineers first planned the facility in 1936, he pointed out, it had recommended a modest flood-control dam at a cost of $9 million. Over the years, the engineers had revised the plans so that by the mid-1950s the estimated cost of the largest water-storage facility in the Northeast had risen to more than $100 million. "That growth is so fantastic it is almost impossible to believe," Saylor lamented.[45]

The Johnstown congressman questioned the need for the mammoth dam. Proponents argued that the facility was necessary to protect Pittsburgh from rampaging floods, but Saylor contended that the eight existing dams offered sufficient protection. He also used Corps of Engineers data and reports from the Pittsburgh Weather Bureau to show that if a dam had existed at Kinzua in 1936, it would have reduced the floodwaters in Pittsburgh by an inconsequential amount, if at all. He maintained that proponents were being disingenuous when they claimed flood control as the primary purpose of the project. The alleged secondary purposes of increased water supply and pollution abatement, he charged, were actually of paramount importance. Impounded water in the Allegheny Reservoir at Kinzua could be released for industrial and municipal use and to help cleanse the river of industrial and human waste near Pittsburgh. "Neither water supply nor pollution control is properly a responsibility of the Federal Government," he held. Saylor did not then see the correlation between preservation and pollution control.[46]

Saylor's stance dumbfounded his Pennsylvania colleagues. Republican Robert J. Corbett of Pittsburgh portrayed him as a nature-loving obstructionist. The Allegheny Valley, Corbett boasted, was becoming the world's industrial heartland, and its businesses would pay in taxes ten times the cost of the project. Rivers could not be left untamed. If Pennsylvania and the nation expected to progress economically and maintain their position of industrial preeminence, then citizens would have to "harness every drop of water that falls in America and use it over and over." Democrat Elmer J. Holland, another member of Congress from Pittsburgh, "was shocked to see a representative from Pennsylvania, and from Johnstown particularly, . . . talk against flood control." He observed that "there is only one member of the entire Pennsylvania group, either Republican or Democrat, that is opposing the building of this dam," noting that this lone dissenter probably did not represent the sentiments of his constituents. Saylor insisted that he was not opposed to flood control but stated that "where a project is for other purposes," then the Pennsylvania delegation should have "the moral courage" to admit it. Some members of Congress outside the Keystone State shared Saylor's concerns but hesitated to "enter the internecine struggle in Pennsylvania" for fear of jeopardizing proposed projects in their own states.[47]

Saylor also frustrated his colleagues by siding with Native Americans. Indeed, he had long been a supporter of Native American causes. In the early 1950s, to the "amazement" of some members of the House Subcommittee on Indian Affairs, he opposed the policy of termination by which Congress repudiated a century-long policy of federal jurisdiction over Native Americans. In the name of economy, states' rights, and self-determination, sixty-one tribes had lost their reservations and federal benefits before the policy was aborted in the 1960s.[48]

Although the Seneca Nation had dodged termination, it faced the probability of losing one-third of its land holdings to the Kinzua reservoir. Cornelius V. Seneca, president of the Seneca Nation, looked to Saylor for assistance and was not disappointed. Saylor argued on the House floor that constructing Kinzua Dam would "violate one of the oldest treaties of the United States and deprive the Seneca Nation [of] their guaranteed treaty rights." Such a violation by Congress would be immoral and dishonorable. It also would be a foreign policy blunder, discrediting the United States in the eyes of the world. How could the United States accuse the Soviet Union of treaty violations if it could not keep its word to the Senecas? How could allies during the Cold War expect the United States to honor its military commitments if it disregarded a treaty that had existed since 1794? "Whether Mr. Saylor's stand was on the side of the angels or an act of treason to the home team depends, of course, on whether you are an Indian or a Pittsburgher," noted a newspaper writer, "but it added spice to the proceedings."[49]

Although Saylor may have been their most outspoken and influential ally, the Seneca Nation also received support for its cause throughout Pennsylvania. The *Sun-Telegraph,* one of Pittsburgh's two major newspapers, ran a series of articles that questioned the need for the dam, and smaller state newspapers also came out against the project. "We need Kinzua Dam about as much as we need a bullet in the head," declared an editorial in the *Sewickley Herald.* The Philadelphia Yearly Meeting of Friends (Quakers), sportsmen's groups, garden clubs, and scores of ordinary individuals, including an employee with the Army Corps of Engineers, denounced the proposal because it would besmirch a treaty. Others criticized the plan because it would be costly; because it would help Pittsburgh polluters at taxpayers' expense; and, in an extreme case, because the huge dam might be targeted by Soviet hydrogen bombs.[50]

On the House floor, Saylor supported an amendment to excise the Kinzua project from the public works bill, but the effort failed by a vote of 43 to 122. A similar move in the upper chamber also proved unsuccessful. While disappointed with the result, the Seneca Nation expressed its thanks to Saylor for attempting to block the appropriation of funds to begin construction of the dam. "Even though the battle was lost," Cornelius Seneca wrote, "my people are gratified with the knowledge that we have a true friend of the Indian in the House of Representatives."[51]

But the Senecas were not done fighting. They pursued legal action, but federal judges, in decisions that eventually reached the U.S. Supreme Court, ruled that the right of eminent domain superseded a treaty. Unsuccessful in the courts, the Senecas continued to court public opinion, made appeals to the White House, and sought out experts to provide an alternative dam site. Through Saylor, the Senecas tried to obtain the services of Luna Leopold of the Interior Department's Geographical Survey. The son of wilderness champion Aldo Leopold, he was a highly respected scientist and generally skeptical of federally engineered water-development projects. But the Interior Department would not permit his involvement on the grounds that federal dam projects in the Eastern states were the responsibility of the Army Corps of Engineers. Consequently, the Seneca Nation hired Arthur Morgan, a private engineer, to review the plans for the Kinzua project.[52]

Morgan possessed impeccable engineering credentials. He had headed more than fifty projects, served as chief engineer and chair of the Tennessee Valley Authority, and was an honorary member and past vice president of the American Society of Civil Engineers. Finding the Kinzua project wanting, he devised an alternative plan that would spare the Seneca lands. The Conewango-Cattaraugus plan, as it was styled, proposed a dam on Conewango Creek northwest of Warren. During floods, excess water could be diverted to Lake Erie by way of Cattaraugus Creek. Besides saving Seneca lands, the Conewango-Cattaraugus plan had the advantage, Morgan claimed, of providing greater flood control for the entire Allegheny River valley, at less cost.[53]

Army engineers claimed that they had considered a similar alternate plan three decades earlier and had rejected it as too costly. Yet Morgan's estimable reputation prevented his recommendation from being dismissed out of hand. Besides, the White House had become involved. President Seneca had complained to Saylor that his appeals to the White House were being routed to the Corps of Engineers for reply, but Saylor's intercession and mounting public support for the Seneca Nation prompted Eisenhower to intervene, albeit cautiously. "The President's position is that the construction of this dam would be wrong if the Indians do not desire it, unless it is essential rather than merely desirable. It is particularly essential that our word be kept with the Indians," wrote Major John Eisenhower following an oval office conference with his father. The president's special adviser on public works, General J. S. Bragdon, asked the Corps of Engineers to investigate alternative plans that would not intrude upon Seneca lands.[54]

Pressed by the White House, the corps asked a civilian engineering firm to review the various plans. The New York firm reported that Morgan's Conewango-Cattaraugus plan would be more costly, flood a larger area, and displace more people (whites instead of Native Americans) than the Kinzua project. Morgan prepared a detailed rebuttal of the firm's findings, requesting a "genuinely impartial" evaluation of the two plans, but to no avail. Saylor later learned that the so-called independent outside firm was hardly impartial: three of its partners had served with the engineers, and the corps was its best customer. This belated discovery added to his ongoing vexation with the Corps of Engineers.[55]

Saylor was also vexed with his government because it seemed to be operating under a double standard: on the one hand, it berated the Russians for mistreating ethnic minorities; on the other, it ignored injustices done to Native Americans. At the request of George Heron, newly elected president of the Seneca Nation, he sent a searching letter to Eisenhower asking how, in the State of the Union address, the president could rebuke the Russians for reneging on their promises relating to Berlin "in view of the action by our own country in its utter disregard for the treaties between our own Nation and some of the Indian tribes." While not condoning Soviet behavior, Saylor pointed out that the Russians were disregarding agreements barely a decade old, while the United States planned to disavow a treaty initiated by the first president that had stood for more than 160 years. Saylor's letter went unanswered.[56]

In January 1959, Warren and several other towns in western Pennsylvania experienced severe flooding. Newly elected governor David Lawrence argued that a dam at Kinzua would have spared the towns, and he and nearly thirty chambers of commerce urged Saylor to expedite appropriations for the dam to prevent future disasters. Saylor pointed out that the regional office of the Corps of Engineers had conceded that a dam at Kinzua would have had only a minimal effect on the floods. Still, he realized that Mother Nature had given "a welcome assist to the proponents of Kinzua Dam."[57]

In spite of pleas from the governor and local business groups, Saylor continued to fight to deny money for the project. But in May 1960, the House voted to spend $4.5 million to begin construction. Saylor then tried to persuade the White House to withhold funds for the project but failed.[58]

Although the outlook looked bleak, the Senecas were heartened by mounting public opposition to Kinzua Dam. A Pennsylvania resident, for example, informed Governor Lawrence that "if there is anyone who knows about the feasibility of dams in this country it is Arthur Morgan. When he testifies that the Corps plan is not the better one, I should think you would give pause." This same correspondent was disturbed by the governor's willingness to break a treaty with the Senecas: "It shows a lack of historical integrity for a governor of the Commonwealth founded by William Penn to appeal for the end of a treaty with Pennsylvania Indians."[59]

Besides ordinary citizens, the Senecas gained support from the American Civil Liberties Union, the Association on American Indian Affairs, and the Indian Rights Association. Newspapers such as the *New York Times,* the *Washington Post,* and the *Buffalo Courier Express* all carried editorials deploring the violation of the Pickering Treaty. Syndicated journalist Eleanor Roosevelt and *New York Times* columnist Brooks Atkinson also expressed support for the Senecas. Hugh Downs brought attention to the controversy on NBC television's *Today Show.* And songwriter Johnny Cash recorded "As Long as the Grass Shall Grow" to protest the government's breach of honor with the Senecas and other Native Americans.[60]

Conservation groups such as the Pennsylvania Federation of Sportsmen's Clubs, the Allegheny Sportsmen's League, and the Izaak Walton League also supported the cause by protesting the loss of fishing and canoeing opportunities. Howard Zahniser of the Wilderness Society considered the upper Allegheny River valley, where he had been raised, "one of the outstanding stretches of rural loveliness" in the nation, and long before the issue became heated he published an article on the glories of the river valley in *Living Wilderness.* Yet a water-development project on the Allegheny, unlike Echo Park, did not threaten any national preserve, so he and other national conservation leaders did not trumpet Kinzua as a major concern. Zahniser always regretted not having done more to kill Kinzua, but he did not want to jeopardize the Wilderness Bill by being perceived as an opponent of all water-development projects.[61]

Democratic presidential candidate John F. Kennedy also gave hope to opponents of Kinzua Dam. During the 1960 campaign, he stated that in his administration there "would be no change in treaty or contractual relationships without the consent of the tribes concerned." Once he became president, however, Kennedy decided not to heed a request by the Senecas for an independent examination of the two Allegheny River dam plans because the courts had ruled that the Pickering Treaty could be broken and Congress had already appropriated money for Kinzua Dam. Saylor and the Senecas pointed out that the Supreme Court had held that the dam *could* be built on reservation land, not that it *had* to be. In all likelihood, Kennedy was playing it safe politically and repaying a debt to Governor David Lawrence, former mayor of Pittsburgh, who had helped deliver Pennsylvania to the Democrats in 1960.[62]

When Kennedy refused to intercede on their behalf, the Senecas were resigned to the loss of their lands. But they hoped to be adequately compensated and looked to Saylor to champion their interests in the House. Holding Saylor in "high esteem" for his "courageous stand on the recent Kinzua Dam battle," they asked him to be a guest speaker at New York State American Indian Day on September 15, 1962. Beginning in Salamanca, New York, Saylor was taken by motorcade through the Allegany Reservation, to the Kinzua dam site, and then to the Cornplanter Grant in Pennsylvania. After a picnic lunch, he gave an address in which he paid tribute to Cornplanter and recounted the generally harmonious relationship between Anglo-American settlers and the Senecas that had culminated in the long-honored Pickering Treaty. At the conclusion of his speech, he was adopted as an honorary member of the Seneca Nation. The host of the festivities also requested that from that day forward all individuals with Seneca blood should refer to the reservoir created by Kinzua Dam as Lake Perfidy.[63]

In January, Saylor and James Haley, chairman of the Subcommittee on Indian Affairs, introduced identical Seneca relocation bills. "As a blood brother of the Seneca Nation," Saylor wrote, "I shall do everything within my power to see that just compensation is made to this tribe for the abrogation of their Treaty of 1794 with our government." Although it took more than a year and a half, Haley's measure, aptly numbered H.R. 1794 to commemorate the date of the Pickering Treaty, recommending $20 million in compensation, was passed by the House. The Senate promptly reduced that payment to $9 million. Saylor scolded the Senate for refusing "to accept its moral responsibility in providing just compensation for the taking of these Indian lands." The Pennsylvania Railroad, he noted, had already been awarded $20 million for having to give up its right-of-way along the river valley. Certainly the Senecas deserved an equivalent sum. In a matter of honor, he said, "the Government of the United States should not haggle about the payment of compensation." House and Senate conferees decided to split the difference between the recommended compensation plans. In late August 1964, shortly before the completion of Kinzua Dam, the Senecas were awarded approximately $15 million in compensatory damages, relocation expenses, and rehabilitation funds. Although grief stricken over the flooding of their ancestral lands, the Seneca Nation expressed its gratitude for the "just" financial settlement by naming a community building on the Allegany Reservation for Haley and a similar structure on the Cattaraugus Reservation for Saylor.[64]

Although the Kinzua project stirred national controversy, it seemed to evoke little reaction from Saylor's constituents. He claimed that the voters of his district were "unalterably opposed" to the dam, but letters would indicate that opposition to the project came mainly from outside, not within, the district. Constituents may have been indifferent toward Saylor's opposition to the dam, but state Republican leaders were not. They had been considering nominating Saylor for the U.S. Senate or governorship in 1958, but his position on Kinzua made him so unpopular in Pittsburgh that election to statewide office seemed unlikely. "I know what's right is right," declared Saylor. "If I have to sacrifice my principles for political expediency, then I haven't any political future." Unable to win his party's endorsement for the U.S. Senate, he ran for reelection to Congress and won handily, defeating Robert Glass, who had also opposed him in 1954.[65]

His 1960 bid for reelection initially appeared to be more challenging. Democrats had gained an edge in the number of registered voters in the district in 1956 and had increased that lead to more than twelve thousand by 1960. Moreover, they nominated an articulate, dynamic candidate who, despite his lack of political experience, seemed capable of unseating an incumbent. Like Saylor, William Patton was a World War II veteran and attorney. After the war, he had married a Johnstown woman, graduated with honors from Princeton University, and taken his law degree from Harvard. He worked in Washington as a special counsel for a Senate subcommittee.[66]

Patton ran a hard-hitting campaign, blaming Saylor and the Eisenhower administration for the district's economic woes. In more than a decade, Republicans had given the district only "headlines, handshakes, and heartaches." Saylor, he said, made promises but rarely delivered. His seniority and experience "have proved worthless to the people of this district." Saylor was a "dinosaur congressman" who practiced "Old Guard Republicanism." His demands for a protective tariff were "so reactionary they could have come from the mouth of Henry Clay in 1824 or William McKinley in 1896. By comparison, they make Herbert Hoover seem like an outright liberal."[67]

Patton challenged Saylor to a series of televised debates. Saylor declined the invitation, accusing his opponent of being a carpetbagger because he worked in Washington, DC, and lived in Maryland: "Your desire to appear on television programs with me is understandable in that you will naturally wish to use every means possible to identify yourself with the 22nd Congressional District. You must, of course, realize that my own time can be devoted to more useful purposes than to share it with a relative stranger to Cambria, Indiana, and Armstrong Counties."[68]

Saylor's familiarity with the issues, ease with voters, and experience proved overwhelming. Interior Secretary Seaton came to Johnstown in July to commemorate Saylor's ten-year congressional anniversary, lauding in particular his conservation record and his efforts to obtain economic relief for distressed mine workers. When Republican presidential candidate Richard Nixon campaigned in Johnstown, Saylor was center stage to introduce him, even though he had supported Nelson Rockefeller for the nomination. Saylor was one of only nine Republican members of Congress nationwide to be endorsed by the United Mine Workers, and Teamsters president Jimmy Hoffa named him as one of only fifty-four House members who were "for labor all the way through." On election day, Saylor defeated his opponent by nearly twenty-two thousand votes for his largest margin of victory up to that time. Saylor was as "strong as ever," noted one newspaper, because he had become "an old hand at following the political rule of 'voting his district,' putting district desires above party and other considerations." Saylor would continue to vote his district, fortunate that his efforts on behalf of wilderness preservation did not often conflict with the interests of his constituency.[69]

eight

The Rainbow Connection

A CRANKY CALIFORNIAN complained to the editor of *National Parks Magazine* that "those nature lovers who place sentiment above public needs for water, in the case of Rainbow Bridge, should all be submerged in the rising waters of the lake!" The editor replied that the rising waters of Glen Canyon Dam would not "submerge conservationists but rather a cornerstone of national park policy." This cornerstone, set in place by the National Park Service Act of 1916 and reinforced by provisions of the Colorado River Storage Project Act of 1956, upheld the inviolability of the national park system. Accordingly, any attempt to intrude upon nationally protected areas such as Rainbow Bridge National Monument in southern Utah would draw fierce opposition from preservationists.[1]

John Saylor shared this sentiment and worked, albeit not very doggedly, to maintain the integrity of Rainbow Bridge National Monument. During the late 1950s, however, he was more concerned with protecting Pennsylvania coal interests from public power projects than he was with defending the natural bridge. The impounded water of Glen Canyon Dam might set a dangerous precedent by intruding upon a national monument, but the movement toward publicly funded electrical power affected the livelihood of his constituents and, if left unchecked, might endanger capitalism itself, Saylor reasoned. So Saylor used his influential position on the House Committee of Interior and Insular Affairs to fight the Burns Creek project on the Snake River in Idaho.

In 1959, both Saylor and Wayne Aspinall accepted leadership positions on the House Interior and Insular Affairs Committee. Under the system of congressional seniority, Aspinall, as the longest-serving committee member of the majority party, took the chair and Saylor became the ranking minority member. The two men would dominate the committee for the next fourteen years.

Both men entered Congress in 1949 and left in 1973. Aspinall represented the western slope of Colorado, which, geographically speaking, approximated the size of the entire state of Pennsylvania. He had been born in Ohio in 1896 but as a young boy moved with his family to western Colorado, where he spent the rest of his life. After graduating from the University of Denver, he taught school in Palisade, near Grand Junction, before embarking upon a political career in the 1930s.

In matters of physical appearance and temperament, the Democratic Westerner and the Republican Easterner were a mismatch. Both wore black-rimmed glasses, but Saylor stood nearly a foot taller and was twelve years younger. Saylor also was more personable, jovial, and impulsive than his cranky, methodical, reserved colleague. Saylor, recalled one House Interior Committee staff member, could be profane, coarse, and loud. He and Representative Dingell had nearby offices, and instead of visiting or communicating by telephone, they would just shout to one another down the hall, their booming voices carrying throughout the Rayburn Office Building.[2]

As chair, Aspinall ran the committee with a strong hand, but he took pains to consult and plan with Saylor in terms of holding hearings, scheduling legislation, appointing subcommittee members, and hiring staff. Both men were bright, hardworking, and serious about their responsibilities, attending nearly every committee and subcommittee hearing. Saylor was a more pugnacious and aggressive interrogator of public officials appearing as witnesses before the committee. He was being only partially facetious when he explained to a Midwestern governor that the House of Representatives was the forge of democracy but that "before a forge can amount to anything, you have to get the metal red hot, and then the blacksmith has to take that hammer and beat the living daylights out of it to get it in the shape he wants it. So that is the seat you are in this morning."[3]

Although their styles differed, Aspinall and Saylor mastered the rules of congressional procedure, recognized where the votes were, and adeptly handled legislation. Once a bill had made it through their committee, the full House invariably passed it. "I'll say this for Congressman Saylor," Aspinall recalled in his later years. "He was a valiant fighter in the committee for the purpose of carrying the position of the minority—or as some would say—the opposition." He and Aspinall "used to go to it in committee meeting, but when we went out of the committee the consensus was determined." Saylor "did his work as an oppositionist on the house floor, but never, never tried to upset the action of the committee." The two leaders, Aspinall recalled, handled more than a thousand pieces of legislation and never lost a vote on the House floor.[4]

Although the two men often disagreed on environmental issues, they never lost respect for one another and maintained a friendly relationship. "We have been on opposite sides of the fence on many occasions," Aspinall wrote Saylor in 1960, "but there has never been any question about your sincerity or your motives. When you thought it necessary you have been a tough opponent, but always an honorable one." Later in life, he wrote that they "knew each other like open books." John Saylor, he said, "was my friend in the highest meaning of such relationship": "I did my best to be a good friend of his. From his many acts of kindness shown to me, I believe that he cherished my friendship also."[5]

At times, both legislators could be stubborn, petty, arrogant, tyrannical, and vindictive. Saylor displayed his vengeful side in the mid-1960s during a party battle to elect a minority House leader. He had been shunned by the incumbent leader, Charles Halleck of Indiana, because six years earlier he had supported Joseph Martin for the position. So in January 1965, he used his influence to convince the Pennsylvania Republican congressional delegation to support Gerald Ford, rather than Halleck, thus becoming a favorite of the new House minority leader. "Just let me tell you what kind of guy Charlie Halleck is," Saylor told his fellow Pennsylvanians. "I'm the ranking Republican on Interior. If he wants something done in the committee, does he call me? Hell, no! He talks to somebody who voted for him. I voted with Joe Martin and I can't get the time of day out of Charlie." After Halleck's loss, Saylor boasted that "Charlie lost it all right in our caucus. It took me a long time to get even, but it was worth it."[6]

Both Aspinall and Saylor jealously guarded their privileges as committee leaders. "John Saylor was a prickly man," recalled a junior colleague. "You could say for both Aspinall and Saylor that power got to them. . . . Saylor and Aspinall were two guys who had spent a lot of time in the House, had gotten the power, and they wielded it." On one occasion, when surgery forced Aspinall to miss a hearing, subcommittee chair Gracie Pfost scheduled the appearance of witnesses without first consulting Saylor. Though this was perhaps an oversight, Saylor decided to make a point. Under the rules, a hearing could not begin without at least one Republican member present, so Saylor let Pfost cool her heels. After nearly an hour's delay, Saylor marched into the committee room to "get a few things squared away." He informed Pfost that he and Aspinall enjoyed "a great working relationship" and had established certain procedures: "We are either going to run this thing the way Mr. Aspinall and I have agreed, or we will not have meetings. It is just that simple."[7]

On another occasion in the mid-1960s, he demeaned a junior Republican who, Saylor believed, had not shown him proper deference, firing off a reproachful letter to Wendell Wyatt of Oregon and mailing copies to the entire House Interior Committee and the Oregon governor. Protective of the prerogatives of seniority, Saylor berated Wyatt for slighting him as the ranking minority member of the committee. He had asked for Wyatt's proxy while Wyatt was in Spain attending a conference on forestry, and instead, Wyatt gave it to Democratic representative Tom Foley of Washington. Saylor regarded this action as a sign of distrust and "a malicious, personal affront": "As long as I am the ranking Republican on the Interior and Insular Affairs Committee of the U.S. House of Representatives, you have ceased to exist on this committee. If you remain as a member of the Committee, you will not be assigned to any subcommittee nor will you be assigned to represent either a subcommittee or the full committee on any field hearings, regardless of how it will affect you politically or otherwise."[8]

Nearly forty years later, Wyatt still felt stung by the rebuke. At the time, he expressed "shock" over the letter, as did some committee members who found it "incredible." Wyatt explained that he planned to vote with Foley on every issue relating to the pending legislation. His constituents, he said, could understand leaving a proxy with a Northwesterner, but not a Pennsylvanian. He believed he had satisfied Saylor with this explanation before leaving for Spain; otherwise he never would have departed. Wyatt further explained his actions personally to Saylor upon his return from Spain, and pressed by Aspinall and the Oregon governor, Saylor eventually lifted his harsh sanction.[9]

With congressional newcomers, Saylor could be both gracious and gruff. Generally, Eastern committee members, whether Republicans or Democrats, found him more accommodating than Westerners. Wyoming Republican John Wold, for example, was no "admirer," as Saylor was too close to unions and conservationists. Politically, Wold gravitated toward Aspinall, who reflected the Western perspective on public resource development.[10]

Other young representatives, especially non-Westerners, found Saylor courteous, kindly, and welcoming. Leo Frey (D-FL) recalled that initially he was somewhat intimidated by Saylor. One day he boarded a subway with the Republican congressman. After they were seated, ash jumped from Frey's cigar and burned a hole in Saylor's pants. "For a while I thought my world was coming to an end," Frey said. But Saylor laughed off the incident and thereafter teased Frey for smoking cheap cigars and being an agent for the garment industry.[11]

Saylor was admired by his personal staff. Richard Gentry described him as "a marvelous man" who treated staff "like members of the family." Aspinall and Saylor also built a dedicated committee staff consisting of a counsel, two assistant counsels, a secretary, and several clerical workers—in all, about a dozen people. One longtime employee described the staff as generally nonpartisan and close-knit. By the late 1970s, however, after the departure of both leaders, the staff had grown to nearly eighty employees and become unwieldy, partisan, and distant.[12]

House committee members in the late 1950s and 1960s, one former assistant recalled, did most of their own preparation for pending legislation, but they were seldom too busy to chat with staff members. Aspinall was generally courteous, but a taskmaster and a stickler for thoroughness, punctuality, and professional decorum. He frowned upon swearing and telling off-color jokes. He was also paternalistic, forbidding women to wear slacks, smoke at their desks, or accompany committee members to field hearings for fear of giving the appearance of sexual impropriety. Both leaders were considered strict and old-fashioned, but both were highly respected. A former counsel described Aspinall as "a schoolteacher at heart and a very caring and decent person." Saylor was occasionally gruff and, when he became angry, would "puff up like a grouse," but he was also "fun and a nice man." Both leaders, an assistant recalled, "knew where they came from, and what their district was, and what the district wanted, and they tried to represent it as best they could. But on land and water issues they disagreed."[13]

As a son of the arid West, Aspinall was a champion of the federal reclamation program. He was also hesitant to lock up valuable timber, grazing, and mineral lands as wilderness, seeing himself as a "practical conservationist" in the mold of Gifford Pinchot and Theodore Roosevelt. "I believe in protecting the environment—the ecological balance of nature and all that whenever you can," he once declared, "but my philosophy is that those natural resources were placed here for the benefit of man." Saylor, by contrast, championed a preservationist perspective, also in the tradition of Theodore Roosevelt, that stressed the importance of setting aside wild places for aesthetic purposes. Saylor's penchant for wilderness preservation rankled many Westerners. Lee McIlvaine, a Coloradan hired by Aspinall to serve as assistant counsel on the House Interior Committee, referred to Saylor as "the fair-haired boy of the Sierra Club" and a "park-barrel" legislator because at every turn he seemed to be sponsoring bills to set aside more wild Western landscapes as national parks and monuments.[14]

Aspinall was a strong supporter of the newly appointed commissioner of the Bureau of Reclamation, Floyd Dominy, considering him "not only the best Reclamation Commissioner I have ever known, but the *only* good Reclamation Commissioner I have known." Accrbic, articulate, intelligent, and politically savvy, Dominy was driven to expand the bureau's dam-building efforts; Saylor was determined to curb Dominy's ambitions. Saylor professed being "a true friend of honest reclamation," but by "honest reclamation" he meant the bureau building dams for irrigation, not hydropower. He liked Dominy personally but considered him dangerous because he supported public power. "The Bureau of Reclamation is no longer a Federal agency for reclaiming and irrigating arid lands of the West," he asserted. "It is now primarily a Government agency devoting most of its time, attention, and money to development of Government electric power." All three men became deeply involved in the controversy surrounding Rainbow Bridge National Monument. By a curious twist, Aspinall and Dominy took an anti-dam position, while Saylor and preservationists advocated the construction of barrier devices to prevent the monument from being abused by the waters of the Glen Canyon Reservoir.[15]

Discovered by whites in 1909 and given federal protection the following year, the 160-acre Rainbow Bridge National Monument is located on the Navajo Indian reservation in southern Utah. Standing 309 feet high and 278 feet across, the splendid sandstone arch straddles Bridge Creek Canyon. Generally dry, Bridge Creek Canyon meanders for three miles, to the point where it joins Aztec Creek, and then goes on for three more miles through Forbidding Canyon to the Colorado River. The few hearty souls who visited the monument each year did so by hiking an arduous six-mile trail from the Colorado River up the two canyons or by riding a mule or horse for twenty miles from Navajo Mountain.[16]

Protection for Rainbow Bridge National Monument became a concern during the debate over the Colorado River Storage Project Act. During that debate, conservationists proposed the construction of a high dam on the Colorado River at Glen Canyon as an alternative to the Bureau of Reclamation's recommendation to build a high dam at Echo Park in Dinosaur National Monument and a low dam at Glen Canyon in northern Arizona. The bureau tried to shore up its case by pointing out that the huge reservoir created by the high dam at Glen Canyon might allow water into Rainbow Bridge National Monument. When the bureau realized that Congress would not approve a dam at Echo Park, it stated that for about $3.5 million it could build a barrier to protect Rainbow Bridge from the water of a high Glen Canyon dam. Conservationists insisted upon adding two provisos before giving their blessing to the Colorado River Storage Project. One stipulated that no national park or monument would be menaced by a dam or reservoir. The other required the interior secretary to have protective works erected to shield Rainbow Bridge National Monument from the sprawling waters of Glen Canyon Dam.[17]

A few nature enthusiasts considered Glen Canyon more majestic than the Dinosaur gorges and wanted to give it federal protection, but most conservationists had not visited Glen Canyon. As David Brower put it in 1954, "if a choice must be made between sacrificing what has already been given national monument protection . . . and another place which has no such protection and certainly a lot fewer advocates, I'm not too optimistic about the chances of the latter." Brower, like many other conservationists, would change his mind after visiting the doomed canyon. He later agonized over his advocacy of a high dam at Glen Canyon, declaring, "I wish I had been struck dead at the time."[18]

Never having visited Glen Canyon, except to fly over it, Saylor expressed no remorse over its loss. Unlike most conservationists, he had never given his support to the CRSP, so he suffered no pangs of guilt. Even when the threat to the national park system had been removed, he could not support the CRSP because it was both frightfully expensive and a public power project, not one designed for irrigation.

The Bureau of Reclamation began construction of Glen Canyon Dam in 1957. When filled to capacity, the 710-foot concrete structure would create a massive reservoir, Lake Powell, that would back water into Rainbow Bridge monument. Indeed, the finger of water that would wiggle up Bridge Canyon would come within 57 feet of the top of the arch. Besides encroaching upon a national monument, the pool of water might abuse the monument structurally by wearing away its great legs and aesthetically by leaving rings of debris and discoloration. Conservationists, therefore, eagerly awaited news of the Interior Department's plans to save the monument from desecration.[19]

The bureau had worked out an elaborate plan to protect the natural bridge. First, it would build a 25-foot-high earthen dam on Bridge Creek above the monument that would first trap and then tunnel runoff water to Aztec Creek one mile to the west. Second, it would construct a concrete barrier dam between 185 and 245 feet tall below the monument to block the intruding water from Lake Powell. Three sites, identified as "A," "B," and "C," would work as water restraints. Site A proved the least desirable because it would be within sight of the arch. Sites B and C, situated a half mile and three miles down the canyon, respectively, were both beyond sight of the bridge. Conservationists generally favored site C because it would spare more of the canyon from drowning.[20]

Although the bureau had detailed plans for protective works, Interior Secretary Fred Seaton was in no rush to implement them. Indeed, some people began to question whether the restraining structures might cause more havoc to the landscape than a placid body of water would. Charles Eggert, whose film had helped save the Dinosaur canyons, once admitted that he "wouldn't mind seeing water" under Rainbow Bridge: "Matter of fact, it would enhance it a bit."[21]

Because so few decision makers and activists had actually seen the monument, Floyd Dominy decided to visit it in the fall of 1958. He and L. F. "Lem" Wylie, the bureau's head engineer for Glen Canyon Dam, took a small plane to the base of Navajo Mountain, where they met a guide who escorted them to the bridge by horseback. Although it was "rather on the rugged side," Dominy later wrote, "I thoroughly enjoyed the opportunity of seeing that part of the country." For three days, he remarked, "I took a lot [of] pictures and wore my ass out on that horse." He concluded that constructing a barrier dam and diversion tunnel would "do far more scenic violence to this natural wonderland" than allowing the water from Lake Powell to crawl under the arch. Not surprisingly, the following year the bureau released a report affirming Dominy's private conclusions: water from Glen Canyon reservoir would not wear away the arch, and it was unnecessary to build a barrier dam that might cost $25 million. Another government agency, the U.S. Geological Survey, reached a similar conclusion.[22]

Following these reports, Wayne Aspinall asked members of the House Interior and Insular Affairs Committee to visit the monument in October 1959. Saylor was occupied with the Dinosaur National Park and C&O Canal Historical Park bills, so he begged off. Aspinall and four other committee members met Dominy and Wylie in Page, Arizona, from which they were helicoptered over the monument. After their tour, Aspinall was noncommittal, but Democrat Walter Rogers of Texas expressed doubt that the protective works would be worth the money. Dominy informed the press that he was opposed to the bookend barrier structures because they would detract from the scenery. Moreover, "the water up under the Bridge would make it a more beautiful sight."[23]

Dominy's views drew a sturdy rebuke from conservation groups. Failure to erect the restraining works, they insisted, would ignore a law; defy the intent of Congress; and, most important, establish a fiendish precedent. "The main issue was not the enhancement of scenery," they instructed Interior Secretary Seaton, but the "protection of a national monument and in turn the whole national park and monument system from encroachments which are foreign to preservation of their natural condition." Allow one intrusion into a nationally protected area, they maintained, and others surely would follow. "It was the 'domino theory' of environmental protection," as one scholar phrased it. Pressed by conservation groups, Seaton announced in February 1960 that he had requested $3.5 million in the Bureau of Reclamation budget to initiate construction of an upstream dam and diversion tunnel and a downstream barrier dam at site B. But Congress refused to authorize the expenditure.[24]

In the summer of 1960, Aspinall asked Saylor and Arizona representative Stewart Udall to inspect the Rainbow Bridge Monument grounds and to report to the committee on whether they believed the protective works should be undertaken. At first, the two committee members planned to tour the monument together, but Udall decided to make a family vacation of the trip, so the two men made separate visits.[25]

Saylor met a Bureau of Reclamation engineer in Page, Arizona, and together the two men flew over the proposed barrier-dam sites. After the flyover, the pilot landed the helicopter in the canyon above the monument, and the men toured the various sites by foot. In his report to Aspinall, Saylor concluded that an earthen dam and diversion tunnel above the monument were essential in order to protect the monument from rubble deposited by rain and runoff. He expressed very little enthusiasm for any of the downstream barrier dams. Site A was "absolutely unsatisfactory": it would be an "eyesore." Site C was also "completely untenable": its construction would necessitate a major disfigurement of the landscape. An earthen dam at site B would be the best alternative, since fill for the structure could be obtained from a nearby mesa with minimal devastation to the landscape.[26]

Udall, who had been a strong supporter of the CRSP, including Echo Park Dam, arrived at a different conclusion. After hiking six miles to the area and spending several hours immersing himself in the scenery, he concluded that none of the protective works was necessary because they would defile a primitive area. "Although the lake water offends a basic principle of park conservation," he wrote, "it is my conviction that the construction of any man-made works within five miles of the present Monument boundaries would do far greater violence to the first commandment of conservation—that the great works of nature should remain in their virginal state whenever possible." But beyond enduring the "intrusion of the lake as the lesser of two evils," Congress should greatly expand the boundaries of the monument through a land-exchange program with the Navajo tribe: "Such action would safeguard this remarkable natural wonder and endure its preservation for all time as a primitive park area."[27]

In spite of Saylor's senior status, Udall's report held more sway with the committee. Its prose sparkled, Udall rhapsodizing about the red-rock landscape, calling it "unquestionably the most awe-inspiring work of natural sculpture anywhere in the United States." Saylor, on the other hand, filed a perfunctory report that displayed more amazement for the rollicking helicopter ride than for the splendor of the sandstone country. And his letter showed no commitment to the precedent of keeping dam waters out of national parks and monuments. Already predisposed toward inertia, the committee probably took satisfaction in the belief that by doing nothing it was safeguarding the pristine beauty of the area.[28]

Meanwhile, resistance to the barrier dams continued to mount. Katie Lee, a frequent visitor to the monument, complained to the National Parks Association that "all this building of tunnels and dams by the Rainbow is going to completely destroy the lovely solitude of the place." Angus Woodbury, an emeritus professor at the University of Utah, published an essay asserting that a protective dam would constitute a "bigger blot on the landscape" than the intruding water of Lake Powell. And photographer Tad Nichols, who had accompanied Udall on his trip, contended that "too much of an issue was being made of the encroaching lake water precedent."[29]

Park protectionists hammered away at the precedent issue because permitting an intrusion would be "a departure from national park standards [that] will stay with us for centuries." They searched for alternatives to the restraining dams; either lowering the height of Glen Canyon Dam or reducing the expanse of the reservoir would prevent water from trespassing across the boundary of the monument. The National Parks Association and the president's Advisory Board on National Parks recommended these alternatives to Seaton, but he was replaced following the presidential election of 1960.[30]

President-elect John F. Kennedy named Stewart L. Udall secretary of the interior. The forty-one year old Democrat from St. John's, Arizona, was a three-term member of Congress and had familiarized himself with conservation issues as a member of the House Committee on Interior and Insular Affairs. His appointment, he later remarked, galled Aspinall, Saylor, and other senior members of the committee. Traditionally, this appointment went to a Westerner, so Saylor, an Eastern Republican who was unfriendly toward the reclamation program, was not considered. Aspinall, however, seemed an ideal choice. But Udall's youth, zeal, and early support for Kennedy's nomination won him the job over more seasoned candidates.[31]

Udall came to the job when the conservation movement was in a state of flux. A traditional agenda that stressed efficient use of resources, public recreation, and federal dam building was being challenged by an emerging environmental outlook that emphasized wilderness preservation, park inviolability, and environmental protection. Determined to build a conservation program "worthy of the two Roosevelts," Udall tried to balance the utilitarian and aesthetic strains of the conservation movement. But in practice, the Kennedy administration generally wed itself to a traditional agenda.[32]

As for Rainbow Bridge, Udall was in a delicate position. As a Westerner and as head of the federal dam-building program, he was committed to the construction of Glen Canyon Dam. But as guardian of the national park system, he was pledged by law and tradition to keep manmade lakes out of federally protected areas. He could not limit the size or storage capacity of Glen Canyon Dam because enough electricity had to be produced to meet demand and pay for the project. Too, because barrier dams and construction works would mar the beauty of the landscape that tugged at him, he was willing to sacrifice the principle of park sanctity. He hoped that expanding the borders of Rainbow would be an acceptable trade-off to conservationists, but he was wrong.

After a mid-February meeting with conservation leaders, Udall realized that they were not about to relent in their efforts to defend Rainbow from the

Glen Canyon impoundment. "There is no doubt in my mind that in their publications and newsletters they will issue a call-to-arms over this so-called 'precedent' and I think it is important to us to plan accordingly," he told Dominy and Conrad Wirth, director of the National Park Service. At an April meeting with conservation activists, he again pitched the idea of expanding the borders of Rainbow monument and invited them to join him on another inspection trip.[33]

Accompanied by sixty people, Udall swooped down on the monument by helicopter in late April. Except for conservation leaders, just about everyone was sold on the idea of enlarging the monument and forgetting about the barrier dams. Park guardians, on the other hand, pressed for an enlarged monument and construction of a restraining dam at site C.[34]

Unable to move Udall, park defenders tried to win over the public and influential members of Congress such as Saylor. "Dear Uncle John," Brower began an appeal. "We urgently need your help in making sure the right solution is implemented in time to protect Rainbow Bridge as promised, and plead that you set aside other things, and yourself make sure that this grave threat to our National Park system is ended at once." Conservationists, he said, were tired of excuses and wanted Congress to honor its CRSP commitment relating to parks and monuments. Brower ended his note with "HELP!"[35]

Saylor agreed that the Interior Department was being remiss in not honoring its pledge to keep parks and monuments sacrosanct. He also agreed that in refusing to authorize funds for the restraining dams, Congress was placing "the entire National Park system in jeopardy." But he did not battle for the cause. Other than writing a letter to the comptroller general demanding funds for the barrier dams, Saylor remained uncharacteristically aloof. He made no angry speeches and inserted no supportive articles, editorials, or statements into the *Congressional Record*. Like other members of Congress, he was distressed by domestic civil rights demonstrations and foreign policy crises in Berlin and Cuba. He also probably realized that politically the Rainbow cause was lost. As it turned out, Udall repeatedly asked Congress to appropriate $20 million to build barrier works, and the House Committee on Appropriations routinely rejected his request. Frustrated, park defenders appealed to the courts but lost.[36]

As historian Mark Harvey has observed, the Rainbow Bridge controversy did not provoke the same sense of outrage among politicians, conservationists, and the public as did the threat to the canyons of Dinosaur monument. After all, Lake Powell would not impair the Rainbow monument structurally.

Nor would the tiny wedge of water that approached the arch mar the scenery. Indeed, it would make the bridge more accessible because visitors would eventually be able to reach it by boat. Then, too, park guardians seemed narrowminded and arbitrary when they insisted upon safeguarding the purity of the monument, but not the equally pristine canyon country surrounding it. But they were right to worry about precedent. Having won at Rainbow, the Bureau of Reclamation set in motion plans to build dams at Bridge and Marble canyons on the Colorado River that would endanger Grand Canyon National Monument. Saylor would be in the forefront of the battle to save the Grand Canyon, but that fight would come later.[37]

For Saylor, the threat to the coal industry from public power was far more grave than the threat to Rainbow Bridge from Lake Powell. A multitude of evils seemed to be conspiring against the coal industry with help from the federal government. From his perspective, lenient trade policies permitted foreign producers to ship oil and natural gasoline to the United States to compete with coal. The government also encouraged the production of electricity through federally funded proposals such as the Burns Creek hydroelectric dam project in Idaho and the atomic reactor plan in Hanford, Washington. Indeed, as far as Saylor was concerned, during the Kennedy administration, creeping socialism in terms of public power had given way to "galloping socialism."[38]

In 1956, the Bureau of Reclamation recommended construction of a 175-foot-high earthen dam on the Snake River in southeastern Idaho. The $45 million project, called Burns Creek, was to be located thirty miles downstream from existing Palisades Dam. Due to the press of other business, the House Subcommittee on Irrigation and Reclamation did not hold hearings on the proposal until late August 1959 and then again in February and March 1960.[39]

The Bureau of Reclamation characterized Burns Creek as a "reregulating" reservoir. In other words, the discharged water from the upstream Palisades Dam would be trapped and reused at Burns Creek for irrigation and power purposes. Backers included the Idaho congressional delegation and state business and civic leaders. Opponents of the proposal came mainly from private utilities, which claimed that they adequately served the area; coal companies and mine workers, especially from neighboring Utah and Wyoming; and members of Congress from coal-producing states.

As he did so often, Saylor represented the interests of private electric companies, mine workers, and coal operators at the hearings. He reminded his colleague, Republican Hamer Budge of Idaho, that under the reclamation law power production was supposed to be incidental to irrigation. Yet the Bureau of Reclamation estimated that 98 percent of the estimated cost of this project was to go for power generation and less than 1 percent for irrigation. "Back in the eastern part of the United States, where it is my privilege to have been born and raised," he sarcastically noted, "when we discuss something incidental, it is usually the smaller part." Saylor also raised the specter of socialized power. The bureau, he insisted, was beginning to believe that it had a responsibility to serve the utility needs of the Western states. "If that is the case, if that is the attitude of the Bureau of Reclamation," he proclaimed, then "we need not worry about Mr. Khrushchev's statement that our grandchildren will live under communism."[40]

Saylor also tore apart other features of the project. The notion of river reregulation disturbed him. If Congress approved Burns Creek, would the bureau return next year with another reregulating proposal for the river? Where would the reregulating stop? He pointed out that the project would bring no new lands under irrigation. The Burns Creek reservoir would merely provide supplemental water for acreage already irrigated by Palisades Dam. And the cost would surely exceed $45 million because in its fifty-eight-year history, he claimed with only slight exaggeration, the bureau had yet to build a project at its estimated cost. "I think the gentleman from Pennsylvania is to be commended on the diligence with which he has pursued his case," Aspinall stated at the end of the hearings. Not surprisingly perhaps, given Aspinall's statement, the subcommittee refused to report the bill to the full committee.[41]

The Subcommittee on Irrigation and Reclamation considered a slightly revised version of the Burns Creek legislation in the spring of 1961. Once again Saylor and, to a lesser degree, James Haley of Florida denounced the project as a reclamation sham. It was, Saylor charged, "strictly a power project." He had supported the Palisades project in 1949 and would happily back other worthy irrigation proposals, but if Westerners continued to mask public power projects as irrigation works, they would endanger the entire reclamation program.[42]

He reiterated his charge that the Burns Creek project would injure the coal industry. Coal miners from the economically distressed community of Kemmerer, Wyoming, would have difficulty selling their product. Indeed, coal experts predicted that the Burns Creek project would replace the need for 250,000 tons of coal annually. The Interior Department should learn that "the people who are producing coal and producing electricity by thermal means are a segment of this country too."[43]

Despite Saylor's spirited opposition, the subcommittee voted thirteen to seven to report the bill to the full committee. Once again, however, Saylor helped derail it. "This was a tough one to lose," said Democratic Idaho representative Ralph Harding, the bill's sponsor. "I regret that John Saylor, the anti-reclamation Republican from Pennsylvania, was able to bring such pressure that not a single Republican voted for Burns Creek."[44]

But the project was not yet dead. With the cooperation of the U. S. Army Corps of Engineers, proponents two months later recast it as a flood-control project and asked Congress to approve it as part of the Omnibus Rivers and Harbors and Flood Control Bill. As a bureau-built flood-control proposal, Burns Creek was assigned to the Public Works Committee rather than to the Committee on Interior and Insular Affairs. Now Saylor-proof, the bill was reported out of committee and sent to the full House. Saylor took to the floor to denounce the legislative end-around as showing a "blatant disregard" for legislative procedure and constituting a "personal affront" to certain members of the House Interior Committee. Once again, he and other opponents managed to excise the Burns Creek proposal from the bill. Proponents pushed the project unsuccessfully for three more years and then finally gave up.[45]

Besides fighting Western projects such as Burns Creek on an individual basis, Saylor worked to discourage the Interior Department from promoting public power as a matter of policy. When Reclamation Commissioner Dominy, in a speech at Rupert, Idaho, bemoaned the loss of Hells Canyon and the blocking of the Burns Creek project, Saylor took him to task. During the Eisenhower administration, he charged, Dominy had won a deserved reputation for fixing ailing irrigation projects, but the Rupert speech revealed "his true colors as an outright proponent of public power."[46]

Saylor went after Dominy again when the commissioner proposed that the Bureau of Reclamation construct the transmission lines for the CRSP. Saylor preferred a plan whereby the bureau would contract with private companies to wheel the electricity to customers. He maintained that private companies could deliver the electricity at a savings of $136 million and would also pay $284 million in taxes. When Dominy referred to those who opposed federal construction of CRSP transmission lines as "obstructionists," Saylor accused him of "totalitarian thinking" and said he was "unfit for office." The bureau, he claimed, was attempting to build "a federal power empire in the reclamation states." He warned his Western colleagues that "if you want to get future

reclamation projects you had better use your influence to break up this un-
holy alliance between the fanatical public power zealots and the Bureau of
Reclamation who are using the reclamation program for the promotion of
subsidized Government power." The bureau eventually contracted with four
private utilities to market the power from Glen Canyon Dam.[47]

Udall's alleged sympathy for public power also drew Saylor's wrath. Indeed,
Saylor had become convinced that the Interior Department had plans to establish a gargantuan national power-grid system that would intertie federal hydroelectric systems from the Pacific Northwest to the Tennessee River Valley. The
creation of such a vast network, he thundered, "would make a Commissar of
power in the Kremlin look like a minor leaguer." When Udall announced that
he, Dominy, and other federal officials were visiting the Soviet Union to inspect their electric installations, Saylor criticized the trip. He advised Udall to
tour his "own backyard" instead of "going over to Russia to learn some new
way to federalize the world's greatest and most efficient electric supply system."
Udall's May 1963 decision to permit a federal agency, the Bonneville Power
Administration, to market electricity in southern Idaho provided additional
evidence to Saylor that the government was attempting to take over the electrical industry. He introduced evidence showing that for the previous five years
Bonneville had run deficits. Daily for a month, he inserted speeches, articles,
editorials, and statements from southern Idahoans who opposed federal intrusion into their state. He also introduced legislation trying to undo Udall's
decision. All to no avail.[48]

While generally unpopular in the West, Saylor's stance on public power
proved popular in Pennsylvania. "Ever since going to Washington," observed
one local newspaper, "Saylor has solidified himself with the folks back home
by 'voting his district.' Voting his district, for Saylor, has meant jumping in
with both feet to save old coal markets and get new ones. The battle has not always been a rewarding one."[49]

Still, while his primary responsibilities were to his district, state, and nation, Saylor also claimed to be "a sincere friend of the West." He would continue
to support reclamation projects that were intended primarily for irrigation. At
the same time, he wanted to protect areas of scenic splendor and wilderness in
the West from "unnecessary and devastating Federal wrecking projects." His
dogged support for the Wilderness Bill brought him into heated conflict with
resource-development advocates like committee chair Wayne Aspinall. It would
prove to be one of his most difficult and ultimately rewarding battles.[50]

nine

Passage of the Wilderness Bill

In 1964, a junior high social studies teacher from Aurora, Colorado, appeared before the House Subcommittee on Public Lands in behalf of the Wilderness Bill. He stated that he had been feeling the pressure of having to pass a comprehensive exam for an advanced degree in history, so he and a companion had backpacked in the Maroon Bells Wild Area of Colorado. After an all-day hike through lush meadows and fir forests they reached their destination of Snowmass Lake. "It was late when we reached it," he said, "and we were hungry. Anything would have tasted good, but it seemed that the trout we caught were the best I'd ever eaten." After dining on mountain-lake trout, he continued, "we sat around the campfire reading Robert Service poems until the fire was glowing coals. Then under a blanket of moonlight, we crawled into sleeping bags." Lying there reliving the day's adventures and listening to the lake lap at the shoreline eased his anxiety and placed events in their proper perspective. Rejuvenated by that wilderness experience, he returned to college and passed the exam.[1]

Most opponents of the Wilderness Bill could identify with the experience of the social studies teacher, but they objected to withdrawing vast forest and mineral tracts from development so that a few elitists could frolic in the wilderness. John Saylor and other backers of wilderness legislation worked diligently to show that, relatively speaking, only a small amount of the public domain would be set aside as wilderness, that just about any able-bodied individual of modest means could access primeval backcountry, and that wilderness had inherent value as an idea even if the vast majority of people never directly experienced it. Still, by the early 1960s, it was evident that a wilderness bill would not be enacted until legislators had satisfactorily addressed three questions. What areas should be set aside? How much commercial development, if any, should be permitted in these areas? And which of the two branches, Congress or the executive, would be empowered to bring future preserves into the system? A champion of wilderness legislation, John Saylor would play a pivotal role in resolving those contentious issues.

Undeterred by previous setbacks, proponents of wilderness legislation introduced several bills early in 1961. Joined by thirteen cosponsors, Clinton Anderson, who had taken over as chair of the Senate Committee on Interior and Insular Affairs, submitted S. 174, a bill that closely resembled a measure that had been stymied the year before. In the House, Saylor introduced H.R. 776, a bill nearly identical to Anderson's. The legislation received support from the new administration when Kennedy, in a special message to Congress on natural resources, became the first president to advocate the establishment of a national wilderness preservation system. Interior Secretary Udall also endorsed the legislation at the seventh biennial wilderness conference of the Sierra Club.[2]

Like Udall, Saylor also spoke in favor of wilderness preservation at the Sierra Club conference. Introduced as the member of Congress who most deserved credit for protecting Dinosaur National Monument from dams, Saylor called the introduction of the first wilderness bill in the House in 1956 "one of the highlights of my life." Reporting on the status of the current bill, he cited several reasons for optimism. It had the support of the president, the Budget Bureau, and the Interior and Agriculture departments. In addition, Clinton Anderson was pushing hard for Senate enactment. Although he made no mention of Aspinall, Saylor cautioned against overoptimism because of the opposition from "selfish interests"—timber, mining, grazing, and reclamation users who believed that preserving primeval landscapes might injure local, state, or regional economies. At issue, he said, were 14 million acres out of 181 million, about 7 percent of all national forestland: "I cannot believe that the American people have become so crass, so dollar-minded, so exploitation conscious that they must develop every last acre of land in this country and destroy that last little bit that still exists." To those people who saw no need for wilderness,

Saylor responded, "Oh, how mistaken can you be?" Primeval backcountry was needed more than ever before to provide solitude, inspiration, adventure, inner peace, and a closer relationship with the Creator.[3]

In September 1961, the Senate passed the Wilderness Bill by a vote of seventy-eight to eight. As amended, the bill made several concessions to commodity users. It permitted grazing in the wilderness system where the practice had already been established, it allowed miners to explore for and develop mineral resources for a period of ten years, and it upheld the authority of the Federal Power Commission to grant licenses to develop hydroelectric dams. The wilderness network would consist immediately of those national forest areas designated "wild," "wilderness," and "canoe," some 6 million acres. An extra 8 million acres of national forestland classified as "primitive" could also be added to the system pending further review by the Forest Service, the president, and Congress. The bill gave the Agriculture Department ten years to evaluate the primitive tracts and forward its recommendations to the president. The president's selections would be made part of the system so long as neither the House nor the Senate disagreed with them.[4]

Keeping a promise to move on the legislation following Senate action, Aspinall scheduled field hearings on the various wilderness bills in late October and early November 1961. The Subcommittee on Public Lands, chaired by Gracie Pfost, held hearings in McCall, Idaho; Montrose, Colorado; and Sacramento, California. Testimony at these hearings, which Saylor did not attend, was dominated by commodity interests voicing their objections to locking up resources. The hearings were supposed to conclude in Washington, DC, but Aspinall delayed scheduling them until after the Outdoor Recreation Resources Review Commission had issued its report on wilderness to the president and Congress on January 31, 1962.[5]

This commission, on which both Saylor and Anderson served, gave a hearty endorsement to the wilderness preservation concept, Saylor inserting excerpts from the commission's report into the *Congressional Record*. "There is widespread feeling, which the Commission shares," it declared, "that the Congress should take action to assure the permanent reservation of suitable areas in National Forests, National Parks, wildlife refuges, and other lands in federal ownership." This statement delighted longtime Wilderness Bill advocates like Howard Zahniser, who had become frustrated by opponents using the issuance of the commission report as a delaying tactic.[6]

Congress had established the Recreation Commission in 1958 to study the recreation needs of present and future generations. After World War II, sub-

urban sprawl had gobbled up open space near urban centers. Increased affluence, more leisure time, and expanded use of the automobile to experience
nature further intensified demands on national and state recreation areas.
Now, in its 243-page summary report, the commission recommended setting
aside more open space near metropolitan areas, providing increased funding
to acquire more recreation lands, establishing a new federal agency to work
with the states in planning future outdoor opportunities, and enacting legislation to establish primitive or wilderness areas that would be free from roads
and "other works of man."[7]

As a member of the commission, Saylor worked mainly on the wilderness
features of the study. He visited some of the proposed wilderness areas, for example taking a horseback tour of Bridger National Forest in Wyoming. He
also read a massive study of wilderness undertaken by the University of California's Wildland Research Center, inserting a summary of this study into the
Congressional Record. The Wilderness Society also reprinted it as a brochure
for distribution to national conservation groups. The university study recommended national "legislation which specifically authorizes establishment of
wilderness areas within Federal agency jurisdictions, and management activities
to perpetuate wilderness conditions." Moreover, the study continued, legislation
"should include restrictions on mineral entry, mining, and water development,
limiting these activities to those clearly in the national interest."[8]

While buoyed by the Recreation Commission's report, Wilderness Bill
backers continued to be exasperated by Aspinall's dawdling. Aspinall wanted
time, he said later, for the House Interior Committee to scrutinize the commission's recommendations. Meanwhile, in early March, President Kennedy
delivered a special conservation message to Congress that included, among its
many recommendations, another request for the establishment of a national
wilderness preservation system. Horace Albright, the venerable former head
of the National Park Service who had made a fortune in the potash industry,
insisted that the Wilderness Bill would not injure the mining industry and
urged Aspinall to act. Pressed by the president, conservationists, journalists,
and concerned citizens, Aspinall finally resumed subcommittee hearings in
Washington, DC, in early May.[9]

At these hearings, Saylor and other House members testified in support
of their bills. Saylor's statement was merely a reiteration of his article "Saving
America's Wilderness," which had appeared in Living Wilderness five years
earlier. While his statement did not go into specifics, his bill approximated
Anderson's, initially bringing into the system areas categorized as wild, wilder-

ness, and canoe, with primitive tracts incorporated after undergoing a review process and nomination by the executive branch. Commercial enterprises would be banned, except when authorized by the president in a national crisis. Several members balked at the exclusion of development, especially mining, from the wilderness system. Walt Horan of Washington, for example, pointed out that the economic well-being of the Pacific Northwest "depends heavily upon the continued wise use development of many resources available in these abundant areas of forest lands." John B. Bennett of Michigan conceded that preserving wilderness was a notable goal, but not at the expense of developing resources: "In other words, I think that you have a dual set of purposes here, and I do not think that one should be permitted to jeopardize the other." Saylor dismissed this argument by declaring that mining would destroy wilderness values. Besides, he pointed out, his bill permitted the president, in a national emergency, to open protected areas to dam building and mining.[10]

Interior Secretary Udall agreed that wilderness and development were mutually exclusive. There was plenty of public land, he insisted, to meet mineral, timber, water-power, and grazing needs. Moreover, the 14 million acres of national forestland that would be set aside in the wilderness system were isolated, inaccessible, and for the most part "unsuited for ordinary commercial enterprises." Though roads and economic development would be banned, other practical purposes would in fact be served. Besides recreation and re-creation, wilderness preserves would protect watersheds, serve as natural scientific laboratories, and provide excellent hunting and fishing opportunities.[11]

Despite the bill's several congressional sponsors, widespread public support, and the backing of the administration, its fate rested with committee chair Wayne Aspinall. "I want it understood that I take second place to none in this room who may be interested in this legislation in the matter of enjoying the great outdoors," he told the committee. But in truth he was a friend of commodity users and was determined to protect their interests. He had informed David Brower in 1959 "that until the sponsors of the wilderness bill are able to get together with the other users of the public lands in the West and assure them that the wilderness bill supporters are not endeavoring to destroy already established uses (which include water resource development, mining, grazing, etc.), I will continue to be opposed to the legislation." His position had not materially changed since that time.[12]

On wilderness legislation, Aspinall did not want to be pushed, but neither did he want to be accused of dragging his feet or obstructing the public will.

Was the committee justified in taking its time? he asked Udall. Unwilling to upset the powerful committee chair, the interior secretary assured him that delay was wise. Was the committee prudent in waiting for the Recreation Commission's report? Again Udall said yes. Aspinall, who considered it "rather ridiculous" for the bill's proponents to criticize him for thoroughly studying the issue before acting, then raised a major objection to the Senate and Saylor bills: he was concerned, as were other members of Congress, that having the executive branch designate wilderness areas, with Congress holding only veto power, would diminish the authority of the legislative branch. He also realized, he said, that less land would be brought into the system, and hence shielded from development, if Congress had to act affirmatively on each recommendation from the president. Udall and Saylor pointed out in response that it was the executive branch that had first established wilderness areas in the national forests. "Thank God for Teddy Roosevelt and Gifford Pinchot," declared Saylor, "because if it had not been for the foresightedness of Mr. Pinchot and Mr. Roosevelt, what we are now praising as our national forest system would not exist." Having amassed more than seventeen hundred pages of testimony, the committee adjourned on May 11. It seemed likely that a bill would be reported, but it was also clear that this would be on Aspinall's terms.[13]

In late June 1962, Aspinall's subcommittee met to consider the various wilderness measures, with Saylor's H.R. 776 selected for markup. Aspinall promptly offered an amendment that nearly obliterated the Saylor bill. Still called H.R. 776, Aspinall's amended version consisted of two parts, Title I and Title II. Title I was an attempt to reassert congressional control over the public domain by proposing the creation of a national commission to review federal land policy. Title II proposed the establishment of a national wilderness system. Unlike the Anderson and Saylor bills, however, Aspinall's excluded from the system national forest primitive areas covering nearly 8 million acres. These tracts might be brought in at a later date, but only after public hearings and only through an affirmative vote by both houses of Congress. About 7 million acres of national forestland designated wild, wilderness, or canoe would be given statutory protection, but these acres would be open to oil drilling and ore extraction for a period of ten years. On August 9, the subcommittee approved the amended bill and forwarded it to the full committee.[14]

The substitute bill disappointed conservation leaders. Zahniser called it a "poor wretch," but "something that we can work with in hopes that we can see sound legislation ultimately enacted." His goal was "to get the legislation out of the committee, where we have no chance at all, onto the floor of the House where we do have a chance of operating." The Citizens Committee on Natural Resources prepared fifteen amendments to the lame Aspinall bill that would have, in effect, restored the intent of the Anderson and Saylor measures but never had an opportunity to present them to the full House.[15]

The full committee, with Saylor dissenting and filing a minority report, then added two amendments to Aspinall's substitute bill. One expanded the time for prospecting and mineral extraction from ten to twenty-five years. The other permitted the construction of a ski resort on 3,500 acres of the San Gorgonio Wild Area near Los Angeles, California. After reporting the bill, the full committee, again over Saylor's objections, instructed Aspinall to submit it under suspension of the rules. When Saylor protested that such a move served as an affront to the chair, Aspinall replied that "the chair does not consider this to be anything derogatory to the chairman's position." The seldom used suspension-of-the-rules maneuver permitted the bill to escape scrutiny by the House Rules Committee. It also limited floor debate, denied members an opportunity to add amendments, and required a two-thirds vote for passage. Aspinall explained that it was late in the session and that there was not sufficient time for the bill to be considered by the Rules Committee and the full House. Additionally, he wanted "to avoid having emotions take over and undo the work of the Committee." In other words, it would be Aspinall's wilderness bill or none.[16]

The actions of Aspinall and the House committee infuriated conservationists, who described the substitute bill as a "travesty" and "mockery." "Your heart must be heavy," a dispirited preservationist wrote Saylor. "This bill is so bad," sneered Spencer Smith of the National Parks Association, "that it is worse than no bill at all. It is a retrogression from the whole concept of wilderness. It is a hunting license for western mining interests." Newspapers also poured on the criticism. The *Denver Post* referred to the Aspinall substitute as a "non-wilderness bill." The *New York Times* labeled it a "sickly substitute" and used phrases such as "sabotage," "betrayal," and "wrecking job" to describe the committee's work. Conservation leaders pressed Speaker of the House John McCormack (D-MA) to deny the request for a suspension of the rules. He complied by instructing Aspinall to follow regular procedure by sending the bill to the Rules Committee. Instead, Aspinall decided to defer action until the following year since he wanted to return to Colorado to campaign for reelection. He instructed the committee not to seek a rule in his absence.[17]

Before leaving for Colorado, however, Aspinall defended the work of the committee, describing the substitute bill as "a logical piece of legislation and a true conservation measure." Historically, he held, "conservation and wise use have been synonymous. To me, that is what conservation has meant: accepting the material resources which nature is capable of providing . . . and developing them for the best use of the people as a whole." Next year, he predicted, the House would enact a wilderness bill similar to the committee's substitute bill.[18]

Stung by the intense criticism, Aspinall even took to the House floor on September 20 to explain to his colleagues and the American people why the wilderness measure had failed to pass. The substitute bill, he said, was an effort to reach middle ground. Unfortunately, he said, "the extremists have now demonstrated that they have no desire to compromise and, in their reckless and ruthless demand to rule or ruin, they have created an atmosphere which makes [im]possible the enactment of any wilderness legislation during this congress." The committee leaders, he noted, had worked diligently on the legislation. Pfost had attended all twenty-nine meetings of the subcommittee and committee, Aspinall twenty-seven, Saylor twenty-one. If preservationists had amendments to improve the bill, why hadn't they suggested them at one of the subcommittee or committee sessions? The reason they had not, he correctly concluded, was because they planned to present them when the legislation reached the House floor. Aspinall, however, did not want the legislation to be considered by the entire House because, in his mind, proponents of a strong bill had created such an emotionally charged atmosphere that members would have been unable to make reasoned judgments.[19]

The next day, however, Saylor provided his colleagues with a different version of the bill's journey through the committee. In effect, he accused Aspinall of lying and refusing to accept responsibility for sabotaging the legislation. No one was being fooled by Aspinall's explanations, he declared. Hostile to wilderness preservation, the chairman had refused to send his resource-user-friendly bill to the full House because it would have been overturned. To say that "debate would be too emotional, appears ludicrous." He charged Aspinall with foot-dragging and deception. The Senate had passed its Wilderness Bill in early September 1961, but the House committee did not conclude its hearings until early May. The Recreation Commission had released its report in late January, but Aspinall waited four months to resume hearings. And when the subcommittee had at last met to consider a bill, it was presented with a substitute that had never been discussed during the hearings, which had covered seventeen hundred pages of testimony.

As for amending the Aspinall substitute, Saylor pointed out, the work of the subcommittee had been conducted in "complete secrecy"; "those of us favoring the original bill," he said, "were precluded from discussing the matter with the outside proponents." Moreover, he had considered it futile to bring the fifteen amendments proposed by conservation groups before the full committee because these changes would have resurrected the original bill, which had just been disemboweled. "No, Mr. Speaker," he concluded, "the Chairman's explanation of the House Interior Committee will not wash. The failure to bring the wilderness bill to the floor for full consideration is the responsibility of the committee leadership. Their refusal is due to the fear, that when the House has the opportunity to work its will, the result will not be to their choosing."[20]

On the same day Saylor criticized Aspinall on the floor, he received a letter from the chairman saying that the committee's work was done for the Eighty-seventh Congress. Aspinall thanked Saylor for his "cooperation and conscientious and diligent attention to the Committee work during the year," pointing out that some of the difficulties the committee had faced occurred because it was an election year. Although he did not say so directly, Aspinall may have been referring to the fact that members of Congress, especially those in the eleven Western states where the proposed wilderness preserves would be located, did not want to alienate powerful economic interest groups. At the bottom of the letter, Aspinall scrawled by hand: "John: We part this time with some fundamental differences separating us. However, I sincerely trust that we shall not let them spoil a personal friendship which I value very much, Wayne."[21]

Aspinall's conciliatory letter, however, did not deter Saylor from continuing to criticize his handling of wilderness legislation. In mid-October he prepared a minority report for the committee decrying the mutilation of his original bill. He was embarrassed, he declared, that the Aspinall substitute bore the same number, H.R. 776, as his own. He also began to refer publicly to the Aspinall substitute as "a bill to protect miners, lumbermen and other enterprising patriots against rampant conservationists trying to preserve 2 percent of the country as God made it."[22]

Saylor's minority views brought a mild rebuke from Aspinall, who said he was "surprised, shocked, and deeply hurt" to learn that Saylor had been embarrassed by the H.R. 776 designation of the substitute bill. He reminded Saylor that he had asked for and received his permission to use that number. This story would remain "off the record," he said, "but we know." Doubtless Aspinall was correct, as he almost always was on technical matters, but it is difficult to believe that Saylor would have been so accommodating had he known that his legislative offspring was about to be butchered.[23]

Following congressional adjournment in mid-October, Saylor returned to Pennsylvania to campaign for reelection. The campaign was interrupted, however, by the Cuban missile crisis. Like the vast majority of his colleagues, he supported Kennedy in that "hour of grave national emergency" and voted for a congressional resolution authorizing the president to take all means necessary to protect the United States from the missile menace in Cuba.[24]

Following the successful resolution of the missile crisis, Saylor returned to the political campaign, opposed by Johnstown attorney Donald J. Perry. Although Democrats outnumbered Republicans in the district by twenty-two thousand registered voters, Saylor had the advantage of incumbency and was endorsed by most district labor groups and newspapers. Even the Democratic *Johnstown Tribune-Democrat*, the newspaper with the largest readership in the region, conceded that Saylor represented the district well. Saylor thus defeated his opponent by nearly twenty thousand votes. In Colorado, Wayne Aspinall also won reelection, although he received only 58 percent of the vote. In Idaho, Gracie Pfost lost her race for election to the U.S. Senate.[25]

During the opening days of the Eighty-eighth Congress, in January 1963, Senator Clinton Anderson and twenty-one cosponsors introduced S. 4, a bill identical to the Senate measure passed in 1962. Once again, the Wilderness Bill breezed through the upper chamber, passing in April by a vote of seventy-three to twelve. Meanwhile, in the House, Saylor and other representatives introduced bills nearly identical to the Senate version, but as usual, Aspinall proved hesitant to move the legislation.[26]

Aspinall was irritated because the Agriculture Department had been reclassifying primitive areas, such as the Selway-Bitterroot National Forest in Idaho, as wild, thus safeguarding them from commercial use. In October, he had written to Kennedy recommending a halt to any redesignation of primitive forestlands until Congress had completed a review of all policies relating to the disposition of federal lands. He also wanted a moratorium on the Wilderness Bill and other conservation-related measures until Congress had finished its study.[27]

Aspinall's proposal outraged backers of the Wilderness Bill because it smacked of blackmail. The Citizens Committee on Natural Resources protested to President Kennedy that conservation measures "should not be suspended simply because Mr. Aspinall has a notion that some new relationship between Congress and the Executive is needed." It also issued a press release stating that Aspinall's "concern about Executive-Legislative relationships, as real as it might be, is a transparent shield at best when it concerns the wilderness bill." Newspapers also blasted the chairman's high-handed tactics. "The arbitrary use of congressional power reached some kind of new peak," noted the *Washington Post*, when Aspinall insisted that the Wilderness Bill be shelved "until an understanding can be reached as to who shall set aside public lands for specific purposes." And Howard Zahniser observed that Aspinall claimed "to be a champion of Congress, but in obstructing the wilderness bill he has been frustrating Congress itself." George Marshall of the Wilderness Society wanted the American public to learn of Aspinall's attempt to pervert the democratic process, suggesting to Zahniser that preservationists get the story into a popular magazine like the *Atlantic* or *Harper's*. He would soon get his wish.[28]

In December 1962, Paul Brooks sought Zahniser's comments for a scathing article he had prepared for *Harper's* entitled "Congressman Aspinall vs. the American People." Zahniser made suggestions, praising the piece to the magazine's editor as "an excellent interpretation" of the Wilderness Bill debate during the previous Congress. It was "unfortunate," he said, "that the article has had to deal with Wayne Aspinall in such a personal way but—also unfortunately—it does seem impossible to understand the situation without such personal understanding of Congressman Aspinall. The article is actually restrained in many respects."[29]

As its title indicates, Brooks's article characterized Aspinall as an autocrat whose sympathy with commercial interests denied the popular will. The Saylor wilderness bill, Brooks wrote, was "hogtied and butchered in committee, and not even the spare ribs got to the House floor." "Like any well-planned murder," he added, "it is not without some morbid interest." The robust victim, Saylor's H.R. 776, had been done in by delay and "parliamentary shenanigans." The American public must not allow Aspinall to victimize future legislation by abusing his power as committee chair.[30]

Meanwhile, Kennedy attempted to mollify Aspinall by endorsing his recommendation for a joint executive-legislative review of public land policies. Kennedy, however, sidestepped the issue of whether the Wilderness Bill had to await this study. Saylor and Zahniser asked the president not to hold up wilderness legislation and to make another statement recommending it. Kennedy made no such statement, but members of his staff assured Saylor that the president had not retreated from his support for a strong wilderness measure. While they did not say so directly, it became clear that an understanding had been reached whereby Aspinall would move on the Wilderness Bill in return for the executive branch's support for the establishment of a public land review committee.[31]

Aspinall also insisted upon one other concession before moving on wilderness legislation, demanding that Congress vote affirmatively on all primitive areas recommended for inclusion in the wilderness system by the executive branch. The administration then asked the Budget Bureau to prepare a bill that would meet Aspinall's demands. Zahniser was prepared "to do anything" to satisfy the committee chair, working behind the scenes with the administration on a draft "so highly confidential that I hardly dare think about it in the presence of anybody here in D.C.," he joked. This draft eventually became H.R. 9162, introduced by John Dingell of Michigan. Meanwhile, Saylor delivered a speech on the House floor saying that preservationists would support any measures that provided "for more positive congressional action" so long as they "insure the protection of the areas provided for in the act until Congress does take further positive action." In other words, primitive areas nominated by the executive branch for inclusion in the wilderness network would be off-limits to commercial use until Congress made a decision one way or the other.[32]

Pressed by conservation groups, the administration, and public opinion, Aspinall gradually gave ground. But he was still combative. "In some respects John," he wrote Saylor in late July, "our goals may not be far apart, but in procedures and in the way that the matter has been handled to date, we have been divided so far that there has been no possibility of our getting together." He confided that he had been in contact on the legislation with members of the White House staff: "To date we have some understanding, but we certainly do not have my agreement." He warned that he would not depart significantly from the substitute he had proposed the year before: "I think after fourteen years of association with me you know I am not an extremist and I can assure you that in this matter I shall continue to refuse to take the side of the extremists."[33]

In the fall, Saylor appeared with Aspinall and Nevada Democrat Walter S. Baring on a Wilderness Bill panel before the American Mining Congress. Baring, who had succeeded Gracie Pfost as chair of the House Subcommittee on Public Lands, was an opponent of wilderness legislation, but both he and Aspinall opened the door for compromise. Aspinall noted that as committee chair he was constantly striving to make House members "aware of the basic constitutional question requiring affirmative action by Congress in the designation of wilderness areas." Baring echoed these sentiments, saying, "If there is going to be a wilderness bill, there will be provisions for affirmative action by Congress" after the executive branch had completed its review and submitted its nominations to Congress. He also observed that progress on wilderness legislation depended upon the willingness of proponents "to move in the direction of the compromise offered by the House Committee last year." In other words, some concessions would have to be made to resource users. These statements, Saylor said later, prompted him "to reconsider some aspects of this important subject" and to prepare a new bill.[34]

After discussions with Aspinall, Saylor introduced H.R. 9070 on November 7, 1963. Like the chairman's 1962 substitute, it instantly brought into the wilderness preservation program only those seventeen national forest tracts already classified as wilderness, wild, or canoe, an area totaling, with recent additions, nearly 9 million acres. After undergoing a careful review, other unspoiled tracts in national preserves could be added to the system with the approval of Congress. Saylor set a five-year limit for completion of the review process.

The Agriculture Department would conduct the review for thirty-six national forest primitive tracts and forward its recommendations to the president. These units would retain their status as primitive until Congress approved or disapproved their participation in the program. The bill permitted the continuation of existing uses—aircraft landings, motorboating, prospecting, and mining—until Congress had reached a decision. Once national forest units had been added to the program, dam building and the extraction of minerals would be forbidden. Hunting, fishing, and grazing, where it had already been established, would be allowed. The measure required the U.S. Bureau of Mines and Geological Survey to evaluate the mineral potential of tracts in the system in case the president was forced to authorize the extraction of minerals in a national crisis.

The procedure was similar for adding primeval portions of national parks, monuments, and wildlife refuges, except the review would be undertaken by the Interior Department. As with national forest primitive areas, Congress had to vote positively before any additions could be made to the wilderness system. The House Interior Committee, Saylor concluded, might offer improvements to his bill, but by and large he was confident that "it meets the criticisms made against its predecessors and meets these in a way to merit its support."[35]

John Dingell, as noted earlier, also introduced a wilderness bill, H.R. 9162, in the fall of 1963. The Dingell or administration bill resembled Saylor's in that it included in the wilderness program only wilderness, wild, and canoe tracts. Likewise, it required congressional approval for any additions to the program. But the Dingell bill made more concessions to commercial interests, especially the mining industry. It allowed ten years for the appropriate federal agencies to review lands for inclusion in the system. During that time, tracts in national forest primitive areas would be open to oil and gas drilling and the extraction of ores. Moreover, if Congress did not add primitive areas within ten years time, they would lose their special status and be thrown open to logging, road building, and other commercial development.[36]

Meanwhile, the White House continued to press Aspinall into action. After meeting with the House chairman in mid-November, White House special counsel Lee White expressed optimism that a compromise bill would be obtained. The administration bill, he believed, had met the chairman's objections and would be agreeable to Senator Anderson and conservation groups. White recommended that the president telephone Aspinall to urge passage of the bill in 1963. Kennedy made this call, two days before his death in Dallas.[37]

In January 1964, the House Subcommittee on Public Lands held field hearings on wilderness legislation in Olympia, Washington; Denver, Colorado; and Las Vegas, Nevada. Foes raised the usual protests—namely, that commodity use was not necessarily contrary to the wilderness ideal—but supporters of the bill had gained traction. When Westerners recommended allowing dams, mining, and lumbering in primeval forest preserves, Saylor reminded them that these uses were inconsistent with wilderness values. When opponents complained that the Agriculture Department was withdrawing too much forestland from development, Saylor commended its decisions. When Democratic committee member Compton White of Idaho observed that the department had made some mistakes, Saylor excused them with the observation that Jesus Christ was "perfect and he could not pick 12 people to agree with him when the chips were down. So I will forgive any Secretary of Agriculture who has made a mistake." When another Westerner wanted the states that contained wilderness expanses to have some control over what lands would be included in the system, Saylor reminded him that the tracts in question were not owned by the states but by the American people. And when a livestock operator asked that all wilderness areas be open to grazing because cattle thrived in the wide-open spaces, Saylor snorted, "In other words, you want to do for cows what you do not want to do for people." According to Zahniser, 295 witnesses testified at the three hearings, 225 expressing support for wilderness legislation. Among Wilderness Bill backers, 121 favored the Saylor measure. Subcommittee chair Baring also acknowledged support for the legislation but predicted that the House Interior Committee would report a bill along the lines of Dingell's H.R. 9162 because it was better suited to the multiple-use concept.[38]

In late April and early May, the hearings shifted to Washington, DC. By then, two dozen bills had been introduced, twenty-three in the House and one in the Senate with numerous cosponsors. The measures generally were separated into three categories: Anderson's S. 4 and House proposals similar to it, Saylor's H.R. 9070 and House measures identical to it, and Dingell's H.R. 9162 and its companions. Because Dingell's bill had been crafted with input from Aspinall, Zahniser, and the federal agencies, it was expected to be reported with amendments.[39]

House members and federal officials who testified for wilderness legislation went out of their way to flatter Aspinall and Baring. Thanks to their cooperation, noted Dingell, opposition to wilderness preservation had nearly disappeared. For his part, Aspinall professed to be an admirer of wilderness. Indeed, he wanted the record to show that the day before Kennedy had departed for Dallas, he had expressed thanks to the committee chair for clearing a path for the legislation.[40]

Aspinall said that he wanted to protect wilderness, but not too much of it. He was concerned that over the past year the amount of national forestland categorized as wilderness and wild had increased from 6.8 to 8.9 million acres. He admitted feeling "very kindly toward the mining producing industry," so he wanted to minimize the amount of public land withdrawn from development and permit mining in wilderness areas for at least ten years. Committee member Compton White wanted mining to be allowed for twenty-five years. Why was it permissible, he wondered, to harvest animals in national forest wilderness areas but not timber and minerals? To White, destroying animals seemed as contrary to wilderness values as destroying landscapes. Another committee member, Republican Mark Andrews of North Dakota, wanted to build parkways, like the eastern Blue Ridge, through wilderness expanses so they would be more accessible to the masses. Still other witnesses pushed for a ski resort in the San Gorgonio Wild Area near Los Angeles. The status of primitive national forest areas was another concern, especially for preservationists who worried that if Congress did not add them to the system within ten years, they would no longer be protected from commercial use. Even Dingell conceded that his bill did not adequately protect primitive areas, proposing an amendment that, like Saylor's measure, gave these tracts protected status until Congress made a decision. While conservation leaders favored either the Anderson or the Saylor bill, they would accept the Dingell compromise if it was amended to protect primitive areas.[41]

Perhaps the most eloquent testimony during the hearings came from Howard Zahniser, the bill's creator, who had worked patiently and painstakingly for eight years trying to reconcile the various perspectives: "It may seem presumptuous for men and women who live only 40, 50, 60, 70, or 80 years, to dare to undertake a program for perpetuity, but that surely is our challenge." The goal, he reiterated, was not to preserve wilderness for a privileged few, but for everyone.[42]

Zahniser's testimony put the subcommittee in a conciliatory mood. Though two days of testimony remained, Baring predicted a positive outcome for the wilderness proposal. Then came another Aspinall snit. He was stung by a *Washington Post* editorial that rebuked him for failing to pass the Wilderness Bill earlier. That editorial, he fumed, "was just about as dangerous, as far as killing wilderness legislation, as any article could be." He was prepared to guide a new bill out of committee, "but if I have to work with individuals who can put before the public such unworthy, untrue statements of conditions as they really are, then, of course, I am about ready to withdraw and let the chips fall where they will." Perhaps he had Saylor in mind when he accused some members of the committee of extremism: "We have some members of this Committee who are absolutely opposed to any wilderness legislation. They have good reason; and we have some members of this Committee who are for any kind of wilderness legislation. They would lock up anybody's property. It would not make any difference whether it upset the economy of a State government, or the economy of a region. They just do not care they are so selfish. Then we have a great many moderates who would like to see some kind of decision arranged." The crotchety chairman let it be known that further criticism would end all hope of obtaining a wilderness bill.[43]

In early May, just a few days after Aspinall's outburst, came the shocking news of Zahniser's death at age fifty-eight from heart failure. Distressed, Aspinall delivered a tribute saying that although "Howard did not live to see"

"Make Yourself Comfy In Our Little Lodge"

This 1963 Herblock cartoon lambasts Wayne Aspinall for opposing the Wilderness Bill. Copyright 1963 by Herblock in the *Washington Post*.

the enactment of the Wilderness Bill, "he knew that his battle had been won." Saylor also paid tribute, praising Zahniser's commitment, perseverance, and kindliness. "As I worked with 'Zahnie,'" he said, "my respect and admiration for him grew and grew. I realized I was truly in the company of one of God's noblemen. My life, and I know the lives of those who worked with Howard Zahniser, is better because of it." Saylor closed by suggesting that there could be no "better tribute to this 'Apostle of the wilderness'" than "to have Congress this year pass Howard Zahniser's dream legislation—a wilderness bill." Enactment of the bill seemed assured, but as usual Aspinall would not be rushed, nor would he be detracted from a spate of other conservation-related legislation.[44]

Aspinall gave highest priority in the Eighty-eighth Congress to the Land and Water Conservation Fund, calling it "of greater significance to the whole of the American public . . . than any measure which our committee is likely to report to the House for a long time to come." Saylor also considered it a "far-reaching" and "important" measure.[45]

An outgrowth of the Recreation Commission report and a pet project of Secretary Udall, the Conservation Fund, as it came before the House Interior Committee in 1963, sought to raise $2 billion over the course of twenty-five years to purchase private property for state or national recreation uses. Revenue would be raised by selling surplus nonmilitary public property; taxing motorboat fuel; and assessing admission and user fees at federal parks, monuments, and recreation areas. Unlike an earlier version, the revised bill called for an annual interest-free loan of $60 million from the third through the eleventh year of the fund's duration. During this time period, 60 percent of the revenue would go as matching grants to states to improve or develop outdoor recreation facilities. The remainder of the money would be available to the federal government to obtain recreation areas with the approval of Congress on a site-by-site basis. After the eleventh year, states would receive 50 percent of the fund, and the national treasury would be apportioned the remainder to repay the interest-free loan. Udall hoped to use the fund to establish additional national parks, lakeshores, and seashores. Congressmen J. Edward "Ed" Edmondson of Oklahoma and Charles Buckley of New York, both Democrats, held up the bill because they strongly opposed user fees, but Aspinall and Saylor pushed the bill through the House Interior Committee and the full House, where it passed by voice vote in July 1964.[46]

Meanwhile, on June 1, approximately one month after Zahniser's death, Aspinall's House subcommittee met in executive session to rework the wilderness measure. Instead of marking up the Dingell bill, as expected, the subcommittee amended Saylor's H.R. 9070, reporting it to the full committee. Their amendment, approved over Saylor's objections, permitted mining for twenty-five years after the establishment of a wilderness program. The full committee, again over Saylor's protests, then further amended the bill, removing the San Gorgonio Wild Area from protection to permit the construction of a ski resort, extending the review period for primitive areas from five to ten years, and authorizing the executive branch to eliminate primitive areas from national forestlands subject to a congressional veto.[47]

Conservation leaders hoped to add their own strengthening amendments on the House floor, but they were wary of being too demanding for fear of jeopardizing passage of the bill. Stewart Brandborg, who had succeeded Zahniser as executive director of the Wilderness Society, believed the "signs were good" for getting a stronger measure. As always, conservation groups worked closely with Saylor and looked to him to lead the fight on the floor. They also sent a letter to each member of Congress suggesting ways the bill could be improved.[48]

The Wilderness Bill was scheduled for debate by the full House on July 30. That morning Saylor told Michael Nadel of the Wilderness Society that Zahniser was still guiding the bill "and will see to it that all the influences will go to the proper places." But even with Zahniser's "presence," Saylor still had "the jitters." Nadel told him that "all great actors become tensed before the big moment, and it improves their performance." "And Saylor's performance," Nadel later informed Zahniser's widow, "was dynamic."[49]

After speaking in behalf of wilderness preservation in general, Saylor introduced two amendments to the legislation, both opposed by Aspinall and Baring. One, proposing the return of the San Gorgonio Wild Area to the wilderness system, passed by a vote of 73 to 39. The second, carried by a vote of 67 to 38, negated the committee's attempt to open primitive areas to commercial development by allowing the agriculture secretary to declassify them during the study period. This Saylor amendment gave Congress sole authority to redesignate primitive areas.[50]

The Saylor bill, as amended on the House floor, passed by a vote of 374 to 1, Saylor hailing it "as the most important landmark in conservation history since the days of Theodore Roosevelt and Gifford Pinchot." He went on to say that "the 88th Congress now is on record that it holds sacred the generous national assets that God has bestowed upon America and that ruthless and unnecessary commercialization will not be tolerated on lands and properties that obviously should and can be preserved in their natural state."[51]

Saylor served as one of ten conferees to work out the differences between the House and Senate versions of the bill. Although the bill was numbered S. 4, it resembled, in its final form, the Saylor measure. Pressed by conservation groups, conferees managed to limit mining in the wilderness system to twenty instead of twenty-five years. The conference report was approved by both houses in mid-August, and President Lyndon Johnson signed the bill into law on September 3, 1964.[52]

Thus, after an eight-year campaign, the wilderness proposal was finally enacted. Congress gave immediate protection to 9.1 million acres of national forestland categorized as wilderness, wild, and canoe regions and protected wilderness values in primitive national forest areas until Congress decided to incorporate them into the system. As one scholar has stated, "The system established was small, but it had the potential to grow." Indeed, by the turn of the century the system had grown to nearly 106 million acres.[53]

Most of the credit for the statutory establishment of a national wilderness system must go to Zahniser and the preservation community. They transformed an idea into legislation, broadcast the cause in their publications and conferences, won over the new administration, agitated the press, pressured members of Congress, and helped shape public opinion. But passage of the legislation may have been delayed even longer or perhaps never occurred had it not been for the strong support of Anderson in the Senate and Saylor in the House. Saylor encouraged and supported Zahniser during the bill's gestation period, introduced it initially and repeatedly in the House, and fought valiantly for its passage for eight years. He alone on the House Interior Committee had the stature and daring to rip into Aspinall for delaying and eviscerating the bill in 1962. In the end, both men gave ground. The final bill was not as pure as Saylor and preservationists would have liked, but it was a considerable improvement over the Aspinall substitute.

Given Saylor's commitment to the cause, it hurt when the press credited the Kennedy administration and the Democratic Congress, especially Anderson and Aspinall, for passage of the Wilderness Bill. When the Scripps-Howard press identified Aspinall as an "architect" of the legislation, Ann Dunbar could not restrain herself. "I am shocked and deeply saddened at the complete and utter lack of recognition to Congressman Saylor by the press for his role in the conservation measures enacted by this Congress," she began a biting letter to Edward M. Meeman, the conservation editor of that newspaper chain. The wilderness measure, she asserted, "was Mr. Saylor's legislation." Moreover, "it was his willingness to compromise his beliefs that insured the passage of a bill in the House of Representatives this year. For eight solid years, Representative Saylor has revised, changed, amended and compromised on his wilderness legislation in order that the members of the House could have an opportunity to vote on the proposal." She scorned Aspinall's efforts: he was an opponent of wilderness preservation and had repeatedly bottled up the legislation in his committee. The press had conveniently "[forgotten] his 'walk' during the 87th congress when he returned to his district, after reporting a bill to the House, leaving implicit instructions that *no* one was to act in his absence in request- ing a rule in order that the bill could be voted upon." She concluded by saying that happily for preservationists, "failure to receive due recognition for his work and efforts will have little if any effect on Mr. Saylor—his is a deep-rooted, long-standing belief in conservation principles."[54]

While written by a biased, dedicated associate, Dunbar's bristling analysis was essentially on the mark. Privately, Meeman had written Saylor stating that "your combination of aggressiveness and patience, which summed up in effec- tive persistence, paid off! I am glad I was here, to see it." He also sent a note to Ann Dunbar: "Rep. Saylor certainly deserves the profound and enduring grati- tude of the country for his dedicated, intelligent, undiscouraged and continu- ing activity for conservation. His service is outstanding and great." For whatever reason, Meeman chose not to commend Saylor publicly. But other editorial writers did, as did House colleagues. Aspinall noted that their disagreements had threatened to destroy the bill, but Saylor, "especially during the last 2 years, has been most cooperative." While cooperative, the Pennsylvanian had always "conscientiously represented the interests of conservation groups who were desirous of getting just as strong wilderness legislation as they could. The gen- tleman had not yielded except where it seemed to be absolutely necessary to yield in order to save the legislation." The bill deserved to be known as the "Anderson-Saylor Act—named after two talented and able conservationists."[55]

The conservation community also hailed Saylor's dedication to the cause of wilderness preservation. In 1963, Zahniser described Saylor as "a continu- ous champion of and hard worker for" wilderness legislation: "The difficulties we have been having are felt by him too, and without him our chance for suc- cess would be much poorer." Other members of Congress, he said, had been supportive, "but Congressman Saylor's service to the wilderness bill has indeed been outstanding." And Stewart Brandborg of the Wilderness Society and Michael McCloskey of the Sierra Club described Saylor's efforts on behalf of national parks and wilderness preservation as unrivaled by those of any other member of Congress.[56]

The battle to preserve the wilderness had been controversial and often acrimonious, but ultimately successful. Saylor would soon find himself in the midst of another contentious issue when Arizonans and other Westerners proposed the construction of two dams on the Colorado River that would intrude upon Grand Canyon.

ten

The Battle to Save Grand Canyon

In late July 1966, tension tugged at members of the House Interior Committee as they completed deliberations on a proposal to build two hydroelectric dams on the Colorado River in Grand Canyon. "You're being selfish," John Saylor snapped at Arizona Democrat Morris Udall, a proponent of the dams. "Nobody's being selfish here," Udall barked back. Saylor resembled a rugged Westerner, one journalist reported, but he was in fact an Easterner who had become the "tireless, redoubtable" leader of the preservationist forces in the House. Preservationists adamantly opposed both proposed dams. One, at the lower end of the great gorge, would back water through Grand Canyon National Monument and into part of Grand Canyon National Park. The reservoir created by the dam at the upper end of Grand Canyon, they asserted, would smooth a raucous river and desecrate its wilderness character.

A descendant of Mormon pioneers whose brother served as interior secretary, Morris Udall usually sided with Saylor on conservation issues. But in this instance he served as the leading proponent of the hydroelectric dams because he believed that they would provide the revenue and power to deliver Colorado River water to central Arizona without maiming the scenic value of Grand Canyon. The dispute between preservationists and reclamationists over dams in Grand Canyon took six years to resolve and became the most contentious conservation issue in the post–World War II decades. As usual, Saylor thrust himself into the thick of the battle.[1]

Arizonans rejoiced in early June 1963 when they learned that the U.S. Supreme Court had ruled in their favor in the case of *Arizona v. California.* For forty years, the two states had been squabbling over the apportionment of the waters of the lower Colorado River. Arizona had refused to approve the Colorado River Compact of 1922, by which six of the seven basin states had agreed to divide the water equally between the upper and lower basins. Estimating the annual flow at 17.5 million acre-feet, the compact apportioned 1.5 million acre-feet to the Republic of Mexico; 7.5 million acre-feet to the upper basin states of Colorado, New Mexico, Utah, and Wyoming; and 7.5 million acre-feet to the lower basin states of Arizona, California, and Nevada. It left it up to the individual states to divvy up the allotment within each basin.

Since the late 1940s, Arizonans had sought congressional approval for the Central Arizona Project. A dream of senior Democratic Arizona senator Carl Hayden, this project proposed to deliver by an open 250-mile aqueduct about 1.2 million acre-feet of Colorado River water yearly to the parched but mushrooming cities of Phoenix and Tucson. The measure passed the Senate in 1950 but stalled in the House Interior Committee, where Californians fought it. In 1951, John Saylor, then a young member of the House Interior Committee, introduced a successful resolution preventing House action on the Central Arizona Project bill until the courts had settled the long-standing dispute between Arizona and California over each state's claim to the lower Colorado River. The next year, Arizona asked the Supreme Court to resolve the issue, and after ten years of fact-finding and testimony, the justices upheld Arizona's claim to 2.8 million acre-feet of water from the main stem of the Colorado River, leaving 4.4 and 0.3 million acre-feet respectively to California and Nevada.[2]

Having won the court case, Arizona's five-member congressional delegation—Carl Hayden and Barry Goldwater in the Senate and Morris Udall, John Rhodes, and George Senner in the House—immediately introduced legislation establishing the Central Arizona Project. The battle to win congressional approval for this project would prove nearly as lengthy and agonizing as the court case had been.[3]

Morris Udall detailed some of the obstacles that had to be overcome. First, a bill had to pass the Senate, where Arizona had an edge because Carl Hayden, though eighty-six years old in 1963, had influence as head of the Appropriations Committee. The measure would also require the support of the executive branch. There too Arizona had an advantage because Interior Secretary Stewart Udall served as the president's chief adviser on federal water projects. But the legislation would draw the wrath of preservationists because it called for the Bureau of Reclamation to construct a high dam at Bridge Canyon, just three miles upriver from the end of Lake Mead. The reservoir formed by this dam would be ninety-three miles long, backing water through forty miles of Grand Canyon National Monument and thirteen miles into Grand Canyon National Park. One leg of the dam would stand on the Hualapai Reservation, so the project would also require the cooperation of the tribe.

But the main battle would be in the House of Representatives, where Arizona held only three seats, compared to thirty-eight for California. On the House Interior Committee, where the legislation would initially be considered, California outnumbered Arizona five members to one. Wayne Aspinall, who chaired the committee, was a strong supporter of the reclamation program, but John Saylor, the ranking minority member, took a more skeptical view. Projects, he insisted, must be economically sound, and their main purpose must be to deliver water, not to produce public power. Moreover, projects must not intrude upon the national park system. Morris Udall characterized Saylor as a "dynamic, resourceful, hard-hitting protagonist" who was highly respected by his House colleagues. "His attitude on our bill could be critical," he observed. "Saylor is a fervent conservationist who has labored hard for the growth of the National Park System and for greater outdoor recreation programs. He is one of the top national advocates of a strong Wilderness Bill. He is adamant about the 'integrity of the national parks' and will have much to say about the proposed Bridge Canyon Dam." Udall cautioned dam proponents not to take Saylor lightly: he had almost engineered the defeat of the Colorado River Storage Project in 1956.[4]

Before Saylor and preservationists could mount a full offensive against Bridge Canyon Dam, they were confronted with a bolder, more ambitious plan to develop the lower Colorado River. Interior Secretary Stewart Udall believed that the CAP would never be realized without the cooperation of California and the other basin states. Moreover, he maintained that the average annual flow of the river was considerably less than 17.5 million acre-feet, so there was not enough water to serve the needs of the upper and lower basins, plus Mexico. Consequently, he instructed his department to consider the possibility of augmenting the river through water imports.

Secretary Udall released a draft of the Pacific Southwest Water Plan (PSWP) in the summer of 1963. Grandiose in scope, it called for the Bureau of Reclamation to construct the Central Arizona Project, plus additional reservoirs in southern Utah, southern Nevada, and western New Mexico. It sought

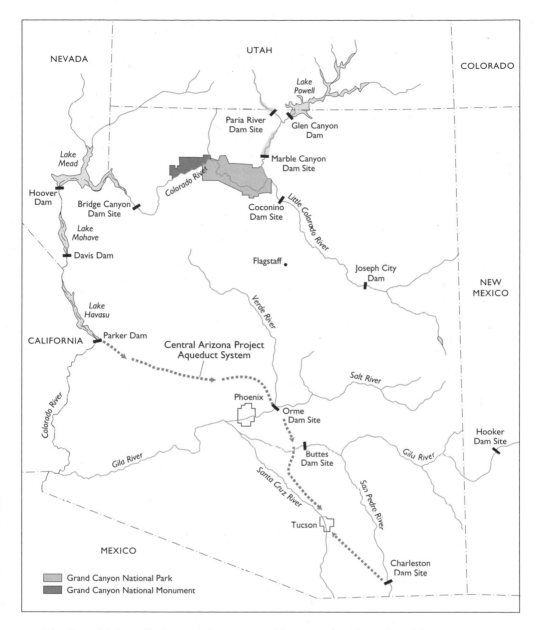

The Central Arizona Project aqueduct system with proposed Bridge and Marble
Canyon Dam sites. The Hualapai Reservation adjoins the Bridge Canyon Site and
Grand Canyon National Monument to the south. The Navajo Reservation borders
the Grand Canyon National Park and Marble Canyon Dam site to the east. Reprinted
with permission from Luther S. Carter, "Grand Canyon Dams Debated," *Science* 152
(July 17, 1966), 1601. Copyright 1966 AAAS.

to augment the supply of water in the lower basin by building desalting plants and channeling water into the Colorado River from streams in northern California or the Pacific Northwest. The cost of the project, estimated at $4 billion, would be met by creating a kitty called the Colorado River Basin Account. Revenues for this fund would come from selling the power generated by two hydroelectric "cash register" dams that would flank both ends of Grand Canyon. Bridge Canyon Dam would be built on the lower end of the canyon, just upstream from Lake Mead. The other facility would be located in Marble Gorge, only sixty miles downstream from Lake Powell. Marble Canyon Dam would flood fifty-three miles of the river but would not impinge upon the national park or monument. Additional money for the basin fund would come from the sale of power at other facilities on the Colorado River such as Hoover Dam, once it was paid for in 1990, and Parker and Davis dams, when they paid out in 2005.[5]

Insisting that his plan had the greater chance of political success, Udall withheld Interior Department support for the basic CAP measure introduced by the Arizona delegation. Udall's actions initially irked Arizona water leaders, except for Stewart's brother Morris, because it sidetracked the CAP. But his stance seemed warranted when Wayne Aspinall in September 1963 announced his support for river augmentation and the regional approach. Aspinall also stated that there would be no bill unless Arizona and the other basin states could agree upon a regional plan.[6]

The PSWP, however, presented problems. First, there was the staggering cost of $4 billion. Second, Henry "Scoop" Jackson, Democratic chairman of the Senate Interior Committee, had made it clear that the Pacific Northwest would not tolerate any pirating of Columbia River water for the lower Colorado River basin. Third, the plan would require the cooperation of at least two Native American tribes: Bridge Canyon Dam would stand partially on Hualapai land, and Marble Canyon Dam would straddle Navajo territory.

Finally, preservationists resisted the plan. They recognized that when Carl Hayden introduced the legislation creating Grand Canyon National Park in 1919, he inserted a clause empowering the interior secretary to build dams. But this provision, they insisted, ran counter to the secretary's obligation to protect scenic values, as detailed in the National Park Service Act. The Sierra Club wanted to protect all 277 miles of the geological Grand Canyon between Lake Powell above and Lake Mead below. His organization, David Brower warned, was preparing "for a knock down drag out fight to keep the Department of the Interior from building any dams in Grand Canyon." As usual, Saylor was expected to lead the charge against the dams in the House.[7]

By late 1963, Saylor had not taken a position on either the PSWP or the CAP. Twelve years earlier, his resolution suspending House Interior Committee action on the CAP bill had probably saved it from defeat. For that reason and because he had not sided with California, some Arizonans considered him friendly toward their cause. In the past, however, as one Phoenix journalist reminded readers, Saylor had opposed dams in Dinosaur National Monument and had "displayed a passionate and often a furiously protective interest in the nation's outdoors." Winning him over might prove difficult, but it would be worth the effort because his "voice reflects the outlook of the populous East toward reclamation in the West."[8]

This characterization of Saylor as friendly toward the West mystified other Arizonans. "In fact," noted one columnist, "it is our guess that insofar as he is concerned the entire West should be declared a wilderness area, locked up forever as a National Park and restricted to a few wealthy hunters and fishermen who could fly out from Pennsylvania and New York occasionally for an outing."[9]

Despite considerable criticism, Secretary Udall did not back away from the PSWP. Early in 1964, he announced a modified version of the plan that eliminated the desalting plants, thus reducing the cost by nearly $1 billion. He recommended studying the feasibility of augmenting the Colorado from streams in northern California but made no mention of tapping into the Columbia River for fear of alienating Scoop Jackson. After considerable cajoling, Udall won over Hayden, the senator reworking his bill to reflect the regional PSWP approach.[10]

But obstacles continued to mount. Conservation groups continued to assail the plan, and Californians balked at the idea of transferring water to the Colorado Basin from their northern watershed, worried about shortfalls in the annual flow of the Colorado River. Presently using 5.1 million acre-feet, they would be required to downsize to 4.4 million. If the river ran short of 7.5 million acre-feet for the lower basin, they feared that the interior secretary would take water for the CAP from California's 4.4 allotment. Worried about a shortage, California senator Thomas Kuchel introduced a bill guaranteeing his state's entitlement of 4.4 million acre-feet in case the Colorado ran short. In other words, in the event of scarcity, California's existing use should prevail over Arizona's future use. With so many obstacles to overcome, Arizonans were not optimistic about the bill's chances for success in 1964.[11]

At the urging of Morris Udall, Aspinall scheduled a hearing on the Central Arizona Project in Phoenix in early November 1964. The CAP was considered the most important issue facing Arizona since statehood, so House dignitaries spent one day flying over the proposed Grand Canyon dam sites and another day listening to testimony relating to the area's water needs.[12]

During the hearings, Arizona witnesses emphasized four points. First, to sustain its booming population and economic growth, Arizona needed more water. Second, it was overdrawing its natural supply of surface and underground water. Third, the project would not contribute to the national crop surplus because water would not be used to irrigate additional lands. Fourth, it would take ten years to construct the aqueduct and pumping plants to bring water to central Arizona. The hearings concluded with the subcommittee promising to reconsider the legislation in 1965.[13]

Overall, Arizonans considered the hearings successful. They had demonstrated their need for water, and both Aspinall and Saylor seemed receptive to the CAP. During the hearings and later over dinner at the Phoenix Country Club, Saylor stated that Arizona deserved the chance to develop her share of the lower Colorado River, but he questioned whether a dam was necessary. If dam builders could violate Grand Canyon Park, he said, they would then want to flood Glacier National Park. Should a dam at Bridge Canyon be necessary, however, he preferred a low one that would not roll water into the national park.[14]

With the opening of the Eighty-ninth Congress in January 1965, Senators Carl Hayden and Thomas Kuchel (R-CA) introduced similar regional bills authorizing federal development of the lower Colorado River. Now entitled the Lower Colorado River Basin Project, instead of the PSWP, the bills established basin accounts, with Bridge Canyon and Marble Canyon dams providing most of the power revenues to pay for the CAP and other projects in the basin. Kuchel's bill and an identical House measure introduced by Craig Hosmer of California carried a provision guaranteeing California 4.4 million acre-feet yearly from the Colorado until at least 2.5 million acre-feet of additional water could be imported into the basin from certain unspecified areas. Hayden agreed to the California 4.4 guarantee so long as the House passed the bill first.[15]

Pressed by environmentalists, Saylor lashed out against both Grand Canyon dams. In March, he inserted into the *Congressional Record* an editorial from the *Washington Daily News* that denounced the dams as "a crime against nature." In his introductory remarks, he pointed out that President Lyndon Johnson had recently addressed the nation on the importance of preserving America's natural beauty, noting that the message had evidently gone unheeded by dam builders, who wanted to deprive future generations of "one of their priceless heritages of scenic beauty."[16]

Saylor's speech prompted a swift reply from Arizona representative George "Duke" Senner, who portrayed Saylor as "brilliant" and "sincere," but wrong on the issue of the dams. Senner said that Grand Canyon was located in his congressional district and that he would be the first to fight any attempt to impair its beauty. Marble Canyon Dam, he asserted, would not encroach upon the national park at all. Bridge Canyon Reservoir would only crawl into the park for thirteen miles, not injuring its "awe-inspiring beauty." Instead, the reservoir would "permit tens of thousands of families to enjoy scenic grandeur where only a small handful of river adventurers dare to journey." By making the area more accessible, he concluded, Bridge Canyon Dam would serve the same purpose as a highway through the scenic Appalachian Mountains of the East.[17]

Saylor was not convinced. In response, he characterized the proposal to construct dams in Grand Canyon as "one of the most unfortunate schemes ever to come out of the darkness of the Bureau of Reclamation." He compared dam proponents to "medicine show pitchmen hawking the snake oil elixir which they claimed would cure all ills; but, in reality would result only in a big headache the next morning." Water could be delivered to central Arizona, he proclaimed, without building either hydroelectric dam. Once they were paid out, Hoover, Parker, and Davis dams could produce the revenue to pay for the CAP, and private, coal-fired steam plants could provide the pumping power to deliver water to Phoenix and Tucson.[18]

Frustrated by the barrage of criticism, dam proponents struck back. In February 1965, the Department of the Interior published a glitzy, twenty-eight-page pamphlet entitled *Lake Powell: Jewel of the Colorado*. With text and photographs provided by Reclamation Commissioner Floyd Dominy, the slender booklet packed a powerful sensual punch. At Glen Canyon, Dominy claimed, the Interior Department had tamed a rambunctious river and improved upon

This 1966 Reg Manning cartoon in the *Arizona Republic* reflects the view, scorned by Saylor and other preservationists, that the proposed Hualapai Dam would have only a minimal impact on Grand Canyon National Monument. Courtesy of the Reg Manning Collection, Arizona Collection, Arizona State University Libraries.

a stark landscape, transforming an inaccessible river gorge experienced by only a few sturdy elitists into a sparkling, sprawling lake that could be accessed and enjoyed by thousands of recreation users. The reservoir also brought individuals closer to Rainbow Bridge National Monument because they could now visit it by boat and a short walk instead of a grueling two-day hike.[19]

The pamphlet ended with a sales pitch for Bridge Canyon and Marble Canyon dams in Grand Canyon. These proposed dams, like Glen Canyon, would provide access and recreational opportunities for the multitudes without impairing the scenic grandeur of the park or monument. They also would serve as "cash registers" to pay for the delivery of water to arid Arizona: "They will ring up sales of electrical power produced by Colorado River water." The Interior Department mailed hundreds of copies of the pamphlet to members of Congress and journalists.[20]

The publication and distribution of the pamphlet infuriated Saylor. The bureau's advocacy of the construction of the Grand Canyon dams, he thundered in a House speech, constituted "one of the most pernicious and blatant illegal lobbying campaigns to influence pending legislation which I have ever seen any executive agency undertake in my 16 years in Congress." He asked the comptroller general of the United States to determine whether public funds had been misused to produce and distribute the booklet and asked the U.S. attorney general to determine whether the final two pages of the "huckster's pitch" constituted a violation of the Lobbying Act of 1913.[21]

Dam proponents tried to embarrass Saylor by showing that the Interior Department had also distributed a spiffy booklet on the proposed Tocks Island National Recreation Area on the Delaware River in Pennsylvania. Fellow Republican John Rhodes privately teased Saylor about this publication, asking if he was going to demand an investigation by the attorney general. Democratic senator Frank Moss of Utah blasted Saylor on the House floor for condemning one publication but not the other.[22]

Saylor then took to the floor to explain the apparent inconsistency. He considered "extensive and expensive lobbying" a threat to the democratic form of government and assured his critics that he vigorously opposed any federal department engaging in illegal lobbying, whether for one of his bills or not. The Tocks Island booklet, he said, was printed with private, not public, funds and did not openly advocate passage of a bill. At any rate, Saylor's charges came to naught when the Justice Department ruled that no violations of the law had occurred.[23]

Uncharacteristically, Dominy maintained a low profile during the booklet controversy. Years later, however, he expressed amusement over the incident and conceded that he had engaged in lobbying: "No doubt about it, that was the purpose of the magazine." Both he and Saylor, he recalled, took strong positions on the bureau's dam-building program, Dominy pushing the merits of hydroelectric power, while Saylor decried public power in general. "John Saylor's position on dam building pure and simple was that if it had hydroelectric in it you didn't want it," Dominy said, because it competed with fossil fuels for the generation of electricity. The public spats between the two men sometimes produced interesting theater. The House hearing room, noted one journalist, was "stuffy and baroque" except when Saylor grilled witnesses. He "delights in baiting Department of Interior witnesses, especially Commissioner Floyd Dominy of the Bureau of Reclamation. Dominy often takes the lure—at any rate, he often becomes very red in the face." Though the two pugnacious men often disagreed, they occasionally enjoyed each other socially. During the Grand Canyon dam controversy, both men were invited to attend the dedication of a reclamation project in South Dakota. There they decided to go pheasant hunting. As they walked side by side through a field, Dominy remembers, he said: "John, I'm going to lag behind a little bit. I don't like the idea of walking next to you when you are carrying a loaded shotgun."[24]

Dam proponents withstood the withering attacks of Saylor and the preservationists, but in early May they suffered a major setback from the Budget Bureau from which they never fully recovered. In his report on the Senate bill, Deputy Director Elmer Staats endorsed the Lower Colorado River Basin Project, but without Bridge Canyon Dam. Because preservationists objected to the encroachment upon Grand Canyon National Park, he recommended deferring the decision to build a dam at Bridge Canyon. He also urged the establishment of an independent commission to investigate national water needs instead of having the Interior Department study the possibility of importing water to the Southwest from the Northwest. Having lost the argument within the executive branch, Stewart Udall publicly had to go along with the Budget Bureau's recommendations, including the decision to drop Bridge Canyon Dam from the project.[25]

Senate and House Interior Committee chairs Henry Jackson and Wayne Aspinall added to the concerns of proponents of the Lower Colorado River Basin Project. Worried about a potential raid on the Columbia River, Jackson added an amendment to a Senate bill in July stating that the Interior Department could not undertake an import-feasibility study without the consent of Congress. Convinced that the Colorado River lacked sufficient water for both the upper and the lower basins, Aspinall proclaimed that there would be no hearing on the bill unless the seven basin states could agree on an import-feasibility study. Delegates from the seven basin states met in August and agreed to work for the inclusion of such a study in the House bill. With this assurance, Aspinall scheduled hearings before the House Subcommittee on Irrigation and Reclamation.[26]

The subcommittee held hearings in late August and early September 1965. Morris Udall, speaking for the Arizona delegation, explained the five main features of the bill. It called for construction of the Central Arizona Project and Hooker Dam in New Mexico. It promised California first call on 4.4 million acre-feet of water in case the Colorado did not yield 7.5 million acre-feet to the lower basin. It proposed that the interior secretary study the water resources of the Columbia and Colorado river basins. It urged the importation of 2.5 million acre-feet yearly into the Colorado Basin from areas with water surpluses. And it defied the Budget Bureau by recommending federal construction of two hydroelectric dams at Bridge and Marble canyons to provide the power revenues that would fund the Central Arizona Project and water imports.[27]

Stewart Udall and Floyd Dominy also testified for the project, but without Bridge Canyon Dam. Marble Dam alone, they said, would produce enough revenue to finance the project, dropping the cost from $1.3 billion to $812 million. Representatives from the Hualapai tribe testified in favor of Bridge Canyon Dam. Since one end of the dam would be anchored on their land, they expected to be handsomely compensated. They insisted that the structure be named Hualapai Dam and threatened to seek a license from the Federal Power Commission to develop on their own a low dam that would not threaten the park if Congress did not authorize the high Bridge Canyon Dam.[28]

Opponents included mainly representatives from the Pacific Northwest and the upper Colorado River basin and preservationists. Northwesterners opposed the import idea. Upper Colorado River basin representatives, especially Wayne Aspinall, worried that the Central Arizona Project would use all the unused flow of the river and that the lower basin would then object to future water projects in the upper basin. Aspinall wanted to be sure that the water would be available when Colorado and the other upper basin states were ready to use it. Augmenting the river by 2.5 million acre-feet yearly seemed the best way to remedy the shortage, and since the Columbia, according to some specialists, had perhaps as much as 160 million acre-feet wasting to the sea each year, it appeared the most likely source for imports.[29]

Saylor joined representatives from numerous conservation groups in opposition to both dams. He shared President Theodore Roosevelt's belief, he said, that Grand Canyon should be left inviolate because humans would only ruin it in their attempts to improve upon it. Because the Interior Department no longer recommended construction of Bridge Canyon Dam, he directed the bulk of his criticism toward the state of California, whose water demands he considered unreasonable and insatiable. Arizona, he declared, had won the Supreme Court decision in 1963 but was bargaining away its victory by caving in to California's demands for water imports and the 4.4 guarantee. Saylor mocked the import idea. Pointing to possible water sources on a large map, he wondered aloud how far California's reach would extend. The Rio Grande? The Arkansas? The Platte? The Missouri? The Kuskokwim in Alaska? Hudson Bay in Canada? Or possibly Hawaii, which had very heavy rainfall?[30]

Morris Udall pointed out that the court victory did not bring water to Arizona's parched lands; only Congress could do that. To the argument that neither dam was necessary for the Central Arizona Project, Udall replied that "we can't go out in the street with a tin cup and get the money to put water into Arizona." To the suggestion that the Reclamation Bureau could construct nuclear-powered or coal-fired steam plants to push the water into Arizona, Udall said that the bureau by law could only build hydroelectric plants, "and it will be over the dead bodies of several of my colleagues on this Committee that you will ever put the Bureau in the steamplant business." After eight days and more than nine hundred pages of testimony, the hearings concluded with the understanding that the committee would resume its work on the bill at a later date.[31]

While awaiting the resumption of the hearings, preservationists and reclamationists both sought to advance their positions on the project with the American public. Working closely with the Sierra Club, Saylor continued to thunder against the dams. In March, he introduced a bill to expand the boundaries of the national park to include all 277 miles of Grand Canyon from Lake Mead to Lee's Ferry. This bill, however, was buried in committee.[32]

Saylor also continued to snipe at Floyd Dominy. In early January 1966, the reclamation commissioner had portrayed preservationists as "zealots" who overstated the injury the dams would do to Grand Canyon. He also tried to persuade *Reader's Digest* to withdraw its commitment to publish Richard

Bradley's article "Ruin for Grand Canyon." Convinced that Dominy had a comeuppance coming, Saylor penned a childish verse:

Hominy Dominy Sat on the Wall,
Hominy Dominy Had a Great Fall
All Udall's Horses and All Udall's Men
Couldn't Put Hominy Dominy Together Again.[33]

The Hominy Dominy poem prompted Bradley to question Saylor's mental stability. "I'm worried that Saylor has outlived his usefulness to conservation; he strikes me as a person who has flipped his lid," he complained to David Brower. "I'm not sure any longer that his statements will be respected in congress." Brower evidently did not agree with Bradley because he continued to work closely with Saylor on the Grand Canyon dams and other environmental issues.[34]

While Saylor and preservationists railed against the impending ruin of Grand Canyon, Aspinall worked to make the bill more palatable to Colorado by adding five water projects. The addition of these projects, he reasoned, would enable Colorado to fully develop its share of the overallocated river and virtually compel water imports. Arizonans considered the demand "blackmail" but went along, knowing they had to gain the chairman's support for the bill. At Aspinall's suggestion, they also agreed to amend the bill to satisfy the demands of the Hualapai tribe. This way, if preservationists continued to oppose Bridge Canyon Dam, they would appear to be anti-Indian. They proved unreceptive, however, to Dominy's suggestion that they compromise with preservationists by agreeing to Saylor's proposal to include Marble Canyon in an expanded Grand Canyon National Park in return for a high Bridge Canyon Dam. With Aspinall's support, they believed that "even with Bridge in and Saylor mustering all possible opposition" the bill would glide through the Interior Committee.[35]

In April, preservationists achieved a public relations coup when *Reader's Digest,* the most widely read magazine in the world, did indeed publish Richard Bradley's "Ruin for Grand Canyon." The article, as its title indicates, argued that either dam would devastate one of America's most valuable natural treasures. To offset the damaging publicity, dam proponents organized a massive letter-writing campaign to the magazine, but to little effect.[36]

Even with the damaging publicity, proponents expected the Lower Colorado River Basin Project to reach the House floor. Once there, however, they realized that they needed to neutralize Saylor, whom they expected to propose an amendment removing both controversial dams. This move might succeed, they believed, unless they added an amendment of their own stating that any power plant that replaced the hydroelectric dams would be federally owned.[37]

Aspinall resumed the hearings on the bill in May 1966, with more than seventy witnesses testifying during the six days of hearings. Morris Udall, the lead witness, explained the revised bill. Retitled the Colorado River Basin Project to reflect basinwide accord, the measure added three main features. First, it incorporated concessions to the Hualapai people, including renaming the dam for the tribe. Second, the interior secretary would be authorized to study the feasibility of augmenting the Colorado River by 8.5 instead of 2.5 million acre-feet yearly. Third, five water projects would be added to permit the upper basin to take advantage of its entitlement to 7.5 million acre-feet of water.[38]

Udall also sought to downplay opposition to the dams from preservationists. By approving both Hualapai and Marble dams, Congress would not ruin Grand Canyon but would "achieve the delicate balance between conservation of scenic and historical values and the full development of the water and power potential of the river to meet pressing human needs." He asserted that if the federal government did not build the Central Arizona Project, the state of Arizona would.[39]

Saylor praised Udall and the Arizona delegation for their able and bipartisan presentation but then said he disagreed with just about all of it. The project, he said, would cost $1.7 billion, plus the untold expense of river augmentation. He reiterated his charge that Arizona had bargained away its Supreme Court victory. It had made concessions to the Hualapai, a tribe it had ignored for decades. It had yielded to California's demand for river augmentation, a 4.4 million acre-feet priority, and a basin account funded by the revenues from two unnecessary dams. And it had agreed to five water projects for Colorado. Sarcastically, he asked, "Why no project for Utah? . . . Why be chintzy?" Why not resurrect the Echo Park Dam proposal and add it to the bill? Udall said that if Saylor proposed an amendment to add Echo Park Dam, he would second it. Unamused, Saylor declared that he opposed all the proposed dams, especially those that would crouch at either end of Grand Canyon.[40]

The Democratic administration, he reminded Udall, opposed Bridge Canyon Dam: "Here I am supposed to be a member of the loyal opposition and in this hearing I am carrying the cross for the White House. There is something wrong in this whole thing." Udall said, "Will the Johnson administration floor leader yield?" Saylor responded, "I will be happy to yield to the rebellious member of the other party." Replied Udall, "I just wanted to commend him for the way he is representing the administration."[41]

Saylor, of course, had allies in criticizing the project. As usual, representatives from the Pacific Northwest voiced opposition to regional water-import studies. They preferred a separate bill establishing a nongovernment panel to examine water needs on a national basis. Geography professor Stephen Jett of the University of California pointed out that the sentiments of the Navajo Nation had been ignored even though Marble Canyon Dam would cover some forty-six miles of their land. In addition, individuals from various conservation groups spoke out against the dams because they would mar Grand Canyon. They supported the Central Arizona Project but insisted that the water could be provided by thermal or nuclear power and that the project could be funded by revenues from existing dams after payoff.[42]

Though usually fair, Aspinall criticized preservationists for being uncompromising. Why not approve one of the dams and save the rest of the canyon as part of an expanded park? he inquired. Saylor asked why the chairman refused to eliminate both dams and preserve the entire canyon. Aspinall replied that maybe a compromise could be reached if Saylor and other preservationists were not so extreme in their views.[43]

By the end of the hearings, the ranking members of the committee had not found ground for compromise. Aspinall insisted upon at least one dam, river-augmentation studies, and five water projects for Colorado. Saylor would not approve any measure that included the damming of Grand Canyon. So they would fight it out before the full committee, where Aspinall, as chair, held the upper hand.

During the early June deliberations of the Subcommittee on Irrigation and Reclamation, the *New York Times* and other national newspapers published two Sierra Club advertisements that helped turn public opinion against the dams. The ads bemoaned the flooding of Grand Canyon and urged readers to write letters of protest to members of Congress, resulting in a flood of criticism to Congress and the Interior Department. On June 10, the day after the ads appeared, the Internal Revenue Service (IRS) announced that it was launching an investigation to determine if the Sierra Club should be deprived of its of tax-exempt status for lobbying against the dams. This announcement brought criticism of violations of free speech and the right to petition, the Sierra Club playing its role as victim to the hilt.[44]

In a speech entitled "Defender of Grand Canyon," Saylor supported Brower and the Sierra Club. He questioned the timing of the IRS investigation and decried the chilling effect it might have on civil liberties. He also tore into Udall for supporting dams in Grand Canyon. "My friend from Arizona has himself established a reputation as a conservationist, so it is all the more puzzling to me why he should not seize the opportunity to free the Central Arizona Project of the albatross of the Grand Canyon dams," he declared. "How can he expect to be effective in the future pleading for the national park system and its expansion when he at this time appeals for an invasion of one of the Nation's oldest and best known parks?"[45]

Besides defending the Sierra Club from what he regarded as unfair attacks and bullying tactics, Saylor peppered the *Congressional Record* with anti-dam speeches and materials. He also mailed a letter to each member of Congress urging them to "save our priceless national heritage—the Grand Canyon— from intrusion." Saylor sent this "Dear Colleague" letter to counter the pro-dam steak luncheons the Arizona delegation was holding in Washington for members of Congress.[46]

The House subcommittee pressed ahead with the markup of the Lower Colorado River Basin bill amid the furor created by the Sierra Club ads and the IRS investigation. Saylor attempted to remove both dams from the bill by offering a substitute authorizing only the Central Arizona Project. It failed. In late June, the subcommittee approved the bill by a count of thirteen to five, Saylor and four representatives from the Northwest voting with the minority.[47]

The bill then proceeded to the full Committee on Interior and Insular Affairs in mid-July 1966. There, Saylor tried to delete the dams and again failed. To retain basin-state accord, Aspinall and Udall prepared what they regarded as a modest alteration to the bill, calling for the establishment of a national water commission and empowering that panel to undertake a reconnaissance study relating to the water-import program. If the reconnaissance review showed a reasonable chance of success, then the Interior Department would automatically follow up with a comprehensive feasibility study.[48]

Saylor denounced their "nefarious legislative shenanigans." As he sat drinking tea from a huge mug, he scolded Udall, who sat across from him at the horseshoe-shaped table: "You have violated the policy of the administration, you have violated the wishes of the President, you have violated the Park Service, you have violated the recommendations of the Bureau of the Budget, and you have violated the recommendations of your own brother." Udall could only shake his head and smile. The next day, on July 28, Saylor introduced an amendment eliminating Bridge Canyon Dam, but it failed sixteen to thirteen. With California's support, the full committee approved the bill as modified by Aspinall and Udall by a vote of twenty-two to ten, forwarding it to the Rules Committee.[49]

As the Rules Committee deliberated, public criticism of the bill continued to surge. The Sierra Club published a now famous full-page ad mocking the argument that the dams would make Grand Canyon more user-friendly. In conspicuous type it asked: SHOULD WE ALSO FLOOD THE SISTINE CHAPEL SO TOURISTS CAN GET NEARER THE CEILING? In early August, the Navajo Tribal Council retracted its 1961 resolution supporting Marble Canyon Dam. After review, the tribe determined that greater economic benefits could be secured by using coal on the reservation to fire the steam plants for the Central Arizona Project, leaving the gorge unimpaired to attract tourists. Saylor also maintained a barrage of criticism in the *Congressional Record* and sent his colleagues a twenty-five-page letter detailing some of the "pertinent facts" relating to the proposed Bridge Canyon and Marble Canyon dams.[50]

Saylor vowed to make a final stand on the House floor if the Rules Committee forwarded the bill. He would offer a substitute bill, in the form of an amendment, that would eliminate the 4.4 million acre-feet guarantee, the import study, the five Colorado water projects, and the two Grand Canyon hydroelectric dams. His streamlined bill would authorize only the Central Arizona Project, with privately produced thermal plants providing the power to pump the water.

With elections only three months distant, members of Congress could not easily dismiss opposition to the dams. Democratic Massachusetts representative Thomas "Tip" O'Neill, a member of the Rules Committee, remarked that "in all my years in Congress, I have never seen so much flak from the conservationists!" Dam proponents also could not readily discount the possibility that Saylor's substitute bill might succeed. Aspinall took pride in the fact that bills reported favorably by the Interior Committee invariably passed the House; he often fought with Saylor over bills in committee, but not on the floor. Consequently, he did not urge the Rules Committee to act.[51]

California water leaders also feared Saylor's streamlined substitute and used the state's two members on the Rules Committee to help Aspinall stonewall the bill. Anxious over the lack of action by the Rules Committee, Morris Udall and John Rhodes met with California's water policy guru, Northcutt Ely, and Senator Thomas Kuchel to seek an explanation, stating that California's congressional leaders had informed them that Saylor "had the horses" to get his "stripped-down" proposal through the House. He could take the position that his substitute bill would deliver water to central Arizona while simultaneously saving $1 billion and Grand Canyon too. And once Saylor's substitute passed the House, Senate Interior Committee chair Scoop Jackson would promptly escort it through the upper chamber, and California would be left without its 4.4 guarantee and its import studies. Udall and Rhodes assured the Californians that their head count indicated that, at best, Saylor's substitute bill stood only a 50 percent chance of success. But the Californians did not wish to go forward in the Rules Committee "with the Saylor problem facing them." Ely suggested ending on a "favorable plateau" and waiting until the following year to get a bill that would satisfy all of the basin states. Before giving up, Rhodes and Udall met with six members of California's congressional delegation, who asserted that Saylor could not be stopped on the floor and recommended approaching him about adding the 4.4 guarantee to the substitute. If he consented, then the Rules Committee would act.[52]

Whether Udall approached Saylor is not clear. But in early September, he learned through a third party that Saylor apparently was willing to make modifications to his substitute bill. He would accept the 4.4 California guarantee, two water projects for Colorado that had been recommended by the Budget Bureau, and the formation of a National Water Commission. Reportedly, Saylor also would also be willing to accept a low dam at Bridge Canyon. Downsized by ninety feet, the shorter dam would produce enough revenue to fund the CAP and other projects without intruding upon the national park. True, it would still back water into the national monument, but this intrusion would be offset by expanding the park's boundaries at the other end to include Marble Canyon.[53]

Though doubtful that they could get any bill through the Rules Committee and both houses so late in the session, Udall and Rhodes pursued the Saylor initiative. They contacted California water leaders, but Northcutt Ely said Saylor's proposal was unacceptable because it failed to include water-import studies. After learning of California's negative response, Aspinall also shunned the alleged Saylor overture. The chairman wanted five water projects for Colorado, not just two, and also insisted upon import studies. He also doubted that the Senate would have time to act on the revised bill even if the House Rules Committee acted favorably. The legislation, he said, was dead until next year.[54]

Historian Byron Pearson argues that political motives, more than environmental concerns over the Grand Canyon dams, derailed the legislation. Relying on Morris Udall's imprecise head-count tallies, Pearson asserts that Saylor did not have the votes to pass a substitute bill and gives this as the reason why he made additional concessions, including a low Bridge Canyon Dam. The political machinations of Northcutt Ely proved pivotal, he says, in spoiling the legislation. Ely used his influence with California political leaders to mire the bill in the Rules Committee. All along, Pearson argues, Ely wanted the legislation to fail and "used the Saylor threat as a pretext to delay implementation of the Supreme Court decision of 1963" so that California could continue to use annually 5.1 million acre-feet of the Colorado River instead of downsizing to 4.4 million acre-feet.[55]

While interesting, Pearson's thesis exaggerates Ely's duplicity and minimizes the threat of Saylor's substitute bill. Granted, Ely persuaded California's representatives to stymie Rules Committee action on the bill, but he did so, as he explained later, because Saylor had the votes for a bill without dams, import studies, or the 4.4 guarantee. Thus Ely helped immobilize the measure to enable California to negotiate a better deal in the next Congress. Moreover, it would have been impossible for California's two representatives on the fifteen-member Rules Committee to block action on the measure without the cooperation of Aspinall, who also believed Saylor had the strength to pass the substitute. Even Morris Udall's top legislative assistant later admitted that Arizona did not have the votes to block Saylor on the floor. "If you quote me, I'll probably have to deny it," Richard Olson wrote, "but I frankly think some of our people in Arizona have totally misread California's actions of last fall in the house. I attended the final 'head count' session, and while I was optimistic about our chances on the floor, I also know that we were far short of the 218 'sure' votes against a Saylor-type substitute. If I had been calling shots for California, I probably would have advised blocking the bill in the Rules Committee as was done. Therefore, I see no villains across the border."[56]

Why then did Saylor make concessions, including support for a low Bridge Canyon Dam? The evidence is not clear that he did; indeed, the existing evidence is hearsay. Udall learned of Saylor's alleged compromise from an unnamed third party: there was no written proposal or communication from Saylor. Udall's detailed notes contain no reference to a conference with Saylor on the so-called concessions, nor is there any public mention of support for a low Bridge Canyon Dam from Saylor himself or from any of the involved parties. Recommending a low dam would have been completely at variance with

Saylor's fervent belief that national parks and monuments were inviolate. Even if Saylor did offer a compromise, however, this does not mean that he did so because he lacked votes for the substitute bill on the floor and acted out of desperation, as Pearson suggests. He may have offered to bend because he wanted to get water for Arizona, an expanded park for Grand Canyon, and committee action on other conservation-related issues.

Bitterly disappointed over the legislative stalemate, Arizonans reassessed their position. The Arizona congressional delegation—Rhodes, Udall, and newly elected Republican Sam Steiger—prepared new legislation and discussed strategy, including how to deal with Saylor. At a Republican breakfast in early January, Rhodes and Saylor had an opportunity to discuss the Central Arizona Project. Saylor, Rhodes reported, appeared to be torn. On the one hand, he felt obliged to transfer water to thirsty Arizona. On the other hand, he disliked "California with a purple passion" and opposed both dams in Grand Canyon. It may be, Rhodes concluded, that Saylor "really feels that the best way to keep dams from being built in the Colorado River is to completely defeat the whole project" through a "strategy of divide and conquer." Whatever his motives, Saylor was "not a person to be ignored and the possibility that he may be a real force in our favor should never be taken lightly."[57]

Secretary Udall proposed a revised federal plan. For practical political reasons, he sought the Central Arizona Project for his home state, believing success depended upon acting before the elderly but politically powerful Carl Hayden retired in 1968. Moreover, environmentally Udall gravitated toward a preservationist perspective, preferring to leave Grand Canyon undammed. Consequently, he recommended federal construction of the Central Arizona Project with coal-fired steam plants on the Navajo Reservation near Page providing the power. The Marble Canyon dam site would be brought into an expanded Grand Canyon National Park. Thus both dams were out under Udall's revised proposal.[58]

To the surprise of many Westerners, Senator Hayden, who had pushed for hydroelectric dams on the river since the late 1940s, endorsed Secretary Udall's proposal and with Paul Fannin introduced a bill in February 1967. Senate interior chair Jackson also gave his support but insisted upon the establishment of a National Water Commission as a precondition to any Colorado River Basin Project. Saylor also supported the new bill.[59]

Rhodes, Udall, and Steiger seemed to be in a no-win situation. To secure House authorization for the Central Arizona Project, they needed allies. But

California and Colorado would not help without the inclusion of a 4.4 guarantee, import studies, upper basin water projects, and a basin fund supplied with revenues from at least one hydroelectric dam on the river. And they could not count on the support of preservationists and the executive branch unless the project were freed from import reviews and dams. "I tried to analyze whether we could put together a combination consisting of Saylor, Arizona, the eastern Democrats, and Saylor's Republican allies from the east as against Colorado and California," Udall agonized. He was doubtful, though, because Aspinall might not schedule the bill for hearings, and if he did California would choke it in the Rules Committee. The Arizonans decided to cast their lot with their sister basin states.[60]

Still, Morris Udall did not expect to go to the House floor with the previous year's bill. Given the administration's change of heart on Marble Canyon Dam, there was an even greater possibility, he cautioned Aspinall, that "a Saylor-style substitute bill without any dams would be adopted" unless they made changes. He recommended that Arizona, California, and Colorado should each be prepared to make concessions. Arizona would give ground on virtually any point to get the central artery. California and Colorado might yield on the issue of import studies in return for the 4.4 guarantee and the five upper basin projects. Above all, though, the three states must stand together.[61]

Besides the administration bill introduced by Hayden and Fannin, Californians in both chambers introduced measures including the 4.4 guarantee and river-augmentation studies. Aspinall submitted a bill calling for a high Hualapai Dam, the Central Arizona Project, five water projects for Colorado, and inclusion of Marble Canyon in an expanded Grand Canyon National Park. Conceding the loss of Marble, but not Bridge Canyon, Arizona House members introduced legislation proposing Hualapai Dam and the Central Arizona Project.[62]

In mid-March, the House Subcommittee on Irrigation and Reclamation held hearings on numerous Colorado River Basin Project bills. Throughout the proceedings, Saylor raged against the Grand Canyon dams. He preferred the administration's bill to all others but urged Secretary Udall to convince the president to issue an executive order annexing Bridge Canyon to Grand Canyon National Monument, scorning the arguments of those who claimed that Hualapai Dam would make the canyon more accessible and only encroach upon a small portion of the park. Any intrusion upon the national park system would be precedent shattering. Instead of the domino theory, he advanced an olive analogy to emphasize his point: store-purchased olives, he said, were so tightly packed that if you turned the jar upside down none of them would come out. But once the first one was pried loose, the rest would come tumbling down. So it would be with the units of the national park system: "I don't propose to see that the national park is invaded by the waters of any dam whether you call it Hualapai, Havasupai, Bridge Canyon, or any other name anybody wants to call it."[63]

Morris Udall used humor to deflect Saylor's strident opposition to Hualapai Dam. When a special-interest group, the National Reclamation Association, testified before the House Interior Committee in behalf of an irrigation project in Nebraska, Udall said that he expected their support, "with Mr. Saylor's assistance, to authorize the Hualapai Dam." Saylor said, "Did I hear you correctly?" Udall responded, "You heard me correctly. I am sure I spoke correctly." "I want to say," Saylor asserted, "I am one of those who still thinks we can build the Central Arizona Project without Hualapai Dam. I just want to inform my friend and members of the committee that if you authorize the Central Arizona Project, I am sure that it will be without the Hualapai Dam." Udall replied, "The gentleman's solicitude for Arizona and my project warms my heart. I thank you."[64]

While the House subcommittee could not reach an accord on the CAP bills, it did favorably report Senator Jackson's bill establishing a National Water Commission. This action, in turn, prompted the Senate Interior Committee to send the Hayden-Fannin bill to the floor for action. In an effort to make the bill more pleasing to California and Colorado, Hayden added amendments granting a 4.4 priority to California for twenty-seven years and five water projects for Colorado. But Californians demanded the 4.4 guarantee in perpetuity, and Aspinall wanted Hualapai Dam to produce the revenue for river augmentation. When Aspinall did not get these concessions, he dallied, believing Saylor had the votes in committee to win approval for a bill similar to Hayden-Fannin. Indeed, Saylor had told the Arizona delegation that he had the votes "to take the Committee away from Aspinall" but that he did not want to embarrass the chairman.[65]

After the Senate passed the Hayden-Fannin bill in early August, pressure mounted on Aspinall to take up the bill. Instead, he and Saylor agreed that the House Interior Committee would adjourn in mid-August without acting on the legislation. The postponement would give Aspinall an opportunity to return to Colorado to confer with state water leaders. In agreeing to the postponement, Saylor obtained two pledges from Aspinall. First, the legislation would be considered early in 1968, and the committee would be given an opportunity to vote it up or down. Second, the committee would also take up the Wild and Scenic Rivers Bill and proposals to establish Redwoods and North Cascades national parks, all measures that were more dear to Saylor than the Central Arizona Project.[66]

Disenchanted, Arizonans denounced the postponement and scurried to get action on the bill. According to some accounts of the controversy, an irate but crafty Carl Hayden used his influence to force Aspinall's hand, threatening, as chair of the Senate Appropriations Committee, to hold up money for the Fryingpan-Arkansas Project in Colorado. He also connived with Morris Udall and Rhodes to thwart House Interior Committee action on the bill. Resorting to a rarely used legislative maneuver, he would attach the Hayden-Fannin bill to a recently passed House appropriations bill that had been forwarded to the Senate. These moves, so the story goes, brought Aspinall scampering back to Washington on October 10, promising Hayden that the House would consider the Colorado River bill next year.[67]

Hayden's actions provoked "bitter resentment" in the House of Representatives. Saylor wrote a long letter to Senator Everett Dirksen (R-IL) denouncing the maneuver as "fundamentally violative of the legislative process." His actions were also unnecessary, he said, because Aspinall had given him assurances weeks earlier that the House Interior Committee would "work its will" on the legislation early in 1968.[68]

Aspinall and Saylor returned to Washington on October 10, not to give Hayden assurances but to explain to the House Interior Committee the arrangement they had made in early August. They also wanted to undermine Hayden's legislative ploy. Once they announced that the committee would vote on the bill, there was little need for the Senate to go ahead with a procedure that would antagonize the other body. Consequently, Hayden withdrew his legislative rider. While wishing that Aspinall and Saylor had shared their arrangement with other members of the committee, Morris Udall "respected the integrity" of both men and accepted their explanation. He also grew optimistic: "At long last," he wrote, "I see light at the end of the tunnel and would privately make anyone a bet giving three to one odds that CAP will become an actuality in 1968."[69]

Early in January 1968, Aspinall met with Morris Udall to plan a course of action for the Colorado River Basin Project, saying he planned to introduce a substitute bill that he hoped the Arizonans would prefer over a simpler measure that Saylor planned to offer. After yet another round of hearings, the Subcommittee on Irrigation and Reclamation would meet to mark up both bills and vote.[70]

With the dams excised from the legislation, the hearings were generally conciliatory. Republican representative Laurence Burton of Utah found it a pleasure "to be relieved of the withering volleys that are fired from John Saylor and Dave Brower" in trying to save the canyon. Secretary Udall remarked that Saylor must be delighted with the decision to use coal instead of falling water to power the project. "Mr. Secretary," Saylor responded, "that is not wax in my ear, that is coal dust." Indeed, Arizonans began to realize that the state's abundant coal resources would attract industry and create jobs. "If you let your fancy race just a little bit," wrote a Phoenix journalist, "you can see a new Pittsburgh rising in the West, belching smoke and making money." If this occurred, he noted, "you can see a delegation of prominent Arizona citizens building a statue to Rep. John Saylor, the Pennsylvania coal-minded congressman who generously provided the impetus for moving lots of industry from the weary East to the eager West."[71]

When the subcommittee met following the hearings, it considered the substitute bills offered by Aspinall and Saylor. Aspinall's proposal contained the Central Arizona Project powered by a coal-fired steam plant at Page, five water projects for Colorado, authorization for a feasibility study to divert 2.5 million acre-feet to the Colorado Basin, and a 4.4 guarantee to California for twenty-seven years. Saylor offered a more streamlined plan calling for the Central Arizona Project, a dam on the Gila River that would not intrude upon the Gila Wilderness Area, two water projects for Colorado, and a 4.4 guarantee to California for ten years. He omitted any reference to river-augmentation studies or the obligation of American taxpayers to finance the delivery of 1.5 million acre-feet of water to Mexico. Unlike Aspinall, Saylor believed that the residents of the seven basin states, not taxpayers at large, had the responsibility to deliver 1.5 million acre-feet to Mexico under the Treaty of 1944. The subcommittee voted seventeen to five for the Aspinall substitute and forwarded it to the full committee. There Saylor offered twenty-nine amendments, but they all failed to carry.[72]

In mid-May, the legislation moved to the House floor, where Aspinall managed the proponents and Saylor the opponents. Aspinall began the debate by explaining the provisions of the bill and recommended its enactment. Representatives from Arizona and California emphasized the point that the bill was a delicate compromise that had taken years to craft, but representatives from the Northwest objected to any raid on the water of the Columbia River. Saylor also spoke in opposition, but he offered only token resistance. He supported the Central Arizona Project, he said, but not in its present form with so many "extorted" add-ons such as the 4.4 California guarantee, the five projects in Colorado, and the Mexican treaty obligation.[73]

Saylor put up a "brave front," an Arizona group noted, but he refused to play saboteur. He lauded proponents and opponents alike for their statesmanship and lack of rancor and declined to offer a substitute bill. With only representatives from the Northwest putting up stiff resistance, the Colorado River Basin Project Bill passed easily by voice vote.[74]

Over the summer, Senate and House conferees, including Saylor, worked out the differences between the two bills. The conferees, with Saylor the lone dissenter, essentially accepted the House version of the bill. Both houses approved the work of the conferees, and President Johnson signed the bill into law on September 30, 1968.[75]

Arizonans beamed with delight. After two decades they had finally obtained delivery of water to their arid heartland. Preservationists, too, were satisfied with the outcome. With the help of a massive publicity campaign and Saylor's relentless efforts in committee, they had managed to protect Grand Canyon by eliminating both dams from the bill. Eventually, they won protection for the entire 277-mile stretch of the canyon as part of an enlarged Grand Canyon National Park.

Long after the controversy had ended, Morris Udall conceded that on the issue of dams in Grand Canyon, the preservationists had been right and he had been wrong. Indeed, both he and his brother, Stewart, would remember Saylor as a "great" preservationist who had dedicated his career to protecting the national park system and wild places. Having helped to preserve Grand Canyon, Saylor would next spearhead legislation to protect other wild rivers from the threat of dams.[76]

eleven

Wild and Scenic Rivers

THE GROWING MOVEMENT to preserve wilderness, including unharnessed rivers, exasperated some Americans. In 1959, a Chicago resident berated the National Parks Association for its hostility toward the proposed Bridge Canyon Dam on the Colorado River in Grand Canyon. "The Association seems to take the view that the only good dam is a non-existent one," he complained. "Why don't you ever consider the practical aspects of a dam and reservoir: electrical power, water supply, flood control, employment, irrigation? This is a growing nation and we must find room for both progress and wilderness. Certainly no dam is built merely to destroy wilderness as some people would have us believe." In reply, the editor of *National Parks Magazine* took the position, as did most conservation groups, that the association did not oppose all dams, just those that threatened protected areas such as national parks and monuments.[1]

But disclaimers aside, many preservationists, including John Saylor, opposed impounding free-flowing rivers in pristine backcountry. Saylor once informed a constituent that he was for wild rivers long before he had entered Congress. His raft trip down the Green River with Wayne Aspinall in 1953 and his later experiences on rivers such as the St. Croix in Minnesota had reinforced his commitment. And he had grown disgusted with the seemingly ceaseless efforts of the Army Corps of Engineers and the Bureau of Reclamation to plug unhindered rivers with dams. "There are certain people in these United States that cannot see two hills come together that they do not get filled with an insatiable desire to fill them with concrete," he fumed to a colleague in 1958. "I happen to be one of those folks that believe that there are certain advantages to keeping a little bit of the rivers that run this country as God made them."[2]

Passage of the Wilderness Act in 1964 gave added protection to some pristine headwaters, but there remained vast stretches of unspoiled rivers that lay outside the national park and wilderness systems. By the early 1960s, preservationist leaders sought legislation, patterned after the Wilderness Bill, that would give national protection to several untamed waterways. Already a champion of the national park system and an architect of the national wilderness program, Saylor eagerly and effectively led the charge in the House of Representatives for the protection of wild and scenic rivers.

While difficult to pinpoint, much of the credit for initiating a grassroots effort to establish a national wild rivers program must go to John and Frank Craighead. These brothers, who became noted wildlife research biologists, began rafting the Snake River in the mid-1930s. After World War II, they turned their attention to Idaho's Salmon River. On that nearly 400-mile-long waterway, they periodically trained U.S. airmen in survival techniques. More often, however, they rafted the Salmon to experience the joy of its primeval landscapes, frothing white water, abundant wildlife, and superb fishing.[3]

On one weeklong adventure in 1955, John Craighead and three companions spotted golden eagles, mule deer, black bears, elk, and bighorn sheep. They ate pemmican stew; wild berries; fruit from abandoned orchards; and freshly caught Dolly Varden, cutthroat, and rainbow trout. Occasionally, they encountered hardy souls such as "Buckskin Bill" and "Gold Dust Hank" who seemed as unencumbered as the river. One rancher's wife informed them that she had been away from the river only once in the past twenty years. Her isolation had been made harder to bear that previous winter because her radio had expired and she had lost her glasses and was unable to read.[4]

Adventures on the Snake, Salmon, and other northwestern rivers convinced the Craigheads that these unspoiled waterways should be protected against development. The right of an American citizen to experience a wild river, they insisted, was as sacred as the right to worship. They pressed their cause in articles, letters, and speeches. Eventually, state and national conservation groups, government officials, and members of Congress such as Saylor rallied to the cause.[5]

In the early 1960s, Interior Secretary Stewart Udall and the Outdoor Recreation Resources Review Committee, on which Saylor served, endorsed the wild rivers concept. Learning that the Craigheads had proposed a method of evaluating the recreational value of rivers in a magazine article, Udall asked Frank Craighead to prepare a similar program for the Interior Department. Craighead's report recommended studying more than 300 waterways and classifying them as "wild," "semi-wild," "semi-developed," or "developed." This recommendation served as the basis for a 1963 joint Interior-Agriculture report that expanded the study list to 650, eventually proposing 22 wild or semi-wild rivers for possible inclusion in any protection program.[6]

Successful efforts to give national protection to unspoiled rivers in the Ozark hills of southeastern Missouri also gave a boost to the wild rivers concept. At the request of the Missouri state legislature, the National Park Service in the late 1950s had begun evaluating the Current, Jacks Fork, and Eleven Point rivers to determine if they merited national protection. The Park Service did recommend protection, and in 1964 Missouri members of Congress introduced successful legislation designating 140 miles of the Current and Jacks Fork rivers a new national preserve: the Ozark National Scenic Waterways Project. This precedent-setting measure gave added impetus to the wild rivers plan.[7]

In 1965, President Lyndon Johnson recommended river stewardship in his State of the Union address. Stewart Udall recalled that after the speech Wayne Aspinall left the floor and told a reporter that wild rivers legislation was a foolish idea. Realizing that Saylor completely supported the wild rivers concept, Udall informed him of Aspinall's comment. "We'll just wear him down," Saylor responded. Udall recalled that Saylor generally was able to "handle" Aspinall and "bring him around" on important conservation issues.[8]

The first national wild rivers bill was drafted by the Interior Department and introduced in March 1965 by Democratic senator Frank Church of Idaho. It sought immediate protection for the entire Suwanee River in Georgia and Florida and segments of five other streams: the Salmon and Clearwater in Idaho, the Rogue in Oregon, the upper Rio Grande in New Mexico, and the Green in Wyoming, all chosen for their remote and near pristine status. Nine other waterways were to be evaluated for inclusion in the system by the secretaries of agriculture and interior in cooperation with officials in the affected states. Cabinet secretaries could also nominate other streams for evaluation.[9]

Some senators supported the concept of wild rivers, but not if the protected streams were located in their states. Senators' interest in economic development usually predominated over scenic preservation. Milward L. Simpson of Wyoming, for example, protested the inclusion of the Green, and senators from Georgia and Florida objected to protection for the Suwanee. But some senators wanted waterways in their states to be included in the system, especially if there were no plans for development. As it played out, wild rivers legislation reflected what political scientist Craig Allin has termed the "pork barrel principle": as with river-development projects, senators and representatives generally got what they wanted in their states and districts. The Senate bill was reworked so that the Green and Suwanee rivers were dropped from the instant-protection category, but the Cacapon and Shenandoah in West Virginia and the Eleven Point in Missouri were added. A total of seventeen rivers, including the west and north branches of the Susquehanna and portions of the Allegheny, were included in the study group. The administration bill passed the Senate by a lopsided vote of seventy-one to one.[10]

Protecting unharnessed rivers seemed to be as popular with the American public as it was with the U.S. Senate. Outdoor magazines such as the *Naturalist, Better Camping,* and *National Wildlife* devoted feature articles or entire issues to the subject, and the *New York Times, Washington Post,* and numerous other newspapers boosted the idea in editorials.[11]

Despite widespread popular support, however, the Wild Rivers Bill swirled eddylike in the House. When it was forwarded for consideration to the House Interior Committee, chairman Wayne Aspinall expressed indifference. Udall reported to President Johnson that Aspinall "has negative views on this legislation and we must use the low-pressure approach if we are to get his support."[12]

Saylor, on the other hand, enthusiastically supported the protection of unspoiled rivers. The experience of wilderness, he believed, enriched the American character, and unruly rivers also allowed citizens to revisit the past of Champlain, Lewis and Clark, and other adventurers. Besides stirring the voyageur in all of us, undisciplined waterways regenerated the human spirit. Saylor quoted Carl Buchheister of the National Audubon Society, who wrote that "the cares and tensions of human society evaporate" for anyone paddling a canoe and that "no sleep is so refreshing as a slumber in a tent or sleeping bag on the banks of a wild river."[13]

Saylor lauded President Johnson for speaking so eloquently for the need to create a rivers system in his conservation message of February 1966, but he had qualms about the rivers bill itself. Those who had prepared the legislation "must not have been listening to their President or they grew fainthearted and beached their canoe before they reached the rapids." The Senate bill, he declared, was "timorous" and "weak-kneed," and the preservation of wilderness could not be gained by "half-baked measures."[14]

Saylor introduced his own measure. Like most of the rivers it sought to protect, the Saylor bill was forceful, sweeping, and rocked a few boats. Prepared with the cooperation of Edward Crafts of the Interior Department's Bureau of Outdoor Recreation, Charles Callison of the National Audubon Society, and other conservation leaders, it was entitled the Scenic Rivers Bill. Saylor insisted upon the name change because the Senate-passed bill seemed too restrictive. Even using the Senate's vague definition, there were few streams that could be legitimately designated "wild." He feared that scenic rivers would be denied protection because they did not qualify as remote or unspoiled. Additionally, protecting accessible scenic rivers would give the bill more mass appeal.[15]

Waterways, unlike Forest Service lands that had been protected by the Wilderness Act, had not already been classified according to their degree of wildness. Saylor thus introduced a scenic river classification system approximating the categories created by the Craigheads. Class I areas consisted of streams that were free of pollution, dams, bridges, roads, and shoreline development. Class II areas comprised waterways with no dams, bridges, or shoreline developments, but some accessibility by roads. Class III rivers had limited shoreline intrusion, were easily accessible by road and rail, and may have had impoundments at one time. Saylor left it to the interior and agriculture secretaries to place a river in one of the three classifications.[16]

The administration or Senate bill seemed tame by comparison. It gave initial protective status to seven waterways; Saylor's measure gave scenic status to sixteen. The Senate named seventeen rivers for possible inclusion in the system; Saylor nominated sixty-six, including five in Pennsylvania. The Senate bill provided no timetable for a decision on the rivers placed in the study category; Saylor provided a schedule that compelled federal and state officials to make a determination within three years for sixteen rivers, including the five in Pennsylvania, and within ten years for the remaining fifty river segments. Both bills prevented the Federal Power Commission from licensing development projects on rivers immediately designated wild or scenic, but Saylor's also prohibited the construction of dams on streams that were in the evaluation process. Both proposals called upon states to initiate river-protection plans on their own, but Saylor's version, unlike the Senate's, prevented federal agencies from building dams on state scenic waterways such as the Allagash in Maine.

The Senate bill had no restrictions on road building, grazing, and commercial timbering; Saylor's legislation outlawed these activities on unsullied streams and restricted them on Class II and Class III rivers. Neither bill had adequate regulations against mining. Saylor's version accommodated mining interests, insisting only that operations not pollute the stream or unnecessarily spoil the landscape. The Senate version placed no limits on mining. Finally, both bills sought to minimize the amount of land taken by eminent domain by recommending scenic easements, a relatively new legal arrangement that permitted owners to retain title to property so long as they kept it in a natural state. The Senate legislation called for scenic easements of one-quarter mile from each shore, while the Saylor proposal sought corridors of two miles from each riverbank. In areas where easements were not suitable, the Senate authorized the acquisition of lands within three hundred feet of each shore, a beltway that Saylor termed "so inadequate as to border on the ridiculous." He called for the acquisition of a scenic pathway of one mile on each side of the waterway.[17]

Saylor's bold bill grabbed national attention. "That nemesis of western reclamation, opponent of public power and ardent wilderness devotee," wrote the political editor of the *Idaho Daily Statesman*, "has come up with a wild rivers bill that makes the one that passed the Senate last year a model of restraint in the field." Letter writers from across the nation thanked Pennsylvania's "voice for wilderness" for standing up to "scenic murderers" and for having the "G-U-T-S to keep America beautiful." One woman wrote that rushing rivers were important to her, but "absolutely necessary to the survival of my husband." In a similar vein, a Michigan physician asserted that without "irreplaceable rivers we have nothing." Correspondents offered additional rivers for inclusion in the system, and Harper and Row Publishers asked Saylor to promote the cause with a book on wild rivers. Saylor passed on the book offer, but he did advance river protection by authoring an article for the popular magazine *Parks and Recreation*.[18]

Reclamation proponents considered Saylor's bill too "far-reaching," especially if it touched anticipated projects in their states. In Tennessee, supporters of the Tennessee Valley Authority's proposed Tellico Dam objected to the inclusion of the Little Tennessee River in the three-year study group. Similarly, the Ohio Department of Natural Resources considered the bill "antithetical" to the state's interests and suggested an amendment permitting dams and roads on scenic streams such as the Little Miami. The proposed amendment would "completely contravene the purposes of the bill," Saylor retorted, and he saw no need to preserve scenic land "if a road or a well built highway follows within five feet of the area." Upset that the legislation had assigned scenic status to the upper Missouri, the Missouri River Development Association proposed making the entire Susquehanna a protected river. All bridges, dams, and shoreline developments would be removed, and Westerners would export thousands of pounds of sagebrush seed, skunks, prairie dogs, elk, and antelope in order to transform the Susquehanna Valley into a wilderness paradise. Saylor initially termed the playful proposal "asinine" but then mused that if his ancestors had taken protective measures, "how happy I would be."[19]

Actually, Saylor had to concern himself more with his Pennsylvania contemporaries than with his antecedents. Several of his colleagues, including fellow Republican Albert W. Johnson from Smethport, preferred development over preservation and were especially upset over the attempt to preserve the Susquehanna's West Branch from Clearfield to Lock Haven and its North Branch from Cooperstown, New York, to Pittston, Pennsylvania. They would create problems for Saylor as the legislation progressed.[20]

Saylor also had to deal with Aspinall. He asked the Coloradan to move on the bill, but the session ended without action. "The chairman apparently didn't understand President Johnson's direct statement in his conservation message earlier this year that the time had come to preserve free-flowing stretches of our rivers," Saylor grumbled to an outdoor writer. Saylor promised to "hit, kick and scratch" in his battle to obtain a scenic rivers bill: "We cannot afford the delay that allows our heritage of free-flowing rivers of beauty to be destroyed." One supporter, appropriately named Jack Bull, offered the use of his nine-foot bullwhip to prod Aspinall. Another proposed ignoring Aspinall and moving ahead. Despite his bravado and bombast, however, Saylor was a realist who understood that he needed Aspinall's support to gain protection for rivers.[21]

Along with thirty-eight cosponsors, Senator Church reintroduced the administration's rivers bill in January 1967. At the same time, Saylor reintroduced his bill in the House. The idea of protecting untamed rivers was popular, and pressure mounted on Congress, especially Aspinall, to move the legislation. Saylor informed a colleague that he had "received more favorable mail on this legislation than any other subject," except for the Bureau of Reclamation's plan to build dams on the Colorado River that would have flooded part of Grand Canyon. To the surprise of preservationists and political observers, Aspinall introduced his own wild rivers bill in April. "He must have owed Saylor some real big favors," recalled Stewart Brandborg of the Wilderness Society. Actually, Aspinall had reached an understanding with Interior Secretary Udall:

Aspinall would support a national rivers system if the administration promised to proceed with water-development projects in Colorado that had been authorized in the CAP legislation.[22]

Of the three proposals, Aspinall's protected the fewest rivers, and Saylor's protected the most. Prepared with the help of Coloradan Joe Penfold of the Izaak Walton League, Aspinall's measure gave instant protection to segments of only four rivers (the Rogue, Rio Grande, Salmon, and Clearwater) and placed portions of twenty others in the review category. The Senate bill preserved nine streams at once and designated thirty-five more for study. Saylor's proposal immediately protected sixteen river segments and assigned sixty-six others for later consideration. The main attraction of Aspinall's bill to conservationists, aside from the hope it gave that some legislation was likely, was its strong regulations against mining along protected waterways.[23]

Saylor was pleased with the Aspinall bill because he believed it would lead to some kind of compromise legislation. Interior Secretary Udall was also "delighted" with the turn of events, to the dismay of preservationists disowning his own bill and coming out in support of Aspinall's measure.[24]

Because it protected more waterways, established a classification system, and set a definite timetable for the inclusion of additional rivers, most conservation groups preferred the Saylor bill. The Senate Interior Committee, no doubt influenced by conservationists, adopted various aspects of Saylor's proposal, principally the classification system. The amended Senate bill immediately designated seven rivers "wild" and another five "scenic," while twenty-seven streams were assigned for review at some future date. In August 1967, the Senate bill passed by a vote of eighty-four to zero.[25]

In the House, on the other hand, rivers legislation stalled yet again. Many members fretted over locking up rivers. Preservationists pointed out that Congress could always unlock a preserved river, but once a waterway had been dammed, the work could not be undone. Perhaps because they were unaware of the bill's details, Pennsylvania congressmen were silent in 1967 over the inclusion in the study group of portions of the Susquehanna, Delaware, Clarion, Allegheny, Pine Creek, and Youghiogheny rivers. Legislators in other states were more vigilant. Republican congressman William Cramer of Florida opposed the bill because the Army Corps of Engineers was considering fifty rivers in his state for development. Saylor showed his disdain for the schemes of government engineers when he assured Cramer that "there is not a river basin or river in the entire United States which does not have a recommended comprehensive plan for optimum multiple use or development by either the Corps or the Bureau of Reclamation."[26]

Owing to the press of other conservation-related issues, especially the threat to Grand Canyon, Aspinall failed to schedule hearings on river legislation in 1967. But Saylor was confident that a compromise river preservation bill would be crafted by the Ninetieth Congress in 1968. He did not anticipate that Pennsylvania politicians would balk and nearly kill the bill.[27]

The House Interior Committee faced a daunting agenda in 1968. Aspinall and Saylor gave river protection priority because it had been in the legislative pipeline longer than bills to establish Redwoods National Park, North Cascades National Park, and a national trails system. Aspinall scheduled four days of hearings on the various river protection bills in mid-March. Roy A. Taylor of North Carolina chaired the Subcommittee on National Parks and Recreation, where the bills were sent, but Aspinall, as was his custom, attended all subcommittee hearings. Saylor helped keep the sessions light with his humor but at times proved a tough interrogator.[28]

Only a few witnesses spoke out against the legislation. Predictably, the National Reclamation Association opposed any bill that would prevent the development of any river. The subcommittee considered this position unrealistic, given the fact that the Senate had unanimously approved a river bill. Other witnesses objected to the fact that they would lose their riverfront property to a grasping government that already held too much land. Despite his abhorrence of socialism, however, Saylor had little sympathy for the views of property owners when it came to the preservation of wildlands. They should yield to what he considered to be the greater good of scenic preservation. When he listened to their harangues against an intrusive government, he began to wonder if he "was some kind of nut." He pointed out that the same right-to-private-property argument had been made against the Blue Ridge Parkway but that "the country is a great deal better off for having it."[29]

Few representatives were more dedicated to individual property rights and private enterprise than Saylor, but he believed just as strongly in the value of wilderness. He held that scenic landscapes and wilderness provided solitude and inspiration that were essential to national well-being; indeed, their loss might sow the seeds of discontent and socialism. He represented a district where mining and farming were "a vital part of our economic welfare," he informed a property-rights critic of the bill. "I have no intention of promoting laws that would threaten imposition of unnecessary roadblocks to the maximum development of these industries." But preserving a few river segments "presents no danger" to overall commercial development: "The fact is that you and I have seen such lawless and irresponsible treatment of our streams and their environs that only through federal law will we be able to protect the aesthetic values and other natural benefits which God bequeathed when he formed those magnificent waterways." Lest there be any misunderstanding of his position, he added: "I assure you I will not relax in my efforts to enact this legislation regardless of how much adverse reaction the crusade may prompt."[30]

Most preservationists at the House hearings wanted to create a "legislative supernova" by merging the best features of the Aspinall and Saylor bills. Initially, however, it seemed that the two authors were unwilling to compromise. Aspinall made it clear that preservationists would not get "the whole pie." When Charles Callison of the National Audubon Society expressed a preference for the Saylor bill because it designated sixteen rivers for instant protection, Aspinall advised him to prioritize "because I can tell you very frankly you are not going to get all 16." Aspinall, to Saylor's dismay, also watered down the bill by permitting members of Congress to remove rivers in their districts from the protected list. He was amenable, for example, when E. C. Gathings protested the inclusion of that stretch of the Eleven Point River that ran through Arkansas. Agitated, Saylor pointed out that Gathings was not up for reelection and should not have "veto" power. Besides, the opinion of the state's two senators, governor, and constituents should be considered. This comment prompted a scolding from Aspinall. He rebuked Saylor for being unyielding and for pushing his version of the bill in Colorado: "He has criss-crossed my State with his proposal like nobody's business. Is he going to give on this?" "It depends on how much I get in return," Saylor shot back. "I am a poker player. I have learned a good many tricks. I have watched him. I have sat at the feet of Gamaliel [a biblical teacher] and I have learned. I hope he does not envy the fact that his student has been more than apt."[31]

Their differences, however, were reconciled during the executive session of the subcommittee. The new bill retained Saylor's river-classification system but incorporated Aspinall's strong restrictions against mining. It granted immediate protection to six rivers that were truly undeveloped: the Salmon and Clearwater (Idaho), Rogue (Oregon), Rio Grande (New Mexico), Wolf (Wisconsin), and St. Croix (Wisconsin and Minnesota). Segments of twenty-eight other streams, including the five in Pennsylvania, were placed on the study list for possible inclusion in the system at a later date. Aspinall recommended that

Saylor be given the honor of introducing the new, clean bill with more than twenty cosponsors. The full committee approved the compromise measure and forwarded it to the House on July 1, 1968.[32]

Presumably because of time constraints—Congress was scheduled to recess in August for the national political conventions—Aspinall and Saylor asked House Speaker John McCormack for a suspension of the rules on scenic rivers and five other bills that had been reported by the House Interior Committee. Normally, a bill is given a rule and then sent to the floor for debate and amendments. Suspending a rule, which requires a two-thirds vote from the members, means that legislation will be sent to the floor but cannot be amended. Waiting for a rule took time, and Aspinall and Saylor may have feared that Congress would adjourn without acting on the bill. Additionally, they may have wanted to suspend the rules so that their colleagues could not gut the bill with amendments; legislators, after all, had been given an opportunity to remove rivers from the bill during the hearings or through correspondence. Another possibility, raised by disgruntled preservationists, is that Aspinall wanted to sabotage the bill and sought this unusual legislative procedure knowing that it would fail. He had used a similar legislative gimmick in 1962 to delay the Wilderness Bill. The more reasonable interpretation, however, is that Aspinall and Saylor had an ambitious conservation agenda, which included a strong scenic rivers bill, and wanted to enact as much legislation as they could before Congress adjourned.[33]

On the evening of July 16, just before adjournment for the summer recess, the decision to suspend the rules came before the whole House. Representatives from Pennsylvania, New York, and a few other states raised objections. In a blow that must have embarrassed Saylor, Pennsylvania congressmen Daniel Flood of Wilkes-Barre (D), Joseph McDade of Scranton (R), and William Green of Philadelphia (D) balked at the procedure because they wanted to add amendments to the bill deleting the Susquehanna and Clarion rivers in Pennsylvania. Their position had been influenced by Governor Raymond Shafer and Maurice Goddard, the state's secretary of forests and waters. Goddard had testified for the bill during the subcommittee hearings but then reversed himself when he realized that water-development projects were banned while a proposed scenic river was under study. Several projects were under consideration for the Susquehanna, including an atomic reactor on the North Branch and interstate highway 80 along the West Branch. And in the western part of the state, the Clarion River Organization for Water Development—CROWD—championed the Corps of Engineers proposal to build the St. Petersburg Reservoir. Saylor must be faulted for not getting his fellow Pennsylvania congressmen on board before being publicly blindsided.[34]

Taken aback, proponents of the Scenic Rivers Bill sought to save it by promising to remove any objectionable river from the study group when House and Senate conferees met to work out their differences. But opponents were not won over because the House might not be able to work its will on the Senate. The vote to suspend the rules failed, and the Scenic Rivers Bill seemed to have been "sunk without a trace."[35]

Embarrassed and angered by the rebuff from Shafer and the Pennsylvania delegation, Saylor was not optimistic about the bill's chances; after all, the session would end in mid-October. Udall and other proponents urged him to salvage the bill by seeking an ordinary rule and then offering amendments removing Pennsylvania's rivers from the study category. Still brooding, Saylor refused. He could not in good conscience withdraw Pennsylvania waterways and retain streams in other states. The legislation, he told Udall, "is defeated for this Congress in my opinion, and I have no intention of seeking a rule to have its further consideration."[36]

Then came a telegram from Shafer. Pennsylvania would withdraw its objections to the bill if amendments were approved that either eliminated the Susquehanna and Clarion rivers or lifted the moratorium on development projects for study streams. Saylor's sarcastic reply indicated that he might satisfy these demands. Was the governor aware, he asked, that the Clarion "is a part of my Congressional District and neither you, your legislative staff nor your department heads have had [the] courtesy to discuss the matter with me?" Did Shafer understand that in committee hearings Pennsylvania's secretary of forests and waters, who he assumed "spoke for" the administration, had endorsed the moratorium on the economic development of study streams, including the Clarion and Susquehanna? Given the governor's parochial preference for "optimum impoundment and river development" over the national perspective of protecting selected untamed waterways, he would offer an amendment, if the bill were revived, removing all Pennsylvania waterways from the study category, but he would take no action until the governor had had the courtesy to consult with him.[37]

It is not clear whether Saylor's offer to remove all Pennsylvania rivers was genuine. Since Representatives McDade, Flood, and Johnson opposed study status for the north and west branches of the Susquehanna, Saylor realized that these streams would be deleted from the bill. The upper Allegheny was in Johnson's district, so that stream too would go. The Clarion, however, was in his own district, and he was reluctant to remove it even though John Murtha, his Democratic congressional opponent, favored development of the waterway. At any rate, Shafer never conferred with him directly, so Saylor considered the arrangement void.[38]

Meanwhile, conservation groups began to mobilize public opinion. Indeed, Saylor told a friend that he had delayed seeking a rule in order to give his conservation friends time to get out the message. And citizens were receptive because it seemed that no river was safe from development. The year before, preservationists, with Saylor at the forefront, had successfully blocked an attempt by the Bureau of Reclamation to construct dams on the Colorado River that would have flooded part of Grand Canyon. Now it seemed that water planners were trying to kill scenic rivers legislation. The *New York Times* blasted those "parochial pork-barrel politicians" who had served a "death warrant" on the Susquehanna River and other unspoiled waterways. Conservation organizations urged Shafer to reconsider his position. The Wilderness Society sought to shame the governor by pointing out that his stance was contrary to the state's "reputation for leadership" in the field of conservation: "The Pinchot tradition has been deep and influential and we feel it is not accidental that one of the outstanding conservationists of our time is a Pennsylvanian and the author of the scenic rivers bill." In a special memorandum entitled "Position of Pennsylvania's Governor Imperils Passage of National Rivers System Bill," it urged its two thousand Pennsylvania members to write Shafer and members of Congress recommending support for the "landmark conservation measure."[39]

Letters streamed into the governor's office. Correspondents were "distressed," "dismayed," and "horrified" by Shafer's "tragic," "lamentable," and "absolutely incomprehensible" position. Even fellow Republican Frank Masland, a nationally respected conservationist who headed the governor's Committee on Natural Resources, implored Shafer to reevaluate his position.[40]

Faced with a public relations fiasco, Shafer's staff scrambled to minimize the damage. Their long-awaited explanation, however, strained belief. In effect, they claimed that the state could better manage Pennsylvania's rivers than the federal government. They wanted to develop some waterways, such as the Allegheny, Clarion, and Susquehanna, and preserve portions of others, such as the Delaware, Pine, and Youghiogheny. They could, they said, move more quickly to protect streams than Congress: "We're moving ahead in Pennsylvania," claimed Goddard, "and we don't want our progress halted."[41]

On September 4, the first day Congress returned from its recess, Aspinall and Saylor requested reconsideration of the bill. The Rules Committee agreed and scheduled the bill for debate under an open rule, which allowed amendments. Conservation groups hailed the decision and endorsed the resurrected bill. So did Shafer, conditionally: Pennsylvania would support the legislation if the Susquehanna and Clarion were removed or if Congress permitted economic development on study streams.[42]

The House took up discussion of the bill on September 12. Aspinall and Saylor reviewed its history, explained its provisions, and recommended passage. Setting aside scenic rivers, Saylor acknowledged, seemed to contradict most people's idea of progress, but "the real challenge of this society is to preserve what we know has been good and useful in our American way of life." A national scenic rivers system would give all citizens, "and especially our children, an opportunity to appreciate: A sense of history, a sense of environment, a sense of national place, and a sense of joy for free-flowing water." Having delivered an emotional plea for rivers, Saylor then left for Johnstown to attend the funeral of his younger brother, Tillman, who had died from a heart attack.[43]

During the floor debate, several amendments were offered affecting six rivers from the study group. At the request of representatives from New York and Pennsylvania, the Susquehanna—both the North Branch and the West Branch—was removed from the bill. Saylor considered the Susquehanna, especially the West Branch, "one of the few scenic rivers left in the East," and he had informed Aspinall that he was going to fight for its inclusion. Aspinall regretted the absence of the river's champion, but he did not want "to upset any State or any group of States" and always deferred to the members of Congress whose districts were affected. The amendments were thus approved, and the Saylor bill, even without its sponsor there to support it, passed by a vote of 265 to 7.[44]

With the passage of the bill, both chambers appointed conferees to work out the differences between the House and Senate versions. Saylor served as one of eight House conferees and was instrumental in shaping the final legislation. Renumbered S. 119 and entitled the Wild and Scenic Rivers Bill, the legislation the conferees crafted essentially followed the House version. Several modifications, however, were added to address the Senate's concerns. Saylor's classification system was changed from the stark Class I, Class II, and Class III zones to the more illustrative "wild river," "scenic river," and "recreational river" areas. As with the House bill, the executive branch would determine a stream's classification, while the legislative branch made the decision to include a waterway in the system. The period allotted for a decision on the rivers placed in the study group was increased from five to ten years. Dam building and mining were prohibited. The conference committee shrank the shoreline corridors from one to one quarter of a mile and slightly reduced the appropriation for the acquisition of river land and scenic easements from $17.3 to 17.0 million.[45]

Some conferees, including Saylor, sought protection for additional waterways. Two rivers, the Eleven Point in Missouri and the Middle Fork of the Feather in California, were switched from the study list to the immediate-designation category, and four streams were added to the study group, including two from Pennsylvania at Saylor's request, the lower Allegheny and a portion of the Youghiogheny. He and Democratic senator Joe Clark of Pennsylvania also sought to reinsert both branches of the Susquehanna in the study group, but Aspinall insisted upon legislative prerogative, and neither river made it. In all, the bill gave instant protection to eight rivers and placed portions of twenty-seven others, including five in Pennsylvania, in the study group. The House and Senate approved the work of the conference committee, and President Johnson signed the bill into law on October 2, 1968.[46]

Aside from the Wilderness Act, after which it was patterned, the National Wild and Scenic Rivers Act was the most sweeping and significant piece of preservationist legislation in the 1960s. Within a decade, nineteen rivers totaling 1,655 miles had been protected. With the expiration of the ten-year study period, additional legislation was passed in 1978 that eventually brought the list to sixty-six waterways covering 7,300 miles. By the early twenty-first century, the list had grown to more than 160 units, totaling over 11,000 miles. Two of these nationally protected river segments, the Allegheny and the Clarion, are located in western Pennsylvania, and a third, the Delaware, forms the border between Pennsylvania and New Jersey.[47]

Saylor had worked closely with conservation leaders to craft an ambitious and effective rivers-protection bill. He was forced to compromise, but the result was still a stronger bill than the administration, the Senate, committee chairman Aspinall, Governor Shafer, and some Pennsylvania congressmen had intended. Recognizing Saylor for being of "inestimable value" in securing the legislation, President Johnson gave him one of the pens at the signing ceremony. The Democratic administration acknowledged privately that it wanted to honor the Republican representative because for a decade he had served "as a lever to push Aspinall into action on 'must' legislation." Congressional colleagues praised Saylor as "Mr. Conservation" for sponsoring a rivers bill that would "mark a place in the history of conservation for all time to come." Conservation organizations also recognized his contributions. He became the first recipient of the Bernard Baruch Conservation Award and also received awards from the Pennsylvania Fish and Game Protective Association and the Izaak Walton League.[48]

Saylor did not live to see all the study rivers brought into the system, but as the tenth anniversary of the bill approached, *National Geographic* devoted a special feature to "America's Wild and Scenic Rivers." It depicted gangly waterways, pavilioned in natural splendor, crawling and rushing to their destinations. Some ran "clean and free, as of old," and others yielded "a respite to the modern soul." In some remote regions, "that purest poetry of nature, the chiming of a mountain stream," could be detected. This precious riverine legacy had been bequeathed to the nation, in large measure, by John Saylor.[49]

twelve

Base Camp

JOHN SAYLOR's involvement with national conservation issues, especially the wilderness preservation movement, did not always sit well with Pennsylvanians. Given the state's economic woes, one vocal couple from the Pittsburgh area, for example, wondered why he devoted so much effort to trying to block the construction of federal dams in the American West. Saylor, they said, was "spending too much time meddling in the affairs of distant parts of our nation and too little time in representing and solving the problems of Pennsylvania." His supporters defended his actions on economic grounds, pointing out that costly federal power projects competed with private enterprise and burdened taxpayers, most of whom lived in the East. And constituents apparently believed that he was doing an acceptable job because they reelected him in 1964 by more than twenty thousand votes.[1]

Perhaps sensing that he was vulnerable to charges of indifference toward the district, Saylor worked hard to advance the interests of his state and region. For Saylor, this meant championing the interests of his district's major employers—the coal industry and the private utility companies that depended upon fossil fuel to generate electricity. It also meant establishing more recreational opportunities for the heavily populated Northeast. Unfortunately, the interests of the coal industry and those of the emerging environmental movement did not always coincide. Moreover, efforts to provide more recreational opportunities for Northeasterners were often manifested as open space along waterways such as the Tocks Island National Recreational Area on the Delaware

River. These efforts did not square with the goal of preserving free-flowing rivers.

In spite of their robust support, constituents struggled to comprehend Saylor's political philosophy. "Saylor is obviously a difficult man to place into any one category," noted a district news reporter. "He doesn't always vote with his fellow Republicans, yet one could not say he was liberal." Independent-minded, Saylor relished his role as a political maverick.[2]

When Barry Goldwater, the conservative Republican presidential candidate, campaigned in Johnstown in 1964, Saylor remained aloof because of the Arizonan's hostility to big labor and federal social programs. Yet the two mavericks agreed on many issues. Both were virulent anti-Communists. Both supported the American commitment in Vietnam. Both sought to remove restraints against the military so the war could be won. Both considered dissent tantamount to treason. Saylor believed that protesters who burned their draft cards or desecrated the flag should be jailed or drafted into the military. When thousands of antiwar protesters marched on the Pentagon in 1967, he considered the demonstration "mutiny" and wished that the "mangy individuals" had been dispersed with teargas. Antiwar protests in Washington, DC, literally made him weep, and he repeatedly referred to dissenters as "degenerates," "loathsome derelicts," and "rebellious filth." His most difficult task as a representative, he declared, was to attend the funerals of young officers whom he had recommended for appointment to one of the military academies.[3]

Always a supporter of the Second Amendment, Saylor opposed attempts to restrict firearm sales or gun ownership, even after President Kennedy's assassination. "Men and boys trained in the use of firearms have formed the nucleus of this country's defenders of freedom from the days of our early settlers," he asserted in a House speech. Because Communist states posed a constant threat to freedom, "we must continue to keep our powder dry and encourage our youth in the use of firearms." Saylor also asserted the importance of states' rights in some issues. He opposed federal aid for education, for example, because he did not want Washington bureaucrats dictating school policy or educational standards. Education, he insisted, should remain a responsibility of the states.[4]

In many ways, Saylor was indeed a traditional conservative. In the Miranda decision of 1966, he asserted, the U.S. Supreme Court had given too much protection to alleged criminals. He also decried Court decisions in the mid-1960s that were permissive toward pornography and restrictive toward religion. He blasted the Engle decision, which outlawed prayer in public schools, and he bristled at attempts by the American Civil Liberties Union to remove "under God" from the Pledge of Allegiance. He also fumed when the Court negated laws preventing avowed Communists from working as teachers and in defense plants. Abhorring judicial activism, he claimed that the Supreme Court headed by Chief Justice Earl Warren "did more to rend the constitutional fabric of this great Republic than did any other Court in any previous 16-year period." He even introduced a constitutional amendment authorizing Congress to override Supreme Court decisions by a two-thirds vote of both houses, although it failed.[5]

However, on many social and labor issues, Saylor took a liberal stance. He supported the Civil Rights Act of 1964; the Voting Rights Act of 1965; and the Twenty-Fourth Amendment, eliminating the Poll Tax. He voted for increased Social Security benefits and the Medicare Bill. A champion of the food stamp proposal, he used his influence to have his district serve as a pilot area for the program. He pushed hard for the Appalachian Aid Bill because it provided job training for unemployed youth and construction of highways in economically deprived coal states. Passed in 1965, the bill provided the funds to build Highway 219 connecting Johnstown with two major interstate highways. Some constituents regarded this as Saylor's greatest achievement as a member of Congress.[6]

Saylor also supported federal funding of the arts and humanities. Owing to the Sputnik scare, he believed, the focus in education had been on science, while the arts had been neglected. Consequently, he and other representatives proposed successful legislation establishing the National Foundation for the Arts and Humanities. Saylor introduced the bill, in part, to combat what he considered the corrupting influence of "junk" music. Even the "Pennsylvania Polka," performed by bandmaster Lawrence Welk, was preferable, he said, to the "jungle gyrations" and "ear-splitting toots and screeches" of rock and roll.[7]

In spite of his occasional liberal tendencies, Saylor always went out of his way to defend the interests of the coal industry, in particular the Rochester and Pittsburgh Company, a major employer in his district. He opposed massive Western dams because these publicly funded "hydrodillies" often invaded wilderness, competed with private utilities, and put coal miners out of work. The Bureau of Reclamation, he declared, should be renamed the "Bureau of Federal Power." Imports of foreign oil were an even more serious threat to coal markets than hydroelectric dams. An ardent protectionist, Saylor pushed for higher tariffs on imported residual oil. For more than two decades, he lamented in a House speech, "jobs of miners and railroaders in the Appalachian region have been sacrificed to the surging seas of foreign residual oil that capture coal's traditional east coast markets." Owing to preservationists' growing aversion toward dams and the abhorrence of socialism by most members of Congress, Saylor's battles against public power projects met with more success than his fight for protectionist trade policies.[8]

Saylor was also a nontraditional conservative in that he served the interests of labor, especially the United Mine Workers of America. In the House, he delivered tributes to long-time UMW president John L. Lewis on the occasion of his eighty-fifth birthday and to John Ghizzoni, retiring president of the local UMW. Saylor further ingratiated himself with unions by supporting a bill that sought to force the implementation of a union shop if the majority of workers in a plant had so voted. When the Taft-Hartley Act was approved in 1947, section 14 (b) permitted states to pass "right-to-work" laws prohibiting the union shop. Since then, nearly twenty states had passed such laws, which Saylor and other labor-friendly representatives believed undercut the union movement. The bill Saylor supported repealing the right-to-work provision of the Taft-Hartley Act passed the House but failed in the Senate.[9]

Saylor also worked hard to rejuvenate the economy of his district. To make Indiana County the "Christmas Tree Capital" of America, he urged growers to donate samples of their product to all members of Congress who requested them. He helped block the proposed Lake Erie–Ohio Canal, referring to this Corps of Engineers project as a "ridiculous scheme" that made less sense than building "a stairway to the ocean floor." Besides the engineering problems and projected expense of $1 billion, the project "would have a devastating effect upon the economy of the 22nd District because railroad and truck haulers would not be able to compete with federally subsidized shipping on the canal."[10]

Though his precise role is unclear, Saylor claimed that he helped persuade Pennsylvania Electric and New York State Electric and Gas to build three massive electric generating plants—Keystone, Conemaugh, and Homer City—in his district. They were planned as mine-mouth facilities, meaning that the power plant would be built near the mouth of the fuel source. The three stations would go on line by the end of the 1960s, providing some economic security to the miners and mine owners. The plants would devour ten million tons of coal yearly; employ two thousand miners; and provide electricity to consumers as far away as Binghamton, New York, more than 170 miles distant. These investor-owned stations, Saylor bragged, would serve customers for the next century and make the Twenty-second District the "energy Capital" of the East. Unfortunately, as residents would eventually learn, the toxic emissions from those plants would instead make the Twenty-second District one of the most contaminated in the nation. Saylor, of course, could not have had the prescience to predict such dire outcomes.[11]

In any case, the district needed more than three generating plants to become economically buoyant. Saylor bristled when a young federal social worker wrote about large patches of poverty in Armstrong County, describing families —mainly unemployed miners—living in ramshackle huts with shattered windows and no plumbing. Nearly 60 percent of the adults she interviewed had less than a ninth-grade education, and she encountered children who had never been to school. Saylor claimed that she had exaggerated but did not dispute the fact that poverty was a problem in his district.[12]

Nevertheless, poverty did not seem to heighten the crime rate, at least in Johnstown. According to FBI statistics, Johnstown enjoyed the lowest crime rate in the nation, less than a tenth than that of the worst offenders, Los Angeles and Las Vegas. Four additional Pennsylvania coal-mining towns also ranked in the ten least crime-prone cities. Saylor attributed the low crime rate in Pennsylvania cities to the fact that coal-mining and steelworking families instilled in their children a respect for God, country, and community.[13]

In his district, Saylor continued to present himself as a man of the people and a representative who took joy in his job. He threw out the first ball to begin the Johnstown Little League season but didn't stay for the game, he said, because he had to go home to mow the lawn. He launched the start of the sap season by hammering a spigot into a maple tree. When the district was redrawn in 1966 to include Clarion and Jefferson counties, he warmed to the task of representing Gobbler's Notch, home of the celebrated groundhog "Punxsutawney Phil." Always accommodating to camera operators, he posed with "Phil" and gladly delivered the annual Groundhog Day speech. And he rarely passed up an opportunity to associate with celebrities. He eagerly participated in ceremonies honoring local athletes who had become nationally recognized, such as major league baseball umpire August "Augie" Donatelli; Michigan State University football coach Duffy Daugherty; and Johnny Weissmuller, the powerful swimmer who went on to star in *Tarzan* movies.[14]

Still, for the most part, his concerns were serious. Representing a major coal- and steel-producing area, Saylor struggled to balance his concern for the environment with his goal of protecting the economic livelihood of his constituents. Coal, of course, was a prime polluter of the air and water, but the danger to humans was not well-known until the mid-1960s. Coal-burning electrical plants spewed sulfur dioxide, carbon dioxide, and other contaminants into the air. Streams meandering through abandoned coal workings carried acid that killed fish and plant life. Saylor readily conceded the dangers of air and water pollution in the coal-mining areas of Appalachia, and he ardently supported the federal Water Quality Act of 1965 and the Air Pollution Control Act of 1967. Yet he rebuked those few critics who advocated the cessation of coal operations: coal mining was vital to the production of electric energy and to the livelihood of thousands of laborers. And in a case of the pot calling the kettle black, he cautioned against looking to the atom to resolve the problem of pollution. Uranium miners were dying prematurely, and atomic plants might leak radiation or explode. Then, too, atomic waste had to be safely discarded. Saylor contended that "the potential danger from a single nuclear plant is far greater than all hazards—actual and suspected—associated with coal in the lifetime of the industry."[15]

Although Saylor was a vigorous defender of the coal, utility, and steel industries, he was hardly a shill. Besides supporting water and air quality bills, he spoke out against the blight of strip mining and pushed hard for a federal study to determine the extent of the problem. As the author of a companion bill establishing Indiana Dunes National Lakeshore on Lake Michigan, he courageously criticized Bethlehem Steel for going forward with Burns Ditch Harbor. Not only would this project destroy dozens of acres of dunes, but the harbor complex would be unsightly and spoil the experience of visiting the nearby national lakeshore. He tempered his criticism of Bethlehem Steel, however, by pointing out that the company had donated more than a thousand acres of land along a mountainside in western Pennsylvania for public recreation. The company was working diligently and investing heavily, he claimed, to find a remedy for air pollution.[16]

Saylor also stood by his preservationist principles when he came out against a proposal to expand the airport in Clarion County. The county commissioner sought to acquire fifty acres for added airport space from the adjoining Crooked Creek State Park, but Saylor used his influence to block the land transfer on the grounds that once acreage had been set aside as a state or federal land preserve it became untouchable, except for a national emergency. The county commissioner considered Saylor unreasonable and "dictatorial," but the park remained undisturbed.[17]

While heedful of the economic interests of his state and district, Saylor seldom wavered in his support for the emerging environmental movement. With the nation becoming increasingly fragmented by the Vietnam War and the Civil Rights Movement, he initially viewed conservation as an issue that might unite Americans. The conservation movement itself, however, was becoming polarized between those who emphasized the prudent use of natural resources and those who stressed the need to preserve wilderness and the health of the planet. By the mid-1960s, only a few members of Congress from either party could be categorized as ardent environmentalists. Saylor, Morris Udall, Phillip Burton (D-CA), John Blatnik (D-MN), and John Dingell headed the cause in the House, while Clinton Anderson, Lee Metcalf, Frank Church, Gaylord Nelson (D-WI), Henry Jackson, and John Chaffe (R-RI) led the effort in the Senate.

Virtually alone among congressional Republicans, Saylor pressed hard for wilderness and environmental quality legislation. In the early 1950s, he believed that water pollution was a local issue, but as the problem became more severe, including the danger of pesticides, he became convinced that only the federal government possessed the financial resources to clean up the environment. While deploring public power as "galloping socialism," he saw nothing inimical about granting public protection to additional pristine landscapes. He pushed for wild rivers legislation and the establishment of Key Biscayne National Monument in Florida, Guadalupe Mountains National Park in Texas, and national lakeshores at Pictured Rocks and Sleeping Bear Dunes in Michigan. With scores of other representatives, conservation leaders, and government officials, he helped the National Park Service celebrate its fiftieth anniversary at the Statler Hilton Hotel in Washington, DC, in August 1965. Worried that the newly created Land and Water Conservation Fund would not have sufficient resources to acquire additional landscapes, he worked unsuccessfully to supplement that fund by using money from offshore oil drilling projects. He also championed the Endangered Species Preservation Act of 1966.[18]

Saylor generally supported legislation to protect historical and cultural landscapes. In 1961, he and Senator Clinton Anderson introduced a bill establishing Piscataway National Park on the Potomac River in Maryland. This legislation blocked construction of an oil tank farm, thus preserving the cross-river view from President Washington's Mount Vernon home. He also used his influence on the House Interior Committee to bring national recognition to two historical sites in Pennsylvania. In 1964, Congress passed his bill setting aside 55 acres in Cambria County as the Johnstown Flood Memorial to commemorate the tragedy that took two thousand lives in 1889. This same measure also designated 950 acres along the former Allegheny Portage Railroad route as a national historical site. Saylor also supported measures designating trading posts, military forts, the St. Louis Arch, and the boyhood homes of Presidents Hoover and Kennedy as national historic sites. On the other hand, perhaps because a private utility would have been inconvenienced, Saylor blasted Secretary Stewart Udall's decision denying permission to the Potomac Edison Company to cross the C&O Canal National Historic Park because its power lines along private lands would have come too close to the Civil War battle-field of Antietam, marring the experience.[19]

Never one to shy away from publicity, Saylor took advantage of every opportunity to capitalize on his growing acclaim as an environmentalist. Stewart Udall, the keynote speaker at the fiftieth anniversary of the Johnstown Sportsmen's Association, heaped praise on Saylor even though he was a member of the opposition party. Saylor, he asserted, was one of the top conservationists in Congress, and the recent work of the Eighty-eighth "Conservation" Congress, in particular, would "be recognized and looked upon as significant 100 years from now."[20]

In the mid-1960s, Saylor's contributions were recognized by several conservation groups. In 1965, he and Aspinall were honored by the National Wildlife Federation as corecipients of the Conservationist of the Year award for their efforts on behalf of the Wilderness Act, the Land and Water Conservation Fund, Canyonlands National Park, Fire Island National Seashore, and the Lower Klamath Pacific Flyway for migratory birds. Saylor was also honored by the Pennsylvania State Fish and Game Department, the Pennsylvania Outdoor Writers Association, and Trout Unlimited. A spokesperson for Trout Unlimited referred to Saylor as one of only a half-dozen members of Congress who could be described as a "dedicated conservationist": "He's the type of guy who doesn't apologize for being regarded as an outspoken conservationist. After a couple minutes with Mr. Saylor, you quickly realize that here's the average kind of guy whom you might encounter fishing for trout on the Davidson River or hunting quail behind a liver-colored pointer."[21]

Saylor also served as the featured speaker at the National Audubon Society's annual convention in 1965, warning preservationists against apathy. They had made progress in their efforts to protect wild creatures and wild terrain. "But every time we take one step forward," Saylor said, "our enemies take two."

He urged members specifically to help block attempts to dam Grand Canyon and to push for passage of the Wild and Scenic Rivers Bill.[22]

Saylor thrived in the limelight, and his constituents seemed to delight in the fact that he enjoyed his job. In Congress, there were "not enough Saylors," lamented the *Punxsutawney Spirit*. Because he had "performed brilliantly" in the field of conservation, he was one of only a handful of 435 representatives specifically recommended for reelection by the *New York Times*. In the election of 1966, Saylor overwhelmed his Democratic opponent, Frank Buck, by fifty-two thousand votes, amassing 67.4 percent of the vote.[23]

Saylor's reelection came on the heels of what was initially considered to be another victory for conservationists, especially those seeking more recreational opportunities along the heavily populated New York–Philadelphia corridor. In 1965, Congress passed Saylor's bill authorizing the establishment of the Tocks Island National Recreation Area (TINRA) along the Delaware River in Pennsylvania and New Jersey. This spacious recreation area would adjoin a reservoir created by Tocks Island Dam, a Corps of Engineers project that Congress had approved three years earlier. The authorization of Tocks Island Dam in 1962 had drawn little attention from the conservation community because it was considered a routine flood-control project that would not intrude upon a national preserve. But by 1965, the growing sentiment to protect free-flowing rivers, a notion that Saylor helped to promote, provoked new controversy over Tocks Island Dam.

Conservationists welcomed the chance to provide citizens more recreational opportunities, but the Tocks area came under fire because it was partnered with a dam. Just as Morris Udall had yielded to political reality in advocating federal dams in Grand Canyon, however, Saylor caved to expediency in his support for the Tocks Island Dam, considering the dam and the adjoining recreation area to be irrevocably connected. Politically and legally, there could be no recreation area, he believed, without the dam. A former member of the Outdoor Recreation Resources Review Committee, he recognized the demand for additional recreation areas near metropolitan areas, especially in the crowded East. The dam would not intrude upon a national preserve, and for Saylor, the demand for recreation in this case superseded the demand for wild rivers. Though it escaped notice, his position was hypocritical: at the very time that he was championing the Wild and Scenic Rivers Bill and denouncing proposals to dam the Colorado River in Grand Canyon National Monument, he was cooperating with efforts to dam the main stem of the Delaware, one of the last unencumbered rivers in the Northeast. Besides local conservationists, property owners along the river criticized the project as "socialistic" because it took their land. All in all, the project became a political, economic, and environmental fiasco, but Saylor survived the controversy with his reputation intact as a dedicated preservationist.[24]

Originating in upstate New York near the town of Hancock, the Delaware River glides southward, forming the border between New Jersey and Pennsylvania before spilling into Delaware and the Atlantic Ocean some 330 miles downstream. Though not one of the nation's longest rivers, the Delaware supplies about 10 percent of the U.S. populace with water.[25]

In the decades prior to World War II, the states of New Jersey and Pennsylvania had made several efforts to dam the Delaware, but for a variety of political, economic, and geological reasons these attempts never materialized. Then, in August 1955, hurricanes Connie and Diane ripped through the Delaware River basin. The rampaging floods and frantic winds claimed at least ninety-nine lives and $100 million in property damage.[26]

Although the loss of life occurred along the river's tributaries, the 1955 floods rekindled interest in the federal government building a dam on the Delaware to prevent future devastation. The U.S. Senate asked the Corps of Engineers to undertake an exhaustive study to determine the merits of building a multipurpose dam on the river. In earlier studies completed in the 1930s, 1940s, and, ironically, in 1955, a month before the devastating floods, the corps had not been able to justify the expense of damming the Delaware.[27]

Now, while the corps prepared yet another study, area residents formed the Delaware River Basin Advisory Committee. With a grant from the Ford Foundation, the committee contracted with Syracuse University to study how the four basin states could coordinate development of the river. The committee also created a public relations group to lobby for federal development of the river basin.[28]

The Syracuse consultants recommended establishing a Delaware River Basin Compact and an interstate commission, with federal representation, to oversee and coordinate river development. Saylor supported a 1961 bill authorizing the establishment of the compact and the interstate basin commission. Meanwhile, the corps' study, released in 1960, recommended the construction of nineteen dams on the river over a fifty-year span. Army engineers proposed eight for immediate construction, including the key facility located at Tocks Island.[29]

Owned by the state of New Jersey, Tocks Island was located about six miles upstream from the Delaware Water Gap, a famed scenic vista where the river had chiseled through the Appalachian Mountains. Coupled to the states of New Jersey and Pennsylvania, the earthen dam would stand 160 feet above the streambed. The reservoir created by the impoundment would cover nearly 13,000 acres and back water upstream for thirty-seven miles to Port Jervis, New York. The facility would provide flood control, water supply, limited hydroelectric power, and recreation. The lake, plus an adjoining 9,500 acres, would provide recreation benefits to perhaps as many as ten million visitors per year.[30]

Tocks Island Dam was one of two hundred public works projects bundled in the Omnibus Rivers and Harbors and Flood Control Bill of 1962. During the floor debate, Saylor said nothing about Tocks Island Dam, preferring instead to use his time to denounce the inclusion in the bill of the Burns Creek project in southeastern Idaho. A year earlier, he had managed to kill that public power project when it came before the House Interior Committee because it would further "Russianize" the utility industry. But determined Westerners, in "blatant disregard for clearly established legislative processes," had managed to add the Burns Creek project to the omnibus bill. Saylor regarded this backdoor maneuver as a "personal affront" and once again helped to derail it. The omnibus bill, with Tocks Dam included, passed by voice vote.[31]

While authorized in 1962, the dam's construction, at an estimated cost of $94 million, was not scheduled until 1967 because the Army Corps of Engineers needed time to conduct field studies to determine the best geological anchor points for the structure. Meanwhile, the National Park Service, which had planned the recreational features of the project, recommended making the 9,500 acres surrounding the proposed reservoir a national recreation area. Having the Park Service administer this area would require separate congressional action.[32]

In 1962, Democratic representative Francis Walter of Easton, Pennsylvania, introduced the first bill proposing a Tocks Island National Recreation Area, but Congress did not have time to consider it. After Walter's death in 1963, Saylor agreed, at the request of Senator Joseph Clark and Representative Fred Rooney, both Pennsylvania Democrats, to assume major responsibility for the legislation in the House. Clark and Rooney claimed that while there were plenty of recreation areas in the West, "here in the Middle Atlantic Metropolitan Seaboard, where 25 million Americans live, we are having an extremely difficult time in obtaining a national recreation area which would serve more

Americans than any other similar facility in the country." In January 1965, Saylor introduced an expanded TINRA bill in the House, and Clark submitted a similar measure in the Senate.[33]

Although supplying more water to Philadelphia, Trenton, and other municipalities was important, Saylor considered recreation the main benefit of the Tocks Island project. The ORRRC report of 1962, he noted, emphasized the need to preserve more open space and recreational opportunities near population centers. Secretary Udall and other resource policy makers shared this goal. In the early 1960s, Congress had established the Cape Cod and Fire Island national seashores in the heavily populated Northeast and Point Reyes National Seashore near San Francisco. President Kennedy had endorsed TINRA during a speech at Milford, Pennsylvania, in 1963, and President Johnson in February 1965 recommended TINRA during a special message to Congress. With strong backing from the administration and Saylor, chairman Wayne Aspinall gave TINRA priority status. He forwarded Saylor's bill to the Subcommittee on National Parks and Recreation and scheduled hearings in Washington, DC, on March 1, 1965.[34]

At the hearings, Saylor explained that his bill, and companion measures, sought congressional authorization to establish TINRA, the first national recreation area east of the Rocky Mountains. The bills sought $37.5 million to purchase an additional 47,675 acres bordering the already approved reservoir and another $18 million to build boat-launching sites, picnic areas, campgrounds, restrooms, parking areas, and hiking trails. In all, the $55.4 million recreation area would total approximately 72,000 acres, including the reservoir and its surrounding recreation land. Located within one hundred miles of thirty million people, TINRA offered crowded Easterners a chance to boat, fish, swim, hike, camp, picnic, and commune with nature. Besides the inspiring vista at Delaware Water Gap, the shorelines and hillsides harbored deer, squirrels, fox, raccoons, beaver, and more than two hundred bird species. Mountain laurel and rhododendron gave vibrancy to the river basin, as did hemlock forests and hardwood trees that flared in the fall. Kittatinny Ridge, which paralleled the river for ten miles on the Pennsylvania side, was topped by ponds and lakes, and from this plateau streams tumbled down gorges and over waterfalls to the river below. If Saylor saw a contradiction between championing a wild rivers bill at the same time he was cooperating with efforts to plug the free-flowing Delaware, he did not mention it. Nor did he give much heed to the fact that hundreds of farm, home, cottage, and small-business owners would be forced to sell and relocate. He urged swift action on the bill before costs soared.[35]

Support for TINRA was overwhelming. Initially, the only opposition came from some local officials who fretted over the loss of taxes on the withdrawn land and property owners who would be displaced through eminent domain. One of these property owners, Nancy Shukaitis, an East Stroudsburg, Pennsylvania, homemaker, scolded the subcommittee for failing to hold hearings close enough for local people to access them. If hearings were held in the affected region, she predicted, there would be far less support for the project. Saylor pointed out that the House Interior Committee handled about 20 percent of all legislation and that time did not allow field hearings in every instance. But when the *Washington Post* and other newspapers shared the homemaker's concern, the subcommittee caved in, scheduling another round of hearings in East Stroudsburg in late April 1965.[36]

Though still a minority, TINRA opponents were more numerous and vocal at the second hearing. Led by Nancy Shukaitis, property owners generally decried the federal takeover as socialistic. Saylor professed sympathy with their position but pointed out that they would be fairly compensated and agreed to support an amendment that would enable them to live on their property for twenty-five years. In some cases, however, property consisted of "hurdy-gurdy" such as filling stations, restaurants, souvenir stands, and motels, which were inconsistent with national park principles. In such instances, owners would be forced to sell immediately, and the businesses would be razed. The establishment of national preserves, he asserted, was one of the few occasions when private property must give way to the public good, and he considered TINRA "one of the most worthwhile projects of its type that has ever been presented to the nation in recent years."[37]

A few witnesses attempted to speak out against the dam, but when they did the subcommittee informed them that they were off target: Congress had already approved it. The Saylor bill dealt exclusively with the establishment of a national recreation area. Still, Frederick W. Egger, a self-described "ardent conservationist," ignored the catch-22 warning and rebuked Congress for destroying the free-flowing Delaware River. How could the grandeur of Kittatinny Ridge be improved, he asked, by having a limpid reservoir at its base? "In the name of so-called progress," he continued, "we have forfeited our irreplaceable heritage." If Congress truly wished to preserve the scenic splendor of the area for the multitudes, it would establish a national recreation area along a free-moving river, not an artificial reservoir.[38]

But the free-flowing Delaware had few defenders in the spring of 1965, and Saylor, one of the national leaders of liberated rivers, cooperated in its demise. For Saylor and the subcommittee, providing water, flood control, and recreational opportunities for thirty million people along the Atlantic seaboard took priority over saving one scenic river. Then, too, Saylor had recommended that the upper portion of the Delaware be studied for possible inclusion in the wild rivers program.

Unanimously approved by the subcommittee and then the full committee, the legislation was forwarded to the full House for action in mid-May 1965. To ensure TINRA's chances for success, the committee also recommended passage of related bills establishing Whiskeytown-Shasta-Trinity National Recreation Area in California, national historic sites at trading posts in Arizona and North Dakota, the first transcontinental railroad juncture in Utah, President Hoover's birthplace in Iowa, and the Ellis Island immigration station in New York. Though each proposal was a separate bill, there is little doubt that the committee intended them to be considered as a package to maximize their chance of success. All of the bills passed separately by voice vote. With the region renamed the Delaware Water Gap National Recreation Area (DWGNRA), Saylor's bill passed on July 12, 1965. A month later, the Senate approved it, and President Johnson signed it into law on September 1, 1965.[39]

Problems, however, soon surfaced. Land values skyrocketed as developers bought up adjacent real estate on which to build homes and tourist businesses. To Saylor's horror, the estimated cost of buying out private owners to establish the recreation area climbed from $37.4 million in 1965, to $56.1 million in 1969, to $65 million in 1972.[40]

Led by Nancy Shukaitis, property owners in the proposed dam and recreation areas formed the Delaware Valley Conservation Association to resist their removal. They filed a class-action suit but lost. Meanwhile, the Corps of Engineers began using what little money had been appropriated for the dam to buy out property owners along the reservoir site. Once the property had been sold and vacated, demolition began. Occasionally, corps bulldozers dropped the wrong house or mistakenly razed a historic building. The corps also had to ask federal marshals, with bulldozers bellowing behind, to remove a community of hippies who had moved into vacated houses along the river.[41]

While most people in the vicinity favored the establishment of a national recreation area, a growing number began to question the need for a dam. Owing to the Vietnam War, the House Appropriations Committee had delayed providing money for dam construction. Meanwhile, the Lennai Lenape League, the

Sierra Club, the Wilderness Society, Trout Unlimited, and other conservation groups used the delay in construction to mount an attack on the dam. Not only would an impoundment, they argued, destroy a free-flowing river, but the reservoir would drown farmland, historic sites, and hundreds of homes and businesses. The reservoir also might reduce the oxygen level and harm fishing.[42]

Even as he clamored for passage of the Wild and Scenic Rivers Bill, however, Saylor refused to join the assault on Tocks Island Dam. Perhaps he did not want to contradict his earlier support for the dam. More likely, he considered the dam and recreation area irrevocably interconnected and feared that the courts might negate any uncoupling of the two projects. Consequently, he said and did nothing that might jeopardize the establishment of a recreation area that would benefit millions of people.

In the mid-1970s, after Saylor's death, several bills were introduced to deauthorize the dam. These measures died in the House and Senate Public Works Committees. Though the dam had lost most of its support and its estimated cost had risen to $1 billion, representatives from Delaware, Pennsylvania, and New Jersey still wanted it built. To get around their blocking action in the Public Works Committees, proponents of deauthorization recommended including both the upper and middle reaches of the Delaware in the National Wild and Scenic Rivers System. Saylor had included the upper Delaware in the study group in his 1968 bill but had been willing to sacrifice the middle section. Both river segments, however, were included in an omnibus parks and rivers bill that became law in 1978. The inclusion of both stretches of the waterway in the National Wild and Scenic Rivers System virtually assured that the dam would never be built. Today, the Delaware Water Gap National Recreation Area, located hard by a free-flowing river, serves as a sylvan retreat of 72,000 acres for millions of yearly visitors.[43]

Saylor poses near Homer City, Pennsylvania, with coal-fired, utility smokestacks in the background.

Saylor campaign flyer with his district superimposed on the state of Pennsylvania.

President Lyndon Johnson presents a pen to Saylor upon signing the Wild and Scenic Rivers Act of 1968.

Saylor embraces GOP minority leader Gerald Ford, who referred to Saylor as the congressional Theodore Roosevelt.

Saylor with Republican presidential nominee Richard Nixon campaigning in Johnstown in 1968.

Saylor posing in front of the Capitol with Punxsutawney Phil.

Saylor greets his colleague and environmental ally Morris "Mo" Udall of Arizona.

Congress salutes Saylor for twenty years of service. Saylor poses with wife Grace, son Phil, and daughter Susan. The cake reads: "Keep Sailing with Saylor."

Saylor and National Park Service Director George Hartzog. The photo caption reads: "For John Saylor—A great park man & valued friend. George Hartzog."

Saylor delivers a playful jab at his nemesis Floyd Dominy, director of the Bureau of Reclamation. The caption on the photo reads: "For John Saylor: An esteemed member of Congress—a Picture symbolic of our association! Floyd Dominy."

President Johnson signs the 1964 Wilderness Bill. Saylor introduced the first wilderness legislation in 1956 and served as its principal champion in the House of Representatives.

Saylor was part of a congressional delegation visiting newly established Lake Powell in Page, Arizona. Saylor stands to the far left in the back of the boat. To his right are Wayne Aspinall, Senator Carl Hayden (in the black hat), and Representative Walter Rogers of Texas.

On horseback, Saylor visits the Bridger Primitive Area in Wyoming, circa 1960.

President John Kennedy signs a 1963 bill widening the powers of the Bureau of Outdoor Recreation.

Saylor greeting Chairman Wayne Aspinall in the meeting room of the House Committee on Interior and Insular Affairs. Note Aspinall's portrait looming in the background.

Saylor's closest congressional colleague, John Dingell (D-MI), helps him celebrate a 1958 award from several national conservation groups "for distinguished service to conservation."

A young Congressman Saylor poses in front of the Capitol.

Saylor poses with President Dwight D. Eisenhower. Saylor was generally critical of Eisenhower's conservation record.

Saylor helps gather potatoes on Gooderham Farm in Pennsylvania.

Saylor bought fishing licenses from several states, carried gear in his car, and occasionally stopped to wet a line. Here he is fishing an unidentified stream.

Saylor belonged to a sportsmen's association and often unwound at "Lost Cabin," a fishing and hunting retreat in Potter County, Pennsylvania.

Saylor with the Dickinson College School of Law graduating class of 1933. Due to the Depression, the college produced no yearbook or photos. The photo here was sent to Saylor by a classmate forty years later.

Saylor visiting proposed Redwood National Park in California, 1968.

thirteen
Greening America

AS THE ENVIRONMENTAL movement began to surge in the late 1960s, so did interest in wilderness, scenic beauty, recreational opportunity, and a contamination-free countryside. Once a pioneer, John Saylor had become a respected and influential old hand in the movement. Like most environmentalists, he stressed quality of life over quantity of goods. Federal resource policy, he insisted, should address posterity, not just prosperity. He equated a green America with a great America and believed that failure to set aside recreation sites and wild and scenic landscapes diminished the nation and deprived future generations of their natural heritage.[1]

Saylor understood that environmental legislation usually required bipartisan support and taxpayer funding. But liberal Democrats were beginning to dominate the movement, and the war in Vietnam was drawing away precious financial resources. Saylor worked to add a stronger environmental statement to the Republican Party platform in 1968 but failed. While never abandoning his support for the war, he worked doggedly to find more revenue to finance outdoor recreation. Although fiscally conservative, Saylor refused to scrimp on either military defense or the acquisition of lands for national preserves and recreation areas.[2]

In 1964, Saylor had helped craft the Land and Water Conservation Fund to finance the purchase of recreation lands. That fund, however, could not meet the demand for more open space. Wayne Aspinall, who chaired the House

Interior Committee that controlled park and recreation bills, stated that without additional funds, "the further authorization of new outdoor recreation facilities will be a senseless gesture." Roy Taylor, chair of the Subcommittee on National Parks, said that "this Committee is pretty much out of business in authorizing new parks." Prodded by Saylor, then, these committee leaders sought to infuse the Conservation Fund with additional revenue. The House, Saylor asserted, was "the forge of democracy," and he hoped it would save the Conservation Fund "and in a sense save the country."[3]

Not all preservation goals were expensive. Adding units to the national wilderness system, for example, required congressional action, but little expense. Under the Wilderness Act of 1964, the Agriculture and Interior departments, within ten years, were required to review 150 wildland units within national forests, national parks, and national wildlife refuges to determine if they merited inclusion in the wilderness system. Inclusion in the wilderness system would further preserve these already protected lands by removing the future threat of timbering, mining, and other commercial development. At least one third of these unit studies had to be completed within three years. After holding hearings in the affected areas, Interior and Agriculture would make their recommendations to the president, who, in turn, could accept, reject, or revise them for final action by Congress.[4]

In early January 1967, President Johnson recommended the 143,000-acre San Rafael Primitive Area in the Los Padres National Forest in southern California as the first addition to the wilderness system. Republican California representative Charles Teague, in whose district the area was situated, then introduced legislation in the House designating it a wilderness area. Saylor, principal architect of the parent Wilderness Act, introduced a companion bill.[5]

At the hearings in late June, Saylor stressed the significance of the legislation. It was important, he said, because "it marks the beginning of a long series of such additions" over the next several years. He expressed the hope that the system would grow from 9 million to 55 million acres. Specifically, the San Rafael area was worthy of protection for four main reasons. First, it would involve minimal cost since it was already held as a national forest unit. Second, it was an area of rugged beauty within two hours' driving distance of six million people in the vicinity of Los Angeles. Third, it was a natural stronghold of the endangered California condor, a rather ignoble vulture with a wingspan of nine feet. And finally, the area held the cultural remnants, including pictographs, of the ancient Chugash Indian people.[6]

Initially, the bill encountered only meager resistance. Never enthusiastic about the establishment let alone expansion of the wilderness program, chairman Wayne Aspinall let it be known that he did not share the preservationists' goal of setting aside as much as 55 million acres. As for the San Rafael unit of 143,000 acres, he wanted assurances that it would be open to mineral development until December 31, 1983, just like the 9 million acres originally covered in the program. A representative from the Interior Department insisted, though, that Congress could ban mining if government scientists determined that a candidate area had scant mining potential. In the case of San Rafael, he continued, eight government scientists had examined rock samples in the summer of 1965 and concluded that the area held little promise of mineral development. Aspinall scoffed at the superficiality of the studies and prevailed upon the committee, including Saylor, to permit prospecting and mining in all additions to the system through 1983.[7]

Having prevailed on the mining issue, Aspinall proved receptive to an amendment adding 2,200 acres to the San Rafael unit. Citizens for the San Rafael Wilderness, a local group from Santa Barbara County, wanted to add acreage, called Area F, along San Madre Ridge in order to protect *potreros* (open, grassy meadows), ancient cave drawings, and the flyways of condors. The Sierra Club, the Wilderness Society, the National Audubon Society, and other conservation groups supported their recommendation. Saylor promised to introduce an amendment, to the delight of a Sierra Club member who praised him as "a distinguished conservationist." Nearly always receptive to flattery, Saylor replied that "after the abuse I take, those words are well received."[8]

As promised, during markup of the bill Saylor argued passionately for the addition of Area F. The House Interior Committee agreed to the Saylor amendment and forwarded the bill to the full House, where it passed by voice vote. Unfortunately, the Forest Service opposed the addition of Area F, arguing that it was needed for a road and a fire-protection zone. The Senate bill, passed earlier in 1967, omitted Area F, so a conference committee was appointed to reconcile the differences between the two measures. Saylor served as one of the conferees.[9]

Friends of the Forest Service emphasized the need for fire protection. Members of Congress, they said, would not wish to be held accountable for the loss of life and property if firefighters were prevented from doing their jobs. Preservationists argued that firefighters could access fires via an abutting jeep road and that the *potreros* served as natural firebreaks. Then, too, five condors had recently been spotted. "The condors like Area F. They need it," declared Robert Easton of the citizens' committee.[10]

The position of preservationists was weakened somewhat when fire raged through the Los Padres National Forest in late 1967. The blaze did not intrude upon the proposed San Rafael wilderness site, but it did swallow 10,000 acres of neighboring timberland. Still, the fire did not deter Saylor and preservationists, who continued to pound away on the need to protect the ecologically distinct *potreros,* aboriginal cave paintings, and condors.[11]

For Saylor, there was also a political principle at stake. When he and other legislators crafted the Wilderness Act of 1964, he declared in a House speech, they wanted citizens to have input in expanding the system; they did not want executive agencies imposing their will on citizens or on Congress. Consequently, the legislation called for administrative field hearings to listen to the recommendations of citizens. The Forest Service now refused to yield on Area F out of arrogance; it did not want common citizens to challenge its authority or expertise on the issue of fire protection. He urged his colleagues to heed the recommendations of citizen preservationists who wished to add Area F.[12]

Despite widespread public support for the inclusion of Area F, however, the conference committee considered it a "monster." California senator Thomas Kuchel, one of the sponsors of the bill, was up for reelection and dared not go against the recommendation of the Forest Service with fires raging in California. Senate conferees insisted upon excluding the controversial area from the bill.[13]

Morris Udall held the pivotal vote among House conferees. Saylor and Laurence Burton of Utah supported the House bill, which included Area F. Walter Baring and Harold Johnson (D-CA) opposed it. Customarily, Udall sided with preservationists, but during the San Rafael controversy, he had been involved with other legislation and had not attended any of the hearings or markup sessions. He was also anxious to please the California delegation because he wanted their support on the Central Arizona Project. So Udall verbally agreed to accept the Senate bill and gave his proxy to Representative Johnson. As a result, the committee approved the Senate version of the bill.

Meanwhile, over the weekend, Udall had a change of heart after being deluged with telephone calls and telegrams from preservationists, who reminded him that someday Arizonans might wish to adjust the boundaries of a proposed wilderness area and would need the support of Saylor and other preservationists. Udall informed Johnson that he had reversed his position and would not sign the conference report. With Udall's refusal to sign and Saylor's decision to fight the conference report on the floor, Aspinall decided to postpone a vote until the next congressional session in 1968.[14]

The San Rafael dispute distressed Aspinall. He detested fights among committee members on the floor. "We try to take care of our differences in Committee discussion, and we usually succeed," he wrote. He blamed the mess on the Forest Service and fired off a scolding letter to its chief, Edward Cliff. The Forest Service, Aspinall said, should have presented its argument for a fire-protection zone in Area F during the House subcommittee hearings: "Mr. Saylor would have more than likely presented his position and, if he had been defeated in the Committee, he would have gone along with us. But the way the matter was handled made an almost impossible situation for him." Saylor had won his case in committee and on the House floor, but then in conference the Forest Service and Udall had sabotaged him; he "had no other alternative but to fight the Conference Report." Aspinall advised Cliff to "make your case before the Committee and not make it after the Committee has finished its deliberations." If future proposed additions to the wilderness system proved as controversial as San Rafael, "there [would] be very few of them authorized."[15]

Meanwhile, Saylor and preservationists mobilized opposition to the conference report. Joined by several colleagues, Saylor sent a letter to House members urging them to reject the report. The San Rafael bill, they said, would be precedent setting for more than one hundred future additions to the system: "Our concern is not only with the biologically and archeologically important 2,000-acre addition to the San Rafael area, but with the basic question as to whether or not citizen conservation organizations and conservationists are to have a voice within the Congress in the final designation of additions to the National Wilderness Preservation System."[16]

Saylor repeated these arguments on the House floor. Several colleagues, including Udall, joined him in urging rejection of the conference report, but their appeal failed. The House voted to accept the Senate bill, which excluded the 2,200 acres, by a vote of 238 to 156. Although Saylor had lost the San Rafael battle, he had enhanced his reputation as a champion of preservation and wilderness values. By fighting for only 2,200 acres, he had also demonstrated his support for grassroots conservation. Gracious in defeat, he sent a thank-you letter to the representatives who had supported him with a reminder that there were other battles for a green America to be won.[17]

Adding other primeval units to the wilderness program proved less time-consuming and controversial than did San Rafael. In 1968, President Johnson recommended the inclusion of twenty-six parcels to the system. Some of these wilderness tracts, such as the Great Swamp of New Jersey and the North Cascades of Washington, were near major population centers and could offer recreation to millions of visitors.[18]

The Great Swamp National Wildlife Refuge was located in Morris County, New Jersey, about thirty miles from Manhattan. The pristine swamp of 3,750 acres sheltered a variety of wildlife, including 175 species of birds. In 1959, the New York Port Authority had sought to acquire the then privately owned area for a jetport, but local conservationists had protested and raised $1 million to buy it. They had then donated it to the American people as a wildlife refuge.[19]

Incorporating the refuge into the wilderness program would scotch future jetport talk and prevent the Interior Department from changing its protected status without congressional approval. The swamp would be the first wilderness tract administered by the Interior Department's Bureau of Sport Fisheries and Wildlife, which had formulated plans to make the area more visitor friendly by building restrooms and trails. It also proposed flyovers to patrol for poachers and survey the waterfowl population. When the House subcommittee learned of the bureau's plans, however, it promptly put an end to them. "I don't expect to see any trails up there; I don't expect to see you people fly over there counting the birds," Saylor admonished the bureau's director. These activities violated wilderness values and would not be condoned. The bureau thus scrapped its plans, and the bill passed the House easily. President Johnson signed the bill into law in early October 1968.[20]

The executive branch also proposed unspoiled areas in Washington for the wilderness program. Called the "American Alps," the North Cascade Mountains offered breathtaking scenery, abundant wildlife, and pristine wilderness. And they were within easy driving range of Seattle. In 1967, several members of Congress from Washington proposed legislation nearly as sweeping as the mountains. They sought to expand the existing Glacier Peak Wilderness Area by 10,000 acres, provide wilderness status for the Pasayten National Forest Primitive Area, authorize the Ross Lake and Lake Chelan national recreation areas, and establish North Cascades National Park. In all, about 1.2 million acres would be protected at minimal cost to taxpayers. Because there was little mining and logging in the area, the measure met little resistance.[21]

Most of the area was national forest administered by the Department of Agriculture. After considerable resistance, that department agreed to transfer control of the lands that would be included in the park and recreation areas to the Interior Department. About $3.5 million would be needed, however, to buy 5,000 acres of privately owned land in the proposed national recreation areas.[22]

Except for an existing state highway that was closed by snow much of the year, the area was roadless. Because the park and recreation areas were so vast and inaccessible, some representatives proposed the construction of tramways to transport visitors. Secretary Udall considered trams preferable to more roads, but Saylor objected. Once aerial trams had been constructed to glide visitors up mountainsides, he said, there soon would be demands to cut swaths down the slopes for skiing. The House rejected the recommendations for trams and additional roads and passed the Senate version of the bill by voice vote. The establishment of such a "vast recreation complex," Saylor noted, "ranks among the most significant and far-reaching conservation measures of this 90th Congress."[23]

As the San Rafael, Great Swamp, and North Cascades measures attest, pristine landscapes could be protected without huge costs. However, other proposals —establishing a system of national trails and a redwoods national park— would entail considerable expense because they required the acquisition of private property.

Saylor and other preservationists sought congressional protection for back-country trails. As with the wild and scenic rivers measure, which was being considered at the same time, the idea was to establish a core group of pathways and design a process for later adding others to the system. At the request of President Johnson, Agriculture and Interior had undertaken a two-year study of several scenic, historic, and recreational trails. Completed in 1967, their report recommended the establishment of different trail categories and specified four units for initial inclusion in the national system. The administration prepared a bill, and several representatives, including Saylor, introduced it in 1967.[24]

The bill recommended four trail types: national scenic trails; national park, forest, and recreational trails; state park, forest, and recreational trails; and metropolitan trails. The first units proposed for protection were national scenic trails: the Appalachian Trail, stretching some 2,000 miles from Maine to Georgia; the Pacific Crest Trail, winding for 3,100 miles from the Canadian to the Mexican border; the Continental Divide Trail, extending some 2,300 miles from Canada to New Mexico; and the Potomac Heritage Trail, which meandered for 825 miles from its source in the hills of Pennsylvania to the Atlantic Ocean. The

Interior Department would administer the Appalachian and Potomac units, and the Agriculture Department would administer the Pacific Crest and Continental Divide pathways. Other trails—mainly historic—would be studied for possible later inclusion by Congress. The estimated acquisition and development costs for the four initial trails were pegged at $30 million.[25]

The House Subcommittee on Public Lands, where the bill was sent, balked at the expense. Aspinall was reluctant to approve such a large expenditure when previously authorized projects such as Cape Cod National Seashore, Point Reyes National Seashore, and the Delaware Water Gap National Recreation Area had not been completely funded. With Saylor in agreement, the Interior Committee favorably reported the bill, but not before making significant changes. To minimize acquisition costs, it recommended only the Appalachian Trail for inclusion in the program. Thirteen other footpaths, including the Pacific Crest, Continental Divide, and Potomac Heritage trails, were recommended for additional study for possible later inclusion by Congress. The Interior Committee proposed $5 million for land acquisition and $1 million for development of the Appalachian Trail. During the floor debate, Saylor pushed the bills for national trails and scenic rivers as complementary: both "could very well become the most popular conservation measures ever passed by the Congress of the United States." The trails bill passed by a vote of 376 to 18.[26]

Earlier in the year, the Senate had passed the $30 million administration bill establishing four national trails. The House-Senate conference committee, which included Saylor, now compromised. It recommended the instant designation of two trails—the Appalachian and the Pacific Crest—and proposed fourteen other routes as possible additions to the program. It also authorized $6.5 million for acquisition and development of the two trails. The House accepted the Conference Report, and the bill became law on October 2, 1968.[27]

During committee hearings on national trails, the North Cascades area, and other bills, Aspinall warned members that unless more revenues were found, proposals to acquire additional lands for national park and recreation purposes would not be authorized. Saylor, of course, understood the nation's financial woes. While fiscally conservative, however, he considered scenic beauty and open space to be as important as national defense and was determined not to reduce expenditures on either. He also wished to save the treasured redwoods of California, an effort that would require perhaps as much as $150 million. Anxious to fund projects that already had been authorized and new ones such as Redwoods National Park, Saylor worked furiously to find ways to augment the Land and Water Conservation Fund, the main revenue source for land acquisition.

Saylor had helped prepare the legislation establishing the Conservation Fund. It derived its revenue from the sale of surplus federal property; a motorboat fuel tax; and entrance and user fees at federal park, monument, and recreation facilities. Since its inception in 1965, the Conservation Fund had provided $88 million to purchase 313,000 acres for national projects and $128 million to fund local projects such as municipal parks. But over the next ten years, according to Secretary Udall, the government would need $3.6 billion to fund already authorized and proposed projects. The fund would yield slightly less than $1 billion, leaving a shortfall of $2.6 billion.[28]

The Conservation Fund produced about $95 million yearly, far less than the $160 million that had been anticipated. Revenues from park-entrance and -user fees proved especially disappointing. Expected to produce $60 million annually, these fees yielded only $10 million. Not all government agencies uniformly collected fees for their facilities. The Corps of Engineers, for example, argued that their taxpayer-funded reservoirs should be available at no charge. The Golden Eagle Passport also fell short of expectations. For $7 yearly, individuals could purchase this passport to attach to a vehicle. For one year from the date of purchase, the sticker allowed unlimited visits to federal parks, monuments, forests, and recreation areas. Sales were soft, however. People would rather spend the money on a bottle of liquor, Aspinall complained, than a park sticker. Saylor noted that car rental agencies could buy stickers for their vehicles, thus permitting thousands of people to gain free admission to national recreation facilities.[29]

Early in 1967, Saylor introduced legislation to amend the Conservation Fund Act. He proposed supplementing the fund with revenues from public land mineral leases and oil and gasoline leases from the Outer Continental Shelf, expecting revenues from these sources to yield between $400 and $500 million yearly. Roy Taylor, chair of the House Subcommittee on Public Lands, proposed a measure that restricted the revenues to oil and gasoline leases for a period of five years. Secretary Udall submitted yet another proposal that was identical to Taylor's except it capped the revenue at $100 million yearly.[30]

Aspinall scheduled hearings on the various proposals before the Subcommittee on Public Lands in 1968. Subcommittee chair Taylor noted that "the importance of this legislation is emphasized by the fact that we took it up as the very first bill this year," and Aspinall called it "one of the most important pieces of legislation we have had for a long, long time." And in a warning clearly meant for Saylor, he added "that if you ask for too much in this legislation, we are not going to get anything."[31]

Saylor took the hint. He said that he was not wed to any particular bill or revenue formula and agreed with Aspinall that it made little sense to continue authorizing recreation projects without providing the money to acquire the land. He lamented the fact that the House Appropriations Committee had made only modest allocations to federal conservation projects. After all, the fund was intended to serve as a supplemental, not the sole, source of revenue for conservation. He also noted that he was provoked "no end" by the Corps of Engineers, which advocated free admission to their facilities.[32]

Secretary Udall pushed the administration bill as a practical solution to the revenue-shortfall problem. The fund required an additional $100 million to meet existing and future needs, and Congress, he said, could not move forward on "such vitally needed conservation bills as the Redwoods National Park bill unless we first have action on this legislation." Continental shelf leases off the coasts of Texas and Louisiana, he noted, would produce $285 million yearly; newly developed wells off the coast of California would yield another annual $215 million. Unlike Saylor's bill, which would have taken the entire $500 million in perpetuity, Udall was willing to settle for $100 million for five years and then revisit the issue. Counting revenue from the shelf leases, the fund would total $200 million yearly, although owing to the nation's financial woes, the Budget Bureau might recommend against spending the entire amount.[33]

Portions of Udall's statement proved unsettling. For one thing, granting priority status to the Redwoods National Park bill irritated Aspinall. The redwoods, he declared, were not more important than previously authorized projects. He conceded that the redwoods had "sex appeal," but they would not receive preferential treatment from the committee. He reminded Udall that the proposal to enlarge the Conservation Fund "should not be considered as a Redwoods National Park bill."[34]

Saylor was also peeved with the secretary. Why would he settle for $100 million when shelf leases would yield $500 million? Udall pointed out that the nation had priorities other than the preservation of natural wonders and recreation. Saylor was also troubled by Udall's assertion that the Budget Bureau might not approve the expenditure of the entire $200 million in the fund. "Very frankly, if I had my way, I don't think we should ever ask you people downtown for a report on a bill," he fumed to Udall. "Confidentially, I don't think it is any of your business. The next thing I would do would be to abolish the Appropriations Committee. The country got along for 150 years without it and I think we ought to abolish it."[35]

Representative Morris Udall echoed Saylor's demand that the country raise and spend more than $200 million on outdoor recreation bills, but he was "not prepared to declare war on the Budget Bureau or abolish the Appropriations committee yet." Saylor thanked Morris Udall for his support but expressed disappointment that he was not willing to join his war: "I would probably say to my colleague that if suddenly the Bureau of the Budget decided to tell the administration that it was against the Central Arizona Project, he would probably be over on my side real fast." "Within 30 seconds," Udall replied. Thereafter, whenever Morris Udall wanted to needle Saylor, he referred to him as the "Ex-Officio Chairman of the Ad-Hoc Committee to Abolish the Appropriations Committee."[36]

The main opposition to the supplemental Conservation Fund measure, however, came from representatives of Texas and Louisiana, where shelf drilling had been successfully developed. They fought any attempt to take revenues from shelf leases. Indeed, Louisiana representatives had introduced legislation proposing that states adjoining shelf wells would acquire 37.5 percent of revenues, with the remainder going to the other states. Saylor pointed out that in the Submerged Lands Act of 1953 Congress had determined that beyond three miles and up to a distance of ten miles the ocean floor and its resources belonged to the American people, not to the residents of the adjoining states. He asked Democratic representative Hale Boggs how Louisiana could lay claim to any share of shelf revenues, given that law. Boggs replied: "I find myself, whenever the interests of my State conflict with the administration, supporting my State." Saylor responded: "I thought that was the reason we fought the War Between the States, to get rid of that concept. . . . I thought a hundred years ago we settled that problem."[37]

Subcommittee chair Taylor cautioned Saylor to be more civil to his Southern colleagues, but Saylor would not back down. He scolded the Louisiana governor for trying to "take something that belongs to the whole 50 States" and asked Democratic representative Edwin Willis if the state of Louisiana would claim 37.5 percent of the minerals if the United States landed an astronaut on the moon.[38]

After taking one last shot at the House Appropriations Committee as "a sterile group" that did "a lousy job," Saylor urged support for the administration bill. He had wanted all $500 million of the annual shelf revenue to go into the Conservation Fund but would settle for $100 million annually for five years. The administration bill was better than nothing, and besides, it would prevent the Gulf States from grabbing the revenue. Morris Udall supported Saylor and sought to conclude the hearings on an upbeat note: "This legislation, as supported by my good friend, Mr. Saylor, hits it about on the head, and I am prepared to follow his leadership as I nearly always do. In fact, I was going to move to suspend the rules and abolish the Appropriations Committee right here this morning. But I am told this would be out of order."[39]

The House Interior Committee sent a bill to the full House that amended the Conservation Fund Act in two major ways. First, the Golden Eagle Passport and user-fee revenue stream were eliminated. Each government agency would determine whether to assess entrance and user fees for lands under its supervision and be responsible for collecting them. These fees would not go into the Conservation Fund, but directly to each agency. This amendment was designed to please representatives who argued that federally financed Corps of Engineers reservoirs and their adjoining recreation lands should be open without fee to the public. Second, receipts from Outer Shelf wells would supplement the fund up to a maximum of $200 million. In other words, if revenue from the sale of surplus federal property and motorboat fuel tax brought in $125 million yearly, for example, then the fund could take only $75 million from Outer Shelf revenue.[40]

Opposition to the bill on the House floor came from two sources. Representatives from coastal states like Louisiana and Alaska insisted that they were being denied their fair share of offshore drilling receipts, and fiscal conservatives opposed designating funds for specific purposes—such as the Conservation Fund—as a dangerous precedent. In only two other cases, they declared, did Congress permit earmarking: payroll taxes for Social Security and gasoline taxes for highway building. Fiscal watchdogs claimed that Outer Shelf revenues should all go into the general treasury to lower the national debt, not to purchase more recreation lands. Saylor countered by arguing that "the need for this legislation cannot be overstated despite the other demands and domestic programs. The conservation of the land and water resources of this nation are most important to the overall posture of this great country if it is to remain strong in every way. You either have this program which the American people want," he continued, "or quit having a recreation program. It is just that simple." With strong backing from Saylor and Aspinall, the bill easily passed the House and became law in 1968.[41]

Saylor and other preservationists were pleased because the fund, for at least five more years, would provide Congress with additional revenue to complete authorized projects and initiate new ones. They were especially anxious to acquire and protect one of the nation's most precious scenic landscapes: the mighty redwoods of northern California.

fourteen
Saving the Redwoods

LED BY REPRESENTATIVES of the Sierra Club, John Saylor, Morris Udall, and three other members of the House Subcommittee on National Parks in mid-April 1968 tramped along lower Redwood Creek in northern California. Owned by timber companies, this remote area held stands of virgin redwood trees being considered for inclusion in a proposed national park. Only five years earlier, a survey team from the National Park Service and the National Geographic Society had discovered old-growth redwoods, the tallest trees in the world, along a bend in the creek. Saylor's field-inspection party visited the Tall Trees and another cluster of virgin timber farther downstream in an area called the Emerald Mile.

Saylor separated from the group and huffed up a slope, where he sat enthralled by the ancient giants. Older than the nation, some of the trees measured more than 15 feet across and 350 feet in height. His colleagues thought he was lost, he remarked a few weeks later, but he "was never in better company" than when he was up there alone among the trees and "wading that creek." California, he said, had preserved some excellent redwood groves, "but some of the area up the Emerald Mile equals anything" in the state system.[1]

Trudging among the redwoods awed Saylor and reinforced his commitment to protect them. Timber companies, however, were equally determined to harvest them. The battle to save the redwoods, along with the fight to spare Grand Canyon from dams, was the last of the great conservation controversies of the 1960s. As usual, Saylor was in the midst of the fray, leading the charge in the House to preserve the redwoods in a spacious national park.[2]

Nourished by rain and fog, redwoods, *Sequoia sempervirens,* grow into giants hundreds of feet tall and hundreds of years old. These cinnamon brown monarchs commanded a narrow sylvan domain that ran for nearly five hundred miles along the coast of northern California. Many of the tall trees had been downed to build San Francisco during the Gold Rush. Four decades later, in the 1880s, more trees were dropped to construct the towns of Oakland and Berkeley. By the early twentieth century, most of the virgin groves were located north of San Francisco in Humboldt and Del Norte counties near the Oregon border. Timber companies acquired most of these in order to mill the rot-resistant lumber into clapboards, fence posts, deck material, picnic tables, and lawn furniture.[3]

In 1901, the first redwoods, about twenty-five miles south of San Francisco, were set aside as California Redwood State Park. Seven years later, William Kent, a member of Congress, donated his stand of mighty trees to the American public as Muir Woods National Monument. In 1918, the Save-the-Redwoods League was established to acquire additional groves as public preserves. Within a decade, the league had raised more than $500,000 to establish four redwood state parks: Humboldt and Prairie Creek in Humboldt County and Jedediah Smith and Del Norte Coast in Del Norte County.[4]

By the 1960s, thanks mainly to the financial donations of the Save-the-Redwoods League, California had preserved 50,000 acres of virgin growth in twenty-eight state parks. These parks were small and scattered. Highways penetrated two of the largest, Humboldt and Jedediah Smith, and another highway threatened to intrude upon Prairie Creek Redwood State Park. Disturbed by the threat of roads and lumbering, preservationists, led by the Sierra Club, sought national protection for the few remaining sizable tracts of old-growth timber. Edgar Wayburn and David Brower of the Sierra Club won over Secretary Stewart Udall, who endorsed the goal of a redwood national park and secured a grant to survey sites for its location.[5]

The location of the park proved to be a complex and contentious issue. The Save-the-Redwoods League preferred a 42,000-acre site along Mill Creek in Del Norte County, where the old-growth trees were owned by the Miller Redwood Company. The Sierra Club, influenced by Martin Litton of *Sunset* magazine, gravitated toward the Redwood Creek area in Humboldt County. This area, Litton insisted, was more remote and contained a larger tract of vir-

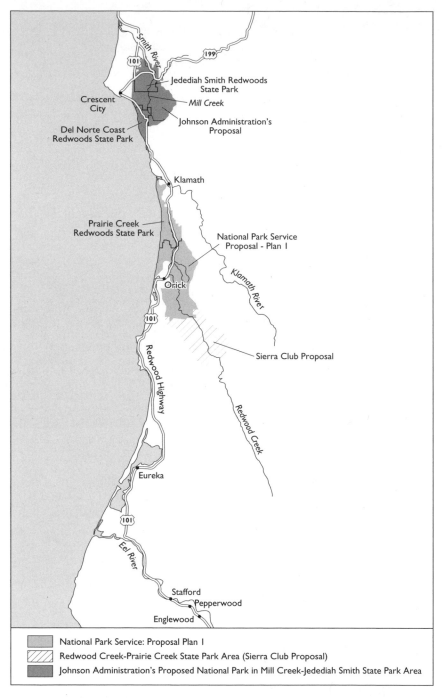

Redwood National Park proposals, 1966. Susan Schrepfer, *The Fight to Save the Redwoods.*
Copyright 1983. Reprinted by permission of the University of Wisconsin Press.

gin timber. The Redwood Creek site took on added appeal after the 1963 discovery of a redwood grove containing the tallest trees in the world, including one giant that stood 367 feet in height. Redwood stands in the Redwood Creek area were owned by three timber outfits: the Arcata Redwood Company, the Georgia-Pacific Corporation, and the Simpson Timber Company. And these companies were not receptive to the establishment of a national park that might ruin their business and cripple the local economy.[6]

In September 1964, the National Park Service recommended the Redwood Creek site for a national park. With Redwood Creek serving as the nucleus, the Park Service actually produced three plans ranging in size from 31,000, to 39,000, to 53,000 acres. The timber companies, especially Arcata and Georgia-Pacific, which owned either side of the creek, protested the park plans, and the redwood industry hired a public relations firm to lobby against the park proposals. The Save-the-Redwoods League favored a park, but not at Redwood Creek. The Mill Creek tract, it asserted, included an entire watershed, possessed superior trees, had only one timber company to deal with, and would be less costly. Fred Smith, an insurance executive with close ties to Laurance Rockefeller and the Redwoods League, warned Secretary Udall that a park in the Redwood Creek region would devastate the local economy and the timber companies. If Udall continued to listen to "conservationist purists" who wanted a sizable park, he could not possibly avoid a "bloody, fruitless battle." Conservationists, Smith continued, should seek measured rather than dramatic gains. If Udall tried to make the 1960s a "CONSERVATION ERA," there would surely be a backlash against environmentalism in the decades to follow.[7]

Though divided, many preservationists pushed for a large park along Redwood Creek. The redwoods, noted one, "are far more valuable to our civilization as cultural and recreational resources than they can possibly be in terms of wood products." The Sierra Club hailed the selection of the Redwood Creek site but considered a park of even 50,000 acres too puny, advocating a substantial park of 90,000 acres at a cost of $140 million. "We are certainly going to have our hands full with the Save-the-Redwoods League," noted one preservationist. "I only hope this conflict doesn't kill off the idea of establishing a worthy area."[8]

Influenced by the Redwoods League and the timber industry, President Johnson cooled toward a national park centered at Redwood Creek. Facing the same corporate pressure, the state of California also scorned the Redwood Creek selection. The Sierra Club, however, pressed their large park plan and persuaded John Saylor and Democratic California representative Jeffery Cohelan to introduce the first redwood national park bills in 1965. These so-called Sierra Club bills were introduced late in the session and failed to move, but the club considered them "instrumental in getting the task under way."[9]

Early in 1966, the administration proposed a compromise bill. Introduced by Senator Thomas Kuchel of California, the measure recommended a 39,000-acre national park made up of the Jedediah Smith and Del Norte Coast state parks; the Mill Creek watershed; and a 1,600-acre Tall Trees tract on Redwood Creek. Secretary Udall wrote privately that "the key issue is the political one. If we had 5 or 10 years in which to have a big battle, obviously we should try for the largest area possible on Redwood Creek. We do not have that much time, for the chain saws are at work every day. Mill Creek is the art of the possible."[10]

Preservationists rebuked the bill as a sellout to lumber interests. The park would be small, consisting mainly of trees already protected in the two state parks. And except for the small Tall Trees cluster, it excluded old-growth trees in the Redwood Creek corridor. They insisted upon a "redwood park to match the redwoods." Some Save-the-Redwoods League members and the timber industry considered the demand for a big park greedy and unrealistic, but the Sierra Club would not retreat from its position. The timber interests, said Ansel Adams, had a complete disregard for unsullied wilderness: "We are set forth as a group of selfish, impractical nuts who are out to 'get' the redwood industry. They do not seem to understand that we do not want to preserve the entire timber resource of California, but only secure an important area before all forest areas are turned into tree farms and second-growth plots." Faced with considerable controversy and a packed conservation calendar, Aspinall refused to hold hearings, and the Eighty-ninth Congress adjourned without acting on the Redwoods Bill.[11]

Meanwhile, throughout 1965 and 1966, timber companies, to the horror of preservationists, continued to log old-growth trees. In Del Norte County, the Miller Company chainsawed a swath of redwoods that bordered Jedediah Smith State Park. Secretary Udall condemned this as "spite cutting." To the south, in Humboldt County, the three timber companies ripped through treasured forests in the Redwood Creek area. Outraged citizens pressed Congress to protect the trees. "We have waited too long to save the redwoods," lamented one writer to the *New York Times*. "The densest and most spectacular forest on the face of the planet is about to vanish." On the House floor, Saylor and other representatives decried the cutting and warned the companies to stop. Due to public outcry and the threat of punitive action by Congress, the lumber companies agreed to a one-year ban on cutting in areas that held strong potential for federal protection, but preservationists realized that unless Congress provided park designation, the old-growth redwoods were doomed. "It's in your hands now, baby," a cheeky Californian informed Saylor.[12]

Early in 1967, during the first session of the Ninetieth Congress, more than fifty Redwood National Park bills were introduced in the House. The measures fell into one of three categories: the Clausen bill, preferred by the lumber companies; the administration measure, promoted by the Save-the-Redwoods League; and the Saylor-Cohelan and companion bills, championed by the Sierra Club. Don Clausen, a Republican who represented the Mill Creek area of Del Norte County, sought national park status for the redwoods without injuring the timber companies or the local economy. He proposed a redwoods-to-the sea plan including five state parks—Jedediah Smith, Del Norte Coast, Prairie Creek, Dry Lagoon, Patrick's Point—linked together by the acquisition of privately held lands along fifty miles of coastline. In all, he proposed a 53,000-acre park, of which 20,000 acres would be privately owned. The downside of the plan from the perspective of Saylor and other preservationists was that it excluded prime, privately owned tracts along Redwood Creek and preserved virtually no additional virgin-growth trees. Additionally, a highway would bisect Clausen's proposed park.[13]

The administration bill, introduced by Aspinall and others, proposed a park of 43,000 acres, nearly all of which would be located in Del Norte County. It would include Jedediah Smith and Del Norte Coast state parks, which would be obtained in return for the existing Muir Woods National Monument and the Kings Range Conservation Area in southern Humboldt County. Additional redwood lands, nearly 25,000 acres along Mill Creek and the coastline, would be acquired from private owners, mainly the Miller Redwood Company. The plan would also include the 1,600-acre Tall Trees tract along Redwood Creek. The administration bill would cost about $60 million.[14]

The Sierra Club bill, introduced by Saylor, Cohelan, and more than thirty other representatives, called for a park of 92,000 acres located in Humboldt County. It would include Prairie Creek State Park and more than 70,000 acres of privately held redwoods along Skunk Cabbage, Lost Man, Little Lost Man, and Redwood creeks. The estimated cost of acquiring groves along the Redwood Creek corridor from the timber companies was pegged at $140 million.[15]

To the relief of Redwood National Park proponents, Aspinall scheduled hearings on the bills before the Subcommittee on National Parks and Recreation in late June and early July 1967. Heretofore he had refused to schedule hearings, he said, because of the crowded conservation calendar. He cautioned park proponents to proceed slowly, to avoid seeking too much, and to keep in mind that previously authorized projects also required funding.[16]

Representatives Clausen and Cohelan explained their respective bills without much reaction from the subcommittee, but when Secretary Udall and his subordinates pushed the administration bill, Saylor aggressively challenged them, especially on the location of the park: "They have vacillated on this matter from one side to the other. I think it is about time we find out what they really want." The Park Service in 1964 had recommended Redwood Creek as the best site for a park, he declared, yet three years later the Interior Department was reversing itself and proposing Mill Creek. Why? Park Service director George Hartzog explained that the department had performed additional studies that showed that Mill Creek held the highest-quality trees; additionally, at Mill Creek an entire watershed could be protected. Saylor was not convinced and accused the Interior Department of submitting a "second-rate program." He argued that the Redwood Creek site would be larger; would preserve 23,000 instead of 7,000 acres of old-growth trees; and would protect three partial watersheds. "You know I am not going to debate this with you because I know of your devotion and your dedication to parks and I am grateful for it," Hartzog replied. But he would not concede that Redwood Creek was a superior site. Saylor asserted that the Park Service was permitting cost considerations and pressure from timber companies, not the quality of the redwoods, to dictate the location of the park: "The public is just beginning to be a bit shaky on whether or not the Park Service has sold out for dollars."[17]

When Charles Luce, undersecretary of the interior, seemed to disparage the Sierra Club bill, Saylor bristled: "You almost sounded like people from the Internal Revenue Service with the castigation and the inference in the tone of your voice." Luce replied that he meant no offense to the club. Later, when another witness implied that the Sierra Club was composed of extremists, Saylor said that "as far as I am concerned, the Sierra Club has never taken any position I could not defend."[18]

Saylor's performance won praise from big-park proponents. "I am all with you," declared subcommittee member Phillip Burton of California. And the Sierra Club devoted an article on Saylor's interrogation of Interior Department representatives in a special redwoods issue of its magazine.[19]

The House subcommittee delayed action on the Redwood National Park bills until it could tour the region during its spring recess of 1968. Meanwhile, the Senate passed a so-called compromise bill in November 1967, Senators

Henry Jackson and Thomas Kuchel proposing a two-unit park of 62,000 acres. The larger, southern complex of 36,000 acres would include Prairie Creek State Park and 20,000 acres of privately owned land in the Redwood Creek drainage region. The northern complex of nearly 26,000 acres would encompass Jedediah Smith and Del Norte Coast state parks, plus private land in the Mill Creek area owned by the Miller Redwood Company. To make allowances for the loss of jobs and tax revenues that would result if the Miller Company was forced out of business, the Senate measure proposed a land transfer. Miller would exchange its age-old redwoods in the Mill Creek region for the Northern Redwood Purchase Unit, roughly 14,000 acres of mainly secondary-growth trees in the nearby Six Rivers National Forest. The projected cost of the plan would be $100 million.[20]

Saylor and the Sierra Club were encouraged by the Senate compromise bill, but they preferred a bigger park and hoped to add 8,000 acres of virgin redwoods along lower Redwood Creek, including the Emerald Mile. Other conservation groups and Agriculture Secretary Orville Freeman were opposed to the Northern Redwood Purchase Unit exchange, deeming it a bad precedent. Privately, Secretary Udall supported the land exchange and eventually won over President Johnson.[21]

The House subcommittee resumed hearings on the Redwood National Park bills in northern California in mid-April 1968. For the committee, the trip to northern California was hardly a junket. It spent one day listening to residents of Del Norte County and another taking statements from residents of Humboldt County. In between, committee members toured portions of the proposed park. Morris Udall explained that Aspinall awakened them at 6:00 A.M.: "We go to breakfast and then we have a meeting and then we dash out in the field and tramp through the Redwoods. We go back to several hundred witnesses until 6:30, then the Chamber of Commerce has a dinner to make some points with us. If there is time between 12 and 1:00 A.M., it's all our own, we can do anything we want."[22]

Residents of Del Norte County generally favored Clausen's bill because the others would result in the loss of jobs and tax revenues. The federal government already owned about 70 percent of the land in the county, and any additional land withdrawals would harm the tax base and prevent the Miller Company from staying in business. Company officials declared that they would oppose any bill that did not include the transfer of the Northern Redwoods Purchase Unit.[23]

Perhaps because only 21 percent of its land was publicly owned, residents of Humboldt County proved receptive to the establishment of a national park in the vicinity of Redwood Creek. The three timber companies, however, insisted that enough redwoods had been preserved in state parks and that there was no real need for them to sell their old-growth giants for a national preserve.[24]

When Saylor and his colleagues on the subcommittee visited the Emerald Mile, they also inspected nearby hillsides where, despite the moratorium, the Georgia Pacific Company had felled ancient trees and scattered them for later pickup like bales in a hayfield. The visitors were sickened by the sight and angered that the carnage had occurred on terrain that Saylor had proposed for inclusion in the park. Company officials said that they had cut some redwoods that were likely to be blown down in a storm and others while "pioneering" for a road. The moratorium, they declared, was voluntary and applied only to lands proposed in the administration and Senate park bills. They later admitted that they had harvested at least two hundred trees. Saylor considered the actions contemptible, adding sarcastically that the company's answer to the "blowdown syndrome" was "if we cut them down, they won't blow down."[25]

Pressed by President Johnson and the American public to act before the opportunity was lost, the House subcommittee concluded its hearings in Washington, DC, in mid-May. At these hearings, Secretary Udall announced that Johnson was eager to establish a park and would support the Senate bill, including the transfer of the Northern Redwood Purchase Unit. The administration, however, did not want this transfer of national forestland to be considered a precedent. Udall also announced that Governor Ronald Reagan and the state of California would go along with the transfer of three redwood state parks to the federal government without getting any public land in return. California, however, did not want any park bill to ruin the timber companies.[26]

Udall reviewed the terms of the bill. It would include Jedediah Smith, Del Norte Coast, and Prairie Creek Redwood state parks, plus timber company–held groves at Mill Creek in Del Norte County and at Skunk Cabbage, Lost Man, Little Lost Man, and Redwood creeks in Humboldt County. In all, about 35,000 acres of the 62,000-acre park would have to be purchased from the timber companies. Udall, however, set a price ceiling for acquiring these lands at $65 million and cautioned that there would be no park unless Congress passed legislation augmenting the Land and Water Conservation Fund.[27]

Aspinall expressed delight that a compromise bill seemed imminent. The administration, the state of California, the timber companies, and preservationists seemed receptive to the compromise bill. Only the Forest Service was resistant because of the land-transfer issue. Saylor also was not won over. Like most preservationists, he supported a spacious park that included the Emerald Mile and additional virgin redwoods along its slopes. He scolded Secretary Udall for capping the estimated cost at $65 million. Instead of recommending an ideal park, he had allowed cost to set the boundaries. Udall stated that the committee could always expand the size of the park. "In other words, Mr. Secretary," Saylor said, ". . . this potato got real hot, and so you have tossed it over to this Committee." Udall replied, "I won't reject the figure of speech."[28]

Saylor painstakingly grilled each of the lumber companies on the extent of their redwood holdings in the proposed park areas, the proportion of old versus secondary growth, their receptivity to the Northern Redwood Purchase Unit exchange, and how the various bills would impact their business. When he finished, he said, "I know that there were some of you who dreamed that I would not be here this afternoon." Before they could answer, Representative William Ryan (D-NY) replied, "that would have been an impossible dream."[29]

More than a month after the conclusion of the hearings, the subcommittee met at a closed session on June 25 to hammer out a bill. Rumors quickly surfaced that the Senate proposal was going to be gutted in favor of a micropark. These rumors proved to be accurate.[30]

The subcommittee proposed a park of only 25,000 acres, including Del Norte Coast and Prairie Creek state parks and a nine-mile ribbon of giants along Redwood Creek. Only 7,000 acres of old-growth trees would be added to the national park system, compared to more than 30,000 acres of virgin redwoods under the Senate plan. The subcommittee scrapped the land-transfer scheme and excluded ancient trees on private lands along the Emerald Mile and Mill, Skunk Cabbage, Lost Man, and Little Lost Man creeks.[31]

Preservationists were stupefied by the subcommittee's decision. The Sierra Club called the downsized plan "shocking in its disregard for park values," pointing out that "it protects even less acreage than the lumber companies have offered to sell." The *New York Times* blasted it as "a craven capitulation to the lumber interests." And Representative Cohelan said that the subcommittee's "pathetic" proposal was so unworthy of the designation "national park" it was like calling "a tricycle a motorcycle."[32]

Sierra Club conservation director Michael McCloskey dogged the Interior Committee to add blocks of virgin redwoods, making the House and Senate proposals comparable. Representative William Ryan of New York, who had inspected Redwood Creek with Saylor, convinced Aspinall to add the Emerald

Mile and its hillsides, an area of about 3,500 acres. His earlier efforts to add the Skunk Cabbage, Lost Man, and Little Lost Man creek stands had failed by a vote of ten to seven. McCloskey asserted later that preservationists had the votes to add those drainages, but Morris Udall and Saylor failed to deliver them for fear of antagonizing Aspinall.[33]

While technically accurate, McCloskey's assessment of the actions of Saylor and Morris Udall is misleading. The evidence clearly suggests that during the subcommittee proceedings Aspinall and Saylor had reached an understanding regarding the handling of the House bill. In short, Saylor and Udall agreed that they would not seek to enlarge the park until it had reached the floor or they were at conference with the Senate.[34]

A number of factors dictated this strategy. First, with adjournment only a few months away, the Interior Committee had to move hastily to establish a Redwood National Park in 1968. Second, the committee faced a punishing conservation agenda that included not just the redwoods but the Central Arizona Project, the National Trails Bill, the supplemental Land and Water Conservation Fund, North Cascades National Park, and the Wild and Scenic Rivers Bill. Third, Aspinall wanted to keep the park limited in size to maintain his standing with the lumber companies and other resource users. Fourth, Aspinall insisted upon keeping the park acquisition costs down pending the outcome of the Conservation Fund bill. Finally, Saylor and Udall hesitated to buck Aspinall in committee for fear of jeopardizing the Redwood National Park Bill and their pet measures such as the Central Arizona Project and the Wild and Scenic Rivers Bill.

The full committee reported a substitute bill calling for a park of 28,500 acres at an anticipated cost of $56 million. Saylor and nine other members of the thirty-three-member committee filed minority reports stating that they intended to propose amendments enlarging the park. They made it clear that they wanted the groves specified in the Senate bill, plus the Emerald Mile and its hillsides. Moreover, Saylor and Udall emphasized to McCloskey that they had gone along with the plan only after Aspinall had "assured them" that the "bill would be reworked" in conference committee and that "they could then expand [the] boundaries."[35]

Pressed by time and abhorring fights on the floor over Interior Committee legislation, Aspinall did not push the redwoods measure with the Rules Committee. After consulting with Saylor and Speaker John McCormack, Aspinall announced that time constraints compelled him to send the bill to the floor under suspension of the rules. By bypassing the Rules Committee, the bill would require a two-thirds vote for approval and could not be amended. Saylor agreed to this procedural maneuver once Aspinall gave his word that he would not oppose expansion of the park when House and Senate conferees met to work out differences between the two bills. Though it appeared that he was backing away from his commitment to a spacious national park, Saylor was, in fact, nudging the legislation along. And his relationship with Aspinall was such that he knew Aspinall would not go back on his word.[36]

Unaware of Aspinall's private assurances to Saylor, supporters of a large park bill expressed outrage over the House committee's recommendation. Newspaper editorials strafed the scrawny redwoods bill as "an unconscionable outrage," "a blatant sham," "a mockery," "pitiful," and "a lumberman's bill." The Sierra Club called it "a stunning blow" and "a travesty on the national park idea." The club also took an indirect shot at Saylor and Morris Udall when it asked, "How could some of our best conservationist congressmen turn their heads away from these projects which they had previously supported so ardently?" Aspinall, in particular, came under fire. "In our system, a single man on a single committee may have enough power to single-handedly call the shots," declared the Sierra Club. The *Denver Post* accused him of a "sell-out." Representatives Phillip Burton, Jeffery Cohelan, Richard Ottinger (D-NY), and William Ryan criticized his maneuvering, which prevented the full House from working its will on the legislation. Burton accused the chairman of the "ultimate hustle." His action, he said, "borders on an abuse of the Committee process and the rules of the House. I submit that representatives of the people of this land have been denied their day and their voice in court on this matter regarding a unique and precious national heritage."[37]

In a classic understatement, Aspinall declared on the House floor that some individuals might object to his methods. However, with adjournment looming, "this is the only sure way we have of getting a redwoods bill passed this Congress." He pledged that he would "try to find in conference the answers by which the acreage can be increased to a reasonable and logical amount."[38]

Saylor defended Aspinall, stating that he was a man of honor who would not renege on a promise. Saylor expressed dissatisfaction with the scaled-down House bill but believed that a substantial park would roar back to life in conference. The goal, he said, was to enact a "meaningful" park bill that would preserve "the grandeur and inspirational qualities of virgin stands of these age-old giants in their natural setting." Realizing the votes were there, Saylor

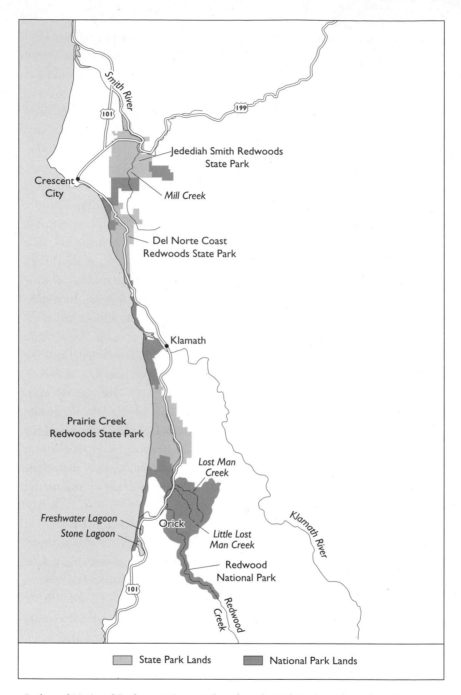

Redwood National Park, 1968. Susan Schrepfer, *The Fight to Save the Redwoods.*
Copyright 1983. Reprinted by permission of the University of Wisconsin Press.

urged support for the puny park bill but could not bring himself to vote for it out of principle. The bill passed by a tally of 389 to 15, with Saylor voting "present."[39]

As expected, the Senate rejected the House redwoods bill, thus necessitating the formation of a conference committee. The House conferees were Aspinall, Roy Taylor, Harold Johnson, Theodore Kupferman (R-NY), and Saylor. Henry Jackson and Thomas Kuchel headed the five-member Senate management team. Realizing that a gigantic park was no longer politically feasible, Saylor worked to save the best stands of privately owned virgin redwoods. He proposed a park of 33,000 acres located exclusively in Humboldt County. His plan, estimated to cost $85 million, encompassed Prairie Creek State Park and Lost Man, Little Lost Man, and Redwood creeks, including the Tall Trees unit and the Emerald Mile.[40]

While satisfied with Saylor's recommendations relating to redwoods protection in Humboldt County, the Senate conferees insisted upon adding coverage in the Mill Creek drainage of Del Norte County. Like the Senate bill, which it closely resembled, the conference committee report was customized to please the Save-the-Redwoods League, preservationists, the state of California, the timber companies, and the major legislative sponsors. Released in early September, it recommended a two-unit national park of 58,000 acres at a projected cost of $92 million. In all, the proposal would protect 10,876 acres of old-growth giants acquired from private owners and 21,000 acres of virgin redwoods in state parks. The state parks would be brought into the national park system upon approval of the California legislature. The northern unit would take in Jedediah Smith and Del Norte Coast state parks and a tract along Mill Creek acquired from the Miller Company. The southern unit of 34,717 acres closely followed Saylor's recommendation. The plan also called for the purchase of a thirty-three-mile coastal greenway linking the various pieces of the park and authorized the transfer of some 14,000 acres of the Northern Redwood Purchase Unit for 10,875 acres of timber-company lands. Finally, the plan authorized "legislative taking," meaning that as soon as the bill became law the private lands would be taken, even before the title had officially changed hands. This provision of the bill protected the redwoods from logging during the title-transfer period.[41]

On September 12, the House considered the conference report. Aspinall recommended approval, stressing the fact that the bill protected thirty-three miles of unbroken coastline in addition to the pristine stands of redwoods.

Saylor was forced to miss the debate to attend the funeral of his younger brother, Tillman, but Aspinall inserted his remarks into the record. The furor over the protection of the redwoods, Saylor stated, was but one example of the "environmental revolution which has aroused the American people to the sudden awareness of the rapid dwindling of its natural resources and the vanishing treasures of our American heritage." He expressed regret that cost considerations prevented inclusion of additional high-quality stands of virgin redwoods in the Redwood Creek corridor. Still, as constituted, the park would be a "notable conservation achievement."[42]

House members generally agreed with these sentiments. Even Phillip Burton and Jeffery Cohelan, two of the harshest critics of the legislative maneuverings of the Interior Committee, expressed praise for the House conferees for an excellent report. The report was approved by a vote of 329 to 1. Three weeks later, with Saylor and other champions of the park proudly looking on, President Johnson signed the Redwood National Park Bill into law.[43]

Along with Secretary Udall, the Sierra Club, and Senators Jackson and Kuchel, Saylor must be considered one of the architects of the Redwood National Park Bill. With Representative Cohelan, he introduced the first redwood park measure in Congress, and throughout the bill's tortuous three-and-a-half-year trek through the House, he steadfastly championed a meaningful park. In the end, his trusting relationship with Aspinall helped produce a satisfactory bill. When it appeared that the bill had been emasculated, Aspinall and Saylor actually agreed upon a maneuver to move the legislation and secure passage of an enlarged bill before adjournment. Although Aspinall never wanted a large park, he realized that public opinion and tenacious legislators like Saylor, Kuchel, and Jackson demanded one. By announcing that he was amenable to changes in the conference committee, Aspinall, in effect, was yielding to public and political pressure for an enlarged park. In committee, Saylor helped exert this pressure.

While some preservationists were unhappy that virgin groves along Skunk Cabbage and Redwood creeks had not been protected, most believed that Congress had produced a worthy bill given the budgetary limitations and the resistance of timber companies. (In 1978, Congress authorized the purchase of an additional 48,000 acres along these two creeks at a cost of $360 million.) A Sierra Club member from Minnesota wrote Saylor that "millions of Americans will be forever in your debt for your determined and courageous efforts which added thirty thousand acres to the Redwood National Park." He added in a postscript: "I feel I have reaped a large dividend on the admittedly small contribution I made to your campaign fund."[44]

After adjournment, Saylor returned to Johnstown to campaign for reelection. He could look back with pride on the conservation achievements he had helped to craft. The Ninetieth Congress had proved nearly as productive as the earlier "Conservation Congress." Besides the Redwood National Park Bill, it had added the first unit to the wilderness system; provided an additional revenue stream for the Land and Water Conservation Fund; and established North Cascades National Park, the Central Arizona Project, and National Trails and Wild and Scenic Rivers systems. A new administration and Congress would be hard-pressed to match these landmark achievements.[45]

fifteen

Congressman for Conservation

NATIONALLY SYNDICATED columnist James Kilpatrick expressed disappointment with conservatives for failing to take an active interest in environmental issues. Conservatives, he wrote in 1969, were growing in number, but they would never prevail politically until they shook their "image as the negative party." Instead of just criticizing, he asserted, they should take the lead in resolving the nation's problems. "One of the most serious problems in American society goes to the quality of life in the world around us," he continued. Rivers and lakes were polluted, cities were shrouded in smog, pesticides had invaded the food chain, and majestic landscapes had fallen to bulldozers: "The problem essentially is a problem of conservation—of conserving some of the great values of America; and conservatives, of all people, ought to be in the vanguard of the fight."[1]

Saylor shared this sentiment. He believed that conservatives, and Republicans in general, had allowed their zeal for financial restraint, small government, and commercial enterprise to blind them to "the deeper and more significant concerns of the Nation at large." He urged Republican leadership to "conscientiously" study Kilpatrick's remarks: "The hope of the party's future must be down the path of more affirmative policies. In my opinion, there is no better way to help change the conservative's image than by assuming leadership of the desire to preserve our natural and national heritage for the future."[2]

Saylor, as always, equated environmentalism with the national interest. Because it provided spiritual, physical, economic, and recreational value, environmental protection, for Saylor, was nearly as important as the preservation of freedom and private enterprise. Defending the environment, like upholding freedom, required constant vigilance, generous financing, and a relentless bipartisan effort. It sometimes proved difficult to be a friend to coal miners and to nature, but Saylor managed to please both the United Mine Workers and the Sierra Club. As a longtime green Republican, Saylor endeavored to serve as his party's environmental conscience and to prod his House colleagues and the Nixon administration into action. He met with only limited success, but his commitment to the cause of environmentalism prompted one of his Democratic House colleagues to refer to him as "the Congressman for Conservation."[3]

Because the year 1968 had been rife with violence—Vietnam, the assassinations of Robert Kennedy and Martin Luther King, street and campus riots, nightsticking at the Democratic National Convention—Saylor and other Republicans were buoyed by their party's prospects in that year's elections. Gaining control of Congress seemed a long shot, but the White House appeared within reach.

Saylor had never been fond of Richard Nixon, the Republican nominee, but he supported him for election. Nixon campaigned in Johnstown, touting Saylor, who accompanied him, for reelection as a stalwart Republican conservationist. John Murtha, a Johnstown attorney, opposed Saylor, attacking him for being out of touch with the district and for championing legislation, such as the Wild and Scenic Rivers Act, that hindered dam building and economic development.[4]

Comprising five counties after redistricting in 1966, the Twenty-second Congressional District held an edge of sixty-six hundred Republicans among registered voters. As usual, Saylor refused to debate on the grounds that it would give his opponent added publicity. He was endorsed by most district newspapers and labor unions. In the national election, Nixon narrowly defeated the Democratic nominee, Hubert Humphrey. The closeness of the popular vote was reflected in the Twenty-second Pennsylvania District, which Nixon carried by only eleven hundred votes. Saylor, on the other hand, defeated Murtha by twenty-seven thousand votes to win his eleventh term in office.[5]

Democrats captured both houses of Congress, so Saylor would not become chair of the House Interior Committee, a position he coveted. Rumors soon surfaced, however, that president-elect Nixon might name Saylor secretary of the interior. He was the party's foremost conservationist and served as ranking minority member on the committee that had produced the previous interior secretary. Other rumored candidates for the post included Representative

Rogers C. B. Morton (R-NC); Senator Gordon Allott (R-CO); and Walter Hickel, the Republican governor of Alaska.[6]

Preservationists relished the possibility of Saylor heading the Interior Department. He was, as one writer put it, "out in front" on the issues, "one of the best friends conservationists have in congress," and even more committed to park and wilderness preservation than former Secretary Udall. Many Westerners, however, shuddered at the thought of Saylor managing much of the nation's natural resources. He was "an arch-conservationist," who had opposed dams in Grand Canyon and was "closer to the Sierra Club than the Department of Reclamation," observed a Utah journalist. "He is unthinkable as secretary of the one agency that has nearly life or death say over the 17 western states, 15 of which went for Nixon.... Politically, it seems impossible that Nixon could name to that post any person not eminently acceptable to the West." This analysis proved prophetic: Nixon selected Walter Hickel of Alaska for the position.[7]

Hickel's nomination drew a flurry of protests from preservationists, especially after he denounced "conservation for conservation's sake" soon after his name had been submitted for Senate confirmation. Conservationists believed that he was too cozy with oil interests and unenthusiastic about environmental preservation. Saylor was cool toward the nomination because Hickel had once told him in a hearing that he believed that some spacious national parks, especially in Alaska, should be opened to mineral and timber development. Though preservationists delayed the Alaskan's confirmation, they were unable to block it.[8]

In spite of his own reservations, Saylor worked, with only limited success, to establish a trusted relationship with Hickel, similar to the one he had developed with Secretary Udall. He invited Hickel to visit his district in June 1969. Eager to win over Saylor, in part because he wanted his support for the Trans-Alaska Pipeline project, Hickel accepted the invitation, along with Alaska's senior Republican senator, Ted Stevens. Accompanied by the presidents of Pennsylvania Electric and the Rochester and Pittsburgh Coal Company, the politicians toured the privately financed, coal-fired Keystone and Conemaugh electric-generating stations. Sporting overalls, hard hats, goggles, miner's lamps, and crawl sticks, they plunged 450 feet underground to observe longwall coal mining near Carrolltown. The purpose of the tour, said Saylor, was to give "the broadest picture of what our mines and electric utilities are doing for the national economy and national security." Hickel said that he was particularly impressed with the efforts being made in the plants to eliminate "fly ash," an air contaminant. And Senator Stevens, in a statement that must have given Saylor pause, stated that he wanted to use western Pennsylvania as a model for resource development in Alaska. All in all, reported an official with the Pennsylvania Railroad, the visit was "quite worthwhile from a PR standpoint."[9]

Saylor also looked for other ways to promote his congressional district. The successful Apollo space program, especially the planned moon landing in July 1969, prompted him to ask the U.S. postmaster general to issue a commemorative stamp that would be sold first in the small town of Apollo, Pennsylvania. The only town in America with the designation Apollo, Saylor noted, was located in Armstrong County, which shared its name with the astronaut who first walked on the moon. Saylor's request was denied, so the town held a moon-landing parade, which Saylor attended, and its postmark became wildly popular. Saylor regarded the moon landing as "perhaps the greatest feat in the annals of time," but he did not want Congress to become enamored with outer space to the neglect of open space on earth.[10]

As always, Saylor mingled with constituents and engaged in self-promotion. He delivered speeches to civic, political, student, and outdoors organizations. He attended the forty-fifth anniversary of his high school graduation in Johnstown. He declined President Nixon's invitation to attend the dedication of Redwood National Park in 1969, he said, because he wanted to visit with constituents: "There is nothing to take the place of meeting the citizens face-to-face and that is what I'll be doing most of the congressional recess."[11]

Saylor was quick to publicize the achievements of state residents, whether they be Scouts, students, beauty contestants, athletes, or a hundred-year-old couple who had celebrated seventy-nine years of marriage. He was photographed with prominent federal officials, astronauts, and of course the famed groundhog, Punxsutawney Phil. He sought to identify with farmers and gardeners by planting and harvesting potatoes on "Saylor's acre," at a local farm. He dramatized his vote against a 42 percent pay hike for members of Congress and other federal officials with a stunt: a Patton, Pennsylvania, hardware store owner advertised that federal officials who patronized his store would be charged an extra 42 percent for their purchases. Saylor then made a production out of buying a box of shotgun shells and paying the "penalty."[12]

Saylor hammered away at issues that seemed to resonate with the majority of his constituents: controlling imports, restricting the spread of pornography, reducing foreign aid, repealing restrictions on gun ownership, and curbing an activist Supreme Court. He sought tax relief for the middle class, railing against tax loopholes that permitted the wealthy to pay minimal federal taxes. He blasted as discriminatory a federal tax code that forced a single head of household to pay higher taxes than a married couple. He cosponsored successful legislation raising the personal federal tax exemption from $600 to $750. Guided, he said, by the pulse of his constituents, he supported a constitutional amendment lowering the voting age to eighteen but resisted another proposing equal rights for women because it would end chivalry.[13]

Saylor also labored assiduously to protect the interests of coal miners. When President Nixon in May 1970 appointed Richard Lucas as director of the Bureau of Mines, Saylor publicly criticized the move. Although Lucas headed the Mining Engineering Department at Virginia Polytechnic Institute, Saylor regarded him as unfit for the Interior Department post because he was heavily invested in mining companies and would likely be insensitive to labor. He asked to meet with Nixon about the appointment, but the president refused to see him. Publicly, Saylor criticized the president's inaccessibility, as would other lawmakers over the years. Eventually, Lucas withdrew his name from consideration after a newspaper columnist divulged that he had plagiarized portions of his doctoral thesis.[14]

Indebted politically to the United Mine Workers, Saylor hesitated to criticize the shady activities of its leaders, especially union president Tony Boyle. In 1969, rumors spread that Boyle had rigged the election against his rival Joseph "Jock" Yablonski. That same year, Yablonski was murdered along with his wife and daughter. Saylor refused to believe that union officials could be involved in murder. In 1972, however, Boyle was convicted of election rigging and misusing union funds by making nearly $50,000 in contributions to political candidates. Saylor was the recipient of an illegal $1,000 donation. In 1974, a year after Saylor's death, Boyle was convicted of having ordered a "hit" on Yablonski.[15]

Representing a district with the second most active coal mines in the state, Saylor recognized the political benefits of advocating legislation to improve the health and working conditions of miners. When conservative lawmakers sought to deny food stamps to striking coal miners in 1969, he joined with liberals to foil the effort. He and other legislators from coal-mining states teamed with liberals again to push for legislation providing monetary benefits to miners who had been disabled by pneumoconiosis. Usually called "black lung," the now rare grievous disease, which steals oxygen from pulmonary blood vessels, is caused by breathing coal dust over several years' time. In a House speech, Saylor recalled in his boyhood observing men with "miner's cough," or "miner's asthma," as it was then called, pausing to battle for breath as they trudged home from work.[16]

Because it was difficult to verify black lung, states usually denied claims for disability payment under the workmen's compensation program. Ultraliberal Phillip Burton, the driving force behind the bill even though his San Francisco district contained no coal mines, singled out Saylor for his zealous efforts. Saylor, Burton noted, was instrumental in persuading many skeptical colleagues that the measure would not establish a precedent for having the federal government assume the states' responsibility for all workmen's compensation claims. The black lung bill was a singular exception. Once coal dust had been eliminated from the mines through ventilation devices, as required in the bill, the disease would be conquered, and the program could be terminated.[17]

Enacted in late December 1969, the Coal Mine Health and Safety Act provided disability payments of $136 per month to disabled miners. If a miner suffered symptoms and X-rays could not detect the disease, it would be presumed that coal dust had caused the illness if a claimant had worked in the mines for at least ten years. Saylor was pleased to report that in its first year the program paid more than $500 million in benefits to nearly 112,000 claimants, 59 percent of whom lived in Pennsylvania.[18]

Saylor also consistently supported federal efforts to regulate coal strip mining. While some environmentalists like Phillip Burton preferred to ban strip mining, Saylor and most other lawmakers insisted that surface coal mining was essential to meet the nation's energy needs. He argued that with stringent regulations and a program to redeem decimated lands, strip mining could dovetail with environmentalism. In 1972, he championed a bill providing federal regulations over surface mining. It required permits from the Interior Department and bonds to insure reclamation of disfigured lands, prohibited strip mining on sharply sloped terrain, and established a $100 million fund to restore previously stripped lands. Opponents of the legislation, like Wayne Aspinall, argued that the regulations and bureaucratic paperwork would drive out small operators and destroy the jobs of thousands of miners. The bill passed the House by a vote of 265 to 75 but died in the Senate. It took five more years for a similar bill to become law.[19]

By the late 1960s, environmentalism had become a raging movement, especially among youth. "Environment May Eclipse Vietnam as a College Issue," read the title of a *Los Angeles Times* column. Saylor was pleased by the mass support for a cause he had long championed, often with few congressional allies. He welcomed young people so long as they did not sully the cause by using violent tactics or advocating socialism. Saylor was distressed by campus unrest. Always fearful of internal subversion, he denounced the New Left as "modern Marxists" who sought to bring down the capitalist system. He believed that the Students for a Democratic Society and other campus radicals who violently protested the Vietnam War should lose their federal scholarships and be expelled from college. When critics assailed J. Edgar Hoover for spying activities that violated the civil rights of student protesters, Saylor defended the FBI director. "The bureau is keeping watch on the activities of the bombers, radicals, revolutionaries, in short, the nuts whose aim is the fabric of American society," he asserted. "Mr. Hoover is worth a legion of lefties."[20]

He warned middle America to "reverse the present trend toward a total, national-pollution caused economic and social breakdown" that might endanger democracy and human survival. At a press conference in early December 1969, Saylor and eight other representatives announced their intent to make the 1970s the Environmental Decade. Without a crash program to clean up the environment, Saylor argued, humankind might become extinct. He promised to prod the administration to request adequate funding to purify the air and water and preserve more open space. While some federal agencies were working to green America, others, such as the Department of Transportation, were "trying to put everything under concrete." The president, he said, needed an advisory group with the power "to knock heads among government agencies to protect our environment."[21]

Saylor strongly supported the National Environmental Protection Act (NEPA). Enacted in late December 1969, this "landmark" measure asserted as a national goal the protection of the environment and the interconnectedness of humans and nature. It established a three-member Council of Environmental Quality (CEQ) to formulate environmental policy in the executive department. NEPA also required federal agencies to prepare and publicize statements detailing the environmental impact of proposed development projects. If citizens were unsuccessful in public hearings, they could challenge in court projects they considered inimical to their environment.[22]

Saylor was heartened when President Nixon in early February 1970 delivered to Congress a special message on the environment. The president called for a national campaign to clean the water, purify the air, beautify the countryside, and acquire more open space. That call to action, Saylor beamed, might become the most momentous speech of the 1970s. He was also pleased when Nixon, by executive order, created the Environmental Protection Agency (EPA) as a complement to the Council of Environmental Quality. The CEQ would shape environment policy, and the EPA would see that its policies relating to pollution abatement were implemented. While pleased with the administration's environmental initiatives, Saylor worried that the momentum would not be sustained. "To date," he said in April 1970, "the environmental concern is a fad. When the American people are asked to pay for cleaning up and restoring the natural landscape, then we will discover if there is a real environmental concern that can move legislation." For Saylor, protecting the environment was more deserving of federal funding than welfare, education, or "foreign-aid giveaways." He feared that it might take the environmental equivalent of a Pearl Harbor or Sputnik "to move Congress and the administration to effective action."[23]

Saylor's commitment to earth stewardship did not go unnoticed by young people. Suddenly, he found himself "discovered" and in demand as a speaker and writer. A group of young Pennsylvania Republicans asked him to contribute an essay on environmental problems to their newsletter. He agreed and urged Republicans to become activists, especially at the grassroots level. "Environmental pollution is first and foremost a local problem," he stated. "Before a stream is dammed, a road built, an airport sited, or a power plant constructed, all options must be weighed, and not just by governmental officials—by you." He asked his reading audience to take a pledge vowing "to identify and overcome all that degrades our earth, our skies, our water, and the living things therein."[24]

Perhaps the most dramatic public expression of the new environmentalism was the celebration of the first Earth Day on April 22, 1970. On that day perhaps as many as twenty million Americans from all walks of life gathered on college campuses, city squares, and town greens to demonstrate their support for earth stewardship. Saylor was asked to be the featured speaker at Pennsylvania State University.[25]

A few days before the Earth Day celebration, the Penn State campus had erupted in violence over the Vietnam War, so Saylor was in a testy mood when he addressed the three hundred students who gathered in the Hetzel Union. "I don't know what you expected of your Earth-Week kick-off speaker," he began. "If you expected him to tell you to man the barricades, burn down billboards, clog telephone lines, occupy buildings, beat-up policemen, carry signs and banners, stage sit-ins or sit-downs, wear gas masks, and other childish nonsense, all in the name of conservation—then you will be disappointed. Very frankly, there is already too much of the revolutionary motif in the student environmental movement to suit my tastes." He urged students not to become "swept up in the oratorical fervor of the New Hitlerites," as he termed the New Left. "The revolutionary underground is not dedicated to saving the environment," he asserted. "The price of revolution is destruction, plain and simple—not preservation, conservation, or ecological balance." He implored his listeners to work within the system: "As I see it, your job as students and beyond student life is to bring middle America around to the point where they, too, see the dangers facing their way of life if uncontrolled pollution is allowed to continue." Sounding at times more like the acerbic vice president, Spiro Agnew, than a passionate environmental advocate, Saylor received a polite but unenthusiastic response. A week later, students at Penn State and more than four hundred other college campuses exploded in anger when Nixon widened the war by ordering an invasion of Cambodia. When four students were gunned down at Kent State University, Saylor callously attributed their deaths not to the Ohio National Guard, but to the American public for being too tolerant of violent dissent.[26]

Saylor gave more heed to the degradation of the environment than he did to the nation's deteriorating position in Vietnam, and he was far more critical of Nixon's environmental policies than of his conduct of the war. Saylor considered water pollution to be the nation's most serious environmental problem. Streams and lakes had become polluted by petroleum, detergents, pesticides, sewage, and mining refuse. Because it was essential to sustain life, clean water, he told a group of constituents, was more valuable than all the coal mined in the state.[27]

A legislative proposal to improve water quality standards earned his enthusiastic support. Passed in 1970, the Water Quality Improvement Act made oil companies and oil-transporting vessels financially liable for spills. It called for criminal penalties for company and vessel authorities who failed to report spills and ordered the interior secretary to establish standards regulating the discharge of human waste from vessels. It demanded permits and assurances from contractors that bridges and power plants would not pollute waterways and provided $412.5 million to study and clean up polluted water.[28]

Two years later, Saylor helped push through Congress another Clean Water Bill, which transferred authority over water pollution abatement from the states to the federal government. It demanded water quality standards by 1981 that would not endanger fish or wildlife and called for the expenditure of $18 billion from 1973 through 1975 to assist states in the treatment of wastewater.

When the president vetoed the measure, Saylor supported the successful congressional override.[29]

Air degradation was another pressing environmental problem. Air quality laws enacted in the mid-1960s had proved ineffective for a variety of reasons. Consequently Congress, in 1970, moved to strengthen them. The legislation set nationwide air quality standards from stationary sources, such as industrial and electrical power plants, and from moving sources such as automobiles. The Environmental Protection Agency would set permissible emission levels for carbon monoxide, nitrogen oxide, ozone, particulate matter, and sulfur dioxide. The legislation also established emission standards for new automobiles. Finally, the measure provided $109 million to help states meet air quality standards. With Saylor in full support, the Clean Air Act amendments were passed and signed into law in late December 1970. "John Saylor will forever be remembered by the Conservation and Environmental organizations for his effective and ardent support of these landmark pieces of legislation," recalled a former environmental leader.[30]

Saylor's support for the Clean Water and Clean Air acts demonstrates his genuine commitment to environmentalism. Representing a district whose mines and smokestacks routinely polluted the environment, he urged the coal and utility industries to work with scientists and environmentalists to find corrective measures. Such measures would be expensive, but "this is one of the prices people must pay for the proper use of our land." Politically, Saylor could take a forthright stand against pollution because district coal and utility operators recognized that even though he was "an avowed conservationist," he was also "the only person that we can get real help from in our [congressional] delegation."[31]

An environmentalist and fiscal conservative, Saylor blasted the administration for recommending federal subsidization of the Supersonic Transport (SST). Designed by Boeing Aircraft, the proposed SST could propel three hundred passengers across the Atlantic Ocean in about two hours. Environmentalists opposed the use of the speedy aircraft because it produced foul emissions and thunderous noise from its engines and a sonic boom. Saylor criticized the project on philosophical and financial grounds. Private investors, not American taxpayers, should finance the "Super Subsidy Transport," as he called it. He also decried as exorbitant the projected cost of $290 million, especially when Congress had authorized less than half that amount to purify the air: "Only $109 million to clean up the air and $290 million to dirty it up again. Really, now, does the administration think that the public will buy a super subsidy for the SST and at the same time believe what they hear about the administration's 'commitment' to cleaning up the environment? I think not, my friends." In what some people regarded as a litmus test for environmentalism, Saylor voted with a narrow majority to deny funding for the project.[32]

Protecting wildlife and its habitat was integral to Saylor's sense of earth stewardship. Like many preservationists who were hunters and anglers, he saw no irony in protecting wildlife so it could be pursued as sport. On one well-publicized occasion, he protected ducks, and the opportunity to hunt them, from a proposed construction project. In the early 1960s, the Teamster's Union had purchased nine acres of marshland at the confluence of Hunting Creek and the Potomac River in Virginia with the idea of filling it and selling it for development of an office complex. The union expected its initial investment of $15,000 to return $1.3 million.

Saylor pounded the project, in part because the marsh was located along a waterfowl flyway that he occasionally hunted. Initially, the Interior Department refused to grant a permit to backfill the property because it served as waterfowl habitat, but succumbing to persistent union pressure, the Interior Department later reversed its decision. When Saylor protested, a union official warned him "to keep your nose out of this affair." Incensed, Saylor telephoned Secretary Hickel and threatened to call for public hearings on the matter. Hickel scuttled the scheme.[33]

Saylor also battled to protect endangered wildlife. He supported successful legislation to safeguard whales, seals, sea lions, and other threatened marine mammals. He also backed another noncontroversial bill to protect wild horses and burros as "living symbols of the West" and fought to protect wolves and other predators.[34]

An NBC television documentary showing men shooting wolves from a helicopter enraged Saylor and the American public. He denounced the "low breed" of humanity who used aircraft to hunt wolves and eagles. "Such activity, he said, "churns the stomach." He and David Obey (D-WI) introduced legislation to prohibit it. On the House floor, Saylor pointed out that only five thousand wolves remained in North America, mainly in Alaska. Over the previous four years, four thousand wolves had been killed in a "blatant crime against nature." In a sarcastic editorial, the *Anchorage Daily Times* thanked "Alaska's congressman from Pennsylvania" for protecting Alaska residents from themselves, accusing him of trying to turn Alaska into a zoo and advising him to tend to Pennsylvania-related wildlife issues. The bill passed the House but died in the Senate.[35]

Undeterred, Saylor, Obey, and several cosponsors reintroduced the bill early in 1971. Only a few days before, NBC had televised another documentary depicting hunters using helicopters to pursue polar bears. A writer with *Field and Stream* accused NBC of trying to "blacken" hunting and blasted Saylor for "grandstanding and headline hunting." But preservationists, including avid hunters, rushed to defend Saylor. "Surely you know what a great job he has done on conservation," wrote the head of Trout Unlimited. If nothing else, he had helped restrain Wayne Aspinall, and "that alone should endear John Saylor to all lovers of the outdoors."[36]

The revised anti–sky hunting bill was nearly identical to the earlier version. It called for criminal penalties for "cowards" who hunted or harassed birds and other animals from an aircraft. Some legislators objected to the measure philosophically because it brought federal intrusion into state wildlife management. Others, mainly Westerners, feared that ranchers would not be permitted to protect their livestock from predators.[37]

But Saylor and other preservationists overcame the opposition by pointing out that over the past year not only wolves but seven hundred bald and golden eagles had been shot in Colorado and Wyoming. Another twenty-three had been inadvertently exterminated by the Interior Department's Division of Wildlife when it distributed poison to kill coyotes. He lashed out at sky hunting and the Interior Department's predator-control program, which purposely poisoned coyotes, wolves, mountain lions, bobcats, and badgers: "The war on predators has been waged with little scientific knowledge of their beneficial roles, or with little moral or ethical consideration for man's responsibility in conserving life as an integral part of the environment." He demanded the termination of the federal predator-control program and swift passage of the anti–sky hunting bill. Given the emotional outcry over the destruction of eagles and wolves, Saylor's bill passed both houses handily in 1971, and the following year President Nixon issued an executive order prohibiting federal agencies from using poison for predator control.[38]

Overall, however, Saylor had begun to question the president's commitment to environmental preservation early on. He was especially disenchanted with policies relating to public land use. When the timber and housing industries complained about lumber shortages, for example, the Agriculture Department moved to open up more national forestland to cutting. Saylor and other preservationists protested this action because it permitted cutting in areas that were being considered for inclusion in the wilderness program. In the Wilderness Act of 1964, Congress had mandated that the Forest Service, over ten years' time, review all sizable federal forest "primitive" and "roadless" tracts for possible preservation. When the Forest Service then authorized cutting in some of these study areas, preservationists obtained a court order to stop it.[39]

Citing sagging supplies and spiraling prices, the timber industry sought legislation to accelerate cutting in 93 million acres of national forestland that were not scheduled for wilderness review. Saylor and other preservationists denounced the proposed Timber Supply Bill because accelerated cutting and haul roads would detract from other uses such as hunting, fishing, recreation, and watershed protection. Moreover, such practices would destroy the hope of establishing any of those corrupted lands as national parks or wilderness areas. "It is incredible that the first environmental bill to be considered by Congress in this decade of the environment is one that will denude major watersheds and rape our great national forests," Saylor thundered in a House speech.[40]

Owing to stiff opposition, representatives from major logging states revised the bill to make it more conservation friendly. The modified bill proposed the establishment of a fund from timber-cutting leases that would be used to serve the multiple needs of recreation, forest growth, watershed protection and soil stabilization. The revised bill, however, did not mollify preservationists. Saylor called it "sick," "half-baked," and a "well-camouflaged attack on the national forests." He denied the existence of a timber crisis. If there were severe shortages, then why would timber companies continue to export lumber to Japan? he asked. The real crisis, said Saylor, was the fact that the Forest Service had given priority to logging instead of balanced use and environmental quality. When the administration endorsed the bill, Saylor accused it of "dancing to the industry's tune." The House killed the bill by a vote of 229 to 150.[41]

Although he rarely rebuked committee chairman Aspinall publicly, Saylor did so when addressing his position on public land use. At a White House ceremony in June 1970, Aspinall delivered to President Nixon *One Third of a Nation*, a lengthy study prepared by the Public Land Law Review Committee (PLLRC). In 1964, Aspinall had demanded the establishment of the PLLRC as a trade-off for his support of the Wilderness Act. Congress had established the PLLRC the following year and instructed it to review public land laws and policies, assess present and future pressures on the 750 million acres in the public domain, and make recommendations on how the lands could be managed to provide optimum benefit to the citizenry.[42]

The commission comprised six specialists appointed by the president; six members of the Senate Interior Committee; and seven members of the House Interior Committee, including Aspinall, who served as chair. Of the thirteen congressional members, only Saylor, Roy Taylor, and John Kyl (R-IA) were non-Westerners, and only Saylor, Morris Udall, and Henry Jackson were committed environmentalists. Aspinall's views toward public resources were well-known: he wanted to reduce executive control, increase congressional authority, grant states with large amounts of public land more input in the formulation of policies and practices, and give priority to resource use over preservation and recreation. Appointing Aspinall chair, noted *Sports Illustrated*, was "a little like letting a rabbit decide the disposition of a lettuce field," practically assuring that the commission would produce a report with a procommercial slant. Indeed, Saylor and Jackson were so dismayed by the body's resource development thrust that they refused to participate in a group photograph for the report as a sign of protest.[43]

Not surprisingly, preservationists pummeled the report after its release. Saylor shared their sentiments but waited nearly a year, perhaps out of respect for Aspinall, before speaking out. The PLLRC was a sham from the outset, he then told the National Audubon Society, because it was composed mainly of Westerners who represented mining, grazing, and timber interests. "On important environmental and conservation issues," he said, "I often felt that I was standing alone." Reflecting a position that had guided him since adulthood, he argued that the public domain was a national treasure that belonged to all Americans and that therefore the commission should have been more nationally representative. For Saylor, the most disturbing recommendation in the report related to timber cutting, particularly the section proposing that federal forests be managed "primarily on the basis of economic factors so as to maximize net dollars return."

While President Nixon did not endorse the PLLRC document, he embraced its recommendation on timber production. After Congress rejected the Timber Supply Bill, Nixon issued an executive order in June 1970 authorizing the secretaries of agriculture and the interior to step up cutting in the national forests to relieve the housing shortage. This directive infuriated Saylor and other preservationists, who accused the president of making an end-run around Congress. The directive, Saylor stated in a letter to each of his House colleagues, was intended "to do by executive fiat what could not be done legislatively." The federal forests, he insisted, were set aside to benefit the American people, not just the timber industry.[44]

Saylor took a similar approach toward livestock grazing on public lands. For decades, ranchers had been allowed to graze their stock on public grassland for a nominal fee. This policy, which Saylor denounced as a giveaway, often led to overgrazing, the destruction of plant life, and soil erosion. Secretary Stewart Udall in 1968 had ordered a three-step increase in grazing fees in order to reflect fair market value. The 1970 PLLRC report accepted the fair-market-value argument without specifically endorsing a fee increase. The policy, however, was unpopular with stock growers, and Secretary Hickel delayed implementing the second scheduled fee hike. Saylor and other preservationists denounced Hickel's moratorium as contrary to the public interest, and eventually, Hickel ordered the increase.[45]

Saylor, enamored with wilderness, also battled to set aside additional pristine areas. The Wilderness Act of 1964 had preserved 9 million acres, but that bill, which he had fought for so furiously, was only a modest initial step. Millions of additional acres, he believed, merited inclusion in the system. But Americans needed to overcome their desire to conquer the wilderness. The remaining wilderness, he argued, was valuable primarily for aesthetic, not economic gain. In wilderness advocacy, he made one of his few attempts to be lyrical: "Who would put a price tag on the stillness of a forest? What is the economic demand for the feel of a forest breeze? Who will give us a cost analysis of the sun shining through the trees at dawn?" Seeing wildlife was always thrilling, but who could forget the sight of a deer "drinking from a stream in the depths of a forest where the only sound is made by the rustle of underbrush against your legs?" Only in wilderness areas, he insisted, could people "hope to find that physical and mental change of pace which produces spiritual renewal."[46]

Saylor was distressed by the fact that only six areas, totaling 1 million acres, had been added to the wilderness program since its inception in 1964. Under the Wilderness Act of that year, the agriculture and interior secretaries were charged with reviewing eligible "primitive" and "roadless" areas and "wildlife refuges" under their jurisdiction and forwarding their recommendations to the president. In all, 140 units totaling 47 million acres qualified for possible inclusion, but the review process, which was to take ten years, had fallen behind schedule. Saylor also pointed out that Congress was acting slowly on the forty areas that had been reviewed and recommended for protection by the president.[47]

In March 1970, Saylor and several colleagues sought to take up the slack by proposing omnibus legislation adding to the system twenty-eight primeval areas that had "tempered and formed our national character." Congress added all but two of these areas to the program. The following year, he sought to safeguard another twenty areas, but that bill failed to carry.[48]

The administration's commercial assault on the national forests prompted Saylor to defend so-called de facto wilderness areas. Because they had not been categorized as "primitive" or "roadless," these national forest tracts had not been designated for review by the Wilderness Act, but Saylor and other preservationists argued that many of these pristine areas deserved protection in the system. At the request of citizen conservation groups, Saylor introduced legislation designating eleven areas totaling 800,000 acres for protection in the system. Ten of these rugged forested areas were situated in the West, and one—the Monongahela—was located in West Virginia. Saylor conceded that these areas had some timber value, but "watershed, wildlife, and wilderness values are clearly paramount." The bill failed to pass mainly because the Forest Service and the logging industry argued that if less than pure lands qualified, then 70 million acres of national forestland, one third of the total, might be brought into the system.[49]

Public opinion, however, favored the preservation of more wilderness. In 1971, Nixon's Council of Environmental Quality prepared an executive order giving temporary protection to de facto wilderness, but Nixon hesitated to sign it. Saylor urged him to shun the advice "of the faceless and nameless sycophants who abound in the depths of the Forest Service." If the president failed to act, he continued, then "conservationists and the public at large will have to believe that which is widely rumored—the timber lobbyists have control of the nation's wilderness system." Nixon never signed the order.[50]

As with the wilderness program, Saylor gave unstinting legislative support to the national park system. He fought for the establishment of new parks, monuments, seashores, and lakeshores such as Apostle Island (Wisconsin), Sleeping Bear Dunes (Michigan), Voyageurs (Minnesota), Cumberland Island (Georgia), and Gulf Islands (Florida and Mississippi). He sought additional appropriations to complete land acquisitions for Cape Cod and Point Reyes national seashores, for the Glen Canyon and Delaware Water Gap national recreation areas, and for Piscataway (Mount Vernon) National Historic Park. He also broke with the president to support the Youth Conservation Corps, a $3.5 million program to hire teenagers between fourteen and eighteen years of age to build campsites and hiking trails in national preserves. Saylor supported this effort because it reminded him of the Civilian Conservation Corps program of the 1930s, which "was one of the best things the Government has ever done."[51]

Saylor's views against dams in national parks were well-known, but he also guarded against other threats such as underfunding, overcrowding, road building, mining, and logging. He denounced "chainsaw cowboys" who clear-cut virgin tracts of redwoods that preservationists hoped to add to the national park system. "The clear-cut area near Skunk Cabbage Creek is one of the most arrogant displays of raw power and disdain for the public by the lumber companies that has been my sad duty to report," he told House colleagues. It would take perhaps two hundred years of growth to hide the scar: "Until that time, the beauty of the Redwood Park area will carry the mark of the profit predators."[52]

Claiming a shortage of lumber for housing, timber companies sought to harvest spruce trees in Washington's Olympic National Park. Saylor and other preservationists would have none of it. In a House speech, Saylor reminded his colleagues that no national park had ever been saved; there would always be attempts to exploit its resources or build more roads. Miners, dam builders, and road builders all threatened the parks, but "the prize for the most persistent assaults on the national park system has to be awarded to loggers. They never give up. As long as there are big trees in a national park, we shall never hear the end of loggers' demands that they be allowed to cut them down."[53]

A proposed airport near Everglades National Park brought screams of protest from the environmental community. Located in southern Florida, the 1.4 million-acre park served as a sanctuary to numerous rare species of wildlife. In 1969, the Dade County Board of Commissioners proposed the construction of a massive airport to handle jet traffic to the booming city of Miami. With runways six miles long, the airport would consume thirty-nine square miles of Big Cypress Swamp, which served as a major water supply for Everglades, just six miles to the southeast. The airport would also produce noise and pollute the air.[54]

When Transportation Secretary John Volpe approved the construction of a training strip for aircraft just north of the park, Saylor telegraphed his disapproval. The decision, he said, demonstrates that the "administration has turned its back on conservation, has broken its pledge to the American people to protect the Nation's environment, has caved in to profit and political pressure." Building the airstrip, he continued, would devastate the fragile ecosystem of a majestic national preserve. He predicted that the "nation's conservationists will rise as a body to trample on [the Department of Transportation] as your decision tramples on the public." Saylor's prediction proved accurate. Owing to overwhelming public opposition, Secretary Hickel and President Nixon came out against the project, and the airport was relocated. Congress also gave Big Cypress Swamp national protection in 1973.[55]

By the early 1970s, Saylor's reputation as a conservationist, while always strong, had reached an all-time high. In Congress, perhaps only Morris Udall and Phillip Burton matched his commitment to earth stewardship. If pressed to name the leading conservationist in the House, said William Springer (R-IL), he would select Saylor. The conservation editor of *Field and Stream* referred to him as "a two-fisted, fire-eating conservationist." And Saylor's colleagues made a point of emphasizing his dedication to environmental preservation when they honored him in 1970 for twenty years' service in Congress.[56]

Saylor also received numerous accolades from conservation groups. The Atlantic Chapter of the Sierra Club honored him in October 1969 for "unique service to the cause of conservation." Keynote speaker Richard Ottinger observed that "as one of the outstanding conservationists in the Congress," Saylor had demonstrated "that conservation can be a truly bipartisan effort and has played a leading role in shaping the most important conservation legislation of the past two decades."[57]

In 1970, the Izaak Walton League presented Saylor with a lifetime membership and its highest honor, the 54 Founders Award. Saylor was credited with helping to preserve millions of acres of pristine streams, lakes, and forests. Two nationally prominent environmentalists—David Brower and Sigurd Olson—were unable to attend the gala but sent congratulatory telegrams. Brower, who had been forced out as executive director of the Sierra Club and then become head of Friends of the Earth, wired that "whenever conservation has needed a friend in Congress, you were there, ready to help. The nation owes you gratitude for saving Grand Canyon and Echo Park, for wilderness and wild rivers and many more—and for giving us hope that Congress can respond to the conservation needs of our time."[58]

Olson, president of the Wilderness Society, wrote in a similar vein, hailing Saylor's "unparalleled contribution to sound conservation policy." "Millions of people have now awakened to the validity of principles you have espoused over many years in expanding our country's system of wilderness areas, national parks and wildlife refuges, in protecting other public land resources, and in your devoted efforts in the fight for clean air and water," he wrote. "It is a tribute to your foresightedness and your high level of awareness that you understood these principles and fought for them long before the general awakening."[59]

Saylor's most satisfying tribute came from the Sierra Club in 1971. That national organization representing seventy-five thousand members recognized him with its highest honor, the John Muir Award. Given to those individuals who had made major contributions to the preservation of scenic and wilderness landscapes, the award, over the course of ten years, had been presented to only one other member of Congress, Senator Henry Jackson.[60]

Saylor's work for environmental preservation represented "the highest quality of consistent legislative performance," noted club president Raymond Sherwin. "There is none who can surpass Congressman John P. Saylor in his record of persistent, effective action on behalf of environmental quality. He is the pioneer in legislation for clean water and clean air and the very practical matter of the adequate funding of such programs." Saylor, he concluded, "was the proper heir of John Muir." No other conservation-related statement could have given Saylor greater satisfaction.[61]

Perhaps because of the national environmental awakening, Pennsylvania newspapers emphasized Saylor's conservation record more than usual during his campaign for reelection in 1970. While the words *environment* and *ecology* were new to many Americans, remarked the *Kittanning Times,* they were familiar to Saylor. And though he had become "a latter-day hero" for his preservation work, he had "never forgotten his constituency." His opponent, Joseph O'Kicki, a Johnstown attorney, claimed that Saylor had passed his prime and should retire. What value was seniority, asked O'Kicki, if Saylor used it "to further conservation projects in the West?" Saylor, he declared, should serve his constituents, "not penguins and sea lions."[62]

As usual, however, Saylor won a decisive victory, outpolling his opponent by twenty-three thousand votes. The vanquished candidate praised Saylor for running a positive campaign and being able to connect with the voters. "Without question," he wrote, "your formula of personal letters to people over the past twenty years, together with your total disregard of the opposition candidate, has proved itself again." Saylor would use his mandate to continue to fight for his constituents and the national conservation interest. As the "congressman for Conservation," his main concern in the upcoming term would be to protect the people's stake in the pristine lands of Alaska.[63]

sixteen
Alaska

THROUGHOUT HIS LIFE, John Saylor had an abiding interest in Alaska. As a youngster, he was captivated by his father's Alaskan hunting experiences. He thrilled to descriptions of Alaska's majestic landscapes, abundant outdoor opportunities, and romantic frontier heritage. As a member of Congress during the 1950s, he eagerly supported statehood for Alaska. Like many Americans, he regarded Alaska as the last frontier—a vast, distant, rugged wilderness. Some of that unspoiled, resource-rich land should be made available for individuals and corporations to exploit economically; other expanses of natural grandeur should be set aside to provide inspiration, beauty, respite, and recreation for future generations. He promised to "champion the conservationist cause until I am satisfied that by tapping Alaskan energy resources we are not foolishly sacrificing irreplaceable values." Like many preservationists, he gave little heed to the fact that aboriginal Alaskans claimed many of these "irreplaceable values" for their own economic and cultural well-being.[1]

During the late 1960s and early 1970s, Congress grappled with two controversial Alaskan issues: the claims of aboriginal people to much of the land and requests from corporations to construct an oil pipeline. In return for rescinding their claim to all 375 million acres of Alaska, Natives—Aleuts, Eskimos, and Indians—sought a combination of land and money. Congress would determine the validity of the claim and the amount of land and money. At the same time, the state of Alaska sought to complete its selection of 104 million acres of public domain granted in the Statehood Act of 1958. Additionally, oil companies wanted an 800-mile sliver of crawl space for a pipeline. The issues took on urgency in the late 1960s because the Interior Department had declared, in effect, that the oil companies would not obtain a pipeline permit and the state of Alaska could not complete its selection of 104 million acres until the Native claims had been settled. Congress, then, had to consider the conflicting interests of Native people; the state of Alaska; oil companies; the American people, who owned nearly 95 percent of Alaska as public domain; and conservationists like Saylor, who wished to safeguard Alaska's pristine environment and preserve additional lands there as national parks and wilderness areas.[2]

Saylor considered resource development a greater threat to Alaska's federal preserves and primitive landscapes than Native land claims. Natives, after all, used the land mainly for fishing, hunting, and trapping, not commercial development. Earlier in the decade, Saylor and other preservationists had denounced the Rampart Dam project. Planned by the Army Corps of Engineers and pushed by Democratic senator Ernest Gruening of Alaska during the early 1960s, the proposal called for federal construction of a massive hydroelectric dam at Rampart Canyon on the Yukon River. The proposed $1 billion dam would stand 530 feet high, produce more electricity than Washington's Grand Coulee Dam, and create a reservoir larger than Lake Erie. It would also stymie salmon runs; flood five Native villages; destroy waterfowl nesting areas; and drown habitat for moose, caribou, and fur bearers.[3]

Senator Gruening pushed the Rampart Dam project as a boon to Alaska's development. Moreover, according to Gruening, it would not intrude upon any national preserve, and the Yukon Flats that would be flooded had little scenic value. But the project encountered stiff resistance both inside and outside Alaska. Natives opposed it, as did state sportsmen's and environmental groups. Nationally, conservation organizations denounced the potential harm to wildlife and the ecosystem. Even the Reclamation Bureau's Floyd Dominy, perhaps the most avid dam builder in America, ripped the project because there would be too few power and recreation users to justify its exorbitant cost.[4]

Saylor led the congressional assault. In a House speech, he called Rampart "North America's most northerly, most extravagant, and most absurd hydroelectric project." He would not support the project even if it could produce as much energy as the Northern Lights themselves. Cheaper, privately funded coal-fired plants could serve Alaska's energy needs for decades to come, he insisted. He and other outraged preservationists managed to kill the project in 1967.[5]

The Native land-claims issue proved to be far more complicated than the Rampart project. Because of its small population and frail economy, Alaska had obtained a generous economic package in the Statehood Act of 1958. One complication to emerge shortly after statehood, however, was that Natives and the state of Alaska claimed some of the same land. Over the span of twenty-five years, according to the Statehood Act, the state could select title, including full mineral rights, to 104 million acres of land that had not been reserved as national forests, parks, monuments, or wildlife refuges. Naval Petroleum Reserve Number Four (Pet 4), an untapped field of 23 million acres set aside by President Warren G. Harding in 1923, was also off-limits. The Statehood Act also granted Alaska 90 percent of the mineral revenue from those unreserved lands retained by the federal government but left hanging the issue of Native proprietary rights.[6]

Shortly after the state began making its land choices, Native groups protested that some selections conflicted with their claims of ownership. Inspired by able leaders and the Civil Rights Movement, Natives organized the Alaska Federation of Natives (AFN) to fight for their ancestral rights. On behalf of fifty-five thousand Natives, about 20 percent of the state's population, the AFN claimed 75 percent of Alaska in 1965. Fearful that Native challenges would disrupt the state's land-selection process and stall economic development, non-Native Alaskans, led by Senator Gruening and Governor Walter Hickel, urged the Interior Department to resolve the issue. Secretary Stewart Udall disappointed them. In December 1966, he imposed a temporary freeze that stopped the state land-selection process with 77 million acres left to complete. The freeze also prevented individuals and industries from using or leasing public land. In short, Udall locked up the public domain pending settlement of the Native claims issue. When the issue had not been resolved by the time he left office in 1968, he extended the moratorium for two more years. Governor Hickel filed suit challenging the land freeze, but the courts failed to overturn it.[7]

Native and non-Native Alaskans alike were heartened when the new president, Richard Nixon, selected Walter Hickel as his secretary of the interior. As governor of Alaska, Hickel had strongly supported swift settlement of the claims issue, even though it meant granting Natives 40 million acres of land. Providing Natives with a generous land base, so long as the acreage was not deducted from the state's share of 104 million acres, would end the land freeze and facilitate economic development, including construction of an oil pipeline. Worried about the pipeline's impact on the environment, conservation groups balked at the choice of Hickel because they did not consider him a dedicated preservationist. He also unsettled them when he stated, shortly after being nominated for the interior post, that if Secretary Udall could impose a land freeze by executive order, he could just as easily rescind it. At the confirmation hearings, Senator Henry Jackson compelled Hickel to guarantee that he would not revoke the land freeze without the approval of the Senate and House Interior Committees.[8]

The discovery of a massive oil field by the Atlantic Richfield Oil Company in February 1968 had intensified demands for a satisfactory and speedy settlement of the claims issue. This find was located on state-owned lands at Prudhoe Bay on Alaska's northern slope. Eighteen months later, the state auctioned drilling rights on the North Slope to various oil companies for $900 million. Atlantic Richfield, British Petroleum, and Humble Oil then formed the Trans-Alaska Pipeline System (TAPS) to deliver the crude oil.[9]

In June 1969, TAPS asked the Interior Department for permission to build an 800-mile-long pipeline, at an estimated cost of $900 million, from the North Slope wells to Valdez, an all-weather, deep-water port in southern Alaska. From Valdez the oil would be shipped by tanker to California. Besides the 100-foot wide, 800-mile-long swath, TAPS also sought a right-of-way for a haul road that would parallel the pipeline. While supportive of the pipeline project, Secretary Hickel passed the request for a right-of-way permit to the Senate and House Interior Committees. But the committees hesitated to recommend the issuance of a pipeline permit until TAPS had provided details on how it planned to safeguard the environment. Additionally, there was not then an energy crisis, so there was no sense of urgency. The resource had been in the ground for millions of years, Saylor said, so Congress should take every precaution to see that the environment was not put at risk in getting the oil to market.[10]

Meanwhile, in August 1969, the House Subcommittee on Indian Affairs considered three Native claims proposals. One, reflecting the interests of the state, proposed conveying 5 million acres to two hundred native villages, along with $100 million from the federal treasury and 10 percent of all revenue produced from oil, gas, and mineral leases on federal land over a period of ten years, an estimated $400 million. A state corporation would be established to control the money and determine who qualified as a Native. Another claims proposal, representing the position of the Interior Department, recommended conveying 10 million acres to two hundred villages, along with $500 million from federal taxpayers paid out over twenty years. A third reflected the views of most aboriginal people. To maintain their ancestral way of life, Natives said they required 40 million acres, which would be parceled out to two hundred villages. They also demanded $500 million and a 2 percent share, in perpetuity, of oil and mineral revenues from federal lands. Moreover, they insisted that twelve regional Native corporations, rather than one state commission, manage the money.[11]

Witnesses at the House subcommittee hearings in Washington, DC, were unanimous in supporting an equitable settlement of Native claims. They differed, however, in their interpretation of what constituted fair terms. Non-aboriginal Alaskans, including Governor Keith Miller, wanted a prompt settlement in order to dissolve the freeze and proceed with state land selection and economic development. Unlike Hickel, Governor Miller wanted to limit the land allocation to between 5 and 10 million acres and the monetary compensation to $500 million. He and most other state officials vigorously opposed the Native proposal that they share mineral revenues. Non-Native hunters, anglers, and trappers feared being denied access to lands granted to Native groups and insisted that the state of Alaska control the harvesting of fish and game. For their part, preservationists worried that large chunks of federal wildlife and forestland would be transferred to Native villages.[12]

Saylor was not very receptive to the Native settlement claims. He insisted that the federal government had gained legal title to all lands when it purchased Alaska from Russia in 1867. He maintained that he and other legislators might not have supported statehood had they realized that additional chunks of the public domain, besides the 104 million acres granted to Alaska, would go to Natives. Still, he wanted to avoid a lengthy legal battle and believed Congress had a moral obligation to compensate Native groups for the loss of their lands. At the same time, he wanted to limit the size of the conveyance because lands that did not go to Natives would be left to the American people. He believed that claims settlement proposals had considered only two constituencies: the Natives and the state of Alaska. But the third and largest constituency was the American people. Two of the three groups required land for economic sustenance, but the third needed it for inspiration and recreation. Alaska was a natural wonderland, a last frontier of wilderness that must be preserved in the national interest. Saylor resisted efforts to return portions of national preserves to Native groups and was reluctant to sacrifice expanses of wilderness that might become new national parks or additions to the wilderness system.[13]

The Senate Interior Committee, headed by Henry Jackson, ended its deliberations in 1969 without reaching an agreement on a bill. In the House, Wayne Aspinall hesitated to conclude without visiting Alaska to take testimony from Aleuts, Indians, and Eskimos. After a five-day tour of Native villages, and a flight over portions of the proposed oil pipeline route, Aspinall, Saylor, and seven other members of the Subcommittee on Indian Affairs held hearings in Fairbanks on October 17 and in Anchorage the following day. Not surprisingly, Native witnesses supported the AFN version of the bill.[14]

Some witnesses believed the bill would enable them to regain land they had lost for federal wildland or wildlife preserves. George King, an Eskimo from the village of Merkoryuk on Nunivak Island off the west coast of Alaska, complained that his people had been dispossessed when the island was designated a refuge for wildlife in 1929. Since that time, the Native people had tried without success to gain a town site on the island. "In other words, the birds, reindeer and musk ox have more rights than the people," he said. The federal government had not consulted the aboriginal people before dispossessing them: "In a way, the Government has treated the musk ox better than they have treated us. We have no land of our own. We cannot hunt reindeer except by permit, and we are only allowed five reindeer a year." The claims bill would enable them to regain control over their lives by granting them 150,000 acres: "That is not quite as much as has been given to the animals, but it is a start."[15]

Saylor commended the witness for an effective presentation but stated that "there is nothing in this bill that would say you would get land on Nunivak Island. You may get 150,000 acres, but it is not necessarily on that island. In all probability it will not be on that island." Representative Ed Edmondson won over the largely Native Alaskan audience when he argued that 150,000 acres of the wildlife refuge should go to Natives. Aspinall found the exchange disagreeable and ended it, then terminated the hearings without acting on any of the bills.[16]

On another front, Saylor expressed serious concerns about construction of the pipeline. He bridled at the arrogance of oil company executives who assumed that Congress would routinely approve their application for a pipeline right-of-way permit. When he flew over the proposed pipeline route in mid-October, he saw a swath of despoliation: oil and gas survey crews had bulldozed into the delicate tundra and scattered debris. "The things the committee saw were enough to raise the hackles on the back of even a bald head," he fumed. "After seeing all the work that's been done up there," he continued, "it's rather like coming to us after the horse has been stolen. The only thing left is to lay the pipe. The rest's been done."[17]

Saylor became further inflamed when he learned that TAPS officials had already purchased the steel pipe from Japan. Ever the trade protectionist, he believed that the pipe should have been purchased from an American company, such as Bethlehem or U.S. Steel. "Even if it cost them more," he said, "the TAPS companies should have bought the steel from American firms because it is going to help U.S. employment." Outraged, he told some TAPS officials that "you've just ruined yourselves as far as I'm concerned. I'm going to fight you every way I know how." When a bank executive reproved Saylor for economic nationalism, he refused to apologize for placing "the economic welfare of my own people and my country above any foreign nation." He later admitted that he had "pleaded" with oil companies to purchase the pipe from Pennsylvania. Domestic plants, he said, were in the process of retooling, but oil executives would not even take the time to explore the possibility that American plants could produce the pipe.[18]

Like most preservationists, Saylor also worried about the pipeline's effects on the ecosystem. Pipeline construction would require the use of heavy equipment and haul roads that would scar and rut the fragile tundra. If buried underground, the pipe would carry heated oil that could thaw the permafrost, producing a gully of goo that might impede caribou migration. An aboveground line might also affect the movement of caribou. There would be litter that would take decades to decompose in the dry, frigid climate; there was the threat of earthquakes; and the recent oil-well blowout off the coast of Santa Barbara, California, had demonstrated the danger of leaks.[19]

Saylor raised numerous red flags regarding the TAPS application for a pipeline permit. The request, he complained to Aspinall, had been submitted without sufficient detail about "what its effect will be upon the fauna and flora in the State of Alaska from Prudhoe Bay to Valdez." Moreover, the oil companies had failed to provide information on "how they expect to construct this line, whether or not it will be buried, or encased, and there is nothing to show what protection they will give to the assets of the Federal Government in Alaska." He recommended withholding approval of the right-of-way request until Congress had obtained satisfactory answers to these questions, taking a similar stand with constituents: "I know that the pressures are mounting to market the oil discovered in the Prudhoe bay area but I fail to see the rush since the impact on the ecology of the State is unknown. I am hoping that the

Interior Department and the oil companies will come up with an alternate route for the construction of the pipeline."[20]

Saylor also grew agitated by rumors that Secretary Hickel planned to open two federal preserves, Pet 4 and the Arctic National Wildlife Refuge, to oil development. He reminded Hickel of an incident in the early 1920s when Interior Secretary Albert Fall opened the Teapot Dome reserve in Wyoming to oil interests. One of the nation's nastiest political scandals, Teapot Dome would seem like a "Sunday school picnic" compared to an intrusion into the Arctic National Wildlife Refuge, Saylor claimed. Hickel assured Saylor that he had no intention of opening preserves in the Arctic Refuge to oil development.[21]

The concerns of Saylor and other preservationists, however, seemed to have little impact. In late 1969, the Interior Committees of both chambers, with Saylor the lone dissenter in the House, voted to modify the land freeze to enable TAPS to obtain a pipeline permit. Just because oil companies had invested heavily, Saylor grumbled, was "no reason for the Congress to lay down and play dead. We are just walking away from what I believe is our serious responsibility." In January, Secretary Hickel announced that he planned to issue the pipeline permit.[22]

In the summer of 1970, Congress revisited the Native claims issue, the Senate passing a bill in mid-July that granted 10 million acres to the Native villages, a $500 million monetary award, and a 2 percent royalty on oil and mineral revenues capped at $500 million. In short, the proposed compensation package totaled 10 million acres and $1 billion.[23]

The Senate-passed bill raised concerns among Native Alaskans and preservationists. Natives wanted more land, at least 40 million acres. Preservationists sought to protect existing national preserves and to prevent Natives and the state from selecting majestic landscapes that might in the future be included in the national park, wilderness, wildlife, or scenic rivers system. To date, no Alaskan lands had been included in the wilderness system. They also worried that revocation of the land freeze would trigger a mad dash for land and haphazard economic development and were distressed by the possibility that the pipeline would be built without stringent environmental safeguards. As usual, they relied on Saylor to voice their concerns in the House.[24]

As a courtesy, Alaska's Howard Pollock in 1970 had introduced three claims bills representing the interests of the state of Alaska, the Interior Department, and the Natives. He was unenthusiastic about all three but did not write his own bill, having announced that he would not seek reelection to the House because he wanted to be governor of Alaska and was challenging the Republican incumbent in the primary. His campaign for the nomination, which proved unsuccessful, took time away from his legislative work.[25]

At an executive session of the Indian Affairs Subcommittee, Aspinall asked Pollock if he had prepared a bill. "As far as I am concerned," the Alaskan replied, "we could modify the Senate bill and it would be perfectly fine—or any of the House bills. I could certainly draw one up, but I think we have to talk about concept. If we can establish a concept in about six or seven areas, then I think we can move very suddenly after that." Aspinall was in no humor to discuss generalities; demanding a bill with specific terms. Since Pollock had not done his job, the chairman asked Lewis Sigler, a Native specialist on the committee staff, to prepare a new bill that would be discussed after the August recess. Saylor supported Aspinall's recommendation.[26]

The subcommittee held several executive sessions in September to consider various claims bills but failed to reach consensus. Despite pressure from oil interests, Native lobbyists, and Alaska's two senators, Aspinall would not consider the Senate bill. And the new, so-called Sigler bill proved unsatisfactory to many subcommittee members because it was not generous enough to the Natives.[27]

When the subcommittee could not produce a bill, Aspinall called a meeting of the full House Interior Committee on September 24 to conclude legislative business for the year. At this meeting, he announced that the next day he was returning to Colorado to campaign. Pollock made a final plea for a claims bill. "I have worked as diligently as I know how to bring this matter to a conclusion," he lamely claimed. With only a "few hours" of additional work, he insisted, the subcommittee could work out its differences and prepare a bill. "Don't point the finger about working," Aspinall scolded. Pollock had returned to Alaska to campaign, and now it was Aspinall's turn.[28]

Saylor then noted that it was noon and that House rules dictated that committees could not meet while there was business on the floor. He abruptly rose and marched toward the door. As he passed Pollock, he snarled, "If you'd tried to help me anywhere along the line during the past four years, you'd have gotten my help." Pollock jumped to his feet and shouted, "You haven't been any leader as far as I'm concerned." Nearly homicidal, Saylor blazed, "I'll be around next year and you won't." Colleagues eventually calmed down both men, but Native claims legislation was dead for the Ninety-first Congress. "What a way for it to end," lamented a lawyer for the Alaska Federation of Natives.[29]

Throughout 1970, a number of factors had an impact on the outcome of claims legislation. Two lawsuits filed in federal district court in Washington, DC, prompted oil companies and the state of Alaska to reevaluate their heretofore strident positions on Native claims. One suit, filed by a firm representing five Native villages along the proposed pipeline, challenged Secretary Hickel's decision to issue a pipeline permit because the villages owned the land. Initially, these villagers had agreed not to claim ownership, but they reneged when oil companies would not put in writing their promise of preferential job treatment. A federal judge issued an injunction halting the issuance of a permit on the grounds that at least one of the villages deserved compensation. Conservation groups filed the other lawsuit, arguing that before construction on the pipeline could begin, TAPS had to file an environmental impact statement with the Interior Department, as stipulated in the recently passed National Environmental Policy Act.[30]

In August 1970, TAPS reorganized as the Alyeska Pipeline Service Company, its new executive officer announcing publicly that a claims settlement bill would be a precondition to a pipeline. Once Alaska business and government officials realized that oil revenues might be jeopardized, they united behind a compromise bill.[31]

Reforms in House procedures also ultimately affected claims legislation. Since the 1950s, junior members of the House had chafed under a system that gave senior members of the majority party almost complete control over committees. Phillip Burton and Lloyd Meeds, young liberal Democrats on the House Interior Committee, considered Aspinall despotic and staged a minirebellion. With the help of young Republicans, their efforts resulted in more autonomy for subcommittees. In other words, subcommittee members would no longer be under the heel of autocratic ranking members like Aspinall, and to a lesser degree Saylor.[32]

New players also emerged. Nick Begich, a Democrat, succeeded Pollock in the House. Alaska's first governor, William Egan, returned to the executive mansion in 1971. Rogers C. B. Morton replaced the headstrong and outspoken Hickel as interior secretary. And Richard Nixon took an active interest by recommending generous settlement terms in the spirit of Indian self-determination.[33]

Congress wrestled with several claims bills in 1971. In the Senate, Jackson submitted a measure calling for a 7.5-million-acre allotment to the villages, $500 million in cash, a possible $500 million in mineral royalties, and a statewide Native corporation to manage the compensation package. This measure also contained a controversial provision that placed a five-year freeze on the public domain that had not been selected by Natives or the state. Anathema to miners, this freeze was imposed to give the Interior Department time to decide what, if any, remaining public lands merited protection as national preserves.[34]

In the House, Aspinall and Haley introduced the Sigler-crafted bill, which essentially lowballed Natives. It proposed 1 to 3 million acres, depending upon the size of the ancient town site; $1 billion, including a $500 million cash–$500 million royalty split; and hunting, fishing, and trapping use, with Interior Department approval, of another 40 million acres. The Natives' bill, introduced in the Senate by Fred Harris (D-OK) and in the House by Lloyd Meeds, recommended $1 billion in money, twelve regional corporations as managers of the funds, and 60 million acres of land. The Natives increased the size of their land demand at the insistence of a disgruntled group called the Arctic Slope Native Association. The administration bill, prepared by the Interior Department, sought middle ground. It recommended a 40-million-acre conveyance and $1 billion to be controlled by a state Native corporation. Native villagers could take land for town sites from national forests and wildlife refuges, but not from national parks and monuments. This bill omitted the five-year hold on mining claims but reserved a twelve-mile-wide corridor from the Arctic Ocean to the Gulf of Alaska for a pipeline. Alaska's Ted Stevens introduced the administration bill in the Senate, and John Saylor submitted it as a courtesy in the House.[35]

James Haley, chair of the Subcommittee on Indian Affairs, held hearings on the Aspinall, Meeds, and Saylor bills in May 1971. At these hearings, Saylor made it clear that he had several reservations about the administration bill he had introduced. First, it was too generous in terms of money and land. He preferred to compensate Alaskan Natives at the same level as Indians in the lower forty-eight states: $1.25 an acre for all of Alaska, or approximately $470 million. Any amount over that figure might prompt Natives in the lower forty-eight states to revisit their claims. He scolded Secretary Morton for quadrupling the land settlement from 10 to 40 million acres. A significant portion of this award, Saylor said, should be deducted from Alaska's statehood grant of 104 million acres. He also objected to the establishment of a statewide Native corporation because it might dominate the state rather than elected officials. He also scorned the idea of twelve regional corporations because, condescendingly, he doubted that Natives had the competence to handle such a large monetary award. Like environmentalists who testified at the hearings, Saylor believed that there should be no settlement until the federal government and state of Alaska had developed a plan for land use.[36]

In late June 1971, more than six weeks after the hearings, James Haley convened the Subcommittee on Indian Affairs to fashion a bill. At the first meeting, Aspinall dismissed the Meeds and administration bills as preposterously extravagant. Saylor shared this view and wanted to proceed with the Aspinall bill. The chairman had made his bill slightly more palatable by increasing the land conveyance to 12 million acres. But Meeds had put together a coalition of Democratic and Republican members who refused to be bulldozed. They insisted upon marking up the administration bill, and Aspinall reluctantly agreed. But when the subcommittee voted down one of his amendments he instructed Haley to halt further sessions.[37]

While committee leaders held the bill hostage, Begich went to work cajoling Aspinall. Like Aspinall, Begich had been a schoolteacher. He was personable, attended meetings faithfully, prepared assiduously, and usually deferred to committee leaders. Wooed by Begich, pressed by the oil lobby, and aware that under the new rules the subcommittee could demand consideration of the bill by the full committee, Aspinall proposed a compromise. If the coalition agreed to support the bill in subcommittee, full committee, and on the floor, he would direct Haley to proceed. The coalition members agreed.[38]

In early August, Aspinall incorporated the compromise into a revised administration bill. It offered Natives 18 million acres of land neighboring their villages, which they had to select within five years. They could obtain another 22 million acres after the state of Alaska had completed its selection of 104 million acres, a process that might take twelve years. It recommended a cash award of $425 million and retained the 2 percent royalty on mineral revenues up to $500 million. Most important, from the standpoint of Native Alaskans, it proposed the establishment of twelve Native corporations to manage their assets. In Saylor's absence, the subcommittee unanimously endorsed the bill. Angered, Saylor chastised Aspinall: "In view of the fact that I have stuck with you on the subject of the Alaskan Native Claims, it is rather astounding to me that you have scheduled an Executive meeting on this legislation to complete Subcommittee action, knowing full well I am unable to be present."[39]

Saylor missed the vote because he had entered Bethesda Naval Hospital for tests that showed he had suffered a heart attack. He kept this medical information private, but his illness concerned preservationists. "No one in American public life," wrote one official, "has done more for conservation, consistently with exceptional judgment, than you have." Regaining his strength, Saylor acceded to a request from the Wilderness Society that he join Morris Udall in proposing a land-use planning amendment when the claims bill came before the full House Interior Committee. This amendment would prohibit the state of Alaska, but not Natives, from proceeding with the land-selection process until the federal government had completed a land-use plan, in five years' time. During this five-year period, the interior secretary could earmark 100 million acres as a study area to determine if it should be given permanent protection as a national park or wildland preserve. The amendment lost by a vote of twenty-six to ten, but Saylor and Udall agreed to reintroduce it when the bill reached the House floor.[40]

Determined to avoid in Alaska the environmental mistakes made in the lower forty-eight states, Saylor and Udall worked on a plan that would save additional expanses of the last frontier. They considered resubmitting the amendment they had brought before the House Interior Committee, but Udall doubted that it was "the horse we want to ride on the House floor." From a conservation standpoint, he said, it made little sense to permit Native groups to proceed with land selection, but not the state. And from a political standpoint, the original amendment lacked appeal because it delayed development for too long—five years for completion of the land-use plan and additional time for Congress to approve it. Despite these known flaws, however, the two men submitted essentially the same amendment. In the new version, however, they outwardly stated that they had no intention of blocking the interior secretary's authority to go forward with the pipeline.[41]

The amendment received avid support from the environmental community and the Eastern press. The *New York Times* urged the House to approve it because it would protect the American people's wilderness heritage in Alaska: "If 19th Century New Yorkers had not had the wisdom to set aside Central Park and the Adirondacks, does anyone suppose they would exist today or could be recreated at less than fantastic cost? The same question can be asked about the heart of Alaska's natural heritage. It is the last great unspoiled piece of America still within man's saving."[42]

When Begich learned of the proposed amendment, on the other hand, he wrote House colleagues urging its defeat because it would "upset the delicate compromise and threaten this legislation." Saylor and Udall responded with a letter of their own assuring colleagues that the amendment would not jeopardize the pipeline and would not reduce the size of the claims settlement. Saylor followed this letter with a House speech charging that the so-called delicate compromise did not protect the public's interest in Alaska. That state, he said, "is the great land, and a fragile, sensitive, easily damaged land. There are, in this great estate, areas of undisputed highest value as new national parks, wilderness areas, wildlife refuges, [and] wild and scenic rivers." Until these pristine regions were studied, it would be irresponsible for Congress to throw them open to commercial development. "Our responsibility," he insisted, "is to act as stewards of these nationally significant areas. This amendment is the vehicle to do just that."[43]

The House debated the claims bill on October 19 and 20, 1971. Aspinall, Haley, Begich, and other members of the House Interior Committee explained its provisions and advocated its approval. In a surprising move, minority leader Gerald Ford of Michigan read a letter from President Nixon urging support for the committee version. Saylor led the opposition, reiterating the arguments he had made in committee. For three years, he said, the administration had recommended a land settlement in the range of 10 million acres. Then suddenly, and for no logical reason, it had upped the award to 40 million acres. The monetary compensation also was too munificent; he wanted to cap it at $500 million. Saylor also criticized Aspinall for supporting a more generous bill without consulting him. Saylor believed the bill would bring devastation to the Native people. Their corporations would mismanage the assets, and Native stockholders would sell their shares after the required twenty-year holding period, leaving them impoverished. He made a strong appeal for a land-use plan and a national land-study area, as specified in the Saylor-Udall amendment. Representatives, he said, had two main responsibilities in the legislation. The first was a moral obligation to settle the Native claims. The second was a legal obligation to protect the public interest: "Alaska is the only place left under the American flag where we can plan before the land has been ruined." Without the Saylor-Udall amendment, he would not support the bill.[44]

Udall also spoke on behalf of the amendment: "You can be for the pipeline and this amendment with perfect consistency." He referred to the amendment as the most important conservation issue to come before Congress in the past decade. Failure to plan for future parks, monuments, refuges, and wilderness areas would be shortsighted because a decade hence, Congress would have to buy these areas from private owners. Why not set pristine areas aside while they were still publicly owned? In the end, the House rejected the Saylor-Udall amendment by a vote of 217 to 178. It then passed the claims bill, with Saylor opposed, by a tally of 334 to 63.[45]

Though the amendment had been spurned, Saylor was not disheartened. He believed that he and Udall had made a strong case for land-use planning and the preservation of additional primeval lands in Alaska. He wrote an upbeat letter to Udall thanking and lauding him for his effort. In praising Udall, Saylor, of course, was also patting himself on the back. "In all the years I have been in Congress," he stated, "this is the first time that I recall of a President personally interceding in a bill being considered by Congress." Indeed, not only the president but the interior secretary, members of the White House staff, the AFL-CIO, the United Auto Workers, the Seafarers Union, and the oil industry had battled them, and still they almost had won. He noted that a reversal "of about 16 votes [actually 21] would have changed the results and even though in a sense we lost we have established a record and in the days to come there will be those who will rise up and call you blessed for having the courage of your convictions and the willingness to fight giants in the cause of right." He concluded by reminding Udall of his belief that "victory only comes to those who are willing to get up off their backs and stand up and fight one time more then [sic] they have been knocked down. As for myself, this morning I am off my back, on my feet and ready to do battle again."[46]

Saylor was buoyed by the possibility that the Senate would pass a bill containing a national land-interest study provision. Indeed, he had helped bring this possibility to fruition. Over the summer, amid heated House subcommittee deliberations, Saylor had contacted National Park Service director George Hartzog, urging him to press an equivalent version of the Saylor-Udall amendment with Senator Jackson. Eager to add more pristine Alaskan landscapes to the park system, Hartzog readily agreed. Jackson seemed sympathetic but hesitated to commit himself without the approval of Alan Bible (D-NV), who headed the Senate Subcommittee on National Parks. Hartzog went to see Bible, who said he had never seen Alaska, so Hartzog invited him for a visit. That summer Hartzog, Bible, and Edgar Wayburn of the Sierra Club toured areas that were being considered as national parks and wildlife sanctuaries. Seduced by the scenery, Bible agreed to propose the amendment so long as it had Jackson's blessing. Upon their return, Wayburn and a colleague went to see Jackson, who asked for Bible's reaction: "He was told and we described the outline of what amounted to the Saylor amendment. He thought about it a moment . . . and then he said 'sounds fine to me.' And essentially that was that."[47]

As promised, Bible added the national land-interest amendment to the bill on the Senate floor. Approved, it required the interior secretary to forward to Congress his suggestions for new national preserves within six months. Congress could take up to five years to act on the recommendations. Meanwhile, Natives and the state could select sites in these potential reserves but would have to swap them for others if Congress designated them as parks or wilderness areas. The amendment set no cap on the acreage to be withdrawn. On November 1, 1971, the Senate bill passed by a vote of seventy-six to five.[48]

House and Senate leaders promptly appointed conferees to thrash out the differences between the two measures. The conference committee met nine times before agreeing. As finally cobbled together, the compromise granted Natives 40 million acres adjoining their villages. Outside the circumscribed Native village areas, the state could proceed with its selections, totaling 104 million acres. The state would provide Natives $500 million from its mineral-leasing revenues. American taxpayers, over the course of eleven years, would provide them with an additional $426.5 million. Fifty percent of the monetary award would go directly to the villages, and the other 50 percent would be managed by the twelve regional corporations. Lawyers' fees were capped at $2 million. The conference committee also established a ten-member Federal-State Land-Use Planning Board but gave it only advisory powers. In addition, it authorized the interior secretary to designate a pipeline construction corridor that was off-limits to Native and state land selection.[49]

In conference, Saylor, Udall, and Bible were successful in their efforts to add the national land interest as section 17. This provision contained two key paragraphs, D-1 and D-2. The first revoked the existing land freeze but permitted the interior secretary to impose a new one for ninety days. During this time, the secretary was empowered to scrutinize all unreserved public lands in Alaska and determine whether any merited permanent national protection. The second paragraph, D-2, authorized the interior secretary, within nine months, to temporarily set aside 80 million acres of public land for review. After nine months, he would forward to Congress specific landscapes that warranted protection in the national park, wildlife, wilderness, or scenic rivers programs. Congress then had five years to act on these recommendations. Natives and the state could make selections from the secretary's study areas but would have to surrender them for others if Congress designated them as national preserves.[50]

Section 17 would prove controversial. Alaska's congressional delegation interpreted the provision to mean that the secretary could withdraw a maximum of 80 million additional acres from the public domain. Saylor and Udall interpreted the provision to mean that within a ninety-day period the secretary could withdraw the 80 million acres and any additional acreage he considered to be in the national interest. In other words, D-1 could be played as a wild card. All the conferees except Saylor signed the conference report. Generally, he was pleased with the report but wanted to give the interior secretary longer than nine months to identify potential park areas, withholding his signature as a sign of protest.[51]

In the closing days of the 1971 session, the conferees sent their report to their respective legislative bodies. In the House, Aspinall controlled the debate for Democrats, Saylor for Republicans. Aspinall, Begich, Meeds, and others championed the conference report in the name of social justice. Saylor supported it in the cause of national wilderness preservation. He began one of his most eloquent and impassioned speeches by criticizing what he considered to be the exorbitant land and monetary settlement terms derived mainly from the lobbying efforts of oil interests. For Saylor, however, preservation, not economic development or social justice, was the transcendent feature of the bill. It gave members of Congress a chance to serve as "true trustees and stewards of the greatest expanse of virtually virgin, unspoiled land anywhere. The public domain in Alaska is the last great frontier over which we can exercise the truest kind of statesmanship, that which secures for all the people for all time, a priceless national heritage." If Congress approved the conference report, he continued, "we will have taken one of the single most historic steps in the annals of conservation in this or any era."[52]

Congress, Saylor insisted, should seize the moment in the tradition of Theodore Roosevelt and Gifford Pinchot at the turn of the century: "Today, we lay the framework for another opportunity of similar vast importance and perhaps even greater ultimate significance." He gushed at the possibilities. Secretary Morton could protect the Gates of the Arctic in the Brooks Range, Yukon Flats, the Wrangell Mountains in southeastern Alaska, and the Alaskan Peninsula. He could expand the size of Mount McKinley National Park and the Arctic National Wildlife Refuge. He concluded by saying that he had not signed the conference report but believed "it is the best we can do." "Very frankly," he said, "I am urging that the Conference Report be adopted."[53]

Morris Udall also emphasized the opportunity for preservation: "Those who stood with John Saylor and me in the fight in the House on the national interest conservation amendment will be pleased to know that, in my judgment, we got about 95 percent of what we were fighting for." John Dingell, another leading preservationist, also recommended adoption of the report and lauded

Saylor, "who once again has demonstrated his full and effective dedication to the cause of conservation and environmental quality." The House adopted the conference report by a vote of 307 to 60. Knowing the bill was out of danger, Saylor voted with the minority to protest the lavish Native compensation package. The Senate also approved the bill, and President Nixon signed it into law on December 18, 1971.[54]

Early in 1972, Saylor and Udall sent Secretary Morton an eight-page memorandum detailing their understanding of section 17 (D). As the primary architects of this section, they wanted the secretary to be cognizant of the "intent of congress" so that there could be "no possible basis for misunderstanding or unnecessary trepidation" when he implemented it. Paragraph D-1 enabled the secretary, within ninety days of the bill's enactment, to withdraw any public lands except those townships eligible for selection by Native villages. By withholding land from private entry or state selection, he could control the pace and extent of development. D-1 lands could be withdrawn in the national interest for an unspecified time period so long as Morton acted by March 16, 1972. They encouraged Morton "to make very broad and extensive withdrawals" under D-1.

Saylor and Udall also pressed Morton to take full advantage of the opportunity presented in the D-2 paragraph. Under this provision, the secretary could set aside as much as 80 million acres for protection in the national park, monument, wildlife, wilderness, and scenic river systems. The secretary had to exercise his option on these lands within nine months of enactment, or by September 18, 1972. He then had another two years to forward his recommendations for permanent protection. Congress, in turn, had five years from enactment, or until December 18, 1978, to act on the secretary's recommendations. Saylor and Udall urged Morton to freeze all 80 million acres. They reminded him that existing reserved areas such as Pet 4 and the Arctic National Wildlife Refuge did not count against the cap. Neither did D-1 lands. Indeed, Morton might choose to propose 20 million acres for a new Gates of the Arctic National Park. He could also set aside, under the D-1 provision, an adjoining 20 million acres in case Congress wanted a larger park. The adjoining D-1 acreage would not count against the 80-million-acres ceiling. They closed by declaring "the prospects immensely exciting" and urged Morton "not to forego this once-in-a-lifetime opportunity."[55]

Morton did not fail them. He withdrew 47 million acres under his D-1 authority and nearly all 80 million acres under D-2. Alaskans howled in protest. Senator Stevens claimed that the conference committee never intended the withdrawal of more than 80 million acres. The state legally challenged the secretary's actions, but in the end they essentially stood. Eventually these withdrawals served as the basis for the Alaska National Interest Lands Conservation Act. Enacted in 1980, seven years after Saylor's death, the measure preserved 104 million primeval acres in Alaska. By insisting upon protecting the nation's interest in wild Alaska, Saylor, Udall, and other preservationists provided an opportunity for a future Congress to craft what one historian has called "the greatest single act of wilderness preservation in world history."[56]

While helpful, passage of the claims settlement bill in December 1971 did not automatically clear the path for construction of the pipeline. Environmental obstacles stood in the way. In mid-January 1971, the Interior Department released a draft report on the environmental impact of the pipeline. This 246-page document recommended going ahead with the project even though it would pose environmental risks and intrude upon unspoiled wilderness, dismissing an alternate route through Canada because it was longer, involved a foreign government, and would only transfer the potential environmental hazard from one nation to another.[57]

The draft statement brought a gush of criticism, especially from environmentalists. They charged that the report failed to give sufficient attention to the possibility of pipeline and tanker spills, permafrost and tundra despoliation, the intrusion upon wilderness, and alternatives such as routing the oil through Canada or delivering it by railroad.[58]

Saylor too promptly ripped into the report. The Interior Department, he charged, had caved in to pressure from "the fattest, most arrogant segment of the American-industrial complex—the oil industry." Somehow oil barons had convinced the executive branch that "despoiling, polluting, and wrecking the wilderness which is Alaska's" was in the national interest. He ridiculed those who argued that the pipeline would destroy only a tiny slice of wilderness. To counter that argument he borrowed an analogy from Theodore Edison, son of the famous inventor, who said "it could be argued that a man could not be much affected by a bullet hole that would leave 99.9 % of his body intact!" Saylor introduced several bills to prevent construction of the pipeline without the express approval of Congress, but they all died in committee.[59]

New to the job, Interior Secretary Morton moved haltingly on the pipeline project. In February 1971, he assigned a task group to prepare a final impact report. Saylor suggested several subjects for the department to consider,

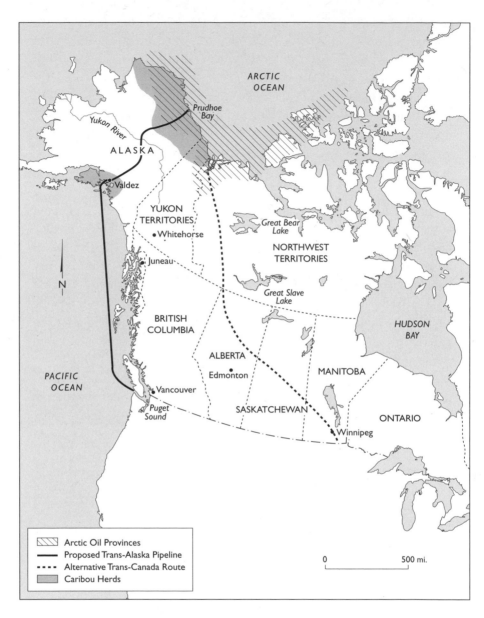

The Trans-Alaska Pipeline, oil tanker passage route to Puget Sound, Trans-Canadian alternative, and location of Arctic oil fields and caribou herds. Peter Coates, *The Trans-Alaska Pipeline Controversy.* Copyright 1991. Reprinted by permission of Lehigh University Press.

·such as the possibility of building railroads to transport the oil; snaking the pipeline through Canada, which would avoid the danger of tanker spills; examining whether the pipeline could survive earthquakes; investigating whether oil companies planned to ship the oil to Japan; and researching how the more experienced Russians built pipeline in permafrost.[60]

More than a year in the making, the final environmental-impact statement became public in March 1972. The nine-volume, 3,500-page study recommended an all-Alaskan pipeline despite the environmental risks and imposition upon wilderness. Preservationists protested, but Secretary Morton announced that he would approve a pipeline permit in May 1972.[61]

Satisfied that the final impact document had met NEPA requirements, the federal district court removed the injunction against the pipeline. Lawyers for preservationist groups promptly appealed the ruling. After several months, the court of appeals in early February 1973 reversed the lower court on the grounds that the Mineral Leasing Act of 1920 set a maximum of fifty-four feet for the width of a pipeline. The proposed line in Alaska was nearly twice the legal size. If the oil companies wanted more pipeline room, they would need the approval of Congress. The appellate court reserved judgment on the worthiness of the impact statement.[62]

With the Watergate scandal and the energy crisis serving as a backdrop, Congress held hearings on pipeline right-of-way legislation in the spring of 1973. From April through mid-June, the House Subcommittee on Public Lands held thirteen days of hearings on various pipeline bills. To relieve shortages, most proponents wanted to establish a line as soon as possible across Alaska. Saylor, Udall, and others on the committee preferred additional studies to determine if the trans-Canadian corridor would be superior from an environmental, engineering, and economic perspective. Because of the crisis atmosphere and frustration over repeated delays, Saylor realized he was fighting a losing battle. "In all probability, I won't be satisfied with what comes out of the Committee," he told his colleagues. "I have been overruled before, but, I have a great deal of faith in the combined judgment of Congress."[63]

On July 17, 1973, the Senate, with Vice-President Agnew breaking a tie vote, approved right-of-way legislation. The Senate bill included an amendment stating that the Interior Department's impact statement had satisfied NEPA regulations. That same day, the House Subcommittee on Public Lands, by a vote of twenty to eighteen, reported a similar bill. Saylor voted with the minority.[64]

Saylor next assailed the bill on the House floor in early August 1973. He conceded the existence of an energy shortage but insisted that the pipeline would not produce enough oil to remedy it. He believed that Americans should buy smaller cars, reduce their driving speed, and drive less often. He reiterated his charge, made in committee, that the bill circumvented the NEPA. He considered the impact statement flawed because the Interior Department was favorably disposed toward the trans-Alaskan route and had failed to adequately consider alternatives. An independent authority, such as the comptroller general, should compare the trans-Alaska and trans-Canadian routes and make a recommendation to Congress. He also urged support for an amendment introduced by John Dellenback (R-OR) and Wayne Owens (D-UT). This amendment sought to uphold NEPA by instructing the court to expeditiously determine the sufficiency of the impact statement. He scolded colleagues who had enthusiastically supported NEPA as landmark legislation a few years earlier but who now wanted to ignore its terms. The Dellenback-Owens amendment, he declared, would serve as a litmus test of whether Congress wished to maintain or only "pay lip service" to environmental values. He would support the bill with the amendment, but not without it. The amendment failed by a vote of 221 to 198.[65]

The bill finally passed, without any major amendments, by a vote of 356 to 60. Saylor voted with the minority. Senate and House conferees, including Saylor, worked out minor differences between the two bills in October amid an energy shortage made worse by the OPEC oil embargo. The conference bill, specifically authorizing the Alaskan pipeline and denying further environmental review, passed easily. President Nixon signed the Federal Land Right-of-Way Bill into law on November 16, 1973. The pipeline and claim settlement proposals would prove to be Saylor's last major environmental battles.[66]

seventeen
Trail's End

PREPARATORY TO THE 1972 congressional election, a popular outdoors magazine endeavored to "Rate the Candidates" for its readership. With assistance from national environmental leaders, Michael Frome, the conservation editor of *Field and Stream,* evaluated the conservation performance of each legislator in the Ninety-second Congress. Senators and representatives were rated principally on their records—whether they had voted "correctly" or "incorrectly" on several key issues. House members, for example, were evaluated on a dozen issues, including SST funding (correct vote—nay), the Timber Supply Bill (correct vote—nay), and the Saylor-Udall amendment to the Alaska Native Claims Settlement Act (correct vote—aye).[1]

Based on the number of times they voted "right," legislators were slotted into one of eight categories ranging from "excellent" to "very poor." Only six senators and eight representatives, including Saylor, earned an "excellent" rating, meaning they voted correctly at least 90 percent of the time. These elite members were described as "out in front" on the issues and worthy of "cheers and support." Nearly half the House members (216) were categorized as "inadequate," "poor," or "very poor." Those candidates, by implication, were unworthy of reelection. One candidate, Wayne Aspinall, scored so poorly he was given a special category, "In a Class by Himself," and targeted as "the man who absolutely must go." Environmentalists would breathe a sigh of relief when Aspinall lost his bid for reelection.[2]

Aspinall's utilitarian perspective had long frustrated preservationists, but defeating him seemed a remote hope until the environmental movement and Colorado's suburbs surged in numbers. In 1972, the Republican-controlled Colorado legislature had redrawn the chairman's western-slope district to include suburbs near Denver. Running as a "sincere conservationist," Alan Merson, a University of Denver law professor, defeated Aspinall in the Democratic primary.[3]

Saylor was surprised and saddened by Aspinall's defeat. At the close of the session in October 1972, he obtained a special order so that he and other colleagues could pay tribute to Chairman Aspinall. Saylor praised his hard work, legislative acumen, integrity, and devotion to duty. The two headstrong committee members had often frustrated each other, but they also respected one another and had remained friends. "Wayne and I have disagreed more times than I like to recall," Saylor declared. "Nevertheless, I like to think that our differing points of view on the great issues that have faced our committee, helped to mold legislation that was beneficial to the whole Nation." Saylor, however, could not resist a gentle criticism of Aspinall's utilitarian stance on public resources. On the House floor, he reminded the chairman that during the mid-1950s some Colorado opponents of the Fryingpan-Arkansas project had voted for him as a write-in opposition candidate to Aspinall: "The issue in that primary concerned the policy of our Nation regarding our natural environment." Saylor did not win that primary, he admitted, but the preservationist position that he represented did ultimately prevail.[4]

Saylor's association with Ann Dunbar, his devoted and skillful legislative assistant of twenty-three years, also came to an end in 1972. Dunbar was Saylor's gatekeeper, sounding board, and most influential adviser on environmental issues. Diagnosed with an inoperable brain tumor, she retired in 1972. The Wilderness Society honored her with a lifetime membership, but she died the following year at age forty-nine. Upon her death, noted environmentalist David Brower wrote a glowing tribute. Dunbar, he averred, had helped make Saylor the leading preservationist in the House. Moreover, she "was a cheerful note that could always be counted on by conservationists who walked the long corridors to defend wild places. . . . But for her faith and friendliness, there would be far less wilderness now than there is."[5]

Like Aspinall, Saylor faced primary and redistricting challenges in 1972. Due to declining population, Pennsylvania had lost two of its twenty-seven congressional seats, and the Democratic-controlled state legislature decided to redraw the districts to the party's advantage. It eliminated a GOP district in Pittsburgh and reconfigured the districts of Saylor and J. Irving Whalley so the two GOP incumbents would be forced to oppose one another in a primary election. Under this plan, Saylor's Twenty-second District would be gutted, part of it, namely Cambria County, merged with the Twelfth District, represented by Whalley. The other part of the old Twenty-second District, Armstrong, Indiana, Jefferson, and Clarion counties, would be folded into the Twenty-third District, represented by five-term Republican incumbent Albert Johnson. The House proposal was announced while Saylor was vacationing in Hawaii. When he learned about it, he threatened, in typical blustering fashion, to mount primary election challenges to Whalley and Johnson in two separate districts.[6]

Fortunately for Saylor, however, Democratic state senator Patrick Stapleton came to the rescue. He argued that the residents of Indiana County did not want to lose Saylor as a representative and pushed a new plan, approved by both houses and the governor, that benefited Saylor and hurt Whalley. The newly constituted Twelfth District would be made up of Somerset, Whalley's home county, plus Cambria, Indiana, Armstrong, Jefferson counties, and part of Clarion, Saylor's old district. Facing a stacked deck, Whalley decided not to seek reelection. A political novice did challenge Saylor in the primary, but he was soundly defeated.[7]

In the 1972 presidential contest, Saylor enthusiastically supported the Nixon-Agnew team. Some GOP legislators wanted to remove the controversial vice-president from the ticket, but Saylor praised his "unparalleled" record of achievement. He touted the administration's environmental efforts and believed that Nixon, unlike Democratic presidential candidate George McGovern, would not "belly crawl" to Hanoi to achieve peace.[8]

Saylor did not anticipate a difficult race for reelection because the redrawn Twelfth District was predominantly Republican. As expected, he overwhelmed his opponent, Joseph Murphy of Ebensburg, by sixty-five thousand votes. Saylor even outran Nixon in the district by nearly ten thousand votes. "I am elated and flabbergasted at the size of my vote and turnout," he declared. He predictably pledged to use his "mandate" to continue to serve the interests of his constituents. It would prove to be his final chance to do so.[9]

The year 1973 began promisingly with news of a peace settlement in the Vietnam War, but on the domestic front evidence began to mount of the president's complicity in the Watergate scandal. Saylor blasted the break-in to Democratic headquarters as a "stupid" idea. He did not "know if President Nixon knew of it or not, but as a member of his party I don't like the way he has handled it." Economic problems compounded the political mess. The economy sputtered due to inflation, high unemployment, an energy crisis, and a gruesome balance-of-payments deficit that Saylor blamed on low tariffs.[10]

Civil disorder also persisted. Campuses had quieted with the waning of the Vietnam War, but Native Americans, like African Americans before them, vented their anger at a system that had oppressed them. In 1969, a group of Native Americans took Alcatraz Island in San Francisco Bay and held it until 1971. The following year another faction, calling itself the American Indian Movement (AIM), temporarily seized the Bureau of Indian Affairs Headquarters in Washington, DC. And in 1973, two hundred AIM militants took over the Oglala Sioux reservation at Wounded Knee, South Dakota. Protesting treaty violations, they took eleven hostages and demanded to negotiate with President Nixon. Saylor decried civil disorders as a blemish on the nation's image and a threat to the democratic system. As a member of the House Subcommittee on Indian Affairs, which investigated the Wounded Knee takeover, he branded AIM leader Russell Means a publicity-seeking renegade who had been repudiated by Oglala tribal leaders: "There is no place in the operation of this Republic for self-appointed hoodlums like the AIM group who represent no tribes and who, by their violent and disruptive revolutionary tactics, do more harm than good for the Indians they falsely claim to represent." After seventy-one days, the standoff ended with the federal government agreeing to review Oglala treaty rights.[11]

While Saylor had no sympathy for violent or lawless tactics, he did sympathize with Native Americans who petitioned Congress for a redress of grievances. He proved particularly receptive to the efforts of the Menominee tribe to end a twenty-year-old federal policy called termination. In 1953, Congress, with Saylor in vigorous dissent, had enacted termination legislation that sought to do away with reservations and federal benefits to Indians. The Menominee Indians of Wisconsin were one of more than sixty tribes affected. Members opted to liquidate the tribe and apportion their assets, mainly rich timberland, to individuals as stockholders in a private corporation. Stock in the corporation could not be sold off for twenty years. Without federal services, the Menominees experienced hard times. Unless federal educational, health, and economic benefits were restored, stockholders would be forced in 1973 to sell off their

timber and lakefront property. Saylor spent his last days in the House successfully working to restore tribal status and federal services to the tribe.[12]

As always, Saylor was also actively engaged in environmental issues. He
continued as ranking member of the House Interior and Insular Affairs Committee while James Haley succeeded Aspinall as chair of that body. A lawyer
and former president of Ringling Brothers, Barnum and Bailey Circus, Haley
was a seventy-four-year-old Floridian who was beginning his eleventh term.
Like Saylor, he was a fiscal conservative and opponent of public power who
had fought federal hydroelectric projects in the West. He was no environmentalist, but he did share Saylor's belief in setting aside more open space in states
east of the Mississippi River.

Saylor and Haley worked together to secure passage of the Endangered
Species Act and the establishment of Florida's Big Cypress National Preserve.
They also introduced legislation to save wilderness in the Eastern United States.
Some Eastern areas, such as the Great Swamp of New Jersey and the Moosehead region of Maine, had been reviewed as required in the Wilderness Act
and brought into the program, but other rugged Eastern national forest tracts
were also deserving of protection but had not been mandated for study by the
original Wilderness Act.[13]

Saylor pooh-poohed the arguments of Forest Service "purists" who claimed
that Eastern areas had been impacted by roading, mining, and lumbering and
therefore fell short of the "untrammeled" standard of the 1964 Wilderness Act.
He held that in at least three instances impacted Eastern areas had already been
added to the system and that there were others where the human imprint was
barely detectable because nature had reclaimed the ground it had once lost.

The Saylor-Haley measure, and a companion bill in the Senate, proposed
to protect as wilderness twenty-eight tracts of national forestland in the East,
South, and Midwest. In all, a total of 471,186 acres would be protected in sixteen states. "I am the author of the Wilderness Act in this House," he blared to
his colleagues. "I know very well what it says and what it intended, and I know
how it was intended to be applied in a practical program." He was not surprised that some individuals were hostile to the wilderness system: "I have
spent more than 25 years of my life doing battle with these people, and I have
been winning right along. If they want to come before me with a lot of hokum
about 'purity' and 'diluting the high standards of the Wilderness Act,' . . . they
are welcome to do so, but I ask them to come with their eyes opened and prepared for battle." He concluded by declaring that wilderness was worth saving

because it provided recreation, solitude, and a humbling reminder that humans are one small part of the web of life. The bill, in slightly different form, passed in 1974.[14]

In general, Saylor had a strained relationship with the Forest Service because that agency, he charged, had allowed cutting to supersede other uses in national forestlands. Indeed, he argued that the purity principle was just a lame excuse to lay open Eastern forestland to the chainsaw. He did, however, avidly support the Forest Service's public relations campaign to combat pollution. The Forest Service had created a lovable mascot, Woodsy Owl, who appeared on posters with the admonition: "Give a Hoot. Don't Pollute." Saylor introduced legislation protecting the symbol, much like Smokey Bear. Grateful for Saylor's support, and no doubt eager to blunt some of his attacks on the department, the Forest Service presented him with a small carved wooden replica of Woodsy Owl. The presentation did not sit well with some representatives of the timber industry, who described Saylor as "among the worst opponents the timber industry has in Congress when it comes to wise use of federal lands."[15]

No member of Congress was more protective of the national park system than Saylor. One of the major problems facing the Park Service in the postwar decades was overvisitation. "Are we loving our parks to death?" asked one outdoor writer. Americans swarmed to Yellowstone, Yosemite, Smoky Mountains, and Grand Canyon. Crowds, traffic, noise, and litter spoiled the park experience and endangered wildlife and the ecosystem. In Grand Canyon National Park one could not break loose from crowds even by rafting down the Colorado River. In 1960, 205 rafters bobbed through the park. By 1972, that number had soared to 16,428. Concern for the biota prompted one young historian to complain that "the parks should not be for people, wilderness preservation is at stake." As a politician, Saylor was discomfited by the concept of wilderness for wilderness's sake. Certainly some areas, such as wildlife refuges, should be protected from human contact, but national parks, even those with designated wilderness areas, existed for the peoples' enjoyment.[16]

In 1971, the National Park Service hired the Conservation Foundation, a private environmental organization, to study the issue of crowding in the thirty-seven national parks. The 254-page study, *National Parks for the Future,* made a number of recommendations, including limiting automobile traffic; eliminating travel by recreational vehicles; and halting the construction of roads, parking lots, and campsites with running water and electrical hookups. In short, the report emphasized preserving the natural landscape rather than accommodating visitors.[17]

Saylor agreed with some of the recommendations, especially relating to regulations on automobiles, but overall he believed the report overemphasized preservation. He insisted that the parks existed to protect the land *and* to serve the recreational needs of the public. "My objection to some of the basic philosophy supporting the recommendations," he declared, "is the ring of 'preservation' first, second and third, with use by the public coming in a poor fourth. Parks are for the people—and you may be assured that members of Congress will not allow that basic assumption to be submerged." He also criticized the report for losing sight of the fact that the parks were controlled by the people through their elected representatives: "Congress—the creator, expander, preserver and funding agent for the system—is mostly treated as a stepchild to the great issues being debated by these groups on the future of the national park system." Saylor sought practical solutions—regulating automobile use, eliminating helicopter and small aircraft flyovers, banning snow machines, and perhaps rationing visitors. He also worked to expand the boundaries of many existing parks (Redwood, North Cascades, Grand Canyon) and to set aside new federal preserves such as Golden Gate National Recreation Area (California), Hell's Canyon Recreation Area (Idaho and Oregon), and Gates of the Arctic National Park (Alaska).[18]

Saylor worried that environmentalism had "gone wild," to borrow a phrase from a newspaper columnist who would address the problem several decades later. To Saylor, some environmentalists in the early 1970s seemed to be sounding an alarm against nearly all resource development projects, thus causing a public backlash against the movement. The Tennessee-Tombigbee Waterway Project in Mississippi was a case in point. Through canals and locks, the Corps of Engineers proposed linking the Tennessee and Tombigbee rivers, thus permitting barges to travel from the Gulf of Mexico to Ohio. By improving transportation and creating jobs, the project would attract industry, create jobs, and be an economic boon to the American Southeast. Congress had authorized the project in 1946 but had not allocated money for construction. When proponents sought funding in 1970, some environmentalists denounced the project because it would damage the ecosystem. Saylor disagreed and accused them of alarmism. "In efforts to halt this project and others like it," he wrote privately, "environmental alarmists have crossed the line separating reasonableness from irrationality. Their 'stop the world, I want to get off' philosophy is totally ridiculous in a modern society." Congress provided $1 million to initiate construction in 1972, and the project was completed twelve years later at a cost of $2 billion.[19]

Before taking a leave of absence to undergo surgery in October 1973, Saylor scrambled to put out political brushfires in his district. He had come under some criticism for helping to block construction of a $375 million flood-control dam on the Clarion River. Besides flood control, the dam would have provided reservoir recreation and a modest amount of hydroelectricity. Saylor and other opponents pointed out that the reservoir would inundate about 10 percent of the land in the county and interrupt the river's flow, thus worsening pollution from acid mine runoff. The cost also seemed exorbitant. Saylor made it clear that he was not likely to reverse his stance: "If I am the only member of Congress from Pennsylvania to take this stand, I will fight alone."[20]

Some district businesses also objected to the strict federal air and water quality standards Saylor had assiduously supported in Congress. Officials with Pennsylvania Electric (Pennelec), who had bragged about their state-of-the-art pollution-control devices during Secretary Hickel's visit in 1969, now found that their generating plants did not meet air quality standards. One Pennelec official estimated that it would cost about $50 million to buy equipment to satisfy pollution standards. It might be cheaper, he said ominously, to import coal with a lower sulfur content from the West. The threat was not lost on the editor of Johnstown's largest newspaper, who observed that "the high cost of pollution control could well make the district coal too expensive to burn. So there is a very real danger of killing off our coal industry . . . and probably even the electric-generating industry itself."[21]

Economic matters were made worse when Bethlehem Steel announced that it was closing its plants in Johnstown and laying off forty-seven hundred workers. The plant closings were caused, in large part, by the fact that the company could not meet pollution-control levels by 1975. Bethlehem also shut down the Cornwall Mine, which had continuously produced iron and other ores for 241 years. A member of Johnstown Area Regional Industries sought to push back the implementation of the new federal air quality standards until 1977. Such a delay might induce Bethlehem to change its mind or at the very least give his organization time to find jobs for displaced workers. He blasted Saylor for being more concerned with the environment than with the economic livelihood of his constituents: "His community needs more than environment right now. I don't want to get into a political debate, but this is not the time to be nice."[22]

Saylor cautioned against inflammatory rhetoric and urged cooperation instead of conflict. He made it clear, however, that there would be no relaxation of air and water quality standards, nor would there be an extension in the implementation of those standards. He would introduce legislation to provide $750 million in low-interest loans for industries in economically deprived areas such as Johnstown to purchase pollution-abatement equipment. Unapologetic for his support of air quality laws, he urged industries to "get into the swing of the environmental decade" and "help clean up America."[23]

Saylor also pushed coal as a possible solution to the nation's energy crisis. In particular, he urged increased federal funding, comparable to that given to the Atomic Energy Commission, for "gasification," a promising process under study by the Office of Coal Research, that would convert coal into clean-burning gasoline.[24]

Grace Saylor had been encouraging her husband to retire so they could spend more time together and live part of the year in Naples, Florida, where they had recently purchased a condominium. But the sixty-five-year-old workhorse showed little inclination to retire. He would, however, need to take some time off to recover from surgery.[25]

In typical dramatic fashion, he purchased time on local television stations to inform his constituents of his pending surgery and to ask their forbearance for taking a couple of weeks to convalesce. He had undergone a physical exam in readiness for a trip to persuade Japanese industrialists to take over Johnstown mills vacated by Bethlehem Steel. During that examination, X-rays had revealed a suspicious shadow on his abdominal aorta. Further tests divulged the existence of a "lemon-sized" aneurysm, which would prove fatal if ignored. The delicate surgery would be performed by renowned heart surgeon Denton Cooley at St. Luke's Hospital in Houston, Texas. Confident of a full recovery, Saylor announced that he planned to seek reelection in 1974.[26]

The four-hour surgery was declared a success. Dr. Cooley patched the damaged aorta and anticipated a complete recovery. Saylor spent the next few days resting and taking light exercise, including short strolls in the hospital hallway with Grace and daughter Susan. But shortly after midnight on October 28, he suffered a heart attack and died.[27]

Tributes poured forth. The flag at the Capitol was lowered to half-mast, as was the flag at Mount Vernon, in gratitude for Saylor's efforts to protect the view by establishing Piscataway National Historic Park. Washington observers could not remember the Mount Vernon flag ever being lowered except for presidents. President Nixon, Pennsylvania governor Milton Schapp, the state legislature, and national and state newspapers publicly mourned his death. The *New York Times* stated that Saylor "battled with good humor and tenacious spirit on behalf of the public interest" and noted that "he had a refreshing idealism about public service and lovable human qualities." Longtime legislative assistant Harry Fox was devastated: "I learned from him, I admired him, I loved him like a father. He was a faithful public servant, always true to his conscience and ideals; there is no blemish on his record. That is a great legacy to leave his family, his friends, and supporters."[28]

Saylor's death stunned his congressional colleagues. On October 30, 30 members delivered eulogies and then adjourned for the day as a further sign of tribute. Over the next few days, 11 senators and 120 representatives inserted eulogies in the *Congressional Record*. Some representatives spoke of his affability, humor, industriousness, and integrity. Others remembered his rugged physique and roaring voice, which seemed to match the expansive landscapes he loved. Still others remembered his advocacy of specific causes—statehood for Alaska and Hawaii, more autonomy for Guam and the Virgin Islands, the restoration of stripped coal lands, black lung legislation, improved conditions for Native Americans, and early support for the food stamp program.[29]

Nearly all eulogists praised his environmental record. His close friend and hunting companion John Dingell called him "one of America's great conservationists. . . . I miss him. I loved him." Thomas "Tip" O'Neill said that on both sides of the aisle Saylor was known as "Mr. Conservation." Ultraliberal Robert Kastenmeier (D-WI) referred to him as "the leading conservationist in the House" and observed that "political ideology did not separate us on environmental issues." House minority leader and soon-to-be vice president Gerald Ford called Saylor "the Congressional Theodore Roosevelt." And Morris Udall, Saylor's longtime ally on the House Interior Committee, said he "had a direct —if sometimes salty—way of expressing himself; no one ever doubted where John Saylor stood." He was a "dominant and powerful" force who would be at or near the top of any list of individuals leading the environmental awakening of the 1960s. "He was truly one of the great legislators of his era."[30]

Similar paeans came from the environmental community. Michael Frome insisted that Saylor "takes his place in history alongside Gifford Pinchot, another Pennsylvanian, and Theodore Roosevelt as one of the Republicans who blazed conservation trails." The Wilderness Society hailed him for setting aside millions of acres of pristine lands and for protecting the national interest in Alaska. David Brower believed that the Wilderness System should be named after Saylor because he and Howard Zahniser had done the most to establish it. Brower was reminded of an Edwin Markum poem that told of a mighty tree falling and leaving an empty place against the sky. New trees would grow in that space, said Brower, but they would be smaller and less noble.[31]

The funeral was held at St. John's United Church of Christ in Johnstown. The modest church could not accommodate the crowds who wished to pay their last respects. Although Saylor was a devoted member of the United Church of Christ, the funeral eulogy was delivered by a Roman Catholic priest who was a close friend. After the service, the body was taken to Grandview Cemetery in Johnstown for burial. The gravesite, marked by hefty stone with the inscription SAYLOR, fittingly commands the high ground.

By any measure—commitment, understanding, effectiveness, leadership—Saylor had a monumental impact on the modern environmental movement. His contemporaries—congressional colleagues and conservation leaders—held him in high regard and considered him an environmental Lancelot. House colleagues dubbed him "Mr. Conservation" or the "Conservation congressman." Conservation leaders considered him "one of us," calling him "St. John" because he was a "go-to" legislator and avid patron of their causes. "Briefly put," wrote one environmentalist, "we relied on him, and he never let us down." "He was a hero of ours," recalled Martin Litton, "always on the right side when it came to saving the Earth." "In the field of conservation," observed still another environmentalist, "John Saylor stood as tall as the Redwoods he spent so much of his life to protect." For twenty-five years, he was the House point man for nearly every conservation battle, and he often entered the fray with few congressional allies. He was "*my & our great champion*," wrote Stewart Brandborg. "In my 20 years [of] association with the Wilderness Society (12 as Executive Director), he was undoubtedly one of the *very best* (and one of the earliest) environmental advocates." He and Ann Dunbar "consistently rallied to the crisis and were always there to lead the charge."[32]

Throughout his career, Saylor's strong sense of patriotism and bipartisanship guided his approach to conservation. He loved America and its land. He considered himself a national representative and believed that it was his congressional and civic duty to protect the peoples' resource heritage and quality of life. To the dismay of the Western bloc in Congress, he championed aesthetic preservation more than wise use of public resources. He was also an early advocate of environmental preservation. Generally, he put aside partisanship to keep the national park system inviolate, preserve wilderness, protect the environment, and prevent special-interest raids on the public estate. "Where conservation was at stake," said his Pennsylvania colleague Frank Clark, "John Saylor was neither Republican nor Democrat—he was American."[33]

Given the fact that his party was never in the majority during his seniority, Saylor was remarkably effective as a legislator. His conservation positions were generally supported by liberal Democrats and ardently pushed by environmental groups. Saylor also got along well with Wayne Aspinall, his powerful counterweight on the House Interior Committee. Aspinall liked and respected Saylor and considered him a "constructive" rather than a "destructive" environmentalist. Together the two men pushed some one thousand committee bills through Congress. Many of those measures—such as the Wilderness Bill, the Wild and Scenic Rivers Bill, and the Redwood National Park Bill—were not as far-reaching or expansive as Saylor had wished, but at least they became law.[34]

Saylor tenaciously supported the national park system. He believed that once a national preserve had been established it was sacrosanct. He first made his mark as a preservationist by opposing a Bureau of Reclamation proposal to build a dam at Echo Park in Dinosaur National Monument. When he did so, his aggressive and critical questioning of federal engineers during House hearings bolstered the belief that those experts might be fallible. He did not oppose all federal dams, just those that violated treaties, as with the Seneca Nation; those with the main purpose of public power rather than irrigation; and those that intruded upon national preserves. His crusade against the construction of dams in Grand Canyon was perhaps his most valiant.

A compilation of Saylor's legislative achievements is impressive. He was the principal House architect of the Wilderness Bill, the Land and Water Conservation Fund, the ORRRC, the Wild and Scenic Rivers Bill, and the anti–sky hunting measure. He also cosponsored legislation establishing Redwood National Park, the C&O Canal National Historic Park, Piscataway National Historic Park, and the National Trails system. He also championed the establishment of Canyonlands, North Cascades, and Voyageurs national parks, plus national lakeshores, seashores, recreation areas, and historic sites. In Pennsylvania, he secured the Johnstown Flood Historic Site, the Allegheny Portage Railroad National Historic Site, the Delaware Water Gap National Recreation Area, the Coal Research Act, and, as a cosponsor, the black lung bill.

As one of the main sponsors of the Wilderness and Wild and Scenic Rivers acts, he worked doggedly to add units to these systems. With Morris Udall he pushed hard to save millions of acres of pristine federal terrain in Alaska for future generations. He also worked to protect endangered and threatened wildlife species, including predators.

Saylor was a friend of the environment, as well as the land. He endorsed the National Environmental Policy Act. He actively supported the Air and Water Quality acts, including full funding for both programs. Worried about environmental damage, he opposed the Alaska Pipeline and sponsored a surface mining bill to restore stripped coal lands.

Few legislators have received so much acclaim for their earth stewardship. In 1954, Saylor became the first legislator to receive the National Parks Association Award. The Izaak Walton League and the Sierra Club presented him with their highest honors, the Founders Award and the John Muir Award, respectively. He was also honored as Conservationist of the Year by the National Wildlife Federation, Trout Unlimited, the Bernard Baruch Foundation, and several Pennsylvania groups.

A Titusville, Pennsylvania, newspaper wrote in 1969 that John Saylor "has made a name for himself as one of the greatest conservationists ever to serve in Congress." This assessment seems reasonable. Among contemporaries—Phillip Burton, John Blatnik, John Dingell, and Morris Udall in the House, and Clinton Anderson, Frank Church, Henry Jackson, Edmund Muskie, and Gaylord Nelson in Senate—perhaps only Udall matches Saylor's achievements. In one study covering the years 1850 to 2000, political scientist David Webber rates Saylor as one of fourteen "outstanding environmentalists of congress."[35]

Soon after Saylor's death, Senator Mark Hatfield (D-OR) suggested naming a wilderness area, wild and scenic river, or recreation area in his honor. This has yet to occur, although Pennsylvanians have established a memorial trail in Windber and a modest park along Black Lick Creek in Indiana County in his honor. The city of Johnstown has no tribute to its native son. Thomas Kimball, former executive director of the National Wildlife Federation, has called Saylor "the most effective and capable environmental advocate in the Congress," but to date Saylor has yet to gain election to that organization's Conservation Hall of Fame, perhaps because few politicians have been so honored. Saylor's main legacy rests in the inspiration he provided and the natural wonders he helped preserve. Minnesota representative John Blatnik wrote that "John Saylor was a man of rare vision and determination, whose legacy is written in countless clear-flowing streams, and in national parks and protected areas across America." Any environmentalist would be pleased with that epitaph.[36]

Abbreviations Used in the Notes

CAP:	Central Arizona Project
CR:	*Congressional Record*
CRSP:	Colorado River Storage Project
DBP:	David Brower Papers
DDEL:	Dwight D. Eisenhower Library
DP:	*Denver Post*
F&S:	*Field and Stream*
GPO:	Government Printing Office
HBP:	Harold Bradley Papers
JFKL:	John F. Kennedy Library
JSP:	John Saylor Papers
LAT:	*Los Angeles Times*
LBJL:	Lyndon B. Johnson Library
LW:	*Living Wilderness*
MUP:	Morris Udall Papers
NPM:	*National Parks Magazine*
NYT:	*New York Times*
PP:	*Pittsburgh Press*
RBP:	Richard Bradley Papers
SCB:	*Sierra Club Bulletin*
SCR:	Sierra Club Records
SLT:	*Salt Lake Tribune*
SUP:	Stewart Udall Papers
WP:	*Washington Post*
WSJ:	*Wall Street Journal*
WSP:	Wilderness Society Papers

Trailblazer

1. Letter to the editor and editor's reply, *National Parks Magazine* (*NPM* hereafter), Sept.–Oct. 2003, 8; William Cronon, "When the G.O.P. Was Green," *New York Times* (*NYT* hereafter), Jan. 8, 2001; rpt. in *ASEH News* 12 (Spring 2001): 1, 5; Keith Easthouse, "The Party That Was Green," *Forest Magazine*, July–Aug. 2001, 14–17; Martha Marks, "The Green Old Party: Republican Conservationists Who Want to Reclaim the GOP," *Sierra* 89 (July–Aug. 2004): 48–52.

2. For an overview of the federal dam-building program in the American West, see Mark W. T. Harvey, "The Changing Fortunes of the Big Dam Era in the American West," in Char Miller, ed., *Fluid Arguments: Five Centuries of Western Water Conflict* (Tucson: University of Arizona Press, 2001), 276–302.

3. John Saylor, *Congressional Record* (*CR* hereafter), 84 Cong., 1 sess., 7986; *Johnstown (PA) Tribune-Democrat,* Aug. 16, 1964; *Kittanning (PA) Daily Leader,* May 25, 1955. Saylor once said that he had to take an interest in conservation: "I was brought up on it." See the *Oil City (PA) Derrick,* Sept. 17, 1969.

4. Editorial, *NYT,* Oct. 8, 1950, qtd. by John Saylor, *CR,* 83 Cong., 1 sess., 5069; John Saylor, "Saving America's Wilderness," *Living Wilderness* (*LW* hereafter) 21 (Winter–Spring 1956–57): 1–12. On nature as the sublime embodiment of the Creator's handiwork, see William Cronon, foreword, Paul Sutter, *Driven Wild: How the Fight against Automobiles Launched the Modern Wilderness Movement* (Seattle and London: University of Washington Press, 2002), vii–viii.

5. Mark David Spence, *Dispossessing the Wilderness: Indian Removal and the Making of the National Parks* (New York: Oxford University Press, 1999).

6. John Saylor to Leo Stormer, June 27, 1972, box 25, John Saylor Papers, Indiana University of Pennsylvania (JSP hereafter); John Saylor, "The Conservation Legacy of Theodore Roosevelt," *NPM,* July–Sept. 1958, 114–16.

7. John Saylor, speech before the Republican Delegations of the Eleven Western States, Eugene, OR, Oct. 13, 1963, box 91, Sierra Club Records, Bancroft Library, University of California, Berkeley (SCR hereafter).

8. John Saylor, *CR,* 84 Cong., 1 sess., 7986; David Brower, "John Phillips Saylor: 1908–1973," *Not Man Apart* 3 (Dec.–Jan. 1973–74): 1.

9. Wayne Aspinall, "A Salute to John Saylor," *CR,* 90 Cong., 2 sess., 10912–13; John Saylor, "The Honorable John McCormack, Speaker of the House of Representatives," *CR,* 89 Cong., 1 sess., 2926–27; John Saylor, "Supporting Members of Congress," *CR,* 92 Cong., 2 sess., 26324.

10. Richard F. Fenno Jr., *Congressmen in Committees* (rpt., Berkeley: Institute of Governmental Studies Press, University of California, 1995), 93, 263–66; Lloyd Meeds, former representative (D-WA), e-mail to author, Oct. 9, 2004.

11. Stewart Udall, "A Congressman Defends the House," *NYT Magazine,* Jan. 12, 1958.

12. John Saylor, *CR,* 87 Cong., 2 sess., 23059; Ben East, "Saylor an Arizona Hero?" *Arizona Republic,* July 25, 1967, rpt. in *CR,* 90 Cong., 1 sess., 20012.

13. Brower, "John Phillips Saylor," 1; Michael McCloskey, interview with the author, July 15, 1997; Stewart Brandborg, interviews with the author, July 11–12, 1998.

Chapter 1. Headwaters

1. Floyd Dominy, interview with the author, July 15, 1997.

2. "The Story of a Real Pennsylvanian: John P. Saylor," campaign pamphlet, box 24, JSP; J. Phillips Saylor, son, interview with the author, Aug. 4, 1993.

3. Martha Bach, "A History of Johnstown, Pennsylvania" (master's thesis, Indiana University of Pennsylvania, 1962); Sharon Brown, *Historic Resource Study: Cambria Iron Company* (Washington, DC: Department of the Interior, National Park Service, 1989); Richard Burkett and George Hand, "Iron and Steelmaking in the Conemaugh Valley," in

Karl Berger, ed., *Johnstown: The Story of a Unique Valley* (Johnstown: Johnstown Flood Museum, 1984), 255–313.

4. David McCulloch, *The Johnstown Flood* (New York: Simon and Schuster, 1968); Robert D. Christie, "The Johnstown Flood," *Western Pennsylvania Historical Magazine* 54 (Apr. 1971): 198–210.

5. "Story of a Real Pennsylvanian"; Anna Catherine Saylor Bennett, sister, interview with the author, Aug. 4, 1997.

6. Bennett, interviews, Aug. 4, Oct. 29, 1997.

7. Bennett, interviews, Aug. 4, Oct. 29, 1997; J. Phillips Saylor, interview, Aug. 4, 1993. In 1957, the First Congregational Church and the Dutch Reformed Church merged to form the United Church of Christ.

8. Bennett, interview, Aug. 4, 1997; David Saylor, nephew, interview with the author, July 14, 1997.

9. Bennett, interview, Aug. 4, 1997; Jean Crichton, "Music and Lights of Main Street," in Berger, *Johnstown*, 667–705; Steve Seman, "Sports in Johnstown," in Berger, *Johnstown*, 643–61.

10. Bennett, interview, Aug. 4, 1997; J. Phillips Saylor, interview, Aug. 4, 1993; David Saylor, interview, July 14, 1997; Susan Saylor Wisor, daughter, interview with the author, July 16, 1997; Harry Fox, legislative assistant, interview with the author, Aug. 25, 1994; John Saylor, qtd. in *CR*, 89 Cong., 1 sess., 2655; John P. Saylor, "Our Outdoors," address to the Wilderness Club of Philadelphia, rpt. in *CR*, 85 Cong., 1 sess., 6017.

11. Stewart Udall, secretary of the interior, 1961–69, telephone interview with the author, June 4, 1997; Fox, interview, Aug. 25, 1994.

12. Bennett, interview, Aug. 4, 1997; David Saylor, interview, July 14, 1997. For Muir, see Stephen Fox, *John Muir and His Legacy: The American Conservation Movement* (Boston: Little Brown and Company, 1981). For nature as the sublime, see Cronon, foreword, vii.

13. J. Phillips Saylor, interview, Aug. 4, 1993; Susan Saylor Wisor, interview, July 16, 1997.

14. Malcolm Cowley, qtd. in Curtis Miner, *Forging a New Deal: Johnstown and the Great Depression* (Johnstown: Johnstown Area Heritage Association, 1993), 17. The files of Howard Zahniser are in the Wilderness Society Papers at the Denver Public Library. I have also benefited from an interview I conducted with his son Edward Zahniser (Aug. 7, 1997). A new biography of Zahniser appeared after this book went into production: Mark Harvey, *Wilderness Forever: Howard Zahniser and the Path to the Wilderness Act* (Seattle: University of Washington Press, 2005). For Carson, see Linda Lear, *Rachel Carson: Witness for Nature* (New York: Henry Holt and Company, 1997). For Abbey's Pennsylvania background, see James M. Cahalan, "'My People': Edward Abbey's Appalachian Roots in Indiana County, Pennsylvania," *Pittsburgh History* 79 (Fall 1996), 92–107: (Winter 1996–97): 160–78.

15. Transcript of John Saylor's high school academic record, Mercersburg Academy Alumni Files, Mercersburg Academy, Mercersburg, PA; *The Spectator, 1924*, Cambria County Public Library, Johnstown, PA.

16. *The Spectator, 1924.*

17. J. Harvey Mickley to William M. Irvine, Apr. 18, June 12, 1924, Mercersburg Academy Alumni Files.

18. Katharine M. Ulery to William M. Irvine, June 14, 1924, Mercersburg Academy Alumni Files.

19. Mercersburg Academy Catalog, 1996–97, 22–23.

20. Donald Dewey, *James Stewart: A Biography* (Atlanta: Turner Publishing, 1996), 78–79; editorial, *Mercersburg (PA) News*, Feb. 6, 1925.

21. Dewey, *James Stewart*, 78; *Mercersburg News*, Sept. 26, 1924; *The Karux* (student yearbook), 1925.

22. *The Karux*, 1925; *Mercersburg News*, Nov. 21, 1924.

23. *Mercersburg News*, Oct. 17, 24, 1924, Apr. 10, 1925.

24. Dewey, *James Stewart*, 79.

25. *Mercersburg News*, Nov. 7, 1924.

26. On "conditions," see *Mercersburg News*, Oct. 10, 1924. For Saylor's academic difficulties, see Registrar, Statement to Dr. W. M. Irvine, Head Master, Aug. 28, 1925, Mercersburg Academy Alumni Files.

27. Tillman K. Saylor to Mercersburg Academy, Aug. 14, 1925, Mercersburg Academy Alumni Files.

28. Registrar, Statement to Dr. W. M. Irvine, Head Master, Aug. 18, 1925, Mercersburg Academy Alumni Files; *Mercersburg Academy Alumni Quarterly* (Summer 1962): 144–45.

29. Ann Keenen, college archivist, telephone interview with the author, Nov. 6, 24, 1997.

30. Keenen, interview, Nov. 6, 24, 1997; editorial, "Twenty Years Growth," May 8, 1929, and editorial, "Our Spirit," Mar. 26, 1930, both in the Franklin and Marshall *Student Weekly*.

31. Editorials, *Student Weekly*, Nov. 7, 21, Dec. 12, 1928, Mar. 13, 20, 29, Apr. 10, 1929.

32. *Oriflamme* (student yearbook), 1928, 1930.

33. *Oriflamme*, 1930.

34. David Saylor, interview, July 14, 1997; anonymous source, University of Michigan Law School.

35. Dickinson School of Law, Catalog, 1930–31.

36. Dickinson School of Law, Catalog, 1932–33.

37. Donald McPherson, "The 'Little Steel' Strike of 1937 in Johnstown, Pennsylvania," *Pennsylvania History* 39 (Apr. 1972): 219–20; Miner, *Forging a New Deal*, 1–7; Morawska, *For Bread with Butter*, 216–21. The Lorain plant of U.S. Steel employed another fourteen hundred employees.

38. Miner, *Forging a New Deal*, 1–7; Morawska, *For Bread with Butter*, 216–21.

39. Bennett, interview, Oct. 28, 1997.

40. Fox, interview, Aug. 25, 1994.

41. Miner, *Forging a New Deal*, 8–11.

42. Miner, *Forging a New Deal*, 8–11, 14–15.

43. Miner, *Forging a New Deal*, 25. Ramon Cooper, *The Flood and the Future: The Story of a Year in City Government at Johnstown, PA, 1936* (Johnstown: McKeown Printing Co., 1936), 48–50, 75–76; McPherson, "'Little Steel,'" 230.

44. Ramon Cooper, *Flood and the Future*, 1–10. The city was flooded again in 1977.

45. McPherson, "'Little Steel,'" 219–38.

46. John Saylor, qtd. in *CR*, 91 Cong., 2 sess., 19750.

47. "Story of a Real Pennsylvanian."

48. "Story of a Real Pennsylvanian"; Bennett, interview, Aug. 4, 1997.

49. "Story of a Real Pennsylvanian."

50. Story of a Real Pennsylvanian"; Ronald H. Spector, *Eagle against the Sun: The American War with Japan* (New York: Free Press, 1985), 500–501.

51. Spector, *Eagle against the Sun,* 500–501.

52. Spector, *Eagle against the Sun,* 500–501.

Chapter 2. Political and Environmental Trailhead

1. For eulogies and a brief biography of Coffey, see *CR,* 81 Cong., 1 sess., 4890, 5005–10.

2. *Johnstown Democrat,* Aug. 24, 1949; unidentified newspaper clippings, n.d., 1949 scrapbook, JSP.

3. *CR,* 81 Cong., 1 sess., index with list of House and Senate members.

4. John Saylor, radio addresses, Aug. 25, Sept. 1, 9, 1949, box 35, JSP.

5. *Johnstown Tribune,* Sept. 14, 1949; unidentified newspaper clippings, n.d., 1949 scrapbook, JSP.

6. John Saylor, radio addresses, Aug. 29, Sept. 5, 1949, box 35, JSP. See also *Baltimore Sunday Sun,* Oct. 14, 1949.

7. John Saylor, radio address, Sept. 12, 1949, box 35, JSP; unidentified newspaper clippings, n.d., John Saylor File, Alumni Records, Franklin and Marshall College, Lancaster, PA; *Philadelphia Inquirer,* Nov. 4, 1973; Manuel Lujan (R-NM), in *Memorial Services Held in the House of Representatives and Senate of the United States, Together with Tributes Presented in Eulogy of John P. Saylor,* 93 Cong., 1 sess. (Washington, DC: Government Printing Office [GPO hereafter], 1974), 64, 124.

8. *Johnstown Tribune,* Sept. 14, 1949; *Johnstown Democrat,* Sept. 14, 1949.

9. *The Truth Shall Keep You Free,* copy courtesy of Susan Saylor Wisor; Joseph Martin qtd. in *Cleveland News,* Sept. 17, 1949; Marion H. Crockett to John P. Saylor, n.d., 1949 scrapbook, JSP; *Chicago Daily Tribune,* Sept. 14, 15 (editorial), 1949; editorial and cartoon, *Philadelphia Inquirer,* Sept. 15, 1949; *New York Herald Tribune,* Sept. 16, 1949; *Baltimore Sun,* Sept. 20, Oct. 14, 1949; *Pittsburgh Press* (*PP* hereafter), Sept. 14, 1949; *San Jose News,* Sept. 14, 1949; *Washington Evening Star,* Sept. 15, 1949; *New York Journal American,* Sept. 22, 1949; editorials with cartoons in the *Chicago Daily News,* Sept. 16, 1949, and the *Catawba (Newton, NC) News-Enterprise,* Sept. 16, 1949.

10. Harry M. Emerick to William French, Sept. 21, 1949, Alumni Records, F&M College. For editorial support for Saylor, see *Johnstown Democrat,* Sept. 12, 1949; *Johnstown Tribune,* Sept. 12, 1949; *Kittanning Leader-Times,* Sept. 12, 1949; *Indiana (PA) Gazette,* Sept. 12, 1949; and others in 1949 scrapbook, JSP.

11. *CR,* 81 Cong., 1 sess., 13461; *Harrisburg (PA) Patriot,* Oct. 2, 1949; unidentified newspaper clippings, n.d., 1949 scrapbook, JSP.

12. *PP,* Oct. 16, 1949; C. W. Dressler in the *Johnstown Tribune,* Oct. 18, 1949.

13. J. Phillips Saylor Jr., interview, Aug. 4, 1993; Susan Saylor Wisor, interview, July 16, 1997; William Lohr, interview with the author, Aug. 5, 1997.

14. Fox, interview, Aug. 25, 1994; *Johnstown Tribune,* Sept. 17, 24, 29, 1949; *Harrisburg Patriot,* Oct. 2, 1949; unidentified newspaper clippings, n.d., 1949 scrapbook, JSP.

15. John Saylor, "A Report to My Constituents," *CR,* 81 Cong., 2 sess., A6873.

16. *Apollo (PA) News-Record,* June 30, 1950.

17. *CR,* 81 Cong., 2 sess., 2780–81, 2947, 9601; "Report to My Constituents," A6875; *Ebensburg (PA) Herald,* Mar. 9, 1950.

18. *Johnstown Tribune,* Feb. 24, 1950; *Washington Evening Star,* May 20, 1949; unidentified newspaper clippings, n.d., 1949 scrapbook, JSP; *CR,* 81 Cong., 2 sess., A6576.

19. *Johnstown Democrat,* Jan. 26, 27, Feb. 18, 1950; editorial, *Apollo News-Record,* Jan. 27, 1950; *Nanty Glo (PA) Journal,* Sept. 14, 1950; *Johnstown Democrat,* Nov. 8, 9, 1950.

20. Eileen Mountjoy Cooper, *Rochester & Pittsburgh Coal Company: The First One Hundred Years* (Indiana, PA: Rochester & Pittsburgh Coal Company, 1982).

21. Marc Reisner, *Cadillac Desert: The American West and Its Disappearing Water*, rev. ed. (New York: Penguin Books, 1993), 136, 140, 145–46; Michael C. Robinson, *Water for the West: The Bureau of Reclamation, 1902–1977* (Chicago: Public Works Historical Society, 1979), 56; William Warne, *The Bureau of Reclamation* (New York: Praeger Publishers, 1973), 17–19, 59–69; Donald C. Swain, "The Bureau of Reclamation and the New Deal, 1933–1940," *Pacific Northwest Quarterly* 61 (July 1970): 137–46.

22. Reisner, *Cadillac Desert*, 134–36; Robinson, *Bureau of Reclamation*, 77–78; Warne, *Bureau of Reclamation*, 86–103. During the late New Deal (1937–41), Congress provided $379 million for reclamation, but during the war years (1942–46), expenditures dropped to $330 million. See Raymond Moley, *What Price Federal Reclamation?* (New York and Washington: American Enterprise Association, 1955), iv.

23. Russell Martin, *A Story That Stands like a Dam: Glen Canyon and the Struggle for the Soul of the West* (New York: Henry Holt and Company, 1989), 47–50.

24. On Straus, see Reisner, *Cadillac Desert*, 137–40. For reclamation expenditures, see Moley, *What Price Reclamation?* iv. For the bureau's development of the Columbia River basin, see testimony of Interior Secretary Oscar Chapman, U.S. Congress, 82 Cong., 2 sess., House Subcommittee on Irrigation and Reclamation, *Hearings on H.R. 5743, Hells Canyon Dam* (Washington, DC: GPO, 1952), 28 (quote), 38–40; also see the testimony of Michael Straus (141–50). See also Elmo Richardson, *Dams, Parks and Politics: Resource Development and Preservation in the Truman-Eisenhower Era* (Lexington: University Press of Kentucky, 1973), 19–38.

25. Unidentified newspaper clipping, n.d., 1955 scrapbook, JSP.

26. William Ashworth, *Hells Canyon: The Deepest Gorge on Earth* (New York: Hawthorn Books, 1977), 80; Hearings, *Hells Canyon Dam*, 1–25.

27. Hearings, *Hells Canyon Dam*, 15. Liberal publications such as the *Nation* and the *New Republic* tended to support public power, while conservative journals like *Newsweek* favored private power. See, e.g., Richard L. Neuberger, "Big Dam in a Big Pit," *Nation*, Mar. 24, 1951, 272–74; Lloyd Tupling, "He Sells America Short," *Nation*, Nov. 1, 1952, 404–6; G. H. R. Taylor, "The Battle of the Snake," *New Republic*, Mar. 17, 1952, 16–17; Raymond Moley, "The Fair Deal in Hells Canyon," *Newsweek*, Aug. 6, 1951, 88.

28. Hearings, *Hells Canyon Dam*, 28–30, 48, 403, 451.

29. Advertisement, *Saturday Evening Post*, May 10, 1952, box 6, folder 20, Harold Bradley Papers, Sierra Club Members Papers, SCR (HBP hereafter); Jordan testimony, Hearings, *Hells Canyon Dam*, 499–503.

30. Hearings, *Hells Canyon Dam*, 650, 686, 735–36.

31. Donald J. Pisani, "Federal Water Policy and the Rural West," in R. Douglas Hurt, ed., *The Rural West since World War II* (Lawrence: University Press of Kansas, 1998), 119–46; Robinson, *Bureau of Reclamation*, 25–32; Warne, *Bureau of Reclamation*, 19; Goodrich Lineweaver, "History of Reclamation," in U.S. Congress, 82 Cong., 1 sess., House Committee of Interior and Insular Affairs, *Hearings, General Study of Irrigation and Reclamation Problems*, Feb. 12, 14, 1951 (Washington, DC: GPO, 1951), 13–14.

32. Lineweaver testimony, Hearings, *General Study of Irrigation*, 19–23. See also "Importance of Power in the Development of Irrigation Projects" (Chapman testimony), Hearings, *Hells Canyon Dam*, 115–16.

33. U.S. Congress, 82 Cong., 2 sess., House Subcommittee on Irrigation and Reclamation, *Hearings on H.R. 5630, H.R. 5489, Repayment Contracts for Frenchtown, Malta,*

and Glascow Irrigation Districts, Montana (Washington, DC: GPO, 1952), 3. Reisner provides a colorful and riveting portrait of Dominy in *Cadillac Desert* (214–54). See also Floyd Dominy, Oral History, Nov. 14, 1968, Lyndon B. Johnson Library, Austin, TX (LBJL hereafter); Floyd Dominy, Oral History, Apr. 6, 1994, Bureau of Reclamation Oral History Program.

34. Hearings, *Repayment Contracts,* 3–5.

35. Hearings, *Repayment Contracts,* 22–26.

36. Hearings, *Repayment Contracts,* 28–30.

37. For a general study, see Rich Johnson, *The Central Arizona Project* (Tucson: University of Arizona Press, 1977); Murdock, qtd. in U.S. Congress, House Committee on Interior and Insular Affairs, 82 Cong., 1 sess., *Hearings on H.R. 1500 and H.R. 1501, the Central Arizona Project,* pt. 1, Feb. 27, 28, Mar. 1,2, 5, 6, 7, 8, 9, 12, 13, 14, 1951 (Washington, DC: GPO, 1951), 9.

38. Hearings, *CAP,* pt. 1, 17–24, 31–37.

39. Hearings, *CAP,* pt. 1, 9. The National Parks Association opposed the CAP from the beginning, while the Sierra Club initially supported it and then reversed its position. See Fred Packard, "Grand Canyon Park and Dinosaur National Park in Danger," *NPM,* Oct.–Dec. 1949, 11–13; Dave Brower to David Brenegar, Jan. 20, 1955, box 65, folder 14, SCR; Martin, *A Story That Stands like a Dam,* 50–51.

40. Hearings, *CAP,* pt. 1, 180–83, 269–71, 291, 548.

41. Norrris Hundley Jr., *Water and the West: The Colorado River Compact and the Politics of Water in the American West* (Berkeley and Los Angeles: University of California Press, 1975), 169–266.

42. Hundley, *Water and the West,* 270–306; Thomas G. Smith, "Lewis Douglas, Arizona Politics, and the Colorado River Controversy," *Arizona and the West* 22 (Summer 1980): 125–62.

43. Robinson, *Bureau of Reclamation,* 55; Norris Hundley Jr., *The Great Thirst: Californians and Water, 1770s–1990s* (Berkeley and Los Angeles: University of California Press, 1992), 192–230.

44. Hearings, *CAP,* pt. 1, 162–63.

45. Hearings, *CAP,* pt. 1, 99.

46. Hearings, *CAP,* pt. 2, Mar. 15, 16, Apr. 9, 10, 11, 12, 13, 18, 1951 (Washington, DC: GPO, 1951), 739, 755–56, 760.

47. John Saylor, qtd. in unidentified newspaper clipping, n.d., 1952 scrapbook, JSP; *CR,* 82 Cong., 2 sess., 8042. For the steel strike, see David McCullough, *Truman* (New York: Simon and Schuster, 1992), 896–901; Robert J. Donovan, "Truman Seizes Steel," *Constitution* 2 (Fall 1990): 48–57.

48. *Johnstown Tribune-Democrat,* Oct. 4, 14, 1952. Johnstown's two dailies, the *Tribune* and the *Democrat,* merged in the fall of 1952.

49. Party platform, qtd. in Richardson, *Dams, Parks and Politics,* 73, and in Robinson, *Bureau of Reclamation,* 79; election results, *NYT,* Nov. 6, 1952. For Eisenhower's visit and endorsements of Saylor, see various newspaper clippings, 1952 scrapbook, JSP.

Chapter 3. Maverick Republican

1. *New York Daily News,* Mar. 16, 1953, *Washington Evening Star,* Mar. 24, 1953. Miller's letter to Saylor appears in Drew Pearson, "The Washington Merry-Go-Round," *Indiana Evening Gazette,* Mar. 23. Eventually Saylor learned that his mother and the pres-

ident shared the same birthday and persuaded Eisenhower to send her birthday wishes every Oct. 14. For Eisenhower's letters to Minerva Saylor, see President's Personal File 28-A, "S," box 715, 716, Dwight D. Eisenhower Papers, Dwight D. Eisenhower Library (DDEL hereafter), Abilene, KS.

2. J. Phillips Saylor, interview, Aug. 4, 1993; Susan Saylor Wisor, interview, July 16, 1997; David Saylor, interview, July 14, 1997.

3. Susan Saylor Wisor, interview, July 16, 1997.

4. Pat Murray, interview with the author, July 14, 1997; Bennett, interview, Aug. 4, 1997; Rep. John Dingell, interview with the author, Nov. 19, 1997; John Saylor's obituary, *Washington Post* (*WP* hereafter), Oct. 29, 1973.

5. Dingell, interview, Nov. 19, 1997; Fox, interview, Aug. 25, 1994; Charles Leppert, House Interior staff member, interview with the author, Jan. 9, 1995; Russell Wisor, son-in-law, interview with the author, Jan. 10, 1995; Richard Gentry, legislative assistant, interview with the author, June 23, 2005.

6. Isabella Hurrell, interview with the author, Aug. 4, 1997; letter to the editor, *Johnstown Tribune-Democrat,* Oct. 29, 1954; Fox, interview, Aug. 25, 1994; David Saylor, interview, July 14, 1997.

7. J. Phillips Saylor, interview, Aug. 4, 1993; tribute to Musial, *CR,* 84 Cong., 2 sess., 12396.

8. Dingell, interview, Nov. 19, 1997; J. Phillips Saylor, interview, Aug. 4, 1993; David Saylor, interview, July 14, 1997.

9. J. Phillips Saylor, interview, Aug. 4, 1997; Susan Saylor Wisor, interview, July 16, 1997; Sam Gilluly, Director, Montana Historical Society, to John Saylor, Aug. 11, 1967, box 33, JSP.

10. Susan Saylor Wisor, interview, July 16, 1997; "Saylor a Native 'Son Of Thunder,'" *Somerset (PA) American,* Oct. 21, 1972, Alumni Files, Dickinson College School of Law, Carlisle, PA.

11. Susan Saylor Wisor, interview, July 16, 1997; J. Phillips Saylor, interview, Aug. 4, 1997. For the visit to Antarctica, see John Cummings in the *Philadelphia Inquirer,* n.d., and John Saylor's account of the adventure in a letter to Robert Hess, Mar. 27, 1958, both in Alumni Files, F&M College. See also numerous newspaper clippings, 1958 scrapbook, JSP.

12. Newspaper clippings, 1950–60 scrapbooks, JSP; D. R. Mathews to John Saylor, May 27, 1954, 1954 scrapbook, JSP.

13. Unidentified newspaper clipping, Jan. 7, 1958, and Minerva Saylor to John Saylor, Jan. 7, [1958], both in 1958 scrapbook, JSP.

14. John P. Saylor in *Johnstown Tribune-Democrat,* Mar. 2, 1954. See also *Nanty Glo Journal,* unidentified newspaper clippings, n.d., 1954 scrapbook, JSP.

15. J. Phillips Saylor, interview, Aug. 4, 1997; Fox, interview, Aug. 25, 1994; Lohr, interview, Aug. 5, 1997; Clifton Jones, Pennsylvania state Republican chairman, interview with the author, Aug. 29, 1997; *Johnstown Tribune-Democrat,* Nov. 5, 1969 (dead cat).

16. Editorial, *Johnstown Tribune-Democrat,* Oct. 29, 1954.

17. Gary Reichard, *The Reaffirmation of Republicanism: Eisenhower and the Eighty-Third Congress* (Knoxville: University of Tennessee Press, 1975), 108–11.

18. Reichard, *Reaffirmation of Republicanism,* 111–12; *CR,* 83 Cong., 2 sess., 2621–22, 3563–64.

19. *CR,* 83 Cong., 1 sess., 6840; 83 Cong., 2 sess., 13805–6.

20. For quote, see *CR,* 83 Cong., 1 sess., 4249–50. See also Saylor's speeches "Importation of Residual Oil," *CR,* 83 Cong., 1 sess., A2012–13; and "American Oil Producers Versus Imported Oil," *CR,* 83 Cong., 1 sess., 8698–99.

21. For Eisenhower's social and welfare policies, see Reichard, *Reaffirmation of Republicanism*, 119–47. For Saylor's votes on social legislation, see *CR*, 83 Cong., 1 sess., 6830–31, 9425 (housing); 83 Cong., 2 sess., 4489–90, 8470, 11109 (housing), 7468 (Social Security), 10093–94 (unemployment benefits). For Saylor and civil rights, see *Johnstown Tribune-Democrat*, Oct. 25, Nov. 1, 1954.

22. *CR*, 83 Cong., 2 sess., 6082; *Johnstown Tribune-Democrat*, May 7, 1954; John Saylor, speech, "Religion and Politics," unidentified newspaper clipping, n.d., 1954 scrapbook, JSP.

23. *Ebensburg Mountaineer Herald*, May 6, 1954; Saylor, "Religion and Politics."

24. *CR*, 83 Cong., 2 sess., 3744–45, 12472–74; John Saylor, speech before the Bituminous Coal Institute, Chicago, *Chicago Daily News*, Dec. 11, 1953, *Chicago Sun Times*, Dec. 12, 1953, 1953 scrapbook, JSP.

25. *Johnstown Observer*, July 23, 1954; C. W. T., letter to the editor, unidentified newspaper clipping, n.d., 1954 scrapbook, JSP; *Johnstown Tribune-Democrat*, Aug. 16, 1954.

26. Eisenhower qtd. in Robinson, *Water for the West*, 79. For the Eisenhower administration's conservation policies, see Reichard, *Reaffirmation of Republicanism*, 148–80; Richardson, *Dams, Parks and Politics*, 71–87, 114–28.

27. Richardson, *Dams, Parks and Politics*, 83–87, 95–96.

28. John P. Saylor to Sherman Adams, Feb. 11, 1953, Adams to Saylor, Feb. 17, 1953, Floyd Dominy, "Riverton Project," memorandum to Commissioner of Reclamation, Dec. 17, 1951, Dominy, "Irrigation in the Heart River Valley, North Dakota," memorandum to Director, Operation and Maintenance Division, Dec. 17, 1951, and Dominy, "Heart River Unit," memorandum to Commissioner Straus, Jan. 3, 1952, all GF-17-E-1, box 313, DDEL.

29. Richardson, *Dams, Parks, and Politics*, 88–100; Robinson, *Bureau of Reclamation*, 80.

30. Dwight D. Eisenhower, *Mandate for Change, 1953–1956* (Garden City, NJ: Doubleday and Company, 1963), 203–8; Reichard, *Reaffirmation of Republicanism*, 149–53; *CR*, 83 Cong., 1 sess., 2557, 2638, 4895, 4898.

31. Minutes of Cabinet Meeting, Apr. 24, 1953, Ann Whitman Cabinet Series, box 2, DDEL; Reichard, *Reaffirmation of Republicanism*, 158, 176; Eisenhower, *Mandate for Change*, 381–84; Richardson, *Dams, Parks and Politics*, 116–20; Elmo Richardson, "The Interior Secretary as Conservation Villain: The Notorious Case of 'Giveaway' McKay," *Pacific Historical Review* 41 (Aug. 1972): 333–45.

32. Reichard, *Reaffirmation of Republicanism*, 164–73; Eisenhower, *Mandate for Change*, 301–2; Charles Alexander, *Holding the Line: The Eisenhower Era, 1952–1961* (Bloomington and London: Indiana University Press, 1975), 40; Keith Hutchinson, "Everybody's Business: The St. Lawrence Seaway, I," *Nation*, Mar. 17, 1951, 253; Keith Hutchinson, "Everybody's Business: The St. Lawrence Seaway, II," *Nation*, Mar. 24, 1954, 279.

33. *CR*, 83 Cong., 2 sess., 5912, 6159–60; Earle D. Chesney, memorandum for the record, June 29, 1954, Ann Whitman Diary Series, box 2, DDEL; John Saylor to Dwight D. Eisenhower, June 17, OF 126-A-2, box 643, Eisenhower Papers; Gerald D. Morgan, Administrative Assistant to the President, to Saylor, July 15, 1954, OF 126-A-2, box 643, Eisenhower Papers; letter to the editor, *Johnstown Tribune-Democrat*, Apr. 21, 1954.

34. Richardson, *Dams, Parks and Politics*, 109–10; Patrick Goldsworthy to John Saylor, Jan. 27, 1954, folder 8, box 66, SCR. Congressman Mike Mansfield pushed the project as early as 1950 because it would provide economic and recreational benefits and "beautify" the park. See Mike Mansfield to Walter C. Nye, Dec. 9, 1950, ser. 7, box 120, Wilderness Society Papers, Denver Public Library (WSP hereafter).

35. Saylor's extended remarks in *CR*, 83 Cong., 1 sess., A5068–69.

36. *CR*, 83 Cong., 1 sess., 435, 663; *Johnstown Tribune-Democrat*, Jan. 23, 1953.

37. Eisenhower, *Mandate for Change*, 391; Richardson, *Dams, Parks and Politics*, 115; Dominy, Oral History, LBJL, 3–4.

38. John Saylor to Douglas McKay, Mar. 6, 1954, qtd. in Richardson, *Dams, Parks and Politics*, 140.

39. Robinson, *Bureau of Reclamation*, 85; Mark W. T. Harvey, *A Symbol of Wilderness: Echo Park and the American Conservation Movement* (Albuquerque: University of New Mexico Press, 1994), 89–91.

40. Harvey, *Symbol of Wilderness*, 184, 211–13. For the connection between the CRSP and the St. Lawrence Seaway project, see Charles G. Woodbury to Richard Leonard, Feb. 9, 1954, and Howard Zahniser to William Voigt, May 5, 1954, both ser. 7, box 120, WSP; Reichard, *Reaffirmation of Republicanism*, 170.

Chapter 4. Dinosaur Canyons

1. Harvey, *Symbol of Wilderness*, 5–16.

2. For the transformation of conservation values and tactics following World War II, see Hal K. Rothman, *The Greening of a Nation? Environmentalism in the United States since 1945* (Fort Worth: Harcourt Brace and Company, 1998); Clayton Koppes, "Efficiency/Equity/Esthetics: Towards a Reinterpretation of American Conservation," *Environmental Review* 11 (Summer 1987): 127–46; Samuel P. Hays, "From Conservation to Environment: Environmental Politics in the United States since World War II," *Environmental Review* 6 (Fall 1982): 1–29; Samuel P. Hays, *A History of Environmental Politics since 1945* (Pittsburgh: University of Pittsburgh Press, 2000).

3. Harvey, *Symbol of Wilderness*, 63.

4. Harvey, *Symbol of Wilderness*, 57–58; Robinson, *Water for the West*, 65–66.

5. For Muir, Leopold, and the emergence of a wilderness philosophy, see Roderick Nash, *Wilderness and the American Mind*, 3d ed. (New Haven: Yale University Press, 1982), 182–271; Susan R. Schrepfer, *The Fight to Save the Redwoods: A History of Environmental Reform, 1917–1978* (Madison: University of Wisconsin Press, 1978), 103–29, 161–70; Craig W. Allin, *The Politics of Wilderness Preservation* (Westport, CT: Greenwood Press, 1982), 60–169; Fox, *John Muir and His Legacy*; Aldo Leopold, *A Sand County Almanac* (New York: Oxford University Press, 1949); Susan L. Flader, *Thinking like a Mountain: Aldo Leopold and the Evolution of an Ecological Attitude toward Deer, Wolves, and Forests* (Columbia: University of Missouri Press, 1974).

6. Harvey, *Symbol of Wilderness*, xv.

7. Harvey, *Symbol of Wilderness*, 130–31.

8. Bernard DeVoto, "Shall We Let Them Ruin Our National Parks?" *Saturday Evening Post*, July 22, 1950, 17–19, 42–48; Harvey, *Symbol of Wilderness*, 155–58.

9. Harvey, *Symbol of Wilderness*, 159–60, 167–69; Stephen Bradley, "Folboats through Dinosaur," *Sierra Club Bulletin* (*SCB* hereafter), Dec. 1952, 1–8; Harold Bradley to Bus Hatch, Oct. 8, 1952, folder 18, box 5, HBP. For the number of boat visitors to Dinosaur, see Jess Lombard, Superintendent, Dinosaur National Monument, to Richard Leonard, July 1, 1953, Conservation Department Records, 1891–1973, folder 20, box 64, SCR.

10. Joe Penfold, guest editorial, *Denver Post* (*DP* hereafter), Aug. 11, 1950. Also see the following sources: Penfold, memorandum to [Izaak Walton League] cooperators,

"Dinosaur Again," July 25, 1951 (quotes); Penfold to "Brownie," memorandum, "Running the River in Dinosaur National Monument," n.d., Penfold to Michael Straus, July 24, 1951, Penfold to Charlotte Mauk, Apr. 9, 1952, Penfold to Conrad Wirth, Oct. 12, 1953, and Penfold, "Dinosaur? No!" *Colorado Conservation* (Spring 1952), all box 7:120, WSP. Also see Penfold to Robert Dally, Dec. 1, 1952, folder 18, box 64, SCR; Penfold to David Brower, July 16, 1953, folder 20, box 64, SCR; Joe Penfold, "Reclamation's Plan for Invasion," *SCB*, May 1952, 10–14.

11. Jess Lombard to Harold Bradley, Sept. 3, 1953, folder 19, box 5, HBP; J. Phillips Saylor, interview, Aug. 4, 1993; Mike Penfold, letter to the author, Aug. 22, 1997.

12. Joe Penfold, confidential memorandum to Bill Voigt, Executive Director, [Izaak Walton League], Aug. 17, 1953, folder 21, box 64, SCR. I am indebted to Steven Sturgeon, an archivist at Utah State University, who brought this memorandum to my attention. Penfold sent copies of the memorandum to Fred Packard, Richard Leonard, Howard Zahniser, and other conservation leaders and asked them to destroy it afterward because he had made what he considered "indiscreet" comments about Saylor and Aspinall. See Joe Penfold to Fred Packard, Dick Leonard, Olaus Murie, Pink Gutermuth, Howard Zahniser, and General U.S. Grant, Aug. 24, 1953, folder 21, box 64, SCR.

13. Joe Penfold, confidential memorandum to Voigt, Aug. 17, 1953; David Brower to Penfold, Sept. 14, 1953, folder 21, box 64, SCR; Penfold to Richard Leonard, Aug. 21, 1953, box 7:120, WSP.

14. For Tudor's description of the raft trip, see "Notes Recorded while Undersecretary," Sept. 12, 1953, Jan. 17, 1954, box 1, Ralph Tudor Papers, DDEL; Tudor to Douglas McKay, Nov. 27, 1953, box 1, Tudor Papers; Tudor to Edgar Wayburn, Jan. 8, 1954, folder 48, box 228, Edgar Wayburn Papers, Bancroft Library, University of California, Berkeley.

15. Department of the Interior, press release, Dec. 12, 1953, OF 155-A-2, box 828, DDEL; Stephen Bradley to John Saylor, Dec. 30, 1953, box 26, JSP.

16. Tudor, "Notes Recorded," Jan. 17, 1954; U.S. Congress, 83 Cong., 2 sess., House Committee on Interior and Insular Affairs, *Hearings on H.R. 4449, 4443, and 4463, Colorado River Storage Project*, Jan. 18, 19, 20, 21, 22, 23, 25, 26, 27, 28, 1954 (Washington, DC: GPO, 1954).

17. Hearings, *CRSP* (1954), 27–29.

18. Hearings, *CRSP* (1954), 30–40, 45.

19. "Dam at Echo Park Blasted by P. A. Solon," *Arizona Daily Star*, Jan. 19, 1954, and Sen. Wallace Bennett (R-UT), Special to the *Vernal Express*, newspaper clipping, n.d., folders 6 and 7 respectively, box 68, SCR. Also see Tudor, "Notes Recorded," Jan. 24, 1954.

20. Larson testimony, Hearings, *CRSP* (1954), 98–184. For the effort to set a time limit for questioning, see Hearings, *CRSP* (1954), 185.

21. Hearings, *CRSP* (1954), 150, 194, 764, 779.

22. David Brower, e.g., remembered a long discussion with Saylor during the Jan. hearings; see David Brower to John Saylor, Mar. 13, 1954, folder 11, box 66, SCR.

23. Hearings, *CRSP* (1954), 36, 645, 647.

24. Hearings, *CRSP* (1954), 438–39, 749, 767.

25. Hearings, *CRSP* (1954), 453, 710, 753, 809.

26. Hearings, *CRSP* (1954), 718–19, 764.

27. Hearings, *CRSP* (1954), 574–80, 594–96, 764–65.

28. Hearings, *CRSP* (1954), 385, 578.

29. Hearings, *CRSP* (1954), 434, 767.

30. Hearings, *CRSP* (1954), 767–85 (Penfold testimony), 799–815 (Packard testimony), 885–901 (Zahniser testimony).

31. Hearings, *CRSP* (1954), 792–94, 797–98.

32. Hearings, *CRSP* (1954), 795–97, 824–25.

33. Robert Dally to John Saylor, Jan. 19, 1954, and Charlotte Mauk to Saylor, Jan. 19, 1954, both folder 8, box 66, SCR; David Brower, confidential memorandum for the files, Jan. 19, 1954, folder 24, box 64, SCR; Richard Leonard to Frank Kittredge, Jan. 25, 1954, folder 29, box 64, SCR; David Bradley to Brower, Feb. 19, 1954, folder 2, box 65, SCR; minutes, Sierra Club Conservation Committee, Jan. 21, 1954, folder 20, box 5, HBP.

34. Brower, confidential memo, Jan. 19, 1954; Sidney L. McFarland to John Saylor, with attachment from Bureau of Reclamation, Feb. 18, 1954, box 26, JSP.

35. Dave Brower to Ric Bradley, Feb. 3, 1954, Bradley to Brower and Howard Zahniser, Mar. 26, 1954, Brower to Bradley, Apr. 2, 1954, and Ann Dunbar to Bradley, Apr. 29, 1954, all box 1, Richard Bradley Papers, Western History Department, Denver Public Library (RBP hereafter); Bradley to Brower, Feb. 8, Mar. 2, 4, 17, 1954, Brower to Bureau of Reclamation, with copy and personal note to John Saylor, Mar. 13, 1954, and Brower to Bradley, Mar. 26, 1954, all folder 3, box 65, SCR.

36. Harvey, *Symbol of Wilderness*, 236. For a sampling of the articles, see Bernard DeVoto, "Parks and Pictures," *Harper's Magazine*, Feb. 1954, 12–17; "Intramural Giveaway," *Harper's Magazine*, Mar. 1954, 10–11, 14–16; Wallace Stegner, "Battle for the Wilderness," *New Republic*, Feb. 15, 1954, 13–15; "Trouble in Dinosaur," *SCB*, Feb. 1954, 3–12; "A Great National Park?—or Two Wasteful Dams" and "Firing Begins in Dinosaur Fight," *SCB*, Mar. 1954, 21–24, 25–30; David Bradley, "Temple in Danger," *Valley News (West Lebanon, NH)*, Apr. 1, 1954, inserted by Saylor in *CR*, 83 Cong., 2 sess., A2668. For some of the letters of protest to the administration, see Joe Penfold to Douglas McKay, Feb. 10, 1954, and Rosalie Edge to McKay, Mar. 29, 1954, both folder 53, box 292, Rosalie Edge Papers, Western History Department, Denver Public Library; Alfred Knopf to President Dwight Eisenhower, Jan. 4, Feb. 5, Apr. 26, 1954, and Howard Zahniser to Eisenhower, Mar. 26, 1954, all box 838, OF 155-E-10, DDEL. For Eisenhower's position on the project, see Eisenhower, memorandum for the Director of the Budget, Feb. 16, 1954, and Eisenhower, memorandum of telephone conversation with Nelson Rockefeller, Mar. 25, 1954, both box 5, Diary Series, DDEL; Eisenhower to E. E. "Swede" Hazlett, July 20, 1954, box 4, Diary Series, DDEL.

37. Ansel Adams to David Brower, Mar. 25, 1954, folder 21, box 12, David Brower Papers, SCR (DBP hereafter); Howard Zahniser to John Saylor, Mar. 30, 1954, Mike Nadel Files, unprocessed, WSP; Roberta, memorandum for Mr. Stevens, Apr. 5, 1954, box 828, OF 155-A-2, DDEL; Saylor to Joseph E. Dodge, Mar. 31, 1954, *CR*, 83 Cong., 2 sess., A2665–66.

38. Saylor to Dodge, Mar. 31, 1954; *CR*, 83 Cong., 2 sess., A2665–66.

39. Carl H. Schwartz Jr., memorandum to the Director of the Budget, Mar. 23, 1954, OF 155-A-2, box 828, DDEL; Joseph E. Dodge to John Saylor, Apr. 13, 1954, *CR*, 83 Cong., 2 sess., 5909–10.

40. Clair Engle to Dave Brower, Mar. 29, 1954, folder 11, box 66, SCR. Aspinall's remark was conveyed to Howard Zahniser by Saylor; see Howard Zahniser to Joe Penfold, Apr. 15, 1954, box 7:120, WSP.

41. Minutes, *Amendments to H.R. 4449 as Considered by the Subcommittee on Irrigation and Reclamation of the House Committee of Interior and Insular Affairs, April 7–May 3, 1954*, box 7:120, WSP.

42. Fred Packard to Rosalie Edge, Apr. 19, 1954, folder 53, box 292, Edge Papers; David Brower to John Saylor, Mar. 13, Apr. 23, 1954, folders 11 and 12, respectively, box 66, SCR; Harold Bradley to John Saylor, Mar. 29, 1954, folder 11, box 66, SCR; Joe Penfold to Saylor, Apr. 29, 1954, folder 12, box 66, SCR; Robert Monahan to Saylor, Apr. 14, 1954, folder 21, box 5, HBP.

43. William Dawson, "Dear Colleague," Jan. 7, 1954, and John Saylor, "Dear Colleague," May 3, 1954, both folder 1767, box 47, Gracie Pfost Papers, University of Idaho, Moscow.

44. Jack Breed, "Shooting Rapids in Dinosaur Country," *National Geographic*, Mar. 1954, 363–90; "River Boat Run through Dinosaur National Monument," *Sunset* 112 (Mar. 1954): 22–23; Don Hatch to John Saylor, n.d., box 7:120, WSP; Hatch to David Brower, Feb. 4, 1954, folder 1, box 65, SCR; Brower to Saylor, Mar. 26, 1954, folder 11, box 66, SCR; Clark Jones to Brower, "Report of Interview with Mrs. Schall," folder 6, box 65, SCR; Charles Eggert to Brower, May 17, 1954, and Howard Zahniser to Hatch, May 19, 1954, both folder 7, box 65, SCR; *CR*, 83 Cong., 2 sess., A3449, A3858–59.

45. Richard Bradley to David Brower, Mar. 22, 1954, folder 3, box 65, SCR; Floyd Dominy to Bradley, Apr. 16, 1954, folder 4, box 65, SCR; W. A. Dexheimer to John Saylor, Apr. 29, 1954, folder 5, box 65, SCR; Dominy, interview, July 15, 1997.

46. David Brower to John Saylor, Apr. 23, 1954, folder 12, box 66, SCR; Richard Bradley to Saylor, May 9, 1954, box 1, RBP; Bradley to Brower, May 11, 1954, folder 6, box 65, SCR; *NYT*, May 9, 1954. Saylor inserted Tudor's admission of mathematical errors to Harrison in *CR*, 83 Cong., 2 sess., 7034. Also see Tudor, "Notes Recorded," June 6, July 18, 1954.

47. *DP*, May 14, 1954; editorial, *NYT*, May 15, 1954; *CR*, 83 Cong., 2 sess., 7034–35.

48. *CR*, 83 Cong., 2 sess., 7034–35. For the minority report, see U.S. Congress, 83 Cong., 2 sess., House Committee on Interior and Insular Affairs, *House Report 1774* (Washington, DC: GPO, July 1954), 30–33; Robert Hansen, "Legislators Hit for Ignoring Error on Dam," *DP*, May 21, 1954.

49. Richard Bradley to John Saylor, May 9, 1954, box 1, RBP; David Brower to Philip Hyde, Apr. 29, 1954, folder 5, box 65, SCR; Penfold address, reprinted in the *Apollo News Record*, June 25, 1954, 1954 scrapbook, JSP.

50. Wayne Aspinall, in the *Grand Junction (CO) Daily Sentinel*, May 18, 1954; editorial, *DP*, May 23, 1954; Dave F. Brinegar to David Brower, Apr. 30, 1954, folder 5, box 65, SCR.

51. Harvey, *Symbol of Wilderness*, 236–37; Joe Penfold to Howard Zahniser ("girding"), Apr. 14, 1954, box 7:120, WSP; John Oakes, "Conservation: The Echo Park Issue," *NYT*, June 6, 1954; Martin Litton to David Brower, May 1, 1954, folder 5, box 65, SCR; Raymond Moley, "Irrigation—Hydropower's Expensive Partner," *Newsweek*, May 17, 1954, 84–85, 88; Bernard DeVoto to David Brower, May 17, 1954, DeVoto to Ansel Adams, June 3, 1954 ("bastard"), and Zahniser to Weldon Heald, May 19, 1954, all folder 7, box 65, SCR.

52. DeVoto to Adams, June 3, 1954; Lowel Sumner to David Brower, May 19, 1954, folder 7, box 65, SCR.

53. Fred Packard, memorandum to conservation organizations, Sept. 23, 1954, Nadel Files.

54. Sigurd F. Olson, "A Tribute to Representative John P. Saylor for Distinguished Service to the National Parks," Oct. 14, 1954, Nadel Files; *Johnstown Tribune-Democrat*, Oct. 15, 1954.

55. Sherley Uhl, in the *PP*, n.d., 1954 scrapbook, JSP. For the concern of conservationists for Saylor's political success, see Horace Albright to David Brower, Aug. 30, 1954,

folder 10, box 65, SCR; Richard Leonard to Howard Zahniser and Fred Packard, Oct. 11, 1954, folder 12, box 65, SCR.

56. *Johnstown Tribune-Democrat,* Oct. 22, 1954; Glass in the *Nanty Glo Journal,* Oct. 25, 1954; John Torquanto, statement to members of the executive committee and district chairmen, *Johnstown Observer,* Oct. 15, 1954.

57. The quote is from the *Portage Dispatch,* Oct. 7, 1954. For newspaper endorsements, see *Johnstown Tribune-Democrat,* Oct. 5, 29, 1954; *Apollo News-Record,* Oct. 29, 1954.

58. DeVoto in the *Barnsboro (PA) Star,* Sept. 23, 1954; John Saylor to Raymond Moley, Oct. 5, 22, 1954, folder 31, box 48, Raymond Moley Papers, Hoover Institution on War, Revolution and Peace, Stanford University; Moley, letter to the editor, *Johnstown Tribune-Democrat,* Oct. 28, 1954. Moley also contributed money to Saylor's campaign.

59. For the election results, see *Johnstown Tribune-Democrat,* Nov. 4, 1954. For the comments of the Democrat, see *Johnstown Observer,* Nov. 12, 1954.

60. Editorial, "Distinguished Service," *Salt Lake Tribune* (*SLT* hereafter), Oct. 22, 1954.

Chapter 5. Big Dam Foolishness

1. *CR,* 84 Cong., 1 sess., 7406. The chapter title derives from a speech by Elmer T. Peterson before the National Wildlife Conference, Mar. 10, 1953, folder 2, box 64, SCR.

2. *CR,* 84 Cong., 1 sess., 7145.

3. For a brief history, see U.S. Congress, House, Hearings before the Subcommittee on Irrigation and Reclamation of the Committee on Interior and Insular Affairs, 83 Cong., 1 sess., *H.R. 236, A Bill to Authorize the Construction, Operation, and Maintenance by the Secretary of the Interior of the Fryingpan-Arkansas Project, Colorado,* June 8, 9, 10, 1953 (Washington, DC: GPO, 1953), 12–19; Arthur Carhart to Richard Leonard, Aug. 25, 29, 1953, folder 12, box 19, DBP.

4. Fred D. Glidden to Frank Young, Dec. 5, 1951, Joe Penfold, letter to the editor, *DP,* Apr. 11, 1952, Pitkin County Water Protection Association Pamphlet, "The Rape of the Roaring Fork—1953 Version," Robert Dally to David Brower, May 19, 1953, and George Jackson to William Henry Harrison, June 29, 1953, all folder 12, box 19, DBP; James H. Smith, Assistant Secretary of the Navy, to Charles Willis, Assistant to the President, July 1, 1954, box 841, OF 155-M, DDEL; J. Edgar Chenoweth, interviews with former members of Congress, Library of Congress, Washington, DC.

5. Beverly Gerbanz, Secretary, Pitkin County Water Protection Association, to Sierra Club, Aug. 20, 1951, and Robert Dally to Charlotte Mauk, Mar. 22, 1953, both folder 19, box 64, SCR; Richard Leonard to Arthur Carhart and Joe Penfold, Aug. 20, 1953, folder 20, box 64, SCR; Dally to David Brower, Sept. 19, 29, 1953, and Dally to Fred Packard, June 29, July 6, Aug. 29, 1953, all folder 12, box 19, DBP.

6. Hearings, *Fryingpan-Arkansas Project* (1953), 31, 269.

7. *DP,* May 18, 1954; *Grand Junction Daily Sentinel,* June 26, 1954; J. Edgar Chenoweth to Frank Hoag Jr., June 29, 1954, folder 24, box 74, J. Edgar Chenoweth Papers, University of Colorado Library, Boulder.

8. U.S. Congress, 83 Cong., 2 sess., House Committee on Interior and Insular Affairs, *House Report 1943 Authorizing the Construction, Operation, and Maintenance by the Secretary of the Interior of the Fryingpan-Arkansas Project, Colorado* (Washington, DC: GPO, 1954), Minority Report, 11-15.

9. Homer H. Gruenther, memorandum to Sherman Adams, July 19, 1954, and Charles F. Willis Jr., memorandum to Adams, July 23, 1954, box 841, OF 155-M, DDEL.

10. *CR*, 83 Cong., 2 sess., 12451–52. The "bed of roses" quote is from Barnet Nover in the *WP*, June 24, 1954.

11. J. Edgar Chenoweth to W. B. Winchell, Aug. 9, 1954, folder 25, box 74, Chenoweth Papers; *CR*, 83 Cong., 2 sess., 12451–52; Chenoweth, address before the Sertoma Club of Pueblo, CO, unidentified newspaper clipping, 1954 scrapbook, JSP.

12. *CR*, 83 Cong., 2 sess., 12453; editorial, *Rocky Mountain News*, July 30, 1954; editorial, *DP*, Aug. 8, 1954, folder 13, box 19, DBP.

13. *DP*, Sept. 16, 1954; *Johnstown Tribune-Democrat*, Sept. 16, 1954; *Pittsburgh Post-Gazette*, Sept. 16, 1954; Richard Leonard to Howard Zahniser and Fred Packard, Oct. 11, 1954, folder 12, box 65, SCR.

14. U.S. Congress, House, Hearings before the Subcommittee on Irrigation and Reclamation of the Committee on Interior and Insular Affairs, 84 Cong., 1 sess., *H.R. 412 to Authorize the Construction, Operation, and Maintenance by the Secretary of the Interior of the Fryingpan-Arkansas Project, Colorado*, May 9, 11, 12, 18, July 1, 16, 1955 (Washington, DC: GPO, 1955), 269. After failing to approve the project in 1956, 1957, and 1958, Congress finally authorized it in June 1962, over Saylor's opposition. The reservoir was completed in 1975. See *CR*, 87 Cong., 2 sess., 10171–74.

15. Bernard DeVoto to Ansel Adams, June 3, 1954, and Weldon Heald to David Brower, June 11, 1954, both folder 8, box 65, SCR; Martin Litton to Dave [Brower] and Dick [Leonard], Sept. 22, 1954, folder 11, box 65, SCR.

16. Howard Zahniser to Weldon Heald, May 19, 1954, folder 7, box 65, SCR; David Brower to Horace Albright, Aug. 27, 1954, folder 10, box 65, SCR; Joe Penfold to Brower, Aug. 30, 1954, folder 11, box 65, SCR.

17. David Brower to Joe Penfold, Aug. 26, 1954, folder 10, box 65, SCR: Penfold to Brower, Aug. 30, 1954.

18. David Brower to John Saylor, Apr. 23, 1954, folder 12, box 66, SCR; Brower to Saylor, "Big Glen Strikes Back," May 12, 1954, folder 18, box 66, SCR; Brower to Richard Bradley, Aug. 27, 1954, and Brower to Raymond Moley, "A Modified Upper Colorado Storage Project," Aug. 31, 1954, both folder 10, box 65, SCR; Fred Packard to Brower, Feb. 2, 1955, folder 15, box 65, SCR; Joe Penfold to Fred Packard, Sept. 8, 1954, box 7:120, WSP. Eggert called that portion of Glen Canyon below the entrance of the San Juan River "the most incredible works of Nature I have ever witnessed!" The landscapes "are of the highest calibre for Park standards and why we have not discovered them before and began crying out long ago, I don't know." See Charles Eggert to Packard, Aug. 2, 1955, folder 19, box 65, SCR.

19. Fred Packard to Dr. W. R. Halliday, Feb. 17, 1954, folder 2, box 65, SCR; Harvey, *Symbol of Wilderness*, 221–25.

20. "Saylor Renews Notice He'll Fight River Project," *DP*, Jan. 13, 1955; James Daniel, "River Project Foes Put Big Ed on Their Side," *Rocky Mountain News*, Jan. 13, 1955.

21. "Saylor Spouts Again," *Grand Junction Sentinel*, Feb. 3, 1955; "Dams v. Dinosaurs," *Time*, Jan. 31, 1955, 14–15; Stewart Udall to Mrs. M. H. Starkweather, Jan. 20, 1955, folder 17, box 66, SCR; *DP*, Jan. 12, 1955; Harvey, *Symbol of Wilderness*, 200, 233–34.

22. Joe Penfold to John Saylor, Jan. 13, 1955, folder 17, box 66, SCR; John Saylor, "Hi, Ho, Aqualantes!" *CR*, 84 Cong., 1 sess., 999.

23. Robert Dally, letter to members of Congress, "The Angrilantes," June 15, 1955, and Eugene Guild, memorandum, "Fool Dams and Dam Fools," both folder 17, box 65,

SCR; Wallace Stegner, ed., *This Is Dinosaur: Echo Park Country and Its Magic Rivers* (New York: Alfred A. Knopf, 1955); Moley, *What Price Reclamation?*; Harvey, *Symbol of Wilderness*, 256–62.

24. Harvey, *Symbol of Wilderness*, 268.

25. U.S. Congress, House, Hearings before the Subcommittee on Irrigation and Reclamation of the Committee on Interior and Insular Affairs, 84 Cong., 1 sess., *H.R. 270, H.R. 2836, H.R. 3383, H.R. 3384, and H.R. 4488 to Authorize the Secretary of the Interior to Construct, Operate, and Maintain the Colorado River Storage Project and Participating Projects, and for Other Purposes*, Mar. 9, 10, Apr. 18, 20, 22, 1955 (Washington, DC: GPO, 1955), 179–201, 976–77.

26. Hearings, *CRSP* (1955), 675–76.

27. Hearings, *CRSP* (1955), 1135.

28. David Brower to John Saylor, June 1, 1955, folder 18, box 66, SCR; Clyde Jones to Saylor, Mar. 6, 1955, folder 17, box 66, SCR.

29. Richard Bradley to John Saylor, Mar. 22, 1955, folder 17, box 66, SCR; William Voigt to Arthur Carhart, May 2, 1955, and David Brower to Ned Graves, May 18, 1955, both folder 18, box 65, SCR; John Saylor, "Who Should Blush over Echo Park?" *CR*, 84 Cong., 1 sess., 6953.

30. Watkins testimony, Hearings, *CRSP* (1955), 704–30; "New Evidence Proves Echo Park Legally Reserved for Dam Site," *Colorado River News*, Aqualante pamphlet, n.d., folder 18, box 65, SCR.

31. Hearings, *CRSP* (1955), 1133–34; Fred Packard to Arthur Watkins, Apr. 7, 1955, Richard Leonard to David Brower, with attachment of draft of letter to Watkins, Apr. 12, 1955, and Leonard, telegram to Sen. Arthur Watkins, Apr. 16, 1955, with copies to Zahniser, the *Christian Science Monitor*, the *NYT*, and Senators Richard Neuberger (OR) and Thomas Kuchel (CA), all folder 17, box 66, SCR.

32. *CR*, 84 Cong., 1 sess., 7918–20.

33. *CR*, 84 Cong., 1 sess., 7986–87.

34. *CR*, 84 Cong., 1 sess., 8543–44, 9530–31.

35. Harvey, *Symbol of Wilderness*, 272–73.

36. *CR*, 84 Cong., 1 sess., 8544.

37. Harvey, *Symbol of Wilderness*, 274–76.

38. Howard Zahniser to John Saylor, July 29, 1955, rpt. in *CR*, 84 Cong., 1 sess., A6209; David Brower to Saylor, Aug. 2, 1955, folder 19, box 66, SCR.

39. Harvey, *Symbol of Wilderness*, 287–94.

40. See, e.g., the tribute to Saylor from *Sports Afield*, in *CR*, 84 Cong., 1 sess., 11102, and editorial, "Rep. Saylor Is Fighting Spirit for Conservation," *Ebensburg Mountaineer Herald*, Mar. 15, 1956.

41. *CR*, 84 Cong., 1 sess., 8881, 8885, 8889; Udall qtd. in the *SLT*, July 4, 1955, folder 5, box 69, SCR.

42. Robert S. Monahan to David Brower, Aug. 5, 1955, folder 19, box 65, SCR.

43. Fred Packard to Dave Bradley, Nov. 2, 1955, folder 20, box 65, SCR; David Brower to John Saylor, Nov. 21, 1955, folder 19, box 66, SCR; Harvey, *Symbol of Wilderness*, 277–78.

44. *CR*, 84 Cong., 2 sess., 3605–6, 3746–47, 3754.

45. Carl O. Gustafson to David Brower, Sept. 26, 1956, folder 20, box 66, SCR; Haley in *CR*, 84 Cong., 2 sess., 4104.

46. For Saylor's speeches against atomic power and imported foreign oil, see *CR*, 84 Cong., 1 sess., 2650, 3568, 13308–9.

Chapter 6. Wilderness and Park Advocate

1. Martin Litton to David Brower, n.d., folder 1, box 65, SCR.

2. Howard Zahniser to John Saylor, July 29, 1955, ser. 7, box 120, WSP.

3. Harvey, *Symbol of Wilderness,* xv, 65–66, 287–92; Mark W. T. Harvey, "Echo Park, Glen Canyon, and the Postwar Wilderness Movement," *Pacific Historical Review* 60 (Feb. 1991): 43–67.

4. Fred Packard to Joseph Carithers, Sept. 22, 1955, folder 1, box 65, SCR. For "true" conservation, see David Brinegar, letter to the editor, *Christian Science Monitor,* Feb. 19, 1955, and Frank Crippa in *Vernal (UT) Express,* Feb. 24, 1955, both folder 22, box 68, SCR.

5. Saylor recalled the legislative origins of the bill in a tribute shortly after Zahniser's death: "A Wilderness Apostle" [1964], ser. 3, box 500, WSP; *CR,* 84 Cong., 2 sess., 12583.

6. Allin, *Politics of Wilderness Preservation,* 31–50; Michael Frome, *Battle for the Wilderness,* rev. ed. (Salt Lake City: University of Utah Press, 1997), 71–72, 114; Nash, *Wilderness and the American Mind,* 132–33, 172.

7. Allin, *Politics of Wilderness Preservation,* 67.

8. Sutter, *Driven Wild.*

9. Arthur Carhart to Olaus Murie, Oct. 19, 1955, box 2, Olaus Murie Papers, Western History Department, Denver Public Library; Allin, *Politics of Wilderness Preservation,* 79; Frome, *Battle for the Wilderness,* 118.

10. Arthur Carhart to Olaus Murie, Oct. 19, Nov. 21, 1955, box 2, Murie Papers; Aldo Leopold, "Wilderness as a Form of Land Use," *Journal of Land and Public Utility Economics,* Oct. 1925, 397–404, box 1, Murie Papers; Aldo Leopold, "Origin and Ideals of Wilderness Areas," *LW* 5 (July 1940): 7–9; Allin, *Politics of Wilderness Preservation,* 69–71; Frome, *Battle for the Wilderness,* 117–20; Nash, *Wilderness and the American Mind,* 182–99.

11. Allin, *Politics of Wilderness Preservation,* 74, 83.

12. The U regulations created thirty "wilderness," forty-two "wild," and two "roadless" areas, totaling 14 million acres. See Robert Sterling Yard, "Saving the Wilderness," *LW* 5 (July 1940): 3–4; John Sieker, "The National Forest Wilderness System," *LW* 5 (July 1940): 5–6; Allin, *Politics of Wilderness Protection,* 80–85; Frome, *Battle for the Wilderness,* 125–26.

13. Benton MacKaye to Stewart Brandborg, Sept. 11, 1974, ser. 3, box 501, WSP; Frome, *Battle for the Wilderness,* 123; Harvey Broome, "Origins of the Wilderness Society," *LW* 5 (July 1940): 13–15; Nash, *Wilderness and the American Mind,* 206–8; Sutter, *Driven Wild,* 3–7, 194–238, 252–55. The other founding members of the Wilderness Society were Harold Anderson, Harvey Broome, Bernard Frank, Aldo Leopold, Benton MacKaye, Ernest Oberholtzer, and Robert Sterling Yard.

14. Frome, *Battle for the Wilderness,* 132–34.

15. Howard Zahniser, memorandum for the files, [Jan. 30, 1952], Fred Packard to Miles Kennedy, Nov. 19, 1952, Zahniser to Arthur E. Newkirk, Mar. 22, 1953, Zahniser, "Need For Wilderness Areas," speech before the National Citizens Planning Conference on Parks and Open Spaces for the American People, May 1955, David Brower to Sen. Hubert H. Humphrey, Apr. 11, 1956, and numerous letters from conservationists commenting on the draft legislation, all ser. 5, box 100, WSP; Brower, confidential memorandum, "A Bill to Establish [a] Wilderness System," Mar. 1, 1956, folder 1, box 9, HBP.

16. *CR,* 84 Cong., 2 sess., 12589–92. National forestlands encompassed three "roadless," fourteen "wild," ten "wilderness," and forty-nine "primitive" areas.

17. *CR,* 84 Cong., 2 sess., 12589–92.

18. *CR*, 84 Cong., 2 sess., 12583–89.

19. Saylor, "Saving America's Wilderness"; Howard Zahniser to Michael [Nadel], July 8, 1956, and penciled notations, July 9, 12, 16, 1956, George Fell to Nadel, Oct. 29, 1956, David Brower to Nadel, Oct. 31, 1956, Nadel to Karl Frederick, Nov. 2, 1956, E. Budd Marter to Nadel, Nov. 14, 1956, Frank Craighead to John Saylor, Nov. 19, 1956, Nadel to Ann Dunbar, Dec. 3, 1956 (48,000 copies), Carl Gustafson to Nadel, Dec. 13, 1956, all ser. 5, box 100, WSP.

20. John Saylor to Friends of Conservation, Nov. 1, 1956, James Munro to Saylor, Dec. 10, 1956, and Howard Zahniser to Saylor, Jan. 30, 1957, all ser. 5, box 100, WSP; Saylor to Harold Bradley, June 7, 1957, folder 2, box 9, HBP.

21. Howard Zahniser to Horace Albright, July 3, 1957, and Zahniser to John Saylor, Jan. 30, 1957, both ser. 5, box 100, WSP; Allin, *Politics of Wilderness Preservation*, 108.

22. Joe Penfold to David Brower and Howard Zahniser, Oct. 20, 1956, Leo Bodine (National Lumber Manufacturers Association) to Hubert H. Humphrey, Oct. 8, 1956, James Mussatti (California water needs) to William F. Knowland, Feb. 18, 1957, Bernard L. Orell (Weyerhaeuser Forest Products) to Zahniser, Feb. 27, May 16, 1957, and Leonard Netzorg (fire, insects, disease) to John P. Saylor, May 31, 1957, all ser. 5, box 100, WSP; Allin, *Politics of Wilderness Preservation*, 111; Frome, *Battle for the Wilderness*, 140.

23. Allin, *Politics of Wilderness Preservation*, 112; Richard Allan Baker, *Conservation Politics: The Senate Career of Clinton P. Anderson* (Albuquerque: University of New Mexico Press, 1985), 110–11.

24. Allin, *Politics of Wilderness Preservation*, 111–12.

25. Arthur Carhart to Howard Zahniser, May 11, 1956, Carhart to John Oakes, Jan. 31, 1957, Devereux Butcher to Hubert Humphrey, June 26, 1956, and Fred Smith to Olaus Murie, Jan. 14, 1957, all ser. 5, box 100, WSP.

26. *CR*, 85 Cong., 1 sess., 1900–1903, 14964–65. Saylor forwarded the letters of support to the Wilderness Society; they may be found in ser. 5, box 100, WSP.

27. Howard Zahniser to John Saylor, Jan. 30, 1957, and D.R.B. [David Brower], "Notes on Wilderness Bill," Mar. 5, 1957, both ser. 5, box 100, WSP.

28. Michael Nadel to Marjorie Hurd, Jan. 31, 1957, Howard Zahniser to Bernard Orell, Mar. 6, 1957, David Brower to William F. Knowland, Mar. 22, 1957, and Zahniser to Thomas Hughes, Apr. 2, 1957, all ser. 5, box 100, WSP.

29. Howard Zahniser to Dave [Brower] and Joe [Penfold], Oct. 23, 1956, Zahniser to Claude Wood, Administrative Assistant to Sen. Clinton Anderson, Feb. 19, 1957, Zahniser to Publisher of the *Seattle Times*, May 6, 1957, and Charles Callison to Editor of the *Seattle Times*, May 13, 1957, all ser. 5, box 100, WSP.

30. *CR*, 85 Cong., 1 sess., 5004, 6017.

31. Sen. Joseph O'Mahoney to John W. Fradet, Jan. 16, 1958, Howard Zahniser to Harvey Broome, Jan. 31, 1958, and David Brower to Harvey Banks, Department of Water Resources, State of California, Feb. 12, 1958, all ser. 5, box 100, WSP; Allin, *Politics of Wilderness Preservation*, 115–16.

32. John Saylor, address before the Lumber Dealers Association of Western Pennsylvania, Feb. 6, 1958, ser. 5, box 100, WSP.

33. David Brower to Howard Zahniser, Dec. 30, 1957, Zahniser to Brower, Feb 6, 1958, Zahniser to Walter Cottam, Feb. 13, 1958, and Sigurd Olson to Zahniser, Aug. 5, 1958, all ser. 5, box 100, WSP; Allin, *Politics of Wilderness Preservation*, 117.

34. Saylor in *CR*, 85 Cong. 1 sess., 6017; Joe Penfold to Dave Brower, with attached draft of bill, Dec. 14, 1956, folder 14, box 74, SCR; Ansel Adams to Gracie Pfost, Aug. 12, 1957, folder 279, box 9, Pfost Papers; Brower to President Dwight Eisenhower, June 18, July 11, 1958, folder 8, box 12, DBP; Rep. Clem Miller to Brower, July 1, 1959, folder 28, box 90, SCR; Baker, *Conservation Politics*, 108–14.

35. *CR*, 86 Cong., 1 sess., 377; Allin, *Politics of Wilderness Preservation*, 119; Olaus Murie to Sen. Joseph O'Mahoney, Feb. 5, 1959, ser. 5, box 102, WSP.

36. Sen. Richard Neuberger to Howard Zahniser, Feb. 24, 1959, Clinton Anderson to Harvey Broome, Apr. 9, 1959, and Anderson to Odd Halseth, May 20, 1959, all ser. 5, box 102, WSP; Baker, *Conservation Politics*, 104, 116–18; Wayne Aspinall to David Brower, Jan. 2, 1959, and Member of Congress Clem Miller to Brower, July 1, 1959, both ser. 5, box 102, WSP.

37. Ann Dunbar to Howard Zahniser, Feb. 16, 1959, Zahniser to Member of Congress George McGovern, Apr. 25, 1959, and Zahniser to Lloyd Tupling, Apr. 29, 1959, all ser. 5, box 102, WSP; John Saylor, "Conservation Legacy of Theodore Roosevelt," 114–16.

38. Erwin D. Cantam, editor, *Christian Science Monitor*, to Dave Brooks, May 12, 1959, editorial, *St. Louis Post Dispatch*, May 21, 1959, and Sen. Joseph O'Mahoney to Olaus Murie, Feb. 16, 1959, all box 1, Murie Papers; O'Mahoney to Sen. James Murray, Aug. 27, 1959, and O'Mahoney to Howard Zahniser, Sept. 1, 1959, both ser. 5, box 102, WSP; Charles H. Porter to John Saylor, Aug. 8, 1959, box 37, JSP.

39. Olaus Murie to Howard Zahniser, Sept. 14, 1959, and Zahniser to Murie, Sept. 21, Oct. 2, 1959, all ser. 3, box 500, WSP.

40. *CR*, 86 Cong., 2 sess., 11711, 11720; Richard McCardle, Chief, U.S. Forest Service, to Olaus Murie, Dec. 16, 1959, box 1, Murie Papers; "Multiple Use Act Is Passed," *LW* 25 (Summer 1960): 27–28; Baker, *Conservation Politics*, 124–25; Frome, *Battle for the Wilderness*, 137.

41. Editorial, *San Francisco Examiner*, Mar. 15, 1960; Trustees for Conservation to Dear Congressman, Mar. 31, 1960, ser. 5, box 102, WSP; John Oakes, *NYT*, May 1, 1960.

42. The Murray-Saylor bill was nearly identical to H.R. 10621, introduced by Rep. Clem Miller of California in Feb. In Apr., O'Mahoney and Sen. Gordon Allott of Colorado offered a substitute bill that was unacceptable to preservationists because it would have safeguarded only 6 million acres. See Howard Zahniser to Peggy and Edgar Wayburn, Aug. 15, 1960, ser. 5, box 102, WSP; *CR*, 86 Cong., 2 sess., 15849; Sen. James Murray, "The Wilderness Bill of 1960," *LW* 25 (Summer 1960): 34–45; Allin, *Politics of Wilderness Preservation*, 122–23.

43. John Oakes, *NYT*, July 3, 1960; editorial, *Saturday Evening Post*, July 16, 1960; Howard Zahniser to Olaus Murie, Oct. 2, 1959, ser. 3, box 500, WSP.

44. David Brower to John Saylor, Apr. 19, 1956, folder 20, box 66, SCR; Joe Penfold to Saylor, Apr. 24, 1956, box 37, JSP.

45. David Brower, memorandum to Anne [?], Mar. 1, 1956, ser. 5, box 100, WSP; Robert Daly to Brower, Oct. 15, 1957, folder 22, box 65, SCR; Brower, untitled memorandum summarizing the two bills, n.d., box 37, JSP.

46. Editorial support: *San Francisco Chronicle*, Apr. 27, 1956, and *NYT*, Apr. 29, 1956; Dawson and Watkins in the *SLT*, Apr. 19, 1956. For Saylor as a foe of reclamation, see *SLT*, Apr. 29, 1956.

47. *CR*, 84 Cong., 2 sess., 7174–75; telegrams, Apr. 24, 1956, to Sen. Arthur Watkins and the *SLT*, from Ira Gabrielson, Citizens Committee on Natural Resources, Fred Smith, Council of Conservationists, Ansel Adams, Trustees for Conservation, David Brower, and

Sierra Club, and Brower, memorandum, "Dinosaur Tiff, Watkins et al.," Apr. 28, 1956, all box 37, JSP.

48. *CR*, 85 Cong., 1 sess., 81; Fred Packard to Fred Smith, Jan. 23, 1957, box 37, JSP; Smith to Gordon Allott, July 15, 16, 1957, and memorandum to WE [staff assistant Warren Elliott] from GLA [Allott], July 16, 1957, all ser. 3, box 5, Gordon Allott Papers, University of Colorado, Boulder; Michael Nadel, memorandum to Zahnie, "telephone call from Fred Smith," July 17, 1957, ser. 7, box 120, WSP.

49. Gordon Allott to E. J. Deshayes Jr., May 21, 1956, ser. 3, box 5, Allott Papers; Howard Zahniser, memorandum for the files, July 18, 1957, ser. 7, box 120, WSP.

50. Memorandum to WE from GLA, July 16, 1957.

51. "Pennsylvanian Charges Insincerity by Echo Park Dam Backers," *DP*, Aug. 9, 1957; McNichols qtd. in *DP*, Aug. 19, 1957, box 37, JSP.

52. Fred Packard to Fred Smith, July 31, 1957, and Devereux Butcher to Smith, Aug. 12, 1957, both box 37, JSP.

53. Fred Smith, memorandum to the Trustees of the National Parks Association, Aug. 2, 1957, box 37, JSP.

54. Fred Packard to Dave Brower, July 25, 1957, folder 23, box 67, SCR; Packard to Olaus Murie, Aug. 20, 1957, box 3, Murie Papers; Packard, memorandum to the Board of Trustees and Cooperating Organizations, Aug. 15, 1957, Packard to Fred Seaton, Aug. 15, 1957, Packard to John Saylor, Aug. 21, 1957, Packard to Sig Olson, Aug. 21, 1957, and Murie to Fellow Members of the Board of Trustees of the National Parks Association, Aug. 12, 1957, all box 37, JSP; Richard Leonard, memorandum to Harold Bradley, "Wilderness Society Council Meeting, August 17–21, 1957," Aug. 26, 1957, Nadel Files; Brower, memorandum to Conservation Cooperators, "The Dinosaur Park Dilemma: An Analysis," Sept. 24, 1957, folder 23, box 5, HBP; Fred Packard, "Dinosaur Park Proposal," *NPM*, Oct.–Dec. 1957, 159–60; "Dinosaur Park Proposal," *SCB*, Sept. 1957, 4.

55. Alfred A. Knopf to Gordon Allott, Aug. 9, 1957, ser. 3, box 5, Allott Papers; David Brower to Fred Smith, Sept. 19, 1957, Smith to Harold Bradley, Sept. 24, 1957, Charles Callison to Smith, Sept. 26, 1957, Bradley to Richard Leonard, Oct. 6, 9, 1957, Howard Zahniser to Leonard, Oct. 10, 1957, Leonard to Harvey Broome ("psychotic"), Oct. 11, 1957, and Robert Daly to Brower ("muddleheaded"), Oct. 15, 1957, all folder 22, box 65, SCR; memorandum of telephone conversation between Zahniser and Allott, Nov. 13, 1957, ser. 3, box 5, Allott Papers; Allott to Fred Seaton, Mar. 26, 1958, and Seaton to Allott, May 12, 1958, both box 37, JSP.

56. Fred Smith to Gordon Allott, Jan. 5, 1959, Wayne Aspinall to Allott, Jan. 12, Apr. 27, 1959, and Allott to Aspinall, Apr. 29, 1957, all ser. 6, box 91, Allott Papers.

57. Fred Smith to David Brower, Aug. 5, 1959, folder 1, box 66, SCR; Horace Albright to John Saylor, Aug. 7, 1959, box 37, JSP.

58. John Saylor to Horace Albright, Aug. 10, 1959, box 37, JSP.

59. Saylor to Albright, Aug. 10, 1959.

60. Fred Smith to John Saylor, Aug. 13, 1959, Horace Albright to Saylor, Aug. 18, 1959, and Gordon Allott to Edward Graves, Aug. 31, 1959, all box 37, JSP; Albright to David Brower, Aug. 25, 1959, and Fred Smith to Brower, Aug. 28, 1959, both folder 20, box 66, SCR; Fred Smith to Graves, Sept. 3, 1959, Nadel Files.

61. For the statements of the governors, see *SLT*, Aug. 8, 1957; *Vernal Express*, Aug. 15, 1957; *DP*, Aug. 8, 1957; and *Durango Herald-News*, Aug. 8, 1957. Also see Ted Moss to Don Hatch, Nov. 3, 1959, folder 23, box 5, HBP; David Brower, confidential letter to

Charles Eggert, Aug. 14, 1959, folder 34, box 10, DBP; Gordon Allott to Ethel Larsen, Aug. 23, 1957, ser. 5, box 120, WSP; Allott to Fred Packard, Sept. 19, 1957, box 6, Nadel Files; Allott to C. Edward Graves, Aug. 31, 1959, box 37, JSP; Allott to R. G. Lyttle, Aug. 14, 1957, ser. 3, box 5, Allott Papers; Warren Elliott to John J. Barnard, Nov. 16, 1959, ser. 6, box 91, Allott Papers.

62. Fred Smith to Howard Zahniser ("Great Dispute"), Sept. 24, 1957, ser. 7, box 120, WSP; Dave Brower to Horace Albright, Apr. 15, 1958, folder 3, box 9, HBP; Spencer Smith, Secretary, Citizens Committee on Natural Resources, to John Saylor, Aug. 22, 1959, Ansel Adams to Saylor, Aug. 23, 1959, Saylor to Adams, Aug. 26, 1959, and Olaus Murie to Saylor, Aug. 26, 1959, all box 37, JSP.

63. Editorial, "Is It Best, Mr. Secretary, to Modify the Dinosaur Bill H.R. 951?" *National Wildlands News*, Jan. 1960, 1; Fred Smith to Devereux Butcher, Jan. 18, 1960, and Smith, memorandum to David Brower and seven other conservation leaders, Jan. 18, 1960, both box 37, JSP; Smith to Gordon Allott, Jan. 18, 1960, ser. 6, box 91, Allott Papers. Smith described Devereux Butcher, editor of the *National Wildlands News*, as an "irresponsible troublemaker" and accused Saylor of being behind the editorial criticizing the Allott bill. He vowed to find a way "of taking care" of Saylor. See Smith to Allott, Jan. 15, 1960, ser. 6, box 91, Allott Papers.

64. *CR*, 86 Cong., 2 sess., 12572–80.

65. *CR*, 86 Cong., 2 sess., 12580–82, 12606, 13598, 14669, 15009, 16700, 17649, 17901, 18482, 18921; U.S. House of Representatives, Report No. 2197, Aug. 25, 1960; Public Law 729, *U.S. Statutes at Large*, vol. 74, 86 Cong., 2 sess., 1960, 857–62.

66. John Saylor to Harold Bradley, Nov. 14, 1957, folder 8, box 87, SCR; David Brower to Fred Smith ("best friends"), Aug. 14, 1959, and Fred Packard to Brower ("leading champion"), Sept. 8, 1959, both folder 1, box 66, SCR.

Chapter 7. Coal, the C&O Canal, and Kinzua

1. U.S. Congress, Hearings before the Subcommittee on Public Lands of the House Committee on Interior and Insular Affairs, 86 Cong., 1 sess, on H.R. 953, H.R. 2331, H.R. 5194, and H.R. 5344, *To Establish the Chesapeake and Ohio Canal National Historical Park and to Provide for the Administration and Maintenance of a Parkway in the State of Maryland, and for Other Purposes* (Washington, DC: GPO, 1959), 206.

2. John Saylor, "Save Our River," *CR*, 86 Cong., 2 sess, 7964–65.

3. *Portage (PA) Dispatch*, Feb. 3, 1955, and *Ebensburg Mountaineer-Herald*, Mar. 17, 1955, both 1955 scrapbook, JSP; "Straight from Washington: Exclusive Interview with Congressman Saylor," *Johnstown Observer*, Apr. 26, 1956; "Why Representative Saylor Opposes So-Called Free Trade," *United Mine Workers Journal*, Apr. 15, 1956; Saylor, press releases, July 11, 18, 1956, 1956 scrapbook, JSP; *CR*, 84 Cong., 2 sess, 11656, 14249, 14262, 14264.

4. U.S. Congress, Hearings before the Special Subcommittee on Coal Research of the Committee on Interior and Insular Affairs, House of Representatives, 85 Cong., 1 sess., *The Establishment of a Research and Development Program for the Coal Industry* (Washington, DC: GPO, 1957), 1–2.

5. Hearings, *Coal Industry*, 3–5.

6. Hearings, *Coal Industry*, 7–9.

7. Hearings, *Coal Industry*, 6, 15–20, 20–37; *CR*, 85 Cong., 1 sess., 16173; 85 Cong., 2 sess., 1581–82.

8. *CR*, 86 Cong., 1 sess., 48, 8709, 10673–703, 14309, 14536, 14714, 17429–30, 19753; 86 Cong., 2 sess., 2525, 2531–2532, 2560, 14432–46, 15844.

9. *CR*, 85 Cong., 1 sess., 6320; 85 Cong., 2 sess., 7911, 18340–44; *Johnstown Tribune-Democrat*, Feb. 18, 1960, 1960 scrapbook, JSP; *Memorial Services Held . . . John P. Saylor*, 124.

10. *CR*, 85 Cong., 1 sess., 9049 (quote), 14308; John Saylor, "Depressed Areas and Foreign Aid," *CR*, 85 Cong., 2 sess., 8669–70; *NYT*, Mar. 11, 1959.

11. John Saylor, "Free Our People from the Foreign-Made Shackles of Unemployment," *CR*, 86 Cong., 1 sess., 3074–75; John Saylor, "Mandatory Control Program on Residual Oil Imports," *CR*, 86 Cong., 1 sess., 6182; John Saylor, "Residual Fuel Oil," *CR*, 86 Cong., 2 sess., 8832–33.

12. *CR*, 85 Cong., 1 sess., 51; 86 Cong., 1 sess., 6046.

13. *CR*, 86 Cong., 2 sess., 9442–43.

14. *CR*, 86 Cong., 2 sess., 10302. For debate on the 1958 Area Redevelopment Assistance Bill, see *CR*, 85 Cong., 2 sess., 17837–904.

15. *CR*, 86 Cong., 1 sess., 1969, A871–72; *Blairsville (PA) Dispatch*, Feb. 9, 1959.

16. Editorial, *Apollo News-Record*, July 3, 1959.

17. *CR*, 86 Cong., 1 sess., 11685–86.

18. See numerous newspaper clippings, 1958, 1959, and 1960 scrapbooks, JSP.

19. See 1958, 1959, and 1960 scrapbooks, JSP.

20. John Saylor, "Stan, the American Man," *CR*, 84 Cong., 2 sess., 12396; "High Court Boots Football," *CR*, 85 Cong., 1 sess., A2081.

21. *Portage (PA) Dispatch*, Apr, 9, 1959; *Indiana (PA) Gazette*, Sept. 19, 1959; *Johnstown Tribune-Democrat*, July 9, 1959; Dwight D. Eisenhower to John Saylor, Aug. 21, 1959, OF 147-E, box 755, Eisenhower Papers.

22. *NYT*, Nov. 14, 17, 18, 19, 1957; *Philadelphia Inquirer*, Jan. 7, 1958; *Johnstown Tribune-Democrat*, Jan. 2, 14, 1958.

23. "Secretary of the Interior Fred A. Seaton Creates Arctic and Two Other National Wildlife Ranges in Alaska," *NPM*, Jan. 1961, 17. The two other wildlife ranges were Kuskokwim and Izembek in western Alaska.

24. *CR*, 85 Cong., 2 sess., 9528; 86 Cong., 1 sess., 9208; 86 Cong., 2 sess., 8430; 87 Cong., 1 sess., 12198–99; 87 Cong., 2 sess., 14412–13, 14424–25.

25. Hearings, *C&O Canal* (1959), 15.

26. Irston R. Barnes, "Historic C&O Canal Threatened by Road," *NPM*, July–Sept. 1953, 113–16, 134–38; Irston R. Barnes, "A New Era for the Chesapeake and Ohio Canal," *NPM*, July–Sept. 1956, 110–16; John Oakes, "Conservation News," *NYT*, May 13, 1956; "Continued Threat to Chesapeake and Ohio Canal," *NPM*, Jan.–Mar. 1957, 20–21.

27. U.S. Congress, Hearings before the Subcommittee on Public Lands of the Committee on Interior and Insular Affairs, House of Representatives, 85 Cong., 2 sess., on S. 77 and H.R. 1145, *To Establish the Chesapeake and Ohio Canal National Historic Park and to Provide for the Administration and Maintenance of a Parkway, in the State of Maryland, and for Other Purposes*, June 30, July 1, 15, Aug. 13, 14, 15, 18, 1958 (Washington, DC: GPO, 1958), 5–7, 14, 138–44, 176–77.

28. Thomas Stokes, "Hells Canyon Dam Legislation," *Washington Evening Star*, July 5, 1957; Hearings, *C&O Canal* (1958), 82, 148–50; editorial, "Temporary Defeat," *NPM*, Oct.–Dec. 1958, 153.

29. *CR*, 86 Cong., 1 sess., 48; Hearings, *C&O Canal* (1958), 1–2.

30. "The Parks and Congress," *NPM*, Apr. 1959, 15.

31. Anthony Wayne Smith, "C and O Canal National Historical Park," *NPM*, Jan.–Mar. 1958, 32–35; Aubrey Graves, "Chesapeake and Ohio Canal Park Hearings," *NPM*, June 1959, 15.

32. Hearings, *C&O Canal* (1959), 26–28.

33. Hearings, *C&O Canal* (1959), 197.

34. Hearings, *C&O Canal* (1959), 39 42.

35. Hearings, *C&O Canal* (1959), 42–44.

36. Hearings, *C&O Canal* (1959), 97–98.

37. Hearings, *C&O Canal* (1959), 147.

38. Hearings, *C&O Canal* (1959), 13, 154–55, 214.

39. Hearings, *C&O Canal* (1959), 76.

40. Hearings, *C&O Canal* (1959), 91.

41. Hearings, *C&O Canal* (1959), 204.

42. "The National Parks and Congress," *NPM*, July 1959, 13; *CR*, 86 Cong., 2 sess., 10710–11.

43. "Conservation News Briefs," *NPM*, Mar. 1961, 16; *CR*, 91 Cong., 2 sess., 34847 (Taylor quote).

44. For general works on the Kinzua controversy, see Joy A. Bilharz, *The Allegany Senecas and Kinzua Dam: Forced Relocation through Two Generations* (Lincoln and London: University of Nebraska Press, 1998); Alvin Josephy Jr., "Cornplanter Can You Swim?" *American Heritage* 19 (Dec. 1968): 4–9, 106–10; Paul Rosier, "Dam Building and Treaty Breaking: The Kinzua Dam Controversy, 1936–1958," *Pennsylvania Magazine of History and Biography* 119 (Oct. 1995): 345–68.

45. *CR*, 85 Cong., 1 sess., 9675.

46. *CR*, 85 Cong., 1 sess., 9705; Colonel H. E. Sprague, District Engineer, U.S. Corps of Engineers, Pittsburgh District, to John Saylor, Jan. 15, 1957, and W. S. Brotzman to John Saylor, Mar. 11, May 29, 1957 (with enclosed reports from Weather Bureau covering nine Pittsburgh floods over fifty years), Jan. 26, 1959, all folder 1, box 39, JSP.

47. *CR*, 85 Cong., 1 sess., 9672, 9705–7.

48. *CR*, 82 Cong., 2 sess., 5450; Douglas Smith in the *PP*, June 23, 1957, box 39, JSP.

49. Cornelius V. Seneca to John Saylor, Mar. 8, 1957, folder 2, box 39, JSP; *CR*, 85 Cong., 1 sess., 9706; *Buffalo Evening News*, June 20, 1957; Douglas Smith in the *PP*, June 23, 1957 (quote).

50. J. Alex Zehner, Assistant Managing Editor, *Pittsburgh Sun-Telegraph*, to John Saylor, Jan. 31, Feb. 6, 1957, and numerous other letters, folders 1 and 2, box 39, JSP. See also editorial, *Sewikley (PA) Herald*, June 27, 1957, box 25, Ann Whitman File, Eisenhower Papers.

51. Cornelius Seneca to John Saylor, June 27, 1957, folder 1, box 39, JSP; *CR*, 85 Cong., 1 sess., 9706.

52. J. Alex Zehner to John Saylor, Jan. 31, Feb. 1, 1957, Saylor to Secretary of the Interior Fred Seaton, Jan. 31, 1957, and Felix Wormser, Assistant Secretary of the Interior, to Saylor, Feb. 21, 1957, all folder 2, box 39, JSP.

53. Memorandum, background on Dr. A. E. Morgan, Feb. 23, 1959, folder 1, box 39, JSP; Arthur Morgan, *Dams and Other Disasters: A Century of the Army Corps of Engineers in Civil Works* (Boston: Peter Sargent, 1971), 340–43, 347–64.

54. Cornelius Seneca to John Saylor, Oct. 1957, Gerald D. Morgan, Special Counsel to the President, to Seneca, Oct. 29, 1957, Seneca to Col. R. E. Smyser, Division Engineer, Corps of Engineers, Nov. 1, 1957, and Edward O'Neill, General Counsel, Seneca Nation of Indians, to Saylor, Nov. 14, 1957, all folder 1, box 39, JSP; J. S. Bragdon, memorandum for the President, July 18, 25, 1957, and John S. D. Eisenhower, memorandum of conference with the President, July 22, 1957, both box 25, Whitman File.

55. Arthur Morgan to Gen. Emerson C. Itschner, Apr. 24, 1958, and Morgan to Robert Abbett, May 8, 1958, both folder 2, box 39, JSP; Morgan, *Dams and Other Disasters*, 321.

56. George Heron to John Saylor, Jan. 12, 1959, folder 1, box 39, JSP; Saylor to President Dwight Eisenhower, Jan. 16, 1959, folder 3, box 39, JSP.

57. David Lawrence to John Saylor, Feb. 4, 1959, Paul Bradigan, President, Kittanning Chamber of Commerce, to Saylor, Feb. 26, 1959, and Saylor to Bradigan, Mar. 5, 1959, all folder 3, box 39, JSP.

58. Arthur E. Morgan, memorandum to the Engineers of the Pittsburgh Region, Mar. 26, 1960, and Morgan, letter to members of Congress with attached memorandum, "Additional Advantages of Conewango-Cattaraugus over Kinzua," Apr. 18, 1960, both *CR*, 86 Cong., 2 sess., 11061–62; John Saylor, memorandum to Jack Anderson, Aug. 26, 1960, and Saylor to Morgan, Sept. 3, 1960, both folder 2, box 39, JSP.

59. Sol A. Jacobsen to David Lawrence, n.d., box 41, ms. group 191, David Lawrence Governors Papers, Pennsylvania State Historical Society, Harrisburg.

60. Editorials: *NYT*, Feb. 22, 1961; *WP*, Apr. 8, 1961; *Buffalo Courier Express*, Apr. 25, 1961, excerpted in Walter Taylor, coordinator, *The Kinzua Dam Controversy: A Practical Solution—without Shame* (Philadelphia: Kinzua Project of the Indian Committee of the Philadelphia Yearly Meeting of Friends, 1961), 16–17. Also see Brooks Atkinson, "Critic at Large," *NYT*, Apr. 21, 1961, folder 3, box 39, JSP; Eleanor Roosevelt, "Moral Issue at Stake in Senecas' Land-for-Dam Fight," *Philadelphia Daily News*, June 8, 1961, folder 40, box 66, SCR; telegrams: Hugh Downs to John Saylor, Jan. 7, 1963, and Saylor to Downs, Jan. 14, 1963, both folder 4, box 39, JSP; Bilharz, *Allegany Senecas*, 55–56.

61. U.S. Congress, Hearings by the Subcommittee on Public Works of the House Committee on Appropriations, 85 Cong., 1 sess., *Public Works Appropriation for 1958* (Washington, DC: GPO, 1957), 676–89; Howard Zahniser to John Saylor, Apr. 3, 1957, with enclosed article by William Fenton, "A Day on the Allegheny Ox-Bow," *LW* 13 (July 1945): 1–8, folder 1, box 39, JSP; Zahniser to George Alexander, May 7, 1957, ser. 6, box 100, WSP; Edward Zahniser, interview, Aug. 7, 1997.

62. Kennedy qtd. in Philadelphia Friends, *Kinzua Dam*, 14; Sen. Joseph Clark to John F. Kennedy, Jan. 3, 1961, and Gov. David Lawrence to Clark, Jan. 10, 1961, both box 41, David Lawrence Governors Papers; John Saylor to Ford Blaney, Oct. 2, 1963, folder 2, box 39, JSP; Bilharz, *Allegany Senecas*, 55.

63. Lee C. White, memorandum for the President, "Kinzua Dam," Aug. 8, 1961, and Pres. John F. Kennedy to Seneca Pres. Basil Williams, Aug. 9, 1961, both box 1, Lee White Papers, White House Staff Files, John F. Kennedy Library (JFKL hereafter); George Heron to John Saylor, Aug. 24, 1962, Saylor to Heron, Sept. 4, 6, 1962, and Program, American Indian Day—New York State, Sept. 15, 1962, all folder 3, box 39, JSP; *Kinzua Planning Newsletter*, Sept. 7, 1962, 4; Saylor, "The Seneca Indians and the Cause of American Freedom," Sept. 14, 1962, "Speeches" folder, box 39, JSP; editorial, *Indiana Evening Gazette*, Sept. 27, 1962.

64. John Saylor to Ford Blaney, Oct. 2, 1963, folder 2, box 39, JSP; *CR*, 88 Cong., 1 sess., 1682; 88 Cong., 2 sess., 2513–14, 5764; *Dunkirk-Fredonia (NY) Evening Observer*, Mar. 3, 1967, 1967 scrapbook, JSP; Bilharz, *Allegany Senecas*, 98.

65. Regis O'Brien to John Saylor, July 1, 1957, and Saylor to O'Brien, July 25, 1957, both folder 3, box 39, JSP; Ed Jordan, "Crossroads Politics: Has Kinzua Dam Stand Hurt Saylor?" *Johnstown Tribune-Democrat*, July 10, 1957 (quote); "Saylor's Running," *PP*, Aug. 4, 1957, *Johnstown Tribune-Democrat*, Nov. 7, 1958.

66. For voting registration figures for 1956, see Ed Jordan in the *Johnstown Tribune-Democrat*, Mar. 31, 1956. For registered voters by county and district in 1960, see *Kittanning Leader Times*, Oct. 26, 1960. For Patton's background, see Ingrid Jewell in the *Pittsburgh Post-Gazette*, Oct. 25, 1960, 1960 scrapbook, JSP.

67. Unidentified newspaper clipping, n.d., and *Johnstown Tribune-Democrat*, Sept. 2, 1960, 1960 scrapbook, JSP.

68. Qtd. in *Blairsville Dispatch*, Sept. 19, 1960, 1960 scrapbook, JSP.

69. Dwight D. Eisenhower to William H. Heslop, written message of tribute to Saylor, n.d., box 696, OF 138, Eisenhower Papers; Fred Seaton to Heslop, June 13, 1960, and notes for Saylor testimonial speech, both box 48, Speech Series, Fred Seaton Papers, DDEL; *Johnstown Tribune-Democrat*, Nov. 10, 15, 1960; *Kittanning News-Leader*, Nov. 9, 1960 (quote), 1960 scrapbook, JSP.

Chapter 8. The Rainbow Connection

1. Charles Greenlaw, letter to the editor and editor's reply, *NPM*, Jan. 1962, 2.

2. For Aspinall's personality and career, see Stephen Sturgeon, *The Politics of Western Water: The Congressional Career of Wayne Aspinall* (Tucson: University of Arizona Press, 2002); Steven C. Schulte, *Wayne Aspinall and the Shaping of the West* (Boulder: University Press of Colorado, 2002); Clay Peters, Republican staff member, House Interior Committee, interview with the author, June 22, 2005.

3. U.S. House, Hearings before the Subcommittee on Irrigation and Reclamation of the Committee on Interior and Insular Affairs, 90 Cong., 1 sess., on H.R. 27 and H.R. 1163, *A Bill to Authorize the Secretary of the Interior to Construct, Operate and Maintain the First Stage of the Oahe Unit, James Division, Missouri River Project, South Dakota, and for Other Purposes* (Washington, DC: GPO, 1967), 258.

4. Wayne Aspinall, interview with Nancy Whistlen, Feb. 15, 1979, Library of Congress, 8. Political scientist Richard Fenno commends Aspinall for his effective handling of the House Interior Committee; see Fenno, *Congressmen in Committees*, 57–64, 92–94.

5. Wayne Aspinall to John Saylor, July 1, 1960, box 35, JSP; Aspinall to Grace Saylor, Oct. 28, 1973, folder 40, box 36, Wayne Aspinall Papers, University of Colorado Library, Boulder.

6. Saylor qtd. in "The Fighting 89th," *Newsweek*, Jan. 18, 1965, 19.

7. Paul ("Pete") McCloskey Jr., "An Environmentalist in Congress: Urging Presidential Action on Point Reyes," transcript of oral history interview by Ann Lage, in *Saving Point Reyes National Seashore, 1969–1970: An Oral History of Citizen Action in Conservation* (Berkeley: University of California Regional Oral History Office, 1993), 316; Hearings, *C&O Canal* (1959), 103–4. I am indebted to historian Stephen Sturgeon for bringing the McCloskey interview to my attention.

8. John Saylor to Wendell Wyatt, June 3, 1966, and Saylor to Wayne Aspinall, June 9, 1966, both box 31, JSP.

9. Wendell Wyatt, telephone interview with the author, Oct. 4, 2002; Wyatt to John Saylor, June 11, 1966, Gov. Mark Hatfield to Saylor, June 22, 1966, and Wayne Aspinall to Saylor, June 30, 1966, all box 31, JSP. Morris Udall described Saylor's letter as "incredible" in an undated, handwritten note to his brother Stewart; folder 3, box 127, Stewart Udall Papers, University of Arizona Library (SUP hereafter).

10. John Wold, letter to the author, Sept. 15, 2004, and telephone interview with the author, Sept. 28, 2004.

11. Frey's recollections are recounted in *Memorial Services Held . . . John P. Saylor,* 108. For Saylor's friendliness toward new members, see H. John Heinz in *Memorial Services Held . . . John P. Saylor,* 20; Bill Burlison (D-MO), letter to the author, Sept. 13, 2004.

12. Murray, interview, July 14, 1997; Gentry, interview, June 23, 2005; Peters, interview, June 22, 2005. For the nonpartisan nature of the committee staff, see Sidney Mc-Farland, Chief Counsel, House Interior and Insular Affairs Committee, to John Saylor, June 15, 1970, box 35, JSP.

13. Murray, interview, July 14, 1997 ("fun" and "district"); Charles Leppert, assistant counsel, House Committee on Interior and Insular Affairs, interview with the author, Jan. 9, 1995 ("schoolteacher"); Lee McIlvaine, assistant counsel, House Committee on Interior and Insular Affairs, interview with the author, Jan. 11, 1995 ("grouse").

14. Aspinall, interview, Feb. 15, 1979; McIlvaine, interview, Jan. 11, 1995.

15. Aspinall qtd. in Reisner, *Cadillac Desert,* 247–48. Saylor qtd. in *CR,* 87 Cong., 2 sess., 9137.

16. For general treatments, see Martin, *Story That Stands like a Dam;* Jared Farmer, *Glen Canyon Dammed: Inventing Lake Powell and the Canyon Country* (Tucson: University of Arizona Press, 1999).

17. Harvey, *Symbol of Wilderness,* 278–83.

18. David Brower to W. R. Halliday, Jan. 16, 1954, folder 24, box 64, SCR; Fred Packard to Halliday, Feb. 17, 1954, folder 2, box 65, SCR; Brower "struck dead" quote in Martin, *Story That Stands like a Dam,* 266.

19. Bruce Kilgore, "The Rainbow Bridge Debate," *NPM,* Oct.–Dec. 1958, 155–59, 182.

20. Kilgore, "Rainbow Bridge Debate"; Hugh M. Miller, Acting Regional Director, National Park Service, and E. O. Larson, Regional Director, Bureau of Reclamation, memorandum of understanding, Oct. 13, 1954, attached to Leo Diederich to Howard Zahniser, Feb. 14, 1955, folder 15, box 65, SCR.

21. Charles Eggert to Fred Packard, Aug. 2, 1955, folder 19, box 65, SCR.

22. L. F. Wylie to Floyd Dominy, Sept. 3, 1958, and Dominy to Lem [Wylie], Oct. 28, 1958, both box 3, Floyd Dominy Papers, American Heritage Center, University of Wyoming, Laramie; Dominy to Neva Miller, June 21, 1966 ("scenic violence"), box 14, Dominy Papers; Dominy, interview, July 15, 1997 ("I took"); Mark W. T. Harvey, "Defending the National Park System: The Controversy over Rainbow Bridge," *New Mexico Historical Review* 73 (Jan. 1998): 50.

23. "Touring Lawmakers Split on Rainbow Bridge Plans," *NPM,* Feb. 1960, 2, 19.

24. Anthony Wayne Smith to Fred Seaton, Jan. 19, 1960, rpt. in *NPM,* Feb. 1960, 17; Harvey, "Defending the National Park System," 46; editorial, "At Rainbow Bridge and Elsewhere Precedent Is Important," *NPM,* Feb. 1960, 2; editorial, "Let's Look beyond the Rainbow," *National Wildland News,* Apr. 1960, 2; Devereux Butcher, "Rainbow Bridge a

Stepping Stone," draft of article, box 2, Devereux Butcher Papers, American Heritage Center, University of Wyoming, Laramie; Seaton to David Brower, Feb. 15, 1960, rpt. in "Interior Announces Rainbow Plans," *NPM,* Mar. 1960, 17.

25. Tad Nichols to J. F. Carithers, Aug. 22, 1960, box 2, Butcher Papers.

26. John Saylor to Wayne Aspinall, Aug. 23, 1960, box 31, JSP; *Grand Junction Daily Sentinel,* Aug. 28, 1960.

27. Stewart Udall to Wayne Aspinall, Aug. 27, 1960, box 19, Dominy Papers.

28. Udall to Aspinall, Aug. 27, 1960; "Rainbow Bridge Visit Leaves Two Solons with Two Opinions," *Arizona Daily Star,* Sept. 13, 1960, and J. F. C[arithers], "The Rainbow Bridge Dilemma," memorandum to Devereux Butcher, Sept. 1, 1960, both box 2, Butcher Papers.

29. Katie Lee, letter to the editor, *NPM,* June 1960, 18; Angus Woodbury, "Ecologist Rips Rainbow Bridge Plan, Cites Alternative," *Salt Lake City Tribune,* Aug. 30, 1960; Tad Nichols to J. F. Carithers, Aug. 22, 1960, box 2, Butcher Papers.

30. Bruce Kilgore to Katie Lee, editor's reply, *NPM,* June 1960, 18; J. F. C[arithers], memoranda to Devereux Butcher, "Rainbow Bridge," and "Rainbow Bridge Dilemma," both Sept. 1, 1960, box 2, Butcher Papers; Anthony Wayne Smith to Fred Seaton, Sept. 28, 1960, rpt. in *NPM,* Nov. 1960, 15; "Parks Advisory Board Makes Recommendations," *NPM,* Jan. 1961, 17.

31. Stewart Udall, interview, Aug. 21, 1986, July 18, 1995; Stewart L. Udall, Oral History, JFKL, 3–5, 9–10, 19–21; Lee White, Oral History #4, JFKL, 9.

32. For a general account, see Thomas G. Smith, "John Kennedy, Stewart Udall, and New Frontier Conservation," *Pacific Historical Review* 64 (Aug. 1995): 329–62.

33. Stewart Udall, memorandum to Conrad Wirth and Floyd Dominy, Feb. 15, 1961, box 22, Dominy Papers; U.S. Department of the Interior, press release, Mar. 28, 1961, box 22, Dominy Papers; "Conservation Leaders Discuss Problems with Secretary," *NPM,* Apr. 1961, 15.

34. Ottis Petersen, memorandum to the Commissioner, "Rainbow Bridge Trip," Apr. 21, 1961, box 23, Dominy Papers; Weldon Heald, "Helicopters over Rainbow Bridge," draft of article, May 22, 1961, box 2, Butcher Papers; editorial, "On Enlarging Rainbow Bridge National Monument," *NPM,* May 1961, 2; editorial, "Protection Comes First at Rainbow Bridge," *NPM,* June 1961, 2, 16; Bruce Kilgore to David D. King, June 9, 1961, Sigurd Olson to Kilgore, June 12, 1961, and Bestor Robinson to Stewart Udall, June 15, 1961, all folder 27, box 68, SCR.

35. Ira Gabrielson to John Saylor, June 14, 1961, box 31, JSP; Anthony Wayne Smith to Saylor, Sept. 7, 1961, box 37, JSP; David Brower to Saylor, Apr. 5, 1962, box 37, JSP. See also David Brower, "Wilderness River Betrayal," *SCB,* Oct. 1961, 19–20; Bruce Kilgore, "Tragedy Waits at Rainbow Bridge," *Outdoor America,* Oct. 1961, 4–5; Matt Dodge, "The End of the Rainbow Trail," *NPM,* Mar. 1961, 8–10; editorial, "A Water-Gate for Rainbow," *NPM,* Jan. 1962, 2; David Brower, "Uneasy Chair: An Open Letter to Secretary Udall," *SCB,* Mar.–Apr. 1962, 2–3.

36. John Saylor to Richard Bradley, June 30, 1961, box 31, JSP.

37. Harvey, "Defending the Park System," 59–64.

38. John Saylor, "Public Power—Galloping Socialism," *CR,* 87 Cong., 2 sess., 9136–40.

39. U.S. Congress, Hearings before the Subcommittee on Irrigation and Reclamation of the Committee on Interior and Insular Affairs, House of Representatives, 86 Cong., 2 sess., on H.R. 1235 and S. 281, *To Authorize the Secretary of the Interior to Con-*

struct, Operate, and Maintain a Reregulating Reservoir and Other Works at the Burns Creek Site in the Upper Snake River Valley, Idaho and for Other Purposes, pt. 1, Aug. 27, 28, 1959, Feb. 15, 16, 17, 1960 (Washington, DC: GPO, 1960), 1–3.

40. Hearings, Burns Creek (1959–60), pt. 1, 57, 92.

41. Hearings, Burns Creek Project (1959–60), pt. 2, Mar. 24, 25, 1960 (Washington, DC: GPO, 1960), 9, 45, 48, 50.

42. U.S. Congress, Hearings before the Subcommittee on Irrigation and Reclamation of the Committee on Interior and Insular Affairs, House of Representatives, 87 Cong., 1 sess., on H.R. 36 and H.R. 378, Bills to Authorize the Secretary of the Interior to Construct, Operate, and Maintain a Reregulating Reservoir and Other Works at the Burns Creek Site in the Upper Snake River Valley, Idaho and for Other Purposes, Mar. 16, Apr. 17, 18, May 18, 1961 (Washington, DC: GPO, 1962), 37.

43. Hearings, Burns Creek (1962), 116–17.

44. "House Body Blocks Burns Creek Start," Salt Lake City Tribune, Feb. 8, 1962.

45. John Saylor, "Burns Creek Must Not Be Included in Any Omnibus Rivers and Harbors Bill," CR, 87 Cong., 2 sess., 2116–20 (quote on 2117); John Saylor, "Omnibus Rivers and Harbors Bill," CR, 87 Cong., 2 sess., 23058–59.

46. John Saylor, "Dominy Shows His True Colors," CR, 87 Cong., 1 sess., A6907–9.

47. John Saylor, "Upper Colorado River Storage Project," CR, 87 Cong., 1 sess., 18601–6 (quotes on 18603–4, 18606). See also John Saylor, "Transmission Lines for the Upper Colorado River Storage Project," CR, 87 Cong., 1 sess., 21740–43.

48. John Saylor, "Berlin and the Hanford Reactor," CR, 87 Cong., 1 sess., 13442 ("Commissar"); John Saylor, "The Secretary of the Interior and the Electric Power Industry in the United States," CR, 87 Cong., 2 sess., 17706–7; 88 Cong., 1 sess., 12759. To sample some of Saylor's insertions, see "Bonneville Losing Millions," CR, 88 Cong., 1 sess., A5765, A5766, A5776, A5778, A5815, A6171, A6172, A6209; "Bonneville Invades Southern Idaho, CR, 88 Cong., 1 sess., A5319, A5372, A5392, A5437, A5464, A5465. Saylor also decried the Hanford project, which proposed using by-product steam from atomic reactors, instead of Washington State coal, to generate electricity. He opposed this first as a federal project and later as a joint venture by public and private utilities. See John Saylor, "Hanford Project," and "Prospects in Power," CR, 87 Cong., 1 sess., 14929, 21854–55. For the debate, see CR, 87 Cong., 2 sess., 13761–809, 18035–36, 19492–96.

49. Editorial, Kittanning Leader-Times, Feb. 9, 1963.

50. John Saylor, "Prospects in Power," CR, 87 Cong., 1 sess., 21855.

Chapter 9. Passage of the Wilderness Bill

1. U.S. Congress, Hearings before the Subcommittee on Public Lands of the Committee on Interior and Insular Affairs, House of Representatives, 88 Cong., 2 sess., on H.R. 9070, H.R. 9162, S. 4, and related bills, To Establish a National Wilderness Preservation System for the Permanent Good of the Whole People, and for Other Purposes, pt. 2, Jan. 10, 11, 1964, Denver, CO (Washington, DC: GPO, 1964), 508.

2. Four other House members introduced separate wilderness measures. See CR, 87 Cong., 1 sess., 51; Allin, Politics of Wilderness Preservation, 123; Baker, Conservation Politics, 132; Thomas G. Smith, "John Kennedy, Stewart Udall," 336–37.

3. John Saylor, "Wilderness: The Outlook from Capitol Hill," in David Brower, ed., Wilderness: America's Living Heritage (San Francisco: Sierra Club, 1961), 146–51.

4. Allin, *Politics of Wilderness Preservation,* 124–25; Baker, *Conservation Politics,* 133–44; John Bird, "The Great Wilderness Fight," *Saturday Evening Post,* July 8, 1961, 8.

5. Hearings, *National Wilderness Preservation System,* pt. 1, Oct. 30, 31, 1961, McCall, ID; pt. 3, Nov. 6, 1961, Sacramento, CA (Washington, DC: GPO, 1962).

6. "A Report on Wilderness," *CR,* 87 Cong., 2 sess., 7482; "Wilderness and the Outdoor Recreation Report," *CR,* 87 Cong., 2 sess., A4132–34; Howard Zahniser to Palmer Hoyt, Feb. 1, 1962, ser. 5, box 103, WSP.

7. *Outdoor Recreation for America: A Report to the President and to the Congress by the Outdoor Recreation Resources Review Commission* (Washington, DC: GPO, 1962), 131. For urban sprawl and the accelerated use of automobile nature touring, see Sutter, *Driven Wild,* 255–63; and Adam Rome, *The Bulldozer in the Countryside: Suburban Sprawl and the Rise of American Environmentalism* (Cambridge: Cambridge University Press, 2001).

8. *CR,* 87 Cong., 2 sess., 7482; Howard Zahniser to Carl Gustafson, July 3, 1962, ser. 5, box 103, WSP; Allin, *Politics of Wilderness Preservation,* 125–26. Saylor inserted "The Report to the Outdoor Recreation Resources Review Commission by the Wildland Research Center, University of California, Summary of Major Findings and Recommendations," in six parts in *CR,* 87 Cong., 2 sess.: pt. 1, "What Is Wilderness," A3251–52; pt. 2, "Wilderness Resources," A3296–97; pt. 3, "Potential Alternative Uses for Wilderness Resources," A3356–58; pt. 4, "Wilderness Values," 7970–71; pt. 5, "Future Supply of Wilderness Resources," A3994–96; pt. 6, "Problems in Administration of Wilderness Resources," A4062–65.

9. Bruce Bowler to Howard Zahniser, Feb. 6, 1962, and Horace Albright to Wayne Aspinall, May 4, 1962, both ser. 5, box 103, WSP; John F. Kennedy, "Special Message to the Congress on Conservation," Mar. 1, 1962, *Public Papers of the Presidents 1962* (Washington, DC: GPO, 1963), 176–84; Julius Duscha, "The Undercover Fight over the Wilderness," *Harper's,* Mar. 1962, 55–59; editorial, "Delay Endangers Wilderness Bill," *NYT,* Apr. 4, 1962. For Aspinall's approach to wilderness preservation, see Schulte, *Wayne Aspinall,* 115–76.

10. Hearings, *National Wilderness Preservation System,* pt. 4, May 7, 8, 9, 10, 11, 1962, Washington, DC (Washington DC: GPO, 1962), 1084–95, 1104 (Horan quote), 1111 (Bennett quote and Saylor response).

11. Hearings, *National Wilderness Preservation System,* pt. 4, 1135–41 (quote on 1137).

12. Hearings, *National Wilderness Preservation System,* pt. 4, 1141; Wayne Aspinall to David Brower, Jan. 2, 1959, folder 26, box 90, SCR.

13. Hearings, *National Wilderness Preservation System,* pt. 4, 1160.

14. Allin, *Politics of Wilderness Preservation,* 127.

15. Howard Zahniser to Eliott S. Barker, Aug. 17, 1962 ("Wretch"), and Zahniser to Hugh Woodward, Aug. 21, 1962, both ser. 5, box 103, WSP.

16. *NYT,* Sept. 16, 18, 1962; *CR,* 87 Cong., 2 sess., 20202 ("emotions").

17. Ansel Adams to Charles M. Teague, Sept. 25, 1962 ("travesty"), box 9, HBP; Ernest Day to John Saylor, Aug. 22, 1962 ("heart"), and Bruce Bowler to Saylor, Aug. 30, 1962 ("mockery"), both ser. 5, box 103, WSP; Spencer Smith qtd. in *NYT,* Sept. 16, 1962; editorial, "House Given a 'Non-Wilderness Bill,'" *DP,* Sept. 2, 1962; editorials in the *NYT:* "A Wrecking Job to Undo," Aug. 22, 1962, "Sabotaging the Wilderness Bill," Aug. 31, 1962 ("sickly"), "Betrayal of the Wilderness Bill," Sept. 14, 1962; Ira Gabrielson to John McCormack, Aug. 21, 1962, Howard Zahniser to John McCormack, Aug. 22, 1962, and Hugh Woodward to McCormack, Oct. 3, 1962, all ser. 5, box 103, WSP; editorial, "Wilderness Not for Trade," *NYT,* Sept. 24, 1962.

18. *NYT*, Sept. 16 (quote), 19, 1962.

19. *CR*, 87 Cong., 2 sess., 20201–3.

20. *CR*, 87 Cong., 2 sess., 20267.

21. Wayne Aspinall to John Saylor, Sept. 21, 1962, box 37, JSP.

22. Citizens Committee on Natural Resources, press release, Oct. 29, 1962, ser. 5, box 103, WSP.

23. Wayne Aspinall to John Saylor, Oct. 15, 1962, box 37, JSP.

24. *Johnstown Tribune-Democrat*, Oct. 24, 1962.

25. Editorial, *Johnstown Tribune-Democrat*, Nov. 2, 1962; *Leechburg (PA) Advance*, Nov. 9, 1962; Sturgeon, *Wayne Aspinall*, 168 n. 44.

26. Allin, *Politics of Wilderness Preservation*, 129–31; Baker, *Conservation Politics*, 199–201; Charles Callison, "Facts about the Wilderness Bill," *LW* 82 (Winter–Spring 1962–63): 11–17.

27. Mike Nadel to John Schmidt, Feb. 12, 1963, and Nadel to Ann Whitehall, June 5, 1963, both ser. 5, box 103, WSP.

28. Stewart Brandborg to Ted Trueblood, July 6, 1962, Ira Gabrielson to John F. Kennedy, Oct. 29, 1962, and Citizens Committee on Natural Resources, press release, Oct. 29, 1962, all ser. 5, box 103, WSP; editorial, *WP*, Dec. 5, 1962; Howard Zahniser, letter to the editor, *WP*, Dec. 12, 1962; George Marshall to Zahniser, Oct. 19, 1962, ser. 3, box 500, WSP.

29. Paul Brooks to Howard Zahniser, Dec. 27, 1962, and Zahniser to John Fischer, Feb. 21, 1963, both ser. 5, box 103, WSP.

30. Paul Brooks, "Congressman Aspinall vs. the People of the United States," *Harper's*, Mar. 1963, 59–63.

31. Wilderness Society, press release, "Wilderness Bill Should Not Be Held Up for Any Public-Land Controversy," Jan. 3, 1963, Howard Zahniser to the President, Jan. 29, 1963, Lee White, assistant special counsel, memorandum for the President, "Meeting with Chairman Aspinall," Feb. 26, 1963, and White to Zahniser, Mar. 1, 1963, all Larry O'Brien Papers, box 1, JFKL; Stewart Udall, Oral History, Feb. 16, 1970, 101, JFKL; John Saylor to the President, Mar. 5, 1963, and Larry O'Brien to Saylor, Mar. 7, 1963, both box 37, JSP.

32. Howard Zahniser to Wayne Aspinall, May 3, 1963 (first quote), and Zahniser to Harvey Broome, May 3, Oct. 2, 1963 (second quote), both ser. 5, box 103, WSP; Zahniser, Confidential Memorandum for Use at a Very High Level, Oct. 10, 1963, box 37, JSP; *CR*, 88 Cong., 1 sess., 11930.

33. Wayne Aspinall to John Saylor, July 24, 1963, box 37, WSP.

34. John Saylor to Wayne Aspinall, with attached bill, Oct. 31, 1963, box 37, JSP; John Saylor, "The New Wilderness Bill," *CR*, 88 Cong., 1 sess., 21430.

35. Saylor, "The New Wilderness Bill"; Douglas Smith, "Pennsylvania Leads Battle to Save Nation's Wilderness," *PP*, Feb. 16, 1964.

36. John Dingell to Wayne Aspinall, Oct. 4, 1963, Ernest Dickerman to Howard Zahniser, Oct. 17, 1963, and Zahniser to Stewart Brandborg, n.d., with attached draft, "The New Wilderness Bill," all ser. 5, box 103, WSP.

37. Lee C. White, memorandum for the President, Nov. 12, 1963, Lee White Papers, box 1.

38. Howard Zahniser to Glenn W. Frum, Feb. 25, 1964, and Zahniser to Norman Hatch, Mar. 3, 1964, both ser. 5, box 103, WSP; Hearings, *National Wilderness Preservation System*, pt. 2, 283, 289, 388; pt. 3, 663; pt. 4, 1129.

39. Hearings, *National Wilderness Preservation System,* pt. 4, 1054–76.

40. Hearings, *National Wilderness Preservation System,* pt. 4, 1120, 1129, 1134. Kennedy made a similar telephone call to Saylor; see *Johnstown Tribune-Democrat,* Dec. 3, 1963.

41. Hearings, *National Wilderness Preservation System,* pt. 4, 1078, 1096, 1109, 1123 (quote), 1126–27, 1137, 1148–49.

42. Hearings, *National Wilderness Preservation System,* pt. 4, 1205.

43. Hearings, *National Wilderness Preservation System,* pt. 4, 1291–92.

44. *CR,* 88 Cong., 2 sess., 10214 (Aspinall's tribute), 11153 (Saylor's tribute).

45. *CR,* 88 Cong., 2 sess., 16520 (Aspinall), 16524 (Saylor).

46. *CR,* 88 Cong., 2 sess., 16520–53, 16826–34; Thomas G. Smith, "John F. Kennedy, Stewart Udall," 350.

47. "Wilderness Bill in Committee Hearing," and "Wilderness Bill Reported," *LW* 85 (Winter–Spring 1964): 30–35; Allin, *Politics of Wilderness Preservation,* 134–35.

48. George Marshall to Stewart Brandborg, July 1, 1964, Brandborg to Harvey Broome, with attachment, "Analysis of the Committee Amendments to H.R. 9070, As Reported by the House Committee on Interior and Insular Affairs, July 1, 1964," July 6, 1964, and C. R. Gutermuth, Charles Callison, Joseph Penfold, and Stewart Brandborg to Members of Congress, July 28, 1964, all ser. 5, box 103, WSP.

49. Michael Nadel to Alice Zahniser, Aug. 3, 1964, ser. 3, box 501, WSP.

50. *CR,* 88 Cong., 2 sess., 17430–34, 17451–57.

51. John Saylor, press release, July 30, 1964, ser. 5, box 103, WSP.

52. *CR,* 88 Cong., 2 sess., 20626–32.

53. Allin, *Politics of Wilderness Preservation,* 136; Web site of the National Wilderness Preservation System: http://www.wilderness.net/nwps.

54. Ann Dunbar to Edward M. Meeman, Scripps-Howard Conservation Editor, Aug. 6, 1964, box 37, JSP.

55. Edward J. Meeman to John Saylor, July 31, 1964, box 38, JSP; Meeman to Ann Dunbar, Aug. 10, 1964, box 37, JSP; editorials, *Philadelphia Evening Bulletin,* July 27, 1964, and *Rocky Mountain News,* July 27, 1964; *CR,* 88 Cong., 2 sess., 20630.

56. Howard Zahniser to Alan McIlheny, July 17, 1963, and Helen Zahniser to John Saylor, May 24, 1964, both ser. 5, box 103, WSP; Brandborg, interview, July 11–12, 1998; McCloskey, interview, July 15, 1997.

Chapter 10. The Battle to Save Grand Canyon

1. William V. Shannon, "The Battle of Grand Canyon Is Joined," *NYT,* July 31, 1966. For Morris Udall, see Donald W. Carson and James W. Johnson, *Mo: The Life and Times of Morris Udall* (Tucson: University of Arizona Press, 2001).

2. Hundley, *Water and the West;* Norris Hundley Jr., "Clio Nods: *Arizona v. California* and the Boulder Canyon Act—A Reassessment," *Western Historical Quarterly* 3 (Jan. 1972): 17–51. The Court also rejected the California argument that the water from the Gila River, which flowed almost entirely in Arizona, should be counted as part of the annual flow of the Colorado River.

3. For excellent treatments of the controversy, see Rich Johnson, *The Central Arizona Project: 1918–1968* (Tucson: University of Arizona Press, 1977); Byron E. Pearson, *Still the Wild River Runs: Congress, the Sierra Club, and the Fight to Save Grand Canyon* (Tucson: University of Arizona Press, 2002); Charles Coate, "'The Biggest Water Fight in

American History': Stewart Udall and the Central Arizona Project," *Journal of the Southwest* 37 (Spring 1995): 79–101; Robert Dean, "'Dam Building Still Had Some Magic Then': Stewart Udall, the Central Arizona Project and the Evolution of the Pacific Southwest Water Plan, 1963–1968," *Pacific Historical Review* 66 (Feb. 1997): 81–99.

4. Morris K. Udall, memorandum, n.d., "Arizona's Water Fight Shifts to Congress," folder 10, box 166, SUP.

5. U.S. Department of the Interior, press releases: "Secretary Udall Announces Actions to Meet Pacific Southwest Water Challenge," June 14, 1963, "Address by Secretary of the Interior Stewart Udall before Town Hall, Los Angeles, California," Aug. 21, 1963, "Secretary Udall Announces Massive Program to Meet Southwest Water Shortage," Aug. 26, 1963, all folder 1, box 1, Central Arizona Project, 88 Cong. (CAP/88 hereafter), John Rhodes Papers, Arizona State University.

6. John Rhodes, letter to the editor, *Arizona Republic*, Aug. 23, 1963, folder 1, box 1, CAP/88, Rhodes Papers; Stewart Udall to Carl Hayden, July 22, Aug. 24, Dec. 19, 30 (telegram), 1963, and Morris Udall to "Dear Aunt," Dec. 23, 1963, all box 476, Morris Udall Papers, University of Arizona Library (MUP hereafter); Hayden to Stewart Udall, Dec. 19, 1963, folder 3, box 167, SUP.

7. Sierra Club, press release, Nov. 16, 1963, folder 13, box 6, HBP; Anthony Wayne Smith, "The Mighty Colorado," *NPM*, Oct. 1963, 2; Weldon Heald, "Colorado River of the West," *NPM*, Oct. 1963, 4–9; Clyde Thomas [Martin Litton], "The Last Days of the Grand Canyon Too?" *SCB*, Oct. 1963, 2–4.

8. Ben Cole, "West Has Strong Friend in Rep. John P. Saylor," *Arizona Republic*, Aug. 1, 1963, box 24, JSP.

9. Ed Emerine, "Between Us," *Arizona Journal*, Aug. 22, 1963, box 24, JSP.

10. Pearson, *Still the Wild River Runs*, 62–63.

11. Carl Hayden to Stewart Udall, Feb. 7, 20, 1964, and Stewart Udall to Hayden, Feb. 12, 1964, all folder 6, box 167, SUP; U.S. Congress, Senate Report 1330, *The Lower Colorado River Basin Project*, 88 Cong., 2 sess., Aug. 6, 1964; David Brower, "The New Threat to Grand Canyon: Action Needed," *SCB*, Jan. 1964, 18; Stephen Raushenbush, "A Bridge Canyon Dam Is Not Necessary," *NPM*, Apr. 1964, 4–8; David Brower, "Gigantic Southwest Water Plan Offers More Reservoirs than Water," *SCB*, Sept. 1964, 12–13; Richard Bradley, "Grand Canyon of the Controversial Colorado," *SCB*, Dec. 1964, 73–79; Richard Bradley, "Udall's Water Plan Attacked," *DP*, Sept. 25, 1964, box 1, RBP; Johnson, *Central Arizona Project*, 147; Pearson, *Still the Wild River Runs*, 55–56, 73–75.

12. John Rhodes, memorandum to Gov. Paul Fannin et al., Sept. 3, 1964, folder 2, box 2, CAP/88, Rhodes Papers.

13. U.S. Congress, House, Hearing before the Subcommittee on Irrigation and Reclamation of the Committee on Interior and Insular Affairs, 88 Cong., 2 sess., on H.R. 6796, H.R. 6797, H.R. 6798, *Bills to Authorize, Construct, and Maintain the Central Arizona Project, Arizona–New Mexico, and for Other Purposes*, Nov. 9, 1964 (Washington, DC: GPO, 1965), 98.

14. Hearings, *CAP* (1964), 25; *Arizona Republic*, Nov. 8, 11, 1964, and Central Arizona Project Association, *Newsletter I*, Nov. 1964, all folder 2, box 2, CAP/88, Rhodes Papers.

15. Pearson, *Still the Wild River Runs*, 88.

16. Richard Bradley to John P. Saylor, Nov. 15, 1964, folder 12, box 21, Sierra Club Members Papers; John Saylor, "Don't Drown the Grand Canyon," *CR*, 89 Cong., 1 sess., 5111.

17. George Senner, "The Grand Canyon Will Not Drown," *CR,* 89 Cong., 1 sess. 7248–49.

18. John Saylor, "The Chips Are Down for Grand Canyon," *CR,* 89 Cong., 1 sess., 8042–44.

19. In late 1964, the Sierra Club published a volume, with photographs by Ansel Adams, extolling the pristine beauty of Grand Canyon and decrying the possibility of defacing it with dams; see Francois Leydet, *Time and the River Flowing: Grand Canyon* (San Francisco: Sierra Club, 1964).

20. U.S. Department of the Interior, *Lake Powell: Jewel of the Colorado* (Washington, DC: GPO, 1965); Pearson, *Still the Wild River Runs,* 89–91.

21. Floyd Dominy to John Saylor, with enclosure of Lake Powell booklet, May 20, 1965, box 36, JSP; John Saylor, "Is the Bureau of Reclamation Guilty of Illegal Activities?" *CR,* 89 Cong., 1 sess., 12643–44; Saylor to Comptroller General of the United States, June 4, 1965, and Saylor to Attorney General of the United States, June 4, 1965, both box 36, JSP.

22. John Rhodes to John Saylor, June 18, 24, 1965, and Saylor to Rhodes, June 22, 1965, all box 36, JSP; Frank Moss, "The Lake Powell Booklet," *CR,* 89 Cong., 1 sess., 14695.

23. John Saylor, "Is the Bureau of Reclamation Guilty of Illegal Activities—Act II," *CR,* 89 Cong., 1 sess., 15178–79; "Lake Powell Booklet Triggers Probe," *SLT,* June 30, 1965; Fred Vinson, Assistant Attorney General, to Saylor, July 29, 1965, and Frank Wentzel, Acting Comptroller General of the United States, to Saylor, Aug. 9, 1965, both box 36, JSP.

24. Charles Turbyville in the *Tucson Daily Citizen,* Feb. 5, 1968; Dominy, interview, July 15, 1997.

25. Elmer B. Staats, Deputy Director, Bureau of the Budget, to Sen. Henry Jackson, May 10, 1965, and U.S. Department of the Interior, news release, "Secretary Udall Supports Authorization of Comprehensive Project Package to Meet Long-Range Water Needs of the Lower Colorado River Basin," May 19, 1965, both box 36, JSP. A major magazine also attacked the cash register dams: see "Grand Canyon Cash Registers," *Life,* May 7, 1965, 4.

26. John J. Rhodes and Morris K. Udall to Wayne Aspinall, June 9, 1965, and Aspinall to Morris K. Udall, June 9, 1965, both box 476, MUP; Pearson, *Still the Wild River Runs,* 96.

27. U.S. Congress, House, Hearing before the Subcommittee on Irrigation and Reclamation of the Committee on Interior and Insular Affairs, House of Representatives, 89 Cong., 1 sess., on H.R. 4671 and similar bills *To Authorize the Construction, Operation, and Maintenance of the Lower Colorado River Basin Project and for Other Purposes,* Aug. 23, 24, 25, 26, 27, 30, 31, Sept. 1, 1965 (Washington, DC: GPO, 1965), 36–50.

28. Hearings, *Lower Colorado River Basin Project* (1965), 100–127, 646–55.

29. Hearings, *Lower Colorado River Basin Project* (1965). For the opposition of the Pacific Northwest to the import plan, see 201–2, 701–10; for Aspinall and Colorado, see 134–40, 337–45; for preservationists, see 710–39.

30. Hearings, *Lower Colorado River Basin Project* (1965), 256, 306–7.

31. Hearings, *Lower Colorado River Basin Project* (1965), 255, 891; John J. Rhodes Reports, *The Central Arizona Project—Past And Present,* Sept. 10, 1965, box 481, MUP.

32. John Saylor, "Looking at Marble Gorge through the *New York Times,*" and H.R. 14176, *CR,* 89 Cong., 2 sess., 547–48, 7363.

33. Bert Hanna, "Dominy Blasts Zealot Critics," *DP,* Jan. 6, 1966, box 1, RBP; John Saylor to Floyd Dominy, Sept. 2, 1965, and Saylor to David Bradley, Mar. 25, 1966, both box 36, JSP. Saylor had first used the poem a year earlier when he and Dominy argued the

value of hydropower to the reclamation program; see John Saylor, "Is Power Really Reclamation's Paying Partner? Or Hominy Dominy Sat on the Wall," *CR*, 89 Cong., 1 sess., 2744–51.

34. Richard Bradley to David Brower, Apr. 12, 1966, folder 33, box 19, DBP. The Bradley family soon would question Brower's mental stability; see Harold Bradley to Edgar Wayburn, July 2, 1967, folder 55, box 4, HBP.

35. John Rhodes, memorandum for the files, Mar. 9, 1966, and Morris K. Udall to Les Alexander, Apr. 26, 1966, both box 476, MUP; Orren Beaty, memorandum for the secretary, "Lower Colorado Basin Project," Mar. 9, 1966, folder 1, box 126, SUP; "Report from the Hill," Apr. 6, 1966, folder 1, box 127, SUP.

36. Richard Bradley, "Ruin for Grand Canyon," *Reader's Digest*, Apr. 1966, 193–98. Earlier the article had appeared in *Audubon*, Jan.–Feb. 1966, 34–41. On the need to offset the damage of Bradley's article, see Les Alexander to Lew Haas, Apr. 13, 1966, box 476, MUP.

37. Ozell Trask, memorandum for the files, "Strategy Conference between Congressman Rhodes and Udall and Ed Davis and Roy Elson," Apr. 29, 1966, box 476, MUP.

38. U.S. Congress, House, Hearings before the Subcommittee on Irrigation and Reclamation of the Committee on Interior and Insular Affairs, House of Representatives, 89 Cong., 2 sess., on H.R. 4671 and Similar Bills *To Authorize the Construction, Operation, and Maintenance of the Lower Colorado River Basin Project, and for Other Purposes,* May 9, 10, 11, 12, 13, 18, 1966 (Washington, DC: GPO, 1966), 975–89.

39. Hearings, *Lower Colorado River Basin Project* (1966), 983.

40. Hearings, *Lower Colorado River Basin Project* (1966), 1002–3, 1010–12, 1015, 1075, 1287.

41. Hearings, *Lower Colorado River Basin Project* (1966), 1568.

42. Hearings, *Lower Colorado River Basin Project* (1966), 1486–92, 1582–83.

43. Hearings, *Lower Colorado River Basin Project* (1966), 1492, 1556–57, 1642–43.

44. "Internal Revenue Service Used as a Weapon against the Sierra Club—and against Grand Canyon," *SCB*, July–Aug. 1966, 5–7; Pearson, *Still the Wild River Runs*, 142–45.

45. John Saylor, "Defender of Grand Canyon," and "Threats Will Not Silence Those Who Want to Preserve the Grand Canyon," *CR*, 89 Cong., 2 sess., 14978, 17782–83.

46. See the following, all by John Saylor: "National Wonder: Permit Destruction of Grand Canyon while Spending U.S. Dollars to Preserve Ancient Ruins in Egypt?" "Engineers Report on Proposed Grand Canyon Dams: 'Poor Use of Federal Funds,'" "The Plan to Defile One of Nature's Great Masterpieces," "The Grand Deception about the Proposed Grand Canyon Dams," "Grand Larceny in the Grand Canyon," "The Indians' Stake in Grand Canyon," all *CR*, 89 Cong., 2 sess., 15303, 15486–87, 15775–77, 15958, 16680–81, 17542–43; John Saylor, "Dear Colleague," July 13, 1966, box 476, MUP.

47. Progress Report No. 4, "Water for the West," folder 4, box 169, SUP.

48. J. A. Riggins, memorandum to the files, "Activities of Tuesday, July 26, 1966," July 26, 1966, Morris Udall to John A. Howard, July 27, 1966, and Udall, memorandum to Howard, Aug. 2, 1966, all box 476, MUP; Ben Cole, "California Walkout Imperils CAP Bill," *Arizona Republic*, July 22, 1966, and Bert Hanna, "Aspinall Tells of Change in Basin Bill," *DP*, July 24, 1966, both folder 6, box 171, SUP.

49. Newspaper clippings: *Arizona Republic*, July 28, 1966 ("violated"), *NYT*, July 28, 1966, and *Wall Street Journal* (*WSJ* hereafter), July 29, 1966 ("nefarious"), all folder 6, box 171, SUP; Robert C. McConnell, memorandum to the Secretary and Orren [Beaty], July 28, 1966, folder 3, box 169, SUP.

50. Jerry Mander, telegrams to David Brower, Aug. 1, 15, 1966, folder 24, box 11, DBP; Orren Beaty, "Notes to SLU," Aug. 5, 1966, folder 1, box 127, SUP; Michael P. Cohen, *The History of the Sierra Club, 1892–1970* (San Francisco: Sierra Club, 1988), 362–63; John Saylor, "Arizonans Plead with You," and "Conservatives Misled on Grand Canyon Dams," *CR,* 89 Cong., 2 sess., A4383, A4582; John Saylor, "Dear Colleague," with attachment, Aug. 29, 1966, box 478, MUP.

51. Thomas O'Neill to Morris Udall, Aug. 4, 1966, box 476, MUP.

52. L. M. Alexander, confidential memorandum to the CAP file, "Meeting with Senator Kuchel, California," Aug. 26, 1966, box 477, MUP; Alexander, memorandum to the CAP file, "Meeting between Arizona and California Congressional Delegation re H.R. 4671 and Proposed Amendments," Aug. 30, 1966, box 476, MUP.

53. Morris K. Udall, memorandum to John S. Rhodes, Sept. 7, 1966, box 476, MUP.

54. Northcutt Ely to Morris Udall, Sept. 9, 1966, and L. M. Alexander, memorandum to CAP Task Force Members and Congressional Delegation, Sept. 15, 1966, both box 476, MUP.

55. Pearson, *Still the Wild River Runs,* 158.

56. Northcutt Ely, "A Californian Looks at the Lower Colorado River Basin Plan," Sept. 21, 1966, box 476, MUP; Richard Olson to Lewis Reid, Feb. 28, 1967, box 481, MUP. Aspinall preferred that the bill endure "a lingering death in the Rules Committee" rather than risk passage of a Saylor substitute on the floor; see "Remarks of Honorable Wayne N. Aspinall before the Annual Meeting of the Colorado State Grange, Cortez, Colorado," Oct. 1, 1966, folder 2, box 4, Central Arizona Project, 89 Cong., Rhodes Papers. Using information obtained from Morris Udall, Udall's assistant Roger Lewis, and Saylor's assistant Ann Dunbar, Joy Coombs, an official with a Colorado conservation group called the Grand Canyon Workshop, asserted that Udall had an understanding with Speaker of the House John McCormack. If Udall could promise to deliver 190 votes, the speaker would pressure the Rules Committee to give a rule to Aspinall's bill with the Hualapai Dam. But Udall could only guarantee 150 votes. See Joy Coombs, memorandum to Bob Weiner, Roger Hansen, and Estella Leopold, "Final Report on H.R. 4671, 89th Congress," Sept. 19, 1966, ser. 6, box 102, WSP.

57. John Rhodes, memorandum to Congressmen Udall and Steiger and CAP Task Force, Jan. 10, 1967, box 481, MUP.

58. Stewart Udall, Weekly Report to the President, Dec. 6, 1966, box 126, SUP; U.S. Department of the Interior, press release, "Revised Lower Colorado River Plan Announced by Udall," Feb. 1, 1967, folder 8, box 169, SUP; editorial, "Victory for Grand Canyon," *NYT,* Feb. 2, 1967.

59. Johnson, *Central Arizona Project,* 194–96.

60. Morris Udall, memorandum to John Rhodes and Sam Steiger, Feb. 7, 1967, box 481, MUP.

61. Morris Udall to Wayne Aspinall, Feb. 8, 1967, box 481, MUP.

62. Johnson, *Central Arizona Project,* 196.

63. U.S. Congress, House, Hearings before the Subcommittee on Irrigation and Reclamation of the Committee on Interior and Insular Affairs, House of Representatives, 90 Cong., 1 sess., on H.R. 3300 and Similar Bills *To Authorize the Construction, Operation, Maintenance of the Lower Colorado River Basin Project, and for Other Purposes,* Mar. 13, 14, 16, 17, 1967 (Washington, DC: GPO, 1967), 324, 337–38.

64. U.S. Congress, House, Hearings before the Subcommittee on Interior and Insular Affairs, 90 Cong., 1 sess., on H.R. 845 and H.R. 427, S. 774 *To Authorize the Secretary of the Interior to Construct, Operate, and Maintain the Nebraska Midstate Division, Missouri River Basin Project, and for Other Purposes,* May 16, 18, 1967 (Washington, DC: GPO, 1967), 85.

65. Morris K. Udall to Foy Holcomb, July 27, 1967, and Rich Johnson, memorandum to the Arizona Interstate Stream Commission, "House Action on Central Arizona Project Legislation," Aug. 9, 1967, both box 481, MUP.

66. Morris K. Udall, memorandum for the file, Oct. 13, 1967, box 481, MUP.

67. Johnson, *Central Arizona Project,* 206–7; Pearson, *Still the Wild River Runs,* 168; John Rhodes with Dean Smith, *John Rhodes: "I Was There"* (Salt Lake City: Northwest Publishing, 1995), 95–96.

68. John Saylor to Sen. Everett M. Dirksen, Oct. 6, 1967, box 481, MUP.

69. Wayne Aspinall, memorandum to all Members of the Committee on Interior and Insular Affairs, Oct. 4, 1967, Morris Udall, memorandum for the file, Oct. 13, 1967, and Morris Udall to William Mathews, Oct. 12, 1967 ("light"), all box 481, MUP.

70. Morris K. Udall, memorandum on conference between Morris K. Udall and Chairman Aspinall, Jan. 2, 1968, box 481, MUP.

71. Hearings, *Lower Colorado River Project* (1967), 891 ("withering"), 795 ("wax"); Ben Cole, "Saylor an Arizona Hero?" *Arizona Republic,* July 25, 1967, rpt. in *CR,* 90 Cong., 1 sess., 20012.

72. Morris K. Udall, "Summary of the Proceedings at the Reclamation Subcommittee," Feb. 8, 1968, and Morris Udall to Rogers C. B. Morton, Mar. 11, 1968, both box 482, MUP.

73. For the floor debate, see *CR,* 90 Cong., 2 sess., 13403–74, 13566–89.

74. Central Arizona Project Association, *Situation Report No. 7,* May 16, 1968, box 482, MUP; *CR,* 90 Cong., 2 sess., 13582, 13567–68, 13575–79, 13584–89.

75. Morris Udall, Note to Editors, Aug. 1, 1968, box 482, MUP; Johnson, *Central Arizona Project,* 225–26. Saylor dissented because the bill permitted construction of Hooker Dam, which would have flooded part of the Gila Wilderness Area in New Mexico. Owing to the opposition of preservationists, Hooker Dam has yet to be built.

76. Morris K. Udall, with Bob Neuman and Randy Udall, *Too Funny to Be President* (New York: Henry Holt and Company, 1988), 48, 70; Carson and Johnson, *Mo,* 117; Stewart Udall, interview, June 4, 1997.

Chapter 11. Wild and Scenic Rivers

1. William Lane, letter to the editor and editor's reply, *NPM,* June 1959, 16.

2. John Saylor to Frank Romeo, Oct. 25, 1966, box 37, JSP; U.S. Congress, House, Hearing before the Subcommittee on Public Lands of the Committee on Interior and Insular Affairs, 85 Cong., 2 sess., on S. 77 and H.R. 1145 *To Establish the Chesapeake and Ohio Canal National Park and to Provide for the Administration and Maintenance of a Parkway in the State of Maryland, and for other Purposes,* June 30, July 1, 25, Aug. 13, 14, 15, 18, 1958 (Washington, DC: GPO, 1959), 149. In this chapter, I draw heavily upon my "Voice for Wild and Scenic Rivers: John P. Saylor of Pennsylvania," *Pennsylvania History* 66 (Autumn 1999): 554–79. I thank the publishers of *Pennsylvania History* for permission to use this previously published material.

3. John Craighead, taped interview with the author, July 13, 1998; John Craighead to Clayton G. Rudd, May 13, 1975, Frank Craighead and John Craighead, "Adventures on

Snake River and Its Tributaries," unpublished manuscript, 1956, and John Craighead and Frank Craighead, "River of Adventure," unpublished manuscript, 1956, all John Craighead Papers, privately held, courtesy John Craighead.

4. John Craighead, "Notes on Salmon River Boat Trip, March 31–April 9, 1955," Craighead Papers.

5. John Craighead and Frank Craighead, "River of Adventure," 22–23; John Craighead to Lee Metcalf, June 11, 1956, John Craighead to Stewart Brandborg, Dec. 12, 1956, and John Craighead to Clifton Merritt, Feb. 7, 1957, all Craighead Papers; John Craighead to Frank Masland, Jan. 26, 1956, folder 11, box 4, Frank Masland Papers, Dickinson College, Carlisle, PA; John Craighead, "Wild River," *Montana Wildlife,* June 1957, 15–20.

6. Thomas G. Smith, "Voice for Wild and Scenic Rivers," 561–62; Frank Craighead Jr. and John Craighead, "A Program to Classify, Inventory, and Evaluate the Recreational Resources of Our River Systems," *Naturalist* 13 (Summer 1962): 3–13; John Craighead to Stewart Udall, Feb. 22, 1961, Frank Craighead Jr., memorandum to Charles Stoddard, Director, Resources Program Staff, Department of the Interior, May 22, 1963, and Stewart Udall to Frank Craighead Jr., July 3, 1963, all Craighead Papers; Department of Agriculture and Department of the Interior, press releases, May 14, Aug. 15, Nov. 15, 1963, box 235, Clinton Anderson Papers, Library of Congress, Washington, DC.

7. U.S. Congress, House, Hearing before the Subcommittee on Interior and Insular Affairs, 88 Cong., 1 sess., on H.R. 1803 and H.R. 2884, *Bills to Provide for the Establishment of the Ozark National Rivers in the State of Missouri and for Other Purposes,* Apr. 9, May 6, 1963 (Washington, DC: GPO, 1963); "History and Legislative Background of Scenic Rivers Bill," memorandum, n.d., box 33, JSP; Leo A. Drey, Ozark Rivers Association, to Olaus Murie, with attached essay "The Controversy over Our Natural Free-Flowing Rivers: Some Reflections and a Solution," Oct. 29, 1962, folder 25, box 4, Murie Papers; Leonard Hall, "Our First National River," *Audubon,* Mar. 1969, 48–52; Stephen N. Limbaugh, "The Origin and Development of the Ozark National Scenic Waterways Project," *Missouri Historical Review* 91 (Jan. 1997): 121–32.

8. Saylor qtd. in Tim Palmer, *Endangered Rivers and the Conservation Movement* (Berkeley: University of California Press, 1986), 145. For Udall on Saylor, see Stewart Udall, interview, June 4, 1997.

9. Stewart Udall to House Speaker John W. McCormack, Mar. 3, 1965, box 37, JSP; *CR,* 89 Cong., 1 sess., 4290.

10. Allin, *Politics of Wilderness Preservation,* 173–74.

11. "Wild Rivers," special issue, *Naturalist* 16 (Autumn 1965); "Wild Rivers," *Better Camping,* Apr. 1966; "The Wild Rivers," *National Wildlife,* Feb.–Mar. 1966; "Free-Flowing Rivers," editorial, *NYT,* Jan. 20, 1966; "Singing Rivers," editorial, *WP,* Jan. 20, 1966; "Saving the Heritage of the Wild Rivers," editorial, *Arkansas Gazette,* Jan. 22, 1966.

12. For Aspinall's indifference, see *NYT,* Jan. 23, 1966; Stewart Udall, Report to the President, Jan. 18, 1966, box 126, SUP.

13. Office of Congressman John P. Saylor, press release, May 9, 1966, box 33, JSP; *CR,* 89 Cong., 2 sess., 10043.

14. *CR,* 89 Cong., 2 sess., 10043.

15. Edward C. Crafts to John Saylor, Feb. 5, 1966, and Charles Callison, memorandum for Ann Dunbar, Feb. 8, 1966, with attached letter to the editor of the *NYT,* Jan. 28, 1966, both box 33, JSP.

16. *CR,* 89 Cong., 2 sess., 10043.

17. *CR*, 89 Cong., 2 sess., 10043; John P. Saylor, address to the Florida Audubon Convention, Jan. 30, 1967, rpt. in *CR*, 90 Cong., 1 sess., 1806–8; Saylor testimony, U.S. Congress, Senate Committee on Interior and Insular Affairs, *Hearings on S. 119* (Washington, DC: GPO, 1967), 35–39.

18. John Corlett in *Idaho Daily Statesman*, May 19, 1966; editorials: *Dayton Journal Herald*, May 25, 1966, and *Grand Rapids Press*, July 17, 1966; Charles Callison, "National Outlook," *Audubon Magazine*, July–Aug. 1966, 226–27; "Scenic Rivers Bill Is Lauded," *Trout*, Jan.–Feb. 1967, 10; Joe H. Simpson to John Saylor, May 16, 1966, Anne La Monte to Saylor, July 14, 1966, Hazen Miller to Saylor, July 14, 1966, John Macrae, Executive Editor, Harper and Row Publishers, to Saylor, Nov. 22, Dec. 19, 1966, and Robert Weeden to Saylor, Dec. 21, 1966, all box 33, JSP; John P. Saylor, "Once along a Scenic River," *Parks and Recreation*, Aug. 1968, 20–22, 57–58.

19. *Knoxville News-Sentinel*, May 10, 1966; Fred E. Morr, Director, Ohio Department of Natural Resources, to Member of Congress Clarence J. Brown Jr., Sept. 26, 1966, Brown to John Saylor, Sept. 30, 1966, Saylor to Brown, Oct. 19, 1966, Harry Burns to Saylor, June 14, 1966, and unidentified newspaper clipping, n.d., all box 33, JSP.

20. Albert Johnson to John Saylor, Feb. 19, 1966, Saylor to Johnson, Feb. 25, 1966, *Tri-City Times-News*, Apr. 24, 1966, George Needle, Manager, Quaker State Oil Refining Corporation, to Saylor, Apr. 25, 1966, Paul Lipsie to Saylor, n.d., Saylor to Lipsie, May 19, 1966, D. C. Soles to Saylor, May 18, 1966, and Saylor to Soles, May 19, 1966, all box 33, JSP.

21. John Saylor to Wayne Aspinall, May 24, 1966, *Sports Afield* clipping attached to R. B. Holtzendorf to Saylor, July 1, 1966, Jack Bull to Saylor, June 29, 1966, and Saylor to Theodore Bingham, June 16, 1966, all box 33, JSP.

22. *CR*, 90 Cong., 1 sess., 97; John Saylor to Wayne Aspinall, Feb. 9, 1967, and Saylor to William Cramer, May 18, 1967, both box 33, JSP; Stewart Brandborg qtd. in Palmer, *Endangered Rivers*, 145; Bill Prime, "Wild Rivers: An Opinion," *American White Water* 12 (Spring 1967): 9. Rep. Henry S. Reuss (D-WI) also introduced a House bill, prepared by the Department of the Interior, which was nearly identical to the Senate bill; see Assistant Secretary of the Interior to the Speaker of the House of Representatives, with attached bill, Feb. 18, 1967, box 33, JSP. For Penfold's contributions to the Aspinall bill, see Saylor to Stephen Bradley, Mar. 11, 1968, box 33, JSP.

23. For an analysis of the various rivers bills, see William Steif in the *Knoxville News-Sentinel*, Apr. 23, 1967; Charles Callison, "National Outlook," *Audubon*, Nov.–Dec. 1967, 70–71; Assistant Secretary of the Interior to John Saylor, with attached memorandum, "Principal Differences between H.R. 8416 [Aspinall], S. 119, H.R. 90 [Saylor], and H.R. 6166 [Reuss]," Sept. 18, 1967, box 33, JSP.

24. John Saylor to Stephen Bradley, June 6, 1967, box 33, JSP; Allin, *Wilderness Preservation*, 175.

25. For the preference of preservationist leaders for the Saylor bill, see Charles Callison (Audubon Society) to Stewart Brandborg (Wilderness Society), June 20, 1967, Daniel A. Poole (Wildlife Management Institute) to Brandborg, June 28, 1967, John Craighead to Brandborg, July 5, 1967, and Frank Craighead to Brandborg, July 13, 1967, all ser. 6, box 100, WSP; *CR*, 90 Cong., 1 sess., 21751. Stephen Bradley blasted the Aspinall bill to Joe Penfold, not realizing that Penfold had authored it; see Stephen Bradley to Joe Penfold, Feb. 21, 1968, box 33, JSP.

26. John Saylor to William Cramer, May 18, 1967, box 33, JSP.

27. John Saylor to O. U. Walling, Dec. 6, 1967, box 33, JSP.

28. House Committee on Interior and Insular Affairs, press release, Feb. 19, 1968, box 33, JSP; U.S. Congress, House Committee on Interior and Insular Affairs, *Hearings before the Subcommittee on National Parks and Recreation on H.R. 8416, H.R. 90, S. 119 and Related Bills*, 90 Cong., 2 sess., Mar. 7, 8, 18, and 19, 1968 (Washington, DC: GPO, 1968).

29. Hearings, *National Parks and Recreation*, 397–408, 399 (quote), 408 (quote).

30. John Saylor to Theodore Bingham, Editor, *Dayton Journal Herald*, June 16, 1966, box 33, JSP.

31. Hearings, *National Parks and Recreation*, 243, 142.

32. Minutes, Executive Session, House Subcommittee on National Parks and Recreation, June 10, 11, 1968, box 33, JSP; U.S. Congress, House of Representatives, 90 Cong., 2 sess., House Report No. 1623, *Providing for a National Scenic Rivers System* (Washington, DC: GPO, 1968).

33. Wayne Aspinall to John W. McCormack, July 9, 1968, box 33, JSP; Allin, *Wilderness Preservation*, 175.

34. Raymond Shafer, telegram to Joseph McDade, July 15, 1968, box 33, JSP. For the debate, see *CR*, 90 Cong., 2 sess., 21450–61. For Goddard's reversal, see Edward Crafts to Maurice Goddard, July 17, 1968, box 33, JSP. For CROWD, see *Derrick*, May 23, July 16, 1968, Ray Pope to John Saylor, July 17, 1968, Don Stroup to Saylor, Aug. 28, 1968, and John McClain to Saylor, Sept. 19, 1968, all box 33, JSP.

35. *CR*, 90 Cong., 2 sess., 21456, 21461.

36. John Saylor to Stewart Udall, July 22, 1968, box 33, JSP. Edward Crafts of the Bureau of Outdoor Recreation and Representatives Robert Kastenmeier and James McClure also urged Saylor to seek an ordinary rule; see Edward Crafts to Saylor and Wayne Aspinall, July 16, 1968, and Robert Kastenmeier and James McClure to Saylor, July 29, 1968, both box 33, JSP.

37. Raymond Shafer to John Saylor, Aug. 1, 1968, and Saylor to Shafer, Aug. 2, 1968, both box 33, JSP; James Van Zandt, Special Representative to the Governor, to Robert Bloom, Secretary to the Governor, Aug. 6, 1968, carton 118, ms. group 209, Raymond Shafer Papers, Pennsylvania State Archives, Harrisburg.

38. Albert Johnson to John Saylor, Sept. 17, 1968, box 33, JSP; Don Stroup to Raymond Shafer, Aug. 28, 1968, and James Van Zandt to Theodore Robb, Sept. 17, 1968, both carton 118, Shafer Papers.

39. John Saylor to Frank Masland, Sept. 23, 1968, box 33, JSP; editorial, *NYT*, July 21, 1968; Daniel Poole (Wildlife Management Institute) to Raymond Shafer, July 29, 1968, Thomas Kimball (National Wildlife Federation) to Shafer, July 30, 1968, Spencer Smith (Citizens' Committee on Natural Resources) to Shafer, July 31, 1968, Stewart Brandborg (Wilderness Society) to Shafer, Aug. 1, 1968, Richard Stroud (National Sport Fishing Institute) to Shafer, Aug. 1, 1968, Brandborg, Special Memorandum to Pennsylvania Members and Cooperators, Aug. 7, 1968, and Allston Jenkins (Philadelphia Conservationists) to Shafer, Aug. 12, 1968, all carton 118, Shafer Papers.

40. Frank Masland to Raymond Shafer, Aug. 9, 1968, J. Stuart Zahniser to Shafer, Aug. 15, 1968, both carton 118, Shafer Papers. The letters quoted are, respectively: Ethel Chubb to Shafer, Aug. 18, 1968, Ned Coates to Shafer, Aug. 30, 1968, Ester English to Shafer, Sept. 3, 1968, Beatrice Fenton to Shafer, Aug. 12, 1968, and Mariana Coleman to Shafer, Sept. 7, 1968, all carton 118, Shafer Papers. Of the scores of letters on this subject, only one supported the governor's actions.

41. James Stevenson, Publisher, *Titusville Herald*, to Robert Bloom, Aug. 21, 1968, Bloom to Stevenson, Aug. 29, 1968, and Stevenson to Bloom, Aug. 31, 1968, all carton 118, Shafer Papers; Goddard qtd. in *PP*, Aug. 25, 1968.

42. Wayne Aspinall and John Saylor to House Rules Committee, Sept. 4, 1968, and Raymond Shafer, telegram to Saylor, Sept. 10, 1968, both box 33, JSP; *Pittsburgh Post-Gazette*, Sept. 10, 1968.

43. *CR*, 90 Cong., 2 sess., 26591–92.

44. *CR*, 90 Cong., 2 sess., 26588–611. Besides the Susquehanna, the other deleted rivers were the Cumberland (TN), Niobrara (NE), and a tributary of the Little Miami (OH).

45. U.S. Congress, 90 Cong., 2 sess., House of Representatives, House Conference Report No. 1917, *National Wild and Scenic Rivers System* (Washington, DC: GPO, 1968).

46. *CR*, 90 Cong., 2 sess., 28016–17; *Pittsburgh Post-Gazette*, Oct. 3, 1968.

47. Memorandum, "River Mileage Classifications for Components of the National Wild and Scenic Rivers System," Oct. 1976, ser. 6, box 100, WPS; U.S. Department of the Interior, National Park Service, *River Mileage Classifications for Components of the National Wild and Scenic Rivers System* (Washington, DC: National Park Service, Division of Park Planning, 1996): http://www.nps.gov/rivers. As the original bill intended, individual states also safeguarded rivers. The state of Pennsylvania, e.g., eventually designated thirteen rivers as scenic, including the Pine. See State of Pennsylvania, Department of Conservation and Natural Resources, *Pennsylvania Scenic Rivers System* (Harrisburg, 1993).

48. Mike Manatos, memorandum for Jim Jones, Oct. 2, 1968, box 86, White House Central Files, Lyndon B. Johnson Papers, LBJL; Joe Skubitz (R-KS) on Saylor in *CR*, 90 Cong., 2 sess., 26595. Rep. Tunney (D-CA) called the rivers bill a "landmark" and "pattern-setting," and Joseph Karth (D-MN) considered it "great" legislation. See *CR*, 90 Cong., 2 sess., 26592, 28015; Charles Callison, "National Outlook," *Audubon*, Nov.–Dec. 1968, 80; editorial, "The Wild Rivers Flowing," *NYT*, Sept. 22, 1968; editorial, "Conservation in the 90th Congress," *LW* 32 (Summer 1968): 2; "A Folio of Conservation Plusses in the Ninetieth Congress," *LW* 32 (Summer 1968): 44–46; M. Rupert Cutler, Assistant Executive Secretary, Wilderness Society, to Daniel Elazar, July 18, 1968, box 33, JSP.

49. "Preserving the Nation's Wild Rivers," *National Geographic*, July 1977, 2–52.

Chapter 12. Base Camp

1. "Saylor Accused of Ignoring Own State, Meddling in Idaho," letter to the editor, *PP*, Aug. 16, 1963; letters to the editor defending his conservation activities, *PP*, Aug. 22, Sept. 3, 1963. Saylor defeated Johnstown business executive James McCaffery in the election of 1964; see *Johnstown Tribune-Democrat*, Nov. 22, 1964.

2. *Apollo News-Record*, n.d., 1964 scrapbook, JSP.

3. For Saylor's coolness toward Goldwater, see *Kittanning Daily Leader-Times*, Oct. 30, 1964. For his views on the Vietnam war, see *Kittanning Daily Leader-Times*, July 8, 1965 ("degenerates"); Saylor, "Where Is the Spirit and Patriotism of Youth Defiant of This Country's Policies in a Time of Crisis?" *CR*, 89 Cong., 1 sess., 13822; Saylor, "Are These Demonstrations Real?" *CR*, 89 Cong., 1 sess., 27757; Saylor, "The Protesters and the Heroes" (remaining quotes), *CR*, 90 Cong., 1 sess., 30256; Lohr, interview, Aug. 5, 1997.

4. John Saylor, "Goodby to Guns," *CR*, 89 Cong., 1 sess., 12423 (quote); "Beware Aiming Hasty Legislation at Guns," *CR*, 89 Cong., 2 sess., A4591–92; "Firearms," *CR*, 90

Cong., 1 sess., 7410; "Federal Aid to Education," *CR*, 90 Cong., 1 sess., 12515–16; "Our Changing Schools," *CR*, 90 Cong., 1 sess., 27246–48.

5. *CR*, 89 Cong., 1 sess., 16853–54, 90 Cong., 1 sess., 5189–90, 91 Cong., 1 sess., 19136 (Warren Court quote); *Kittanning Daily Leader-Times*, July 7, 1965, Mar. 21, 1967; *Reynoldsville (PA) Star*, Mar. 9, 1967.

6. For civil rights, see *CR*, 89 Cong., 1 sess., 15637–43, 16281–85; Saylor speech to Cambria County Young Republicans Club, Feb. 14, 1964, unidentified newspaper clipping, 1964 scrapbook, JSP. See also *CR*, 89 Cong., 1 sess, 7443–44 (Medicare), 3040–41, 4029–30 (antipoverty bill); *Johnstown Tribune-Democrat*, Apr. 9, 1964; *CR*, 88 Cong., 2 sess., 7140–44, 7307–8 (food stamps). For the importance of Highway 219, see Fox, interview, Aug. 25, 1994.

7. *CR*, 89 Cong., 1 sess., 23946 (quote), 23980–81.

8. John Saylor, address to the National Reclamation Association, Palm Springs, CA, *Kittanning Daily Leader-Times*, Nov. 14, 1964; *CR*, 89 Cong., 1 sess., 6751. Saylor managed to add an amendment to the urban transit bill of 1964 requiring the purchase of buses, railroad cars, engines, rails, glass, and wire from domestic manufacturers; see *CR*, 88 Cong., 2 sess., 14975.

9. *CR*, 89 Cong., 1 sess., 2647, A638 (tributes), 18639–46 (Taft-Hartley).

10. *CR*, 89 Cong., 2 sess., 23411; 89 Cong., 1 sess., 6751.

11. John Saylor, "The Energy Center of the East," *CR*, 89 Cong., 1 sess., A4306–7. For the problem of air contamination, see Don Hopey, "Environment: Pennsylvania Power Plants Called 3rd Dirtiest in the Nation," *Pittsburgh Post-Gazette*, Dec. 5, 2003.

12. *Kittanning Daily Leader-Times*, Feb. 9, 16, 1967; *Leechburg Advance*, Feb. 15, Mar. 22, 1967.

13. John Saylor, "Women Walk Their Neighborhood Streets Unafraid in Johnstown," *CR*, 89 Cong., 2 sess., 12174–75.

14. *Johnstown Tribune-Democrat*, July 10, 1965, Feb. 14, 21, 1967; *Kittanning Daily Leader-Times*, Mar. 18, 1966; *Indiana Gazette*, Feb. 1, 1967; *Punxsutawney Spirit*, Feb. 2, 1967.

15. *CR*, 90 Cong., 1 sess., 10350 (quote). Saylor inserted several speeches and articles pointing out the dangers of atomic energy; see *CR*, 90 Cong., 1 sess., 14897, 20811, 28735–37, 33259–62. For his support of the Water Quality Bill, see *CR*, 89 Cong., 1 sess., 8658, 24592; 90 Cong., 1 sess., 10071. For his support of the Air Quality Bill, see *CR*, 90 Cong., 1 sess., 30999.

16. For Saylor on strip mining, see *CR*, 89 Cong., 1 sess., 3041; 89 Cong., 2 sess., 2100. For his position on Indiana Dunes, see *CR*, 89 Cong., 2 sess., 26112–14, 26202–11, 26917; 90 Cong., 1 sess., 10720–23.

17. *Kittanning Daily Leader-Times*, Feb. 22, 1966; editorial, *Valley Daily News*, Mar. 1, 1966.

18. *CR*, 89 Cong., 1 sess., A5390–91; 89 Cong., 2 sess., 13662, 14977–78, 22883–87; Saylor, address to the Michigan Bear Hunters Association, *Flint (MI) Journal*, Jan. 23, 1967.

19. *CR*, 88 Cong., 2 sess., 12035, 17810–11; 89 Cong., 1 sess., 16370–91, 25793; 90 Cong., 1 sess., 36446–53.

20. Unidentified newspaper clipping, n.d., 1965 scrapbook, JSP.

21. *Washington Daily News*, Mar. 8, 1965; *Asheville (NC) Citizen Times*, Oct. 1, 1967.

22. Saylor in the *Boston Globe*, Oct. 3, 1965; John Saylor, "The Many-Headed Dragon," *Audubon* 68 (Jan.–Feb. 1966): 52–53.

23. Editorial, "Not Enough Saylors," *Punxsutawney Spirit,* rpt. in *CR,* 90 Cong., 2 sess., 10913; editorial, "Quality in the House," *NYT,* Nov. 4, 1966. For Saylor's margin of victory, see *NYT,* Nov. 13, 1966. Saylor's total vote was significantly higher in 1966 because two counties had been added to his district.

24. For the best treatment of the controversy, see Richard C. Albert, *Damming the Delaware: The Rise and Fall of Tocks Island Dam* (University Park and London: Pennsylvania State University Press, 1987).

25. Albert, *Damming the Delaware,* xiii.

26. Albert, *Damming the Delaware,* 51–52.

27. Albert, *Damming the Delaware,* 53–54.

28. Albert, *Damming the Delaware,* 57–58.

29. *CR,* 87 Cong., 1 sess., 11808–16.

30. Water Resources Association of the Delaware River Basin, "The Facts about Tocks Island" (Philadelphia, 1962), box 41, JSP.

31. *CR,* 87 Cong., 2 sess., 21116–20, 22816–18, 23058–59.

32. Albert, *Damming the Delaware,* 70–71, 75.

33. Joseph Clark and Fred Rooney to John Saylor, Nov. 16, 1963, box 41, JSP; *CR,* 88 Cong., 1 sess., 1042; 89 Cong., 1 sess., 64, 16364–67.

34. John F. Kennedy, address at the Pinchot Institute for Conservation Studies, Milford, PA, Sept. 24, 1963, *Public Papers of the Presidents* (1963), 704–6; Lyndon B. Johnson, special message to the Congress on Conservation and Restoration of Natural Beauty, Feb. 8, 1965: http://www.lbjlib.utexas.edu/johnson/archives.hom/speeches.hom/650208.asp.

35. U.S. Congress, House, Hearings before the Subcommittee on National Parks and Recreation of the Committee on Interior and Insular Affairs, 89 Cong., 1 sess., on H.R. 89 and Related Bills *To Authorize Establishment of the Tocks Island National Recreation Area in the States of Pennsylvania and New Jersey, and for Other Purposes,* Mar. 1, 1965, Apr. 22, 1965 (Washington, DC: GPO, 1965), 16–19.

36. Hearings, *Tocks Island* (Mar. 1, 1965), 80–84.

37. Hearings, *Tocks Island* (Apr. 22, 1965), 134, 155 (quote), 158–61, 170, 177, 180–81.

38. Hearings, *Tocks Island* (Apr. 22, 1965), 203.

39. *CR,* 89 Cong., 1 sess., 16362–68.

40. *CR,* 89 Cong., 2 sess., 17543; Albert, *Damming the Delaware,* 87.

41. Albert, *Damming the Delaware,* 135–42.

42. Albert, *Damming the Delaware,* 113–31.

43. Albert, *Damming the Delaware,* 147–49, 171.

Chapter 13. Greening America

1. The title of this chapter has been borrowed from Charles A. Reich, *The Greening of America* (New York: Random House, 1970). In his best-selling book, Reich advocates the overthrow of corporate capitalism, a goal that would have horrified Saylor. I use the term to mean acquiring more open space and the money with which to purchase it.

2. Historian Adam Rome argues that the 1960s environmental movement was driven by three groups: liberal Democrats, middle-class women, and youth of the counterculture; see "'Give Earth a Chance': The Environmental Movement and the Sixties," *Journal of American History* 90 (Sept. 2003): 525–54.

3. For Aspinall quote, see *CR,* 90 Cong., 2 sess., 14623. The Taylor and Saylor quotes are from U.S. House, Hearings before the Subcommittee on National Parks and Recre-

ation of the Committee on Interior And Insular Affairs, 90 Cong., 2 sess., on H.R. 1311 and Related Bills *To Establish a Redwood National Park in the State of California,* pt. 3, May 20, 21, 22, 1968, Washington, DC (Washington, DC: GPO, 1968), 791 (Saylor), 812 (Taylor).

4. The president could recommend boundary revisions but could not expand the size of the proposed addition by more than 5,000 acres. See sections 2 and 3 of the Wilderness Act, rpt. in U.S. Congress, House, Hearing before the Subcommittee on Public Lands of the Committee on Interior and Insular Affairs, 90 Cong., 1 sess., on H.R. 5161, H.R. 5494, and S. 889, *To Designate the San Rafael Wilderness, Los Padres National Forest, in the State of California,* June 19, 20, 21, 1967 (Washington, DC: GPO, 1967), 2.

5. *CR,* 90 Cong., 1 sess., 3499.

6. Hearings, *San Rafael,* 22–23.

7. Hearings, *San Rafael,* 119.

8. Hearings, *San Rafael,* 89–93.

9. Fred Eissler to John Saylor, July 19, Aug. 2, 1967, and Wayne Aspinall to John Mc-Cormack, Sept. 21, 1967, all box 48, JSP; *CR,* 90 Cong., 1 sess., 28962–63.

10. John Callaghan, Secretary-Manager, California Forest Protective Association, to Wayne Aspinall, Sept. 25, 1967, attached to Charles Teague to John Saylor, Oct. 3, 1967, Robert Easton, Chairman, Citizens Committee for the San Rafael Wilderness, An Important Message for the Conservationists of America, n.d., Robert Easton to Brandy [Stewart Brandborg], Sept. 16, 1967, Easton to Saylor, Oct. 20, 1967, Saylor to Arthur Arndt and Kenneth Malloy, Oct. 12, 1967, and Stewart Brandborg, Executive Director, Wilderness Society, special memorandum to conservationists, Nov. 1, 1967, all box 48, JSP.

11. *San Francisco Chronicle,* Oct. 18, 20, 1967, attached to E. Lewis Reid, memorandum to Members of Conference Committee on San Rafael Wilderness, Oct. 26, 1967, box 48, JSP.

12. John Saylor, "San Rafael Wilderness Bill Conferees Should Affirm Principle of Citizen Participation in Wilderness Review Process," and "Roads Versus Condors," *CR,* 90 Cong., 1 sess., 35112–13, 35206–10.

13. For favorable newspaper comments, see editorials: *NYT,* Dec. 1, 1967; *Santa Barbara Times,* Dec. 11, 1967. For "monster" and Kuchel's predicament, see Richard Olson, memorandum to Morris Udall, Nov. 3, 1967, folder 15, box 108, MUP.

14. Morris Udall to Harold Johnson, Dec. 11, 1967, box 48, JSP.

15. Wayne Aspinall to Edward Cliff, Mar. 7, 1968, box 48, JSP.

16. John Saylor and John Dingell et al. to Dear Colleague, Mar. 1, 1968, editorial, *WP,* Feb. 10, 1968, Stewart Brandborg, "An Urgent Call for Action to Wilderness Committee Members and Cooperators," Jan. 5, 1968, and Brandborg, "A Report from the Executive Director, Wilderness Society," Jan. 19, 1968, all box 48, JSP.

17. *CR,* 90 Cong., 2 sess., 5237–71; Douglas Scott to John Saylor, Jan. 15, 1967 [1968], Warren Evans to Saylor, Jan. 25, 1968, and Saylor to Dear Colleague, Mar. 11, 1968, all box 48, JSP. Years later nearly 50,000 acres, including Area F, were added to the San Rafael unit, and thirty-three miles of the Sisquoc River, which flowed through it, were designated wild and scenic.

18. "News and Commentary: A Cornerstone for the Wilderness System," *NPM,* July 1968, 21.

19. Theodore Edison, "Great Swamp of New Jersey: Jetports and 'Progress,'" *NPM,* May 1967, 18–19.

20. Saylor qtd. in *NYT,* June 4, 1968; *CR,* 90 Cong., 2 sess., 27024–28.

21. Stephen F. Arno, "The North Cascades," *NPM*, June 1967, 4–9; Paul Brooks, "The Fight for America's Alps," *Atlantic*, Feb. 1967, 87–99; Allan Sommarstrom, "Wild Land Preservation Crisis: The North Cascades Controversy" (Ph.D. diss., University of Washington, 1970).

22. *CR*, 90 Cong., 2 sess., 27034–41.

23. Saylor qtd. in *CR*, 90 Cong., 2 sess., 27037. For the exchange with Secretary Udall concerning trams, see U.S. Congress, House, Hearings before the Subcommittee on National Parks and Recreation of the Committee on Interior and Insular Affairs, 90 Cong., 2 sess., on H.R. 8970 and Related Bills, *A Bill to Establish the North Cascades National Park and Ross Lake National Recreation Area, to Designate the Pasayten Wilderness and to Modify the Glacier Peak Wilderness, in the State of Washington, and for Other Purposes*, July 25, 26, Sept. 4, 1968, Washington, DC (Washington, DC: GPO, 1968), 957.

24. *CR*, 90 Cong., 1 sess., 3499; Allin, *Politics of Wilderness Preservation*, 176–78.

25. Allin, *Politics of Wilderness Preservation*, 177.

26. *CR*, 90 Cong., 2 sess., 21426–36 (quote 21431).

27. *CR*, 90 Cong., 2 sess., 27316–21. At the turn of the twenty-first century, the National Trail System totals twenty-four units; see http://www.nps.gov/nts/.

28. U.S. Congress, House, Hearing before the Subcommittee on National Parks and Recreation of the Committee on Interior and Insular Affairs, House of Representatives, 90 Cong., 2 sess., on H.R. 8578 and Related Bills *To Amend Title I of the Land and Water Conservation Fund Act of 1965, and for Other Purposes*, Feb. 6, 7, 21, Mar. 4, 1968 (Washington, DC: GPO, 1968), 28–31.

29. Hearings, *North Cascades*, 459.

30. *CR*, 90 Cong., 1 sess., 1158; Hearings, *Conservation Fund*, 9–10.

31. Hearings, *Conservation Fund*, 18 (Taylor quote), 10–11(Aspinall quotes).

32. Hearings, *Conservation Fund*, 11–12.

33. Hearings, *Conservation Fund*, 22–31.

34. Hearings, *Conservation Fund*, 39.

35. Hearings, *Conservation Fund*, 49–50.

36. Hearings, *Conservation Fund*, 52–53, 167.

37. Hearings, *Conservation Fund*, 130.

38. Hearings, *Conservation Fund*, 131, 144, 153.

39. Hearings, *Conservation Fund*, 165–66.

40. *CR*, 90 Cong., 2 sess., 14620–24.

41. *CR*, 90 Cong., 2 sess., 14626–27, 14654. In 1977, Congress amended the Conservation Fund law, raising its spending ceiling to $900 million.

Chapter 14. Saving the Redwoods

1. Hearings, *Redwood National Park*, pt. 3, 780.

2. The best works on the redwoods controversy are Michael McCloskey, "The Last Battle of the Redwoods," *American West* 6 (Sept. 1969): 55–64; Edward C. Crafts, "Men and Events behind the Redwood National Park," *American Forests*, May 1971, 20–28, 58; and Schrepfer, *Fight to Save the Redwoods*.

3. Schrepfer, *Fight to Save the Redwoods*, 6–8.

4. Schrepfer, *Fight to Save the Redwoods*, 18–37, 52, 65. In 1920 and again in 1938, the Interior Department proposed national parks in Del Norte County, but neither effort materialized.

5. Harold Gilliam, "The Redwood Totem," *Nation,* Sept. 7, 1964, 91–93; McCloskey, "Last Battle," 56.

6. Schrepfer, *Fight to Save the Redwoods,* 117–18.

7. Schrepfer, *Fight to Save the Redwoods,* 120–22; McCloskey, "Last Battle," 57; Fred Smith to Stewart Udall, Dec. 9, 1964, folder 15, box 155, SUP.

8. Anthony Wayne Smith to George F. Hartzog Jr., Nov. 13, 1964, folder 34, box 11, DBP; Russ Butcher to David Brower, June 4, 1965, folder 32, box 11, DBP.

9. *CR,* 89 Cong., 1 sess., 27785; Mike McCloskey to John Saylor, Nov. 8, 1965, box 42, JSP.

10. Stewart Udall, penned message to Brooks Atkinson, n.d., folder 15, box 155, SUP.

11. Editorials: *NYT,* Feb. 24, Mar. 3, 1966, *WP,* Dec. 31, 1965, Feb. 28, 1966; Edgar Wayburn, Vice President, Sierra Club, to Edward Crafts, Director, Bureau of Outdoor Recreation, Jan. 27, Dec. 16, 1966, folder 15, box 155, SUP; Horace Albright to David Brower, Aug. 5, 1966, folder 3, DBP; Ansel Adams to Brower, Sept. 2, 1966, folder 2, box 10, DBP.

12. Editorial, *NYT,* Mar. 3, 1966, and letter to the editor, *NYT,* Mar. 30, 1966; Harold Miller to Stewart Udall, Aug. 18, 1966, and Stewart Udall to Miller, Aug. 19, 1966, both folder 15, box 155, SUP; "A War against Redwoods Park," *San Francisco Chronicle,* Aug. 20, 1966; "Udall Accuses Lumbermen in Park Dispute," *Los Angeles Times* (*LAT* hereafter), Aug. 21, 1966; Merlo J. Pusey, "Murder in the Redwoods Groves," *WP,* Aug. 28, 1966; editorial, "Rescue the Redwoods," *WP,* Sept. 3, 1966; John Saylor, "Redwood National Park," *CR,* 89 Cong., 2 sess., 20756–57; M. Guillen to John Saylor, n.d., box 42, JSP; Schrepfer, *Fight to Save the Redwoods,* 140–42.

13. Clausen's plan actually consisted of northern, central, and southern units. The northern unit included the redwoods. The central unit sought to link together the Kings Range conservation area and a half-dozen state parks in Humboldt and Mendocino counties. The southern unit included Point Reyes National Seashore and nearly a dozen additional state parks and reserves in Marin, Sonoma, and Napa counties. Clausen also sought funding—perhaps as much as $40 million—to complete the land acquisition for Point Reyes National Seashore. See Don H. Clausen, "Redwoods to the Sea—A New Philosophy in Conservation," text of a speech before the National Wildlife Federation, Mar. 11, 1967, rpt. in *CR,* 90 Cong., 2 sess., 21393–96.

14. Department of the Interior, press release, Mar. 12, 1967, folder 15, box 155, SUP.

15. *CR,* 90 Cong., 1 sess., 122; Hearings, *Redwood National Park,* pt. 1, Washington, DC, June 27, 28, 29, July 12, 19, 1967 (Washington, DC: GPO, 1967), 1–4.

16. Hearings, *Redwood National Park,* pt. 1, 50.

17. Hearings, *Redwood National Park,* pt. 1, 50, 87, 149–52.

18. Hearings, *Redwood National Park,* pt. 1, 141; pt 3, 806.

19. Hearings, *Redwood National Park,* pt. 1, 158; "Congressman John Saylor," *SCB,* Aug. 1967, 14–18.

20. Schrepfer, *Fight to Save the Redwoods,* 148–50; McCloskey, "Last Battle," 61.

21. Sierra Club Conservation Alert—Redwoods, Oct. 20, 1967; five conservation groups, press release, Oct. 27, 1967, Stewart Udall to Sen. Henry Jackson, Oct. 31, and Stewart Udall to Orville Freeman, Oct. 31, 1967, all folder 15, box 155, SUP; Sierra Club, "A New Proposal for a Redwood National Park: What People Are Saying about the Senate Interior Committee's Plan," Oct. 23, 1967, box 42, JSP; "Bill on Redwoods Backed by Udall," *NYT,* Dec. 1, 1967; editorial, "Dangerous Precedent," *Houston Post,* Dec. 1, 1967.

22. Udall explained the routine a few days after the event during hearings in Washington State on North Cascades National Park. See Hearings, *North Cascades*, 614.

23. See, e.g., Hearings, *Redwood National Park*, pt. 2, Apr. 16, 1968, Crescent City, CA, Apr. 18, 1968, Eureka, CA (Washington, DC: GPO, 1968), 275–81, 303–15, 335, 390–92, 417–18.

24. Hearings, *Redwood National Park*, pt. 2, 439–40, 486–500.

25. Thomas F. Mitchell, Executive Representative, Georgia-Pacific Corporation, to Wayne Aspinall, May 1, 1968, box 42, JSP; Hearings, *Redwood National Park*, pt. 3, 808. Both Cohelan and Saylor had decried the cutting in Nov. on the House floor. Due to public outrage, the company eventually agreed to stop lumbering on proposed parklands until the end of the congressional session. For the comments of Cohelan and Saylor, see *CR*, 90 Cong., 1 sess., 34389.

26. Michael McCloskey to John Saylor, June 12, 1968, box 42, JSP; Michael McCloskey, "House Committee Takes Up Redwood Bill," *SCB*, June 1968, 19.

27. Hearings, *Redwood National Park*, pt. 3, 725–30.

28. Hearings, *Redwood National Park*, pt. 3, 745.

29. Hearings, *Redwood National Park*, pt. 3, 909.

30. Editorial, "Redwoods Decision," *WP*, June 25, 1968.

31. McCloskey, "Last Battle," 62–63.

32. Editorial, "Truncated Redwoods," *NYT*, June 26, 1968; Jeffrey Cohelan, press release, June 26, 1968, box 42, JSP.

33. Mike McCloskey, memorandum to Dear Member of the Committee on Interior and Insular Affairs, June 26, 1968, box 42, JSP; McCloskey, telegram to W. Lloyd Tupling, July 1, 1968, folder 4, box 113, Sierra Club Members Papers, Michael McCloskey; McCloskey, "Last Battle," 63.

34. See, e.g., Leo Rennert in the *Sacramento Bee*, July 5, 7, 8, 10, 1968, rpt. in *CR*, 90 Cong., 2 sess., 21401–3; comments of Aspinall and Saylor in *CR*, 90 Cong., 2 sess., 21387–89.

35. For the minority reports, see *CR*, 90 Cong., 2 sess., 21399.

36. See Saylor's remarks in *CR*, 90 Cong., 2 sess., 21387–88; John McCormack to Harold C. Smith, July 27, 1968, folder 4, box 113, Sierra Club Members Papers, McCloskey.

37. Several critical newspaper editorials are reprinted in *CR*, 90 Cong., 2 sess., 21400–403. For quotes see *NYT*, July 14, 16, 1968; Edgar Wayburn, "President's Message: Of Park and Politics," *SCB*, July 1968, 2; editorial, *DP*, July 19, 1968; *CR*, 90 Cong., 2 sess., 21397 (Burton), 21398–99 (Cohelan), 21407 (Ottinger), 21408–9 (Ryan).

38. *CR*, 90 Cong., 2 sess., 21387.

39. *CR*, 90 Cong., 2 sess., 21388, 21414.

40. Saylor Proposal for Conference Committee, "A Redwood National Park," July 24, 1968, box 42, JSP.

41. *CR*, 90 Cong., 2 sess., 26576–79.

42. *CR*, 90 Cong., 2 sess., 26579–80.

43. *CR*, 90 Cong., 2 sess., 26585, 26588.

44. Edward C. Crafts, the director of the Bureau of Outdoor Recreation, who pushed the legislation for the Interior Department, declared that Redwood National Park was "a monument to seven men." Besides Saylor, the other members of the magnificent seven were Aspinall; Secretary Udall; President Johnson; Phillip Hughes, deputy director of the Budget Bureau; and Senators Jackson and Kuchel. See Edward C. Crafts, "Men and Events behind the Redwood National Park," *American Forests*, May 1971, 20; Chauncey Greene, Secretary, Sierra Club, Great Lakes Chapter, to John Saylor, Sept. 15, 1968, box 42, JSP. On the disaffected preservationists, see Alfred A. Knopf to Martin Litton,

Nov. 30, 1968, folder 16, box 11, Sierra Club Members Papers, David Brower; and Martin Litton, "New Redwood Park Is Not the Victory It May Become," *Sunset* 142 (May 1969): 90–91.

45. Spearheaded by Phillip Burton, who chaired the House Subcommittee on National Parks, Congress in 1978 enlarged Redwood National Park by 48,000 acres. The newly protected areas included Skunk Cabbage Creek and additional lands along Redwood Creek. The cost of acquiring the lands totaled nearly $360 million. In addition, workers who lost their jobs in the timber industry would be compensated for six years to the tune of $33 million. Another $30 million was appropriated to restore parts of Redwood Creek that had been logged. See Schrepfer, *Fight to Save the Redwoods*, chap. 11; John Jacobs, *A Rage for Justice: The Passion and Politics of Phillip Burton* (Berkeley: University of California Press, 1995), chap. 15.

Chapter 15. Congressman for Conservation

1. James Kilpatrick, "Call for Action," *PP*, rpt. in *CR*, 91 Cong., 1 sess., 28791.

2. John Saylor, "Conservatives Should Be Supporting Conservation Efforts," *CR*, 91 Cong., 1 sess., 28791. Saylor and other Republicans also believed that a failure to act might strengthen the socialist agenda of the New Left. See Frank Masland to Gov. Raymond Shafer, with attachment "Conservation: High Priority," Apr. 15, 1970, box 9, ms. group 209, Shafer Papers. For the environmental policies of the Nixon administration, see J. Brooks Flippen, *Nixon and the Environment* (Albuquerque: University of New Mexico Press, 2000); and Russell Train, "The Environmental Record of the Nixon Administration," *Presidential Studies Quarterly* 26 (Winter 1996): 185–96.

3. See the remarks of Richard Ottinger, "Congressman Cited for Conservation Efforts," *New Bethlehem (PA) Leader-Vindicator*, Oct. 15, 1969.

4. Editorial, *Apollo News-Record*, Oct. 23, 1968.

5. *Johnstown Tribune-Democrat*, Oct. 14, Nov. 22, 29, 1968; *Leechburg Advance*, Oct. 9, 1968; *Indiana Gazette*, Oct. 18, 22, 1968.

6. "Waiting for Nixon," *Newsweek*, Dec. 9, 1968, 28–29; *NYT*, Nov. 21, 1968.

7. *Anchorage Daily Times*, Nov. 21, 1968; *Deseret News*, Dec. 19, 21, 1968; *Johnstown Tribune-Democrat*, Dec. 13, 1968; Flippen, *Nixon and the Environment*, 21–24.

8. Flippen, *Nixon and the Environment*, 23–24; *Johnstown Tribune-Democrat*, Jan. 8, 1970.

9. *Indiana Gazette*, June 7, 1969 (Saylor and Hickel quotes); *Kittanning Times*, June 7, 1969; *Altoona Mirror*, June 12, 1969; Bill Baird to Ann Dunbar (PR quote), July 25, 1969, 1969 scrapbook, JSP.

10. *Apollo News-Record*, Apr. 30, 1969 (quote); *CR*, 91 Cong., 1 sess., 14463, 18989.

11. *Johnstown Tribune-Democrat*, June 12, 1969; *Leechburg Advance*, Aug. 22, 1969 (quote).

12. *CR*, 92 Cong., 1 sess., 35387; *Patton (PA) Union Press-Courier*, Oct. 8, 1969; numerous news clippings, 1969 and 1970 scrapbooks, JSP.

13. *CR*, 91 Cong., 1 sess., 7072, 7894 (voting age), 15041 (pornography), 9428–29, 14094–99, 17133, 19136–38 (judicial activism), 8891, 9238, 12730, 14975–77, 16205, 17288–89, 19637, 26653–54 (tax reform), 23823–24 (guns), 25120 (moratorium on foreign aid); 91 Cong., 2 sess., 24085–87 (imports), 28199 (Equal Rights Amendment).

14. *Johnstown Tribune-Democrat*, May 16, 1970; *NYT*, May 17, 1970; *Kittanning Times*,

May 26, 1970; *Johnstown Observer,* July 2, 1970; *Barnesboro Star,* July 11, 1970; Saylor, letter to the editor, *Apollo News-Record,* June 17, 1970, 1970 scrapbook, JSP.

15. *Valley Daily News,* Jan. 17, 1970; *NYT,* Mar. 3, 1971; Victor Riesel, "Inside Labor: The Day Boyle Ordered Murder," *Indiana Gazette,* Oct. 29, 1973; http://www.en.wikipedia.org/wiki/United_Mine_Workers.

16. *CR,* 91 Cong., 1 sess., 31610.

17. *CR,* 91 Cong., 1 sess., 31610.

18. *Blairsville Dispatch,* Dec. 23, 1970. In all, between 1969 and 1981, when the program was barely alive, the federal government contributed more than $9 billion to some 400,000 coal-mining families who resided mainly in Pennsylvania, West Virginia, and Kentucky. See Jacobs, *Rage for Justice,* 197.

19. *CR,* 92 Cong., 2 sess., 35038–42.

20. Saylor qtd. in *Johnstown Tribune Democrat,* Apr. 26, 1971; *LAT* column, rpt. in *CR,* 91 Cong., 1 sess., 36886–87. For the surging environmental movement, see "The Ravaged Environment," *Newsweek,* Jan. 26, 1970, 3, 30–47; "Fighting to Save the Earth from Man," *Time,* Feb. 2, 1970, 56–63; Ben East, "The No. 1 Endangered Species—You," *Outdoor Life,* Apr. 1970, 32–34, 157–159; editorial, "The Audubon View," *Audubon* 72 (May 1970): 109.

21. Saylor qtd. in *Johnstown Tribune Democrat,* Dec. 5, 1969, and *Raleigh News and Observer,* Dec. 7, 1969, 1969 scrapbook, JSP.

22. *CR,* 91 Cong., 1 sess., 26580, 26590, 40925–26.

23. *CR,* 91 Cong., 2 sess., 3137, 10346; Flippen, *Nixon and the Environment,* 85–89.

24. John Saylor, "Environment: The Big Issue Is a Local Issue," *Republican,* Mar. 1, 1970, 1970 scrapbook, JSP.

25. Flippen, *Nixon and the Environment,* 1–2, 7–9; Kirkpatrick Sale, *The Green Revolution: The American Environmental Movement, 1962–1992* (New York: Hill and Wang, 1993), 24–25; "Enthusiasm Mounts for Teach-In," *NPM,* Feb. 1970, 18; Michael Frome, "Reflections on Youth and the Teach-In," *Field and Stream* (*F&S* hereafter), Apr. 1970, 46, 48.

26. Doug Struck in the *Daily Collegian* (Pennsylvania State University), Apr. 18, 1970; John Saylor, "The Environment: Your Attitude Is Critical," Earth Day Address at Pennsylvania State University, published in *Leechburg Advance,* Apr. 29, 1970, 1970 scrapbook, JSP; John Saylor, "The Kent State Tragedy: Where Lies the Blame?" with inserted article, Lawrence Lee, "Blindness to Anarchy Killed Kent Student," *CR,* 91 Cong., 2 sess., 15230. Historian Adam Rome argues that young people gave an important push to the environmental movement in the late 1960s and early 1970s. Saylor, however, remained detached from young environmentalists because they too often used lawless tactics. See Rome, "'Give Earth a Chance,'" 525–54.

27. *Clarion (PA) News,* Sept. 17, 1969.

28. *CR,* 91 Cong., 2 sess., 9325–33.

29. *CR,* 92 Cong., 2 sess., 10264, 37054; Flippen, *Nixon and the Environment,* 180–83.

30. *CR,* 91 Cong., 2 sess., 19230–36, 19244; Flippen, *Nixon and the Environment,* 65, 115–16; Thomas Kimball, letter to the author, n.d. [July 1997].

31. Freeman Bishop, "Interview with Rep. John P. Saylor," *Mining Congress Journal,* June 1972, 72–73; C. J. Potter, Chairman, Rochester & Pittsburgh Coal Company, to Sen. Hugh Scott, Apr. 13, 1973, box 28, JSP; Douglas Smith, "The Many Sides of Rep. Saylor," *PP,* Feb. 23, 1969.

32. Saylor in *CR,* 91 Cong., 2 sess., 15640, 20248 (quotes).

33. Victor Riesel, "Inside Labor: Teamsters Lose Battle to Ducks," *Indiana Gazette,* Apr. 23, 1969.

34. *CR,* 92 Cong., 1 sess., 34782. In the Eisenhower, Kennedy, and Johnson administrations, Saylor introduced unsuccessful legislation restricting the commercial hunting of polar bears, sea otters, and walruses on the high seas; see John Saylor to Robert S. Waters, Chairman, Boone and Crockett Club, Feb. 17, 1965, box 31, JSP.

35. *CR,* 91 Cong., 2 sess., 40205; editorial, "Saylor to the Rescue," *Anchorage Daily Times,* Mar. 18, 1970.

36. Editorial, Clare Conley, *F&S,* Apr. 1971, n.p., and Martin Bovey, Chief Executive Officer, Trout Unlimited, to Don Cullimore, Executive Director, Outdoor Writers Association of America, n.d., both 1971 scrapbook, JSP; R. Theodore Godshall, Associate Editor, *Pennsylvania Game News,* to Editor, *Anchorage Daily Times,* Mar. 23, 1970, and John Saylor to Godshall, Apr. 8, 1970, both box 48, JSP.

37. *CR,* 92 Cong., 1 sess., 1519–20, 5635 ("coward"), 5636, 15193–97.

38. John Saylor, "Butchered Wildlife: A Preventable Tragedy," *CR,* 92 Cong., 1 sess., 30172–74; Flippen, *Nixon and the Environment,* 162. Saylor also introduced legislation to ban the killing of animals from motorized vehicles; see John Saylor to W. M. Kanago, Apr. 16, 1970, box 48, JSP.

39. Flippen, *Nixon and the Environment,* 32; Frome, *Battle for the Wilderness,* 160.

40. *CR,* 91 Cong., 2 sess., 2312.

41. *CR,* 91 Cong., 2 sess., 5113, 5117.

42. Schulte, *Wayne Aspinall,* 236.

43. Schulte, *Wayne Aspinall,* 236–41; Flippen, *Nixon and the Environment,* 96 (quote). Senators Clinton Anderson and Henry Jackson generally supported environmental positions, but Anderson was sick and rarely attended meetings. For criticism of the report and Saylor's refusal to pose for a group picture, see Michael Frome, "A Powerful Congressional Group Moves Backward into the Future," *F&S,* Oct. 1970, 38, 145.

44. Saylor qtd. in E. W. Kenworthy, "Conservationists Say Nixon Bypasses Congress to Increase Timber Cutting," *NYT,* June 22, 1970.

45. *CR,* 91 Cong., 2 sess., 1571–74; Flippen, *Nixon and the Environment,* 96–97.

46. John Saylor, "Preserving Our Nation's Wilderness Areas," *CR,* 91 Cong., 1 sess., 23644.

47. John Saylor, "Wilderness Proposals," *CR,* 91 Cong., 2 sess., 5773. The six wilderness additions to the system were San Rafael (CA), San Gabriel (CA), Great Swamp (NJ), Mount Jefferson (OR), Ventara (CA), and Desolation (CA).

48. *CR,* 91 Cong., 2 sess., 32747–55; 92 Cong., 1 sess., 31996, 32135–36.

49. *CR,* 91 Cong., 2 sess., 36757–59.

50. *CR,* 92 Cong., 1 sess., 28176; editorial, "Shadow over the Wilderness, *NYT,* July 18, 1971. While public pressure failed to sway the president, it did influence the Forest Service to accelerate its planned study of roadless areas. The first review was done hastily and was criticized by preservationists for omitting several areas that might qualify as wilderness. A second review, completed in 1979, recommended that 15.4 million acres be added as wilderness. See Allin, *Politics of Wilderness Preservation,* 160–64; Frome, *Battle for the Wilderness,* 162–63.

51. *CR,* 91 Cong., 2 sess., 3139–40 (Point Reyes), 7400 (Cape Cod), 4355, 18694–95, 19044 (Mount Vernon), 19749–50 (Youth Conservation Corps and quote), 31224 (Gulf Islands), 31232–33 (Apostle Islands), 33145–46 (Sleeping Bear Dunes), 34880–81 (Voyageurs);

92 Cong., 2 sess., 34649–50 (Cumberland Island), 36096–97 (Glen Canyon), 36105–6 (Delaware Water Gap).

52. John Saylor, "Lumber Industry Practices 'Chainsaw Legislation' in Redwoods National Park," *CR*, 92 Cong., 1 sess., 31814–16. Saylor introduced unsuccessful legislation to add virgin groves along Skunk Creek and the unprotected side of the Emerald Mile along Redwood Creek.

53. John Saylor, "Constant Vigilance—The Price of Saving Olympic National Park," *CR*, 92 Cong., 2 sess., 19510–11.

54. Flippen, *Nixon and the Environment*, 31–32; editorial, "Fight for the Everglades," *NPM*, Jan. 1970, 2; Paul Brooks, "Superjetport or Everglades Park?" *Audubon* 71 (July 1969): 4–11; Jack Davis, "'Conservation Is Now a Dead Word': Marjory Stoneman Douglas and the Transformation of American Environmentalism," *Environmental History* 8 (Jan. 2003): 53–76.

55. John Saylor, telegram to John Volpe, Nov. 20, 1969, rpt. in *Pittsburgh Post-Dispatch*, Dec. 5, 1969, 1970 scrapbook, JSP; Flippen, *Nixon and the Environment*, 39–41, 56. Saylor introduced legislation with several cosponsors calling for an appropriation of $154 million to purchase 500,000 acres of Big Cypress Swamp. This measure failed in 1972, but a similar bill, sponsored by James Haley of Florida, succeeded the following year. See *CR*, 92 Cong., 2 sess., 3282–83, 93 Cong., 1 sess., 32833–41.

56. William Springer qtd. in *CR*, 91 Cong., 2 sess., 34332; Michael Frome qtd. in *American Forests*, June 1970, 60; reception for Saylor reported in *Leechburg Advance*, May 13, 1970.

57. "Congressman Saylor Cited for Conservation Efforts," *New Bethlehem Leader-Vindicator*, Oct. 15, 1969.

58. David Brower, telegram to John Saylor, Oct. 20, 1970, and *Johnstown Tribune-Democrat*, Oct. 21, 1970, both 1970 scrapbook, JSP.

59. Sigurd Olson, telegram to John Saylor, Oct. 20, 1970, 1970 scrapbook, JSP.

60. Besides Saylor and Jackson, the other award recipients were William Colby, Olaus Murie, Ansel Adams, Walter Starr, Francis Farquhar, Harold Bradley, Sigurd Olson, and George Marshall.

61. Copy of remarks, Raymond J. Sherwin to John Saylor, Oct. 5, 1971, 1971 scrapbook, JSP.

62. "Saylor Makes Impact beyond State Lines," *Harrisburg Patriot-News*, Nov. 16, 1969; "More Saylors Needed," *Latrobe (PA) Bulletin*, Mar. 19, 1970; editorial, "We Like Saylor," *Kittanning Times*, Oct. 29, 1970; Joseph O'Kicki in *New Bethelem Leader-Vindicator*, Oct. 14, 1970, 1970 scrapbook, JSP.

63. Joseph O'Kicki to John Saylor, Nov. 5, 1970, 1970 scrapbook, JSP.

Chapter 16. Alaska

1. Bennett, interview, Aug. 4, 1997; John Saylor to Leo Stormer, June 27, 1972, box 25, JSP. For the topic of wilderness and the dispossession of Native Americans, see Spence, *Dispossessing the Wilderness*.

2. For overviews of the Native claims-settlement issue, see Allin, *Politics of Wilderness Preservation*, 207–67; Donald Craig Mitchell, *Take My Land, Take My Life: The Story of Congress's Historic Settlement of Alaska Native Land Claims, 1960–1971* (Fairbanks: University of Alaska Press, 2001); Nash, *Wilderness and the American Mind*, 272–315. For

the Alaskan pipeline controversy, see Mary Clay Berry, *The Alaska Pipeline: The Politics of Oil and Native Land Claims* (Bloomington and London: Indiana University Press, 1975); Peter A. Coates, *The Trans Alaska Pipeline Controversy: Technology, Conservation, and the Frontier* (Bethlehem, PA: Lehigh University Press, 1991).

3. George Sundberg, "The 'Biggest Dam' on the Mighty Yukon," *Rural Electrification* 17 (July 1959): 15–17; Richard Starnes, "The Rampart We Watch," *F&S*, Aug. 1963, 64–66; Terry Brady, "Rampart Dam: White Elephant of the Yukon Flats," *NPM*, Oct. 1965, 4–7; Paul Brooks, "The Plot to Drown Alaska," *Atlantic Monthly*, May 1965, 53–60; Stephen Spur, "Rampart Dam—A Costly Gamble," *Audubon*, May–June 1966, 172–75; Ginny Hill Wood, "Rampart—Foolish Dam," *LW* 29 (Spring 1965): 3–7.

4. Editorial, "World's Biggest Boondoggle," *NYT*, Mar. 8, 1965; Wood, "Rampart," 4–6; Brooks, "Plot to Drown Alaska"; Brady, "Rampart Dam."

5. *CR*, 89 Cong., 1 sess., 4441.

6. Allin, *Politics of Wilderness Preservation*, 209.

7. Department of the Interior, press release, "Secretary Udall Moves to Preserve Status Quo in Alaska Lands Pending Congressional Action on Native Land Claims," Dec. 11, 1968, folder 5, box 153, SUP; *NYT*, Jan. 3, 1969; Mitchell, *Take My Land*, 11–12, 144. Before leaving office, Udall urged President Johnson to use his executive authority to enlarge Mount McKinley by 2.2 million acres and establish a new 3.5-million-acre Arctic Circle National Monument in Alaska's Brooks Range; see Mitchell, *Take My Land*, 436–39.

8. David Sanford, "Hickel's Pickle," *New Republic*, Jan. 18, 1969, 11–12; "Hickel Rips Udall 'Freeze,'" *Seattle Post Intelligencer*, Dec. 14, 1968; Mitchell, *Take My Land*, 176–78, 191–95.

9. Paul Friggens, "The Great Alaska Oil Rush," *Reader's Digest*, July 1969, 66–70; Berry, *Alaska Pipeline*, 91–100.

10. Coates, *Trans-Alaska Pipeline*, 168–69.

11. U.S. Congress, House, Hearings before the Subcommittee on Indian Affairs of the Committee on Interior and Insular Affairs, 91 Cong., 1 sess., on H. R. 13142 and H. R. 10193, *Bills to Provide for the Settlement of Certain Land Claims of Alaska Natives and for Other Purposes*, pt. 1, Aug. 4, 5, 6, Sept. 9, 1969, Washington, DC (Washington, DC: GPO, 1969), 80–91, 177–240.

12. Hearings, *Alaska Native Land Claims*, pt. 1 (1969), 132–76, 287–90, 291–95.

13. Saylor first demonstrated his lack of enthusiasm for the Native claims during the hearings of 1968; see U.S. Congress, House, Hearing before the Subcommittee on Indian Affairs of the Committee on Interior and Insular Affairs, 90 Cong., 2 sess., on H.R. 11213, H.R. 15049, and H.R. 17129 *To Settle the Land Claims of Alaska Natives, and for Other Purposes* (Washington, DC: GPO, 1968), 97–100.

14. Hearings, *Alaska Native Land Claims*, pt. 2, Oct. 17, 1969, Fairbanks, AK, Oct. 18, 1969, Anchorage, AK (Washington, DC: GPO, 1970), 365–67; Wayne Aspinall, memorandum to all members, Subcommittee on Indian Affairs, Sept. 4, 1969, and Alaska Rep. Howard Pollock to James Haley, Oct. 23, 1969, both container 2, James Haley Papers, Florida Southern University, Lakeland; Lewis A. Sigler, Counsel and Consultant on Indian Affairs, memorandum to members, Subcommittee on Indian Affairs, Sept. 24, 1969, container 3, Haley Papers. The ten subcommittee members who went to Alaska were Wayne Aspinall (D-CO), James Haley (D-FL), Ed Edmondson (D-OK), Roy Taylor (D-NC), Lloyd Meeds (D-WA), E. Y. Berry (R-SD), Howard Pollock (R-AK), John Camp (R-OK), Manuel Lujan (R-NM), and Saylor.

15. Hearings, *Alaska Native Land Claims*, pt. 2 (1969), 557.

16. Hearings, *Alaska Native Land Claims*, pt. 2 (1969), 558.

17. Saylor qtd. in Berry, *Alaska Pipeline*, 113. Saylor asked Secretary Hickel to arrest those culprits who had defaced the landscape, but without result: see John Saylor to Walter Hickel, Oct. 21, 1969, box 26, JSP.

18. *Christian Science Monitor*, Nov. 10, 1969 ("employment'); Berry, *Alaska Pipeline*, 105 ("ruined"); L. J. Mulkern to John Saylor, Nov. 13, 1969, and Saylor to Mulkern, Nov. 25, 1969, both box 26, JSP. On trying to get the pipe manufactured in Pennsylvania, see U.S. Congress, House, Hearings before the Subcommittee on Public Lands of the Committee on Interior and Insular Affairs, 93 Cong., 1 sess., on H.R. 9130 *To Amend Section 28 of the Mineral Leasing Act of 1920, and to Authorize a Trans-Alaska Oil and Gas Pipeline, and for Other Purposes*, pt. 1, Apr. 11, 18, 19, 30, May 1, 2, 1973, Washington, DC; pt. 2, May 17, 21, 22, 24, 1973, Washington, DC; pt. 3, June 15, 18, 1973, Washington, DC (Washington, DC: GPO, 1973), pt. 1, 173.

19. Editorial, "Alaskan Prospect," *NPM*, Sept. 1969, 2; "Conservationists Could Clog Giant Alaskan Pipeline," *LAT*, Oct. 26, 1969; Michael Frome, "Hickel and the Arctic," *F&S*, Nov. 1969, 12–14, 16, 20, 22–23, 28; Barry Weisberg, "The Ecology of Oil," *Ramparts*, Jan. 1970, 25–33; Ben East, "Is It TAPS for Wild Alaska?" *Outdoor Life*, May 1970, 43–46, 86, 88–89; Richard Starnes, "Can the Arctic Be Saved?" *F&S*, July 1970, 16–17, 82.

20. John Saylor to Wayne Aspinall, July 29, 1969, W. Lloyd Tupling, Washington Representative, Sierra Club, to Aspinall, Oct. 1, 1969, and Saylor to Margaret Buskwalter, Feb. 19, 1970, all box 26, JSP.

21. John Saylor to Walter Hickel, June 18, 1970, and Hickel to Saylor, June 30, 1970, both box 26, JSP.

22. Berry, *Alaska Pipeline*, 115. Saylor qtd. in *Christian Science Monitor*, Dec. 18, 1969.

23. Allin, *Politics of Wilderness Preservation*, 212–13; Mitchell, *Take My Land*, 293–300.

24. Allin, *Politics of Wilderness Preservation*, 213–14.

25. Mitchell, *Take My Land*, 310–11.

26. Mitchell, *Take My Land*, 313.

27. Ramsey Clark to John Saylor, July 22, 1970, Sen. Fred Harris to Saylor, July 28, 1970, Sen. Ted Stevens to Saylor, Sept. 14, 1970, and Eben Hobson, AFN Executive Director, to Wayne Aspinall, Sept. 24, 1970, all box 26, JSP. Howard Pollock qtd. in Mitchell, *Take My Land*, 332.

28. Mitchell, *Take My Land*, 333.

29. Mitchell, *Take My Land*, 334; Berry, *Alaskan Pipeline*, 137. Decades later, Pollock recalled that he and Saylor "never got along." Howard Pollock, telephone interview with the author, Oct. 4, 2004. For a slightly different and expanded version of the Saylor-Pollock exchange, see the *Valley (PA) Daily News*, Sept. 25, 1970, 1970 scrapbook, JSP.

30. Coates, *Trans-Alaska Pipeline*, 189–90.

31. Coates, *Trans-Alaska Pipeline*, 193.

32. Meeds, e-mail, Oct. 9, 2004; Jacobs, *Rage for Justice*, 219–21; Fenno, *Congressmen in Committees*, 285–86.

33. Berry, *Alaska Pipeline*, 141, 162.

34. Berry, *Alaska Pipeline*, 151.

35. Berry, *Alaska Pipeline*, 151–52.

36. U.S. Congress, House, Hearings before the Subcommittee on Indian Affairs of the Committee on Interior and Insular Affairs, 92 Cong., 1 sess., on H.R. 3100, H.R. 7039,

and H.R. 7432, *To Provide for the Settlement of Certain Land Claims of Alaska Natives, and for Other Purposes,* May 3, 4, 5, 6, 7, 1971 (Washington, DC: GPO, 1971), 66–67, 96–103.

37. Mitchell, *Take My Land,* 410–11.

38. Nick Begich, Lloyd Meeds, John Kyl, and Sam Steiger, memorandum to Chairman Aspinall and Subcommittee Chairman Haley, July 26, 1971, Ed Edmondson, memorandum to Chairman Aspinall and Subcommittee Chairman Haley, July 26, 1971, and Wayne Aspinall to James Haley, July 30, 1971, all container 2, Haley Papers; Mitchell, *Take My Land,* 413, 421–24.

39. John Saylor to Wayne Aspinall, Aug. 3, 1971, box 25, JSP; Berry, *Alaska Pipeline,* 179–81.

40. George L. Collins, Conservation Associates, to John Saylor, Aug. 9, 1971, box 25, JSP; Mitchell, *Take My Land,* 444–46.

41. Morris Udall, memorandum to John Saylor, with attached "Saylor-Udall Fallback Position," Sept. 28, 1971, and Saylor to George Klingelhofer, Oct. 4, 1971, both box 25, JSP.

42. Editorial, "A Piece of America," *NYT,* Oct. 19, 1971.

43. Nick Begich, "Dear Colleague," Oct. 18, 1971, and John Saylor and Morris Udall, "Dear Colleague," Oct. 19, 1971, both box 25, JSP; John Saylor, "Protecting the National Interest in Alaska," *CR,* 92 Cong., 1 sess., 36561–63.

44. *CR,* 92 Cong., 1 sess., 36850–51, 36858–61.

45. *CR,* 92 Cong., 1 sess., 36861–62, 37074, 37090–91, 37096–97.

46. John Saylor to Morris Udall, Oct. 21, 1971, box 25, JSP. Saylor wrote a similar letter of encouragement to Stewart Brandborg of the Wilderness Society, and together Saylor and Morris Udall wrote a note of thanks to each of their colleagues who had supported the amendment. See Saylor to Stewart Brandborg, Oct. 21, 1971, and Saylor and Morris Udall to Dear first name of colleague, Oct. 28, 1971, both box 25, JSP.

47. Qtd. in Mitchell, *Take My Land,* 468. See also Edgar Wayburn, "Sierra Club Statesman, Leader of the Parks and Wilderness Movement: Gaining Protection for Alaska, the Redwoods, and Golden Gate Parklands," interview with Ann Lage and Susan Schrepfer (Berkeley: Regional Oral History Office, University of California, 1985), 407–9.

48. Mitchell, *Take My Land,* 468–70.

49. Joint Statement of the Committee of Conference, n.d., container 2, Haley Papers; Mitchell, *Take My Land,* 478–79.

50. Allin, *Politics of Wilderness Preservation,* 216 17; Jonas V. Morris, "Alaska Land Settlement," *NPM,* Feb. 1973, 16–17; Peggy Wayburn and Edgar Wayburn, "Alaska—The Great Land," *SCB,* June 1973, 16.

51. For the controversy involving section 17, see Allin, *Politics of Wilderness Preservation,* 218; Berry, *Alaska Pipeline,* 211–12. Saylor introduced unsuccessful legislation seeking to give the interior secretary an extra six months, or a total of fifteen months, to determine which lands held potential as national preserves. See John P. Saylor, "To Amend the Alaska Native Claims Settlement Act," *CR,* 92 Cong., 2 sess., 27691.

52. *CR,* 92 Cong., 1 sess., 46782.

53. *CR,* 92 Cong., 1 sess., 46783–84.

54. *CR,* 92 Cong., 1 sess., 46787, 46790; Flippen, *Nixon and the Environment,* 154–55.

55. John Saylor and Morris Udall to Rogers C. B. Morton, Jan. 11, 1972, box 25, JSP.

56. Department of the Interior, press release, Mar. 15, 1972, container 2, Haley Papers; Nash, *Wilderness and the American Mind,* 272.

57. Coates, *Trans-Alaska Pipeline Controversy,* 196.

58. Coates, *Trans-Alaska Pipeline Controversy,* 199–200, 217.

59. *CR,* 92 Cong., 1 sess., 7624. For Saylor's bills, see 386, 7642, 10657.

60. John Saylor to Rogers C. B. Morton, June 9, 1971, box 26, JSP.

61. Coates, *Trans-Alaska Pipeline Controversy,* 225–35.

62. Berry, *Alaska Pipeline,* 254–59; Paul Friggens, "The Great Alaska Pipeline Controversy," *Reader's Digest,* Nov. 1972, 125–29.

63. Hearings, *Oil and Natural Gas Pipeline Rights-of-Way,* pt. 2 (1973), 718.

64. John Saylor to L. Joseph Gray, Aug. 2, 1973, box 25, JSP.

65. *CR,* 92 Cong., 1 sess., 27650–51.

66. Flippen, *Nixon and the Environment,* 208.

Chapter 17. Trail's End

1. Michael Frome, "Rate Your Candidate," *F&S,* Sept. 1972, 58–65; Michael Frome, interview with the author, Apr. 11, 2005.

2. Frome, "Rate Your Candidate," 65; J. G. D., "A Battler for Conservation," *LW* 37 (Autumn 1973): 4.

3. Schultz, *Wayne Aspinall,* 268–77.

4. *CR,* 92 Cong., 2 sess., 36980. Saylor also persuaded his colleagues to contribute money to purchase a glass-carved pheasant as a retirement gift for Aspinall. See John Saylor, memorandum to all members of the Committee on Interior and Insular Affairs, 92 Cong., "Aspinall Reception and Gift," Jan. 22, 1973, folder 20, box 656, MUP; Saylor to Wayne Aspinall, Feb. 27, 1973, folder 40, box 36, Aspinall Papers.

5. *Johnstown Tribune-Democrat,* Aug. 23, 1972; D. R. B., "Ann Dunbar, 1924–1973," Friends of the Earth, newspaper clipping, n.d., 1973 scrapbook, JSP. Also see obituaries in the *Washington Post* and the *Washington Star-News,* Sept. 25, 1973.

6. *Indiana Gazette,* Dec. 2, 1971; *Valley News Dispatch,* Jan. 5, 1972.

7. *Punxsutawney Spirit,* Jan. 25, 27, 1972; editorial, "Strange Bedfellows," *Somerset Daily American,* Jan. 25, 1972; "Saylor Labored for Constituents," *Indiana Gazette,* Jan. 29, 1972; *Johnstown Tribune-Democrat,* Feb. 2, 1972; *Kittanning Leader-Times,* Apr. 26, 1972.

8. *CR,* 92 Cong., 2 sess., 24564; 93 Cong., 1 sess., 2325.

9. *Johnstown Tribune-Democrat,* Nov. 22, 1972; *Kittanning Leader-Times,* Nov. 27, 1972 (quote).

10. *Blairsville (PA) Dispatch,* Apr. 9, 1973, box 24, JSP.

11. *CR,* 93 Cong., 1 sess., 13928.

12. *CR,* 93 Cong., 1 sess., 34302.

13. *CR,* 93 Cong., 1 sess., 30167–68, 42915 (endangered species), 32833–41 (Big Cypress). For the introduction of the Haley-Saylor Eastern wilderness bill, see Alice Meyers, memorandum to James [Haley] relating to telephone message from Michael Frome, Jan. 12, 1973, and Michael Frome to James Haley, Feb. 27, 1973, both container 72, Haley Papers.

14. *CR,* 93 Cong., 1 sess., 849–50; Allin, *Politics of Wilderness Preservation,* 186–93. Saylor challenged the purity principle again in 1973 by submitting a measure designating twenty-nine additional national forest tracts in the East for study by the Agriculture Department. He offered this proposal because he and other preservationists were displeased with the results of a Forest Service study—the Roadless Area Review Evaluation (RARE)—

because it had refused to consider areas in the East on the grounds of ecological impurity. See *CR*, 93 Cong., 1 sess., 1833–35.

15. *Ebensburg Mountaineer-Herald*, Sept. 28, 1972; editorial, "The Woodsy Owl Bird," *Western Timber Industry*, Oct. 1972, box 24, JSP.

16. Michael Frome, "Are We Loving Our Parks to Death?" rpt. in *CR*, 92 Cong., 2 sess., 19509–10; Roderick Nash to Nat Reed, Assistant Secretary of the Interior, Nov. 13, 1972, folder 439, box 70, Sam Steiger Papers, Northern Arizona University Library, Flagstaff.

17. Editorial, "Guarding the Wilderness," *Philadelphia Evening Bulletin*, Sept. 25, 1972, box 24, JSP.

18. Saylor in *NYT*, Sept. 25, 1972; editorial, *Audubon* 74 (Nov. 1972): 120.

19. Nicholas Kristof, "Environmental Movement Gone Wild," *Worcester (MA) Telegram and Gazette*, Mar. 15, 2005; John Saylor, "Anti-Environment Backlash Develops," *Oil City Derrick*, Jan. 29, 1972; John Saylor to Ingrid Jones, Aug. 30, 1972 (quote), box 40, JSP. For the Tennessee-Tombigbee controversy, see Jeffrey Stine, *Mixing the Waters: Environment, Politics, and the Building of the Tennessee-Tombigbee Waterway* (Akron: University of Akron Press, 1993); Jeffrey Stine, "Environmental Politics in the American South: The Fight over the Tennessee-Tombigbee Waterway," *Environmental History Review* 15 (Spring 1991): 3–14.

20. Saylor qtd. in *Valley News Dispatch*, Sept. 15, 1972; George W. "Heap" Alexander, "An Open Letter to the editor of the *Clarion News*," *New Bethlehem Leader-Vindicator*, Nov. 1, 1972, and Tom T. Andrews Jr., "From the Publisher's Viewpoint: Dam Proposal Major Issue," *New Bethlehem Leader-Vindicator*, n.d., both box 24, JSP.

21. Editorial, "Coal Industry Threatened," *Johnstown Tribune-Democrat*, Aug. 20, 1973.

22. "Saylor Criticized over Extensions," *Johnstown Tribune-Democrat*, Sept. 25, 1973.

23. Editorial, "Reason, Not Rhetoric, Will Ease the Job Loss," *Johnstown Tribune-Democrat*, Oct. 4, 1973; Saylor in *Somerset Daily American*, Oct. 14, 1973.

24. John Saylor, "Coal Gasification—Process of Future—Probable Solution to the Energy Crisis," *CR*, 92 Cong., 2 sess., 6989; Gene Smith, "A 'New' Fuel: Coal—Process Would Convert It to Gas," *NYT*, Feb. 27, 1972, rpt. in *CR*, 92 Cong., 2 sess., 6989–90.

25. Fox, interview, Aug. 25, 1994.

26. Text of Saylor television address published in *Ebensburg Mountaineer-Herald*, Oct. 25, 1973. The surgery was riskier than it is today because there were no beta blockers and other drugs to prevent clotting and heart attacks. Dr. Daniel Guilbert, interview with the author, Jan. 6, 2005.

27. *Indiana Gazette*, Oct. 29, 1973.

28. *Somerset Daily American*, Oct. 30, 1973. For newspaper tributes, see *NYT*, Oct. 30, 1973, and editorial of Nov. 5, 1973; *WP*, Oct. 29, 1973, and editorial of Nov. 5, 1973; editorial, *Honolulu Star-Bulletin*, Oct. 30, 1973; editorial, *Philadelphia Inquirer*, Nov. 4, 1973; and several other Pennsylvania newspaper tributes in box 24, JSP.

29. See the comments of Herman T. Schneebeli (2–3), Gerald Ford (3–4), Joseph McDade (7–8), Pattsy Mink (23), Won Pat (48–49), Carl Albert (54), Leonor Sullivan (103–4), Ron de Lugo (123–24), Manuel Lujan (124–26), and Don Young (146), all in *Memorial Services Held . . . John P. Saylor*. I am indebted to Saylor's successor, Rep. John Murtha (D-PA) for giving me a copy of this volume.

30. *Memorial Services Held . . . John P. Saylor*, 3–4 (Gerald Ford), 22 (Robert Kastenmeier), 29, 58 (John Dingell), 27, 67 (Thomas O'Neill), 109–10 (Morris Udall). See also Morris Udall to Grace Saylor, Nov. 1, [1973], folder 21, box 656, MUP.

31. J. G. D., "Battler for Conservation," 4; David Brower, "John Phillips Saylor, 1908–1973: A Wide Empty Place against the Capital Sky," *Not Man Apart* 3 (Dec.–Jan. 1974): 1; Michael Frome, "The Clock Strikes Twelve," *F&S*, Feb. 1974, 49, 152–53. When Frome published *Battle for the Wilderness*, he dedicated it to Saylor.

32. Clifton Merritt, letter to the author, Feb. 13, 1998; Martin Litton, interview with the author, July 7, 2005; Stewart Brandborg, letter to the author, Dec. 10, 1997 (emphasis Brandborg's); Brandborg, interviews, July 11–12, 1998; McCloskey, interview, July 15, 1997; Spencer Smith Jr., Secretary, Citizens Committee on Natural Resources, "A Big Loss of a Big Man," *Memorial Services Held . . . John P. Saylor,* 43–44 ("Redwoods"); Clayt Dovey, "Saylor's Passing Is Nation's Loss," *Johnstown Tribune-Democrat,* Oct. 30, 1973.

33. *Memorial Services Held . . . John P. Saylor,* 72.

34. On Aspinall's distinction between a "constructive" and a "destructive" environmentalist, see "Ruler of the Land," *WSJ,* Jan. 21, 1972.

35. Editorial, *Titusville (PA) Herald,* June 16, 1969; Daniel J. Webber, *Outstanding Environmentalists of Congress* (Washington, DC: Capitol Historical Society, 2002), courtesy of Sen. Gaylord Nelson.

36. Hatfield and Blatnik in *Memorial Services Held . . . John P. Saylor,* 131, 153; Kimball, letter, n.d. [July 1997]. Of the twenty-eight inductees in the National Wildlife Federation's Conservation Hall of Fame, the only members of Congress are Morris Udall and George Perkins Marsh, who was selected mainly as an author. The other politicians are Theodore Roosevelt and Gifford Pinchot; see http://www.nwf.org/about/inductees.cfm.

Unpublished Personal Papers and Records

Ansel Adams Papers, Bancroft Library, University of California, Berkeley

Sherman Adams Papers, Dartmouth College Library, Hanover, NH

Gordon Allott Papers, University of Colorado, Boulder

Clinton Anderson Papers, Library of Congress, Washington, DC

Wayne Aspinall Papers, University of Colorado, Boulder

Wayne Aspinall Papers, University of Denver

Harold Bradley Papers, Bancroft Library

Richard Bradley Papers, Western History Department, Denver Public Library

David Brower Papers, Bancroft Library

Devereux Butcher Papers, American Heritage Center, University of Wyoming, Laramie

Arthur Carhart Papers, Western History Department, Denver Public Library

J. Edgar Chenoweth Papers, University of Colorado, Boulder

Frank Church Papers, Boise State University, Boise, ID

John Craighead Papers, privately held

Floyd Dominy Papers, American Heritage Center, University of Wyoming, Laramie

Rosalie Edge Papers, Western History Department, Denver Public Library

James Haley Papers, Florida Southern University, Lakeland

Izaak Walton League Papers, Western History Department, Denver Public Library

Bruce Kilgore Papers, Bancroft Library

Richard Leonard Papers, Bancroft Library

Martin Litton Papers, Bancroft Library

Frank Masland Papers, Dickinson College, Carlisle, PA

Michael McCloskey Papers, Bancroft Library

Olaus Murie Papers, Western History Department, Denver Public Library

Gracie Pfost Papers, University of Idaho, Moscow

John Rhodes Papers, Arizona State University, Tempe

Ross Rice Papers, Arizona State University, Tempe

John Saylor Papers, Indiana University of Pennsylvania, Indiana

Sierra Club Records, Bancroft Library

Sam Steiger Papers, Northern Arizona University, Flagstaff

Morris Udall Papers, University of Arizona, Tucson

Stewart Udall Papers, University of Arizona, Tucson

Edgar Wayburn Papers, Bancroft Library
Wilderness Society Papers, Western History Department, Denver Public Library

Papers and Records at Presidential, State, City, and College Libraries

Dickinson College Law School, Carlisle, PA
Course Catalogs
Yearbooks

Dwight D. Eisenhower Library, Abilene, KS
John S. Bragdon Papers
Fred Seaton Papers
Ralph Tudor Papers
Dwight D. Eisenhower Papers, Ann Whitman File

Franklin and Marshall College, Lancaster, PA
College Newspaper
Saylor Academic File
Yearbooks

Lyndon B. Johnson Library, Austin, TX
White House Central Files

Johnstown Public Library, Johnstown, PA
Yearbooks, Johnstown High School

John F. Kennedy Library, Boston, MA
President's Office Files
Lee White Files

Mercersburg Academy, Mercersburg, PA
Admissions Records
Saylor Academic File
School Newspaper
Yearbooks

Richard Nixon Materials, College Park, MD
Pre-presidential Transitional Task Force Reports
White House Central File

Pennsylvania State Archives, Harrisburg
Merle Deardorff Papers
Governor David Lawrence Papers
Governor Raymond Shafer Papers

Oral Histories, Interviews, and Letters

Wayne Aspinall, Former Members of Congress Project, Library of Congress
Wayne Aspinall, Lyndon B. Johnson Library
Wayne Aspinall, John F. Kennedy Library
David Brower, Bancroft Library
John Carver, John F. Kennedy Library
J. Edgar Chenoweth, Former Members of Congress Project, Library of Congress
Wesley D'Ewart, Columbia University, New York
Floyd Dominy, Bureau of Reclamation Oral History Project, Bureau of Reclamation Library, Denver, CO
Floyd Dominy, Lyndon B. Johnson Library
Michael McCloskey, Bancroft Library
Paul "Pete" McCloskey, Bancroft Library
John Rhodes, Ross Rice Collection, Arizona State University
Sam Steiger, Sharlott Hall Museum, Prescott, AZ
Stewart Udall, Former Members of Congress Project, Library of Congress
Stewart Udall, Lyndon B. Johnson Library
Stewart Udall, John F. Kennedy Library
James E. Van Zandt, Former Members of Congress Project, Library of Congress
Edgar Wayburn, Bancroft Library
Lee White, John F. Kennedy Library

Interviews Conducted by the Author

Anna Catherine Saylor Bennett, sister, August 4, 1997
Stewart Brandborg, former executive director, Wilderness Society, July 11, 12, 1998
John Craighead, wildlife biologist, July 13, 1998
John Dingell (D-MI), telephone interview, November 19, 1997
Floyd Dominy, former director, U.S. Bureau of Reclamation, July 15, 1997
Harry Fox, legislative assistant, August 25, 1994
Michael Frome, former *Field and Stream* columnist, telephone interview, April 11, 2005
Richard H. Gentry, legislative assistant, telephone interview, June 23, 2005
Isabelle Hurrell, assistant to Representative John Murtha (D-PA), August 4, 1997
Clifton Jones, former chair, Pennsylvania State GOP, August 29, 1997
Charles Leppert, former minority counsel, House Interior Committee, July 9, 1995
Martin Litton, environmental activist, telephone interview, July 7, 2005
William Lohr, assistant to John Saylor, August 5, 1997
Michael McCloskey, former executive director, Sierra Club, July 15, 1997
Lee McElvain, former counsel, House Interior Committee, January 11, 1995
Pat Murray, former assistant, House Interior Committee, July 14, 1997
Clay Peters, former GOP staff member, House Interior Committee, June 22, 2005

Howard Pollock (R-AK), telephone interview, September 22, 2004
David Saylor, nephew, July 14, 1997
J. Phillips "Phil" Saylor, son, August 4, 1993
Douglas Scott, environmental activist, March 3, 1998
Theodor Swem, environmental activist, September 17, 1997
Stewart Udall, interior secretary, telephone interview, July 18, 1995, June 4, 1997
Russell Wisor, son-in-law, January 10, 1995
Susan Saylor Wisor, daughter, July 16, 1997
John S. Wold (R-WY), telephone interview, September 28, 2004
William Worf, environmental activist, July 13, 1998
Wendell Wyatt (R-OR), telephone interview, October 4, 2002
Ed Zahniser, environmental activist, telephone interview, August 7, 1997

E-mails and Letters to the Author

Stewart Brandborg, December 10, 1997, April 20, 2005
William D. Burlison (D-MO), September 13, 2004
Louis Clapper, environmental activist, July 30, 1997
Harry Crandell, environmental activist, December 15, 1997
Thomas Kimball, former executive director, National Wildlife Federation, n.d.
      [July 1997]
Michael McCloskey, June 13, 1997
Lloyd Meeds (D-WA), October 9, 2004
Clifton Merritt, environmental activist, February 13, 1998
John B. Oakes, former conservation editor, *New York Times,* June 10, 1997
Mike Penfold, environmental activist, August 22, 1997
Thurman Trospa, environmental activist, n.d. [December 1997]
John S. Wold (R-WY), September 15, 2004
Ed Zahniser, August 8, 1997, December 1, 1997

Published U.S. Government Documents

Congressional Record, 1949–73.
*Memorial Services Held in the House of Representatives and Senate of the United States, To-
      gether with Tributes Presented in Eulogy of John P. Saylor.* 93 Congress, 1 Session.
      Washington, DC: Government Printing Office, 1974.
Outdoor Recreation Resources Review Commission. *Outdoor Recreation for America.*
      Washington, DC: Government Printing Office, 1962.
Public Papers of the Presidents, Dwight D. Eisenhower.
Public Papers of the Presidents, John F. Kennedy.
Public Papers of the Presidents, Lyndon B. Johnson.
Public Papers of the Presidents, Richard M. Nixon.
U.S. Congress. House. Committee on Appropriations, Hearings on *Public Works Appro-
      priations for 1958* [Kinzua Dam]. 85 Congress, 1 session, 1957.

U. S. Congress. House. Committee on Interior and Insular Affairs. *Hearings before the Subcommittee on National Parks and Recreation on H.R. 8416, H.R. 90, S. 119 and Related Bills.* 90 Congress, 2 session, 1968.

————. Hearings on *A Bill to Authorize the Secretary of the Interior to Construct, Operate and Maintain the First Stage of the Oahe Unit, James Division, Missouri River Project, South Dakota, and for Other Purposes.* 90 Congress, 1 session, 1967.

————. Hearings on *Bills to Authorize the Secretary of the Interior to Construct, Operate, and Maintain a Reregulating Reservoir and Other Works at the Burns Creek Site in the Upper Snake River Valley, Idaho and for Other Purposes.* 87 Congress, 1 session, 1961.

————. Hearings on *Bills to Provide for the Settlement of Certain Land Claims of Alaska Natives.* Part 1, 91 Congress, 1 session, 1969; part 2, 91 Congress, 2 session, 1970.

————. Hearings on *Hells Canyon Dam.* 82 Congress, 2 session, 1952.

————. Hearings on *Repayment Contracts for Frenchtown, Malta, and Glascow Irrigation Districts, Montana.* 82 Congress, 2 session, 1952.

————. Hearings on the *Alaska Native Land Claims Settlement Act.* 90 Congress, 2 session, 1968.

————. Hearings on the *Burns Creek Project, Idaho.* Parts 1 and 2. 86 Congress, 2 session, 1960.

————. Hearings on the *Burns Creek Project, Idaho.* 87 Congress, 1 session, 1961.

————. Hearings on the *Central Arizona Project.* Parts 1 and 2. 82 Congress, 1 session, 1951.

————. Hearings on the *Central Arizona Project.* 88 Congress, 2 session, 1964.

————. Hearings on the *Colorado River Basin Project.* 90 Congress, 1 session, 1967.

————. Hearings on the *Colorado River Basin Project.* 90 Congress, 2 session, 1968.

————. Hearings on the *Colorado River Storage Project.* 83 Congress, 2 session, 1954.

————. Hearings on the *Colorado River Storage Project.* Parts 1 and 2. 84 Congress, 1 session, 1955.

————. Hearings on the *Establishment of a Research and Development Program for the Coal Industry.* 84 Congress, 2 session, 1956.

————. Hearings on the *Fryingpan-Arkansas Project, Colorado.* 83 Congress, 1 session, 1953.

————. Hearings on the *Fryingpan-Arkansas Project.* 84 Congress, 1 session, 1955.

————. Hearings on the *Fryingpan-Arkansas Project.* 85 Congress, 1 session, 1957.

————. Hearings on the *General Study of Irrigation and Reclamation Problems.* 82 Congress, 1 session, 1951.

————. Hearings on the *Land and Water Conservation Fund.* 87 Congress, 2 session, 1962.

————. Hearings on the *Land and Water Conservation Fund.* 88 Congress, 1 session, 1963.

————. Hearings on the *Lower Colorado River Basin Project.* 89 Congress, 1 session, 1965.

————. Hearings on the *Lower Colorado River Basin Project.* 89 Congress, 2 session, 1966.

————. Hearings on the *Oahe Unit, Missouri River Project.* Part 1, 90 Congress, 1 session, 1967; part 2, 90 Congress, 2 session, 1968.

————. Hearings *To Amend the Land Water Conservation Fund Act.* 90 Congress, 2 session, 1968.

―――. Hearings *To Authorize a Trans-Alaska Oil and Gas Pipeline.* 93 Congress, 1 session, 1973.

―――. Hearings *To Authorize the Secretary of the Interior to Construct, Operate, and Maintain a Reregulating Reservoir and other Works at the Burns Creek Site on the Upper Snake River Valley, Idaho, and for Other Purposes.* Part 2, 86 Congress, 2 session, 1960.

―――. Hearings on the *Tocks Island National Recreation Area.* 89 Congress, 1 session, 1965.

―――. Hearings *To Designate the San Rafael Wilderness.* 90 Congress, 1 session, 1967.

―――. Hearings *To Establish a National Scenic Rivers System.* 90 Congress, 2 session, 1968.

―――. Hearings *To Establish a National Wilderness Preservation System.* Parts 1, 2, and 3, 87 Congress, 1 session, 1961; part 4, 87 Congress, 2 session, 1962.

―――. Hearings *To Establish a National Wilderness Preservation System.* Parts 1, 2, 3, and 4, 88 Congress, 2 session, 1964.

―――. Hearings *To Establish a Nationwide System of Trails.* 90 Congress, 1 session, 1967.

―――. Hearings *To Establish a Redwood National Park.* Part 1, 90 Congress, 1 session, 1967; parts 2 and 3, 90 Congress, 2 session, 1968.

―――. Hearings *To Establish the Chesapeake and Ohio Canal Historical Park.* 85 Congress, 2 session, 1958.

―――. Hearings *To Establish the Chesapeake and Ohio Canal Historical Park.* 86 Congress, 1 session, 1959.

―――. Hearings *To Establish the North Cascades National Park and Ross Lake National Recreation Area.* 90 Congress, 2 session, 1968.

―――. Hearings *To Provide for the Settlement of Certain Land Claims of Alaska Natives.* 92 Congress, 1 session, 1971.

―――. *House Report 1774.* 83 Congress, 2 session. Washington, DC: GPO, July 1954.

U.S. Department of the Interior. *The Character of a Steel Mill City: Four Historic Neighborhoods of Johnstown, Pennsylvania.* Washington, DC: Government Printing Office, 1989.

―――. *Historic Resource Study: Cambria Iron Company.* Washington, DC: Government Printing Office, 1989.

―――. *Lake Powell: Jewel of the Colorado.* Washington, DC: Government Printing Office, 1965.

―――. *A Legacy of Coal: The Coal Company Towns of Southwestern Pennsylvania.* Washington, DC: Government Printing Office, 1989.

Articles

"Administration Power Policy." *Commonweal,* July 5, 1957, 341–42.

Arno, Stephen. "The North Cascades." *National Parks Magazine,* June 1967, 4–9.

Asmussen, Dennis G., and Thomas P. Bouchard. "Wild and Scenic Rivers: Private Rights and Public Goods." In Richard Conley and Geoffrey Wandesforde-Smith, eds., *Congress and the Environment,* 163–74. Seattle: University of Washington Press, 1970.

Aspinall, Wayne. "The Public Land Law Review Commission: Origins and Goals." *Natural Resources Journal* 7 (1967): 149–52.

Barnes, Irston R. "Historic C&O Canal Threatened by Road." *National Parks Magazine,* July–September 1953, 113–16, 134–38.

———. "A New Era for the Chesapeake and Ohio Canal." *National Parks Magazine,* July–September 1956, 110–16.

Bishop, Freeman. "An Interview with Rep. John Saylor." *Mining Congress Journal* (June 1972): 72–73.

Boyle, R. H. "America down the Drain." *Sports Illustrated,* November 16, 1964, 78–80.

Bradley, Richard. "Attack on Grand Canyon." *Living Wilderness* 30 (Winter 1964–65): 3–6.

———. "Grand Canyon of the Controversial Colorado." *Sierra Club Bulletin,* December 1964, 73–78.

———. "Ruin for the Grand Canyon." *Audubon* 68 (January–February 1966): 34–41.

Bradley, Stephen. "Folboats through Dinosaur." *Sierra Club Bulletin,* December 1952, 1–8.

Brady, Terry. "Rampart Dam: White Elephant of the Yukon Flats." *National Parks Magazine,* October 1965, 4–7.

Brooks, Paul. "Congressman Aspinall vs. the People of the United States." *Harper's Magazine,* March 1963, 60–63.

———. "The Fight for America's Alps." *Atlantic Monthly,* February 1967, 87–99.

———. "The Plot to Drown Alaska." *Atlantic Monthly,* May 1965, 53–60.

———. "Superjetport or Everglades Park?" *Audubon* 71 (July 1969): 4–11.

Broome, Harvey. "Origins of the Wilderness Society." *Living Wilderness* 5 (July 1940): 13–15.

Brower, David. "Gigantic Southwest Water Plan Offers More Reservoirs than Water." *Sierra Club Bulletin,* September 1964, 12–13.

———. "John Phillips Saylor: 1908–1973." *Not Man Apart* 3 (December–January 1973–74): 1.

———. "The New Threat to Grand Canyon: Action Needed." *Sierra Club Bulletin,* January 1964, 18.

Butcher, Devereux. "Resorts or Wilderness." *Atlantic Monthly,* February 1961, 45–51.

———. "Stop the Dinosaur Land Grab." *National Parks Magazine,* April–June 1950, 61–65.

———. "This Is Dinosaur." *National Parks Magazine,* October–December 1950, 122–36.

Cahalan, James M. "'My People': Edward Abbey's Appalachian Roots in Indiana County, Pennsylvania." *Pittsburgh History* 79 (Fall 1996): 92–107; (Winter 1996–97): 160–78.

Cahn, Robert. "Alaska: A Matter of 80,000,000 Acres." *Audubon* 76 (July 1974): 3–13, 66–81.

"California's David Brower, No. 1 Conservationist: Knight Errant to Nature's Rescue." *Life,* May 27, 1966, 37–38, 40, 42.

Callison, Charles. "Facts about the Wilderness Bill." *Living Wilderness* 82 (Winter–Spring 1962–63): 11–16.

Carhart, Arthur. "The Menaced Dinosaur National Monument." *National Parks Magazine,* January–March 1952, 19–30.

Carter, Luther S. "Grand Canyon Dams Debated." *Science,* June 17, 1966, 1600–1605.

Christie, Robert D. "The Johnstown Flood." *Western Pennsylvania Historical Magazine* 54 (April 1971): 198–210.

Clements, Kendrick. "Politics and the Park: San Francisco's Fight for Hetch Hetchy, 1908–1913." *Pacific Historical Review* 48 (May 1979): 185–215.

Coate, Charles. "'The Biggest Water Fight in American History': Stewart Udall and the Central Arizona Project." *Journal of the Southwest* 37 (Spring 1995): 79–101.

Coates, Peter. "Project Chariot: Alaskan Roots of Environmentalism." *Alaska History* 4 (Fall 1989): 1–31.

"Colorado Dam Controversy." *Scientific Monthly,* April 1957, 199–200.

Crafts, Edward C. "Men and Events behind the Redwood National Park." *American Forests,* May 1971, 20–28, 58.

Craighead, Frank, Jr., and John Craighead. "River Systems—Recreational Classification, Inventory and Evaluation." *Naturalist* 13 (Summer 1962): 1–13.

Crevelli, John P. "The Final Act of the Greatest Conservation President." *Prologue* 12 (Winter 1980): 173–91.

Cronon, William. "The Trouble with Wilderness; or, Getting Back to the Wrong Nature." *Environmental History* 1 (January 1996): 7–28.

"Dam Flap." *Time,* May 13, 1957, 93.

Davis, Jack. "'Conservation Is Now a Dead Word': Marjory Stoneman Douglas and the Transformation of American Environmentalism." *Environmental History* 8 (January 2003): 53–76.

Dean, Robert. "'Dam Building Still Had Some Magic Then': Stewart Udall, the Central Arizona Project and the Evolution of the Pacific Southwest Water Plan, 1963–1968." *Pacific Historical Review* 66 (February 1997): 81–99.

Deane, J. G. "Battler for Conservation." *Living Wilderness* 37 (Autumn 1973): 4.

DeVoto, Bernard. "Parks and Pictures." *Harper's Magazine,* February 1954, 12–17.

Donovan, Robert J. "Truman Seizes Steel." *Constitution* 2 (Fall 1990): 48–57.

Drew, Elizabeth. "Dam Outrage: The Story of the Army Engineers." *Atlantic Monthly,* April 1970, 51–62.

Duscha, Julius. "Undercover Fight over the Wilderness." *Harper's Magazine,* April 1962, 55–59.

East, Ben. "The Angry Men: Alaska's Dark Hour." *Outdoor Life,* December 1970, 31–33, 118–21.

———. "Is It TAPS for Wild Alaska?" *Outdoor Life,* May 1970, 43–45, 86, 88–90, 94.

Easthouse, Keith. "The Party That Was Green." *Forest Magazine,* July–August 2001, 14–17.

"Ecology, the New Mass Movement." *Life,* January 30, 1970, 22–31.

Edison, Theodore. "Great Swamp of New Jersey: Jetports and 'Progress.'" *National Parks Magazine,* May 1967, 18–19.

Ewert, Sara E. Dant. "Evolution of an Environmentalist: Senator Frank Church and the Hells Canyon Controversy." *Montana: The Magazine of Western History* 51 (Spring 2001): 36–51.

"Fighting to Save the Earth from Man." *Time,* February 2, 1970, 56–63.

Fleming, Donald. "Roots of the New Conservation Movement." *Perspectives in American History* 6 (1972): 7–91.

Friggens, Paul. "The Great Alaska Oil Rush." *Reader's Digest,* July 1969, 66–70.

———. "The Great Alaska Pipeline Controversy." *Reader's Digest,* November 1972, 125–29.

Frome, Michael. "Alaska: Trouble on the Last Frontier." *Field and Stream,* September 1968, 34, 108–10.

———. "Clock Strikes Twelve." *Field and Stream,* February 1974, 49, 152–53.

———. "Hickel and the Arctic." *Field and Stream,* November 1969, 12–14, 16, 20, 22–23, 28.

———. "A Powerful Congressional Group Moves Backward into the Future." *Field and Stream,* October 1970, 38, 145–46.

———. "Rate Your Candidate." *Field and Stream,* September 1972, 58–65.

————. "Reflections on Youth and the Teach-In." *Field and Stream*, April 1970, 46, 48.

Gilliam, Harold. "The Redwood Totem." *Nation*, September 7, 1964, 91–93.

Grahame, Arthur. "Dams for Eastern Rivers." *Outdoor Life*, December 1957, 25.

Harvey, Mark W. T. "Architect of the Wilderness Act." *Wilderness* (2004–5): 30–31.

————. "The Changing Fortunes of the Big Dam Era in the American West." In Char Miller, ed., *Fluid Arguments: Five Centuries of Western Water Conflict*, 276–302. Tucson: University of Arizona Press, 2001.

————. "Defending the Park System: The Controversy over Rainbow Bridge." *New Mexico Historical Review* 58 (January 1998): 45–67.

————. "Echo Park, Glen Canyon, and the Postwar Wilderness Movement." *Pacific Historical Review* 60 (February 1991): 43–67.

Hauptman, Laurence H. "General John S. Bragdon, the Office of Public Works Planning, and the Decision to Build Pennsylvania's Kinzua Dam." *Pennsylvania History* 44 (July 1986): 189–93.

Hays, Samuel P. "From Conservation to Environment: Environmental Politics in the United States since World War II." *Environmental Review* 6 (Fall 1982): 14–41.

Heald, Weldon. "Colorado River of the West." *National Parks Magazine*, October 1963, 4–9.

————. "The Squeeze Is on the National Parks." *National Parks Magazine*, January–March 1950, 3–4.

Huggard, Christopher J. "America's First Wilderness Area: Aldo Leopold, the Forest Service, and the Gila of New Mexico, 1924–1980." In Christopher Huggard and Arthur Gomez, eds., *Forests under Fire: A Century of Ecosystem Mismanagement in the Southwest*, 133–79. Tucson: University of Arizona Press, 2001.

Hundley, Norris, Jr. "Clio Nods: Arizona v. California and the Boulder Canyon Act—A Reassessment." *Western Historical Quarterly* 3 (January 1972): 17–51.

————. "Water and the West in Historical Imagination." *Western Historical Quarterly* 27 (Spring 1996): 5–31.

Josephy, Alvin, Jr. "Cornplanter Can You Swim?" *American Heritage* 19 (December 1968): 4–9.

Jubler, Eric. "Let's Open Up Our Wilderness Areas." *Reader's Digest*, May 1972, 125–28.

Kilgore, Bruce. "The Rainbow Bridge Debate." *National Parks Magazine*, October–December 1958, 155–59, 182.

Koppes, Clayton. "Efficiency/Equity/Esthetics: Towards a Reinterpretation of American Conservation." *Environmental Review* 11 (Summer 1987): 127–46.

Leopold, Aldo. "The Conservation Ethic." *Journal of Forestry* 31 (October 1933): 634–43.

Limbaugh, Stephen N. "The Origin and Development of the Ozark National Scenic Riverways Project." *Missouri Historical Review* 91 (January 1992): 121–31.

Margolis, Jon. "Our Country 'Tis of Thee, Land of Ecology." *Esquire*, March 1970, 124, 172–77.

Marks, Martha. "The Green Old Party." *Sierra*, July–August 2004, 48–52.

McCloskey, Michael. "Four Major New Conservation Laws." *Sierra Club Bulletin*, November 1968, 4–10.

————. "The Last Battle of the Redwoods." *American West* 6 (September 1969): 55–64.

————. "Wilderness Movement at the Crossroads, 1945–1970." *Pacific Historical Review* 41 (August 1972): 346–61.

McPherson, Donald. "The 'Little Steel' Strike of 1937 in Johnstown, Pennsylvania." *Pennsylvania History* 39 (April 1972): 219–20.

Melosi, Martin V. "Lyndon Johnson and Environmental Policy." In Robert Divine, ed., *The Johnson Years.* Volume 2, *Vietnam, the Environment, and Science,* 113–49. Lawrence: University of Kansas Press, 1987.

Mercure, Delbert V., and William M. Ross. "The Wilderness Act: A Product of Congressional Compromise." In Richard A. Cooley and Geoffrey Wandesforde-Smith, eds., *Congress and the Environment,* 47–64. Seattle and London: University of Washington Press, 1970.

Moley, Raymond. "Irrigation—Hydropower's Expensive Partner." *Newsweek,* May 17, 1954, 84–88.

Morris, Jonas V. "Alaska Land Settlement," *National Parks Magazine,* February 1973, 16–17.

Nash, Roderick. "The American Invention of National Parks." *American Quarterly* 22 (Fall 1970): 726–35.

Neel, Susan R. "Newton Drury and the Echo Park Dam Controversy." *Forest and Conservation History* 38 (April 1994): 56–66.

Neuberger, Richard. "Westerner against the West." *New Republic,* December 7, 1953, 11–12.

Packard, Fred. "Dinosaur Park Proposal." *National Parks Magazine,* October–December 1957, 159–60.

———. "Echo Park Dam? Not by a Damsite!" *National Parks Magazine,* July–September 1955, 99–100, 122.

———. "Grand Canyon Park and Dinosaur Monument in Danger." *National Parks Magazine,* October–December 1940, 11–13.

Penfold, Joe. "Reclamation's Plan for Invasion." *Sierra Club Bulletin,* May 1952, 10–14.

Pesonen, David E. "An Analysis of the ORRRC Report." *Sierra Club Bulletin,* May 1962, 6–9, 12–13.

Pisani, Donald J. "Federal Water Policy and the Rural West." In R. Douglas Hurt, ed., *The Rural West since World War II,* 119–46. Lawrence: University of Kansas Press, 1998.

Raushenbush, Stephen. "A Bridge Canyon Dam Is Not Necessary." *National Parks Magazine,* April 1964, 4–8.

"The Ravaged Environment." *Newsweek,* January 26, 1970, 3–47.

Reilly, P. T. "The Lost World of Glen Canyon." *Utah Historical Quarterly* 63 (Spring 1995): 122–34.

Richardson, Elmo. "Federal Park Policy in Utah: The Escalante National Monument Controversy of 1935–1940." *Utah Historical Quarterly* 33 (Spring 1965): 109–33.

———. "The Interior Secretary as Conservation Villain: The Notorious Case of 'Giveaway' McKay." *Pacific Historical Review* 41 (August 1972): 333–45.

Righter, Robert W. "National Monuments to National Parks: The Use of the Antiquities Act of 1906." *Western Historical Quarterly* 20 (August 1989): 281–301.

Robinson, Michael C. "The Relationship between the U. S. Army Corps of Engineers and the Environmental Community." *Environmental Review* 13 (Spring 1989): 1–41.

Rome, Adam. "'Give Earth a Chance': The Environmental Movement and the Sixties." *Journal of American History* 90 (September 2003): 525–54.

Rosier, Paul. "Dam Building and Treaty Breaking: The Kinzua Dam Controversy, 1936–1958." *Pennsylvania Magazine of History and Biography* 119 (October 1995): 345–68.

Roth, Dennis. "The National Forests and the Campaign for Wilderness Legislation." *Journal of Forest History* 28 (July 1984): 112–25.

Sanford, David. "Hickel's Pickle." *New Republic,* January 18, 1969, 11–12.

Saylor, John. "The Conservation Legacy of Theodore Roosevelt." *National Parks Magazine,* July–September 1958, 114–16.

———. "The Many-Headed Dragon." *Audubon* 68 (January–February 1966): 52–53.

———. "Once along a Scenic River." *Parks and Recreation,* August 1968, 20–22, 57–58.

———. "Saving America's Wilderness." *Living Wilderness* 21 (Winter–Spring 1956–57): 1–12.

Sieker, John. "The National Forest Wilderness System." *Living Wilderness* 5 (July 1940): 5–6.

Smith, Anthony Wayne. "Campaign for the Grand Canyon." *National Parks Magazine,* April 1962, 12–15.

———. "C and O Canal National Historical Park." *National Parks Magazine,* January–March 1958, 32–35.

Smith, Roland. "The Politics of Pittsburgh Flood Control, 1936–1960." *Pennsylvania History* 44 (January 1977): 3–24.

Smith, Thomas G. "John Kennedy, Stewart Udall and New Frontier Conservation." *Pacific Historical Review* 64 (August 1995): 329–62.

———. "Lewis Douglas, Arizona Politics, and the Colorado River Controversy." *Arizona and the West* 22 (Summer 1980): 125–62.

———. "Voice for Wild and Scenic Rivers: John P. Saylor of Pennsylvania." *Pennsylvania History* 66 (Autumn 1999): 554–79.

Spur, Stephen. "Rampart Dam—A Costly Gamble." *Audubon,* May–June 1966, 172–75.

Stansfield, Charles A., Jr. "The Tocks Island Dam Controversy." *Parks and Recreation,* March 1972, 29–33, 53–54.

Starnes, Richard. "Can the Arctic Be Saved?" *Field and Stream,* July 1970, 16–17, 82.

———. "The Rampart We Watch." *Field and Stream,* August 1963, 12, 64–66.

Stegner, Wallace. "Battle for the Wilderness." *New Republic,* February 15, 1954, 13–15.

———. "It All Began with Conservation." *Smithsonian,* April 1990, 35–43.

———. "Quiet Crisis or Lost Cause?" *Saturday Review,* September 19, 1964, 28, 50.

Stine, Jeffrey. "Environmental Politics in the American South: The Fight over the Tennessee-Tombigbee Waterway." *Environmental History Review* 15 (Spring 1991): 3–14.

Strong, Douglas H. "The Rise of Esthetic Conservation: Muir, Mather and Udall." *National Parks Magazine,* February 1970, 5–9.

Sundberg, George. "The 'Biggest Dam' of the Mighty Yukon." *Rural Electrification,* July 17, 1959, 15–17.

Swain, Donald. "The Bureau of Reclamation and the New Deal, 1933–1940." *Pacific Northwest Quarterly* 61 (July 1970): 137–46.

———. "The National Park Service and the New Deal, 1933–1940." *Pacific Historical Review* 41 (August 1972): 312–32.

Swetnam, George. "Labor-Management Relations in Pennsylvania's Steel Industry, 1800–1959." *Western Pennsylvania Historical Magazine* 62, no. 4 (1979): 321–32.

Train, Russell. "The Environmental Record of the Nixon Administration." *Presidential Studies Quarterly* 26 (Winter 1996): 185–96.

Udall, Stewart. "Wilderness Rivers: Shooting the Wild Colorado." *Venture,* February 1968, 62–70.

Wayburn, Peggy, and Edgar Wayburn. "Alaska—The Great Land." *Sierra Club Bulletin,* June 1973, 16.

Weisberg, Barry. "The Ecology of Oil: Raping Alaska." *Ramparts* 8 (January 1970): 25–33.

White, Richard. "American Environmental History: The Development of a New Historical Field." *Pacific Historical Review* 54 (August 1985): 297–335.

Wood, Ginny Hill. "Rampart—Foolish Dam." *Living Wilderness* 29 (Spring 1965): 3–7.

Yard, Robert Sterling. "Saving the Wilderness." *Living Wilderness* 5 (July 1940): 3–4.

Zahniser, Howard. "The Need for Wilderness Areas." *National Parks Magazine*, October–December 1955, 161–66, 187–88.

Books and Miscellaneous

Abbey, Edward. *The Journey Home: Some Words in Defense of the American West.* New York: Plume, 1977.

Albert, Richard C. *Damming the Delaware: The Rise and Fall of the Tocks Island Dam.* University Park: Pennsylvania State University Press, 1987.

Alexander, Charles. *Holding the Line: The Eisenhower Era, 1952–1961.* Bloomington and London: Indiana University Press, 1975.

Allin, Craig. *The Politics of Wilderness Preservation.* Westport, CT: Greenwood Press, 1982.

Ashworth, William. *Hells Canyon: The Deepest Gorge on Earth.* New York: Hawthorn Books, 1977.

August, Jack L., Jr. *Vision in the Desert: Carl Hayden and Hydropolitics in the American Southwest.* Fort Worth: Texas Christian University, 1999.

Bach, Martha. "A History of Johnstown, Pennsylvania and the Influence of the Iron and Steel Industry on the City's Growth and Development," Master's thesis, Indiana University of Pennsylvania, 1962.

Baker, Richard Allan. *Conservation Politics: The Senate Career of Clinton P. Anderson.* Albuquerque: University of New Mexico Press, 1985.

Berger, Karl, ed. *Johnstown: The Story of a Unique Valley.* Johnstown, PA: Johnstown Flood Museum, 1984.

Berry, Mary Clay. *The Alaska Pipeline: The Politics of Oil and Native Land Claims.* Bloomington and London: Indiana University Press, 1975.

Bilharz, Joy A. *The Allegany Senecas and Kinzua Dam: Forced Relocation through Two Generations.* Lincoln and London: University of Nebraska Press, 2001.

Bolling, Frank. *House Out of Order.* New York: E. P. Dutton, 1965.

Brooks, Paul. *The Pursuit of Wilderness.* Boston: Houghton Mifflin, 1971.

Brower, David R. *For Earth's Sake: The Life and Times of David Brower.* Salt Lake City: Gibbs-Smith, 1990.

———, ed. *Wilderness: America's Living Heritage.* San Francisco: Sierra Club Books, 1961.

Carson, Donald W., and James W. Johnson. *Mo: The Life and Times of Morris Udall.* Tucson: University of Arizona Press, 2001.

Coates, Peter. *The Trans-Alaska Pipeline Controversy: Technology, Conservation, and the Frontier.* Bethlehem, PA: Lehigh University Press, 1991.

Cohen, Michael. *The History of the Sierra Club, 1892–1970.* San Francisco: Sierra Club, 1988.

Cooley, Richard A., and Geoffrey Wandesforde-Smith, eds. *Congress and the Environment.* Seattle and London: University of Washington Press, 1970.

Cooper, Eileen Mountjoy. *Rochester & Pittsburgh Coal Company: The First One Hundred Years.* Indiana, PA: Rochester & Pittsburgh Coal Company, 1982.

Cooper, Ramon. *The Flood and the Future: The Story of a Year in City Government at Johnstown, PA, 1936.* Johnstown, PA: McKeown Printing Co., 1936.

Dewey, Donald. *James Stewart: A Biography.* Atlanta: Turner Publishing, 1996.

Dunlap, Thomas. *Saving America's Wildlife.* Princeton: Princeton University Press, 1990.

Eisenhower, Dwight. *Mandate for Change, 1953–1956.* Garden City, NJ: Doubleday and Company, 1963.

Farmer, Jared. *Glen Canyon Dammed: Inventing Lake Powell and the Canyon Country.* Tucson: University of Arizona Press, 1999.

Fenno, Richard F., Jr. *Congressmen in Committees.* Rpt., Berkeley: Institute of Government Studies, University of California, 1995.

Flader, Susan L. *Thinking like a Mountain: Aldo Leopold and the Evolution of an Ecological Attitude toward Deer, Wolves, and Forests.* Columbia: University of Missouri Press, 1974.

Flippen, J. Brooks. *Nixon and the Environment.* Albuquerque: University of New Mexico Press, 2000.

Fox, Stephen. *John Muir and His Legacy: The American Conservation Movement.* Boston: Little Brown, 1981.

Fradkin, Philip. *A River No More: The Colorado River and the West.* New York: Alfred A. Knopf, 1981.

Frome, Michael. *Battle for the Wilderness.* Rev. ed. Salt Lake City: University of Utah Press, 1997.

Gould, Lewis. *Lady Bird Johnson and the Environment.* Lawrence: University of Kansas Press, 1988.

Hamby, Alonzo. *Man of the People: A Life of Harry Truman.* New York: Oxford University Press, 1995.

Hartzog, George B. *Battling for the National Parks.* Mount Kisco, NY: Moyer Bell Limited, 1988.

Harvey, Mark W. T. *A Symbol of Wilderness: Echo Park and the American Conservation Movement.* Albuquerque: University of New Mexico Press, 1994.

Hays, Samuel P. *Beauty, Health, and Permanence: Environmental Politics in the United States, 1955–1985.* New York: Cambridge University Press, 1987.

———. *A History of Environmental Politics since 1945.* Pittsburgh: University of Pittsburgh Press, 2000.

Hundley, Norris, Jr. *The Great Thirst: Californians and Water, 1770s–1990s.* Berkeley and Los Angeles: University of California Press, 1992.

———. *Water and the West: The Colorado River Compact and the Politics of Water in the American West.* Berkeley and Los Angeles: University of California Press, 1975.

Hurt, R. Douglas, ed. *The Rural West since World War II.* Lawrence: University of Kansas Press, 1998.

Jacobs, John. *A Rage for Justice: The Passion and Politics of Phillip Burton.* Berkeley: University of California Press, 1995.

Johnson, Rich. *The Central Arizona Project, 1918–1968.* Tucson: University of Arizona Press, 1977.

Lear, Linda. *Rachel Carson: Witness for Nature.* New York: Henry Holt, 1997.

Leopold, Aldo. *A Sand County Almanac.* New York: Oxford University Press, 1949.

Leydet, Francois. *Time and the River Flowing: Grand Canyon.* San Francisco: Sierra Club, 1964.

Martin, Russell. *A Story That Stands like a Dam: Glen Canyon and the Struggle for the Soul of the West.* New York: Henry Holt, 1989.

McCulloch, David. *The Johnstown Flood.* New York: Simon and Schuster, 1989.

———. *Truman.* New York: Simon and Schuster, 1992.

McPhee, John. *Encounters with the Archdruid.* New York: Farrar, Straus, and Giroux, 1971.

Merchant, Carolyn, ed. *The Columbia Guide to American Environmental History.* New York: Columbia University Press, 2002.

Miles, John C. *Guardians of the Parks: A History of the National Parks and Conservation Association.* Washington, DC: Taylor and Frances, 1995.

Miller, Char, ed. *Fluid Arguments: Five Centuries of Western Water Conflicts.* Tucson: University of Arizona Press, 2001.

———. *Gifford Pinchot and the Making of Modern Environmentalism.* Washington, DC: Island Press, 2001.

Miner, Curtis. *Forging a New Deal: Johnstown and the Great Depression, 1929–1941.* Johnstown, PA: Johnstown Area Heritage Association, 1993.

Mitchell, Donald Craig. *Take My Land, Take My Life: The Story of Congress's Historic Settlement of Alaska Native Land Claims, 1960–1971.* Fairbanks: University of Alaska Press, 2001.

Moley, Raymond. *What Price Federal Reclamation?* New York and Washington: American Enterprise Association, 1955.

Morgan, Arthur. *Dams and Other Disasters: A Century of the Army Corps of Engineers in Civil Works.* Boston: Porter Sargent, 1971.

Nash, Roderick. *Wilderness and the American Mind.* 3d ed. New Haven: Yale University Press, 1982.

Opie, John. *Nature's Nation: An Environmental History of the United States.* Fort Worth, TX: Harcourt Brace, 1998.

Palmer, Tim. *Endangered Rivers and the Conservation Movement.* Berkeley and Los Angeles: University of California Press, 1986.

Pearson, Byron. *Still the Wild River Runs: Congress, the Sierra Club, and the Fight to Save Grand Canyon.* Tucson: University of Arizona Press, 2002.

Porter, Eliot. *The Place No One Knew.* San Francisco: Sierra Club Books, 1963.

Pyne, Stephen J. *How the Canyon Became Grand: A Short History.* New York: Viking, 1998.

Reich, Charles A. *The Greening of America.* New York: Random House, 1970.

Reichard, Gary. *The Reaffirmation of Republicanism: Eisenhower and the Eighty-Third Congress.* Knoxville: University of Tennessee Press, 1975.

Reisner, Marc. *Cadillac Desert: The American West and Its Disappearing Water.* New York: Viking, 1986.

Rhodes, John, with Dean Smith. *John Rhodes: "I Was There."* Salt Lake City: Northwest Publishing, 1995.

Richardson, Elmo. *Dams, Parks and Politics: Resource Development and Preservation in the Truman-Eisenhower Era.* Lexington: University of Kentucky Press, 1973.

Robinson, Michael. *Water for the West: The Bureau of Reclamation, 1902–1977.* Chicago: Public Works Historical Society, 1979.

Rome, Adam. *The Bulldozer in the Countryside: Suburban Sprawl and the Rise of American Environmentalism.* New York: Cambridge University Press, 2001.

Roth, Dennis. *The Wilderness Movement and the National Forests*. College Station, TX: Intaglio Press, 1988.

Rothman, Hal. *The Greening of a Nation? Environmentalism in the United States since 1945*. Fort Worth: Harcourt Brace, 1998.

Runte, Alfred. *National Parks: The American Experience*. 2d ed. Lincoln: University of Nebraska Press. 1987.

Sale, Kirkpatrick. *The Green Revolution: The American Environmental Movement, 1962–1992*. New York: Hill and Wang, 1993.

Schrepfer, Susan R. *The Fight to Save the Redwoods: A History of Environmental Reform, 1917–1978*. Madison: University of Wisconsin Press, 1983.

Schulte, Steven C. *Wayne Aspinall and the Shaping of the American West*. Boulder: University Press of Colorado, 2002.

Sellers, Richard West. *Preserving Nature in the National Parks: A History*. New Haven: Yale University Press, 1997.

Shabecoff, Philip. *A Fierce Green Fire: The American Environmental Movement*. New York: Hill and Wang, 1993.

Smith, Frank. *Congressman from Mississippi*. New York: Pantheon Books, 1964.

Sommarstrom, Allan. "Wild Land Preservation Crisis: The North Cascades Controversy." Ph.D. dissertation, University of Washington, 1970.

Spector, Ronald H. *Eagle against the Sun: The American War with Japan*. New York: Free Press, 1985.

Spence, Mark David. *Dispossessing the Wilderness: Indian Removal and the Making of the National Parks*. New York: Oxford University Press, 1999.

Stegner, Wallace. *The Sound of Mountain Water*. New York: Dutton, 1980.

———, ed. *This Is Dinosaur: Echo Park Country and Its Magic Rivers*. New York: Alfred A. Knopf, 1955.

Stine, Jeffrey. *Mixing the Waters: Environment, Politics, and the Building of the Tennessee-Tombigbee Waterway*. Akron: University of Akron Press, 1993.

Strohmeyer, John. *Crisis in Bethlehem: Big Steel's Struggle to Survive*. Pittsburgh: University of Pittsburgh Press, 1994.

Sturgeon, Stephen C. *The Politics of Western Water: The Congressional Career of Wayne Aspinall*. Tucson: University of Arizona Press, 2002.

Sutter, Paul S. *Driven Wild: How the Fight against Automobiles Launched the Modern Wilderness Movement*. Seattle and London: University of Washington Press, 2002.

Taylor, Walter, coord. *The Kinzua Dam Controversy: A Practical Solution—without Shame*. Philadelphia: Kinzua Project of the Indian Committee of the Philadelphia Yearly Meeting of Friends, 1961.

Topping, Gary. *Glen Canyon and the San Juan Country*. Moscow: University of Idaho Press, 1997.

Udall, Morris, with Bob Neuman and Randy Udall. *Too Funny to Be President*. New York: Henry Holt, 1988.

Udall, Stewart. *The Quiet Crisis*. New York: Holt, Rinehart and Winston, 1963.

Warne, William. *The Bureau of Reclamation*. New York: Praeger, 1973.

Webber, David. *Outstanding Conservationists of Congress*. Washington, DC: Government Printing Office, 2002.

White, Richard. *The Organic Machine: The Remaking of the Columbia River*. New York: Hill and Wang, 1995.

Wilson, Edmund. *Apologies to the Iroquois.* New York: Vintage Books, 1960.

Winks, Robin. *Laurance S. Rockefeller: Catalyst for Conservation.* Washington, DC: Island Press, 1997.

Wirth, Conrad. *Parks, Politics and the People.* Norman: University of Oklahoma Press, 1980.

Worcester, Donald. *Rivers of Empire: Water, Aridity, and the Growth of the American West.* New York: Pantheon Books, 1985.

Aandhal, Frederick: on evaporation loss figures for Echo Park Dam, 86

Abbey, Edward: *Appalachian Wilderness*, 12; *Desert Solitaire*, 12

Adams, Ansel, 70; *This Is the American Earth*, 108; on timber interests, 254

Adams, Sherman, 81

Advisory Board on National Parks: recommendations to protect Rainbow Bridge, 152

AFL. *See* American Federation of Labor

AFL-CIO, 299

Agnew, Spiro T., 274; vote on pipeline right-of-way legislation, 305

Agriculture Department: supports wilderness preservation system, 159; reclassifies primitive areas as wild, 167; and Wilderness bill, 170; reviewing land for wilderness system, 238; administers Pacific Crest and Continental Divide trails, 244

Air Pollution Control Act of 1967, 227

Air Quality Act, 319

Alaska, 285–306; Saylor supports statehood for, 29, 49, 125, 285, 316; and claims of aboriginal peoples, 285–90; Statehood Act of 1958, 286–87; and oil pipeline, 288, 290–91, 294, 303, 305–7, 319

Alaska Federation of Natives (AFN), 287, 294

Alaska National Interest Lands Conservation Act, 303

Alaska Native Claims Settlement Act: Saylor-Udall amendment to, 307

Albright, Horace, 115; and Dinosaur National Park legislation, 113; and preservation, 115; supports Wilderness bill, 161

Alcatraz: seized by Native Americans, 310

Aleuts: claims of, 285–86, 288–90. *See also* Eskimos

Allegany Reservation, 140; threatened by Kinzua Dam, 133

Allegheny Portage Railroad: National Historical Site, 229, 319

Allegheny River, 12; Saylor opposes Corps of Engineers project on, 120; Flood Control Act authorizes dams on, 133

Allegheny Sportsmen's League: supports Seneca Nation, 138

Allin, Craig, 97; pork barrel principle in river preservation, 209

Allott bill: for Dinosaur National Park, 111, 114; Interior Dept. concerns, 116

Allott, Gordon, 109, 268; and reservations over Wilderness bill, 109; submits Dinosaur National Park legislation, 111, 113; position on Echo Park Dam, 111, 113–15; on conference committee for Dinosaur National Park bill, 117

Alyeska Pipeline Service Company, 294

American Civil Liberties Union: supports Seneca Nation, 138

American Federation of Labor (AFL), 25

American Indian Movement (AIM): seizes Bureau of Indian Affairs, 310

American Mining Congress: Saylor and Aspinall appear at, 169

American Society of Civil Engineers, 136

Anderson, Clinton, 228, 319; conservationist, 1; and Wilderness bill, 104, 159, 161, 167, 171, 177; on Wilderness Preservation Council, 107; chair of Senate Committee on Interior and Insular Affairs, 159; member of Outdoor Recreation Resources Review Commission, 160

Andrews, Mark: and Wilderness bill, 172

Antiquities Act of 1906, 97

anti-sky hunting bill, 277, 318

Apostle Island Park, 281

Appalachian Aid bill, 224

Appalachian Trail, 243–44; administered by Interior Dept., 244

Aqualantes. *See* Upper Colorado River Grass Roots, Inc.

Arcata Redwood Company, 253

Arctic National Wildlife Refuge, 301–2; Saylor opposes drilling in, 6; establishment of, 125, 126; opposition to, 126; possible opening of, 292

Arctic Slope Native Association, 295

Area Redevelopment bills, 123

Arizona v. California: Supreme Court rules in favor of Arizona, 41, 181, 192, 194

Arkansas River Valley, 78–79

Armstrong County, Pennsylvania, 24, 26, 28, 141; and decline of coal industry, 121; poverty in, 226; and redistricting, 309

Army Corps of Engineers, 54, 67, 69, 120, 206; and public power plants, 4; builds Bonneville Dam, 31; plans for "cash register dams," 31; and Columbia River projects, 32; and dam on Flathead River, 53; proposes Glacier View Dam, 60; projects on Potomac and Allegheny Rivers, 120, 123; C&O Canal bill, 129–30; and Kinzua Dam, 133–34, 137; reclassifies Burns Creek Dam, 156; and rivers in Florida, 213; proposed St. Petersburg reservoir, 217; and Lake Erie-Ohio Canal, 225; and Tocks Island Dam, 230–32; studies multipurpose dam for Delaware River, 231; and Delaware Water Gap National Recreation Area, 235; and revenues, 245, 246, 248; develops Rampart Dam project, 286

Aspinall, Wayne, 82, 143, 197, 201, 258, 259, 277; joins Saylor on Yampa and Green Rivers, 57, 62; on CRSP, 63, 86; on dams in Dinosaur National Monument, 66, 110; on Echo Park Dam, 71, 74, 80, 90, 111; supports Fryingpan-Arkansas Project, 80; pro-resource development, 83, 146, 157, 162, 308; and Wilderness bill, 102, 104, 108, 159, 161, 172, 176; chairs House Interior Committee, 107, 113, 143; and Dinosaur National Park legislation, 111, 118; introduces Coal Research bill, 121; health of, 129, 144; relationship with Saylor, 142–43, 145–46; relationship with Wold, 145; Roosevelt and Pinchot serve as models for, 146; supports Dominy, 147; visits Rainbow Bridge, 149–50; on appointment of Stewart Udall as Secretary of the Interior, 152; and Wilderness bill, 160, 163, 164, 167–71; and ORRRC report, 163; Saylor criticizes, 165–66; reelection of, 167; Brooks on, 168; appears with Saylor at American Mining Congress, 169; *Washington Post* criticizes, 173;

Aspinall, Wayne *(cont.)*,
    pushes through Land and Water Conservation Fund,
    175, 237–38, 245–46; and Central Arizona Project, 182,
    186, 191; and Pacific Southwest Water Plan, 184; and
    Lower Colorado River Basin Project, 190–91, 193, 196,
    204–5; criticizes preservationists, 195; and water im-
    port studies, 198; meets with Morris Udall on Col-
    orado Basin Project, 203–4; on wild rivers bill, 208–9;
    and Scenic Rivers bill, 212–16, 219–20; Conservation-
    ist of the Year, 229; gives Tocks Island priority in
    committee, 233; postpones vote on San Rafael, 241;
    annoyed with Forest Service, 241; and expense of Na-
    tional Trails bill, 244; and Redwood National Park
    bills, 255–56, 260, 263–64; visits redwood forests, 257;
    suspension of Rules for Redwood National Park bill,
    261; opposes strip-mining legislation, 271; position
    on public land use, 278; and Native Alaskan claims,
    290, 293, 295, 296, 298, 301; poor rating from *Field
    and Stream*, 307; defeated by Merson, 308
Association on American Indian Affairs: supports Seneca
    Nation, 138
Atkinson, Brooks: supports Seneca Nation, 138
Atlantic Richfield Oil Company: finds oil field in Alaska,
    288; and Trans-Alaskan Pipeline System, 288
Atomic Energy Commission, 120; and construction of
    public power plants, 4; ordered to deal with private
    power companies, 52
atomic power plants: Saylor generally opposes, 4
Audubon Society. *See* National Audubon Society

Baring, Walter S.: on Wilderness legislation, 169–70,
    172–73, 176; and San Rafael controversy, 240
Begich, Nick, 294; and Aspinall, 296; on Native Alaskan
    Claims bill, 297–98, 301
Bennett, John B.: on Wilderness bill, 162
Bennett, Wallace: supports Echo Park Dam, 66
Bernard Baruch Foundation: Saylor receives Conserva-
    tion Award, 221; names Saylor Conservationist of the
    Year, 319
Bethlehem Steel, 8, 20; impact of Depression on, 19; client
    of Saylor's firm, 20; accepts unions, 21; and Burns
    Ditch Harbor, 227; closes Johnstown plant, 314
Bible, Alan, 299
Big Cypress National Preserve (Swamp), 282, 311
black lung disease (pneumoconiosis), 270–71, 319; and
    workmen's compensation, 271
Blatnik, John, 228, 319
Blue Ridge Parkway, 214
Boggs, Hale: and submerged lands revenues, 247
Bonneville Dam, 32; and sale of hydroelectric power
    from, 31
Bonneville Power Administration: permitted to market
    electricity, 157
Boulder Dam. *See* Hoover Dam
Boundary Waters Canoe Area, 98
Boyle, Tony, 270
Bradley, Harold, 61; on Saylor, 71
Bradley, Kim, 87
Bradley, Richard, 73; and evaporation loss figures for Echo
    Park Dam, 69, 71; "Ruin for Grand Canyon," 193
Bragdon, Gen. J. S.: and alternative to Kinzua Dam, 136
Brandborg, Stewart, 5; on Wilderness bill, 176; on Saylor,
    179, 317; on Aspinall, 212
Brant, Irving, 55; on Army Corps of Engineers, 130
Bridge Canyon Dam, 31, 184, 187; and Central Arizona
    Project, 38; Saylor on, 38, 182, 197, 198, 201; opposition
    to, 41, 193; Dept. of Interior publication supports, 189
Bridger National Forest: Saylor visits, 161
Brinegar, David, 74, 75

British Petroleum: drilling rights on North Slope and
    Trans-Alaskan Pipeline System, 288
Brooks, Paul: on Aspinall and Wilderness bill, 168
Brower, David, 3, 5, 75–76, 107, 193, 204; conversations with
    Saylor, 65; opposes Echo Park Dam, 68, 91; and Bureau
    of Reclamation errors in evaporation rates, 68, 74; on
    Saylor, 68–69, 71, 87, 90–91, 118, 283, 317; and Dinosaur
    National Monument, 83, 112, 148; and Glen Canyon
    Dam, 84; and need for preservation, 96, 115; and
    Wilderness bill, 105–6; protecting Grand Canyon, 185,
    195; and redwood preservation, 251; on Dunbar, 308
Brown's Park: possible dam at, 67, 70
Buchheister, Carl, 209
Buck, Frank: runs against Saylor, 230
Buckley, Charles: delays Land and Water Conservation
    Fund bill, 175
Budge, Hamer: and Burns Creek Dam, 155
Bureau of Indian Affairs: headquarters seized by mem-
    bers of American Indian Movement, 310
Bureau of Mines, 270
Bureau of Reclamation, 7, 35, 54, 69, 286, 318; Saylor
    blocks dam projects of, 2, 30; and hydroelectric
    plants, 4, 34–35; and "cash register dams," 31, 35; proj-
    ects of, 32, 36, 67, 154, 187, 224; established, 34; Saylor
    attitude toward, 34, 55, 62, 78, 80, 91, 92; and payment
    for projects, 36, 37, 81; and Central Arizona Project,
    37, 182, 192; and Colorado River system water appor-
    tionment, 39, 40; constructs Parker Dam, 40; miscal-
    culates Colorado River flow, 40; Straus heads, 50;
    downsizing of, 51; and Hells Canyon Dam, 52; and
    project on Flathead River, 53; and Colorado River
    Storage Project, 55; and Colorado-Big Thompson
    project, 59–60; and dams in Dinosaur National
    Monument, 59, 99; and Bridge Canyon Dam,
    60; evaporation loss errors, 69, 72–73; develops
    Gunnison-Arkansas plan, 79; and Echo Park Dam,
    86, 148; and protection of Rainbow Bridge, 90,
    148–50; and Saylor bill on Dinosaur National
    Monument, 116; Dominy appointed Commissioner
    of, 147; and construction of Glen Canyon Dam, 148;
    and Burns Creek Dam, 154–55; Saylor on support
    of public power projects, 157; and Pacific Southwest
    Water Plan, 182; Grand Canyon dam projects
    blocked, 218
Bureau of the Budget, 70, 246; Circular A-47, 51; reports
    favorably on Colorado River Storage Project, 70; and
    Fryingpan-Arkansas Project, 81; supports wilderness
    preservation system, 159; prepares Wilderness bill,
    169; and Lower Colorado River Basin bill, 190, 198;
    and revenue for Land and Water Conservation Fund,
    246–47; Morris Udall on, 247
Burns Creek Hydroelectric Dam: opposition to, 142,
    154–55, 232; supporters of, 154; costs of, 155; redesig-
    nated flood control project, 156
Burns Ditch Harbor, 227
Burton, Laurence, 204; and San Rafael controversy, 240
Burton, Phillip, 283, 319; and redwood conservation, 256,
    261, 264; workmen's compensation for black lung
    disease, 271; rebels against Aspinall's leadership, 294
Butcher, Devereux: concerns over Wilderness bill, 103

C&O Canal bill: Saylor sponsors, 126–27; District of Co-
    lumbia and Corps of Engineers dissatisfied with, 128;
    objectives of, 128–29; possible dam at River Bend,
    128; supporters, 132
C&O Canal National Historic Park, 127, 129, 130–31, 229,
    318; and Army Corps of Engineers, 120; Saylor spon-
    sors, 126–27; construction of, 126; federal govern-
    ment purchases, 126; section given to National

Capital Parks, 126; section given to National Park Service, 127; objectives of bills, 128

California Redwood State Park, 251

Callison, Charles, 5; on Scenic Rivers bill, 210, 215

Cambria County, Pennsylvania, 8, 24, 26, 141; and decline of coal industry, 121; and redistricting, 309

Cambria Iron Company, 8, 9

Canyonlands National Park, 229, 318

CAP. *See* Central Arizona Project

Cape Cod National Seashore, 126, 233; Saylor introduces legislation to protect, 126; funding of, 244, 281

Carhart, Arthur, 97; designs structures for Forest Service, 98; recommends against development in forest reserves, 98; concerns over Wilderness bill, 103

Carson, Rachel: *Silent Spring*, 12

Cash, Johnny: supports Seneca Nation, 138

Cattaraugus Reservation, 140

Central Arizona Project (CAP), 40, 74, 182, 204, 240; irrigation its main objective, 37; planned by Bureau of Reclamation, 37; and Lake Havasu, 37–38; and Parker Dam, 38; endorsed by Sierra Club, 38; Californians object to, 38; cost of, 38; Saylor on, 40, 75, 181, 186, 200, 202–5, 247; hearings on, 186; Morris Udall and, 201; Aspinall and, 212–13; various versions of, 213; Saylor and Stewart Udall support Aspinall version, 213

Central Valley (California) project, 35

Chaffee, John, 228

Chapman, Oscar, 32, 36; and Hells Canyon project, 32, 33, 52; hearings on Colorado River Storage Project, 55

Chenoweth, J. Edgar, 79, 80; introduces Fryingpan-Arkansas project, 78, 79, 83

Chesapeake and Ohio National Historic Park. *See* C&O Canal National Historic Park

Chugash Indians, 238

Church, Frank, 228, 319; conservationist, 1; and wild rivers legislation, 208; and Scenic Rivers bill, 212

CIO. *See* Congress of Industrial Organizations

Citizens Committee on Natural Resources: oppose Echo Park Dam, 85; offers amendments to Wilderness bill, 164; protests moratorium request, 167–68

Civilian Conservation Corps: Saylor on, 21, 53, 282

Civil Rights Act of 1964, 224

Clarion County, Pennsylvania: redistricting, 309

Clarion River: proposed dam, 213; and scenic rivers program, 216–20; Saylor opposes dam on, 314

Clarion River Organization for Water Development (CROWD), 216

Clark, Frank: on Saylor, 318

Clark, Joseph: and Tocks Island Recreation Area, 232–33

Clausen, Donald, 256; and redwood preservation, 255

Clausen Bill: for redwood preservation, 255; supporters of, 257

Clean Air Act, 275

Clean Water Bill, 274–75

Cleveland, Grover: adds to forest reserves, 97

Cliff, Edward, 241

Coal Mine Health and Safety Act: disability payments for miners, 271

Coal Research Act, 121, 319

Coffey, Col. Robert, Jr., 24

Coffey, Curry: runs against Saylor, 24, 26

Cohelan, Jeffery, 256, 264; and redwood preservation bills, 253, 255, 256, 259; on Aspinall and redwood legislation, 261

Collbran formula: for repayment of reclamation projects, 81

Colorado-Big Thompson Plan, 59

Colorado Iron and Coal Company, 82

Colorado River Basin Project Bill, 205

Colorado River Compact of 1922: Arizona refuses to participate in, 39, 181; and Supreme Court, 40, 181; approved by Arizona, 40; on hydroelectric dams, 84

Colorado River Storage Project (CRSP), 55, 68, 71, 80, 92, 111, 148, 156, 182; and construction of ten dams, 32, 55; retained some private enterprise, 55; support of, 63, 65–67; and irrigation, 64; errors in evaporation figures, 64, 65, 68, 70, 73, 86; opposition to, 68, 69, 74, 85; Bureau of the Budget recommends, 70; Martin refuses to call to the floor, 75; Saylor and, 63, 71, 76–78, 90; and issue of Echo Park Dam, 67, 80, 84, 87, 93; editorials against, 75; and water storage and hydroelectric power, 84; conference committee on, 93; provisions reinforce inviolability of national parks, 142; protection of Rainbow Bridge, 147

Columbia River, 31, 32, 35; Grand Coulee Dam on, 31, 32, 35; plans for dams on, 31

Committee on Natural Resources (Pennsylvania), 218

condors, 239–40

Conemaugh Electrical Plant, 268; mine-mouth generating facility, 225

Conemaugh Township, Pennsylvania, 8

Conewango-Cattaraugus plan: alternative to Kinzua Dam, 136–37

Congressional Record: Saylor inserts articles and comments in, 69, 72, 91, 103, 111, 160–61, 187, 196; Saylor's eulogies included in, 316

Congress of Industrial Organizations (CIO), 21, 25

Conservation Foundation: prepares *National Parks for the Future*, 312

Continental Divide Trail, 243, 244; Agriculture Dept. administers, 244

Corbett, Robert J.: on Saylor's opposition to Kinzua Dam, 134

Cornplanter Grant: threatened by Kinzua Dam, 133; Saylor visits, 139

Cornwall Mine: closed, 314

Council of Conservationists, 111; oppose Echo Park Dam, 85

Council of Environmental Quality (CEQ), 272–73; and wilderness protection, 281

Cowley, Malcolm, 12

Crafts, Edward: and Wild Rivers bill, 210

Craighead, Frank, 207–8

Craighead, John, 207

Cramer, William, 213

Crooked Creek State Park, 227

Cross Mountain Dam, 71, 84

CRSP. *See* Colorado River Storage Project

Cuban missile crisis, 167

Cumberland Island Park, 281

Curecanti Dam, 84

Davis Dam: and sale of power, 184, 187

Dawson, William, 63, 72; supports Echo Park Dam, 66; on Westerners' attitude toward loss of Echo Park Dam, 110

Delaware River Basin Advisory Committee, 231

Delaware River Basin Compact, 231

Delaware Valley Conservation Association, 235

Delaware Water Gap National Recreation Area, 319; Johnson signs bill, 235; funding of, 244, 281. *See also* Tocks Island Dam; Tocks Island National Recreation Area

Dellenback, John, 306

Del Norte Coast State Park, 251, 255, 257–58, 263

Department of Agriculture: provides surplus food for the needy, 29; U.S. Forest Service established, 97; Zahniser heads Division of Information, 100; land administration, 242–44; transfers land to Interior Dept., 243; and opening land for foresting, 277

Department of the Interior, 55, 73, 79 132, 242; expanding role of Bureau of Reclamation, 30; establishes Reclamation Service, 34; and Hells Canyon project, 32; McKay appointed Secretary, 50; and private power projects, 52; and creation of National Park Service, 59, 97; and potential hydroelectric sites, 88; and Dinosaur National Monument legislation, 111, 116; and coal research, 121–22; Geographical Survey, 136; and protection of Rainbow Bridge, 148; pledges to preserve national parks, 153; supports wilderness preservation system, 159; publishes *Lake Powell: Jewell of the Colorado*, 187, 189; and "cash register" dams, 189; booklet on Tocks Island project, 189; and method of evaluating rivers, 208; and wild rivers legislation, 208; Bureau of Outdoor Recreation, 210; and land acquisition, 238; Bureau of Sport Fisheries and Wildlife, 242; administers Potomac Heritage and Appalachian trails, 244; and Mill Creek, 256; Saylor suggested for Secretary of, 268; and strip mining, 271; and Teamster's land purchase, 276; Division of Wildlife, 277; and predator control program, 277; and Alaskan Native claims, 287; and Trans-Alaskan pipeline, 288, 294, 303; and freeze on Alaskan lands, 295; and Sigler bill, 295

Department of Transportation, 272, 282–83

Devil's Tower: declared national treasure, 97

DeVoto, Bernard, 75; on national park system, 61; endorses Saylor, 77; opposes CRSP, 83; on defeat of Echo Park Dam, 91

D'Ewart, Wesley, 36

Dewey Dam, 71

Dexheimer, Wilbur, 54, 65; heads Bureau of Reclamation, 51; Saylor on, 55, 63; visits Dinosaur National Monument, 63; and hearings on Echo Park Dam, 86; and Rainbow Bridge National Monument, 86

Dickinson College School of Law, 18; Saylor graduates from, 10

Dingell, John, 227, 319; relationship with Saylor, 44, 143, 316; and provisions for primitive areas, 173; and Wilderness bill, 169, 171; Native Alaskan claims bill, 301

Dinosaur National Monument, 66–67, 79, 83, 85, 95, 153, 318; Saylor helps block dam projects at, 2, 67, 76, 87, 90, 185; Saylor visits, 3; proposed construction of dams in, 55, 60, 67, 99; established, 57; Penfold opposes dams in, 61; expansion of, 88, 110; and Echo Park Dam, 89, 110; and assurances of protection of, 93, 118; designation as national park, 109; in Aspinall's district, 110; efforts to make a national park, 110–11, 113, 116; legislation reintroduced, 111; conference committee on, 116–17; bill enacted, 117; and controversy during CRSP debate, 148

Dirksen, Everett, 203

District of Columbia, 129; dissatisfied with C&O Canal bill, 128; water needs of, 130; and issues of water quality, 131–32

Dixon-Yates Company, 52

Dodge, Joseph: and evaporation loss figures, 70

Dominy, Floyd, 7, 35, 51, 54, 153; head of Bureau of Reclamation, 7; favors public hydroelectric dams, 7, 190; and Rainbow Bridge, 149, 150; Saylor on, 147, 156, 192–93; and transmission lines for CRSP, 156; on Lake Powell, 187; on Glen Canyon, 187; testifies on Lower Colorado River Basin Project, 191; opposes Rampart Dam, 286

Downs, Hugh: supports Seneca Nation, 138

Drury, Newton: opposes dam construction in Dinosaur National Monument, 55

Dry Lagoon State Park, 255

Dunbar, Ann, 317; on Saylor's staff, 5, 28; on Saylor's role in wilderness legislation, 177–78; death of, 308; honored by Wilderness Society, 308

Earth Day, 273

Easton, Robert: on condors, 240

Ebensburg, Pennsylvania, 28, 121, 309

Echo Park Dam, 61, 62, 71, 84, 87, 93, 95; hydroelectric project, 31; part of Colorado River Storage Project, 32, 55, 80; and Dinosaur National Monument, 55, 148; Tudor endorses, 63; and evaporation loss figures, 64, 69, 86; and opposition to, 64, 68, 75, 83, 86, 91; Saylor opposes, 65, 66, 76, 77, 89, 91, 115, 127, 283, 318; and possible improvement of park, 89; deleted from House bill, 90; Aspinall and Engle withdraw support for, 90; defeat of, 90, 115; impact of on Dinosaur National Park bill, 110; Allott on, 114–15; Bureau of Reclamation recommends, 148

Edmondson, J. Edward, 120; on Saylor, 121; delays Land and Water Conservation Fund bill, 175; on Native Alaskan claims, 290

Egan, William, 294

Egger, Frederick W.: on impact of Tocks Island project to Delaware River, 234

Eggert, Charles, 84; and preservation of Dinosaur canyons, 149

Eisenhower, Dwight D., 46, 52; visits Johnstown, 41–42; policies of, 43, 47, 48, 50, 54; on resources and power development, 50, 92; first State of the Union address, 50, 54; appoints McKay Secretary of the Interior, 50; and ownership of offshore lands, 51; supports St. Lawrence Seaway, 53; supports Colorado River Storage Project, 55, 85; lobbied by pro-conservationists, 69; vetoes Coal Research Bill, 121; restricts oil imports, 122; vetoes Area Redevelopment bills, 123; designates section of C&O Canal a national monument, 132; on Kinzua Dam project, 136

Eleven Point River, 208

Ellis Island, 235

Ely, Northcutt: on California water policy, 197–98; political maneuvering of, 199

Emerald Mile, 250, 257, 259, 260, 263; congressmen visit, 258

Endangered Species Preservation Act of 1966, 228, 311

Engle, Clair, 39, 40, 78, 107; and CRSP, 71, 86; withdraws support from Echo Park Dam, 90; and Trinity River Project, 92

Environmental Protection Agency, 305; establishment of, 272–73; and air quality, 275

Eskimos: claims of, 285–86, 288–90. *See also* Alaska, Aleuts

Evans, Lewis: Saylor defeats in election, 30

Everglades National Park, 53; proposal for nearby airport, 282

Fannin, Paul, 200, 201

Federal Land Right-of-Way Bill: passage of, 306

Federal Power Commission, 52, 191; and potential hydroelectric sites, 88; granting licenses for hydroelectric dams in wildernesses, 160, 210

Fenno, Richard F., 4

Fire Island National Seashore, 229, 233

Fish and Wildlife Service, 47

Flaming Gorge Dam, 31, 71, 84, 90; part of Colorado River Storage Project, 32

Flathead River: Saylor opposes dam on, 53

Flood, Daniel: on Scenic Rivers bill, 216, 217

Flood Control Act of 1936, 133

Foley, John: and C&O Canal bill, 128, 129, 132

food stamp program: Saylor supports, 21, 29, 122, 224, 270, 316

Ford, Gerald, 27, 298; Saylor supports for minority leader, 144; on Saylor, 316

Ford Foundation, 231

Forest Service: designates categories of forest reserves, 99; concern with timber production, 99; and wilderness bill, 102, 104–5; reduces Three Sisters Wilderness, 103; opposes Area F in San Rafael, 240; Aspinall on, 241; on Redwood National Park bill, 259; authorizes cutting timber, 278; and review of lands under Wilderness Act of 1964, 278, 281; relationship with Saylor, 312; Woodsy Owl mascot of, 312

Fox, Harry, 5, 28; on Saylor, 316

Franklin and Marshall College, 16, 17; Saylor graduates from 10; meets wife at, 22

Freeman, Orville: opposes Northern Redwood Purchase Unit, 257

Frey, Leo: relationship with Saylor, 146

Friends of the Earth, 283

Frome, Michael, 307; on Saylor, 317

Fryingpan-Arkansas project, 78, 91, 92; Saylor opposes, 18, 78, 80, 81, 83, 85; local opposition to, 79; and Hayden, 203

Gabrielson, Ira, 76

Gates of the Arctic National Park, 301, 313

Gathings, E. C., 215

Gentry, Richard, 28; on Saylor, 146

Georgia-Pacific Corporation, 253; cutting redwoods, 258

Ghizzoni, John: Saylor tribute to, 225

Gila National Forest, 98

Gila Wilderness Area, 204

Glacier National Park, 54, 67; proposed dam in, 53, 54, 60

Glacier Peak Wilderness Area: expansion of, 242

Glacier View Dam: proposed, 60

Glass, Robert: runs against Saylor, 76–77, 140

Glen Canyon Dam, 31, 66, 90,153; part of Colorado River Storage Project, 32, 62; and evaporation loss figures for, 69, 73; potential impact on Rainbow Bridge National Monument, 84, 90, 93, 142, 147, 148; Saylor questions, 84–86; cost of, 86; conservationists prefer to high Echo Park Dam, 148; construction of, 148; creates Lake Powell, 148

Goddard, Maurice: on Scenic Rivers bill, 216, 218

Golden Eagle Passport: and funding for Land and Water Conservation Fund Act, 245, 248

Golden Gate National Recreation Area, 313

Goldwater, Barry, 181, 223

Grand Canyon National Park and Monument, 1, 31, 38, 67, 180–205, 313; Saylor helps block dam projects at, 2, 205, 218, 230–31, 268, 283; and mineral resources, 59; impact of Bridge Canyon Dam, 60; planned dams would endanger, 154; expanded, 201; over-visited, 312

Grand Coulee Dam, 31, 32, 286; and sale of hydroelectric power, 31, 35; Saylor opposes, 32

Grand Tetons, 90

Grant, Ulysses, III: and evaporation loss figures for Echo Park Dam, 69

Great Depression, 19; and federal dam construction, 30; impact on National Parks, 59

Great Swamp National Wildlife refuge, 242–43, 311

Greeley, William B.: orders study of wilderness areas, 98

Green River, 57; Saylor rafts down, 3, 57, 62; visitors to, 61

Green, William: on Scenic Rivers bill, 216

Gruening, Ernest, 287; and Rampart Dam project, 286

Guadalupe Mountain National Park, 228

Guam, 29, 316

Gulf Islands, 281

Gunnison-Arkansas project, 81, 82; transfer of water to Arkansas River Valley, 79

Haley, James, 140, 296, 311; on Saylor, 93–94; introduces Seneca relocation bill, 139; opposes Burns Creek Dam, 155; and Native Alaskan claims bill, 295, 298; chairs House Committee on Interior and Insular Affairs, 311

Halleck, Charles, 27, 144

Hanford Nuclear Reactor: Saylor opposes, 154

Harding, Ralph: on Saylor and Burns Creek, 156

Harrington, Michael: *Poverty in America*, 123

Harris, Fred, 295

Harrison, Benjamin, 97

Harrison, William Henry, 63, 65, 73

Hartzog, George, 299; testifies on Redwood National Park, 256

Harvey, Mark W. T.: on Dinosaur National Park, 60, 96; on defeat of Echo Park Dam, 91; and Rainbow Bridge controversy, 153

Hatch, Bus, 3, 62

Hatch, Don, 62, 72, 115

Hatfield, Mark, 319

Hawaii: Saylor supports statehood for, 29, 49, 125

Hawaiian Volcanic National Park, 67

Hayden, Carl, 201, 203; and Central Arizona Project, 181, 200; chairman of Senate Appropriations Committee, 181; introduces legislation creating Grand Canyon National Park, 184; on modified PSWP, 185; introduces Lower Colorado River Basin Project, 186

Hayden-Fannin bill, 201–3; and Aspinall, 203

Heart River irrigation project, 51

Hells Canyon, 32, 34, 63; dam project developed by Bureau of Reclamation, 32; and hydroelectric power, 32–33; and flood control, 33; and Idaho Power and Light, 33; issue of public/private development, 33, 52; Saylor on, 33, 127, 130; Recreation Area, 313

Herling, Albert: and C&O Canal bills, 130–31

Heron, George, 137

Hetch Hetchy Dam, 59, 67; Saylor sees as mistake, 89, 90

Hickel, Walter, 276, 314; appointed Secretary of the Interior, 268; and Trans-Alaska Pipeline, 268, 288, 294; and livestock grazing fees, 280; and Native claims in Alaska, 287; opposes airport near Everglades National Park, 283; possible opening of Federal reserves, 292

High Desolation Canyon Dam, 71

Hoffa, Jimmy: endorses Saylor, 141

Holland, Elmer J., 134

Homer City: mine-mouth generating facility, 225

Hoover, Herbert, 51

Hoover Dam, 30, 32, 39, 40, 184, 187

Horan, Walt: on exclusion of development by Wilderness bill, 162

Hosmer, Craig: opposes Fryingpan-Arkansas project, 81; on water allotments, 186

House Appropriations Committee: refuses funds for barriers at Rainbow Bridge, 153; delays money for Delaware Water Gap Recreation Area, 235; and allocations for conservation projects, 246; Saylor and Udall on, 247

House Committee on Interior and Insular Affairs, 38, 53, 57, 78, 177, 216, 227, 288; Saylor on, 4, 28; jurisdiction of, 4; and Colorado River Storage Project, 71, 73, 86, 90, 202; approves Glen Canyon, Flaming Gorge, and Navajo Dams, 90; approves irrigation works, 90; and Trinity River Project, 91; hearings on wilderness bill, 102; and Dinosaur National Park legislation, 116; and C&O Canal bill, 132; and Burns Creek project, 142, 232;

House Committee on Interior and Insular Affairs *(cont.)*, considers Land and Water Conservation Fund, 175, 248; and Central Arizona Project, 181–82, 203, 204, 260; National Reclamation Association testifies before, 202; and Wild Rivers bill, 209, 260; and passage of Tocks Island bill, 234, 235; and passage of Whiskey-Shasta-Trinity National Recreation Area, 235; and Area F in San Rafael, 239; and national trails, 244, 260; and Redwood National Park bill, 260, 264; North Cascades National Park, 260; members serve on Public Land Law Review Committee, 278–79

House Committee on Public Lands: Saylor assigned to, 27, 28, 30

House Public Works Committee: considers Burns Creek Dam, 156; and Delaware Water Gap Recreation Area, 236

House Rules Committee: approves C&O Canal bill, 132; Lower Colorado River Basin Bill, 197, 198, 199; and Scenic Rivers bill, 219; and Redwood National Park bill, 260

House Subcommittee on Coal Research and Development, 120, 121

House Subcommittee on Indian Affairs, 310; and Seneca relocation bill, 139; and Native Alaskan claims, 288–89, 290, 293, 295, 296; and Sigler bill, 293; Saylor opposes policy of termination, 134–35, 310

House Subcommittee on Irrigation and Reclamation, 35, 73, 86, 195; and Colorado River Storage Project, 63, 68, 71; on Fryingpan-Arkansas project, 80; considers Burns Creek Dam, 154, 155; on Lower Colorado River Basin Project, 190–91, 194, 201, 203–4

House Subcommittee on National Parks and Recreation: and hearings on Scenic Rivers bill, 214; protects rivers, 215; and Tocks Island, 233, 234; proposed Redwood National Park, 255–56, 257, 259

House Subcommittee on Public Lands: hearings on C&O Canal National Historic Park, 127, 129; hearings on Wilderness legislation, 158, 160, 161, 171; Pfost chairs, 160; delays caused by Outdoor Recreation Resource Review Committee, 160; expense for National Trails bill, 244; on revenues from oil and gas leases, 245; and hearings on funding Land and Water Conservation Fund, 245–46; hearings on Alaska pipeline right-of-way, 305

Hualapai Dam, 191, 201, 202

Hualapai tribe, 194; reservation, 182, 184; and Lower Colorado River Basin Project, 194

Humble Oil: drilling rights on North Slope, 288

Humboldt County, California, 251, 254, 257, 258, 263

Humboldt State Park, 251

Humphrey, Hubert H., 267; sponsors national wilderness system with Saylor, 96, 100; resubmits wilderness bill, 102, 106

Hungry Horse Dam, 32

Idaho Power and Light: and Oxbow facility, 33; and Hells Canyon project, 33–34, 52

Imperial Valley, California, 39

Indiana County, Pennsylvania, 12, 24, 26, 30, 141; and decline of coal industry, 121; redistricting, 309

Indiana Dunes National Lakeshore, 227; Saylor introduces legislation to protect, 126

Indian Rights Association: supports Seneca Nation, 138

Internal Revenue Service, 195, 196

Izaak Walton League, 5, 45, 57, 76, 87, 106, 213; opposes Echo Park Dam, 68; honors Saylor, 118, 221, 283, 319; supports Seneca Nation, 138

Jacks Fork River, 208

Jackson, Henry, 1, 228, 284, 319; opposes aspects of Pacific Southwest Water Plan, 185; adds amendment to Lower Colorado River Basin Project, 190–91, 198; support for National Water Commission, 200; and Redwood National Park, 257, 263, 264; and Native Alaskan claims, 295; and Senate amendment, 299

Jedediah Smith State Park, 251, 254, 255, 257, 258, 263

Jefferson County, Pennsylvania: redistricting, 309

Jett, Stephen, 195

Johnson, Albert W., 309; and river development, 212, 217, 218

Johnson, Edward: and hydroelectric dams, 84

Johnson, Harold: and San Rafael controversy, 240; on Redwood National Park conference committee, 263

Johnson, Leroy: and Dinosaur National Monument, 83

Johnson, Lyndon: signs Wilderness Bill, 177; on preservation, 187; signs Colorado River Basin Project bill, 205; recommends river stewardship, 208; recognizes Saylor, 220; recommends Tocks Island National Recreation Area, 233; signs Delaware Water Gap National Recreation Area bill, 235; recommends San Rafael Primitive Area, 238; recommends additions to wilderness program, 242; authorizes Agriculture and Interior departments to study scenic, historic and recreational trails, 243; and redwood preservation, 253, 258; signs Redwood National Park legislation, 264

Johnstown, Pennsylvania, 8, 28, 219, 226, 269; and iron, coal and steel industries, 8; and floods, 8, 19, 21, 22; recreation and entertainment in, 10; traditionally Republican city, 20; Chamber of Commerce, 20; labor relations in, 21; Eisenhower visits, 41–42; chronic unemployment in, 122; crime rate in, 226

Johnstown Area Regional Industries, 314

Johnstown Flood Historic Site, 228, 319

Johnstown High School, 9

Johnstown's Sportsmen's Association: on Saylor, 229

Jones, John T., 77

Jordan, Len, 34

Kastenmeier, Robert: on Saylor, 316

Kennedy, John F., 27, 167, 223; signs Area Redevelopment bills, 123; on Kinzua Dam, 138; refuses to intercede for Seneca Nation, 139; appoints Stewart Udall Secretary of the Interior, 152; approach toward conservation, 152; special messages to Congress, 159, 161; advocates national wilderness preservation system, 159; and Wilderness bill, 168–69; endorses Tocks Island National Recreation Area, 233

Kent, William: donates Muir Woods to the nation, 251

Kent State University, 274

Key Biscayne National Monument, 228

Keystone Electrical Plant, 225, 268

Kilpatrick, James, 266

Kimball, Thomas, 319

King, George, 290

Kings Range Conservation Area, 255

Kinzua Dam: Saylor opposes, 133, 134; Seneca Indians oppose, 133, 136; support for, 133–34; Morgan hired to review, 136, 137; and Pennsylvania flooding, 137; does not threaten national preserves, 138. *See also* Pickering Treaty of 1794

Knopf, Alfred: and Dinosaur National Park legislation, 112

Kuchel, Thomas: and water allotments, 185–86; introduces Lower Colorado River Basin Project, 186; and California water policy, 198; and Area F in San Rafael, 240; and Redwood National Park, 254, 257, 263

Kyl, John, 279

Lake Chelan, 242

Lake Erie-Ohio Canal: Saylor blocks, 225
Lake Havasu, 37, 38. *See also* Central Arizona Project
Lake Mead, 89, 182, 184, 192; created by Hoover Dam, 89
Lake Powell, 151, 184; created by construction of Glen
    Canyon Dam, 148; possible impact on Rainbow
    Bridge 148, 149, 153, 189
Land and Water Conservation Fund, 228, 229, 237, 260,
    265, 318; receives priority in committee, 175; out-
    growth of ORRRC report, 175; support for, 175, 238;
    revenue for, 245; supplemental measure for, 228, 245,
    247–49; hearings on, 245–46; needed for Redwood
    National Park, 258
Lankford, Richard: and C&O Canal bill, 128
Lassen Volcanic Peak: declared national treasure, 97
Laurel Highlands, 8
Lawrence, David, 139; on Pennsylvania flooding and
    Kinzua Dam, 137; and opposition to Kinzua Dam,
    137–38
Lee, Katie: opposes barriers at Rainbow Bridge, 151
Lennai Lenape League: opposes Tocks Island dam, 235–36
Leonard, Richard, 88
Leopold, Aldo, 60, 101; champions preservation, 97; rec-
    ommends preservation of wilderness in Gila Na-
    tional Forest, 98
Leopold, Luna, 136; and evaporation loss figures for Echo
    Park Dam, 69
Lewis, John L., 21; Saylor tribute to, 225
Lineweaver, Goodrich, 50, 51
Little Conemaugh River, 8; South Fork Dam crumbles, 8
Litton, Martin, 95, 317; opposes Echo Park Dam, 75; op-
    poses CRSP, 83; and redwood preservation, 251
Lohr, William, 27
Los Padres National Forest: San Rafael Primitive Area in,
    238; fires in, 240
Lower Colorado River Basin Project, 193–94, 198, 201, 205;
    replaces Pacific Southwest Water Project, 186; and
    Bridge Canyon Dam, 186, 190; and Marble Canyon
    Dam, 186; Jackson and Aspinall add amendments to
    190–91; hearings on, 191, 194; opposition to, 191, 195;
    revised and retitled Colorado River Basin Project,
    194, 196; adjustments to, 196; Udall and Aspinall meet
    on, 203–4
Lower Klamath Pacific Flyway, 229
Low Grey Canyon Dam, 71
Lucas, Richard, 270
Luce, Charles, 256

Mammoth Cave National Park, 67
Marble Canyon Dam, 184, 189, 193, 195, 200, 201; Senner
    on, 187, "cash register" dam, 189; and Saylor, 197, 198;
    administration shift on, 201
Markum, Edward, 317
Marshall, George: opposes Aspinall's delay of Wilderness
    bill, 168
Marshall, Robert, 101; champions preservation, 97, 98, 99;
    cofounder of Wilderness Society, 99
Marshall Plan: Saylor on, 28, 48
Martin, Edward, 77
Martin, Joseph L., 27; on Saylor's victory, 26; House Minor-
    ity Leader, 27; angry with Saylor, 27, 43; refuses to call
    Colorado River Storage Project to the floor, 75–76
Masland, Frank, 218
Matthews, D. R., 46
McCarthy, Joseph, 28, 46, 50
McCloskey, Edward, 20
McCloskey, Michael, 5; on Saylor, 179; and redwood preser-
    vation, 259, 260; on Saylor and Morris Udall, 260
McCormack John, 164, 216, 260
McDade, Joseph, 216, 217

McIlvaine, Lee: on Saylor, 147
McKay, Douglas, 51, 54; Secretary of the Interior, 50; and
    certain private power projects, 52; defends Olympic
    National Park, 53; and Colorado River Storage Pro-
    ject, 55, 63; and dams at Dinosaur National Monu-
    ment, 63, 89, 93; lobbied by pro-conservationists, 69
McNichols, Stephen: on Saylor and reclamation, 112
Means, Russell, 310
Meeds, Lloyd, 294–95; and conference bill on Native
    Alaskan claims, 301
Meeman, Edward M., 178
Menominee tribe: and issue of termination, 310–11
Mercersburg Academy, 13, 15, 16; Saylor attends, 13
Merson, Alan: defeats Aspinall for election, 308
Metcalf, Lee, 54, 228; supports dam on Flathead River, 53
Metropolitan Water District of California, 40
Mickley, J. Harvey, 13
Midvale Steel and Ordnance, 8
Mill Creek: and redwood tract, 253, 254, 257–59, 263; and
    Clausen, 255; and Dept. of the Interior, 256
Miller, A. L., 43, 62, 73; supports Fryingpan-Arkansas
    project, 81–82
Miller, Keith, 289
Miller Redwood Company, 251, 255, 257, 263; cuts red-
    woods, 254
Millersville University of Pennsylvania, 9, 22
Milliken, Eugene: supports Fryingpan-Arkansas project, 80
mine-mouth facilities, 225–26
Mineral Leasing Act of 1920, 305
Missouri River Development Association, 211
Moley, Raymond: opposes Echo Park Dam, 75, 86, 91; en-
    dorses Saylor, 77; *What Price Reclamation*, 86
Moosehead region (Maine), 311
Morgan, Arthur, 138; Seneca Nation hires to review
    Kinzua project, 136; develops Conewango-Cattarau-
    gus alternative plan, 136, 137
Morse, Wayne, 50
Morton, Rogers C.B., 268, 301; Secretary of the Interior,
    294; on Alaskan claims bill, 302; protects Alaskan
    lands, 302–3; on Alaska pipeline project, 303
Moss, Frank, 189
Moss, Ted, 115
Motorboat Fuel Tax: and Land and Water Conservation
    Fund Act, 248
Mount McKinley National Park, 102, 301
Mount Vernon, 227, 316
Muir, John, 101; belief in stewardship, 11; cofounder of
    Sierra Club, 11, 60; and Yosemite National Park, 60
Muir Woods National Monument, 251, 255; declared na-
    tional treasure, 97
Multiple Use-Sustained Yield proposal, 108
Murdock, Thomas, 32, 40; sponsors Central Arizona Pro-
    ject, 37; chaired Committee on Interior and Insular
    Affairs, 38
Murie, Olaus: and National Wilderness Preservation
    Council, 107; on Wilderness bill, 108
Murphy, Joseph, 309
Murray, James: and Wilderness bill, 109
Murray, Pat, 44
Murtha, John, 218, 267
Muskie, Edmund, 319
Mutual Defense Assistance Bill: Saylor's first vote, 28

Nadel, Michael, 176
National Audubon Society, 5, 45, 209, 210, 215, 279; "Land
    Forever Wild," 108; Saylor speaks at convention, 229;
    and Area F in San Rafael, 239
National Capital Parks: manages section of C&O Canal,
    126, 133

National Environmental Policy Act, 319; and impact statement on Trans-Alaskan pipeline, 294
National Environmental Protection Act, 272
National Foundation for the Arts and Humanities, 224
National Geographic Society: and redwoods, 250
National Labor Relations Act. *See* Wagner Act
national monuments, 110; Saylor believes sacrosanct, 2
National Park Service (NPS), 63, 66, 113, 153, 161, 299; Saylor supports funding, 6; opposes dam construction in Dinosaur National Monument, 55; established, 59, 97; impact of Great Depression, 59; and Wilderness bill, 103, 104, 106; and Mission 66, 103, 106; opposes Allott bill, 116; and C&O Canal, 127, 129; Wirth director of, 153; evaluates Current, Jacks Fork and Eleven Point rivers, 208; fiftieth anniversary, 228; and Tocks Island Recreational facility, 232; and redwood preservation, 250, 253, 256; over-visitation of parks, 312; and *National Parks for the Future*, 312
national parks, 110; inviolability of, 2, 142; problem of overuse, 96. *See also park names*
National Parks Association (NPA), 45, 65, 71, 88, 119, 164; objects to reclamation projects, 59–60; and inviolability of national parks, 68; honors Saylor, 76, 319; awards Brower, 91; conflict with developers, 96; opposes Allott bill, 112; recommendations for protecting Rainbow Bridge, 151, 152; and Bridge Canyon Dam, 206
National Park Service Act of 1916, 142, 184
National Parks for the Future: recommendations of, 312–13
National Reclamation Act (Newlands Act), 34
National Reclamation Association: testifies at House Interior Committee, 202; opposes Scenic Rivers bill, 214
national scenic trails, 243, 244, 260; Appalachian trail, 243; Pacific Crest Trail, 243; Continental Divide Trail, 243; Potomac Heritage Trail, 243
National Trails system, 214, 265, 318
National Water Commission, 198, 200, 202
National Wild and Scenic Rivers Act, 220
National Wild and Scenic Rivers system, 2, 236
National Wilderness Preservation Council, 101; opposed by Forest Service and Park Service, 102; representation on, 107; provisions of, 107; delayed for action on ORRRC, 107; eliminated in revised Wilderness bill, 109
National Wilderness Preservation System, 241; Saylor supports, 2, 209–10, 212, 214–17, 222
National Wildlife Federation, 5, 45; opposes Echo Park Dam, 68; Conservationist of the Year Award, 229, 319; Conservation Hall of Fame, 319
National Wildlife Refuges, 97
National Wildlife Week: Saylor at celebration, 104
Native Alaskan claims, 285–90, 294; Sigler bill, 293, 295; Native bill, 295; administration bill, 295; conference committee on, 300; include national land interest provision, 300–301. *See also* Alaska, Aleuts, Eskimos
Native Americans, 2, 29, 107, 310; Saylor and, 2, 3, 4; displaced by National Parks, 3; land and wilderness bill, 102; and federal policy of termination, 134–35, 310
Navajo Dam, 84, 90
Navajo Nation, 195; reservation, 200
Naval Petroleum Reserve Number 4 (Pet 4), 287, 302; possible opening of, 292
Nelson, Gaylord, 228, 319
Neuberger, Richard, 33
New Moab Dam, 71
New York State American Indian Day: Saylor speaks at, 139
New York State Electric and Gas: builds generating plants, 225
Newlands Act. *See* National Reclamation Act
Nichols, Tad: opposes barriers at Rainbow Bridge, 151

Nixon, Richard M., 27, 267, 274, 277, 287; Saylor defends, 41; campaigns in Johnstown, 141; delivers special message on the environment, 272; bans poison for predator control, 277; on timber policy, 279; opposes airport near Everglades National Park, 283; and Native Alaskan claims bill, 294, 298, 302; signs Federal Land Right-of-Way bill, 306; honors Saylor, 316
Norris, William, 88
North Atlantic Treaty Organization (NATO): Saylor supported, 28
North Cascades National Park: establishing, 203, 214, 242–43, 260, 265, 318; issues of roads and tramway, 243; expansion of, 313
Northern Redwood Purchase Unit, 257, 259, 263; Johnson supports, 258

Oakes, John: opposes Echo Park Dam, 75; on opposition to preservation, 109
Obey, David, 276, 277
Office of Coal Research, 315
offshore lands. *See* tidelands
Ohio Department of Natural Resources: and Scenic Rivers bill, 211
O'Kicki, Joseph, 284
Olsen, Richard, 199
Olson, Sigurd, 76, 119; on Saylor, 283–84
Olympic National Park, 53, 60; proposal for harvesting trees in, 282
O'Mahoney, Joseph, 109; and reservations over Wilderness bill, 108–9
Omnibus Public Works Bill of 1957: funding Kinzua Dam, 133
Omnibus Rivers and Harbors and Flood Control Bill: Burns Creek added to, 156
Omnibus Rivers and Harbors and Flood Control Bill of 1962: and Tocks Island Dam, 232
O'Neill, Thomas, 197; on Saylor, 316
One Third of a Nation (Public Land Law Review Committee), 278; criticized by preservationists, 279
Oregon Dunes: Saylor introduces legislation to protect, 126
ORRRC. *See* Outdoor Recreation Resources Review Commission
Ottinger, Richard, 261; on Saylor, 283
Outdoor Recreation Resources Review Commission (ORRRC), 230, 318; established, 106, 160; Saylor and Anderson on, 160, 161; supports Wilderness bill, 160; report of, 165, 233; endorses wild river concept, 207–8; Outer Continental Shelf: revenues from for Land and Water Conservation Fund, 245, 246, 248
Ozark National Scenic Waterways Project, 208

Pacific Crest Trail, 243; Agriculture Dept. administers, 244
Pacific Southwest Water Plan: includes Central Arizona Project, 182; funded by Colorado River Basin Account, 184; and "cash register" dams, 184; cost of, 184; opposition to, 185; renamed, 186
Packard, Fred, 65, 76, 88, 112; opposes Echo Park Dam, 71, 84; on park overuse, 96; and Allott on Echo Park Dam, 115; on Saylor, 118
Padre Island National Seashore, 126
Palisades Dam, 32, 154; Saylor on, 155; Haley supports, 155
Parker Dam, 40; and Central Arizona Project, 38; and sale of power, 184, 187
Pasayten National Forest Primitive Area, 242
Patrick's Point State Park, 255
Pearson, Byron: on Grand Canyon dams, 199, 200
Penfold, Joe, 5, 63, 83, 102; arranges river trip for Saylor and Aspinall, 57, 61, 62; opposes dam construction in

Dinosaur National Monument, 61; on Miller, 62; on Aspinall, 62; on Saylor, 71; honors Saylor, 76; initiates Outdoor Recreation Resource Review Commission, 106; and Aspinall version of Scenic Rivers bill, 213

Penfold, Michael, 62

Pennsylvania Department of Health: and burning coal slag, 124

Pennsylvania Electric Company, 268; builds generating plants, 225; and pollution control, 314

Pennsylvania Federation of Sportsmen's Clubs: supports Seneca Nation, 138

Pennsylvania Fish and Game Protective Association: presents award to Saylor, 221

Pennsylvania Outdoor Writers Association: honors Saylor, 229

Pennsylvania Railroad, 269; and Saylor's firm, 20; and compensation for Kinzua Dam land, 139

Pennsylvania State Fish and Game Departments: honors Saylor, 229

Pennsylvania State University: Saylor speaks at, 273–74

Perry, Donald J.: runs against Saylor, 167

Pet 4. See Naval Petroleum Reserve Number 4

Petrified Forest: Saylor visits, 11; declared national treasure, 97

Pfost, Gracie: and C&O Canal bill, 129, 130; relationship with Saylor, 145; and Wilderness bill hearings, 164; loses reelection bid, 167

Philadelphia Yearly Meeting of Friends: opposes Kinzua Dam, 135

Phillips, John (maternal grandfather of John P. Saylor), 8, 9

Pickering Treaty of 1794: Seneca Nation cites in opposition to Kinzua Dam, 133; and violation of, 138; Supreme Court ruling on, 138–39; Saylor on, 139. See also Kinzua Dam

Pictured Rocks National Monument, 227

Pinchot, Gifford, 163, 176, 218, 301, 317; friend of T. Saylor, Sr., 11; chief of forestry under T. Roosevelt, 11, 97; and efficient use of national resources, 59, 97, 115, 146

Piscataway National Historic Park: preserves view from Mt. Vernon, 227, 316, 318; funding for, 281

Pitkin County: residents oppose Fryingpan-Arkansas project, 81, 83

Pitkin County Water Protection Association: opposes Fryingpan-Arkansas project, 78

Pittsburgh, Pennsylvania, 8; flood in 1936, 133

Pittsburgh Weather Bureau: Saylor uses data of, 134

Point Reyes National Seashore, 126, 233; Saylor introduces legislation to protect, 126; funding of, 244, 281

Pollock, Howard, 294; and Alaskan claims bills, 292–93

postal workers: Saylor supports wage increases for, 49

Potomac Edison Company, 229

Potomac Heritage Trail, 243, 244; administered by Interior Dept., 244

Potomac River: Saylor opposes Corps of Engineers project on, 119–20

Potomac River Protective Association, 130, 131

Poulson, Norris, 40, 75

Prairie Creek State Park, 251, 255, 257, 258, 263

PSWP. See Pacific Southwest Water Plan

public housing: Saylor supports, 49

Public Land Law Review Committee (PLLRC): One Third of a Nation, 278; Aspinall calls for establishment of, 278; membership of, 279

Puerto Rico, 29; nationalists attack House of Representatives, 46

Pyle, Howard, 40

Railway Workers Union: endorses Saylor, 77

Rainbow Bridge National Monument: impact of Glen Canyon Dam, 84, 86, 90, 142; possible protection of, 84, 93, 147, 150, 151–52; Saylor works to protect, 142, 149, 153; Aspinall and Dominy oppose dams in, 147; on Navajo reservation, 147; in debate on CRSP, 147; Lake Powell and, 148, 189; congressional visit to, 150

Rampart Dam project, 287; hydroelectric dam, 286; opposition to, 286

Rayburn, Sam, 27

Reagan, Ronald: and redwood preservation, 258

Reciprocal Trade Agreements Act: Saylor opposes, 48, 77

Reclamation Law of 1939, 36

Redwood Creek, 250–54, 257, 263; and Arcata Redwood Company, Georgia-Pacific Corp., and Simpson Timber Company, 253; as site for national park, 253, 255, 257–59, 263; and old growth stand, 254; Tall Trees tract, 254, 255

Redwood League, 253

Redwood National Park, 203, 214, 244, 318; funding for, 246; supporters, 255; bypassed Rules Committee, 261; conference committee, 263; dedication of, 269; expansion of, 313

redwoods: preservation of, 251–65. See also Redwood National Park; Redwood Creek; Mill Creek, Skunk Cabbage Creek, Tall Trees

Regan, Ken, 66

Regulation L-20, 98–99

Regulation U-1, 98–99

Regulation U-2, 98–99

Republican party, 5; and environmental issues, 1, 237, 266

Republic Steel: accepts unions, 21

Rhodes, John, 68, 189, 203; and Central Arizona Project, 181, 200–201; and Lower Colorado River Basin Project, 197

Rio Grande River: plans for dams on, 31

River Bend: possible hydroelectric dam at, 130–32

Riverton irrigation project, 51

Roaring Fork River, 79

Robinson, Michael, 55

Rochester & Pittsburgh Coal Company, 30, 53, 224, 268

Rockefeller, Laurance, 253

Rocky Mountain National Park, 60, 67

Rogers, Walter: and protecting Rainbow Bridge, 150

Rooney, Fred: and Tocks Island Recreation Area, 232–33

Roosevelt, Eleanor: opposes Echo Park Dam, 75; supports Seneca Nation, 138

Roosevelt, Franklin, 30, 152; establishes and expands Dinosaur National Monument, 57, 66, 88–89, 110; authorizes Colorado-Big Thompson Plan, 59

Roosevelt, Theodore, 1, 101, 147, 163, 176, 316; Saylor's hero, 3; and efficient use of natural resources, 11, 59, 146; adds to forest reserves, 97; proclaims national treasures, 97; establishes national wildlife refuges, 97; and preservation of Grand Canyon, 192

"Ruin for Grand Canyon" (Bradley), 193

Russell, Charles, 45

Ryan, William, 259, 261; and redwood preservation, 259

Salt River Valley: and Central Arizona Project, 37

San Gorgonio Wild Area, 164, 172, 176

San Rafael Primitive Area, 238, 239, 241; and mining issue, 239; and Area F, 239–41; concerns over fire, 239–40; and conference report on, 241

Save-the-Redwoods League, 251, 263; prefers Mill Creek site for national park, 253; on large park, 254

"Saving the Wilderness" (Saylor), 108

Saylor, Anna Catherine (sister of John P. Saylor), 9, 10

Saylor, Christian (ancestor of John P. Saylor), 8

Saylor, Grace Doerstler (wife of John P. Saylor), 22, 27, 45, 315

Saylor, John (paternal grandfather of John P. Saylor), 9

Saylor, John Phillips: champion of conservation and environmental issues, 1, 5, 7; believes national parks and
monuments sacrosanct, 2, 7, 64–65,142, 200; environmentalism rooted in religion and patriotism, 2, 5 11;
and Frederick Jackson Turner, 2; strives for balance
between use and preservation, 3, 123, 227, 267; bipartisanship of, 4; opposed federal hydroelectric and
atomic power plants, 4, 7, 22, 30, 32, 75, 120, 154, 156;
supports air and water quality legislation, 5, 124, 227;
ancestors, 8; childhood and education of, 9, 10, 12, 13,
16–18; visits Yellowstone and Petrified Forest with father, 11; and belief in stewardship, 11; joined father's
law firm, 18; supports organized labor, 21, 41; supports public housing, 22, 49; supports anti-poverty
campaign, 22; on irrigation, 22, 30, 35, 70, 84, 157;
naval service of, 22–23, 46, 125; provided flag raised
on Iwo Jima, 23; election of, 24–26; concerned about
communist threat, 28; protectionist, 29, 48, 53, 120,
225; uses appointments to military academies, 29;
support for striking coal miners, 29–30; fiscal conservative, 30, 93; supports coal industry, 30, 53, 120, 122,
142, 154, 222, 224, 227, 270; equates public hydroelectric power programs with socialism, 31; opposes
multipurpose dams, 32; supports mine-safety bill, 41,
77; on steel strike, 41; defends vice-presidential candidate Nixon, 41; endorsements, 42, 77, 141; and
recreation, 45, 46; visits both poles, 46, 125; supports
wage increases for postal workers, 49; supports civil
rights, 49, 153, 224; adds "under God" to pledge of allegiance, 49; and civil liberties, 49; and Joseph Mc-
Carthy, 50; speeches in defense of national parks, 54;
preservationists praise, 68–69, 93; honored by preservationists, 76; combined sectional and local interests
with preservation, 94; "Save the Wilderness" speech,
101, 104, 108, 161; celebrates National Wildlife Week,
104; distinguishes between preservation and conservation, 104; and definition of wilderness, 105; "The
Conservation Legacy of Theodore Roosevelt," 107;
opposes "promiscuous" dam building, 119; opposes
flood-control projects in East, 119–20; and preservation of Arctic wilderness, 120; and economic assistance for district, 122; health of, 124–25, 296–97, 315;
introduces legislation to protect shorelines, 126; visits
Allegany Reservation, Kinzua site and Cornplanter
Grant, 139; and personal staff, 146; concerned with
foreign policy issues, 153; article in Parks and Recreation, 211; recognized by President Johnson, 220;
awards received, 221, 229; works to increase recreational facilities in Northeast, 222; and Vietnam War,
223, 227; supports Second Amendment, 223; supports
states' rights, 223; on Miranda decision, 223; supports
Voting Rights Act of 1965; supports Twenty-Fourth
Amendment, 224; Groundhog Day speech, 226; opposes expansion of Clarion County airport, 227; and
off-shore drilling, 228; supports historic sites, 228; issues of environment and Republican party, 237, 266;
and revenues from oil leases, 246; refuses to debate
opponents, 267; distressed by campus unrest, 272;
importance of funding environmental programs,
273; works to protect endangered wildlife, 276; disap-
proves of One Third of a Nation, 279; on livestock
grazing fees, 280; and opening of federal reserves,
292; primary and redistricting challenges, 308–9; on
Watergate, 310; receives replica of Woodsy Owl, 312;
on issue of over-visitation of national parks, 313;
takes leave of absence, 314; sees coal as solution to
energy crisis, 315; death of, 315–17
Saylor, John Phillips, Jr. (son of John P. Saylor), 22
Saylor, Margaret (sister of John P. Saylor), 9

Saylor, Minerva Phillips (mother of John P. Saylor), 9, 43,
46, 76
Saylor, O. Webster (uncle of John P. Saylor): mayor of
Johnstown, 20
Saylor, Susan Kathleen (daughter of John P. Saylor), 23
Saylor, Tillman (father of John P. Saylor), 9, 16; city solici-
tor of Johnstown, 9, 20; outdoorsman, 10, 11, 285;
established sportsmen's association, 11; visits Yellow-
stone, 11; and Gifford Pinchot, 11; delegate to Repub-
lican national convention, 13; death of, 22
Saylor, Tillman, Jr. (brother of John P. Saylor), 9, 10; death
of, 219, 264
Saylor-Cohelan bill, 255
Saylor-Haley preservation measure, 311–12
Scenic Rivers Bill, 212–13, 217, 220, 230; introduced by
Saylor, 210; classification system 210; Senate version,
210–11; and Federal Power Commission, 210; and re-
strictions, 210, 211; and vote to suspend rules, 217
Schapp, Milton: honors Saylor, 316
Scripps-Howard Press: credited Aspinall with wilderness
legislation, 177
Seafarers Union, 299
Seaton, Fred, 126; recommends establishment of Arctic
National Wildlife Range, 125; visits Johnstown, 141;
and protection of Rainbow Bridge, 149, 150, 152
Selway-Bitterroot National Forest, 167
Senate Appropriations Committee, 203; and Fryingpan-
Arkansas Project, 203
Senate Committee on Interior and Insular Affairs, 184;
hearings on wilderness bill, 102, 107–8; and Echo
Park legislation, 115; Anderson chairs, 159; reports out
Hayden-Fannin bill, 202; and Public Land Law Re-
view Committee, 279; and Trans-Alaskan pipeline,
288; and Native Alaskan claims, 290
Senate Subcommittee on National Parks, 299
Seneca, Cornelius: letter to Saylor, 135
Seneca Nation: impact of Allegheny River project on, 120;
cites Pickering Treaty in opposition to Kinzua Dam,
133; thanks Saylor for support, 135; opposes Kinzua
Dam, 136, 137; hires Morgan to review Kinzua project,
136; support of, 138; compensation for land taken for
Kinzua Dam, 139–40. See also Pickering Treaty of 1794;
Kinzua Dam
Senner, George; and Central Arizona Project, 181; on Say-
lor, 187; on Grand Canyon Dams, 187
Sequoia National Park, 68
Shafer, Raymond: on Scenic Rivers bill, 216, 217, 218, 220
Shasta Dam, 31; and hydroelectric power, 35
Shenandoah National Park: and mineral resources, 59
Sherman Anti-Trust Act: and football, 125
Sherwin, Raymond, 284
Shields, Daniel, 20
Shukaitis, Nancy, 234; forms Delaware Valley Conserva-
tion Association, 235
Sierra Club, 3, 5, 87, 90, 179, 267, 283; Muir cofounds, 11,
60; Saylor supports, 45, 69, 159, 268; opposes CRSP,
63; opposes Echo Dam, 63–64, 68; on inviolability of
national parks, 88; endorses Central Arizona Project,
38; and McKay, 53; Conservation Committee, 69;
evaporation figure errors, 73; honors Saylor, 76, 118,
283; and Fryingpan-Arkansas plan, 79; and defeat of
Echo Park Dam, 91; conflict with developers, 96; and
wilderness preservation system, 159; and Grand
Canyon, 184, 192; advertisements opposing dams, 195,
197; Saylor defends, 196; opposes Tocks Island Dam,
236; and Area F in San Rafael, 239; and redwood
forests, 250, 251; and Redwood National Park, 253–57,
259, 264; supports Saylor-Cohelan bill, 255; presents
John Muir Award to Saylor, 284, 319

Sigler, Lewis: and Native Alaskan claim bill, 293, 295
Simpson, Milward L., 208
Simpson Timber Company, 253
Skunk Cabbage Creek: and Redwood National Park, 255, 258, 259, 264
Sleeping Bear Dunes Lakeshore, 228, 281
Smith, Fred, 253; and Allott bill, 111, 112; and Dinosaur National Park legislation, 111, 114; opposes Packard, 112
Smith, James, 79
Smith, Spencer, 164
Smoky Mountain National Park: over-visitation of, 312
Social Security, 224; Saylor wants to expand, 22, 49
Somerset County, Pennsylvania 10; and redistricting, 309
Special House Subcommittee on Coal Research and Development, 120; first hearing at Ebensburg Courthouse, 121
Spence, Mark, 2
Split Mountain Dam, 61, 62, 65; and Colorado River Storage Project, 55, 68; in Dinosaur National Monument, 55; Tudor on, 63
Springer, William, 283
SST. See Supersonic Transport
Staats, Elmer: defers decision on Bridge Canyon Dam, 190
Stapleton, Patrick: ensures Saylor's seat in Pennsylvania redistricting, 309
Statehood Act of 1958 (Alaska), 287
Stegner, Wallace: This is a Dinosaur, 85; role in defeat of Echo Park Dam, 91
Steiger, Sam, 200–201
Stevens, Ted, 268, 269, 295
St. John's United Church of Christ, 9; Saylor's funeral at, 317
St. Lawrence Seaway, 52–53; Saylor opposes, 77
Strank, Michael: helps raise flag on Iwo Jima, 23
Straus, Michael, 55; heads Bureau of Reclamation, 31, 50; and Hells Canyon project, 32
Stringfellow, Douglas, 72
strip mining, 123, 316; Saylor requests study of, 124; legislation on, 271
Students for a Democratic Society, 272
Submerged Lands Act of 1953; and ownership of land, 247
Sullivan, Lenor K., 122
Sumner, Col. George: on C&O Canal bills, 130
Superior National Forest, 98
Superior Roadless Area: first national wildlife preserve, 98
Supersonic Transport: Saylor opposes, 275, 307
Supreme Court. See U.S. Supreme Court
Sutter, Paul: and formation of wilderness crusade, 97

Taft-Hartley Act, 25, 225
Tall Trees: stand of redwoods, 250, 254, 255, 263
Taylor, Roy A., 238, 245, 279; credits Saylor for C&O National Historic Park, 133; and Scenic Rivers bill, 214; and Saylor, 247; on Redwood National Park conference committee, 263
Teague, Charles, 238
Teamster's Union: and land purchase, 276
Teapot Dome Reserve, 292
Tennessee-Tombigbee Waterway Project: Saylor on, 313–14
Tennessee Valley Authority, 52, 136; proposes Tellico Dam, 211
Thoreau, Henry David, 101
Three Sisters Wilderness, 103
tidelands: ownership of, 51, 52
timber industry, 6, 53, 60, 254, 264, 278; and ban on cutting redwoods, 254–55; and redwood preservation, 258; and Nixon policy on, 279; and shortages, 282
Timber Supply Bill, 278, 279, 307; and revenues from leases, 278

Tocks Island Dam, 230; and Omnibus Rivers and Harbors and Flood Control Bill of 1962, 232
Tocks Island National Recreation Area, 222–36; Interior Dept. booklet on, 189; Walter proposes, 232; support for, 234, 235; opposition to, 234; approved by committee, 235; renamed Delaware Water Gap National Recreation Area, 235
Trans-Alaska Pipeline System, 288, 303; requests permission for pipeline, 288; application for permit, 291; Saylor concerned over, 290–92, 305–7; and environmental impact statement, 294, 305; renamed as Alyeska Pipeline Service Company, 294
Trappers Lake, 98
Treaty of Paris: establishes off-shore boundaries, 52
Trinity River Project, 91–92
Trout Unlimited, 277; honors Saylor, 229, 319; opposes Tocks Island Dam, 236
Truman, Harry S., 25; Saylor on administration, 28, 29, 41
Trustees for Conservation: oppose Echo Park Dam, 85
Tudor, Ralph, 64, 73, 81; issues of evaporation figures and CRSP, 63, 64, 73
Turner, Frederick Jackson, 2, 101

Udall, Morris, 196, 205, 260, 279, 283, 319; conservationist, 1; and Central Arizona Project, 181, 186, 192, 194, 203; supporter of hydroelectric dams on Colorado River, 180; on Saylor, 182, 202, 316; and Lower Colorado River Basin Project, 194, 197, 200–201; and Grand Canyon dams, 230; and San Rafael controversy, 240, 241; and proxy, 240–41; and funding for outdoor recreation bills, 247; on Budget Bureau and Appropriations Committee, 247; on Land and Water Conservation Fund, 248; visits redwoods, 257; and Redwood National Park bill, 261; and Native Alaskan Claims bill, 297, 299, 302; on Alaskan oil pipeline, 305
Udall, Stewart, 92, 152, 163, 208, 229, 258, 268; inspects Rainbow Bridge, 150; supports CRSP, 151; on Echo Park Dam, 151; on barriers for Rainbow Bridge, 151, 153; balancing utilitarian and aesthetic elements of conservation, 152; appointed Secretary of the Interior, 152; recommendations on Rainbow Bridge National Monument and Glen Canyon Dam, 152–53; and interest in public power projects, 157; and Bonneville Power Administration, 157; endorses wilderness preservation system, 159; on wilderness and development, 162; waiting for ORRRC report, 163; supports Land and Water Conservation Fund, 175, 245–46; and Central Arizona Project, 181, 184, 200; drafts Pacific Southwest Water Plan, 182, 185; accepts elimination of Bridge Canyon Dam, 190; on Saylor, 205; endorses wild river concept, 207–8; on Aspinall, 209; on Scenic Rivers and Central Arizona Program, 212–13; and recreation areas, 233; and trams in North Cascades National Park, 243; on revenues from oil and gas leases, 245; endorses Redwood National Park, 251, 253–54, 256, 258; on cutting in redwoods, 254; sets price ceiling for acquiring redwood lands, 258, 264; and livestock grazing fees, 280; and temporary freeze on Alaska land selection, 287–88
Ulery, Kathryn, 13
Ullman, Al: opposed to Saylor's position on Western dams, 127–28; and maximizing use of natural resources, 128; and C&O Canal proposals, 129, 130, 132; believes in multipurpose water development projects, 130
UMW. See United Mine Workers
Union Theological Seminary: Saylor married at, 22
United Auto Workers, 299

United Mine Workers, 25, 267; endorses Saylor, 77, 141; and hearings of Subcommittee on Coal Research, 121; relationship with Saylor, 225, 270
University of California Wildland Research Center, 161
University of Michigan Law School, 9, 18
Upper Colorado River Grass Roots, Inc. (Aqualantes): supports CRSP, 85; Saylor on, 85
U.S. Bureau of Mines and Geological Survey: and Wilderness bill, 170
U.S. Forest Service, 99; established, 97
U.S. Geological Survey, 69, 149
U.S. Steel: accepts unions, 21
U.S. Supreme Court: and tidelands, 51, 52, 224; rulings in Kinzua Dam case, 136; ruling on Pickering Treaty, 138–39; rules in *Arizona v. California*, 41, 181, 192, 194
U.S.S. *Missoula*, 22–23, 28

Voigt, William, 87
Volpe, John: and proposed airport near Everglades National Park, 282–83
Voting Rights Act of 1965, 224
Voyageurs National Park, 281, 318

Wagner Act, 21
Walter, Francis: proposes Tocks Island National Recreation Area, 232; death of, 232
Warren, Earl: Saylor on, 224
Washington Aqueduct: supplies water to District of Columbia, 131
Water Quality Act of 1965: Saylor supports, 227, 319
Water Quality Improvement Act of 1970, 274
Watkins, Arthur, 89; on Echo Park Dam, 88: on Dinosaur National Park legislation, 110; and loss of election, 114
Wayburn, Edgar: and redwood preservation, 251; visits Alaska, 299
Webber, David, 319
Whiskey-Shasta-Trinity National Recreation Area, 235
White, Compton: on Wilderness bill, 171, 172
White, Lee: presses Aspinall to take action on compromise Wilderness bill, 171
White River National Forest, 98
Wild and Scenic Rivers Bill, 208–9, 260, 265, 267, 318; and pork barrel principle, 209; and conference committee, 219; and classification system, 219; Saylor on, 236
Wilderness Act of 1964, 210, 220, 229, 311, 318; protects some headwaters, 207; and land acquisition, 238; and citizen input, 240; mandates examination of lands for possible preservation, 278; and reviewing process of, 280, 281
Wilderness bills, 101, 158–79; opposition to, 102–3, 105; support for, 103–7, 138, 172; concerns over areas on Indian reservations, 103–4; need for master plan, 104; and Outdoor Recreation Resources Review Commission legislation, 106, 108, 160; resubmitted, 106–7; slowed by Multiple Use-Sustained Yield proposal, 108; changes to, 109; conflict between Saylor and Aspinall, 157; Kennedy and, 159, 168–69; Udall endorses, 159;

Senate passes, 160, 167; provisions of, 160, 170, 177; granting concessions in, 160; Aspinall's maneuvers, 161, 163–64, 167, 169, 170; Senate and Saylor versions, 163; Saylor's amendments, 176; passage of, 176; conference committee for, 177; Johnson recommends additions to, 242
Wilderness Club of Philadelphia: Saylor attends, 104
Wilderness Council: Saylor on, 103
Wilderness Society, 65, 76, 108, 176, 179, 212, 283; Saylor associated with, 5, 45; conflict with developers, 96; formation of, 97, 99; distributes Saylor's speech on wilderness, 101; and modifications to National Wilderness Preservation Council, 107; honors Saylor, 118, 317; supports Seneca Nation, 138; and Scenic Rivers bill, 218; and Area F in San Rafael, 239; and Native Alaskan claims bill, 297; honors Dunbar, 308
Wildlife Management Institute, 76
Willis, Edwin, 247
Wilson, Charles, 77
Wirth, Conrad: visits Dinosaur National Monument, 63; director of National Park Service, 153
Wold, John: relationship with Aspinall and Saylor, 145
Wonder Lake, 102
Woodbury, Angus: opposes barriers at Rainbow Bridge, 151
Wounded Knee: Oglala reservation, 310
Wyatt, Wendell: relationship with Saylor, 145
Wylie, L. F.: visits Rainbow Bridge, 149, 150

Yablonski, Joseph, 270
Yampa River, 57, 66; Saylor rafts down, 3; visitors to, 61; Saylor-Aspinall trip on, 62
Yellowstone National Park, 98, 125; creation displaced Native Americans, 3; Saylor visits with father, 11; establishment of, 96–97; over-visitation of, 312
Yorty, Sam, 39, 40
Yosemite National Park: establishment of, 60, 97; and Hetch Hetchy Dam, 59, 89; and mineral resources, 59; over-visitation of, 312
Young, Clifton: on Lake Mead, 89
Youth Conservation Corps, 281–82
Yukon Flats, 286, 301

Zahniser, Howard, 5, 12, 65, 76, 88, 96; executive secretary of Wilderness Society, 12; on Saylor, 90, 178; and preservation, 96, 99; discusses preservation with Saylor, 96; writer for U.S. Fish and Wildlife Service, 99; heads Division of Information in Department of Agriculture, 100; suggests national wilderness system to Saylor and Humphrey, 100; editor of *Living Wilderness*, 100; on wilderness legislation, 102–3, 105–7, 160, 317; and definition of wilderness, 105; health of, 108; attempt to reconcile House and Senate Dinosaur Park bills, 113; supports Seneca Nation, 138; on Aspinall's request for moratorium on Wilderness bill, 168; pushes through Land and Water Conservation Fund bill, 175; death of, 176; credited with establishment of national wilderness system, 177; work with Saylor, 317